Public Management

Second Edition

For all those who practice, teach, study, and value effective public management.

⑤SAGE | 50 YEARS

SAGE was founded in 1965 by Sara Miller McCune to support the dissemination of usable knowledge by publishing innovative and high-quality research and teaching content. Today, we publish more than 850 journals, including those of more than 300 learned societies, more than 800 new books per year, and a growing range of library products including archives, data, case studies, reports, and video. SAGE remains majority-owned by our founder, and after Sara's lifetime will become owned by a charitable trust that secures our continued independence.

Los Angeles | London | New Delhi | Singapore | Washington DC

Public Management

Thinking and Acting in Three Dimensions

Second Edition

Carolyn J. Hill
Georgetown University and MDRC

Laurence E. Lynn, Jr.
University of Chicago

Los Angeles | London | New Delhi
Singapore | Washington DC

Los Angeles | London | New Delhi
Singapore | Washington DC

FOR INFORMATION:

CQ Press

An Imprint of SAGE Publications, Inc.

2455 Teller Road

Thousand Oaks, California 91320

E-mail: order@sagepub.com

SAGE Publications Ltd.

1 Oliver's Yard

55 City Road

London EC1Y 1SP

United Kingdom

SAGE Publications India Pvt. Ltd.

B 1/I 1 Mohan Cooperative Industrial Area

Mathura Road, New Delhi 110 044

India

SAGE Publications Asia-Pacific Pte. Ltd.

3 Church Street

#10-04 Samsung Hub

Singapore 049483

Acquisitions Editor: Sarah Calabi

Editorial Assistant: Katie Lowry

Production Editor: Bennie Clark Allen

Copy Editor: Michelle Ponce

Typesetter: C&M Digitals (P) Ltd.

Proofreader: Wendy Jo Dymond

Indexer: Mary Mortensen

Cover Designer: Anupama Krishnan

Marketing Manager: Amy Whitaker

eLearning Editor: Allison Hughes

Printed in the United States of America

Library of Congress Cataloging-in-Publication Data

Hill, Carolyn J.

Public management : thinking and acting in three dimensions/Carolyn J. Hill Georgetown University and MDRC, Laurence E. Lynn, Jr.—Second edition.

pages cm
Includes bibliographical references and index.

ISBN 978-1-4833-4432-4 (pbk.: alk. paper)

1. Public administration—United States. 2. United States—Politics and government. I. Lynn, Laurence E., 1937- II. Title.

JK421.H55 2015
351.73--dc23   2015028500

This book is printed on acid-free paper.

15 16 17 18 19 10 9 8 7 6 5 4 3 2 1

Contents

Tables, Figures, and Boxes

TABLES

FIGURES

Preface to the Second Edition

Public Management: Thinking and Acting in Three Dimensions was born of two convictions: (1) effective public management and competent public managers are essential to achieving the duly authorized goals of public policies at all levels of government, and (2) trustworthy public management is a sustaining factor in the legitimacy of public administration within America's constitutional scheme of governance. By the term *public management,* we mean the decisions and actions of public officials in managerial roles to ensure that the allocation and use of resources available to governments are directed toward the achievement of lawful public policy goals.

Imparting a sense of urgency to this project is the steady outpouring of stories of public mismanagement and incompetence in recent years. Policies, organizations, and public officials have too often failed the public, with consequences ranging from unfortunate to tragic. Such failures further diminish Americans' trust in their government to, as public opinion pollsters put it, "do what is right.[i]" Excuses that cavalierly explain mismanagement as "stuff happens" hardly mollify citizens who justifiably resent misuses of their tax dollars.

Yet chronic failure is far from the whole story of American public management. In this book, we highlight examples of successful policies, organizations, and individuals. These stories exemplify how the daily business of government at all levels is performed with commendable competence by officials dedicated to effective public service. That the American administrative state ever or even often works well attracts little media, interest group, or citizen attention. "Another good day at the office" is not a compelling story.

Public management in our democracy can be dauntingly challenging. Doing what is right is hard work. Indeed, to manage effectively in a regime of separated powers and checks and balances entails intellectual and practical challenges that are exceptional among modern industrial democracies. Educating people to understand and to meet these challenges is the goal of public affairs education in general, and it is our reason for writing this book. We aim

- to educate readers to be informed citizens concerning how government works, what is involved in implementing complex public policies, and how managerial leadership and skill can contribute to achieving effective public policy outcomes, and

---

[i]Pew Research Center for People and the Press, "Trust in Government Nears Record Low, but Most Federal Agencies Are Viewed Favorably," Survey Report, October 18, 2013, Retrieved from http://www.people-press.org/files/legacy-pdf/10-18-13%20 Trust%20in%20Govt%20Update.pdf.

- to prepare students to participate as professionals by helping them acquire critical analytical and rhetorical skills appropriate to addressing public management's distinctive challenges, through adherence to a guiding principle of the rule of law and through deliberative processes informed by the multiple dimensions of public management.

THE BOOK'S PREMISES

This textbook's argument is developed from the following premises:

- The topic of public management is about much more than just what tasks managers do and how they do those tasks. Instead, it is fundamentally about *why* public managers do what they do.
- A public manager in a particular situation confronts and must sort through many details. Many of these details may seem inconsequential, but they are often of great importance to an accurate understanding of what matters. As the saying goes, "the devil is in the details." A manager needs to be able to identify the most important among all these details. That requires, in turn, knowing the right questions to ask in order to focus on the key facts.
- Situations that public managers face, and, therefore, the right questions to ask, will differ depending on factors that include

  o the level of government (federal, state, local),
  o politics and political institutions,
  o characteristics of the organizations where public managers work and the type of work the organization does,
  o the organization's institutionalized values and cultures/subcultures,
  o the personalities and skills of the individual managers themselves, and
  o the context of the organization's work.

- The real challenges that public managers face typically have no single best response. Instead, relying on analysis—a way of thinking about and approaching problems—is a more robust approach than searching for a textbook answer or resorting to a one-size-fits-all best practice.
- An analytical approach typically involves

  o choosing a framework for viewing public management problems: in this book, that framework comprises three dimensions: structure, culture, and craft, and
  o adopting a systematic process for thinking about the problem or challenge: in this book, that process is the model deliberative process.

- There is more rational, or at least systematic, thinking in public affairs than may be apparent from media accounts. The institutional framework of American governments tends toward reasoned explanations and justifications for policies and budgets. Making persuasive arguments does matter in practice, and, to the extent it does, that is healthy for democratic governance.

WHY THREE DIMENSIONS?

We believe that managing in the public sector requires an understanding of three distinct dimensions of public action:

- Structure: administrative structures and processes,
- Culture: organizations and their cultures, and
- Craft: individual public managers and their skills and values.

These three dimensions interact in complex ways to produce results that approximate what citizens and their representatives expect from their governments.

The three dimensions encapsulate the typical ways in which citizens and lawmakers tend to think about and react to government: as public agencies that serve the public in particular ways (i.e., structure), as the values institutionalized in public bureaucracies that are reflected in the ways employees do their work (i.e., culture), and as the individuals who hold positions of authority and responsibility in government and should be held accountable for how well or poorly government performs (i.e., craft).

The three-dimensional framework is embedded in James Madison's constitutional scheme of American governance that comprises the rule of law: a separation of powers among legislative, executive, and judicial branches; checks and balances; federalism; and pluralism. Public management is not a thing apart from politics and policy but an integral, inseparable part of making our democratic institutions work for "the people."

TEACHING PUBLIC MANAGEMENT WITH THIS BOOK

The pedagogical approach underlying this book draws on the authors' combined half century of experience teaching both public management and policy analysis to students in professional master's degree programs (experience that, in turn, was grounded on a decade of public service).

The book aims to demonstrate that effective public management in the real world will benefit in significant ways from critical analysis and the manager's ability to incorporate such analysis into managerial actions and strategies and to bring the need for such intellectual skills to vivid life through the liberal use of cases, examples, and insightful anecdotes of public management in actual practice.

A further aspect of our approach is its emphasis on the rule of law. Many texts, whatever methods they use to prepare professionals for practice, view laws, rules, courts, and legality as specialized topics, thus giving short shrift to how the rule of law permeates professional work. These texts may deal with particular laws, lawsuits, and court decisions in the context of considering specific managerial problems, but they do not sufficiently illuminate the relationship of managerial practice to lawfulness and to upholding the Constitution, which the public manager's oath of office explicitly requires. In this book, adhering to the rule of law is regarded as the foundation of public management, and we consider in detail what that proposition means for practice.

Public management is not only thoughtful, analytical deliberation and the lawful action that proceeds from it, however. It is also rhetoric, the ability to use language effectively in political and organizational contexts to bring superiors, peers, and subordinates to agreement, action, and cooperation. The "method" of this book, then, is argument based on ideas fully developed in the book's appendix. We believe that the ability to make persuasive arguments is fundamental to the practice of public management (indeed, it is fundamental to all forms of public service) in a democracy. The intellectual and verbal skills needed for argument—the ability to reason, explain, and persuade—are not always given appropriate emphasis in the teaching of public management, where behavioral skills—supervision, teamwork, motivation, conflict management, and leadership—are often featured. These behavioral skills *are* essential, and our hope is that students are given opportunities to develop such skills in their professional training. But reasoned persuasion is a too-little-recognized *sine qua non* for managerial effectiveness. It is, moreover, a skill that can be practiced and effectively developed in the classroom.

OUR ARGUMENT FOR THIS BOOK

We make a straightforward claim: Public managers who are able to use all three dimensions of public management to address the issues and problems they confront, whether routine or extraordinary, will perform more effectively than will those who cannot distinguish these dimensions or who use them inappropriately. Three-dimensional public management is better public management.

The reason for making this claim is also straightforward. Because the administrative system is embedded within complex political and legal processes having constitutional origins, public officials in managerial roles have neither the broad discretion nor the clear bottom line that provide a focus for business management. Public managers cannot simply resort to "technical rationality" or rely on "leadership" to ensure "profitability." Instead, their decisions are constrained by laws, policies, organizational cultures, and legal precedents, and their actions and the consequences they produce are subject to critical scrutiny from legislators, interest groups, courts, the media, and their own employees. A three-dimensional approach helps bring this kaleidoscopic complexity into a clearer focus for action.

Readers of this book will find the evidence for this claim and the reasoning supporting it in the scores of examples, case studies, stories, and references that are included or cited throughout the text. From the analyses of the structural, cultural, and craft elements of real-world managerial activity emerges a strong sense of their specific importance, used singly or in combination, to effective management. Public managers who, *in extremis,* have the ability to consider all three dimensions of public management are, the evidence suggests, more likely to cope with a crisis, reform an agency, or reach a politically and legally satisfactory resolution to a vexing problem.

The warrant or theory justifying the link between the book's claim and its evidence is in the logic of governance discussed in Chapter 4 and the theoretical reasoning on which it is based. That body of theory postulates that citizens are linked to the activities and performance of their governments through layers of institutions established according to general principles of delegation and control and accountability. No approach to public management that fails to incorporate the resulting logic of governance into its analysis and prescriptions will adequately recognize the kinds of pressures that constitute the reality of day-to-day public management.

The preceding elements of our argument are subject to qualifications, however. As we discuss in the next section, available texts offer many other approaches to the teaching and practice of public management, and there is value in all of them. Behavioral and experiential and best practices approaches yield important insights in how to manage in the public sector. We believe they are useful supplements to, not substitutes for, a three-dimensional approach.

HOW THIS BOOK DIFFERS FROM OTHER TEXTBOOKS

This book differs in significant ways from other textbooks used in introductory courses on public administration and management in professional master's degree programs.

One reason for differences among texts is that authors have different disciplinary orientations. Instructors whose backgrounds differ from ours—we consider ourselves to be political economists—might not agree with our emphasis, for example, on the hierarchical nature of governance or on the analytic value of the principal-agent model. Anticipating this reality, we have tried to let the practical challenges of public management, rather than the preoccupations of our own academic field, govern our selection of concepts, heuristics, and examples. Although the assumption of bounded rationality can be insightful in certain applications, we also discuss insightful kinds of psychosocial considerations that affect decision making. We think that applications of principal-agent logic, suitably qualified, can enlighten practice, but we include other models of human interaction as well. We cannot expect instructors to change their academic stripes, but we do hope they will consider the pedagogical value of concepts that they may not use as scholars.

We also acknowledge the differences in how instructors conceive of the nature of professional education, that is, on the answer to the question: How can students at the master's level best be prepared for the professional practice of public management? Our approach is based on our answer: by helping students acquire critical analytical and rhetorical skills appropriate to addressing public management's distinctive challenges, through adherence to a guiding principle of the rule of law, and through deliberative processes informed by the multiple dimensions of public management.

Some instructors consider the goal of master's education in public management to be familiarizing students with research literature related to specific areas and topics associated with public administration and management. Such familiarity may suggest applications of the theories and empirical findings of that literature to public management. Their students are encouraged, in effect, to think like applied social scientists. As practicing social scientists, we have the utmost respect for rigorous research and the findings it produces; this book introduces and draws heavily on them. We believe, however, that master's-level graduates of a professional program who are not familiar with *all* that is known about a topic are nevertheless able to think critically and analytically about public management problems. Knowing and applying research literature is a means to an end for practice, not an end in itself. Mastery of an insightful heuristic, together with intellectual curiosity about where helpful answers to managerial challenges may lie, is more likely to assist real-time thinking than mere mastery of the full realm of academic knowledge.

Yet another view of the purpose of master's education in public management is that it should familiarize students with the administrative state's architecture and functions, which constitute the context for professional practice and the profession of public administration. As with rigorous social science, we do not stint in our respect for the importance of a working knowledge of the institutions of American governance and the critical importance of public service values. But we believe that being able to describe institutions is of less immediate import to professional practice than knowing how the details of institutions can be a source both of management problems and of solutions to them.

A third view of the purpose of master's-level education in public management is that it should show how individual personality, skill, aspiration, and character—enlightened by knowledge of practices of successful managers—can contribute to effective governmental performance. Many books take a nuts-and-bolts orientation to management, emphasizing popular topics such as handling the press, working with politicians, dealing with unpleasant people, managing one's boss, fostering teamwork, negotiating, and the like. These behavioral skills are important and may enable a particular public manager to handle a situation successfully. But teaching these skills typically involves constructing principles of effective practice from the analysis of cases, examples, and personal experience. Such case-based and experience-based analyses often take institutional and organizational constraints as given.

Our analyses of cases and personal experience assume that management is three-dimensional and must not overemphasize individual managers, however charismatic they may be. We are also skeptical of the value of universal principles of effective practice; good managers will violate them as the situation requires. Knowing when and why to violate them is what is important to managerial effectiveness. Our approach emphasizes the acquisition of critical analytical skills that are appropriate for addressing public management's distinctive challenges in our constitutional scheme of governance.

TEACHING AND LEARNING WITH THIS BOOK

This book is designed for a semester-long course (or a two-quarter course sequence) on public management at the master's degree level. Supplemented by other readings, the book also might be suitable for a doctoral seminar on the subject and, possibly, for advanced undergraduates studying American politics and government. The book is appropriate for precareer students and those with some or even considerable experience in the public sector (many of whom return to school to develop conceptual foundations for their careers), as most contemporary public management classes include both types of students. Although the emphasis is on management in the public sector, students whose interests lie primarily in the nonprofit sector also will find material of value to them because of its public service orientation and sections specifically about nonprofit organizations and management. We intend for this book to be used as a platform for different types of applications and different types of pedagogical strategies.

In developing the text, we confronted two additional issues. First, where do topics that many instructors regard as important to public management belong? Our choice of emphasis, analytic framework, and text organization inevitably means that familiar topics such as budgeting, human resources administration, outsourcing, and decision making are woven across the three dimensions. Frequent cross-references appear throughout the book, emphasizing the multidimensional nature of particular topics. This treatment reflects our view that the appropriate use of specialized functions is intrinsic to managing in three dimensions rather than an end in itself. Presenting such topics in this way, we have found, makes material that can seem tedious in a traditional descriptive and functional format far more engaging for students because they can see the topics in the broader context of public management's distinctive challenges.

Second, how should we choose from among the wide array of concepts and heuristics that can be applicable to public management? We attempted to balance a number of criteria: significance, analytical value, and what works well in the classroom. Citations include additional resources that a reader might find useful. Other topics and readings that appeal to individual instructors can be incorporated in a syllabus at appropriate points in the course. Some instructors may choose a different balance and spend an entire class period discussing contracting (for example), while others may devote less time to this structural feature and instead emphasize networks and network management strategies (for example).

To facilitate an interactive, experiential process of teaching and learning, each chapter offers some ideas for class discussion. They include numerous examples of varying lengths to illustrate how concepts are relevant to practice. These examples are based on media accounts, official reports, and, in some cases, academic research publications. Instructors might consider developing preclass assignment questions based on the examples or encouraging students to find others.

An issue that always arises in selecting examples is the balance to strike between successes and failures. This is a subject of lively controversy, with some arguing that failures are more enlightening and others that successes are more inspiring. We like the anecdote about the Dutch national soccer team's persistent failure to win important matches because of its inability to make penalty kicks. After a coaching strategy of having players study film of successful kicks did not improve matters, team officials decided—with better results—to study film of failed kicks and point out why they failed. While we include both successes and failures throughout the book, we did not hesitate to choose failures—often referred to in the literature as "fiascos"—as a basis for drawing lessons from complex situations.

The examples in the text tend to be weighted somewhat more toward national or federal government issues than toward state or local issues. Although a somewhat more even balance is in principle desirable, the actual balance reflects the fact that public management issues at the federal level and situations occurring in cities such as New York, Los Angeles, and Washington, DC, tend to be more widely publicized, better documented, and more accessible and even familiar to students in many different settings. We hope that instructors will supplement our examples with ones from state and local settings that reflect local interests and concerns.

Following the main text of each chapter is a fully developed case of public management at the federal, state, or local level of government. Each case is accompanied by a series of questions that may be assigned as preparation for class discussion or as the basis of a written assignment. In general, readers are asked to analyze the case using the concepts presented in the chapter or elsewhere in the book.

For class discussions and assignments, students can be encouraged to exercise the method of the course—that is, use the model deliberative process described in Chapter 1 along with the method of argument described in the appendix or to develop their own arguments as they analyze examples and cases.

We have found it helpful to maintain an explicit relationship between the flow of course material and the real world of public management. Students tend to react well to regular discussions of public management in the news, based on current events that illustrate course themes and ideas. Students might be asked to submit news items for inclusion in this segment of class discussion. Involvement and interaction among students outside of class may be enhanced by using a course-based online learning platform to post and discuss such items.

Although we emphasize the skill of making rational arguments, we know that emotions, deeply held convictions and ideologies, and prior experience and beliefs matter, too. They affect choice and action in all branches and at all levels of government. Incorporating this reality into managerial analysis and argument does not mean that managers should appeal to emotions instead of to common sense and considerations of efficiency and effectiveness. It means that managers should understand how particular arguments are likely to be filtered through the values and emotions of citizens, legislators, and public officials. As the account in Chapter 11 shows, Paul Vallas was effective because his arguments reflected a causal understanding of school improvement that was persuasive.

When all is said and done, public management is about making good on those values and commitments that have been given expression in public policies and laws, about satisfying citizens' expectations that their governments will perform honestly and effectively. Doing so is a matter of personal character and democratic values, about caring and serving, but it is more than that. Public managers are at the vortex of America's uniquely complex constitutional scheme, with the intense cross pressures created by its separation of powers and checks and balances. To be effective requires intellectual, behavioral, and emotional strengths of a high—in many cases an extraordinary—order. But that is the kind of challenge the Founders of the Republic created. And there are few deeper satisfactions than meeting such challenges successfully.

Acknowledgments

In addition to those acknowledged in the first edition, we are grateful to Meredith Freed for research and documentation assistance as we prepared the second edition.

From CQ Press, we thank Charisse Kiino for her faith in this project and for guidance and good advice from start to finish; Matthew Byrnie, Sarah Calabi, and Suzanne Flinchbaugh for editorial guidance on the second edition; Katie Lowry and Bennie Clark Allen for their help and patience in preparing this book for publication and seeing it through production; Allison Hughes for her guidance on ancillaries; and Amy Whitaker for her efforts and advice concerning marketing. Thanks also to Michelle Ponce for her copyediting and Mary Mortensen for her superb craft in preparing the indexes.

Finally, the forbearance and sustained support of our spouses, Patricia R. Lynn and Andreas W. Lehnert, enabled us to concentrate on preparing both editions of this book. We thank and love them.

About the Authors

Carolyn J. Hill is associate professor of public policy at the McCourt School of Public Policy at Georgetown University and a senior fellow at MDRC. Her research focuses on whether and why public programs are effective and how they can be improved. Her work has been published in the *Journal of Public Administration Research and Theory,* the *Journal of Policy Analysis and Management,* the *Review of Economics and Statistics,* and other journals. With Laurence E. Lynn, Jr. and Carolyn J. Heinrich, Hill is the author of *Improving Governance: A New Logic for Empirical Research.*

Laurence E. Lynn, Jr. is the Sydney Stein, Jr. Professor of Public Management Emeritus at the University of Chicago. His research focuses on governance, public administration, and public management. His books include *Public Management as Art, Science and Profession, Madison's Managers: Public Administration and the Constitution* (with Anthony M. Bertelli), and *Public Management: Old and New,* and he is co-editor of the *Oxford Handbook of Public Management.* He has received the John Gaus lectureship award from the American Political Science Association, the Dwight Waldo and Paul Van Riper awards from the American Society for Public Administration, and the H. George Frederickson Award from the Public Management Research Association.

PART I ANALYZING PUBLIC MANAGEMENT'S CHALLENGES

The Fundamentals

Public management ... is a world of settled institutions designed to allow imperfect people to use flawed procedures to cope with insoluble problems.[i]

—James Q. Wilson
Bureaucracy: What Government Agencies Do and Why They Do It

Virtually all of us are aware of government: the federal, state, and local legislatures, agencies, commissions, and courts which make, administer, and enforce the laws that govern and serve us. We have probably studied American history and civics in school. Most of us know about our government through necessary interactions with governments and public employees face-to-face, online, and through the mail. Most of us vote. The news media inform us about elections, policy issues and debates, and the decisions of lawmakers, public officials, and judges. For tens of millions of us, our livelihoods depend on government, and we may understand much more about how government works because we are, or know, public employees, government contractors, participants in nonprofit or civil society organizations, or engaged, activist citizens.

Despite these types of familiarity, most of us may nonetheless view the government as distant and amorphous: it is "them", not "us." It is "city hall," "Washington," "the bureaucracy." And most of us don't trust it.

The government is made up of both elected and unelected officials (the infamous unelected bureaucrats). Do their decisions and actions reflect our society's values and meet our needs and expectations? Can we trust government to perform effectively? Our opinions about these questions may vary widely, depending on how much we are affected by or involved in government. Yet a sobering fact is that most

---

[i]James Q. Wilson, *Bureaucracy: What Government Agencies Do and Why They Do It* (New York, NY: Basic Books, 1989), 375.

> At the heart of government are public officials whose job is public management. They work for the departments, bureaus, agencies, and offices of federal, state, and local governments, and they are responsible for transforming the goals and objectives of policymakers into tangible operating results.

Americans do not trust government "to do what is right."[ii] Distrust of "big government," reflected early on in the Boston Tea Party, has grown in recent years as the United States has experienced the Vietnam War, Watergate, Iran-Contra, Hurricane Katrina, the 2008 financial crisis and the subsequent "Great Recession," and National Security Agency surveillance revelations. We have duties as citizens to understand our governments at a level beyond a Twitter feed, headline, or sound bite. We all have an interest in building governments that reflect our values, meet our expectations, and earn our trust. A large part of this responsibility is developing a greater understanding of public management. This book aims to develop that understanding and to improve the chances that public managers' decisions and actions reflect our society's values, perform effectively, and earn the people's trust.

At the heart of government are public officials whose job is public management. They work for the departments, bureaus, agencies, and offices of federal, state, and local governments, and they are responsible for transforming the goals and objectives of policymakers into tangible operating results. "We the people" base our opinions about government on these results. Yet most public managers are largely invisible to us unless they make mistakes. They are the unelected bureaucrats we both depend on and distrust.

Public management is hard work. Unlike managers in the corporate sector, public managers often operate in highly charged, uncertain, and hostile political environments. Elected representatives make the laws that create public agencies and provide their budgets. Bargaining and compromise over the conflicting interests of politicians and their constituencies influence the responsibilities of public managers and the structures and resources of the organizations for which they work, seldom resulting in technically rational organizations that can be managed efficiently and effectively. Yet at the same time, politicians demand efficient and effective performance of the technically irrational organizations they created. Often public managers have been given wrenches to pound nails, gloves that don't fit, maps leading to different destinations.

Public managers must make the best of it. They must be capable of reconciling the tensions between political rationality and technical rationality. They must do so, moreover, in environments where organizations, people, and resources constrain what they can do, instead of enable what they could do if they were managing in the private sector. The jobs of public managers are often regarded as impossible: no matter what they do, critics will say they should have done something else.

So how can public managers do the impossible? One thing above all is essential: their guiding principle must be accountability to and within the rule of law. Accountability means, in the first instance, legality: finding and complying with the laws governing a situation. Most agencies are governed by numerous statutes, regulations, court rulings, and administrative guidelines. Exactly what the law is may not always be clear, however; court rulings and interpretations may be in conflict. The manager must make every effort to know and be answerable to lawmakers, even when the law may change from one legislative session or court session to the next.

Accountability is about more than observing the letter of the law, however. It is also about acting in accordance with the spirit of the law: minding the public and community interests that the rule of law is intended to serve. As citizens, we obey the letter of the law when driving a car on public roadways. We obey the law not only to avoid

---

[ii]Pew Research Center for People and the Press, "Trust in Government Nears Record Low, but Most Federal Agencies are Viewed Favorably," Survey Report, October 18, 2013. Retrieved from http://www.people-press.org/files/legacy-pdf/10-18-13%20Trust%20in%20Govt%20Update.pdf.

getting a ticket but also because safety is in the community's interest as well as our own. Likewise, a public manager's lawfulness, while a personal interest, also serves public interests—in public health, an educated citizenry, fairness in law enforcement, the protection of civil rights—that inspired enactment of the laws. In Aristotelian terms, lawfulness means managing in the interests of collective justice.

Public managers must have the capacities to make decisions, manage people, and cope with the stress that is associated with uncertainty, ambiguous authority, limited resources, and political conflict. Beyond these abilities, public managers must have the capacity to think critically and analytically about what the law, the task, common sense, and collective justice require. By doing so, they are more likely to perform effectively and produce results that earn the public's trust.

PUBLIC MANAGEMENT'S THREE DIMENSIONS

This book lays out a framework for analyzing the challenges faced by public managers. The framework conceptualizes three distinct but interrelated dimensions of public management:

- **Structure:** the lawfully authorized delegations to administrative officials of the authority and responsibility to take action on behalf of policy and program objectives;
- **Culture**: the norms, values, and standards of conduct that provide meaning, purpose, and motivation to individuals working within an organizational unit; and
- **Craft:** the manager's own individual efforts in goal setting, taking appropriate actions, leading, and explaining and justifying what the organization is doing.

This framework draws on many concepts and tools derived from the social sciences and public policy analysis. It fully encapsulates public managers' dual roles as both creatures of their political environments and creators of the capacity to implement public policies that arise within those environments.

Each dimension is evident in responses to Hurricane Katrina. In August 2005, Hurricane Katrina overwhelmed the City of New Orleans and the U.S. Gulf Coast, creating the costliest natural disaster in American history to that point. Hurricane Katrina was public management's perfect storm: a confluence of events, politics, policies, and personalities that pushed America's Constitutional scheme of governance, like New Orleans's levee system, beyond its breaking point. What happened during and following the storm, while revealing acts of responsible and selfless heroism, also exposed fundamental weaknesses in our governing institutions.

The story of Hurricane Katrina is partly about politics, such as the politics of public works spending by the U.S. Army Corps of Engineers, and partly about policy, such as the federal government's responsibilities for responding to emergencies and assisting state and local governments to confront them. It is foremost, however, a story about what officials with managerial responsibilities did prior to, during, and after the storm—and why they did it.

The story of public management in the aftermath of Hurricane Katrina constitutes an appropriate touchstone for the issues and ideas in this book. The introductions to Parts II through V include examples, through the lens of each dimension, of how the Katrina emergency was managed. The source of these examples is the U.S. Senate report on the response of governments to the unfolding emergency.[iii]

[iii]U.S. Senate, *Hurricane Katrina: A Nation Still Unprepared: Special Report of the Committee on Homeland Security and Governmental Affairs* (Washington, DC: Government Printing Office, 2006), http://www.gpoaccess.gov/serialset/creports/ katrinanation.html.

PART I OVERVIEW

Part I of this book comprises three chapters:

- Chapter 1 describes the domain of public management and its distinctive challenges, the basic logic of public management in the three-dimensional framework, and a model deliberative process for public management analysis.
- Chapter 2 describes the fundamental role of public managerial accountability to the rule of law, the meaning of the rule of law, the practice of lawful and accountable public management, and the importance of thinking institutionally.
- Chapter 3 presents a case study of the events surrounding revelations in 2013 and beyond of U.S. National Security Agency surveillance of private communications. Immersion in the case's details is an opportunity to apply the ideas and analytical frameworks from Chapters 1 and 2 and to confront the complexity of many intersecting features of public governance in the United States.

This part of the book provides answers to three questions:

1. **What do public managers do and why?**

2. **How are unelected public managers held accountable to citizens affected by what they do?**

3. **What insights might be gained into the fundamental issues of democratic governance and of managerial responsibility by studying the dauntingly confusing case of what leaked classified documents revealed about the U.S. government's surveillance of Americans' private communications?**

1 Public Management's Three Dimensions

Structure, Culture, Craft

PUBLIC MANAGERS AND THE DOMAIN OF PUBLIC MANAGEMENT

Public managers are all around us. They work in the departments, agencies, bureaus, and offices of federal, state, and local governments. The responsibilities of public organizations vary from providing basic public services, such as education, fire fighting, and law enforcement, to regulating environmental pollution and the safety of coal mines, gathering and analyzing intelligence needed for national security, and providing health care to military veterans. The characteristics of public organizations vary as well, in terms of budgets and personnel, diversity of mission, complexity of tasks, degree of centralization or decentralization, extent and sources of political support. But the secretary of defense and the official in charge of a local animal control office have one thing in common: they are both public managers.

Across all these settings, public managers are responsible for translating the goals and objectives of policymakers into tangible operating results. Public management is the process of ensuring that the allocation and use of resources available to governments are directed toward the achievement of lawful public policy goals. What does this mean in practice? What factors determine the purposes and responsibilities of public managers' roles? How much discretion do they have in deciding how to do their jobs?

Broadly speaking, public managers may be thought of as both **creatures** of their political environments and **creators** of capacities needed to achieve results for themselves and their organizations. Put another way, they are both constrained and enabled in how they implement public policies.

Characterizations of public management that emphasize its creature aspects focus on structural arrangements such as organizational hierarchies. In these accounts, the emphasis may be on elements such as bureaus, offices, job descriptions, and reporting relationships. An essay written by Luther Gulick for President Franklin D. Roosevelt's "Committee on Administrative Management" in 1937 illustrates this perspective, in which public managers were depicted as obediently carrying out specific functions

> **Public management is the process of ensuring that the allocation and use of resources available to governments are directed toward the achievement of lawful public policy goals.**

necessary for the operation of public departments and bureaus: planning, organizing, staffing, directing, coordinating, reporting, and budgeting, functions (POSDCORB).[1] An early doctrine in American public administration, the **politics-administration dichotomy** held that politics and administration could (and should) be separate and distinct activities.[2] This sentiment reflected in part a desire to eliminate corruption and partisanship from the administration of public programs and in part a view that administration was a scientific, not a political, activity.

Characterizations of public managers as creators tend to assume that managers (especially senior officials) have considerable latitude to exercise their own judgment. Public managers create opportunities, policy, direction, administrative structures, and organizational relationships within their spheres of influence. For example, in *The Functions of the Executive*, Chester Barnard argued that a primary task of the organization's leader is to create and shape a culture that can unify employees and improve organizational performance.[3]

This book's definition of public management views the public manager both as creature—of politics, law, structures, and responsibilities—and as creator—of strategies, capacity, and results. The reality of how governments work does not support a politics-administration dichotomy: Politics and policymaking result in mandates that are often ambiguous, subject to conflicting interpretations, politically controversial, and inadequately supported with resources and structures of communication and cooperation. As a consequence, public management necessarily completes policymaking by making concrete decisions within the limits of delegated authority and motivating subordinates and organizations to act in appropriate ways. Thus, in addition to the directive activities uniquely associated with managing, the job of a public manager often involves the realms of politics, policymaking, and institutional leadership. Each of these roles, depicted in Figure 1.1, has a distinctive influence on public policy outcomes.

The domain of **politics** is concerned principally with the distribution and use of control over government resources, summed up nicely in the title of political scientist Harold Lasswell's book *Politics: Who Gets What, When, How.*[4] According to the U.S. Constitution, citizens have sovereign power, and their wishes are given expression through elected representatives in the political branches of government. Politics gives expression to citizen preferences, traditionally referred to as "the public will" and allocates resources among political jurisdictions, interests, policies, processes, and programs in order to express that will.

The domain of **policymaking** is concerned with defining substantive goals of politics and choosing from among alternative courses of action that reflect the values, interests, and facts of given situations and actors. Policymaking involves the subject matter of governmental activity, the making of specific choices concerning the substantive content of statutes, appropriations, organizations, regulations, budgets, strategies, and precedent-setting decisions. Policymaking is inevitably influenced by political values and processes, but the reverse is also true: as political scientist E. E. Schattschneider observed, "new policies create a new politics."[5]

In the context of a particular setting, situation, program, policy, or deliberation, certain individuals assume the responsibility for clarifying purposes and inspiring others to take action toward a focused goal. According to historian and political scientist James MacGregor Burns, **leadership** occurs "when persons with certain motives and purposes mobilize, in competition or conflict with others, institutional, political, psychological, and other resources so as to arouse, engage, and satisfy the motives of followers . . . in order to realize goals mutually held by both leaders and followers."[6] Leadership is essential when purposes are unclear, when a sense of direction is absent, when the situation is characterized by confusion and conflict, or when motivation is lacking.

In the following sections of this chapter, additional ideas and concepts that are central to this book's argument are explained: historical origins of public management as a distinctive function of societal governance; essential

FIGURE 1.1	The Domain of Public Management

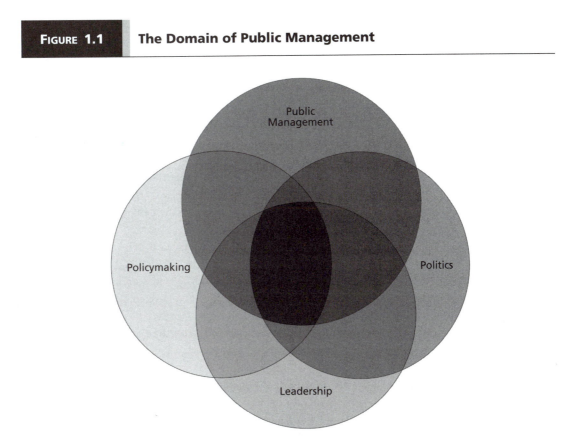

differences between public and private management; distinctive challenges of public management; necessity for managerial accountability to the rule of law; a three-dimensional analytic framework—structure, culture, and craft—by which public management issues and problems can be understood and confronted; and a model deliberative process for public management analysis.

HISTORICAL ORIGINS OF PUBLIC MANAGEMENT

Only in recent decades has public management become a recognized field of research, teaching, and practice around the world. The origins of the field's ideas are, however, ancient.[7] Broadly construed, **public administration and management**, the term used by many scholars, have characterized the earliest quests for order, security, wealth, and civilization.

Examples of bureaucratic government, codified administrative doctrines, and best practices appeared in ancient Chinese, Greek, and Roman civilizations. Confucius argued that the "conductor of government should 'hold the mean'" by which he meant "to approach a problem by seeking the widest differences of opinions and by making the most careful study of the facts in the spirit of absolute impartiality and unselfishness, and then to solve it moderately, practicably, and logically, in accordance with the best ethical rules."[8] Ancient Chinese administrative doctrines influenced public administration in medieval Europe, evident in the thirteenth to seventeenth centuries, where recognizable corporate and bureaucratic forms of public management were adopted in several regimes.[9]

Some scholars trace the emergence of modern public administration and management to a more recent period, however. These accounts regard public management as "the sum of persons and bodies who are engaged, under the direction of government, in discharging the ordinary public services which must be rendered daily if the system of law and duties and rights is to be duly 'served.'"[10] This kind of management grew in Europe, following two critical developments:[11]

- First, beginning in 1640, a succession of German rulers created an absolutist state (central and absolute power, typically of a monarch, unchecked by other institutions). It broke with medieval tradition by instituting administration by trained and competent civil servants acting on behalf of a "public interest" rather than out of narrow dynastic loyalties. Public service was a duty to the people rather than to the feudal nobility. The consequence was the emergence of a field of study and practice termed **cameralism**. (The word refers to the room or place [*kammer*] where the domain is ruled.) Cameralism was "the academic counterpart of modern bureaucratic administration and, hence, in its essence was administrative science."[12]
- Second, beginning in the late eighteenth century, intellectual and political developments leading to national sovereignty would culminate in the emergence of bureaucracies. Servants of the monarch became public officials, government by officials became known as bureaucracy, and bureaucracy became both powerful and controversial. With state building largely accomplished on the continent, "the struggle for legalizing or constitutionalizing these great administrative mechanisms" began.[13] The popular revolutions in the United States, France, and continental Europe established the constitutional foundations for the governance of what became today's advanced industrial democracies.

By the end of the nineteenth century, the field of public administration and management had become preoccupied with the *de facto* separation of policy (that is, politics and policymaking) and administration. That development resulted in tensions between an institution (bureaucracy, with its proclivities toward overreach) and the revolutionary idea of popular sovereignty (with its expectation of the democratic accountability of public administrators). Law and economics eclipsed the older administrative sciences of cameralism in intellectual discourse. The dominant intellectual contribution of the era, however, is Max Weber's analysis of bureaucracy (discussed in Chapter 5), which colors contemporary professional discussions of bureaucratic institutions.

The role of a stabilizing governance institution was served by centralized bureaucracies in Europe and by Parliament in England. In the United States, the Constitution has served this role since the institution of judicial review was established in 1803. But separation of powers and the superordinate role of the courts in the United States also greatly complicate the matter of establishing a legitimate role for "unelected bureaucrats." The field of public administration and management in the United States, and the challenges of conceptualizing managerial responsibility, directly reflect the unique constitutional tensions between executive, legislative, and judicial branches of government.

PUBLIC AND PRIVATE MANAGEMENT: HOW SIMILAR? HOW DIFFERENT?

Is managing a government department or agency fundamentally different from managing a private corporation? Answering this question requires looking beyond individual managers' styles, decisions, and strategies to a broader landscape that encompasses the purposes, interests, and opportunities of the public and private sectors and the respective environments, constraints, and authority affecting public and private management.

Nọ
Gain

Arguing that the interests of public and private organizations are fundamentally different, political scientist Frank Goodnow noted in 1893: "In transacting its business, [the government's] object is not usually the acquisition of gain but the furtherance of the welfare of the community. This is the great distinction between public and private business."[14] Later, political scientist Graham Allison acknowledged that some similarities exist between public and private management, but the differences are far more important.[15] More recently, on the basis of exhaustive review of research on similarities and differences between the sectors, public management scholars Hal Rainey and Young Han Chun argue that differences between the sectors exist, but they should not be overemphasized lest the generic aspects of "management," that is, tasks that all managers must perform, be obscured.[16]

Fundamental Differences in the Public and Private Sectors

Underlying the differences in public and private management are two characteristics of the sectors in which they work. First, public sector organizations exist for the "furtherance of the welfare of the community" because market failures occur: the tendency of free markets to over- or underproduce goods and services the public wants and needs. Second, public sector organizations embody the political and legal processes that created them.

When Markets Fail

The first characteristic differentiating the public and private sectors is the presence of what economists call **market failures,** the tendency of profit-seeking firms to allocate resources in ways that are efficient from the firm's perspective but inefficient from society's perspective. The most common examples, discussed in this section, are the for-profit sector's failure to provide public goods; choices of production methods that have beneficial or harmful externalities; information asymmetries and other problems that lead to phenomena called moral hazard and adverse selection; and the distributional consequences of goods and services such as education and health care.[i]

Public goods are those goods and services for which consumption by one person does not affect the amount that others can consume, that is, they are **nonrival in consumption**. Often, these goods are **nonexcludable** as well, meaning that it is difficult or impossible to restrict the availability of the good to everyone once it is made available to anyone. Familiar examples of public goods are the safety and protection of property afforded by police officers and firefighters or the availability of public roadways and their illumination by streetlights. If the public depended on the market to produce goods like public safety or roads, people who benefit from them might not pay for them because they would expect others to pay; that is, they would **free ride** on the outlays of payers. As a consequence, private providers, uncertain of profitably, would be reluctant to produce these kinds of goods. In such cases, elected representatives are asked step in and arrange for provision by government.

Many goods exhibit varying degrees of nonrivalry or nonexcludability, and thus the appropriateness of government's supplying them may be less clear; for example, National Public Radio and the Public Broadcasting Service are politically controversial. Some goods or services, such as education or health care, are provided by both government and the private sector; these goods, in turn, afford both public and private benefits.

Externalities are additional benefits or costs that occur from producing or consuming a good or service but that are not fully reflected in its price. Goods with positive externalities, such as vaccinations against contagious diseases like polio or the flu, result in benefits that are not fully reflected in the vaccine price. Thus, private producers tend to underproduce them; many people might not be able to get vaccinated, thus exposing others to a communicable

---

[i]Many public finance or public economics textbooks address these topics. See, for example, Harvey S. Rosen and Ted Gayer, *Public Finance,* 10th ed. (Boston: McGraw-Hill Irwin, 2013).

disease. Goods with negative externalities, such as the emission of greenhouse gases and the use of polychlorinated biphenyls (PCBs) in production processes, result in costs or harms that are not fully borne by the producer or consumer and tend to be overproduced. Here, too, government may step in to regulate producers of negative externalities or to subsidize producers such as those who provide green energy with reduced harmful emissions.

Information problems—in particular, **information asymmetries**—occur when the parties involved in a transaction, such as the exchange of work effort for a salary or the sale of insurance against the high costs of illness or the loss of employment, have different information about why and how the transaction should be completed. The problem is that it may be impossible or costly for each party to know everything the other knows such as an employer's exact expectations and a worker's actual skills and motivation. **Moral hazard** exists when, for example, individuals insured against the costs of illness or against income loss from unemployment are careless about their health or less determined to remain or become employed. **Adverse selection** occurs, for example, when insurers lack information about applicants that would influence their decisions about whether to issue the insurance or how to set premiums. Governments step in to regulate information availability and how information may or may not be used, such as credit worthiness or preexisting medical conditions.

Information problems also arise in cases where it may be impossible or costly for consumers to become well-informed about the choices they face or whether they have received what they have paid for. Private sector producers might exploit information asymmetries or imperfect information in ways that are dangerous or harmful, leading to a role for government in overcoming such information problems. The Consumer Product Safety Commission (CPSC) and the Food and Drug Administration (FDA) play such roles. The CPSC is empowered to ban dangerous consumer products, to recall products already on the market and to research potential hazards associated with consumer products, from baby cribs to lawnmowers. In recent years, the FDA has been under pressure to ensure that pharmaceutical manufacturers supply consumers of already-approved prescription drugs with up-to-date information concerning harmful side effects—information that manufacturers may be reluctant to provide voluntarily.

Distributional inequity may occur even when markets are performing efficiently. The public's preferences regarding the fair distribution of income and wealth, or access to particular goods and services such as primary health care, are not guaranteed even if classic market failures are absent. Private producers have little or no incentive to address issues of poverty or wealth inequality or, more specifically, to create an adequate supply of affordable housing or affordable health insurance. Therefore, a potential role is created for the public sector either in subsidizing the production of such goods or, as is the case with the federal Medicare program, in actually providing them.

Public organizations are often created to do what markets cannot or will not, do, that is, to provide public goods, ameliorate information problems, and ensure distributional equity. Public organizations rebalance and redirect resource use in ways that are thought by their proponents to secure higher levels of social welfare than what unregulated private markets, driven by material self-interest, would produce. The choice between private and public organizations need not be a matter of either-or, however. Nonprofit organizations, which are part of the private sector but legally precluded from distributing any surplus revenues to officers or members, also respond to market failures. (Nonprofits are discussed further in Chapter 5.) In addition, policymakers and private resource owners may rely on forms of organization or policy tools, such as vouchers or performance contracts, which are intended to combine the advantages of government authority with market choice and competition: the power of public authority to marshal resources and set terms for their use and the power of interest-driven voluntary choice to direct resources to their best uses.

> **Public organizations are often created to do what markets cannot or will not, do, that is, to provide public goods, ameliorate information problems, and ensure distributional equity.**

When Public Bureaucracies Fail

The second characteristic differentiating the public and private sectors is the legal authority underlying public sector organizations. As political scientists Donald Kettl and James Fesler put it, "Public organizations exist to administer the law, and every element of their being—their structure, staffing, budget, and purpose—is the product of legal authority."[17] The nature of this authority is determined by political processes: public organizations are constrained and governed by incentives that are basically political.

Insight into the interplay of public management with politics and public policymaking has been the focus of political scientist Terry Moe's research.[18] As explained in Chapter 5, Moe develops a theory of public bureaucracy in which public organizations are characterized by four elements not found in private, for-profit organizations:

- Public organizations are governed by public authority.
- Public organizations have a political rather than a technical/economic basis for organizational design.
- Public organizations are subject to the uncertainties of political processes.
- Public organizations reflect a necessity for political compromise.

Together, these four characteristics result in organizations, programs, and managerial roles that result from bargaining among politicians, interest groups, and bureaucrats. In other words, they reflect **political rationality**, not the **technical rationality** found in profitable private firms. Each agency, whatever the technical requirements of effective organization might be, is a structural reflection of its unique politics.[19] As a result, the public manager "may have to deal with inadequate resources, unreasonable or unrealistic workload or reporting requirements, inconsistent guidance, or missions defined so as to be virtually unachievable."[20]

Although market failures provide justification for what has been called **positive government**, economist Charles Wolf has emphasized the occurrence of **nonmarket failures** (sometimes called *pathologies* by other scholars) by public organizations that regulate or produce goods or services.[21] Wolf points to four primary sources of nonmarket failures:

- disconnects between the raising and spending of revenues;
- internalities, that is the subordination of the public interest to organizational interests such as budget growth and information control;
- derived externalities, which are the unintended consequences of government programs, such as the urban sprawl associated with public highway construction; and
- government-created distributional inequities, which are both intentional and unintentional and may result, for example, from the need to ration publicly financed goods and services because of budget constraints.

These problems arise, Wolf argues, because of the supply and demand characteristics of government output. Measures of public policy outcomes are often so hard to define that feedback and signaling from consumers of public services are lacking or unreliable. Thus, internal decision making by nonmarket organizations cannot be informed by these sources. Furthermore, incentives controlling costs that are created by competition are often weak or nonexistent for public agencies. Under these circumstances, nonmarket agencies often develop standards of performance that do not bear a clear or reliable connection with the ostensible public purpose that the agencies are meant to serve.[22]

Wolf argues that nonmarket failures reflect a number of other aspects as well:

- the political processes that create public organizations,
- the separation of payment for and receipt of benefits provided by the public sector,

- the difficulties of measuring output,
- the production of such goods by a monopolistic public agency,
- uncertainties regarding production technologies for many goods provided by the public sector, and
- the absence of assured processes for terminating ineffective programs that have politically influential constituencies.

Together, these characteristic features of the public sector—the work of public organizations in responding to market failures and the reflection in public organizations of the political processes that created them—substantially shape the internal and external environments of public managers.

What Do We Know from Research?

In his foundational study of the differences between public and private management, Graham Allison argued that the two types of management are "fundamentally alike in all unimportant respects." He compared three primary aspects of management in each sector:

- strategy (establishing organizational objectives and operational plans);
- internal components (organizing and staffing, personnel management systems, and measuring performance); and
- external constituencies (communicating and coordinating with internal units, external organizations, the press, and the public).

By informally comparing the jobs of a public and private manager—the Environmental Protection Agency (EPA) director and the chief executive officer of American Motors—Allison concluded, "public and private management are at least as different as they are similar, and . . . the differences are more important than the similarities."[23] He argued that public management could best be improved by specific research on the subject, lesson-drawing from actual practice, and selective application of private sector management practices and principles to the public sector.

A persistent belief dating back to the U.S. industrial revolution holds that competitive free enterprise is inherently superior to government in meeting societal needs. More recently, the push to improve government performance has been sustained by arguments that public organizations can be, and should be, run more like businesses. In other words, public and private management may in fact be different, but they should not be as different as they are. In this view, running government more like a business involves practices such as "steering instead of rowing," decentralizing authority, maintaining a focus on the customer, measuring performance and concentrating on outcomes rather than outputs, and using economic incentives instead of being guided by rules and regulations.[24] Many of the ideas associated with this perspective were reflected in New Public Management reforms around the world, the Clinton Administration's Reinventing Government initiative that was launched in 1993, and the passage of the Government Performance and Results Act in 1993.

Since the 1980s, empirical research has examined the basis for claims of similarities or differences of the efficiency and effectiveness between the sectors. Barry Bozeman developed a framework reflecting **degrees of publicness**.[25] He argued that sectoral distinctions—public, nonprofit, for-profit—based on legal distinctions are not as significant as the source of organizational authority. In particular, it matters that authority comes primarily from consumers, politicians, or founders and donors (as in nonprofits).

An important source of evidence regarding the differences between public and private management is empirical research conducted by Hal Rainey and Young Han Chun.[26] The authors first describe the differences between the sectors that researchers and practitioners often report. One difference is the environments in which public and private managers operate: Public organizations seldom sell a product or service, and they have few incentives for efficient production. Another difference lies in the greater scrutiny of public organizations by legislators, watchdog groups, the Government Accountability Office (GAO), and the like. The differences are also evident in organizational roles, structures, and processes (such as expectations for accountability and fairness); diverse and unclear goals; constraints on authority imposed by political actors; red tape and procedural delays; incentive structures; and values and attitudes.

Rainey and Chun's review of the empirical research literature finds conflicting conclusions across studies: Some claims about differences between the sectors are supported by empirical evidence, such as more red tape and personnel administration problems in the public sector. Other claims are not supported. For example, Rainey and Chun find mixed evidence whether public sector managers have higher or equal levels of work satisfaction than managers in the private sector. Public manager work satisfaction is as high as their counterparts in the private sector, but public managers tend to express specific dissatisfactions with work.[27] For both public and private managers, being able "to make a difference" in the work of their organization shows a strong relationship to job satisfaction.[28]

Are Public and Private Management Different?

Senior executives in all types of complex organizations have common preoccupations with goals, people, organizational resources, task accomplishment, and constituencies. They must spend time meeting with people with whom they must compromise to achieve their goals, they must choose a leadership style that motivates subordinates, and they must deal with substantive and organizational complexities. Yet Rainey and Chun conclude,

> Numerous studies have found that public managers' general roles involve many of the same functions and role categories as those of managers in other settings but with some distinctive features: a more political expository role, involving more meetings with and interventions by external interest groups and political authorities; more crisis management and "fire drills"; greater challenge to balance external political relations with internal management functions.[29]

Where does this mass of evidence, claims, and counterclaims leave those who are trying to understand the differences and similarities between the sectors and why they matter? There is no simple answer; comparisons must necessarily be qualified. Laurence Lynn sums up:

> The two sectors are constituted to serve different kinds of societal interests, and distinctive kinds of skills and values are appropriate to serving these different interests. The distinctions may be blurred or absent, however, when analyzing particular managerial responsibilities, functions and tasks in particular organizations. The implication of this argument is that lesson drawing and knowledge transfer across sectors is likely to be useful and should never be rejected on ideological grounds.[30]

EIGHT DISTINCTIVE CHALLENGES OF PUBLIC MANAGEMENT

In every public and private sector organization, managers encounter routine problems related to resources, personnel, priorities, technology, and task organization that are within their power to solve. For these problems, managers do not need the support of other organizations to take effective action. In such circumstances, managerial focus and accountability are primarily to their own employees and stakeholders. In the public sector, however, even decisions about "routine" managerial tasks can have wider consequences, which may range from merely regrettable to dire.

For example, during the relatively routine activity of moving a spacecraft at Lockheed-Martin (a National Aeronautics and Space Administration [NASA] contractor)[31]

- employees ignored several of the procedures and checks in place;
- only six people were present instead of the required eleven;
- the NASA quality assurance team member arrived late and signed off on already completed steps he had not observed;
- the cart to be used to move the spacecraft was not inspected at the time of the move; and
- the visual observation by one employee that "something looked different" about the cart was ignored.

The cart collapsed when the spacecraft was loaded onto it, causing $200 million in damage.

For "routine" problems like these, business executives can take steps to prevent future occurrences of similar problems by reallocating internal resources, arranging for additional training, or punishing lax performance, perhaps terminating employees. Managerial actions such as these almost certainly will ensure that such adverse events do not happen more often. Public managers, however, do not have the same tools that business managers do. They will face external pressures to explain what happened, who was responsible, and what they propose to do, and they may or may not be given the tools and resources to preclude future occurrences. Because of partisan politics, even routine matters can become crises.

> In the public sector, however, even decisions about "routine" managerial tasks can have wider consequences, which may range from merely regrettable to dire.

Potential consequences of managerial action are compounded, moreover, when public managers operate in situations that are beyond their ability to resolve solely on their own authority. In these circumstances, which are far more common in government than in business, actions of public managers can have social, economic, and public policy implications that may include the well-being of individuals and communities, the security of the nation, prospects for life and death, and the reputation of government for competence in accomplishing public purposes. A number of **distinctive challenges of public management** often characterize these more complex situations (Box 1.1).

Box 1.1 | **DISTINCTIVE CHALLENGES OF PUBLIC MANAGEMENT**

1. Confronting situations where solutions are beyond the manager's span of control.
2. Being responsive to powerful actors whose preferences and expectations are in conflict.
3. Ensuring accountability when control is lacking.
4. Learning about serious problems from outside sources.
5. Operating under constant critical scrutiny.
6. Making consequential decisions with partial information.
7. Contending with employees' ingrained values and beliefs.
8. Responding in a timely fashion to shifts in priorities.

1. **Confronting situations where solutions are beyond the manager's span of control.**

   Public managers may confront situations whose causes and solutions lie beyond their formal authority and their direct influence: they cannot increase their own budgets, nor can they direct the actions of another organization's employees whose assistance may be essential. Managers may require extensive voluntary cooperation from other officials who may have different interests and priorities. In order to develop a full assessment of a situation, they may need to obtain information from or share information with many organizations or jurisdictions. Doing so would enable them, for example, to "connect the dots" in tracking a serial killer or spy network.

2. **Being responsive to powerful actors whose preferences and expectations are in conflict.**

   Public managers may be under pressure to satisfy the preferences and meet the expectations of powerful actors—legislators and legislative committees, elected executives, judges, and interest groups—that are often in conflict. The EPA, for example, has conducted years of study and public comment solicitation regarding cleanup of PCBs that pollute the Hudson River in New York State. The General Electric Company (GE), source of the PCBs, initially opposed an EPA plan for dredging the river. GE challenged the scientific evidence on the harmfulness of PCBs and argued that natural processes would be sufficient to flush them out. The debate eventually involved lawsuits, administrative law hearings, and elected and appointed officials at the local, state, and federal levels. After years of argument, the EPA undertook a successful dredging project with GE's participation. Doing so required sustained efforts by public managers to overcome many obstacles in trying to accomplish what they believed to be their mission.

3. **Ensuring accountability when control is lacking.**

   Public managers must often ensure the accountability of subordinate agents over whom their authority, formal and informal, may be ill-defined or even nonexistent. For example, when reconstruction of war-damaged property began in Iraq, the United States relied on hastily arranged, opportunistic relationships with dispersed networks of local ministries and contractors. These relationships lacked formal accountability structures and blurred the distinction between assistance and occupation and between public and private liability. When projects went awry, numerous investigations were carried out by the Office of the Special Inspector General for Iraq Reconstruction, the Defense Contract Audit Agency, the GAO, and the inspectors general of agencies involved in reconstruction projects. Their findings of malfeasance and mismanagement have led to arrests and convictions and damaged the reputations of many public officials and private companies.

4. **Learning about serious problems from outside sources.**

   Public managers often learn about serious problems from media reports or legislative inquiries based on information leaked by their own employees, uncovered by investigative journalists using Freedom of Information Act authority, or legally provided by whistleblowers inside their own organizations. Managers may be put on the defensive and be expected to respond before they can assess situations that may be spinning out of their control. For instance, reports of the death of Buumba, a zebra at the National Zoo in Washington, DC, set in motion a series of allegations, investigations (including one by the National Academy of Sciences), and damaging revelations of internal management policies and actions. The zoo director, who had to accept responsibility for circumstances leading to the animal's death, never recovered from being put on the defensive and had to resign amid considerable controversy.

5. **Operating under constant critical scrutiny.**

   Public managers operate in an environment where their actions and statements are under constant scrutiny. As the Affordable Care Act's HealthCare.gov website was made accessible to the public on October 1, 2013, problems were reported immediately as some potential enrollees were unable to access the site at all, and others could not complete the process required to sign up for an insurance plan. Obama administration officials immediately came under fire for their failure to ensure a workable system that would operationalize the administration's signature policy initiative. News stories were constant for many months as public managers tried to recover from this embarrassing failure. Every action and explanation was subject to intensely critical and partisan scrutiny. Though the federal health insurance exchange eventually became functional and enrollment goals were met, the administration's reputation for competence was permanently damaged. The resignation of the Secretary of the Department of Health and Human Services months later was widely attributed to the poor public management that occurred during her tenure.

6. **Making consequential decisions with partial information.**

   Public managers may receive warnings of immediate but poorly defined threats to and vulnerabilities of their operations. They must decide whether and how to act in situations where the costs of acting, the uncertainties associated with any action, the consequences of being wrong, and the potential costs of inaction, are all extraordinarily high. For example, telecommunications workers inspecting a cable running through an obsolete concrete drainage tunnel under the Chicago River discovered a leak described as "a tree-like piling piercing through the tunnel roof with a mound of mud slowly growing at its base."[32] The damage may have been caused by construction work at a nearby bridge. The workers forwarded a videotape to the supervisor at Chicago's Department of General Services, who judged it to be a low priority and placed it in his desk drawer. Officials claimed that the situation was not serious and that they did not want to spend $10,000 maintaining a tunnel that was never used. Nevertheless, they began a bid process to repair the tunnels. While these managers were planning to contract for repairs following established procedures, the leak widened and finally ruptured, flooding the central business district (the famous Chicago Loop). The damage required expensive repairs and cleanups and provoked reprisals by the mayor against those (notably the acting transportation commissioner, a 30-year city employee) held responsible for failure to take timely action.

7. **Contending with employees' ingrained values and beliefs.**

   Public managers may have to contend with their permanent employees' ingrained values and beliefs that can be resistant even when change is desired by senior officials and the public. For example, investigations of the Columbia space shuttle accident and of intelligence collection and analysis activities prior to the U.S. invasion of Iraq focused on how the institutionalized values of agency personnel—the organizational cultures of NASA, the Federal Bureau of Investigation, the Central Intelligence Agency, and other agencies—influenced their assumptions and judgments. Employees tended to filter out dissonant information that did not fit prevailing patterns of belief—judgments that had disastrous, possibly preventable, consequences.

8. **Responding in a timely fashion to shifts in priorities.**

   Public managers may be in a situation where priorities or tasks shift suddenly or sharply. When the Federal Emergency Management Agency (FEMA) was incorporated into the newly formed Department of Homeland Security, for example, its focus was abruptly reoriented away from its traditional priorities of assisting states and communities with the consequences of emergency weather events, toward homeland security and combating terrorism. New federal policies governing FEMA's responses to weather emergencies were slow to be put in place. When Hurricane Katrina flooded New Orleans in 2005, FEMA managers were caught off-guard, and federal assistance to states damaged by the storm was neither timely nor well-coordinated. FEMA's administrator ultimately resigned, and the administration of President George W. Bush, which had initiated the policy shift and appointed FEMA's director, was badly damaged.

These kinds of complex public management challenges underlie most high-profile public affairs media coverage of the U.S. federal government in recent years: prisoner abuse at Abu Ghraib, Guantánamo Bay, and other U.S. detention facilities; a second fatal accident in NASA's space shuttle program; ongoing and seemingly irresolvable management problems at the Internal Revenue Service (IRS) and the Federal Bureau of Investigation (FBI); intelligence failures preceding the 9/11 terrorist attacks and the U.S.-led invasion of Iraq; the management of war and reconstruction in Afghanistan and Iraq; the revelations concerning National Security Agency (NSA) surveillance programs; and continuing controversies associated with implementation of the Affordable Care Act. Efforts by policymakers to effectively address these as well as the less dramatic challenges that arise throughout U.S. governments at all levels require sophisticated analysis and public managers who can think through, formulate, and execute complex strategies of amelioration and solution.

Their efforts are vindicated by numerous public management success stories: the largely effective management of the anthrax crisis by officials of the U.S. Postal Service in 2001; the success of Mayor Rudolph Giuliani's administration, particularly, Chief of Police William Bratton, in developing the Compstat system, which was associated with reducing crime in New York City; Oklahoma's use of an innovative performance contracting scheme, which brought about a dramatic transformation in the philosophies of nonprofit agencies serving profoundly disabled people and significantly improving their quality of life; and the success of James Lee Witt, director of the then-cabinet-level FEMA from 1993 to 2001, in transforming the agency from a political backwater into a widely respected emergency services organization.

These and other successful public management cases illustrate how—even in the face of the distinctive challenges of public management—combinations of effective enabling structures, deliberate attention to the transformation of organizational cultures, and skilled craftsmanship can bring about transformative changes in public policy outcomes.

MEETING THE DISTINCTIVE CHALLENGES OF PUBLIC MANAGEMENT

Analytical public managers and informed citizens aim to understand past failures and successes of public organizations and public managers. They aim to understand how current and future distinctive challenges of public management can best be met. Their efforts rest on three fundamental practices: referring to the rule of law as a guiding principle; thinking and acting in multidimensional terms of structure, culture, and craft; and analyzing likely causes and effects through a deliberative analytical process.

A Guiding Principle of Public Management: The Rule of Law

As public managers chart a path through both the routine tasks as well as the distinctive challenges they face, they are guided by the principle that they must act in ways that sustain faith in the rule of law. Citizens, elected officials, and judges place their faith in public managers because managers are accountable to constitutional principles and institutions: elected legislatures, elected executives, the courts of law that review political and administrative acts for their lawfulness, and the institutional checks and balances created by elected executives and legislatures. With respect to public management, the *rule of law* means that written principles and policies, created using recognized and accepted processes and procedures, are the basis for the legitimate exercise of managerial authority. The rule of law is a protection against arbitrary, capricious, and nontransparent acts by public managers.

Operationally, public management necessarily reflects the tensions inherent in three features of the American constitutional scheme: the Madisonian interplay of faction and power, the separation of powers, and checks and balances (discussed in Chapter 4). Public managers must live with and respond creatively to the challenges presented by these tensions.[ii]

First, the interplay of faction and power establishes the political context of public management. After political deliberation in which compromise is reached among contending individuals, parties, and interests, legislatures delegate responsibility and provide resources to public organizations and their managers. It is largely accidental if partisan debate, negotiation, compromise, or interventions by judges create public agency structures and processes that support technically rational management. Public managers must play the hands they are dealt by the political and judicial branches of government.

Second, separation of powers among the legislative, executive, and judicial branches means that public managers must balance the legitimate concerns and interests of legislators, elected executives, and judges who generally compete for control of public administration. Contests are common between public executives and legislative bodies over the release of information that executives assert is privileged. Such contests often spill over into the courts. Tensions between executives and legislators, on one hand, and each with the courts, on the other, are also common and play out in the confirmation of judicial nominees or in legislative restraints on the authority of the courts. Administrative law scholar Phillip J. Cooper suggests that Alexis de Toqueville's "observation that almost all important political problems in America sooner or later are recast as legal problems" might be brought up to date in the following way: "Sooner or later most important political problems in America are transformed into administrative problems which, in turn, find their way into the courts."[33]

The third feature of the constitutional scheme is a broad array of checks and balances that encroaches upon managerial discretion. Investigations by departmental inspectors general and the GAO, critical reports by watchdog groups, and information made available through leaks or Freedom of Information Act requests affect the environment in which public managers operate. Public managers cannot simply define the scope of their own authority, choose their own goals, and employ whatever organizations, personnel, strategies, and resources they think necessary to achieve their purposes. They cannot, as corporate managers can, freely choose the business they are in, the customers they wish to serve, the goods and services they provide, and the prices, quantities, and qualities of what they produce. Those kinds of choices are made by, subject to the approval of, or subject to the

---

[ii]For additional discussion of managing according to the rule of law, see Yong S. Lee with David H. Rosenbloom, *A Reasonable Public Servant: Constitutional Foundations of Administrative Conduct in the United States* (Armonk, N.Y.: M. E. Sharpe, 2005); and Anthony M. Bertelli, "Strategy and Accountability: Structural Reform Litigation and Public Management," *Public Administration Review* 64, (2004): 28–42.

review of, other internal authorities (such as budget or personnel offices) or external authorities (such as elected officials or the courts).

Lawmakers do not scrutinize every decision or every discretionary action by public managers. Legislative oversight often occurs only when something goes wrong. Courts can rule only on cases brought before them. Most of the time the legal bases for managerial activities are well in the background or have been institutionalized in accepted agency routines and practices and in taken-for-granted norms and standards of conduct.[34] But the rules, guidelines, applicable statutes, and judicial decrees are never far away, and controversies over their possible violation may erupt unexpectedly and with little warning. The occasional failure by a child welfare worker to conduct a home visit will ordinarily raise no concerns unless that child becomes a high-profile victim of violence. When that happens, the worker's superiors may find themselves in court answering for the worker's dereliction of duty.

For public managers, as political scientist Herbert Kaufman put it, "the slate is not clean."[35] What's on the slate? Thousands of pages of written directives and guidance, in statutes, government-wide regulations, departmental and bureau regulations, opinions and judgments by courts, the GAO, the Office of Personnel Management, and legislative hearings and floor debates.

Public managers have ample opportunity to exercise their judgment, that is, to be creators. In doing so, they are not free agents; they are creatures managing according to the rule of law. Thus, they are required to have a well-developed ethic of accountability to the institutions that enforce the rule of law.

> Public managers cannot simply define the scope of their own authority, choose their own goals, and employ whatever organizations, personnel, strategies, and resources they think necessary to achieve their purposes.

Thinking and Acting in Three Dimensions: Structure, Culture, Craft

Responding to the distinctive challenges of public management is likely to require a combination of interorganizational cooperation, satisfaction of diverse expectations, accountability to various stakeholders, coping with unexpected and unwelcome developments, evaluating advice of uncertain quality and reliability, and mobilizing skeptical employees to cooperate with managerial goals. Consider the following examples of substantive challenges that managers in the public sector must confront:

- ensuring that urban police departments under pressure to control crime also respect the civil rights of the citizens they are sworn to protect;
- changing the missions of federal and state agencies responsible for homeland security from prosecuting criminals to preventing acts of terrorism;
- introducing new information technologies to improve the effectiveness of organizations whose employees might perceive the change as threatening to their security and importance to the organization;
- achieving an appropriate balance between protecting children from harm and strengthening and unifying troubled families in the administration of child welfare policies and programs that call for removing children from homes if circumstances justify it; and
- managing regulatory agencies to achieve a reasonable balance between promoting and negotiating voluntary compliance with regulations and impartially detecting and punishing violators in areas such as aviation, mining, and consumer products.

Workable solutions that have a reasonable likelihood of success usually are not obvious or easy. Do the policies governing agency operations allow or impede needed change? Are assignments of responsibilities to and within the agency and the resources available—financial, human, and technical—adequate to meeting organizational objectives? Will agency personnel accept new directions or must internal resistance be overcome? Do public managers have the motivation, knowledge, and skills to discover and accomplish what needs to be done to reach the objectives?

Successfully meeting the distinctive challenges of public management requires appropriate levels of delegation and oversight by policymakers, organizations whose employees can adapt to new circumstances while maintaining or improving reliability and quality of service, and high levels of political and administrative skill, commitment, and creativity on the part of public managers.

In responding to the many challenges they face, public officials must figure out how to reflect society's values, perform effectively, and earn the public's trust. Political savvy and an engaging managerial personality will help, but they are not enough. Managers can do better than "muddling through"[36] or "managing by groping along."[37]

This book argues that informed citizens and public managers themselves can gain appreciation for the challenges of public management and can gain insight skills for addressing those challenges by acquiring the habit of thinking in terms of public management's three distinct but interdependent dimensions: structure, culture, and craft (Figure 1.2). Three-dimensional analysis helps an engaged citizenry understand the challenges and possibilities of public management and will materially assist public managers to recognize what the law, the task, common sense, and collective justice require of them.

> Informed citizens and public managers themselves can gain appreciation for the challenges of public management and can gain insight skills for addressing those challenges by acquiring the habit of thinking in terms of public management's three distinct but interdependent dimensions: structure, culture, and craft.

A three-dimensional approach that invokes aspects of structure, culture, and craft relates well to public debates about the performance of public agencies. The structure dimension—the organizational structures and processes that distribute information, responsibility, and resources in ways that further policy and organizational goals—is similar to the rational/legal perspective on authority first set forth by Max Weber. It is also the basis for policymakers' preference for organizational solutions to management problems.[38] The culture dimension—employees infused with beliefs, values, and motivation that enhance the organization's reputation for reliability and for skilled and conscientious performance—reflects the growing popularity of the idea that governing involves far more than demanding compliance with directives by public employees who have minds, motives, interests, and values of their own. The craft dimension—responsible judgment by individual public managers concerning priorities, strategies, and methods to advance the achievement of those goals and to build organizational capacity—reflects the tendency in the United States to assign responsibility for success and failure to specific individuals and to create narratives featuring heroes and scapegoats when things go right or wrong.

The Structure Dimension

The early twentieth-century study of public administration and management focused on the importance of organizational structures that would ensure efficient performance by America's rapidly emerging administrative state. Following that tradition, a typical analysis of structure is concerned with how responsibilities are assigned and how processes of communication, deliberation, and decision making are enabled and constrained. The **unit of analysis** for this approach (that is, the entity for which information is collected and analyzed) is the organization or the system as a whole.

As a dimension of public management, **structure** is defined as lawfully authorized delegations to administrative officials of the authority and responsibility to take action on behalf of policy and program objectives. In

| FIGURE 1.2 | **Public Management's Three Dimensions** |

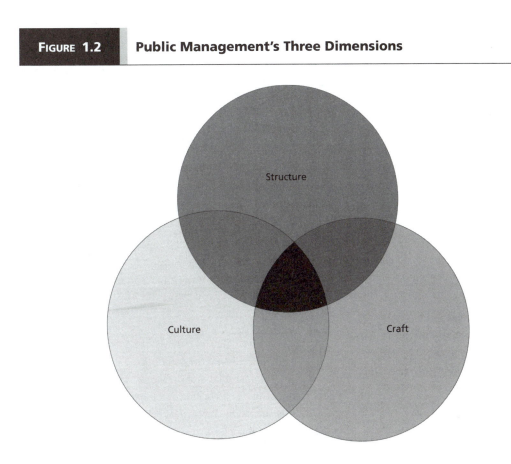

practice, structures are defined in the provisions of authorizing statutes; in approved legislative budgets; in executive orders, regulations, and rules that have the force of law; in decisions and directives by executives and managers within their spheres of authority; and in injunctions and consent decrees (agreements reached by plaintiffs and defendants pursuant to settling lawsuits and approved by courts).

Structures both enable and constrain what public agencies and public managers can do. Delegated responsibilities and authorities may include creating additional administrative structures; establishing planning, decision-making, and communication processes; prescribing specific standards for the performance of functions and tasks; and allocating specific levels of personnel and budgetary resources to agency offices and activities, together with rules and guidelines for their use.

The Culture Dimension

The culture dimension of public management began to emerge as the study of organizations became more sophisticated beginning in the 1930s. A typical analysis of culture focuses attention on the beliefs, values, and norms that govern and motivate employee behavior. First termed the "informal organization," these aspects of an organization can either inhibit or advance the fulfillment of the public's interests as expressed by actions and decisions of its elected representatives. In this approach, the unit of analysis may be either the organization's employees, who are seen as individuals with aspirations and values of their own, or the organization as a whole when **institution-alized values** can be identified.

As a dimension of public management, **culture** is defined as the norms, values, and standards of conduct that provide meaning, purpose, and motivation to individuals working within an organizational unit. Culture is institutionalized: members of an organization "acquire values that go beyond the technical requirements of organizational tasks."[39] In another expression of this concept, institutionalization is "the emergence of orderly, stable, socially integrating patterns out of unstable, loosely organized, or narrowly technical activities."[40] Institutionalized values constitute a unifying source of meaning and purpose that formal structures of authority and assignments of responsibility cannot provide by themselves.

In the context of organizations, it is common to talk about institutionalized values as organizational cultures. The dedication and seeming selflessness of public school teachers, emergency room doctors and nurses, and those who place themselves in danger in service to others are widely admired. Organizations may be spoken of as having high morale, a strong sense of mission, or a "can-do attitude." However, institutionalized values may impede organizational goal accomplishment or a manager's efforts to respect and balance differing values. Organizational cultures may or may not reflect or even acknowledge values prevailing in the community or in the wider society. When this is the case, for example, in the cases of racial profiling by police departments, tensions between public agencies and those who depend on them may arise.

The Craft Dimension

The craft dimension is concerned with how executives and subordinate managers can manage more effectively within their given political and organizational environments. In this approach, the individual manager is the primary unit of analysis. As a dimension of public management, **craft** is defined as the decisions and actions by which individual public managers exert an influence on the achievement of public policy outcomes

Even when delegations of authority to subordinate officials are definitive, the necessity for managers to exercise their own judgment is inevitable:

- Officials are explicitly expected to make judgments when legislators lack the expertise or inclination to be specific in their authorizations.
- Statutory delegations may be ambiguous, incomplete, or inconsistent, leaving public managers little choice but to exercise judgment concerning how policy and program implementation will proceed.
- Even when the rules and standards governing managerial behavior are clear, whether and how to apply them to specific cases or contexts may require managerial or supervisory judgment.

The craft perspective recognizes that public managers' personal judgments and skills—or the lack thereof—have demonstrable consequences for their organizations. Their qualities of mind, temperament, and character and their capacity for analysis and reasoned judgment can have life and death implications, affect the distribution of rewards and punishments among citizens, and influence communications and the flow of information. These processes are at the heart of policymaking and the successful promotion of organizational change. Within frameworks of formal authority, moderated by appropriate institutionalized values, individual managers can affect whether, what, when, and how policy and program implementation occurs.

Each of public management's three dimensions can affect organizational effectiveness and the achievement of public purposes. But public management hardly ever consists of just one dimension. Adequately addressing managerial problems typically requires awareness and use of all three dimensions. This kind of three-dimensional thinking about complex management challenges, intended to provide the intellectual foundations for managerial practice, is the goal of public management analysis.

> **Public management analysis involves the habitual resort to three-dimensional thinking and the insightful use of theories and heuristics. Doing so can lead to a more thorough, in-depth understanding of the role of structure, culture, and craft in causing specific management challenges and in addressing them.**

Analyzing Public Management: A Model Deliberative Process

When confronting the distinctive challenges of public management, responsible public officials must think systematically and analytically about the origins or causes of the problems they face. They must formulate and weigh alternative solutions in terms of their likely consequences for public policy outcomes. They must articulate reasons for the strategies and actions that they believe are appropriate in given situations. And they must diagnose and respond to unfolding events and analyze past situations.

Effective public managers think analytically about topics ranging from whether and how to contract out the production of public services, how to recruit and motivate employees, how to organize successful collaborations, how to allocate scarce budgetary resources, and how to manage a specific program or project. Their analyses support informed decisions regarding courses of action on these and many other matters.

Thinking analytically and arguing persuasively are complementary skills. The skills needed to think analytically, public policy scholar Giandomenico Majone points out in his book *Evidence, Argument, and Persuasion in the Policy Process,* "are not algorithmical [reducible to rote, routine procedure] but argumentative: the ability to probe assumptions critically, to produce and evaluate evidence, to keep many threads in hand, to draw for an argument from many disparate sources, to communicate effectively."[41] The processes of argument and analysis are inextricably related: Analysis supports arguments, and arguments are the outcomes of analysis. Understanding the structure of argument or reason substantially adds to the public manager's toolkit. The Appendix of this book describes philosopher Stephen Toulmin's approach for developing and articulating arguments.[42]

The goal of analytical thinking is, first, to identify the underlying causes of situations requiring managerial attention and, then, to identify relationships that link actions to likely consequences. Next, the analyst creates arguments based on logic and evidence. Public management analysis involves the habitual resort to three-dimensional thinking and the insightful use of theories and heuristics. Doing so can lead to a more thorough, in-depth understanding of the role of structure, culture, and craft in causing specific management challenges and in addressing them.

The basic steps of a model deliberative process that supports analytical thinking and action involve examining a situation through the three dimensions of structure, culture, and craft.[iii]

> Step 1. ***Gather facts, form initial opinions and ideas***. When presented with a situation or set of facts, an analyst might form opinions, supported by reasons, based on his or her own prior experiences or knowledge or on some facts in the case that strike him or her as particularly telling or revealing.

[iii]For additional material on reframing, see Lee G. Bolman and Terrence E. Deal, *Reframing Organizations: Artistry, Choice, and Leadership,* 3rd ed. (San Francisco, CA: Jossey-Bass, 2003), esp. chapters "Integrating Frames for Effective Practice" and "Bringing It All Together: Change and Leadership in Action"; Jonathan R. Tompkins, "Excellence in Government," in *Organization Theory and Public Management* (Belmont, CA: Thomson Wadsworth, 2005); Ian Palmer and Richard Dunford, "Reframing and Organizational Action: The Unexplored Link," *Journal of Organizational Change Management* 9 (1996): 12–25; Christine M. Pearson and Judith A. Clair, "Reframing Crisis Management," *The Academy of Management Review* 23 (1998): 509–576.

Box 1.2	**MODEL DELIBERATIVE PROCESS FOR PUBLIC MANAGEMENT ANALYSIS**

1. Gather facts, form initial opinions and ideas.

2. Analyze facts through lens of three dimensions (3D: structure, culture, craft).

3. Develop and synthesize insights from 3D analysis, drawing on specific theories and frameworks. Use counterfactual analysis to identify potential causal mechanisms.

4. Formulate specific strategies based on 3D analysis.

5. Form persuasive arguments for internal and external audiences.

Step 2. *Analyze facts through lens of three dimensions (3D)*. An analyst uses each of the three dimensions—structure, culture, craft—as a lens through which to examine the facts of the situation: the formal structural and procedural aspects, the facts that reveal an organization's institutionalized values and norms, and the potential contribution of managerial style, skill, and judgment.

Step 3. *Develop and synthesize insights from 3D analysis*. The analyst integrates and synthesizes insights from the three dimensions, drawing not only on the broad ideas of structure, culture, and craft but also on specific frameworks, concepts, theories, and ideas within each dimension illustrated in this book. The analyst considers questions such as

→ How might the formal organization enable and constrain individual public managers to support organizational objectives more effectively?

→ Are some classes of structures and techniques likely to be more effective than others in overcoming the specific problems at issue and, if so, why?

→ How does the organization's culture affect the prospects for success of restructuring?

→ What type of leadership and direction will be needed to promote organizational change efforts, both cultural and structural?

The analyst can use counterfactual analysis, discussed later in this section, to identify potential causal mechanisms.

Step 4. *Formulate specific strategies based on 3D analysis.* The analyst formulates strategies to address the challenges at hand. Potentially effective strategies may emphasize one, two, or all three of the dimensions of public management. If employees are likely to see needed change as consistent with their values, cultural resistance may not be a factor. If the strategy is primarily a matter of changing employee commitments, restructuring may not be necessary. If the strategy is a matter of replacing a particular subordinate, then craft alone may be all that is needed. Good strategic choices, however, will be grounded on a consideration of how all three dimensions are or might be employed effectively.

Step 5. ***Form persuasive arguments for internal and external audiences.*** After arriving at this stage through internal analysis and argument, the analyst formulates persuasive arguments intended for internal or external consumption to support these strategies. Arguments with different emphases might be used in different forums—employees, executive branch budget reviews, legislative testimony, public statements, internal advocacy—to build momentum for the strategy's adoption.

The insights and lessons from three-dimensional analysis are suitably intuitive for addressing management problems in the public sector. Further, this type of analysis enhances appreciation of the different sources of public management knowledge:

- experiential knowledge derived from the actual experiences of public managers;
- normative or ideological knowledge derived from principled belief systems or from established norms and standards; and
- academic or empirical knowledge derived from theory-based analyses of quantitative and qualitative data. Its academic sources can be research that is based in social and behavioral science disciplines and fields, such as economics, political science, sociology, organizational theory, cultural anthropology, and social and cognitive psychology, among others.

In addition to being multidimensional, public management analysis is inherently multimethod and interdisciplinary; no one type of knowledge or understanding will suffice to comprehend and resolve complex problems. The model deliberative process can be employed by informed citizens and public managers to develop judgment and skill as they synthesize insights from diverse sources. The examples discussed throughout the book and the cases presented at the end of each chapter provide opportunities for practicing this set of skills.

An understanding of causality and causal mechanisms can further hone analytical skills in the model deliberative process, especially the third and fourth steps. In the physical sciences, a causal relationship is present when a cause is both necessary and sufficient for producing the effect. A necessary condition "must be present for an event to occur" and a sufficient condition "guarantees that the event will occur whenever it is present [but] the event may occur in its absence."[43] In the social sciences, it is extremely difficult (if even possible) to identify both necessary and sufficient conditions linking a purported cause and its effect(s). An alternative and relatively straightforward concept of causality that can be useful to analytical managers, articulated by sociologist Paul Lazarsfeld, points to three elements:

1. The cause must happen before the effect.

2. An empirical association (based on experience or observation) must exist between the cause and the effect.

3. Other explanations of the cause-effect relationship must be eliminated (that is, spurious or confounding factors must be ruled out).[44] If one can think of an additional characteristic or factor that is not accounted for in the analysis, and if it is related both to the characteristic being considered and to the outcome, then a causal relationship between the hypothesized cause and the observed effect cannot be established.

To see how these ideas might apply in managerial analysis, consider the following. A public elementary school principal (a public manager) wants to improve the performance of students in her school. By reviewing the last year of data, the principal notices that students whose teachers attended the state's flagship public university tend to score higher on standardized tests than do students whose teachers attended other universities. The principal initially concludes that if she hires only graduates from the state flagship university, the performance of students in her school will be higher.

To analyze whether the relationship between the purported cause (a teacher attends the state's flagship university) and effect (average student performance is higher) is causal, the principal can use Lazarsfeld's criteria:

- The first criterion holds because teachers attend the state university before they teach at the school and therefore before student performance is assessed.
- The second criterion also holds because the principal's analysis detects an empirical association between teachers' degree institutions and students' performance.
- The third criterion likely does not hold, however. It may be the case that better-performing students are placed in the elementary classrooms of the state university teachers to begin with. Or perhaps particular types of individuals whose characteristics lead them to be more effective teachers choose to go to, or are admitted to, the state flagship university. So it is not necessarily the state flagship university education per se, but the characteristics of individuals who choose to go there, that is linked to student performance. Or perhaps the state university has a particularly effective approach to elementary education; other universities that use the same approach produce equally effective teachers, but teachers from those universities don't happen to be in the principal's school at the time. All of these situations describe spurious factors that invalidate the conclusion that a cause-effect relationship exists between a teacher graduating from a particular university and improved student performance in that teacher's classroom.

Lazarsfeld's criteria for causality provide a helpful frame for identifying a causal relationship (or its absence). Yet James Bradley and Kurt Schaefer argue that a "mechanism" or "conceptual framework" that justifies an expected relationship between a cause and its effects is really needed for understanding such relationships in the social sciences in particular.[45] Such explication of causal mechanisms provides a guide for action. Furthermore, the need for describing such mechanisms is arguably greater still when it is not possible to establish Lazarsfeld's criteria, a very common state of the world in the social sciences, especially in public management, where it can be extremely difficult to identify causal relationships. Thus, the door is opened for the theories and frameworks of the social sciences, which provide an important resource for developing hypotheses about causes and effects.

These ideas, incorporated into the model deliberative process, can be used to gain analytic traction and to identify the most important aspects of structure, culture, and craft in a situation.

Another useful concept for considering causal mechanisms is the **counterfactual**: what would the outcome have been in the absence of the hypothesized cause? For example, what would student performance have been if the students and their teachers had been the same in all respects *except* that the teachers with flagship university degrees had instead earned their degrees at another institution? This question is literally unanswerable because the same person cannot simultaneously experience two different states of the world. For this reason, the field of program evaluation is focused on constructing approximations of the true counterfactual so that the potential causal effects of programs, policies, and other interventions can be identified.

From that field's literature, it is well established that the ideal counterfactual estimate is approximated through conducting a random assignment experiment. Even though most situations encountered by public managers will not have the benefit of experimental evidence to establish counterfactuals, public managers can still use the concept of the counterfactual to consider critically the relationship between specific evidence or causes and presumed effects, as will be illustrated in Chapter 3.

Because public managers operate in spheres of political rationality, both values and analytic concepts necessarily play a role in analysis and argument. Arguments for action may be based on different interpretations of the same information or "facts," especially when causal relationships are unclear or unspecified. In an analysis of program performance assessments made by the federal Office of Management and Budget, for example, public management scholar Donald Moynihan concluded, "performance information is used, but the meanings assigned to such data are subjective and will be interpreted and debated among different actors consistent with their values, training, motivations, partisan positions, and cognitive characteristics."[46]

> Because public managers operate in spheres of political rationality, both values and analytic concepts necessarily play a role in analysis and argument.

These differing interpretations are not necessarily a bad thing, however. The task of policymaking and public management is not only to put arguments forward but also to critique the arguments of others in the policymaking process in order to expose their biases, flaws in reasoning, and faulty evidence. Such policy debates, whether conducted within or between the branches of government can lead to greater enlightenment for the public as to what is at stake in taking a proposed course of action. The alternative would be a debate based solely on values and beliefs with no attempt by any actors in the process to put forward reasons or evidence of any kind.

ORGANIZATION OF THE BOOK

This book characterizes public management as a multifaceted endeavor. It emphasizes the fundamental dimensions—structure, culture, craft—that define, enable, and constrain the practice of public management. It traces the authority of public management to the rule of law, emphasizes management analysis that uses the method of argument, and describes frameworks and concepts upon which informed citizens and practitioners can draw. The primary goal of this book is to improve the practice of public management by helping readers better prepare for its intellectual and practical challenges.

The book is divided into four major parts:

Part I comprises Chapters 1, 2, and 3, which lay the foundations for analyzing public management's distinctive challenges. Chapter 1 provides an analytic framework for understanding the domain of public management, distinguishing it from private sector management, explaining its foundation as the rule of law, and setting up an expectation for analytical public management. Chapter 2 further explains how the legitimacy of public management is derived from and is ultimately accountable to institutions—elected legislatures, elected executives, and judicial institutions—all of which are both prescribed by the Constitution and operate under its aegis. The applicability and implications of the ideas in Chapters 1 and 2 are examined in a case, set forth in Chapter 3, that provides an account of a quintessential public management story: how the electronic surveillance conducted by the NSA became known to the U.S. public because an employee of an NSA contractor leaked a trove of classified documents to the press.

Part II (Chapters 4, 5, 6, and 7) is concerned with the structure dimension, or the concrete expressions of public policy. It addresses the enabling and constraining structures and processes that are formally mandated in legislation, guidelines, regulations, and court orders, and the resultant realities and incentives faced by public managers and their subordinates. Chapter 4 addresses structures arising from a constitutional scheme of governance, including checks and balances and federalism. It also discusses local and regional governments.

Chapter 5 addresses the politics of administrative structures, the bureaucracy as direct government, and externally authorized structures that enable and constrain the work of public managers. Chapter 6 considers structural tools that managers use within their spans of control to enable and constrain others in policy and program implementation. Chapter 7 discusses regulations and rules, including the evolution of regulation and a depiction of the regulatory state.

Part III (Chapters 8 and 9) is concerned with the culture dimension, or the institutionalized values and organizational cultures that emerge within organizations. Discussed here are the values, ethics, and motives unique to individuals in their own right (Chapter 8) as well as the shared norms, values, and understandings that provide meaning, purpose, and motivation to individuals in their roles as employees of an organizational unit (Chapter 9).

Part IV (Chapters 10 and 11) is concerned with the craft dimension, taking an actor-focused view of public management that considers individual decision, choice, and behavior. The discussion of managerial styles in Chapter 10 considers type, personality, and leadership. Then the discussion of managerial heuristics in Chapter 11 addresses deliberation and decision making, learning, and strategy.

Part V, Chapter 12, brings together the essential and interactive aspects of the three dimensions of public management. Do citizens prefer to have public managers who are entrepreneurial and visionary, who take risks on behalf of creating public value? Or, do they prefer public managers to take care that the laws are faithfully executed, minimizing instability and emphasizing reliability and transparency? Popular rhetoric may favor the former, but individuals in their roles as citizens and taxpayers are likely to favor the latter. What are the tensions inherent in such preferences, and how do they play out in specific situations? How can current and future public managers balance these tensions? Chapter 12 builds on previous chapters to illustrate these tensions and discusses **three-dimensional (3D) public management**.

Because the vast majority of public managers are employed by organizations, the text adopts the organization as the primary unit of analysis. *Organization* in this sense does not solely connote formally separate entities. It may also refer to entities such as departments, agencies, bureaus, offices, contractors, or nonprofit organizations. Ideas such as coordinated or networked management are explored, but interorganizational issues are viewed from the perspective of organizational participants and their motivations and incentives to participate (or not) in such arrangements.

Throughout the text, the ideas are illustrated with examples from real public management situations, case materials, academic research, and official reports and documents drawn from national, state, and local levels of government. Some of the problems and their illustrations are broad or high level—reforming the FBI, ensuring safe space shuttle operations, ensuring service quality and effectiveness by child welfare agencies—to illustrate the multidimensional character and importance of the sociopolitical context in which public managers operate. Other problems and illustrations have more instrumental or operational orientations—instituting performance measurement, contracting, interagency coordination—to illustrate the managerial dilemmas that arise within a hierarchical yet decentralized, pluralistic political system. The examples describe both successes and failures. Successes can inspire, motivate, and exemplify. But, as it is often easier to learn from failure than from success, the examples are weighted toward the former.

As emphasized in the Part I introduction, it is the responsibility of informed citizens to develop a greater understanding of and appreciation for public management. By doing so, together we can improve the chances that public managers' decisions and actions reflect our society's values, perform effectively, and earn the people's trust.

KEY CONCEPTS

Creatures
Creators
Politics-administration dichotomy
Politics
Policymaking
Leadership
Public administration and management
Cameralism
Market failures
Public goods
Nonrival in consumption
Nonexcludable
Free ride
Externalities
Information asymmetries
Moral hazard

Adverse selection
Distributional inequity
Political rationality
Technical rationality
Positive government
Nonmarket failures
Degrees of publicness
Distinctive challenges of public management
Unit of analysis
Structure
Institutionalized values
Culture
Craft
Counterfactual
Three-dimensional (3D) public management

CASE ANALYSIS: COULD "THE SYSTEM" HAVE SAVED THE CHILDREN OF BANITA JACKS?

On January 9, 2008, the bodies of four young girls (ages 5, 6, 11, and 16) were found in a Washington, DC, house by U.S. marshals. The officers were performing a routine search as they served an eviction notice to its occupant, Banita Jacks. Jacks—the mother of the four girls—was charged with their murder. Authorities estimated she had been living in the house with the girls' corpses since at least September 2007, and perhaps as long as 8 months, since May 2007. Early on, it seemed obvious that Jacks was responsible for the death of the girls (and she would be convicted on four counts of murder in July 2009).

Could "the system" have saved the four girls?

A Tragedy

Banita Jacks had raised her four daughters—Brittany Jacks, Tatiana Jacks, N'Kia Fogle, and Aja Fogle in the DC Metro and Maryland areas. The timeline released by Mayor Adrian Fenty's office would indicate that interactions with DC government were recorded as early as December 2005 (when Banita Jacks applied for housing assistance). The timeline shows other interactions with DC government in 2005 and 2006: applications for the Temporary Assistance For Needy Families (TANF) program, Medicaid, food stamps, residence at the DC hypothermia shelter, enrollment of the children in charter schools, reports to the Child and Family Services Agency (CFSA), well child visits. But reports indicate that when Nathaniel Fogle Jr., the father of the two younger girls, died in hospice in February 2007, "troubles spiraled" for Banita Jacks and her daughters.[47]

(Continued)

(Continued)

The bodies of the girls were found by the U.S. marshals on January 9, 2008:

> The eviction proceedings were set in motion in August when a mortgage loan company filed a complaint in DC Superior Court seeking a judge's order to take over the home after a foreclosure. Aurora Loan Services bought the property at a foreclosure sale in May, court papers show. After no one responded to the complaint, a judge granted the court order in October, clearing the way for the eviction action.[48]

The marshals were "met at the door by a calm woman who offered no clue about what would be found inside the house."[49]

The Mayor's Office Responds

Two days after the bodies were found, Mayor Fenty released a timeline that began in December 2005 and ended in January 2008 (Figure 1.3). It described contacts between the family and five DC government agencies:

- The CFSA
- The DC public schools (DCPS)
- The DC Metropolitan Police Department (MPD)
- The Department of Human Services (DHS)
- The Department of Health (DH)

And on January 13, demonstrating his pledge to "create a more responsive, accountable government," Fenty fired six child welfare workers because they "just didn't do their job."[i]

FIGURE 1.3	**Memo from Mayor Adrian Fenty and Timeline for DC Government Contact with the Jacks/Fogel Family**

Government of the District of Columbia
Executive Office of the Mayor

Immediate Release
January 11, 2008

Contact: Dena Iverson
202.727.6914
dena.iverson@dc.gov

Fenty Presents Timeline of District Government Contact with Jacks Family
Outlines initial efforts to ensure child welfare accountability

Washington, DC—Following a critical case review by City Administrator Dan Tangherlini and Interim Attorney General Peter Nickles, Mayor Adrian M. Fenty laid out a timeline of the District government's case

---

[i]Petula Dvorak and David Nakamura, "Fenty Fires 6 in Girls' Deaths," *The Washington Post*, January 15, 008, p.1, http://www.washingtonpost.com/wp-dyn/content/article/2008/01/14/AR2008011401001.html.

history with members of the family of Banita Jacks. Jacks was arrested on January 9 in connection with the discovery of four bodies, preliminarily identified as her daughters, in her Southeast Washington home.

The daughters of Ms. Jacks have been identified as Brittany Jacks, 17, Tatiana Jacks, 11, N'Kia Fogle, 6, and Aja Fogle, 5. The family had contact with DC government agencies dating back to December 2005. Initial review determines five District agencies had contact with the family of Banita Jacks:

- Child and Family Services Agency
- DC Public Schools
- Metropolitan Police Department
- Department of Human Services
- Department of Health

A full and formal review continues to be conducted by the City Administrator and the Attorney General offices, and they have been instructed by Mayor Fenty to take appropriate personnel action with any employees responsible for failures in the case, to include employment termination.

"While the loss of any life is tragic, this case is particularly devastating," said Mayor Fenty. "We will not rest until we have done everything possible to make sure that policies and procedures are in place to make sure that something like this never happens again."

Mayor Fenty committed to the following actions to address issues raised in this case:

- Review every CFSA case closed with a status of "incomplete" to ensure everything possible was done to resolve the case. The Jacks' case was deemed incomplete and closed without confirmation that the family had left the jurisdiction.
- Revamp policies for CFSA social workers regarding cases work completion
- Establish system that facilitates better tracking and monitoring of "home school" families
- Strengthen the ability to track children as they move from school to school within DCPS and Public Charter Schools by fully integrating and implementing well as those that leave District schools through the longitudinal data warehouse currently being developed
- The City Administrator and Attorney General will meet with the Office of the Inspector General to present all the facts gathered and request a full inquiry by the office.

Timeline for DC Government Contact with the Jacks/Fogel Family

December 6, 2005 – DCHA:
Banita Jacks applies for housing assistance on December 6, 2005. At the time of her application, she listed her address as 933 - 3rd Street, N.W. She listed Nathaniel Fogel as her spouse and four female children. It appears that she had never been an active participant in any DCHA housing program.

December 14, 2005 – DHS:
The Jacks/Fogel family entered DC General Hypothermia Shelter on 12-14-05 and exited on 4-9-06. This appeared to have been the family's first and only use of the shelter system. Their destination upon exiting shelter was to live with family/friends. Ms. Jacks entered shelter with her significant other-Nathaniel Fogel and 4 daughters.

(Continued)

FIGURE 1.3 (Continued)

December 21, 2005 – DHS:
The Jacks/Fogel family applies for TANF, Medicaid, and Food Stamp and gives 1900 Mass Ave, SE (DC General Hypothermia Shelter) as their address.

January 13, 2006 – DCPS:
Brittany Jacks enrolls at Eastern High School.

January 18, 2006 – DCPS:
Tatianna Jacks enrolls at Watkins Elementary School.

April 9, 2006 – DHS:
The Jacks/Fogel Family leaves DC General Hypothermia Shelter on 4-9-06 to "live with family and friends."

June 16, 2006 – DOH:
Banita Jacks has a behavioral health Medicaid visit.

July 12, 2006 – CFSA/DOH:
CFSA receives report from a nurse at the family's Medicaid health plan that Mr. Fogel checked himself out of George Washington Hospital where he was apparently receiving treatment for leukemia. Both parents are said to have substance abuse issues and the family is reportedly living in a van. The caller could not provide an address, and CFSA could not follow-up on the inquiry.

August 30, 2006 – Charter School Board:
Brittany Jacks enrolls at Booker T. Washington PCS.

September 5, 2006 – DCPS:
Aja Fogel and Tatianna Jacks enroll at Meridian PCS.

September 6, 2006 – DOH:
Tatianna Jacks and Aja Fogel have a well child Medicaid visit.

September 20, 2006 – DOH:
N'Kiah Fogel has a well child Medicaid visit.

October 5, 2006 – DCPS:
N'Kiah Fogel enroll at Meridian PCS.

November 30, 2006 – DHS:
The Jacks/Fogel family Food Stamp benefits were terminated on 11/30/06 for failure to provide requested information. Failure to recertify for food stamps results in an automatic systems termination every six months.

December 7, 2006 – DOH:
The Medicaid health plan spoke to Banita Jacks on the phone to encourage her to come in for care.

January 14, 2007 – MPD
Banita Jackson arrested by MPD for driving an unregistered vehicle, improper use of tags, and failure to exhibit permit.

<u>February 19, 2007:</u>
Nathanial Fogel died in a hospice in Maryland.

<u>March 3, 2007 – Charter School Board:</u>
Brittany Jacks last attends Booker T. Washington PCS.

<u>March 21, 2007 – Charter School Board:</u>
Tatianna Jacks, N'Kiah Fogel and Aja Fogel are unenrolled from Meridian PCS.

<u>April 27, 2007 – CFSA:</u>
A social worker at Booker T. Washington PCS called CFSA hotline to report an "educational neglect" case because the Brittany Jacks missed 33 days of school and hadn't been to school since March 2, 2007. Booker T. Washington social workers attempts to visit home, but mother would not let her in.

<u>April 28, 2007 – CFSA:</u>
CFSA's social worker attempted to contact the reporter and was informed by recorded message that the reporter was not available.

CFSA social worker visited the home of Ms. Banita Jacks (4249 6th Street SE) to complete an initial assessment. No one answered the door and the social worker left written information requesting client to contact the social worker.

<u>April 30, 2007 – Charter School Board/MPD/CFSA:</u>
Booker T. Washington social worker visits Jacks home again and speaks with Banita Jacks, but is denied entry. She calls MPD to come to home and alerts CFSA social worker and reported that the mother appeared to have mental health issues and was possibly holding Brittany hostage by refusing to allow her to attend school.

MPD officers visit home of Ms. Jacks and report to CFSA social worker. Officer reported that he visited the home and saw the children at home. According to the Officer, the children appeared to be well and healthy. When the Officer inquired why the children were not in school, Ms. Jacks informed him that the children were being home schooled. Jacks told officers that without warrant, MPD could not enter.

The Officer informed her of the proper procedure for home schooling children in the District of Columbia. The Officer reported that he observed books that Ms. Jacks had for the children.

<u>May 1, 2007 – CFSA/MPD:</u>
CFSA social worker along with Police Officer attempted to reenter the home; however, after repeated knocks by the Officer, no one answered.

<u>May 2, 2007 – CFSA:</u>
The social worker attempted a third time to contact Ms. Banita Jacks and no one answered.

The social worker confirmed with Penn Attendance Intervention Center that the children were not currently enrolled in DCPS.

<u>May 4, 2007 – MPD:</u>
Officer Scott made contact with Penn Attendance Intervention Center to inquiry if Penn Center could intervene.

(Continued)

| **FIGURE 1.3** | **(Continued)** |

May 5, 2007 – CFSA/DCPS:

CFSA social worker contacted DCPS to inquire about the home schooling policy. He was informed that DC has no law governing home schooling. He stated that all a parent had to do is to request a form from their school. DCPS will then authorize the parent to proceed with home schooling.

May 11, 2007 – CFSA:

The CFSA social worker completed a referral to the Diligent Search Office to locate the Jacks family.

May 16, 2007 – CFSA:

The CFSA Diligent Search Office reports an address that was used by Banita Jacks of an individual they believed to be a relative in Waldorf, MD.

The social worker wrote to Charles County after first speaking to an intake person and subsequently confirmed that Charles County also attempted to visit the family and were unable to contact them. The social worker submitted for case closure on May 16, 2007, and the Supervisor approved closure on May 16, 2007, based information received from Diligent Search Office, which indicated that the family was believed to have moved out of jurisdiction.

June 13, 2007 – Charter School Board:

Brittany Jacks is unenrolled from Booker T. Washington PCS.

June 14, 2007 – CFSA:

Received letter from Charles County child welfare restating attempt to locate but was unable to locate the family.

October 31, 2007 – DHS:

The Jacks/Fogel Family TANF benefit terminated 10/31/07 for failure to recertify. All benefits on the EBT card have been exhausted. TANF recertification is annual but the termination requires worker intervention.

January 2008

The Jacks family is enrolled in Medicaid. Medicaid recertification is 12 months and is extended for four months beyond the termination date, unless the customer dies, moves out of the District, or voluntarily withdraws from the program.

No known contact with DMH, APRA, DYRS, DHS/EEAC.

Source: http://www.washingtonpost.com/wp-srv/metro/documents/jackstimeline011108.pdf.

Was It "The System"?

News reports filled in details about some of the interactions in the timeline:

- The first alarming report . . . came in July 2006, when the nurse contacted the child protection agency. Fogle had checked himself out of the hospital, and the caller was concerned that one or maybe both parents had substance abuse problems, Fenty said. The caller said the family was living in a van. "Unfortunately, that call went into a CFSA hotline, and the hotline worker immediately closed the case because the family did not have a fixed address," Fenty said. "We have already investigated that as an incident that was not handled properly."[50]

- Tapes of a phone call involving Kathy Lopes, the social worker from Booker T. Washington Public Charter School, showed her to be "increasingly frustrated." In a call on April 30 with police, she reported: "From what I could see, the home did not appear clean. . . . The children did not appear clean, and it seems that the mother is suffering from some mental illness, and she is holding all of the children in the home hostage."[51]
- In a phone call to the CFSA hotline, Lopes said, "The parent was home. She wouldn't open the door, but we saw young children inside the house. . . . Her oldest daughter, who is our student, was at home. She wouldn't let us see her."[52] In response to that hotline call, *The Washington Post* reported:

  > The operator took the information and reminded Lopes, who was clearly distraught that she could not talk to Brittany, that Jacks did not have to let her inside the home. When Lopes called again April 30, she talked with a police nonemergency, 311 operator. "I've been transferred all over. I need someone to go out to a home where I believe abuse and neglect is occurring, and I don't want to be transferred to someone else," Lopes said. "It's an urgent matter. CFSA is pretty much sitting on it, and I would like someone to go to the home and check out the home, 'cause I wasn't allowed in it."[53]

- The girls' enrollment in charter schools is listed on the timeline. But laws and administrative processes were in place that prevented further follow-up after Banita Jacks withdrew the girls from these schools:

  > The school system's home-school office requires parents to fill out a form to obtain approval to withdraw their children from the schools. But the charter schools have no such policy.

  > "When a parent chooses to withdraw their student, a charter school must honor their request, and the charter school does not have the authority to certify the parent's capacity to home-school," said Nona Mitchell Richardson, spokeswoman for the Public Charter School Board. "The parent does not have to provide where the student is going when he withdraws."

  > According to the Home School Legal Defense Association, the District and 14 states provide "low regulation" of home-schooling. Maryland and Virginia, like 17 other states, provide "moderate regulation."[54]

- In response to Fenty's firing of the six CFSA staff, Richard Wexler, the executive director of the National Coalition for Child Protection Reform, pointed out the legal restrictions on the CFSA caseworkers:

  > Even though the police found nothing wrong, a caseworker returned—with police—the following day, but no one answered the door. The next day the worker tried again.

  > What else should the CFSA have done?

  > o Break down the door? That's illegal in America.
  > o Get the police to break down the door? Still illegal.
  > o Get a search warrant and then break down the door? On what grounds? There's no evidence of abuse or neglect—a school social worker's assessment of cleanliness is not evidence. It's not even clear that the children are truant, because apparently, there are few rules about removing children from charter schools and home-schooling them.

(Continued)

(Continued)

> Most important, doing more in this case, such as canvassing the neighbors, would steal precious time from a lot of other cases that, without benefit of hindsight, probably looked more serious.[55]

- Union representatives also responded to the firing of CFSA caseworkers, citing a "flawed" system in which future tragedies would only be avoided if the policies were changed.[56]
- Mayor Fenty already had some structural changes in mind:

> Fenty said no case in which child neglect or abuse is alleged should be closed before the child is located and "appropriate action taken to ensure that he/she is safe."
>
> In such cases, he said, he wants at least three visits to a last-known address at different times of the day or night. He said that child welfare cases that are deemed "incomplete" will be reviewed and that a system will be created to track home-schooling families.[57]

- But the executive director of DC Action for Children, Kate Sylvester, pointed out that even though CFSA had made some structural changes, things had improved somewhat and now "what we need to change is the culture of some workers in the agency."[58]
- In scheduling a DC Council committee hearing on the matter, council member Tommy Wells said he "wants to determine whether this is 'an individual failing or a systemic failing.'"[59]

Discussion Questions

Use the model deliberative process described in this chapter to analyze whether "the system" could have saved Brittany Jacks, Tatiana Jacks, N'Kia Fogle, and Aja Fogle.

1. What aspects of formal structure, organizational culture, and managerial competence and judgment do you observe in this case? As part of answering this question, identify the public managers and the frontline workers, where they work, and the roles they play.

2. What role does the rule of law play in this case?

3. Reflecting on your answers to the previous questions, consider the following:

   a. Did any DC government agency have the power to prevent the deaths of the four girls? Why or why not?

   b. Which of the distinctive challenges of public management, discussed in this chapter, are illustrated by this case?

   c. Would the outcome have been the same had the private sector (for-profit or nonprofit organizations) run the agencies with which the family interacted? Why or why not?

   d. Who should be held accountable for the girls' deaths? Why?

4. Drawing on your analysis above, what changes can realistically be implemented to reduce the likelihood of tragedies like this happening again? Can the possibility of such tragedies be completely eliminated?

NOTES

1. Luther Gulick, "Notes on the Theory of Organization," in *Papers on the Science of Administration,* ed. L. Gulick and L. Uric (New York, NY: Institute of Public Administration, 1937), 3–13.

2. Woodrow Wilson, "The Study of Administration," *Political Science Quarterly,* Vol.2, No. 2 (June 1887), 197–222; Frank J. Goodnow, *Politics and Administration: A Study in Government* (New York, NY: Russell and Russell, 1900).

3. Chester Irving Barnard, *The Functions of the Executive* (Cambridge, MA: Harvard University Press, 1938).

4. Harold D. Lasswell, *Politics: Who Gets What, When, How* (New York, NY: Whittles House, 1936).

5. E. E. Schattschneider, *Politics, Pressures and the Tariff* (Hamden, CT: Archon Books, 1963 [1935]), 288.

6. James MacGregor Burns, *Leadership* (New York, NY: Harper and Row, 1978), 18.

7. Dwight Waldo, *The Administrative State: A Study of the Political Theory of Public Administration*, 2nd ed. (New York, NY Holmes and Meier, 1984).

8. A. Lepawsky, *Administration: The Art and Science of Organization and Management* (New York, NY: Alfred A. Knopf, 1949), 83, quoted from Shih-Lien Hsü, *The Political Philosophy of Confucianism: An Interpretation of the Social and Political Ideas of Confucius, His Forerunners, and His Early Disciples* (New York, NY: Dutton, 1932).

9. H. Rosenberg, *Bureaucracy, Aristocracy and Autocracy: The Prussian Experience, 1660-1815* (Boston, MA: Beacon Press, 1958).

10. E. Barker, *The Development of Public Services in Western Europe: 1660-1930* (London, UK: Oxford University Press, 1944), 3.

11. Ibid.; J.A. Merkle, *Management and Ideology: The Legacy of the International Scientific Management Movement* (Berkeley: University of California Press, 1980).

12. Carl Friedrich, "The Continental Tradition of Training Administrators in Law and Jurisprudence," *The Journal of Modern History 11* (1939): 130-131.

13. Ibid., 132.

14. Frank J. Goodnow, *1902 Comparative Administrative Law: An Analysis of the Administrative Systems, National and Local, of the United States, England, France, and Germany* (New York, NY: G. P. Putnam's Sons), 10, quoted in Lynn, "Public Management," 19.

15. Graham T. Allison, *Public and Private Management: Are They Fundamentally Alike in All Unimportant Respects?* (proceedings for the Office of Personnel Management Public Management Research Conference, Washington, DC, November 19–20, 1979), 27–38.

16. Hal G. Rainey and Young Han Chun, "Public and Private Management Compared," in *The Oxford Handbook of Public Management,* 72–102. See also Jack Knott, "Comparing Public and Private Management: Cooperative Effort and Principal-Agent Relationships," *Journal of Public Administration Research and Theory* (1993); Christopher Pollitt, "Public Sector, Private Sector—Where Would We Be Without a Few Good Stereotypes?" in *The Essential Public Manager* (Maidenhead, Barks, UK: Open University Press, 2003), 1–25; Hal G. Rainey, *Understanding and Managing Public Organizations* (San Francisco, CA: Jossey-Bass, 2003); Wilson, *Bureaucracy.*

17. Donald Kettl and James Fesler, *The Politics of the Administrative Process* (Chatham, NJ: Chatham House, 1996), 10.

18. Terry Moe, "The Politics of Structural Choice: Toward a Theory of Public Bureaucracy," in *Organization Theory: From Chester Barnard to the Present and Beyond,* ed. Oliver E. Williamson (New York, NY: Oxford University Press, 1990), 116–153.

19. Ibid., 143.

20. Laurence E. Lynn Jr., "Public Management," in *Handbook of Public Administration, Second Edition,* ed. B. Guy Peters and Jon Pierre (London, UK: Sage, 2012), 26.

21. Charles Wolf Jr., *Markets or Governments: Choosing Between Imperfect Alternatives,* 2nd ed. (Cambridge, MA: MIT Press, 1993). In a related work, Barry Bozeman calls such phenomena "bureaupathologies." Barry Bozeman, *Bureaucracy and Red Tape* (Upper Saddle River, NJ: Prentice Hall, 2000).

22. Wolf, *Markets or Governments,* 69–70.

23. Allison, *Public and Private Management: Are They Fundamentally Alike in All Unimportant Respects?,*15.

24. Michael Barzelay and Babak J. Armajani, *Breaking Through Bureaucracy* (Berkeley: University of California Press, 1992); David Osborne and Ted Gaebler, *Reinventing Government* (Reading, MA: Addison-Wesley, 1992).

25. Barry Bozeman, *All Organizations are Public: Bridging Public and Private Organizational Theories* (San Francisco, CA: Jossey-Bass, 1987).

26. Rainey and Chun, "Public and Private Management Compared," 72–102.

27. Ibid.

28. Santa Falcone, "Self-Assessments and Job Satisfaction in Public and Private Organizations," *Public Productivity & Management Review* 14, no. 4 (1991): 385–396.

29. Rainey and Chun, "Public and Private Management Compared," 93.

30. Lynn, "Public Management," 17.

31. Marty Davis, "Managing the Unexpected," *ASK* magazine, November 2004, http://appel.nasa.gov/ ask/issues/20/20s_managing_ davis.php

32. David Anderson, "The Great Chicago Flood," *Horizon* Magazine, August 1999, 2; see also Transit Cooperative Research Program and National Cooperative Highway Research Program, *Making Transportation Tunnels Safe and Secure,* TCRP Report 86/NCHRP Report 525, Transportation Security, vol. 12 (Washington, DC: National Academies/National Research Council, Transportation Research Board, 2006), 37–39.

33. Phillip J. Cooper, *Public Law and Public Administration,* 3rd ed. (Itasca, IL: F. E. Peacock, 2000).

34. Herbert Kaufman, "The Confines of Leadership," in *The Administrative Behavior of Federal Bureau Chiefs* (Washington, DC: Brookings Institution, 1981), 91–138.

35. Ibid., 91.

36. Charles E. Lindblom, "The Science of "Muddling Through,"" *Public Administration Review* 19, no. 2 (Spring 1959): 79-88.

37. Robert D. Behn, "Management by Groping Along," *Journal of Policy Analysis and Management* 7, 4 (1988): 643-663.

38. Max Weber, *Economy and Society,* ed. G. Roth and R. Wittich (Berkeley: University of California Press, 1978).

39. Jean-Claude Thoenig, "Institutional Theories and Public Institutions: Traditions and Appropriateness," in *Handbook of Public Administration,* ed. B. Guy Peters and Jon Pierre (London, UK: Sage, 2003), 129.

40. Philip Selznick, *TVA and the Grass Roots,* quoted in Jane E. Fountain, *Building the Virtual State: Information Technology and Institutional Change* (Washington, DC: Brookings Institution Press, 2001), 92.

41. Giandomenico Majone, *Evidence, Argument, and Persuasion in the Policy Process* (New Haven, CT: Yale University Press, 1989), 21–22.

42. Stephen E. Toulmin, *The Uses of Argument,* updated ed. (Cambridge, MA: Cambridge University Press, 2003); Stephen Toulmin, Richard Rieke, and Allan Janik, *An Introduction to Reasoning,* 2nd ed. (New York, NY: Macmillan, 1984).

43. W. James Bradley and Kurt C. Schaefer, *The Uses and Misuses of Data and Models: The Mathematization of the Human Sciences* (Thousand Oaks, CA: Sage, 1998), 162.

44. Ibid., 164.

45. Bradley and Schaefer, *The Uses and Misuses of Data and Models,* 164–171.

46. Donald P. Moynihan, "What Do We Talk About When We Talk About Performance? Dialogue Theory and Performance Budgeting," *Journal of Public Administration Research and Theory* 16, no. 2 (2006): 167.

47. Allison Klein, Keith L. Alexander, and Sue Anne Presley Montes, "SE Woman Says Four Daughters Were 'Possessed': Girls Might Have Died in May," *The Washington Post,* January 11, 2008, A01, http://www.washingtonpost.com/wp-dyn/content/article/2008/01/10/AR2008011001174.html

48. Allison Klein and Joshua Zumbrun, "Bodies of 4 Girls Found in SE Home: Deaths Treated as Homicides," *The Washington Post,* January 10, 2008, A01, http://www.washingtonpost.com/wp-dyn/content/article/2008/01/09/AR2008010901413.html

49. Ibid.

50. Sue Anne Pressley Montes, "Fenty Describes Missteps Before Girls Died: After Efforts to Help, Agency Erred in Closing Cases, Mayor Says," *The Washington Post,* January 12, 2008, A01, http://www.washingtonpost.com/wp-dyn/content/article/2008/01/11/AR2008011101761.html.

51. Dvorak and Nakamura, "Fenty Fires 6 in Girls' Deaths," *The Washington Post,* January 15, 2008, p. 1, http://www.washingtonpost.com/wp-dyn/content/article/2008/01/14/AR2008011401001.html.

52. Ibid.

53. Ibid.

54. Sue Anne Pressley Montes, "Fenty Describes Missteps Before Girls Died: After Efforts to Help, Agency Erred in Closing Cases, Mayor Says."

55. Richard Wexler, "Fenty's Unthinking Ax," *The Washington Post,* January 16, 2008, A15, http://www.washingtonpost.com/wp-dyn/content/article/2008/01/15/AR2008011502862.html

56. Dvorak and Nakamura, "Fenty Fires 6 in Girls' Deaths."

57. Ibid.

58. Ibid.

59. Ibid.

2 First Principles

Managerial Accountability to the Rule of Law

INTRODUCTION

The United States is "a government of laws, not of men." This precept was the guiding principle of the Founders of America's republican—that is, representative—democracy. In Thomas Paine's words, the law is king, the king is not law.[1]

But who decides what the law is? That might seem elementary: the laws are made by the legislatures that enact the statutes and the elected executives who sign them. These elected officials also provide administrative direction, with the force of law, to public departments and agencies concerning how to implement those laws. And, of course, the Supreme Court and the high courts of the states say what the law is in cases of disputes over a law's meaning.

But abiding by the rule of law is anything but straightforward, as the following example demonstrates.

On May 31, 2014, President Barack Obama announced that he had secured the release of Bowe Bergdahl, a U.S. Army enlisted man who had been held captive by the Taliban for 4 years. In exchange for Bergdahl, the president had agreed to release five Taliban fighters captured in Afghanistan and held for many years at the U.S. detention facility at Guantanamo Bay. This prisoner swap was controversial for many reasons: Had the president negotiated with terrorists? Had he paid too high a price for Bergdahl? Was Bergdahl really a deserter who had not served his country with honor? But one thing seemed clear to the president's critics: he had broken the law.[i]

Section 1035 of the National Defense Authorization Act (NDAA) for Federal Fiscal Year 2014 required the president to notify congressional intelligence committees 30 days in advance of any proposed release of prisoners from Guantanamo Bay.[2] In the case of Bergdahl, the secretary of defense had not notified Congress at all. Was this a clear violation of law by President Obama, a former law school professor?

---

[i]One discussion of the issues raised by the president's action can be found at http://thedailybanter .com/2014/06/right-left-attack-obama-signing-statement-rationale-bowe-bergdahl-swap/.

The president's justifications for his apparent violation of the law were statements he had made on December 13, 2013, when signing the NDAA into law. Some provisions of the act "would, in certain circumstances, violate constitutional separation of powers principles" by restricting presidential authority to "act swiftly" when conducting negotiations with foreign countries, such as negotiating prisoner exchanges.[3] The president was claiming, in effect, that the president of the United States can disregard specific provisions of a duly enacted law that he regards as unconstitutional. However, this claim has no basis in the Constitution and has not been recognized in U.S. court rulings.

In response to a request from a Senate committee, the Government Accountability Office (GAO) responded that failure to notify Congress of the release of prisoners in exchange for Bergdahl did indeed violate the law. The GAO went further: "In addition, because [Department of Defense] DOD used appropriated funds to carry out the transfer when no money was available for that purpose, DOD violated the Antideficiency Act. The Antideficiency Act prohibits federal agencies from incurring obligations exceeding an amount available in an appropriation."[4] On both issues, the GAO and DOD were in sharp disagreement.[ii]

In fact, a number of seeming anomalies arise in administering the rule of law in this and many other situations:

- On signing into law a bill passed by Congress, the president may issue a signing statement such as the one President Obama issued when signing the NDAA in 2013. Frequently used by recent administrations, presidential signing statements may indicate that the president regards certain provisions in the law to be unconstitutional and that the administration will not enforce them. While these statements are considered authoritative instructions to executive branch officials on how to administer the law, their legal status is unclear, and their use has been condemned by the American Bar Association as undermining the rule of law.[5]

- On July 22, 2014, two U.S. Circuit Courts of Appeal issued diametrically opposed decisions on implementation of the Affordable Care Act. A number of lawsuits filed in federal courts claimed that the Affordable Care Act authorized subsidized premiums for health insurance plans purchased on exchanges created by the states but not for plans purchased on the exchange created by the federal government, contesting an Internal Revenue Service ruling that allowed subsidies for plans on the federal exchange. A panel of the U.S. Circuit Court of Appeals for the District of Columbia ruled 2-1 that the IRS ruling was invalid. A similar panel of the U.S. Court of Appeals for the Fourth Circuit in Richmond, Virginia, ruled unanimously that the IRS ruling was valid. If the Supreme Court ultimately invalidated the IRS ruling, millions of U.S. residents who had purchased plans on the federal exchange would lose their subsidies.[6]

- Unanimous U.S. Supreme Court decisions may mask sharp ideological differences among the justices and may avoid the most controversial and divisive issues raised by a case.[7] One view is that such decisions reflect strategic leadership by the chief justice; another view is that rather than settling the core issues, the strategy simply postpones their resolution.

- The actual administration of certain areas of law, such as the administration of the Internal Revenue Code, may be inconsistent with or violate general duly promulgated administrative law standards. The justification for nonstandard or exceptional tax regulations is that the constitutional authority of regulators permits it and practical considerations necessitate it.[8]

[ii]In March 2015, following an investigation, the U.S. Army charged Bergdahl with one count of desertion and one count of misbehavior before the enemy.

- In many instances, state governors and attorneys general have refused to defend in court or to otherwise enforce legislative enactments concerning morally charged and divisive issues such as same-sex marriage, immigration, abortion, and gun control. These refusals often reflect these officials' views on the constitutionality as well as the morality of controversial laws.
- Individuals and organizations in both the public and private sectors have refused to comply with laws, such as those concerning the reproductive rights of women, to which they object on religious or moral grounds. Examples include pharmacists who refuse to fill prescriptions for contraceptives, physicians who refuse to comply with laws that impose procedural obstacles to abortions, and religious organizations that refuse to provide employees with insurance benefits that, while required by law, are contrary to their religious beliefs.[iii]

Situations like these that arise in administering the law illustrate how the meaning of *the rule of law* can be ambiguous and controversial. The reason for such confusion is the nature of the legal system created by the Founders. Following the Declaration of Independence, the framers of the first state constitutions insisted upon dividing state authority among three separate departments, or branches, of government. One of the best-known expressions of

> The rule of law is a protection against arbitrary, capricious, and nontransparent acts by public managers.

the principle behind the rule of law in America was drafted by John Adams for the constitution of the Commonwealth of Massachusetts to provide a rationale for a **separation of powers**:

> In the government of this commonwealth, the legislative department shall never exercise the executive and judicial powers, or either of them: the executive shall never exercise the legislative and judicial powers, or either of them: the judicial shall never exercise the legislative and executive powers, or either of them: *to the end it may be a government of laws and not of men* [emphasis added].[9]

Thus, in the U.S. legal tradition, the rule of law is viewed in the first instance as a protection against tyranny in the form of an overly powerful central government.[iv] With respect to public management, the **rule of law** means that duly promulgated written principles and policies are the basis for the legitimate exercise of managerial authority. The rule of law is a protection against arbitrary, capricious, and nontransparent acts by public managers.

An ironic consequence of America's constitutional scheme is that the legitimacy of the rule of law depends on an unwritten and unenforceable faith in law and lawful institutions. As legal scholar Michael Mullane put it,

> The rule of law only exists because enough of us believe in it and insist that everyone, even the nonbelievers, behave as if it exists. The minute enough of us stop believing, stop insisting that the law protect us all, and that every single one of us is accountable to the law—in that moment, the rule of law will be gone. . . . . It is the rule of law that governs us, that protects each one of us when we stand alone against those who disagree with us, or fear us, or do not like us because we are different. It is the strongbox that keeps all our other values safe.[10]

[iii]A Supreme Court decision in June 2014 upheld the right of "closely-held corporations" to refuse on religious grounds to comply with the Affordable Care Act's requirement that company-provided insurance cover the costs of contraceptives, a decision which raised many more issues than it resolved.

[iv]A useful online source of definitions related to the rule of law is at http://www.quickmba.com/ law/sys/. Articles from the electronic journal of the former United States Information Agency offer a comprehensive overview of how the U.S. court system works. See http://usinfo.state .gov/ journals/itdhr/0999/ijde/ijde0999.htm. Access to a comprehensive body of informative links for the federal government, the states, and other sources of law is at http://www.lawsource.com/also/ # [United%20States].

Public managers, therefore, must always act in ways that sustain the public's faith in the rule of law. The authority and the legitimacy of public management—the faith placed in it by citizens, elected officials, and judges—are ultimately derived from public managers' sense of responsibility to constitutional principles and institutions. These institutions include elected legislatures, elected executives, the courts of law that review political and administrative acts for their lawfulness, and the institutions and conventions created by elected executives and legislatures (these conventions are checks and balances, which are discussed further in Chapter 4).

This chapter explains how the rule of law functions as the framework for public management, in all of its three dimensions: structure, culture, and craft. The next section discusses the meaning of the term *rule of law* in practice and in principle. Then, the rule of law is viewed from a managerial perspective: finding the laws that govern choices and decisions in particular managerial contexts and the sources of those laws. Next is a discussion of the conceptual and practical challenges of being accountable, which is the ultimate source of legitimacy for lawful public management. The concluding section ties these ideas together and argues that the concept of *thinking institutionally* should be the ethos of public management practice in governments at all levels.

WHAT IS MEANT BY *THE RULE OF LAW*?

Public management in America is, and must be, lawful. Its ambiguities aside, what does that mean, in practice and in principle?

The Rule of Law in Practice

The law is the framework for public management practice in America's constitutional scheme of governance, enabling and constraining discretion by public managers.

> *Example: Performance-Based Organizations in the Clinton Administration's "Reinventing Government" Initiative*

One element of the highly publicized Reinventing Government initiative sought to imitate Great Britain's Next Steps reform, an initiative of British prime minister Margaret Thatcher. Next Steps aimed to give the heads of government agencies the incentive and authority to perform efficiently. Next Steps created agencies (organizations headed by chief executive officers or CEOs) to administer specific governmental functions and activities under the supervision of ministries (organizational units in Britain that are equivalent to U.S. cabinet-level departments). Over 130 agencies were created; examples are the Education Funding Agency and The Royal Parks. The CEOs were bound by performance agreements setting out specific measures and targets. Although the CEOs were civil servants, their pay was based on meeting performance targets, and they could be fired for poor performance. The Clinton administration called its version of such agencies **performance-based organizations** (PBOs).

Public administration scholars Andrew Graham and Alasdair Roberts have shown that America's constitutionally defined separation of powers meant that, unlike Great Britain, "an influential third party—Congress—threatened to complicate negotiations over the content of annual performance agreements."[11] Such agreements were to commit future Congresses to provide budgets for PBOs. But future Congresses cannot legally be bound by the decisions of a sitting Congress, and power and politics can change from one Congress to the next.

An additional issue was that public managers in the United States do not have access to management strategies that are available to many foreign governments or to private sector executives who do not confront separate centers of power. For example, the Next Step agreements specified conditions for CEO termination. In the U.S. system of governance, Congress "may not limit the ability of the President to remove appointees, unless those appointees exercise quasi-legislative or quasi-judicial functions that require some independence from the administration."[12] The three PBOs ultimately created were thus denied significant flexibilities and were a pale reflection of the British model.

Example: Civil Rights Violations by Local Law Enforcement Agencies

Local law enforcement agencies such as police departments, especially those in large metropolitan areas, have long been vulnerable to complaints by citizens about police misconduct that violates their civil rights, frequently resulting in class action lawsuits. Parts of the Violent Crime Control and Law Enforcement Act of 1994 addressed this problem. Section 210401, "Cause of Action", states

a. UNLAWFUL CONDUCT.—It shall be unlawful for any governmental authority, or any agent thereof, or any person acting on behalf of a governmental authority, to engage in a pattern or practice of conduct by law enforcement officers or by officials or employees of any governmental agency with responsibility for the administration of juvenile justice or the incarceration of juveniles that deprives persons of rights, privileges, or immunities secured or protected by the Constitution or laws of the United States.

b. CIVIL ACTION BY ATTORNEY GENERAL.—Whenever the Attorney General has reasonable cause to believe that a violation of paragraph (1) [*sic*] has occurred, the Attorney General, for or in the name of the United States, may in a civil action obtain appropriate equitable and declaratory relief to eliminate the pattern or practice.[13]

This law authorizes federal intervention in the management of local law enforcement agencies engaged in patterns of conduct that violate citizens' civil rights. The first consent decrees, beginning with Pittsburgh in 1996, prescribed systems to identify misconduct (and those likely to engage in it) and supervision and training to change police behavior.

In May 2013, a civil society organization called the Police Executives Research Forum (PERF)[v] issued a report entitled "Civil Rights Investigations of Local Police: Lessons Learned."[14] This report reviews the history of suits brought against local police departments. Following investigations by the Civil Rights Division of the U.S. Department of Justice, these suits typically result in consent decrees that prescribe actions for police departments in order to come into compliance with federal laws. Actions taken by police department officials to comply were monitored by a court-appointed official for a period initially required to be 5 years but usually extended for many more.

The decrees require police administrators to establish systems to identify problematic behavior (and those likely to engage in it) and "pathways to correction." The Pittsburgh decree established 14 categories of behavior for which the department would be required to collect data. The decree did not, however, "specify what degree of unacceptable behavior would trigger supervisor involvement or what to do with miscreants." Significant latitude was left to police department managers and supervisors as to how to create incentives to comply and to create a culture of compliance with civil rights laws.

---

[v]The Police Executives Research Forum provides research and management services, technical assistance, and executive-level education to support law enforcement agencies; http://www.policeforum.org/home/.

Pittsburgh's police chief at the time, as have executives from other cities, welcomed the investigation and consent decree because the need to comply can put pressure on city councils and on labor unions to provide funds and support bringing the department into compliance. The department created the Performance Assessment Review System, which became "a model early intervention system throughout the country." This management tool "compares officers' behavior to a peer group within their unit and shift, and it identifies positive behaviors as well as negative behaviors."[15]

Consent decrees are not guaranteed to produce compliant behavior. The reasons are many: "insufficient resources, unclear or unfocused mandates, or police resistance to federal oversight." Many police chiefs assembled at a PERF conference identified the department's relationships with the monitor appointed to oversee the compliance process as "a critical factor in how swiftly reforms can be made and a consent decree ended." Thus, a department's administrators are accountable not only to the city's legislators but also to an official with the power to determine whether they met the Justice Departments objectives.

Over time, according to the PERF report, the Justice Department has become more aggressive with respect to the terms it will accept for consent decrees. The decrees cover a wider range of issues and remedies, including officer interactions with suspects who have mental health issues and the manner in which sexual assault complaints are handled. For example, the decree for New Orleans "is a 122-page document that mandates hundreds of police department policy changes dealing with use of force, searches and seizures, arrests, interrogations, performance evaluations, misconduct complaints, off-duty work assignments, and more." Specific requirements are included, such as "respecting that bystanders to public-police interaction have a constitutional right to observe and record officer conduct, and creating a policy to guide officers' interactions with gay, lesbian, bisexual and transgender citizens."[16]

Many other government agencies providing individual and social services have similar constraints imposed on them by the rule of law. Public managers now must comply with written contracts (that is, consent decrees) enforced essentially by an individual (the monitor) who is, in turn, accountable to a judge. In New Orleans, the monitor is a team from the law firm Sheppard, Mullin, Richter, and Hampton, appointed by a federal district judge. The team includes a former deputy monitor of the consent decree for the Washington, DC, police department.[17] Public managers must become skilled at negotiating the terms of the decree and at maintaining productive relationships with the teams of lawyers in addition to meeting the many other pressures that the local political context creates.

> **Managerial discretion is a fundamental aspect of the rule of law, not an exception to it.**

The Rule of Law in Principle

The above examples demonstrate how the law—even in its most exalted form, the Constitution—shapes and constrains the managerial prerogatives of American governments at all levels. No consequential matter requiring managerial discretion lies beyond the law's actual or potential influence.

The necessity for managers to exercise discretion and judgment, however, is by no means extinguished by the rule of law. Managerial discretion is a fundamental aspect of the rule of law, not an exception to it.

Justice Scalia wrote in *Printz,*

> Executive action that has utterly no policymaking component is rare, particularly at an executive level as high as a jurisdiction's chief law enforcement officer. Is it really true that there is no policymaking involved in deciding, for example, what "reasonable efforts" shall be expended to conduct a background check? It may well satisfy the Act for a CLEO to direct that (a) no background checks will be conducted that divert personnel

time from pending felony investigations, and (b) no background check will be permitted to consume more than one half hour of an officer's time. But nothing in the Act *requires* a CLEO to be so parsimonious; diverting at least *some* felony investigation time, and permitting at least *some* background checks beyond one half hour would certainly not be *un*reasonable. Is this decision whether to devote maximum "reasonable efforts" or minimum "reasonable efforts" not preeminently a matter of policy? It is quite impossible, in short, to draw the Government's proposed line at "no policymaking," and we would have to fall back upon a line of "not too much policymaking." How much is too much is not likely to be answered precisely; and an imprecise barrier against federal intrusion upon state authority is not likely to be an effective one.[18]

In other words, it is difficult to know where to draw the "no policymaking allowed" line when carrying out a public responsibility. Thus, managerial discretion is inevitable. But it must be disciplined by constitutional principle.

The lawmaking and fiscal powers assigned to legislatures and the powers assigned to the courts by Articles I and III of the U.S. Constitution, elaborated since the founding by countless U.S. Supreme Court decisions, result in a hierarchical fiscal and administrative framework, or backbone, that structures American public management. Apart from the powers expressly assigned to the executive by Article II (as interpreted by federal courts), managerial judgment in the executive branches of American governments is formally, and conditionally, checked by the powers assigned to the other two branches.

Legality is not the only source of legitimacy for managerial conduct, however. The Constitution, after all, is a means to a broad societal end, as its Preamble makes clear: "We the People of the United States, in Order to form a more perfect Union, establish Justice, insure domestic Tranquility, provide for the common defense, promote the general Welfare, and secure the Blessings of Liberty to ourselves and our Posterity, do ordain and establish this Constitution for the United States of America."[19] Legitimacy is conferred on public management by evidence of managerial commitment to forming a more perfect Union, by managerial respect for individual liberties and for members of society as citizens, and by personal qualities of character and integrity that inspire trust. Yet the constitutional backbone operates even when public managers derive power and influence from sources beyond statutory mandates, including

- the decentralized nature of policy and program administration in states and communities,
- the creation of networks linking public and private agencies, and
- the various forms of direct democracy, such as public consultation, advisory bodies, and power-sharing arrangements with citizens.

A manager's discretionary actions may be oriented toward community values, guided by the policy preferences of superiors, influenced by the interests of particular constituencies, or reflective of conscience and ethical promptings. No matter how well-intentioned, the legitimacy of managerial conduct is ultimately reviewable, at the behest of citizens, by legislatures and courts.

But what if the law is silent, incomplete, or ambiguous? What is the relationship between the exercise of **delegated authority**—that is, the authorized discretion to use one's best judgment—and the rule of law? What if laws appear to be in conflict with one another? What if elected executives and legislators disagree on how a law should be interpreted or carried out? Obedience to the rule of law is not straightforward for public managers. Discretion and judgment are needed.

A sufficient test of lawfulness is that the public manager's actions do not violate clearly established statutory or constitutional rights that a reasonable person in his or her position would have known.[20] A superficial grasp of

end 1

what lawfulness requires is insufficient for reasonable and responsible public service: Public managers must make the effort to educate themselves about the lawful foundations of the activities for which they are responsible.

start 2

PRACTICING LAWFUL PUBLIC MANAGEMENT

Writing in 1933, political scientist and public administration scholar Marshall Dimock advocated "a more realistic, a more complete development of public administration."[21] He observed, "Law is not something outside [the administrator's] work, boring in on him. Rather, it is an integral part of his unfolding plan and strategy of accomplishment."[22] Dimock emphasized the importance for public administrators of "finding the law."[23] He depicted a logical process based on his experience while drafting an administrative manual for field officials in the Immigration Service. The process involves answering six basic questions (Box 2.1).

Box 2.1	A PUBLIC MANAGER'S GUIDE FOR FINDING THE LAW

1. What is our statutory authority?

2. What is the ruling case law as found in court cases that serve as precedents?

3. What are our own sub-legislative or policy interpretations of statutory authority by means of which we give effect to steps in the administrative unfolding of the law not specifically provided in the words of the statute?

4. Behind the statutory authority and controlling and limiting it, what is our constitutional authority?

5. What standards of fairness as found in administrative due process of law are we expected to observe?

6. What internal standards of administration are we prepared to follow in order to give fuller effect to the foregoing?

Source: Marshall E. Dimock, *Law and Dynamic Administration* (New York: Praeger, 1980), 31–32. Public Administration Review © 1987 American Society for Public Administration. Reprinted with permission from John Wiley and Sons, Inc.

Managers' actions are of course subject to judicial review. Public administration scholar Yong S. Lee elaborates on the implications for lawful public management. A **doctrine of objective reasonableness** has emerged to govern the conduct of public officials under the rule of law:

> The concept of objectively reasonable conduct is measured by reference to clearly established law. The conduct of a public official is deemed objectively reasonable and, hence, deserving of the defense of qualified immunity [from individual tort liability], if and when the [official's] conduct does not violate sufficiently clearly established statutory or constitutional rights that a reasonable person in that position would have known.[24]

Other sources provide guidance for lawful public management beyond the doctrine of objective reasonableness. For example, public law scholar Philip Cooper's work provides a comprehensive discussion of administrative responsibility that resonates with Dimock's more realistic and complete public administration.[25] Public management scholars Anthony Bertelli and Laurence Lynn argue that the rule of law in the American constitutional scheme of governance calls for public administrators to act in accordance with an axiomatic **precept of managerial responsibility**: the balanced and reasonable exercise of judgment, which defines accountability and earns legitimacy in the constitutional scheme.[26]

Sources of Law

The Founders were moved by precepts of natural law in declaring U.S. independence and creating republican institutions. As a practical matter, however, as the above discussion suggests, "the law" has come to refer to **positive law**, or rules of administrative conduct found in constitutions, statutes, lawful administrative directives and guidelines, common law, and international law. Positive law both enables and constrains the work of public managers. It enables by delegating discretion to act. It constrains by imposing substantive and procedural restrictions on their choice making.

> Positive law both enables and constrains the work of public managers. It enables by delegating discretion to act. It constrains by imposing substantive and procedural restrictions on their choice making.

Rule in the term *rule of law* refers to the "supervising mechanisms" employed to audit the use of managerial discretion and ensure that it conforms to the law.[27] These mechanisms are not confined to the judicial branch. They also include political mechanisms that have an important bearing on the exercise of administrative discretion. Such political mechanisms include elections and checks and balances that are defined in or derived from the Constitution (discussed further in Chapter 4).

The Constitution is not the only source of law, but it is the most important among five distinct sources: constitutional law, statutory law, administrative law, common law, and international law.

Constitutional Law

Constitutional law is the body of law that codifies the decisions of the U.S. Supreme Court and of state higher courts of review.[vi] Legislative and executive branches make decisions and take actions that ultimately are subject to review and reversal by the U.S. Supreme Court or by equivalent state courts. These decisions define and interpret the meaning and implications of the formal constitutional provisions. The body of constitutional law resulting from judicial review carries considerable weight in subsequent decision making, though precedents are sometimes overturned. Consider the far-reaching public management effects of *Brown v. Board of Education* (1954), which overturned *Plessy v. Ferguson* (1896).

Statutory Law

The second and most widely recognized source of law is **statutory law.** It is the body of law that codifies the enactments (subject to signature by the executive) of the U.S. Congress and of state and local legislatures. The power to legislate is not unconstrained. All acts of Congress must be presented to the president for approval and are subject to veto (although vetoes may be overridden). Article I of the U.S. Constitution enumerates the legislative powers of Congress and the limitations on those powers. Article I, Section 7, for example, states that "All Bills for raising Revenue shall originate in the House of Representatives; but the Senate may propose or concur with Amendments as on other Bills."

[vi]For an annotated text of the U.S. Constitution, see http://www.law.cornell.edu/constitution/index.html.

Administrative Law

The third source of law is **administrative law,** which consists of rulemaking and the adjudication of alleged rules violations by administrators in executive agencies such as the Environmental Protection Agency (EPA) and the Federal Aviation Administration (FAA) and by independent regulatory agencies such as the Federal Trade Commission, the Federal Labor Relations Board, and the Federal Mine Safety and Health Review Commission.[28]

Rulemaking—the issuance of regulations to accomplish the agency's purposes—can be both substantive and procedural. Administrative law scholar David Rosenbloom cites the example of the director of the FAA issuing rules concerning child safety aboard airplanes.[29] The failure to issue rules may also be consequential. Ten states sued the EPA for its alleged failure to issue rules on carbon dioxide emissions. Administrative law concerns the procedures for the lawful issuance of such rules and for their application in specific cases: the rules for issuing and applying rules.

Adjudication of alleged rules violations by administrators takes the form of court-like proceedings in which individual petitions for relief are heard and decided by an administrative law judge or a hearing examiner, positions authorized by the Administrative Procedure Act (APA) of 1946. David Tatel, a judge on the U.S. Circuit Court of Appeals for the District of Columbia argued,

> Doctrines of administrative law are not barriers erected by activist judges to prevent agencies from exercising their natural authority to make public policy. Just the opposite. These doctrines exist for a compelling constitutional reason: they keep agencies tethered to Congress and to our representative system of government. They ensure that the complex administrative state of the twenty-first century functions in accordance with the constitutional system established in the eighteenth. . . . The fundamentals of administrative law really do matter, and they should be understood as engines of administrative policymaking, rather than merely obstacles cluttering the road.[30]

Executive authority is of considerable importance in administrative law. An **executive order** is a declaration issued by the president or a governor that has the force of law. Executive orders are usually based on existing statutory authority and require no action by Congress or a state legislature to become effective. At the federal level, executive orders are published in the Federal Register as they are issued and then codified in Statutes at Large and Title 3 of the *Code of Federal Regulations* each year.[31]

Common Law

The fourth source of law is the body of case law that makes up American **common law.** According to the common law, a citizen may sue another individual or organization for the harm or injury (termed a *tort*) to plaintiffs that the defendants allegedly have caused and be awarded compensation or damages if a judge or jury agrees with the plaintiff. Under the common law doctrine of sovereign immunity, the state, and those operating on its behalf, may not be sued for causing harm unless sovereign immunity has been waived or the courts have recognized a specific exception. If the state and its officers cause injury, the individual's usual recourse is to persuade a legislature to specifically authorize compensation for such injury.

Congress and state legislatures have passed various tort claims acts that waive sovereign immunity in certain circumstances, allowing citizens to make claims of negligence against public officials. An alternative—allowing unlimited legal liability—is not regarded as feasible because it would provide incentives for bringing claims and result in the legislature reducing public services and qualified professionals being hesitant to enter public service. The U.S. government, through the Tucker Act of 1887, has waived its sovereign immunity in specific circumstances, such as lawsuits arising out of contracts to which it, or one of its agencies, is a party. Congress has also passed civil rights acts that allow suits against officers acting under the authority of state law who violate constitutional and statutory rights intentionally or through negligence.

International Law

The fifth source of law is **international law** incorporated in duly-ratified treaties and conventions, such as the North American Free Trade Agreement, the U.S.-Canada Agreement on Air Quality, and the Geneva Conventions defining the laws of war. If a treaty and a federal statute are in conflict, the more recent or more specific will typically take precedence. Treaties, moreover, are often implemented by federal statutes.

American public management may also be affected by the decisions of regional and international judicial institutions. In May 2006, the European Union's (EU) highest court ruled that the EU had overstepped its authority by agreeing to give the United States personal details about airline passengers on flights to the United States in an effort to fight terrorism. The decision forced the two sides to renegotiate their agreement at a time when European concerns for infringements of civil liberties were rising.

Together, these five sources of law—constitutions, statutes, administrative directives, case law, and international agreements—create an extensive, complex, and intrusive environment for public management.

WHAT IS MEANT BY *ACCOUNTABILITY?*

The rule of law implies that public officials are accountable to the people and their representatives. Yet accountability is one of most elusive issues in public management. How can "the people" and their elected representatives hold public managers accountable to duly constituted authority? How in turn can managers hold their employees accountable as they exercise their own delegated authority? What should managers do if demands for accountability come from several sources whose expectations are in conflict? Because the execution of policies and programs must be delegated, and because public managers and their subordinates must inevitably exercise judgment and discretion, accountability is a fundamental challenge for public management. Indeed, many of the distinctive challenges of public management described in Chapter 1 are directly concerned with ensuring accountability.

Accountability in Historical Perspective

Accountability is deeply rooted in constitutional principle. Defined by Alexander Hamilton as "due dependence on the people in a republican sense," the idea of accountability has been central to public administration's claim to constitutional legitimacy from the beginning of the Republic.[32] As James Madison expressed in *Federalist No. 37*, "the genius of republican liberty seems to demand . . . not only that all power should be derived from the people, but that those entrusted with it should be kept in dependence on the people."

Often referred to as the accountability clause, Article I, Section 9, Clause 7, of the Constitution states, "No Money shall be drawn from the Treasury, but in Consequence of Appropriations made by Law; and a regular

Statement and Account of the Receipts and Expenditures of all public Money shall be published from time to time." This clause focuses on financial accountability, but many other constitutional provisions bear on accountability, including, but not limited to, the following:[33]

- Congress is required to keep and publish a journal of its proceedings.
- The president is required to report to Congress on the state of the Union and to publish reasons for vetoing legislation.
- Criminal defendants must be tried in public.
- Public officers may be impeached and removed from office for cause.

State constitutions contain similar provisions, as well.

In the largely prebureaucratic America between 1789 and the beginnings of the Progressive era in the late 1800s, accountability was direct, personal, and haphazard.[34] Extensive delegation of authority was unnecessary because of the practice at the time of specifying in detail the expectations of the legislature for administrative actors. As James Hart described that era,

> With the theory abroad in the land that the legislature should legislate as little as possible, it was entirely possible for it to debate and prescribe every minute detail and try to anticipate every contingency. And with problems before them of relative simplicity and stability, the laymen who are chosen by popular elections could with less absurdity than today attempt to decide in detail for future events.[35]

But some contingencies could not be foreseen. Coping was left to administrative officers (many of them elected) to function independently of executive authority, with legislatures appropriating funds directly to their offices.[36] According to public administration scholar Dwight Waldo, "the lack of a strong tradition of administrative action [i.e., supervision] . . . contributed to . . . public servants acting more or less in their private capacities."[37] A **spoils system** (to the victor belongs the spoils or privileges of office) of rotation in office with each election dominated nineteenth-century selection and control of administrators so that officials were beholden to political parties. Legislators, political parties, and the courts exercised intermittent oversight of administration.[38]

The issue of accountability first became urgent in the latter part of the nineteenth century. Governments at all levels expanded rapidly to meet the needs, expressed politically, of an industrializing, urbanizing, demographically changing United States. The most prominent of Progressive-Era administrative reforms involved separating politics from administration in an effort to rescue municipal governments from the spoils system's corrupt machines and to professionalize the management of urban services. The most significant innovation was the **city-manager form of government** in which city councils hire or remove a professional city manager on the basis of merit. That form of government contrasts with the **mayor-council form of government** where administrative authority rests with the elected mayor. The goal in city-manager governments was, and still is, accountability that is less political and corruptible, with administration conducted in compliance with impersonal and lawful rules by qualified professionals.

But the politics-administration dichotomy was not the dominant orthodoxy that many public administration scholars have claimed it was. Woodrow Wilson is credited with advocating a politics-administration dichotomy as doctrine in his famous 1887 essay, "The Study of Administration." But his more important observation in that essay was "there be no danger in power if only it be not irresponsible."[39] In other words, because the Founders' political doctrines predated the emergence of American bureaucratic institutions, the doctrines proved inadequate to resolve the issues of accountability raised by widespread delegation of authority to administrators. It fell to the emerging professions of public administration and public law to develop new doctrines for the rapidly emerging government bureaucracies.

In traditional public administration literature, the concept of responsibility emphasized by Wilson is often equated with accountability. Public administration scholar Frederick C. Mosher observed, "responsibility may well be the most important word in all the vocabulary of administration, public and private."[40] Noting the importance of "responsibility and accountability of the agencies of administration," public administration scholar Wallace Sayre identified a common concern: how to reconcile the great, unprecedented growth of administrative power with democratic government.[41] Although no regime of rules can eliminate possibilities for self-interested behavior by subordinate officials, argued public administration scholar John Millett in 1954, "management guided by [the value of responsibility] abhors the idea of arbitrary authority present in its own wisdom and recognizes the reality of external direction and constraint."[42]

In traditional public administration, the function of democratic institutions is to preserve an appropriate balance between administrative flexibility in serving the public interest, on the one hand, and the accountability of administrators to democratic authority, and especially to representative and judicial institutions, on the other.[43]

Accountability Institutions

The inevitable emergence of new structures and processes of public management carries with it a constant redefinition of an ideal balance between administrative discretion and accountability. Such developments often lengthen and weaken the chains of delegation that link citizens, their elected representatives, and the delivery of publicly supported services. These new structures and techniques include the service and regulatory agencies and administrative technologies created during the legislatively active Progressive, New Deal, and Great Society periods. They also include special districts, local-regional corporations at the state and local levels, government corporations, government-sponsored enterprises, and quasi-governmental organizations created since World War II to ensure a businesslike distance between politics and service delivery. In recent times of budgetary stringency and heightened legislative scrutiny, popular movements toward decentralization, deinstitutionalization, devolution, privatization, and outsourcing have necessitated new structures and processes for meeting public needs (discussed in Chapter 5).

Similar to the innovative idea of professional city management, new accountability institutions often rely on professional and legal forms of accountability. "Using the corporate device . . . involves trusting board members and executives after giving them a firm mandate and discretion."[44] But accountability and the rule of law may be weakened under these arrangements. Therefore, new institutions concerned with accountability have long accompanied the expansion of new structures and processes of public management.

> **New institutions concerned with accountability have long accompanied the expansion of new structures and processes of public management.**

- Among the earliest of these accountability institutions were the Progressives' innovative forms of **direct democracy**: initiative, referendum, and recall, which allow citizens to propose and vote on laws and constitutional amendments and to remove officials from office, thereby directly holding elected officials accountable for their performance.

  The initiative and the referendum are popular in many states, especially California, where a 2003 recall vote resulted in Governor Gray Davis being removed from office.

- Another early accountability institution is the **General Accounting Office**, now called the **Government Accountability Office** (GAO). Created by the Budget and Accounting Act of 1921 to audit an executive branch swollen by Progressive reforms and World War I, the GAO, whose chief executive is the comptroller general of the United States with a 15-year term, is an agency of the U.S. Congress.

  The GAO has substantial discretion to investigate fraud, waste, and abuse in the executive branch and to publish reports containing its findings and recommendations. "The comptroller general retains from his heritage, and has gained by statute, elements of authority that in any other national jurisdiction are lodged with executive officials."[45]

- Some accountability institutions emphasize **transparency** as a way to promote accountable action by public agencies. These institutions include laws, such as the federal Freedom of Information Act, which "establish a public right to information held by government agencies. Such institutions establish a presumption that government documents should be publicly accessible and provide methods for compelling officials to comply with its requirements."[46]

  Other transparency institutions include the Federal Advisory Committee Act of 1972, which requires meetings of federal advisory committees to be open to the public, and the Government in the Sunshine Act of 1976, which requires meetings of federal commissions to be open to the public. Each act contains exemptions for material relating to national security or to certain personnel or law enforcement matters.

- In 1978, Congress created the **office of inspector general** (IG) in many federal agencies. By 2014, there were 74 statutory IG offices.[47] IGs are empowered to conduct and supervise audits of the programs and operations of their agencies with the purpose of identifying and recommending solutions for waste, fraud, and abuse.

  IGs report to their agency heads, but they are appointed by the president, confirmed by the Senate, and formally protected from political interference: "Neither the head of the establishment nor the officer next in rank below such head shall prevent or prohibit the Inspector General from initiating, carrying out, or completing any audit or investigation, or from issuing any subpoena during the course of any audit or investigation."[48]

  The President's Council on Integrity and Efficiency and the Executive Council on Integrity and Efficiency were established by Executive Order 12805, on May 11, 1992, to "address integrity, economy, and effectiveness issues that transcend individual Government agencies, and increase the professionalism and effectiveness of IG personnel throughout the Government."[49]

- Protections for **whistleblowers** constitute another venerable accountability institution. Whistleblowers are individuals who report misconduct in their agencies or organizations. The first federal legislation with the intent to protect whistleblowers was the Lloyd-La Follette Act of 1912, which guaranteed the right of federal employees to furnish information to Congress.

  Whistleblower protection became popular in the late twentieth century, especially in the new regulatory agencies such as the Environmental Protection Agency and the Occupational Safety and Health Administration. In the Civil Service Reform Act of 1978, Congress established the Office of Special Counsel, an independent federal investigative and prosecutorial agency, "to safeguard the merit system by protecting federal employees and applicants from prohibited personnel practices, especially reprisal for whistleblowing."[50]

end (handwritten, left margin)

In 1989, Congress enacted the Whistleblower Protection Act "to strengthen and improve protection for the rights of Federal employees, to prevent reprisals, and to help eliminate wrongdoing within the Government."

Because of America's separation of powers and steadily evolving and increasingly complex system of checks and balances (discussed further in Chapter 4), accountability and accountability institutions will also evolve and become more complex as the executive, the legislature, and the courts interpret accountability's requirements and create new forms to ensure them.

Future (handwritten)

Start 4 (handwritten, left margin)

Frameworks for Analyzing Accountability

The difficulties in pinning down accountability are evident in historical concerns for responsible action by unelected bureaucrats. The evolving, complex institutions of public management mean that holding organizations and individuals accountable is, as emphasized, not a straightforward matter. Competing pressures and expectations from different sources introduce further complications.

Public management scholar Robert D. Behn has observed, "To 'hold people accountable' has become a cliché" yet its meaning is not consistent among those who use the term.[51] William T. Gormley, Jr., another public management scholar, has argued that accountability is a "procedural value" that, along with other procedural values such as responsiveness, leadership, effectiveness, and fairness, should be invoked only when it is possible to "define them more precisely, to defend them more persuasively, and to place them in the context of other values."[52]

Thus, an analysis of accountability first seeks clarity regarding the meaning of accountability in a given situation. Next, it engages in systematic inquiry, informed by the model deliberative process described in Chapter 1. Accountability concerns span the three dimensions of public management. Structure is the dimension most often used in attempts to ensure accountability. Though they are more difficult for external authorities to influence, culture and craft are fundamental as well. To support an analytical approach to accountability, the remainder of this section reviews different meanings of accountability from the literature. In so doing it illustrates the difficulty of operationalizing a concept that at first may seem straightforward.

- Public administration scholar Mark Bovens suggests that public accountability serves five essential functions in a representative democracy:

    - assuring democratic control,
    - enhancing integrity,
    - improving performance,
    - maintaining legitimacy, and
    - providing catharsis after tragedy or failure.[53]

- Behn points to three typical targets of accountability:

    - for finances,
    - for fairness, and
    - for outcomes.

    He argues that the first two targets "reflect concerns for *how* government does what it does," and the third target reflects a concern for "*what* government does—what it actually accomplishes."[54]

- Public administration scholars Herbert A. Simon, Victor A. Thompson, and Donald W. Smithburg define accountability as "the enforcement of responsibility." They emphasize *responsibility* as "the extent to which administrators are responsive to other persons or groups, in and out of the bureaucracy." They identify other meanings of *responsibility* as well: "as a synonym for legal authority," "to denote the compliance with generally accepted moral obligations," or as "responsiveness to other people's values."[55]
- Frederick C. Mosher defined accountability in relation to what he termed **objective responsibility**, which "connotes the responsibility of a person or an organization *to* someone else, outside of self, *for* some thing or some kind of performance. It is closely akin to accountability or answerability."[56] He distinguished objective responsibility, which reflects the structure dimension of public management, from **subjective responsibility,** which is more closely associated with the culture dimension, in the sense that it focuses on "identification, loyalty, and conscience" and "hinges more heavily upon background, the processes of socialization, and current associations in and outside the organization than does objective responsibility.[57]
- Public administration scholars Barbara S. Romzek and Melvin J. Dubnick offer a definition of accountability that reflects Mosher's conceptualization of objective responsibility: "a relationship in which an individual or agency is held to answer for performance that involves some delegation of authority to act."[58]

Romzek and Dubnick develop a framework for analyzing public accountability. They delineate four types of accountability systems based on the source of control over an agency's action: whether control originates within or outside the organization and the degree of that control (see Table 2.1).

- **Bureaucratic (or hierarchical) accountability** is characterized by hierarchical relationships within an organization that are accompanied by and characterized by rules and clearly defined expectations. These types of relationships correspond with structures that are further discussed in Part II.
- **Legal accountability** is concerned with "a formal or implied fiduciary (principal/agent) agreement between the public agency and its legal overseer" and by definition is imposed by formal authorities external to the organization. Like bureaucratic accountability, legal accountability tends to be manifested in structures.
- **Political accountability** is concerned with representativeness and responsiveness of the public manager or organization to a constituency. "Constituencies include the general public, elected officials, agency heads, agency clientele, other special interest groups, and future generations."[59]
- **Professional accountability** is concerned with discretion and deference to the expertise of professionals in an organization. This type of accountability reflects Mosher's concept of subjective responsibility and the culture dimension of public management.

TABLE 2.1	**Types of Accountability Systems**	
Degree of Control Over Agency Actions	**Source of Agency Control**	
	Internal	**External**
High	1. Bureaucratic	2. Legal
Low	3. Professional	4. Political

Source: Barbara S. Romzek and Melvin J. Dubnick, "Accountability in the Public Sector: Lessons from the *Challenger* Tragedy," *Public Administration Review* 47, no. 3 (May/June 1987): 229.

- Political scientist Judith E. Gruber focuses on ensuring accountability in democracies. The task is not unique to governments or to democracies, but it takes on special urgency in democracies because unaccountable power flies in the face of the central norms of such political systems. When the legitimacy of a government derives from the consent of the governed, the problem becomes not merely an inability to get the governmental apparatus to act in ways the leaders or citizens wish but also a challenge to the fundamental nature of that government.[60]

Gruber is concerned with issues of democratic control of the bureaucracy—that is, control that stems from citizens. Bureaucratic behaviors, she argues, exhibit two dimensions for which they can be held accountable: the procedures they use and the substance of decisions they make. The combination of these dimensions results in four idealized types of bureaucratic actors: autonomous actors, end achievers, procedure followers, and clerks. Each has a corresponding system for ensuring accountability through democratic control (Table 2.2).

TABLE 2.2	**Idealized Perspectives of Bureaucratic Democracy and Approaches to Democratic Control**	
	Substantive Constraint	
Procedural Constraint	**Low**	**High**
Low	Actor: Autonomous actor Approach: Self-control	Actor: End achiever Approach: Public interest
High	Actor: Procedure follower Approach: Participatory	Actor: Clerk

Source: Adapted from Figures 1 and 2 in Judith E. Gruber, *Controlling Bureaucracies: Dilemmas in Democratic Governance* (Berkeley: University of California Press, 1987), 15, 18.

- **Self-control approaches** apply in situations characterized by both low substantive and procedural constraints.
- **Participatory approaches** apply in situations characterized by low substantive but high procedural constraints.
- **Public interest approaches** apply in situations characterized by high substantive but low procedural constraints.
- **Accountability approaches** apply when substantive constraints are low, and when procedural constraints span from moderate to high. These approaches focus on "guaranteeing that decisions are made in an 'appropriate fashion' with only peripheral concern for what the decisions are."
- **Clientele-oriented approaches** apply when both substantive and procedural constraints are moderate. These approaches "are more concerned with the substance of decisions made in administrative agencies than with the procedural fact that they are made solely by administrators."[61]

The use of analytic frameworks like the ones described in this section can support public management analysis by helping to clarify the meaning of accountability in a given situation and among different actors with different interests. Incorporated into a model deliberative process, these frameworks can support analysis of accountability issues by informed citizens and public managers alike.

THINKING INSTITUTIONALLY

Managing under the rule of law—finding the law—might be construed as requiring the drawing of distinctions between "the unambiguously expressed intent of Congress" (or of any legislative body) and "the interstices created by statutory silence or ambiguity" and then using common sense in those interstices. Indeed, Supreme Court Justice Sonia Sotomayor recently stated, "The government must be allowed to handle the basic tasks of public administration in a manner that comports with common sense."[62]

The reality, however, is that the unambiguously expressed intent of a legislature, not to mention what constitutes common sense, may be ambiguous, or at least so it may be claimed by elected executives and their appointees in managerial roles. In the American scheme of governance, the process of judicial review resolves conflicting claims about managerial discretion.

Some in public administration and management wish it were otherwise. They dream of a public administration with greatly enhanced power and autonomy, able to define its own mission and take risks guided by, but not subordinate to, lawmakers, policymakers, and lawyers. It is not hard to imagine that the design of policies to control air pollution would be the business of highly trained scientists and policy analysts empowered to make technically rational choices subject to peer review and to ultimate approval by the people's representatives.

The danger is that, if not held in check by the rule of law, those who possessed such autonomy—whether they are members of the American Society for Public Administration or of the Federalist Society[vii]—could be prone to making judgments that subordinate the rule of law to their own preferences, perhaps even with the backing of respectable values and scientific sanction. Doing so could deprive administration of the only legitimacy that ultimately counts: that which adheres to the constitutional scheme.

> Thinking institutionally means more than knowing the rules of the game: that is, the rule of law as legality and constraint. It means respecting the game you are playing: the rule of law as a principle of responsible administration.

The implication of this argument is that public management's practitioners, scholars, and teachers must internalize a commitment to the law by exercising the habit of what political scientist Hugh Heclo calls "thinking institutionally" about public administration and management. Thinking institutionally means more than knowing the rules of the game: that is, the rule of law as legality and constraint. It means respecting the game you are playing: the rule of law as a principle of responsible administration.

Someone who thinks institutionally exhibits "a coherent, sensitive awareness in making judgments," in this case about fulfilling the constitutional scheme. Institutional thinking is infused with value that "stretch[es] the time horizon backward and forward [and] senses the shadows of both past and future lengthening into the present."[63] Without this type of thinking, Heclo argues, institutions—legislatures, agencies, courts—are little more than empty formalities. Without it, the rule of law is little more than legality.

Responsible management, then, is management that reflects the habit of thinking institutionally with respect to the rule of law, which, after all, an administrator's oath of office requires. As a report to the American Society for Public Administration, a committee led by public administration scholar Nicholas Henry put it,

> The profession's central commitment must be to give specific and principled meaning to the oath of office and what it means to be accountable to that oath. Public administrators are thus required to follow constitutional,

---

[vii]The Federalist Society for Law and Public Policy Studies is an organization that promotes conservative and libertarian interpretations of the Constitution.

statutory, and administrative law, plus decisions and orders of the courts. Within this framework, the defining practice of governance is the interpretation and exercise of public authority.[64]

Not only are public officials sworn to govern lawfully, the separation of powers guarantees that failure to exercise good judgment concerning the meaning of *lawful* invites the other branches to constrain the exercise of official discretion. These constraints may undermine administration's capacity to contribute effectively to democratic governance, further disempowering the profession that "runs the Constitution."

Law is the root system of public management. Public management that ignores its roots will be rightly seen as a parasite.

KEY CONCEPTS

Separation of powers
Rule of law
Performance-based organizations
Delegated authority
Doctrine of objective reasonableness
Precept of managerial responsibility
Positive law
Constitutional law
Statutory law
Administrative law
Rulemaking
Executive order
Common law
International law
Spoils system
Direct democracy
Government Accountability Office/General Accounting Office

Transparency
Office of inspector general
Whistleblowers
Objective responsibility
Accountability
Subjective responsibility
Bureaucratic (or hierarchical) accountability
Legal accountability
Political accountability
Professional accountability
Self-control approaches
Participatory approaches
Public interest approaches
Accountability approaches
Clientele-oriented approaches
Chevron deference
Expertise-forcing

CASE ANALYSIS: THE RULE OF LAW IN ACTION: *MASSACHUSETTS V. ENVIRONMENTAL PROTECTION AGENCY*

Public law scholar Phillip Cooper observes, "sooner or later, most important political problems in America are transformed into administrative problems which, in turn, find their way into the courts."[65] A clear-cut example of this process is how the ongoing problem of air pollution and climate change are addressed politically, administratively, and, ultimately, legally.

Responding to the growing power of the environmental protection movement, Congress passed the Clean Air Act of 1970 (CAA), which authorized the creation of the Environmental Protection Agency (EPA). It "gave authority to EPA to designate air pollutants, determine acceptable concentrations of those pollutants, review state implementation plans for regulation of stationary emissions sources, and directly regulate mobile source emissions."[66] Section 202(a)(1) of the CAA required the EPA administrator to

(Continued)

(Continued)

establish standards, "applicable to the emission of any *air pollutant* from . . . new motor vehicles or new motor vehicle engines, which in [his or her] judgment *cause, or contribute to*, air pollution which may reasonably be anticipated to *endanger* public health or welfare" [emphasis added].[67]

In subsequent years, mounting scientific evidence suggested that global warming was occurring, and that an important cause was the man-made greenhouse gases (GHGs). Although some climate scientists demurred from the emerging consensus, support grew for regulating emissions of GHGs. Proposals to do so were politically controversial, however, because of opposition from firms and industries responsible for those emissions. Nonetheless, pressure on EPA to use its authority under the CAA to take action increased among environmentalists. Concerns focused on CO_2, a pollutant caused by the use of carbon-based fuels by energy producers and by mobile sources such as automobiles.

Arguments for No Regulation

In 1998, in response to the political pressure, EPA administrator Carol Browner asked EPA's general counsel, Jonathan Cannon, to provide an authoritative statement concerning the EPA's legal authority to regulate CO_2 under the CAA. Although CO_2 met the law's definition of a pollutant, Cannon argued that the EPA could not regulate it because the administrator had not issued a legally required finding that public health and welfare were endangered by CO_2 emissions.[68]

This judgment by the EPA's top lawyer caused political controversy to focus on the issuance of such a finding. The International Center for Technology Assessment (ICTA), a bipartisan nonprofit research organization, submitted a petition to compel the EPA (under CAA section 202(a)(1)) to regulate the emissions of four GHGs: CO_2, methane, nitrous oxide, and hydro-fluorocarbons, all of which are emitted by new mobile sources.

In September 2003, the EPA, then under a Republican administration, published a denial of ICTA's petition. In a reversal of Cannon's judgment, EPA general counsel Robert Fabricant argued that GHGs were *not* pollutants under CAA. The agency, he said, "must determine that Congress intended for the grant to give the agency authority to regulate in that specific area."[69] Fabricant also argued that "Congress did not intend the CAA to give EPA authority to regulate GHG emissions from mobile sources." Further, even if CAA gave authority to regulate carbon emissions, the EPA had no obligation to determine whether those emissions "cause, or contribute to, air pollution which may reasonably be anticipated to endanger public health or welfare," that is, the EPA had no obligation to issue an "endangerment finding."

The Massachusetts Complaint

The ICTA had failed to convince the U.S. Court of Appeals for the District of Columbia Circuit to reject the EPA's arguments. Then on March 2, 2006, the State of Massachusetts filed a petition for a writ of certiorari—a request for a Supreme Court review of the lower court's ruling. Certiorari was granted on June 26, 2006. Massachusetts sought the high court's review of the EPA's interpretation of its statutory authority under the CAA.

Specifically, the Commonwealth of Massachusetts argued that CAA section 302(g) defines an air pollutant as an "air pollution agent or combination of such agents, including any physical, chemical, biological, radioactive substance or matter that is emitted into or otherwise enters the ambient air." Because CO_2 and other GHGs are chemicals emitted into the ambient air by new motor vehicles, they are air pollutants that can be regulated under section 202(a)(1) of the CAA.[70] The state argued that the EPA had misapplied prior Supreme

Court rulings that the EPA believed restricted its authority. Moreover, the EPA was incorrect to interpret the CAA's use of the words "in [administrator's] judgment" to mean that the EPA "had no obligation" to regulate.

The EPA argued in response that the State of Massachusetts had no standing to file this lawsuit. That is, it could not demonstrate that the EPA's judgments in this matter had caused harm to the state, that GHG emissions from vehicles were not significant enough to harm the state's climate. It argued, further, that Congress had not intended to authorize regulation of pollutants if doing so had significant "economic and political consequences."[71]

The Supreme Court Rules

On April 7, 2007, the Supreme Court ruled, in a narrow 5–4 decision, that the state of Massachusetts had standing to file its complaint. On the merits of the complaint, the Court ruled that "the plain meaning" of the CAA's broad language was that the EPA had the authority to regulate GHGs. Moreover, the EPA had not reasonably explained its decision.[72] The Court reasoned,

> As we have repeated time and again, an agency has broad discretion to choose how best to marshal its limited resources and personnel to carry out its delegated responsibilities. See *Chevron U. S. A. Inc. v. Natural Resources Defense Council, Inc., 467 U. S. 837*, 842–845 (1984). That discretion is at its height when the agency decides not to bring an enforcement action. Therefore, in *Heckler v. Chaney, 470 U. S. 821* (1985), we held that an agency's refusal to initiate enforcement proceedings is not ordinarily subject to judicial review.[73]

In this case, however, the "affected party" had "an undoubted right to file" a complaint, and a refusal to promulgate rules is susceptible to judicial review, albeit a review that is extremely limited and highly deferential to the agency. As the agency clearly had the authority to promulgate rules controlling GHG emissions, denial that such authority existed and that, even if it did exist, promulgating such rules would conflict with "other administration priorities," the Court must hold such a denial to be "arbitrary and capricious, an abuse of discretion, and otherwise not in accordance with law."[74]

> The implication was that it was not reasonable for the EPA to argue that the science underlying global warming claims was contested, that regulating GHGs would have harmful economic consequences, and thus to justify the decision not to regulate.

Although the EPA's administrators could take "scientific uncertainty" into account in declining to regulate, the Court declared that the uncertainty must be "so profound" that a decision not to regulate is reasonable. To say that uncertainty, along with other factors such as conflicting priorities, is a reason for declining to regulate is not reasonable. The implication was that it was not reasonable for the EPA to argue that the science underlying global warming claims was contested, that regulating GHGs would have harmful economic consequences, and thus to justify the decision not to regulate.

Managerial Discretion and Its Limits

Public administrators are entitled to deference from the courts when their actions and decisions are "reasonable." This doctrine, known as **Chevron deference**, was first promulgated by the Supreme Court in its ruling on *Chevron U.S.A. vs. Natural Resources Defense Council* in 1984. That ruling provided a two-step test for an agency's entitlement to judicial deference:

(Continued)

(Continued)

(1) First, always, is the question whether Congress has directly spoken to the precise question at issue. If the intent of Congress is clear, that is the end of the matter; for the court as well as the agency must give effect to the unambiguously expressed intent of Congress.

If, however, the Court determines that Congress has not directly addressed the precise question at issue, the court does not simply impose its own construction of the statute . . . Rather,

(2) If the statute is silent or ambiguous with respect to the specific question, the issue for the court is whether the agency's answer is based on a permissible construction of the statute.[75]

More recent Supreme Court decisions have clarified the doctrine of judicial deference to administrative judgment. For example, a regulation promulgated under the "notice and comment" provisions of § 553 of the Administrative Procedure Act (APA) would likely receive Chevron deference. The notice-and-comment procedure "was expressly fashioned by Congress in 1946 to legitimize the broad delegation of administrative authority that began during the New Deal" on the condition that the exercise of such delegated authority was subject to "robust judicial review."[76]

Agencies are required to provide the public with adequate notice of a proposed rule followed by a meaningful opportunity to comment on the rule's content. Although the APA sets the minimum degree of public participation the agency must permit, '[matters] of great importance, or those where the public submission of facts will be either useful to the agency or a protection to the public, should naturally be accorded more elaborate public procedures.'[77]

Yet some agency interpretations of statutes and rules are made outside the regular rule-making process. For example, the Securities and Exchange Commission (SEC) might send a letter to a particular firm saying that no administrative action will be taken. "Although the SEC addresses no-action letters to particular recipients, because the letters are publicly disseminated on the SEC website, they have the effect of encouraging SEC-favored actions by other similarly situated entities and securities practitioners."[78] The Courts have not exercised "strong Chevron deference" with respect to nonlegislative rules such as the SEC no-action letter but instead have applied a less stringent test for deference.[79] In general, according to Judge Tatel,

Congress delegates authority to administrative agencies not to authorize any decision at all, but to permit agencies to apply their expertise. The reason-giving requirement allows courts to determine whether agencies have in fact acted on the basis of that expertise. . . . At a minimum, the requirement of reasoned justification ensures that the best arguments that can be marshaled in favor of a policy are enshrined in the public record, so that anyone seeking to undo the policy will have to grapple with and address those arguments. In this way, the reason-giving requirement makes our government more deliberative. And even when it slows agency action, it makes government more democratic.[80]

Politics or Expertise?

When public managers use their delegated discretion to implement public policies, their decisions are inevitably political. That is, they affect "who gets what, when, and how." Yet judicial review may hold public managers accountable to standards of technical rationality rather than political rationality. The exercise of managerial discretion is legitimate to the extent that it reflects the application of the agency's expertise free of political pressures. It is the application of expertise that was the reason for creating the agency in the first place and for delegating to it the implementation of public policies. This **expertise-forcing**, however, is arguably

> in tension with one leading rationale of the *Chevron* doctrine, a rationale that emphasizes the executive's democratic accountability and that sees nothing wrong with politically inflected presidential administration of executive branch agencies. . . . expertise-forcing has its roots in an older vision of administrative law, one in which politics and expertise are fundamentally antagonistic.[81]

From that perspective, *Massachusetts v. EPA* suggests that "the Court has at least temporarily become disenchanted with executive power and the idea of political accountability and is now concerned to protect administrative expertise from political intrusion."[82]

The Saga Continues

In December 2009, with the EPA under a Democratic administration, the EPA administrator reversed the earlier assessment regarding GHGs:

> the current and projected concentrations of the six key well-mixed greenhouse gases—carbon dioxide (CO_2), methane (CH_4), nitrous oxide (N_2O), hydrofluorocarbons (HFCs), perfluorocarbons (PFCs), and sulfur hexafluoride (SF_6)—in the atmosphere threaten the public health and welfare of current and future generations [and that] the combined emissions of these well-mixed greenhouse gases from new motor vehicles and new motor vehicle engines contribute to the greenhouse gas pollution which threatens public health and welfare.[83]

Active EPA rulemaking followed for both stationary (electric power plants) and mobile (light-duty trucks) sources of GHG emissions. One new regulation required new or modified "major emitting facilities" such as power plants subject to the CAA's "prevention of significant deterioration" (PSD) provisions to obtain permits for emissions exceeding limits. The limits were measured in tons per year of a regulated pollutant. The EPA added four GHGs to the list of regulated pollutants, including CO_2.

However, the EPA also made a significant change in public policy. Instead of imposing the statutory limits of 250 tons per year for PSD facilities and 100,000 tons per year for other sources on the newly added GHGs (the limit beyond which a permit was required for previously regulated pollutants), the EPA changed the threshold for the new GHGs to the 100,000 tons per year appropriate for major polluters. The reason was straightforward: thousands of previously unregulated small to medium facilities emit 100 to 250 tons of the newly added GHGs per year, and the EPA did not want to extend its regulatory reach so dramatically.

The EPA's decision provoked a rash of lawsuits by states and industries. Plaintiffs again contested whether the CAA authorized the regulation of GHGs but also challenged the EPA's policy decision to lift the emission thresholds, saying that the EPA was trying to "design its own climate-change program."[84]

(Continued)

(Continued)

On June 22, 2014, the Supreme Court announced its decision in one of these lawsuits, *Utility Air Regulatory Group v. Environmental Protection Agency*.[85] The court upheld the EPA's authority to regulate GHGs in accordance with its 2007 decision in *Massachusetts v. EPA*. It also ruled, however, that the EPA was not authorized to require permits based solely on GHG emissions or for facilities that do not have other emissions above threshold levels. The Court indicated that a quantitative limit could not be used that was different from the one in the statute. The ruling noted that EPA could thus control 83 percent of GHGs, not the 86 percent the EPA design proposed to control.

The Supreme Court's decision in *Utility Air Regulatory Group v. Environmental Protection Agency* was about the extent of public managers' discretion—in this case, that of the EPA administrator—to design their own policy implementation strategies. The EPA claimed it had exercised its legally recognized "discretion" to make a court-recognized "reasonable construction of the statute." The court rejected this claim, however, saying,

> Even under *Chevron's* deferential framework, agencies must operate "within the bounds of reasonable interpretation." And reasonable statutory interpretation must account for both "the specific context in which . . . language is used" and "the broader context of the statute as a whole." . . . Thus, an agency interpretation that is "inconsisten[t] with the design and structure of the statute as a whole, "does not merit deference. . . . Agencies exercise discretion only in the interstices created by statutory silence or ambiguity; they must always "give effect to the unambiguously expressed intent of Congress."[86]

Discussion Questions

1. Analyze the EPA's actions in this case through the lens of Justice Scalia's comment in the *Printz* decision, excerpted in this chapter.

2. Judge David Tatel, quoted at different points in this chapter, has commented, "when reading a set of briefs or listening to oral argument, I sometimes wonder whether the agency consulted its lawyers only after it found itself in court."[87] Consider Dimock's guidelines for "finding the law." Presumably the EPA had skilled attorneys during the different administrations described in this case. Was the difficulty in this case "finding the law"? Or was it something else?

3. Of the different sources of law described in this chapter, which are evident in this case (including those directly involved in the lawsuits)?

4. What does *accountability* mean in the context of this case? Which accountability institutions are evident?

5. Discuss what it means for an EPA public manager to *think institutionally* concerning the issues raised in this case.

6. What are the tensions between technical rationality and political rationality evident in this case?

NOTES

1. Thomas Paine, *Common Sense* (Philadelphia, PA: W. and T. Bradford, 1791), http://www.earlyamerica.com/earlyamerica/milestones/commonsense/text.html.

2. The notification requirement in Section 1035(d) of the NDAA states, "The Secretary of Defense shall notify the appropriate committees of Congress of a determination of the Secretary under subsection (a) or (b) not later than 30 days before the transfer or release of the individual under such subsection." http://www.gpo.gov/fdsys/pkg/BILLS-113hr3304enr/pdf/BILLS-113hr3304enr.pdf.

3. "Statement by the President on H.R. 3304," *The White House*, http://www.whitehouse.gov/the-press-office/2013/12/26/statement-president-hr-3304.

4. Government Accountability Office, "Department of Defense—Compliance with Statutory Notification Requirement" (B-326013), August 21, 2014, http://www.gao.gov/assets/670/665390.pdf.

5. American Bar Association, Task Force on Presidential Signing Statements and the Separation of Powers Doctrine, July 24, 2006, http://www.americanbar.org/content/dam/aba/migrated/leadership/2006/annual/dailyjournal/20060823144113. Congressional Research Service, "Presidential Signing Statements: Constitutional and Institutional Implications," January 4, 2012, http://fas.org/sgp/crs/natsec/RL33667.pdf

6. Brent Kendall and Stephanie Armour, "Appeals Courts Issue Conflicting Rulings on Health-Law Subsidies," *The Wall Street Journal*, July 22, 2014, sec. US, http://online.wsj.com/articles/key-section-of-health-care-law-struck-down-by-appeals-court-1406309685?mod=WSJ_hp_LEFTTopStories.%20%20See%20also%20http://www.washingtonpost.com/opinions/ruth-marcus-the-supreme-court-may-not-protect-obamacare-this-time/2014/07/24/7d414bcc-1353-11e4-8936-26932bcfd6ed_story.html?hpid=z2. See also Ruth Marcus, "Supreme Court May Not Protect Obamacare This Time," *The Washington Post*, July 24, 2014, http://www.washingtonpost.com/opinions/ruth-marcus-the-supreme-court-may-not-protect-obamacare-this-time/2014/07/24/7d414bcc-1353-11e4-8936-26932bcfd6ed_story.html?hpid=z2.

7. Adam Liptak, "Compromise at the Supreme Court Veils Its Rifts," *The New York Times*, July 1, 2014, http://www.nytimes.com/2014/07/02/us/supreme-court-term-marked-by-unanimous-decisions.html.

8. Gene Magidenko, "Tax Exceptionalism: Wanted Dead or Alive," *Michigan Journal of Law Reform*, March 6, http://mjlr.org/2012/03/06/tax-exceptionalism-wanted-dead-or-alive-2/

9. Constitution of the Commonwealth of Massachusetts, Preamble, Art. XXX (1780).

10. Michael Mullane, "The Rule of Law," *NPR Morning Edition*, June 5, 2006.

11. Andrew Graham and Alasdair Roberts, "The Agency Concept in North America: Failure, Adaptation, and Incremental Change," in *Unbundled Government: A Critical Analysis of the Global Trend to Agencies, Quangos and Contractualisation,* ed. Christopher Pollitt and Colin Talbot (London, UK, and New York, NY: Routledge, 2004), 146.

12. Ibid., 147.

13. Violent Crime Control and Law Enforcement Act of 1994, Pub.L. 103–322, 108 Stat. 1796, 1994.

14. The Police Executives Research Forum provides research and management services, technical assistance, and executive-level education to support law enforcement agencies. http://www.policeforum.org/home/.

15. Ibid.

16. Ibid., p. 3.

17. Ramon Antonio Vargas, "NOPD Consent Decree Monitor Chosen: Sheppard Mullin Gets Contract," *NOLA.com*, July 5, 2013, http://www.nola.com/crime/index.ssf/2013/07/nopd_consent_decree_monitor_ch_1.html.

18. *Mack and Printz v. United States*, 521 U.S. 898 (1997).

19. U.S. Constitution, Preamble.

20. Gary Wamsley et al., "Public Administration and the Governance Process: Shifting the Political Dialogue," in *Refounding Public Administration,* ed. Gary L. Wamsley et al. (Newbury Park, CA: Sage, 1990), www.cpap.vt.edu/current/wamsley_etal.pdf.

21. Marshall E. Dimock, "The Development of American Administrative Law," *Journal of Comparative Legislation and International Law* 15 (1933): 35.

22. Ibid., 32

23. Marshall E. Dimock, *Law and Dynamic Administration* (New York, NY: Praeger, 1980), 31.

24. Yong S. Lee with David H. Rosenbloom, *A Reasonable Public Servant: Constitutional Foundations of Administrative Conduct in the United States* (Armonk, NY: M. E. Sharpe, 2005), 36; Yong S. Lee, "The Judicial Theory of a Reasonable Public Servant," *Public Administration Review* 64 (July 2004): 425.

25. Phillip J. Cooper, *Public Law and Public Administration,* 4th ed. (Itasca, IL: F. E. Peacock, 2006).

26. Anthony Bertelli and Laurence E. Lynn Jr., *Madison's Managers* (Baltimore, MD: Johns Hopkins University Press, 2006), 206.

27. Martin Shapiro, "Discretion." *Handbook of Regulation and Administrative Law*, David H. Rosenbloom and Richard D. Schwartz eds. (New York, NY: Marcel Dekker, 1994), pp. 501-17.

28. On administrative law, see David H. Rosenbloom, *Administrative Law for Public Managers* (Boulder, CO: Westview Press, 2003); Phillip J. Cooper, *Public Law and Public Administration,* 4th ed. (Itasca, IL: F. E. Peacock, 2006).

29. Rosenbloom, *Administrative Law for Public Managers.*

30. David S. Tatel, "The Administrative Process and the Rule of Environmental Law," *Harvard Environmental Law Journal* 34, (2010): 7.

31. Congressional Research Service, "Executive Orders: Issuance, Modification," April 16, 2014, http://fas.org/sgp/crs/misc/RS20846.pdf.

32. Bertelli and Lynn, *Madison's Managers,* 206.

33. Robert S. Barker, "Government Accountability and Its Limits," *Issues of Democracy* 5, no. 2 (August, 2000).

34. Laurence E. Lynn Jr., *Public Management: Old and New* (London, UK: Routledge, 2007).

35. James Hart, *The Ordinance Making Powers of the President of the United States*, reprinted in *Johns Hopkins University Studies in Historical and Political Science*, vol. XLIII, no. 3 (Baltimore, MD: Johns Hopkins University Press, 1925), 1–359, 268.

36. Laurence E. Lynn Jr., "The Myth of the Bureaucratic Paradigm: What Traditional Public Administration Really Stood For," *Public Administration Review* 61(2001): 144–160.

37. Dwight Waldo, *The Administrative State: A Study of the Political Theory of American Public Administration*, 2nd ed. (New York, NY: Holmes and Meier, 1984), 11.

38. Lynn, "The Myth of the Bureaucratic Paradigm," 144-160.

39. Woodrow Wilson, "The Study of Administration," *Political Science Quarterly* 2 (1887): 197–222, 213.

40. Frederick C. Mosher, *Democracy and the Public Service* (New York, NY: Oxford University Press, 1968), 7.

41. Wallace S. Sayre, "Trends of a Decade in Administrative Values," *Public Administration Review* 11 (1951): 1–9, 5; Bertelli and Lynn, *Madison's Managers.*

42. John D. Millett, *Management in the Public Service: The Quest for Effective Performance* (New York, NY: McGraw-Hill, 1954), 403.

43. Lynn, "The Myth of the Bureaucratic Paradigm"; Bertelli and Lynn, *Madison's Managers.*

44. Marshall C. Dimock, "Review: Government Corporations," *Public Administration Review* 49, (1989): 85.

45. Harvey C. Mansfield Sr., "Review: The Quest for Accountability," *Public Administration Review* 41, (2001): 397–401, 397.

46. Alasdair Roberts, *Blacked Out: Government Secrecy in the Information Age* (Cambridge, MA: Cambridge University Press, 2006), 14.

47. All are members of the Council of Inspectors General on Integrity and Efficiency, at http://www.ignet.gov.

48. 5 U. S. C. App. § 3(a).

49. "IGNET," accessed November 7, 2014, https://www.ignet.gov/.

50. U.S. Office of Special Counsel, https://osc.gov/.

51. Robert D. Behn, "What Do We Mean by Accountability, Anyway?" in *Rethinking Democratic Accountability* (Washington, D.: Brookings Institution Press, 2001), 6. See also Mark Bovens, "Public Accountability," in *The Oxford Handbook of Public Management,* ed. Ewan Ferlie, Laurence E. Lynn Jr., and Christopher Pollitt (Oxford, UK: Oxford University Press, 2005), 182–208.

52. William T. Gormley Jr., "Institutional Policy Analysis: A Critical Review," *Journal of Policy Analysis and Management* 6, no. 2 (1987): 153–169, 155, 161.

53. Mark Bovens, "Public Accountability," in *The Oxford Handbook of Public Management,* 191–192.

54. Robert D. Behn, *Rethinking Democratic Accountability* (Washington, DC: Brookings Institution, 2001), 9–10.

55. Herbert A. Simon, Victor A. Thompson, and Donald W. Smithburg, *Public Administration* (New Brunswick, NJ: Transaction, 1991), 513.

56. Mosher, *Democracy and the Public Service*, 7.

57. Ibid., 8.

58. Barbara S. Romzek and Melvin J. Dubnick, "Accountability," in *The International Encyclopedia of Public Policy and Administration,* ed. Jay M. Shafritz (Boulder, CO: Westview Press, 1998), 6–11.

59. Barbara S. Romzek and Melvin J. Dubnick, "Accountability in the Public Sector: Lessons from the Challenger Crisis," *Public Administration Review* 47 (May/June 1987): 227–238, 229.

60. Judith E. Gruber, *Controlling Bureaucracies: Dilemmas in Democratic Governance* (Berkeley: University of California Press, 1987), 5.

61. Ibid., 20, 22–23.

62. Wheaton College v. Sylvia Burwell, Secretary of Health and Human Services, 573 U. S. _____ (2014), http://s3.documentcloud.org/documents/1212608/wheaton-vs-burwell.pdf, 16.

63. Cooper, *Public Law and Public Administration*, (2006, 733, 737).

64. Lynn, Laurence E., Jr., "Restoring the Rule of Law to Public Administration: What Frank Goodnow Got Right and Leonard White Didn't." *Public Administration Review* 69, 5 (2009):803-813.

65. Cooper, *Public Law and Public Administration*, 2006.
66. "Regulation of Greenhouse Gases under the Clean Air Act.," *Wikipedia, the Free Encyclopedia*, accessed November 7, 2014, http://en.wikipedia.org/wiki/Regulation_of_greenhouse_gases_under_the_Clean_Air_Act; Michael Sugar, "Massachusetts V. Environmental Protection Agency," *Harvard Environmental Law Review* 31 (2007): 532.
67. 42 U.S.C. § 4521(a)(1). Retrieved from http://www.law.cornell.edu/uscode/html/uscode42/usc_sec_42_00007521----000-.html.
68. Sugar, "Massachusetts V. Environmental Protection Agency," 533.
69. Ibid., 534.
70. Ibid., 535.
71. Ibid., 537.
72. Ibid., 537.
73. *Massachusetts v. Environmental Protection Agency*, 549 U.S. 497 (2007).
74. 5 U.S.C. § 706. Retrieved from http://www.law.cornell.edu/uscode/text/5/706.
75. *Chevron U.S.A. v. NRDC*, 467 U.S. 837, 842–843 (1984).
76. Tatel, "The Administrative Process and the Rule of Environmental Law," 3.
77. Congressional Research Service, "A Brief Overview of Rulemaking and Judicial Review," January 4, 2011, http://www.wise-intern.org/orientation/documents/CRSrulemakingCB.pdf.
78. Thomas J. Fraser, "Interpretive Rules: Can the Amount of Deference Accorded Them Offer Insight Into the Procedural Inquiry?" *Boston University Law Review,* 90 (2010): 1309.
79. Ibid., 1303–1329.
80. Tatel, "The Administrative Process and the Rule of Environmental Law," 5, 7–8.
81. Jody Freeman and Adrian Vermeule, "Massachusetts v. EPA: From Politics to Expertise," *Supreme Court Review,* August 2007, 53.
82. Ibid., 54.
83. Endangerment and Cause or Contribute Findings for Greenhouse Gases under Section 202(a) of the Clean Air Act, last modified November 22, 2013, http://www.epa.gov/climatechange/endangerment/.
84. Dana Milbank, "Dana Milbank: At the Supreme Court, a Royal Mess for 'King Barack,'" *The Washington Post*, February 24, 2014, http://www.washingtonpost.com/opinions/dana-milbank-at-the-supreme-court-a-royal-mess-for-king-barack/2014/02/24/4de3ac46-9dae-11e3-9ba6-800d1192d08b_story.html?hpid=z2.
85. Supreme Court of the United States, "Utility Air Regulatory Group v. Environmental Protection Agency, 573 U.S." ___(2014),, http://www.supremecourt.gov/opinions/13pdf/12-1146_4g18.pdf.
86. Ibid., 19, 24.
87. Tatel, "The Administrative Process and the Rule of Environmental Law," 7.

3 National Security Agency Surveillance

Reflecting Society's Values, Performing Effectively, Earning Trust?

INTRODUCTION

Beginning in early June 2013, media accounts revealed that the U.S. National Security Agency (NSA) was engaged in a vast program of electronic surveillance that collected information on the personal communications of millions of people, including American citizens. These revelations were based on highly classified documents leaked to the British newspaper *The Guardian* and shared with other news organizations by Edward J. Snowden, who was employed by a private company under contract to the NSA. He had gained access to information on the agency's clandestine efforts, which were a response to the terrorist attack on the World Trade Center in New York City on September 11, 2001. Their purpose was to identify actual or potential terrorist threats to the national security of the United States. This chapter tells the story of the revelations and events that rocked American and global politics during a 7-month period in 2013.

Underlying these revelations and events are deep roots of public management. The details of this case reveal how, why, and by whom an immensely complex activity gets done by public agencies and their managers. On display is the panoply of organizations, procedures, and mechanisms available to formulate and implement national counterterrorism policy. The details of the case reveal the consequences of how and why that work is done.

In terms of this book's progression, this chapter's case serves as a waypoint. Chapters 1 and 2 outline the main ideas of the book: public managerial accountability to the rule of law and three-dimensional management analysis supported by a model deliberative process. Analytic frameworks, such as ones that address accountability, have been discussed as well. This chapter provides an opportunity to analyze the NSA case in depth, using the concepts and tools covered so far. Then, Parts II, III, and IV of the book discuss specific theories, frameworks, heuristics, and concepts from the social sciences that can be used to strengthen public management analysis through the lens of each of the three dimensions. With these additional tools, the NSA case can be analyzed in even greater depth.

This work gets done in an age in which politics can be intensely partisan and investigative journalists must feed an insatiable 24-hour news cycle. The managers of public welfare, environmental protection, health, and law enforcement agencies may find themselves dealing with operational challenges and public controversies similar to those confronted by the NSA.

The case of NSA surveillance reveals how policymakers and public managers can be tempted to shield what they are doing from prying legislative, journalistic, and public eyes. The case also shows that the accountability of government to "the people" under the rule of law is essential if government is to fulfill the Founders' promise of "liberty and justice for all" as well as how very difficult it is to actually accomplish this.

The NSA case is organized as follows:

- "A Leak, A Crisis" describes how the situation began to unfold and summarizes events during the 7 ensuing months.

- "National Security Agency Surveillance: The Building Blocks" provides background on the systems in place to protect the United States from terrorist attacks:

  o the agencies;
  o the laws that govern these agencies;
  o the surveillance technologies agency officials use;
  o the private sector firms that work under contract to the surveillance agencies;
  o other government organizations that depend on surveillance information; and
  o the public managers at the heart of the story, in particular the director of the NSA and the director of National Intelligence.

- "Revelations of U.S. Surveillance Unfold" describes the responses of an intertwined set of public and private sector actors to the barrage of revelations:

  o the leaker, Edward Snowden;
  o the media organizations that gained access to the leaked documents and to other privileged information;
  o the administration of President Barack Obama, which was caught off balance by the unrelenting stream of media stories;
  o the U.S. Congress, in particular the Senate Select Committee on Intelligence and the House Permanent Select Committee on Intelligence;
  o individual critics of the U.S. government's bulk surveillance programs in Congress, in civil society, and in the legal community; and
  o foreign governments and international organizations involved and caught up in U.S. surveillance activities.

- The case analysis section presents a strategy for systematic approach to the facts of the case. It describes the model deliberative framework as well as specific questions about the public managers and broader governance questions.

Although the chapter includes rich details, they are only a subset of the vast information about NSA surveillance that continued to pour forth. As conveyed here, the same detail or event may appear at different points to emphasize how it fits with different perspectives or actors. The details afford an opportunity to conduct a public management analysis at the end of the chapter. Concepts from the first two chapters are woven through the case.

As has been stressed, public managers throughout American government face issues of proportionate urgency to those raised by this chapter's case. They must reconcile tensions between, for example, parental rights and the best interests of the child, environmental protection and property rights or economic growth, delegation and control of authority to make decisions, efficiency and equity in delivering public services, and rehabilitation and punishment of criminal offenders.

Analysis of the NSA case reveals a major, ongoing, and instructive public management story. That same kind of analysis is suited to all kinds of issues at the local, state, national, and international levels of public governance.

A LEAK, A CRISIS

In early June, 2013, the British newspaper *The Guardian* claimed that the NSA was spying on U.S. citizens using a vast database of telephone and other communications records. Ever since the terrorist attacks of September 11, 2001, the protection of Americans from terrorist attacks had been of overriding importance to the U.S. government. The existence of NSA's secret surveillance programs was known to legislators because their authorization by House and Senate Intelligence Committees was required. But the American people knew very little about the programs.

They learned a little in December 2005, when *The New York Times* revealed that the NSA was authorized by President George W. Bush to conduct warrantless wiretaps of domestic telephone calls. This revelation ignited a major political controversy. Most Americans had since come to tolerate, albeit warily, the need for constant surveillance by U.S. intelligence agencies in order to identify and obstruct foreigners who might wish to harm Americans and America's interests.[1] That such activities had to be conducted in secret so America's enemies could not foil them was also understood. In countering terrorist threats, the government was given the benefit of the doubt because it was the communications of foreigners, not American citizens, which were being collected.

The new revelations by *The Guardian* were remarkable against this backdrop. *The Guardian* reported that a secret federal court had authorized the NSA to obtain from Verizon (a major telephone company) the metadata—records of who was calling whom and when—on U.S. domestic telephone calls through a program called PRISM. *The Guardian* also revealed that the NSA had direct access to the records of Google, Facebook, Apple, and other U.S. Internet service providers (ISPs) with the companies' agreement. Every American, the stories implied, was, or could be, under surveillance by the NSA.[2]

The world was learning these things because Edward J. Snowden, a 30-year-old employee of Booz Allen Hamilton, a private consulting firm under contract to the NSA, had stolen and given to journalists an unknown number of highly secret internal government documents on U.S. surveillance programs. The handover of these digital files, moreover, had been to a foreign newspaper, *The Guardian*, at a secret location in The People's Republic of China (soon to be revealed as a hotel room in Hong Kong).

These revelations turned out to be only the beginning. A drawn-out series of stories in several media outlets followed during 2013 and into 2014. These stories were based on Snowden's leaked documents, and each contained new, stunning revelations. The U.S. government had been creating a vast, sophisticated surveillance system for a wide variety of intelligence missions, including some (such as money laundering) unrelated to counterterrorism. The unpredictable timing and content of these stories were unnerving for the public, the Congress, the administration of President Obama, and foreign governments around the world. Revelations of U.S. government surveillance of its closest allies drew furious condemnations from foreign leaders, roiling U.S. foreign policy. Some members of congressional intelligence oversight committees who knew about these programs (but could say nothing about them because the information was classified) began indicating that more astonishing revelations were yet to come.[3]

President Obama and senior members of his administration galloped to stay ahead of the relentless outpouring of leaked information. Officials repeatedly denied invasions of Americans' privacy, justified efforts to foil terrorists, declassified documents suggesting that there was proper oversight of the NSA, promised—and delivered—greater transparency of intelligence community (IC) activities and strengthened institutional checks on surveillance programs to ensure respect for Americans' privacy rights. Under criticism from members of Congress, privacy advocates, and the media, layers of secrecy were peeled away from U.S. spying. But, as one journalist put it, when it comes to adhering to the rule of law, "the NSA is losing the benefit of the doubt."[4]

NATIONAL SECURITY AGENCY SURVEILLANCE: THE BUILDING BLOCKS

Conducting surveillance on behalf of U.S. national security is a responsibility of the executive branch of the federal government. Its activities are subject to congressional authorization, appropriation, and oversight and to rulings by federal courts concerning what the Constitution and statutory law—in this case, the Foreign Intelligence Surveillance Act (FISA) and the USA Patriot Act[i]—require. These statutes, as well as executive orders and regulations, are the sources of formal authority that lawfully delegate authority over intelligence activities to public officials.

The Agencies

Three agencies are central to conducting electronic surveillance of foreigners who might be engaged in terrorism-related activities: the NSA itself, the Foreign Intelligence Surveillance Court (FISC), and the Office of the Director of National Intelligence (ODNI).

The **NSA** was created in 1951 by an executive order issued by President Harry S. Truman. Operating under the authority of the Department of Defense and the ODNI, NSA collects foreign and military intelligence by intercepting signals (that is, communications transmitted by various technical methods: audio, video, digital, sonar, radar, and other devices). Headquartered at Fort Meade, Maryland, the NSA has facilities and operations in Colorado, Georgia, Hawaii, Texas, and Utah, as well as in Australia and Great Britain.

Once best known for gathering information to assess nuclear threats from the Soviet Union during the Cold War, the NSA's missions have been dominated in recent decades by military needs for battlefield intelligence in Iraq and Afghanistan. Activities include locating signals associated with targets of the Central Intelligence Agency's (CIA) armed drone aircraft and U.S. military Special Operations units (including locating Osama bin Laden and al Qaeda operatives in the tribal regions of Pakistan).

---

[i]The USA Patriot Act's title is the Uniting and Strengthening America by Providing Appropriate Tools Required to Intercept and Obstruct Terrorism Act of 2001, enacted in the immediate aftermath of the 9/11 terrorist attacks.

A major portion of the information for the President's Daily Brief (PDB) on threats to national security is collected by the NSA.[5] According to NSA officials, "in carrying out its signals intelligence mission, N.S.A. collects only what it is explicitly authorized to collect. Moreover, the agency's activities are deployed only in response to requirements for information to protect the country and its interests."[6]

The NSA and private companies working for it under contract develop and use sophisticated computers and software tools to obtain and analyze signals that might contain information relevant to its battlefield support and counterterrorism missions. The NSA also compels or obtains the cooperation of private communications companies to obtain metadata on various forms of communication. The agency's Special Source Operations unit, described by Snowden as the "crown jewel" of the NSA, manages surveillance programs that rely on "corporate partnerships."[7] Most information about the agency's capabilities and how they are used is highly classified. Little would be known by the public about NSA's operations were it not for leaked documents and for revelations by often anonymous individuals who have been employed by or associated with the agency.

FISC was created by Congress in 1978 to hold agencies such as the CIA and the Federal Bureau of Investigation (FBI) accountable to the rule of law. The CIA and the FBI are required to obtain a judicial warrant from the FISC before they conduct electronic surveillance and gather intelligence within the United States. The Chief Justice of the U.S. Supreme Court appoints 11 federal judges to the FISC. They serve staggered terms of up to 7 years. It wasn't until January 17, 2007 that the Justice Department transferred oversight of the counterterrorism surveillance program from the NSA to the FISC in response to criticism that NSA wiretapping lacked judicial oversight.[8]

Applications for warrants are reviewed by three FISC judges assigned by the court's presiding judge. Unlike other courts in the federal judicial system, FISC proceedings are not adversarial; no one represents those who might oppose an application on privacy grounds. All rulings, which may include "novel interpretations of constitutional law,"[9] are conducted in secret, although the U.S. Attorney General is required to report to Congress summary data on cases and their disposition. Virtually all applications for warrants have been approved, although there are significant exceptions, noted later in this chapter.[10] According to a *New York Times* report,

> unlike traditional, narrowly tailored search warrants, those granted by the intelligence court often allow searches through records and data that are vast in scope. The standard of evidence needed to acquire them may be lower than in other courts, and the government may not be required to disclose for years, if ever, that someone was the focus of secret surveillance operations.[11]

What little could be learned about the FISC, including the names of the court's judges, was monitored by, among others, the Federation of American Scientists.

ODNI was created by the Intelligence Reform and Terrorism Prevention Act of 2004 to oversee and coordinate the intelligence activities of 15 federal agencies, including the CIA (see Figure 3.1). The DNI directs the National Intelligence Program, which comprises all programs, projects, and activities of the IC. The DNI also serves as principal advisor to the president, the National Security Council, and the Homeland Security Council concerning intelligence matters related to national security. Presidential Policy Directive 19, issued in October 2012, assigned responsibility for whistleblower and source protection to the DNI under the supervision of the IC's Inspector General. Following the Snowden leaks, the DNI was the president's highest-ranking spokesman concerning revelations of the bulk surveillance of U.S. citizens by the NSA.

FIGURE 3.1	**Office of the Director of National Intelligence–Organization Chart**

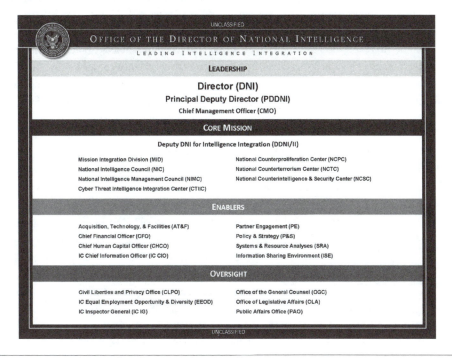

Source: http://www.dni.gov/files/OrgChart_for_DNI_unclass_site.pdf.

The ODNI was created in response to recommendations by the National Commission on Terrorist Attacks Upon the United States (the "9/11 Commission") to enable the IC to understand the relationships among the many bits and pieces of information gathered by its nearly two dozen separate agencies. Because of skepticism on the part of legislators and intelligence experts that a new layer of bureaucracy would be an effective solution to the kind of intelligence failures leading up to the 9/11 terrorist attacks, considerable logrolling and infighting accompanied the structuring of the ODNI.[12] When Robert Gates, former CIA director and future secretary of defense, was asked to become the first DNI, he is reported to have declined, saying that the new organization was "doomed to fail."[13]

The Rule of Law

The NSA, FISC, and ODNI are accountable for operating within the rule of law. Specifically, they were accountable in 2013 to (1) the provisions of Section 215 of the USA Patriot Act, which authorized the seizure of communications records to protect against international terrorism, (2) Section 702 of the FISA Amendments of 2008, which authorized "the targeting of persons reasonably believed to be located outside the United States to acquire foreign intelligence information,"[14] and (3) Executive Order 12333, which governed "United States intelligence activities" pursuant to statutory authorizations.[15]

The U.S. Supreme Court clarified the scope of the 2008 FISA amendments in *Clapper v. Amnesty International* in 2013. In a 5–4 decision reflecting the court's ideological division between conservative and liberal justices, the

Court ruled that individuals who had not proved they had been harmed in tangible ways by the government's surveillance programs (individuals who, like the plaintiffs, were bringing suit on the basis of the existence of the surveillance programs) had no standing to bring suit against the government for violations of their Fourth Amendment protection against unreasonable searches.

That ruling left unclear whether surveillance statutes were beyond judicial review altogether. The answer might be revealed in future litigation in which a U.S. citizen charged with espionage (a tangible harm) cited as a defense that prosecutors had obtained evidence through a dragnet surveillance conducted by the NSA. The U.S. Justice Department filed a case in October 2013 that relied on this kind of evidence and thus deliberately invited a Supreme Court test of the 2008 law's meaning.[16]

The Technologies

Enabling the NSA's surveillance activities are highly sophisticated computers, software programs, and servers designed to enable collection, analysis, and storage of communications information that might contain clues to threats to U.S. citizens and U.S. interests. For example, a communication by cell phone or e-mail may reveal the exact location of a suspected terrorist. A pattern of telephone, e-mail, and Internet communications might reveal the existence of an international terrorist or arms-trafficking network.

> After 9/11, the number of private companies the NSA depended on more than tripled, from 150 to almost 500.

Behind its veil of secrecy, the NSA developed technologies to access virtually all communications entering, leaving, or electronically transiting the United States on fiber-optic cables. Access is obtained using computerized filters installed on the telecommunications infrastructure facilities throughout the country. The filters are placed at switches, or key junction points. The NSA also has intercepted communications at and between the data centers of private communications firms located in foreign countries. Additional data were shared with the NSA by foreign government intelligence agencies, notably by Britain's General Communications Headquarters and by numerous telephone and Internet service providers.

Staff analysts can access these private communications without a warrant.[17] NSA analysts, from their desks at headquarters in Fort Meade, Maryland, or around the world, can insert selectors (names, e-mail addresses, key words, or other indicators) by remote control into contractor-maintained computer systems. Based on information in Snowden's leaked documents, the public learned about the numerous software programs used for analyzing the data, with codenames such as PRISM, XKEYSCORE, BULLRUN, MUSCULAR, and UPSTREAM.

The Contractors

As the counterterrorism missions of the NSA expanded, so too did its dependence on the private companies of an information/cyber industrial complex.[ii] After 9/11, the number of private companies the NSA depended on more than tripled, from 150 to almost 500.[18]

The complex includes many famous (and infamous) defense contractors who provided support for the wars in Iraq and Afghanistan, then supported the NSA's expanding surveillance ambitions. For example, Booz Allen Hamilton, Snowden's employer, a blue-chip consulting firm, describes itself:

> We are fully integrated across all organizations of NSA providing a diverse range of services and solutions such as
> DoD acquisition support; SIGINT technical intelligence analysis; information assurance; information operations

---

[ii]A Web site called "Black Hat" has information on the activities of this complex. https://www.blackhat.com.

strategy, policy analysis, and operations; systems engineering and technical assistance; IT analysis and strategy; and network and telecommunications. We have over thirty active contracts with a footprint that spans the entire NSA including: SIGINT, Information Assurance and Technology Directorates, as well as Research, the NSA/CSS Threat Operations Center, NSA/CSS Commercial Solutions Center, FAD, HR, NCS, and Acquisition.[19]

Being employed by this firm, it would seem, was virtually the same as being employed by the NSA.

Another NSA contractor, Narus, specializes in big data analytics. Established in Israel and now owned by the airplane manufacturer Boeing, "Narus specializes in spyware, equipment that examines both the metadata—the names and addresses of people communicating on the Internet—and the content of digital traffic such as e-mail as it zooms past at the speed of light."[20] One of the company's directors is a former NSA deputy director.

Many NSA contractors' activities were highly classified. For example, Endgame Systems, established in Atlanta in 2008 as a start-up backed by a number of venture capital firms, produces a worldwide map of every device connected to the Internet.[21] Its "vulnerability researchers" search for weaknesses in software programs for which patches have not been developed.[iii] An Endgame Systems official observed in a leaked email, "We've been very careful not to have a public face on our company." Said another, "We don't ever want to see our name in a press release."[22]

The Federal Bureaucracy

As Dana Priest of *The Washington Post* observed, "The story of the NSA's growth, obscured by the agency's extreme secrecy, is directly tied to the insatiable demand for its work product by the rest of the U.S. intelligence community, military units, and the FBI."[23] NSA officials said, repeatedly, that access to its surveillance data and tools was limited to those with a high priority "need to know." The FBI was the most likely to have a need to know when it came to counterterrorism and espionage. Agencies tasked with different kinds of missions requiring intelligence information, including those working to curb drug trafficking, cyber-attacks, money laundering, counterfeiting, and copyright infringement, claim a need to know justifying access to NSA's resources, but agencies complained that access was often denied despite a 2008 presidential executive order intended to increase inter-agency sharing of intelligence information.[24] NSA officials retained discretion to restrict access to those requests for access that agency officials deemed to be of high priority. NSA and FBI officials both said that other agencies sometimes exaggerated their need to have access to surveillance capabilities.

Alternatively, "if a link to national security is considered legitimate, the FBI will at times simply take over an agency's case itself and work it with the NSA."[25] For example, after a case of smuggling cigarettes was developed by the Bureau of Alcohol, Tobacco, Firearms, and Explosives, the FBI became interested because it might have been tied to financing terrorist groups. A drug agency spokeswoman said that her agency had no objections to allowing the NSA (and the FBI) to take the lead in seeking surveillance warrants from the FISA Court. "We don't have the authority [to seek warrants], and we don't want it, and that comes from the top down."[26]

Officials in the ODNI worried about broadening the surveillance process beyond the NSA and FBI. They "have been 'burned' by past wiretapping controversies and know the political consequences if they venture too far afield," commented one former intelligence officer, further stating, "I would have been very uncomfortable if we had let these other agencies get access to the raw NSA data."[27]

[iii]A patch is software code designed to be inserted into an executable program in order to fix errors in, or update the program or its supporting data.

The Public Manager

In August 2005, General Keith B. Alexander became the director of the NSA. A West Point graduate, he spent spent his career almost entirely in military intelligence assignments. Along the way, he earned several masters degrees, most in technical subjects. He had never served in combat. He rose rapidly through military intelligence ranks, earning a reputation as a capable manager. His overarching objective was made clear in a statement he made in 2001: "We have to stay out in front of our adversary. . . . It's a chess game, and you don't want to lose this one."[28]

As Alexander assumed leadership of the NSA, U.S. soldiers in Iraq were being killed by improvised explosive devices (IEDs). Hundreds of NSA analysts were searching for information snippets that might help commanders thwart these attacks. At Alexander's direction, a collection plan called Real Time Regional Gateway (RTRG) was implemented that, by 2008, had significantly reduced the IED threat. RTRG exemplified the philosophy by which Alexander confronted all threats to Americans, whether on the battlefield or in the homeland, whether from terrorists or from cyber attackers. According to an observer, "Rather than look for a single needle in the haystack, his approach was, 'Let's collect the whole haystack. Collect it all, tag it, store it. . . . And whatever it is you want, you go searching for it.'"[29] The strategy didn't just happen: "Alexander has pushed hard for everything he can get: tools, resources and the legal authority to collect and store vast quantities of raw information on American and foreign communications."[30]

> The strategy didn't just happen: "Alexander has pushed hard for everything he can get: tools, resources and the legal authority to collect and store vast quantities of raw information on American and foreign communications."

Those sympathetic toward the NSA's aggressive collection efforts insist it was all done under the watchful eyes of congressional intelligence committees and the FISC and in accordance with all laws governing the NSA's activities. Without the American people knowing how, their security was being safeguarded by Alexander's NSA. Alexander has said, "Everyone . . . understands that if we give up a capability that is critical to the defense of this nation, people will die."[31]

In 2010, Alexander's power was greatly expanded when he assumed command of U.S. Cyber Command, newly created to defend against and engage in cyber warfare, that is, attacks on a military or political opponent's communications and command and control systems. Of the power Alexander now possessed, the publication *Wired* commented,

> The forces under his command were now truly formidable—his untold thousands of NSA spies, as well as 14,000 incoming Cyber Command personnel, including Navy, Army, and Air Force troops. Helping Alexander organize and dominate this new arena would be his fellow plebes from West Point's class of 1974: David Petraeus, the CIA director; and Martin Dempsey, chair of the Joint Chiefs of Staff.[32]

In a hearing before a House committee, Alexander reflected on his new leadership of U.S. Cyber Command, "the only way to counteract both criminal and espionage activity online is to be proactive. If the U.S. is taking a formal approach to this, then that has to be a good thing."[33]

A probable example of General Alexander's use of proactive cyber warfare—the attack has never been officially confirmed or denied—is an NSA project named Stuxnet. Designed in cooperation with the CIA and Israeli intelligence to destroy physical equipment, Stuxnet was software that disrupted computer operations. It "was aimed at Iran's nuclear facility in Natanz. By surreptitiously taking control of an industrial control link known as a Scada (Supervisory Control and Data Acquisition) system, [Stuxnet] was able to damage about a thousand centrifuges used to enrich nuclear material."[34] At some point in the future, activities such as Stuxnet, some believe, might be considered "acts of war" under international law. At the very least, Stuxnet indicates a willingness to take significant risks.[iv]

Admirers say Alexander is creating "an enduring legacy—a position of far-reaching authority and potentially Strangelovian powers."[35] The *Wired* article on Alexander published at the moment of *The Guardian*'s first revelation based on Snowden's leaked documents summed up Alexander's reputation this way:

> Inside the government, the general is regarded with a mixture of respect and fear . . . . 'We jokingly referred to him as Emperor Alexander—with good cause, because whatever Keith wants, Keith gets,' says one former senior CIA official who agreed to speak on condition of anonymity. 'We would sit back literally in awe of what he was able to get from Congress, from the White House, and at the expense of everybody else.'[36]

Alexander's aggressive management style began to draw critics. According to one intelligence committee member, Alexander's evasive statements to the committee made "a mockery of congressional oversight."[37] Commenting on the behavior of Alexander's NSA at the conclusion of a 4-year investigation of an NSA employee who allegedly leaked classified information to a reporter, a federal judge said, "That's four years of hell that a citizen goes through . . . . It was not proper. It doesn't pass the smell test . . . . [U]nconscionable. Unconscionable."[38]

Of his own management style, Alexander said in 2012, "In one sentence, I will share the best advice I've learned from one of my mentors: communicate, communicate, communicate."[39] The irony in that statement became clear as the public learned more and more about the government's highly secret surveillance programs.

REVELATIONS OF U.S. SURVEILLANCE UNFOLD

On May 26, 2011, more than 2 years before Snowden's historic leak, Ron Wyden, a Democratic U.S. senator from Oregon and a member of the Senate Intelligence Committee, stated: "When the American people find out how their government has secretly interpreted the Patriot Act, they will be stunned and they will be angry."[40] Members of both Senate and House Intelligence Committees had been secretly briefed on NSA surveillance programs, but they were precluded by law from discussing classified information with other members of Congress, much less with their constituents.

The growth and details of the NSA's surveillance programs might still be unknown to the general public and even to congressional intelligence committees were it not for Snowden's information leaks. Press reports based on them provoked intense debate in a variety of forums as President Obama, administration officials, congressional intelligence committee chairs and members, and longtime opponents of NSA surveillance sought to influence public opinion. Watchdog organizations such as the Electronic Frontier Foundation, the Federation of American Scientists, and the Center for Democracy & Technology began assembling and publicizing all available information on what was popularly termed "NSA spying."[v]

[iv]Citing anonymous Obama administration officials, *The New York Times* reported that Stuxnet had an unintended effect: its malware had begun replicating itself and migrating to computers in other countries. Cyber-security detectives were thus able to detect and analyze it. By the summer of 2010 some experts were pointing fingers at the United States as its instigator.

[v]Timeline at https://www.eff.org/nsa-spying/timeline ; Center for Democracy & Technology on NSA spying at https://www.cdt.org/content/nsa-surveillance; *The Washington Post* surveillance timeline from 2001 up to June 7, 2013 at http://apps.washingtonpost.com/g/page/national/electronic-surveillance-under-presidents-bush-and-obama/213.

The Leaker

With a GED but no college degree, Edward Snowden is a self-described "computer wizard" whose career began in 2005 at a private research center in a job requiring a top secret security clearance.[41] In 2006 he took a position at the CIA, where he was trained as a technology specialist. In 2009, he became a contractor for Dell, Inc., where he was assigned to an NSA facility in Japan and consultant to the CIA as a cyberstrategist.

According to federal investigators, while Snowden was working for Dell he began copying the classified documents he would later leak to journalists. This copying continued after he was reassigned in May 2012 as lead technologist for the NSA's information-sharing office in Hawaii. While in Hawaii Snowden "may have persuaded between 20 and 25 fellow workers . . . to give him their logins and passwords by telling them they were needed for him to do his job as a computer systems administrator."[42] In early 2013, Snowden left Dell to become a system administrator for the NSA while working for the management consulting firm Booz Allen Hamilton.

The leak had been carefully planned by Snowden. Because they were likely to be sympathetic to his purposes, Snowden had chosen the two individuals to whom he would leak documents: Glenn Greenwald of *The Guardian* and Laura Poitras, a documentary filmmaker then making a film on NSA surveillance programs.[43] After convincing them of his credibility, the documents were handed over on June 6. On June 9th, in a film clip made by Poitras, Snowden identified himself as their leaker.

Later, further details about Snowden's work history and clearances came to light. In 2009, Snowden's supervisor at the CIA wrote a derogatory evaluation of Snowden, noting "a distinct change in the young man's behavior and work habits" and, moreover, that he "suspected that Mr. Snowden was trying to break into classified computer files to which he was not authorized to have access."[44] Snowden, according to these sources, was "sent home," although this was disputed by the CIA. The negative report was either ignored or overlooked in later applications for his access to highly classified information.

It also was revealed that Snowden's clearance for access to top secret information had been processed by a little-known private sector contractor, U.S. Investigations Services, LLC (USIS), the largest security background check firm, which worked almost exclusively for the U.S. government's Office of Personnel Management.[45] Once a government agency, USIS was privatized in 1996 and became a proprietary firm owned by Providence Equity, LLC. In 2012, it came under scrutiny by a federal grand jury because of allegations by former employees that they were continually pressured to "flush" background checks, that is, push incomplete checks through the system even if questions had been raised about the individual being checked.

Following the June 2013 leaks, Snowden was charged by federal prosecutors with espionage and theft of government property.[46] In Hong Kong, Snowden was thus a fugitive, and after being turned away by several countries, he was eventually granted temporary asylum in Russia.

Snowden claimed to have done nothing wrong. In his view, no effective judicial checks and balances were in place to assure that the targeting of an American had been approved by a FISA court order and not just by NSA employees. He believed the public had a right to know about this. "I do not want to live," he said, "in a world where everything I do and say is recorded."[47] "My sole motive is to inform the public as to that which is done in their name and that which is done against them."[48] Many around the world, including former president Jimmy Carter, saw him as a legitimate whistleblower, even a patriot, and they applauded what he had done.

The News Media

Freedom of the press in the United States is guaranteed by the First Amendment to the Constitution. But what does this mean when the press receives and publishes classified information that was illegally disclosed by someone like Edward Snowden (or, before him, by WikiLeaks or by Daniel Ellsberg, who leaked what became known as "The Pentagon Papers")?[49] Using their constitutional freedom, the news media are able to become an influential player in American politics and public management.

> Using their constitutional freedom, the news media are able to become an influential player in American politics and public management.

Media coverage of the NSA's post-9/11 spying had begun well before Snowden's leaks. In 2005, as noted earlier, the *The New York Times* reported, "according to government officials," that the Bush administration had interpreted the USA Patriot Act to allow NSA to "eavesdrop on Americans" without the obtaining warrants to do so by the FISC.[50] The ensuing public controversy culminated in a 2006 renewal of the Patriot Act but with greater specificity in the language of its Section 215.

Press reporting on NSA surveillance was unrelenting following the Snowden leaks. Over a period of weeks and months, the contents of Snowden's documents were revealed to stunned publics around the world. Investigative reporters from print and online media probed all aspects of the story. Many of these reports were labeled by Washington insiders as "game changers" and included revelations about specific surveillance programs, legal loopholes exploited by the NSA, how FISC authority was exercised, the rationales for each program in the so-called black budget, and eavesdropping on foreign allies.

The initial reports, posted in *The Guardian* on June 5th and in both *The Guardian* and *The Washington Post* on June 6, 2013, revealed, based on leaked documents, the existence of a surveillance program called PRISM. Throughout June, *The Guardian* reported a steady stream of revelations:

- Britain's counterpart to the NSA, the Government Communications Headquarters (GCHQ), had intercepted the communications of participants in the 2009 G20[vi] summit conference held in Pittsburgh.
- The FISA Court approved of the NSA's using domestic communications information obtained inadvertently as a result of NSA's broad surveillance activity.
- The GCHQ had access to the network of cables that carry the world's phone calls and Internet traffic and was processing the vast streams of sensitive personal information it shared with the NSA.

At the end of June, the German news magazine *Der Spiegel* added to the revelations, reporting that the United States had been spying on European Union and United Nations offices in the United States.

Beyond these stories, the news in June and in July was dominated by stories on the whereabouts, thinking, and possible fate of Snowden as he wended his way from Hong Kong to Moscow International Airport and into Russia. In August, once Snowden was settled in Moscow, more details on NSA surveillance poured forth from media outlets:

- *The Guardian* published a story that the domestic communications of Americans in contact with a foreign "target" were collected without a warrant due to "incidental [i.e., inadvertent or unintended] collection."[51] The story was based in part on Snowden's leaked glossary from the NSA's Special Source Operations division, a unit that was responsible for many surveillance programs (including PRISM), and involved private

---

[vi]The website for the Group of Twenty (G20) is https://www.g20.org/. It is a forum for the political leaders and central bank governors of 20 of the world's largest economies.

companies. The glossary included details of "minimization procedures" to protect individuals' privacy. For example, "analysts may NOT/NOT [not repeat not] implement any USP [US persons] queries until an effective oversight process has been developed by NSA and agreed to by DOJ/ODNI."

- *The Washington Post* reported that the NSA had broken privacy rules "thousands of times" each of the five years following 2008.[52]

- The *Post* reported limitations on the authority of the FISC as described by the FISC's own chief judge, Reggie B. Walton: "The FISC is forced to rely upon the accuracy of the information that is provided to the Court. . . . The FISC does not have the capacity to investigate issues of noncompliance, and in that respect the FISC is in the same position as any other court when it comes to enforcing [government] compliance with its orders."[53]

- The *Wall Street Journal* revealed new details on the NSA's ability to monitor Americans' Internet communications: "The programs, code-named Blarney, Fairview, Oakstar, Lithium and Stormbrew, among others, filter and gather information at major telecommunications companies [using] complex algorithms."[54]

- Various news media reported that the NSA's e-mail surveillance program had been disapproved by the FISA Court in 2011, and that the court had several times rebuked the NSA for repeated misrepresentations and inaccurate statements concerning its surveillance programs (a decision obtained under a FOIA request). FISC judge John D. Bates stated "Contrary to the government's repeated assurances, N.S.A. had been routinely running queries of the metadata using querying terms that did not meet the standard for querying." A ruling in 2009 had observed that requirements were "so frequently and systematically violated that it can fairly be said that this critical element of the overall . . . regime has never functioned effectively."[55]

- *The Guardian* reported that the NSA paid Internet service providers' costs of complying with Judge Bates' 2011 decision.

- Citing a classified NSA inspector general report, *The Guardian* reported that U.S. intelligence analysts chose to ignore the minimization procedures designed to protect privacy. [56]

- Regarding press reports of U.S. surveillance of foreign governments, *The New York Times* quoted *Der Spiegel* as pointing out the reports "added extensive new detail to what had previously been reported, and it may compound the frictions developing between the United States and its allies over the issue—especially with Germany, where Chancellor Angela Merkel is in the midst of an election campaign."[57]

- Under banner headlines at the end of August, *The Washington Post* published major reporting of something the public and most members of Congress had never seen before: the federal budget for the entire U.S. intelligence community.[58] Based on a 178-page document leaked by Snowden, the $52.6 billion budget summarizes budgetary data for each of the IC's 16 agencies and over 100,000 employees. Successes and failures are assessed against goals established for them by the president and the Congress. The reporting revealed that the budget for the CIA was significantly higher than had been thought and over 50 percent higher than the budget for the NSA.

- As President Obama arrived in St. Petersburg, Russia, for a G20 Summit meeting on September 5, *ProPublica* reported on the existence of an NSA program called "Bullrun" (along with a similar program of the British surveillance agency GCHQ): "The [NSA] has circumvented or cracked much of the encryption, or digital scrambling, that guards global commerce and banking systems, protects sensitive data like trade secrets and medical records, and automatically secures the e-mails, Web searches, Internet chats and phone calls of Americans and others around the world."[59]

- Media reports revealed another target of NSA surveillance programs: the agency was eavesdropping on the personal telephone calls of German Chancellor Angela Merkel and nearly three dozen other heads of state, many of them close American allies.[60]
- *The Washington Post* added a twist to the story of ISPs cooperating with the NSA: What the NSA didn't get voluntarily, it simply took anyway.[61] Both the NSA and the GCHQ, in a project called MUSCULAR, "are copying entire data flows across fiber-optic cables that carry information between the data centers" of Google and Yahoo from undisclosed interception points.[62] PRISM was collecting some information from ISPs through voluntary agreements; MUSCULAR was sweeping up everything else.[63] If intercepted in the United States, the MUSCULAR actions would be illegal but not if intercepted in foreign data centers, "where the NSA is allowed to presume that anyone using a foreign data link is a foreigner" under the terms of Executive Order 12333.[64]
- The NSA was "gathering nearly 5 billion records a day on the whereabouts of cellphones around the world . . . enabling the agency to track the movements of individuals—and map their relationships."[65] The NSA had been authorized to spy on Britain and other allies "even though those English-speaking countries have long had an official non-spying pact."[66] The NSA "is secretly piggybacking on the tools that enable Internet advertisers to track consumers, using 'cookies' and location data to pinpoint targets for government hacking and to bolster surveillance."[67]

The public had become inured to these stories. Other issues—negotiating a nuclear deal with Iran, the difficulties of implementing President Obama's health insurance reforms—had drawn the attention of official Washington. But policymakers and civil society critics of the NSA could not ignore efforts to "collect the whole haystack" that were coming to light.

The Obama Administration

Reaction to the Snowden leaks and to the deluge of stories based on them was swift. But political damage control proved difficult for the Obama Adminstration. First came an effort to reassure U.S. citizens that they need not fear for their privacy. At a press conference the day after *The Guardian* revealed details of PRISM, President Obama said

> Now, with respect to the Internet and e-mails, this does not apply to U.S. citizens and it does not apply to people living in the United States. And again, in this instance, not only is Congress fully apprised of it, but what is also true is that the FISA Court has to authorize it.[68]

As the big picture of NSA surveillance emerged, the president and other administration officials reacted in a variety of forums:

- testimony and letters to Congress;
- press conferences and releases;
- informal comments in media interviews;
- prepared statements, including the release of newly declassified documents;
- directives to government agencies and entities;
- new Web sites; and
- statements by "sources who requested anonymity."

These responses seemed tactical rather than strategic, and at times, improvised or inconsistent. Because the administration did not know what information Snowden had leaked, it could not anticipate the timing or content of press reports or head off damaging revelations.

The administration attempted to counter the revelations with a number of overarching arguments.

Argument: Surveillance Programs Are Essential

One of the administration's arguments emphasized that NSA's surveillance programs were essential and effective for countering threats to U.S. national security:

- Administration intelligence officials argued early on that "the breadth of the collection is necessary to ensure all relevant information is available to the government and can be identified through searches in NSA's database, rather than having more focused collection that might miss relevant information."[69]
- The Justice Department argued that "it was necessary for the N.S.A. to collect such large volumes of domestic telephone data to perform the analysis necessary to identify suspected terrorist activity."[70] Supporting this claim was evidence that surveillance efforts had "helped prevent over 50 potential terrorist events," of which four specific examples were provided to a congressional committee.[71]
- With the revelation of the NSA's MUSCULAR program in early September, the administration needed to justify NSA surveillance again. It issued a short statement on icontherecord.tumblr.com that read in part,

> it should hardly be surprising that our intelligence agencies seek ways to counteract our adversaries' use of encryption. Throughout history, nations have used encryption to protect their secrets, and today, terrorists, cybercriminals, human traffickers and others also use code to hide their activities. Our intelligence community would not be doing its job if we did not try to counter that.

> While the specifics of how our intelligence agencies carry out this cryptanalytic mission have been kept secret, the fact that NSA's mission includes deciphering enciphered communications is not a secret, and is not news. Indeed, NSA's public website states that its mission includes leading "the U.S. Government in cryptology . . . in order to gain a decision advantage for the Nation and our allies."[72]

Argument: Surveillance Programs Complied With the Law

A second administration argument emphasized that NSA surveillance programs were subject to rigorous and effective oversight and fully complied with all relevant legal authority:

- At a June 18, 2013 hearing of the Permanent Select Committee on Intelligence of the House of Representatives, General Alexander stated, "Ironically, the documents that have been released so far show the rigorous oversight and compliance our government uses to balance security with civil liberties and privacy."[73]
- On August 9, the Justice Department released a legal argument for why it was lawful under Section 215 of the Patriot Act to collect and store logs of every phone call dialed or received in the United States. Simultaneously, the NSA released a seven-page document describing the legal authorities the agency uses for its information collection. It also described guidance for the NSA's surveillance procedures, as well as the internal controls that limit collection.[74]

- The White House issued a statement saying: "NSA documents being reported on today ... demonstrate that the NSA is monitoring, detecting, addressing and reporting compliance incidents."[75]
- The *New York Times* reported, "The administration released a partly redacted semiannual report about 'compliance' incidents, or mistakes involving the privacy rights of Americans or people in the United States. It found that there had been no willful violations of the rules, and that less than 1 percent of queries by analysts involved errors."[76] Furthermore, "the document also showed that the government recently changed the rules to allow NSA and CIA analysts to search its databases of recorded calls and e-mails using search terms designed to find information involving American citizens, not foreigners."[77]
- NSA Compliance Director John DeLong repeatedly claimed in a conference call with reporters that the NSA took compliance seriously and emphasized the importance of keeping the violations in perspective given the large volume of database queries (20 million per month): "I do think in a lot of the headlines and other things, there's people talking about privacy violations or abuses or willful violations, right, it is important for people to understand, NSA has a zero tolerance policy for willful misconduct. Zero. That's our tolerance, it's very simple."[78] When he was asked about the number of privacy violations, DeLong responded, "They are extremely rare. . . . The number of willful violations is miniscule, I mean tiny. . . . I don't have the exact numbers, but a couple over the past decades."[79]
- According to *The Wall Street Journal*, NSA spokeswoman Vanee Vines said, "if American communications are 'incidentally collected during NSA's lawful signals intelligence activities,' the agency follows 'minimization procedures that are approved by the U.S. attorney general and designed to protect the privacy of United States persons.'"[80]
- Referring to the illegal collection rebuked by the FISC, ODNI general counsel Robert Litt said the collection "stemmed from a technological problem the NSA itself uncovered."[81] "The NSA devised a new set of procedures for handling the Internet traffic in question. It also purged its databases of all the data—domestic and foreign—collected under those programs during the 3 years of unlawful collection."[82]
- CNN interviewer Chris Cuomo asked President Obama if he was "confident that you know everything that's going on within that agency and that you can say to the American people, 'It's all done the right way'?" The president asserted that he was. "Because there are no allegations, and I am very confident—knowing the NSA and how they operate—that purposefully somebody is out there trying to abuse this program or listen in on people's email."[83]
- The president did acknowledge, however, that "I think there are legitimate concerns that people have that technology is moving so quick that, you know, at some point, does the technology outpace the laws that are in place and the protections that are in place? ... [D]o some of these systems end up being like a loaded gun out there that somebody at some future point could abuse?"[84]

Argument: Lawmakers Knew About Surveillance Programs and Supported Them

A third administration argument emphasized that lawmakers had been fully informed about the NSA surveillance programs and had voted to continue them:

- In his February 12, 2013 State of the Union Address, President Obama stated, "my administration has worked tirelessly to forge a durable legal and policy framework to guide our counterterrorism efforts. Throughout, we have kept Congress fully informed of our efforts."[85]

- Following Snowden's leaks in early June, Attorney General Eric Holder told a Senate Committee, "Members of Congress have been fully briefed as these issues, these matters have been underway," but that he was "not really comfortable in saying an awful lot more than that" in an unclassified setting.[86]
- On June 9, however, the following exchange occurred between DNI James Clapper and NBC News correspondent Andrea Mitchell: [87]

Andrea Mitchell: Director Clapper, thank you very much for letting us come out here and interview you on the subject of all these leaks and how it has affected American intelligence gathering. Does the intelligence community feel besieged by the fact that these top secret documents are getting out?

James Clapper: Well, I think we're very, very concerned about it. For me, it is literally—not figuratively, literally gut-wrenching to see this happen because of the huge, grave damage it does to our intelligence capabilities. And of course for me, this is a key tool for preserving, protecting the nation's safety and security. So every one of us in the intelligence community, most particularly the great men and women of NSA are very—are profoundly affected by this.

Andrea Mitchell: Senator Wyden made quite a lot out of your exchange with him last March during the hearings. Can you explain what you meant when you said that there was not data collection on millions of Americans?

James Clapper: First—as I said, I have great respect for Senator Wyden. I thought, though in retrospect, I was asked, "When are you going to start—stop beating your wife" kind of question, which is meaning not—answerable necessarily by a simple yes or no. So I responded in what I thought was the most truthful, or least untruthful manner by saying no.

- The phrase "least untruthful manner" undercut the claims of his superiors and on June 21, Clapper apologized for remarks made at a March 2013 hearing on the NSA's surveillance program.[88]
- At an August 9 press conference, President Obama again argued that "lawmakers were fully informed of the surveillance program and voted to keep it in place as recently as 2011."[89]

Argument: Balancing Secrecy and Transparency Is Difficult

A fourth administration argument emphasized that finding the right balance between secrecy and transparency is difficult:

- The Obama administration struggled with the tradeoffs between transparency and secrecy. In a set of statements in August 2013, Obama seemed to emphasize transparency: "What I'm going to be pushing the [intelligence community] to do is rather than have a trunk come out here and leg come out there and a tail come out there, let's just put the whole elephant out there so people know exactly what they're looking at."[90]
- At the same time the president announced a new transparency mechanism, www.icontherecord.tumblr .com, which "will serve as a hub for further transparency, and this will give Americans and the world the ability to learn more about what our intelligence community does and what it doesn't do, how it carries out its mission, and why it does so."[91] ODNI maintained the website, and it included content categories for "Official Statements," "Declassified Documents," "Testimony," "Speeches & Interviews," "Fact Sheets," and "Oversight & Compliance."

- Later in August, DNI Clapper posted a statement on icontherecord.tumblr.com that provided a precise description of his commitment to transparency. The details seemed less ambitious than the president's initial description:

  DNI has determined, with the concurrence of the IC, that going forward the IC will publicly release, on an annual basis, aggregate information concerning compulsory legal process under certain national security authorities.

  Specifically, for each of the following categories of national security authorities, the IC will release the total number of orders issued during the prior twelve-month period and the number of targets affected by these orders:

    - FISA orders based on probable cause (Titles I and III of FISA and sections 703 and 704)
    - Section 702 of FISA
    - FISA Business Records (Title V of FISA)
    - FISA Pen Register/Trap and Trace (Title IV of FISA) National Security Letters issued pursuant to 12 U.S.C. § 3414(a)(5), 15 U.S.C. §§ 1681u(a) and (b), 15 U.S.C. § 1681v, and 18 U.S.C. § 2709

  Our ability to discuss these activities is limited by our need to protect intelligence sources and methods.

    - FISA and national security letters are an important part of our effort to keep the nation and its citizens safe, and disclosing more detailed information about how they are used and to whom they are directed can obviously help our enemies avoid detection.[92]

- After the MUSCULAR program was revealed, the brief statement by the administration on icontherecord .tumblr.com also included this statement:

  The stories published yesterday, however, reveal specific and classified details about how we conduct this critical intelligence activity. Anything that yesterday's disclosures add to the ongoing public debate is outweighed by the road map they give to our adversaries about the specific techniques we are using to try to intercept their communications in our attempts to keep America and our allies safe and to provide our leaders with the information they need to make difficult and critical national security decisions.[93]

- As DNI, Clapper constantly confronted the tension between secrecy and transparency. He had once argued that the country needed the equivalent of a "secretary of intelligence."[94] "By seeking consensus rather than issuing directives," said *The Washington Post* columnist David Ignatius, "Clapper is beginning to figure out a way to make the fuzzy DNI structure work after all."[95] Working in "an intelligence culture that rewards protection of secrets," Clapper, tilting toward transparency, insisted that NSA counsel Litt reduce the amount of material redacted from a declassified FISC decision, believing the NSA was "suppressing too much."[96] Clapper supported the Defense Department's desire to cancel one of two overlapping satellite imaging programs on behalf of streamlining the NSA's overambitious collection approaches. Ignatius concluded, "The intelligence community is still way too big and turf-conscious, and it combines the worst features of bureaucracy and secrecy. But at least someone is trying to manage this secret empire." [97]

Argument: The President Provided General Policy Direction, Not Specific Oversight

A fifth administration argument emphasized that the president provided policy direction to the NSA but he relied on National Security Council (NSC) staff to monitor specific surveillance programs.

- In early fall, President Obama was fending off the resentment of the presidents of Brazil and Mexico over revelations that the NSA had been spying on sensitive political communications. At a press conference held in St. Petersburg, Russia, President Obama said,

  > [O]ur intelligence agency's job is to gather information that's not available through public sources. . . . [W]hat we do is similar to what countries around the world do with their intelligence services. . . . The nature of technology and the legitimate concerns around privacy and civil liberties means that it's important for us on the front end to say, all right, are we actually going to get useful information here? . . . On Brazil and Mexico. I said that I would look into the allegations . . . we get these through the press and then I've got to go back and find out what's going on with respect to these particular allegations . . . what I assured President Rousseff [of Brazil] and President Peña Nieto [of Mexico] is . . . that I take these allegations very seriously. . . . we will work with their teams to resolve what is a source of tension.[98]

- In follow-up stories containing new revelations, some based on briefings by White House officials, a claim reemerged that

  > President Barack Obama went nearly five years without knowing his own spies were bugging the phones of world leaders. Officials said the NSA has so many eavesdropping operations under way that it wouldn't have been practical to brief him on all of them. They added that the president was briefed on and approved of broader intelligence-collection "priorities," but that those below him make decisions about specific intelligence targets. . . . "These decisions are made at NSA," the official said. "The president doesn't sign off on this stuff." [99]

- The president himself confirmed the gist of this view, while at the same time calling for a "review" of the processes: "We give them policy direction. But what we've seen over the last several years is their capacities continue to develop and expand, and that's why I'm initiating now a review to make sure that what they're able to do doesn't necessarily mean what they should be doing."[100] The external review, by a five-member Review Group on Intelligence and Communications Technology, would, according to the White House,

  > bring to the task immense experience in national security, intelligence, oversight, privacy and civil liberties. The Review Group will bring a range of experience and perspectives to bear to advise the President on how, in light of advancements in technology, the United States can employ its technical collection capabilities in a way that optimally protects our national security and advances our foreign policy while respecting our commitment to privacy and civil liberties, recognizing our need to maintain the public trust, and reducing the risk of unauthorized disclosure.[101]

- Meanwhile, unnamed intelligence officials revealed, "certainly the National Security Council and senior people across the intelligence community knew exactly what was going on, and to suggest otherwise is ridiculous."[102]

- On October 29, DNI Clapper was asked during testimony before the House Intelligence Committee whether the White House knew about the eavesdropping on foreign leaders. He replied, "They can and do," although "I have to say that that does not extend down to the level of detail. We're talking about a huge enterprise here, with thousands and thousands of individual requirements."[103] When asked whether wiretapping friendly foreign leaders should be reported to the intelligence committees" Clapper replied that the agencies had "lived up to the letter and spirit of that requirement."

The United States Congress

Many lawmakers were realizing that the privacy of Americans' communications might have been breached through intentional abuses of access to their communications and through "inadvertent" capture of their information:

- The cascade of surveillance revelations put the House and Senate Intelligence Committees, as well as committees on the judiciary and on homeland security, on the spot responding to the Obama Administration's claim that these committees had been "fully informed" of the NSA's bulk surveillance programs. If that was true, the question arose as to whether the intelligence committees had practiced due diligence (that is, conscientious investigation) in their oversight with due regard to the rights to privacy of American citizens. Four congressional hearings on NSA surveillance activities were held in June and July 2013:

  o House Intelligence Committee: Disclosure of National Security Agency Surveillance Programs, June 18, 2013;
  o Senate Homeland Security and Governmental Affairs Committee: Safeguarding our Nation's Secrets: Examining The Security Clearance Process, June 20, 2013;
  o House Judiciary Committee: Oversight of the Administration's use of FISA Authorities, July 17, 2013; and
  o Senate Judiciary Committee: Strengthening Privacy Rights and National Security: Oversight of FISA Surveillance Programs, July 31, 2013.

- A statutory amendment was fast-tracked to a vote in the House of Representatives in late July 2013 that would have prevented the NSA, the FBI, and other agencies from relying on Section 215 of the Patriot Act "to collect records, including telephone call records, that pertain to persons who are not subject to an investigation under Section 215."[104] The amendment was narrowly defeated in a bipartisan vote after intense opposition by President Obama and NSA director Alexander.
- Many lawmakers, including Senator Wyden, were nonetheless pleased that the issue of NSA surveillance had finally reached policymakers' agendas. He said that a "culture of misinformation" and a lack of transparency sustained the bulk collection of telephone records.[105]
- Legislative views on sensitive intelligence issues generally divided along party lines: civil-rights-minded Democrats and security-minded Republicans. The Senate Intelligence Committee included the main protagonists on either side of the merits of NSA surveillance, and both were Democrats. Senator Wyden was a longtime critic of what he saw as weak oversight of U.S. surveillance programs. Senator Diane Feinstein of California, the committee chair, was a strong supporter of the NSA's mission and programs.
- As the NSA controversy continued, Wyden argued, "The public was not just kept in the dark about the Patriot Act and other secret authorities, the public was actively misled."[106] He publicly observed that the 2011 change in the rules governing the NSA's minimization procedures amounted to a "'backdoor search' through Americans' communications data. Section 702 [of the FISA Amendments] was intended to give

the government new authorities to collect the communications of individuals believed to be foreigners outside the US, but the intelligence community has been unable to tell Congress how many Americans have had their communications swept up in that collection."[107]

- Along with his Intelligence Committee colleague Mark Udall, a Democrat from Colorado, Senator Wyden warned about the ability of the IC to look at the communications of U.S. citizens. They sent a letter to General Alexander pointing out inaccuracies in a fact sheet released by the NSA in the wake of the initial PRISM revelations.[108]

- Wyden's colleague Senator Feinstein initially defended the NSA, arguing, "The committee has never identified an instance of intentional abuse by the NSA" but also said that the committee "can and should do more to independently verify that NSA's operations are appropriate."[109] Later, after revelations concerning the NSA's rule violations, Feinstein said, according to a *New York Times* account, that the violations were unacceptable but that the NSA had an oversight system that worked, despite the problems.[110]

- Along with the partisan and ideological divisions among legislators over where to strike the balance between security and privacy was the question whether Congress had indeed been "fully informed" about the extent of NSA surveillance. The meaning of *oversight*, and how it was and should be conducted, turned out to be controversial. The briefings of congressional intelligence committees had necessarily followed procedures governed by the need to maintain security. "Unlike typical congressional hearings that feature testimony from various sides of a debate," *The Washington Post* reported, "the briefings in 2010 and 2011 on the telephone surveillance program were by definition one-sided affairs, with lawmakers hearing only from government officials steeped in the legal and national security arguments for aggressive spying."[111]

- Congressman James Sensenbrenner, a Wisconsin Republican who helped write the law authorizing bulk data surveillance, nonetheless called the NSA's briefings of lawmakers a "rope-a-dope operation" designed to silence "those who are on the trail of something that isn't right."[112] Briefers, it was said, were evasive, informing committee members in the "least untruthful way," as Clapper had put it.

- Many ranking members of the intelligence committees disagreed with colleagues who complained that they were kept in the dark, saying that critics turned down invitations to get more information because they didn't have the time for it. According to one report, "a recent briefing by senior intelligence officials on surveillance programs failed to attract even half of the Senate, showing the lack of enthusiasm in Congress for learning about classified security programs."[113]

- Former congressman Lee Hamilton, an Indiana Democrat and a longtime member of the House Intelligence Committee who cochaired the 9/11 Commission, observed, "I am astounded that so many members of Congress could be informed about the specifics of the program and fail to see the urgent need for public discussions." But, he noted ruefully, even those legislators who knew and were skeptical, like Wyden, "were simply unable to get it into the open. It took a leaker to do it."[114]

- A Senate Judiciary Committee hearing on July 31 put into the record several significant political reservations about the effectiveness of congressional oversight:

  o Senator Charles E. Grassley, a Republican from Iowa, asked skeptical questions about the legal basis for the program while criticizing DNI Clapper for making inaccurate statements to Congress about it in March, even though he had already apologized for doing so.

- o Senate Judiciary Committee chair Patrick Leahy, a Democrat from Vermont, challenged the administration's claims that its bulk surveillance was effective in thwarting terrorist plots. Saying he had seen a classified list of "terrorist events" detected through surveillance, Leahy said the list did not show that "dozens or even several terrorist plots" had been thwarted by the domestic program. "If this program is not effective it has to end. So far, I'm not convinced by what I've seen."[115]
  - o Senator Sheldon Whitehouse, a Democrat from Rhode Island, "charged that the administration's response to the NSA leak revelations has been slow from the beginning, reflecting a culture of secrecy that grants the executive branch an inherent advantage over the checks of the legislative branch." Whitehouse was quoted as saying, "It all came out in response to the leaker."[116]

- The firestorm of European criticism in late October 2013 prompted additional congressional hearings and a possible change of heart among Senate leaders. In a public statement, Senator Feinstein stated, "I do not believe the United States should be collecting phone calls or emails of friendly presidents and prime ministers."[117] Her committee, she said, would begin "major review of all intelligence collection programs." This was an even bolder stance than the Obama Administration's cautious "may curtail" speculations concerning such eavesdropping. One staff member commented, "She believes the committee was not adequately briefed on the details of these programs, and she's frustrated . . . . In her mind, there were salient omissions."[118]
- In the Republican-led House, it was a different story. The chair of the House Intelligence Committee, Congressman Michael Rogers of Michigan, considered "the DNI structure under Clapper 'vastly improved' from where it was a few years ago, including 'much better' fusion of intelligence in the president's daily brief."[119] Rogers argued, "We need to focus on who the bad guys are . . . And the bad guys, candidly, are not U.S. intelligence agencies. They're the good guys at the end of the day."[120] Rogers supported "Clapper's efforts to disclose more information about NSA programs" where it could be done "without damaging security. 'We've got to have some confidence-builders and show the public that these programs are as transparent as they can get while still being effective.'"[121]

The issue of Americans' privacy rights was now on Congress's agenda, however. In a "tectonic shift toward boosting privacy and curbing government surveillance,"[122] the Senate on May 31, 2015 allowed key parts of the Patriot Act to expire as of June 1, 2015. Following intense debate, Congress enacted the USA Freedom Act on June 2, 2015. While reauthorizing many Patriot Act provisions, the new act imposed some restrictions on the bulk collection of metadata on Americans' telecommunications, a sharp change in post-9/11 priorities.

Civil Society Watchdogs and Experts

Revelations concerning NSA surveillance programs intensified advocacy efforts by civil society organizations. A number of organizations monitored government intelligence activities with goals of promoting transparency about these activities and protecting the privacy of Americans guaranteed by the Fourth Amendment to the Constitution:

- The Electronic Frontier Foundation (EFF), for example, had long been a source of information and criticism of NSA surveillance. According to its Web site, "Blending the expertise of lawyers, policy analysts, activists, and technologists, EFF achieves significant victories on behalf of consumers and the general public. EFF fights for freedom primarily in the courts, bringing and defending lawsuits even when that means taking on the U.S. government or large corporations."[123]

- In response to the administration's claim that terrorist plots had been foiled by the NSA's surveillance efforts, Kenneth Roth, executive director of Human Rights Watch and a former federal prosecutor, commented, "Upon scrutiny, however, many of these plots appear in fact to have been uncovered not because of these mass collection of our metadata but through more traditional surveillance of particular phone numbers or e-mail addresses—the kinds of targeted inquiries that easily would have justified a judicial order allowing review of records kept by communications companies or even monitoring the content of those communications."[124]

- The Federation of American Scientists, a civil society monitor of government secrecy and surveillance, pointed to a paper by Army signals intelligence officer Major Dave Owen in which he argued that the structures of oversight governing NSA surveillance [for example, the FISA Court] "have formed and continuously reinforce an NSA culture that is extremely adverse to any issue that may be construed as collecting on American citizens."[125] As Owen put it, "exploiting American citizens' communications seemed to be a normal part of operations."[126]

- In November 2013, a group of civil society organizations concerned with consumer and privacy rights and civil liberties requested the Federal Trade Commission (FTC) to open an investigation. The question was whether companies that provided the NSA with metadata and other information had failed to comply with lawful orders by the FTC to protect individuals' privacy rights. Groups making this request included the Electronic Privacy Information Center, the Center for Digital Democracy, the Privacy Rights Clearinghouse, the Consumer Federation of America, and Public Citizen. "The Commission should pursue this investigation," the signatories said, "because it routinely holds itself out as the defender of consumer privacy in the United States. It is inconceivable that when faced with the most significant breach of consumer data in U.S. history, the Commission could ignore the consequences for consumer privacy."[vii]

- Two former judges who served on the FISA court, in their capacity as private citizens, called for structural reforms of oversight institutions. One former judge suggested that the Privacy and Civil Liberties Oversight Board might be restructured to provide a further check. He also proposed the creation of an advocate, with appropriate security clearances, to argue against the government's filings with the FISA court.[127] In a *New York Times* op-ed, another former judge argued for a similar type of representation.[128]

Pressure from watchdog organizations and experts continued to carry weight and keep the pressure on public discourse over the NSA's surveillance activities.

World Leaders

Revelations that the NSA's bulk surveillance included the communications of foreign governments and international institutions drew caustic criticism from many of America's closest allies.

[vii] EPIC to Federal Trade Commission, "NSA Data Collection from US Companies," November 13, 2013, http://epic.org/privacy/nsa/Priv-Grps-to-FTC-re-NSA.pdf. Lawsuits filed by civil society organizations under the Freedom of Information Act (discussed in Chapter 2) often lead to court orders requiring federal agencies to release documents relating to surveillance programs. Such disclosures add to the volume of information available to legislators and citizens for evaluating public policies and programs.

- The issue of "spying on your friends" came to a head when it was revealed in October 2013 that the NSA had tapped the telephones of 35 world leaders, including German chancellor Angela Merkel's cell phone. A political firestorm of foreign criticism ensued.
- It soon became known, however, that the governments of Great Britain, Italy, France, and Spain had their own surveillance programs and shared information collected by these programs with the NSA. As a result, bulk surveillance became a domestic political issue in Europe.
- As the revelations continued, officials of America's European allies as well as foreign business executives wanted the same no-spying agreements that the United States had with Great Britain, Canada, Australia, and New Zealand, collectively known as the Five Eyes. Said one U.S. official, "There are other types of agreements you could have: cooperation, limits on intelligence, greater transparency. The countries on the top of the list for those are close European allies."[129]
- There was, moreover, a commercial backlash against the NSA's collection methods. Some executives suggested that the global Internet be segmented in order to prevent communications signals from being intercepted as they pass through the United States.[130]
- U.S. officials, including NSA director Alexander, seemed to back away from defending politically fraught information collection from foreign governments. "What's more important?" Alexander asked. "Partnering with countries may be more important than collecting on them."[131] Jeopardizing partnerships aimed at defending America and its allies against cyber-attacks might be unwise, he suggested.
- Senator John McCain, an Arizona Republican, called for a "wholesale housecleaning" at the NSA and suggested that General Alexander "should resign or be fired."[132] An Obama adviser commented, "The only way the president is going to get a fresh start with the allies is to present them with a new team."[133]

In official Washington, it was generally understood that nations spy on each other even if they are close allies. Elected officials could not, however, ignore the criticism of their citizens and businesses. Official delegations from U.S. allies began behind-the-scenes discussions with U.S. officials about restricting the more intrusive forms of collection.

CASE ANALYSIS: NATIONAL SECURITY AGENCY SURVEILLANCE

An analysis of the decisions and actions by public managers and policymakers during this 7-month period in 2013 provides a number of insights into public management practice, even as the events and repercussions of this case continue to unfold. To support such an analysis, this section is divided into two parts: the first part introduces an analytic structure for considering the many issues that arise, and the second part poses a number of specific questions that could be considered within that analytic structure.

Conducting a 3D Analysis Using the Model Deliberative Process

Using the model deliberative process outlined in Chapter 1, an analyst can systematically consider the facts of this NSA case.

(Continued)

(Continued)

1. *Gather facts and form initial opinions and ideas.*

This chapter includes many details of the unfolding story of NSA domestic surveillance.[i] Rich facts, details, and observations are the primary data that an analyst needs to build a solid analysis. The analyst builds initial opinions based on these data and on his or her prior experiences and knowledge.

2. *Analyze facts through the lens of public management's dimensions—structure, culture, and craft.*

The three-dimensional framework provides a structure for interpreting the primary data. Some facts are relevant to multiple dimensions. The three-dimensional framework provides a way to gain traction on the mass of information:

- Information about the structure dimension is provided in details about reporting relationships, organizational structures, laws, executive orders, FISC operations, contracting out and contractors, the technology and processing of data collected from it, accountability requirements between and within branches of government, and more.
- Information about the culture dimension is provided in details about interactions between branches, within branches across IC actors, within the Obama administration, and about interactions with the public and with news outlets.
- Information about the craft dimension is provided in details about DNI Clapper's management style, his operating paradigm, his response to reporters' questions, and his adaptation to changing circumstances and information revelations. Information about the craft of other actors, such as President Obama, is evident as well.

3. *Develop and synthesize insights from the three-dimensional analysis, drawing on specific theories and frameworks. Use counterfactual analysis to identify potential causal mechanisms.*

The three-dimensional framework provides a structure for interpreting the primary data. Some facts are relevant to multiple dimensions. The three-dimensional framework provides a way to gain traction on the mass of information.

This step aims to engage in an analytical process and produce an "informed diagnosis" with respect to a particular question or problem. Relevant ideas and frameworks presented in Chapters 1 and 2 can be used to analyze the facts of the case. These include market failures, the politics of bureaucratic structure, "finding the law," and types of accountability systems.

Parts II, III, and IV of the book discuss additional theories and frameworks that can illuminate issues raised in this case. For example, consideration of "inherently governmental activities," principal-agent relationships, transaction costs, and incomplete contracts (Chapter 6) provide frameworks for analyzing the NSA's reliance on contractors. Consideration of ethics, neutral competence, and "high-reliability" organizations (Chapter 8 and 9) provide frameworks for analyzing the NSA's culture. Consideration of leadership theories, strategy, and learning styles (Chapters 10 and 11) provide frameworks for analyzing DNI Clapper's managerial craft.

---

[i]More details of this time period and beyond relevant to the case are included in a number of sources, such as Glenn Greenwald's book *No Place to Hide: Edward Snowden, the NSA, and the U.S. Surveillance State*, as well as original source material such as press briefings and interviews, some of which are cited here.

Initial counterfactual analysis is possible at this point. In retrospect, what if specific facts or processes had been different in this case? Might a problematic sequence of events have been forestalled or led to a different outcome? In such a complex case, many avenues for analysis are possible. But the key to a good counterfactual analysis is its plausibility and its focus on the most important of the many possible alternatives. Fanciful conjectures about unrealistic possibilities are ruled out. For example, in the NSA case, one might ask,

- What if . . . the managers of intelligence programs had insisted that a rigorous investigation be conducted prior to issuing a security clearance? That would have been fully consistent with the prevailing view in the IC that danger lurked in every corner. Snowden aroused the suspicions of at least one CIA supervisor. If those suspicions had been taken seriously, the leaks might not have occurred. Such a rigorous investigative process for every security clearance could be very expensive. Should haste or scarce resources undermine an essential, politically sensitive administrative process of such paramount importance?
- What if . . . IC managers had consistently communicated to their employees that the bearers of bad news or idealistic potential whistleblowers would not be punished but, instead, would be given a fair hearing? President Obama said that Edward Snowden was wrong to go public with revelations about secret surveillance programs because "there were other avenues available for somebody whose conscience was stirred and thought that they needed to question government actions."[ii] But Snowden must have believed that to going through these avenues would have been futile. Protections for whistleblowers in cases of sexual assault, fraud, and waste have been effective. Why were they not effective in this case?
- What if . . . IC leaders, such as the DNI and the Director of NSA had taken the initiative to release information about surveillance programs and their governance, instead of being on the defensive as information was leaked? This counterfactual might seem implausible given the secretive ethos of the IC culture. Yet a former NSA director from the Cold War era, Bobby R. Inman, said of the NSA's post-Snowden predicament, "My advice would be to take everything you think Snowden has and get it out yourself. It would certainly be a shock to the agency. But . . . the sooner they get it out and put it behind them, the faster they can begin to rebuild."[134] Would managers have been better served by thinking like a chess master instead of a boxer: looking ahead several moves, assessing possible countermoves, and being proactive concerning the release of information?
- What if . . . President Obama and his administration had reacted more consistently and strategically to the ongoing revelations in the news media by either putting forward a strong but nuanced explanation and justification for NSA's bulk surveillance programs or taken a more conciliatory stance toward Snowden in keeping with Obama's long-held commitment to transparency and democratic accountability? The administration's efforts to limit damage and the resulting statements seemed to compound, instead of reduce, the damage.

Some other possible counterfactual scenarios are less insightful for *management analysis* because they suggest no plausible alternatives for the managers who are confronting the situation (though these questions may be of interest to historians and public management reformers). What if the FISC had been designed to incorporate an adversarial process? What if someone other than Alexander—there were other, less openly zealous candidates for the position—had been chosen to head the NSA? What if a nonmilitary

[ii]Barack Obama, "Remarks by the President in a Press Conference," White House, August 9, 2013, https://www.whitehouse.gov/the-press-office/2013/08/09/remarks-president-press-conference%20.

(Continued)

(Continued)

candidate had been chosen to be the DNI? What if President Obama had maintained closer, more cordial relationships with key congressional leaders of both parties, including the heads of congressional intelligence committees? Posthoc counterfactual analysis can provide valuable insights into what might work in public management. Drawing on theories, heuristics, and frameworks such as those described in this book helps illuminate the critical issues.

4. *Formulate specific strategies based on the three-dimensional analysis.*

Using the diagnoses and insights obtained through the previous step, the analyst develops conclusions or strategies. For example, an analysis of contracting out may conclude that reliance was too extensive on private contractors for intelligence collection and analysis. The analyst would develop and communicate the findings of his or her analysis, with specific steps and implications. The analyst could use the method of argument (see Appendix) or some other rhetorical framework to organize and support the analysis.

5. *Form persuasive arguments for internal and external audiences.*

Different formats and forums might be used for communicating the findings of the analysis, depending on a number of factors (see Appendix).

The model deliberative process provides a roadmap for absorbing the raw data of a case or situation. It provides a method for analyzing these data and helps to identify the most important dimensions of structure, culture, and craft in a particular case, either ex post or ex ante. The next section poses some questions that might be considered, using the model deliberative process.

Reflecting Society's Values, Performing Effectively, Earning Trust

In balancing the constitutional imperatives of national security and individual freedom, how can public managers ensure that our governments reflect our society's values, perform effectively, and earn the people's trust? This case raises a number of questions concerning public managers' responsibilities in a democratic society, as well as broader questions of governance. For many questions, there is no single correct answer, but analyses should be supported with argument. That is, they must provide a compelling answer of *why?* in each response.

Discussion Questions

Public Managers' Responsibilities, Decisions, Actions

1. What does accountability to the rule of law mean for public managers in this case?

2. Did the public managers in this case practice "lawful public management," using the concepts and frameworks described in Chapter 2?

3. What aspects of market failures are evident in this case? What are the implications for the design and management of public programs?

4. Identify at least one instance of each of the eight distinctive challenges of public management evident in this case.

5. Does the challenge arise primarily due to structure, culture, or craft?

6. How did the public manager respond to the challenge? Could he or she have reasonably made a different choice? If so, what was that choice? Could it have changed the course of events?

7. What are the ethical responsibilities of public managers in this case?

8. Under what circumstances and to what extent is deference to experts and expertise preferable to reliance on partisan and adversarial processes of deliberation and choice?

9. What are the roles of different accountability institutions (described in Chapter 2) in this case? Were these institutions effective in ensuring accountability?

10. Consider the four types of accountability systems identified by Romzek and Dubnik (discussed in Chapter 2): hierarchical, legal, political, and professional. What types of accountability systems were relied on, implicitly or explicitly, in this case? Were any of these systems particularly effective or ineffective?

11. How should General Alexander be evaluated as a public manager?

12. Who—elected officials, senior political executives, professional staff, technical experts—should know what, when, and how much in matters of national security? How should information be shared?

Governments and Governance in a Democratic Society

This book is about public management, but necessarily broader issues of governance arise in the cases and examples included throughout this book. Public managers and citizens at large need to engage with these kinds of questions and understand the importance of their views on such matters for the stability of American democracy.

1. Does this case suggest that the government's efforts to balance national security and civil liberties were successful?

   a. Was too much weight given to the need for secrecy? Or was too much weight given to the need for transparency?

   b. Who should decide where the balance is between transparency and the need for secrecy? To what extent is trust in government (elected officials, unelected officials) to make these decisions justified? How should or can citizens be involved in deciding where this balance rests?

2. How can trust and legitimacy be earned by lawmakers and public administrators? General Alexander told an information security industry conference that only 35 NSA analysts could "query a database" of phone records when it is lawful to do so.[135] Can U.S. citizens trust General Alexander? Can they trust the 35 NSA analysts, who could conceivably violate policy without his knowing it? Can they trust those who, like Edward Snowden, had high-level security clearances and unauthorized access to metadata? Can they trust Snowden himself, whose sincerity in believing that, in the depths of surveillance programs, large numbers of individuals are in a position to "defy policy" and jeopardize our privacy and our security?

3. In the light of their potentially far-reaching consequences, what risks are U.S. citizens willing to take, and what risks are they willing to have government take, to secure freedoms? For example, James Bamford in *Wired* quotes a former NSA director for information assurance as saying: "If you

(Continued)

are engaged in reconnaissance on an adversary's systems, you are laying the electronic battlefield and preparing to use it."[136] Indeed, General Alexander "now says the possibility of 'zero-day exploits' [attacks which exploit a previously unknown information system vulnerability] falling into the wrong hands is his 'greatest worry.'"[137]

4. What is the role of a free press where the nation is threatened by enemies who operate outside of any recognized regime or rule of law? In light of the media's freedom to keep a story alive, or to drop it, or to negotiate its content with public officials, should the media be trusted to do the right thing?

NOTES

1. Masuma Ahuja, "Electronic Surveillance under Presidents Bush and Obama," *The Washington Post*, June 7, 2013, http://apps.washington post.com/g/page/national/electronic-surveillance-under-presidentsbush-and-obama/213.

2. Glenn Greenwald, "NSA Collecting Phone Records of Millions of Verizon Customers Daily," *The Guardian*, June 5, 2013, sec. World News, http://www.theguardian.com/world/2013/jun/06/nsa-phone-records-verizon-court order.

3. Spencer Ackerman, "NSA Revelations of Privacy Breaches 'the Tip of the Iceberg'—Senate Duo," *The Guardian*, August 13, 2013, sec. World News, http://www.theguardian.com/world/2013/aug/16/nsa-revelations-privacy-breaches-udall-wyden.

4. Ruth Marcus, "Ruth Marcus: The NSA Is Losing the Benefit of the Doubt," *The Washington Post*, August 22, 2013, http://www .washingtonpost.com/opinions/ruth-marcus-the-nsa-is-losing-the-benefit-of-the-doubt/2013/08/22/16e5a740-0b4f-11e3-b87c-476db8ac34cd_story.html.

5. Dana Priest, "NSA Growth Fueled by Need to Target Terrorists," *The Washington Post*, July 21, 2013, http://www.washingtonpost.com/world/national-security/nsa-growth-fueled-by-need-to-target-terrorists/2013/07/21/24c93cf4-f0b1-11e2-bed3-b9b6fe264871_story.html.

6. Charlie Savage, "N.S.A. Said to Search Content of Messages To and From U.S.," *The New York Times*, August 8, 2013, sec. U.S., http://www.nytimes.com/2013/08/08/us/broader-sifting-of-data-abroad-is-seen-by-nsa.html; As discussed later, NSA officials have considerable discretion over "operational" decisions, such as "target selection."

7. Ewen MacAskill, "NSA Paid Millions to Cover Prism Compliance Costs for Tech Companies," *The Guardian*, August 22, 2013, sec. World News, http://www.theguardian.com/world/2013/aug/23/nsa-prism-costs-tech-companies-paid.

8. "Foreign Intelligence Surveillance Court Orders," *Electronic Frontier Foundation*, accessed September 26, 2014, https://www.eff.org/issues/foia/07403TFH.

9. The Editorial Board, "More Independence for the FISA Court," *The New York Times*, July 28, 2013, sec. Opinion, http://www.nytimes .com/2013/07/29/opinion/more-independence-for-the-fisa-court.html.

10. Even Perez, "Secret Court's Oversight Gets Scrutiny," The Wall Street Journal, June 9, 2013, http://www.wsj.com/articles/SB100014241 27887324904004578535670310514616; Matt Sledge, "FISA Court: We Only Approve 75 Percent of Government Warrants without Changes," The Huffington Post, October 15, 2013, http://www.huffingtonpost.com/2013/10/15/fisa-court_n_4102599.html.

11. Eric Lichtblau and Michael S. Schmidt, "Other Agencies Clamor for Data N.S.A. Compiles," *The New York Times*, August 3, 2013, sec. U.S., http://www.nytimes.com/2013/08/04/us/other-agencies-clamor-for-data-nsa-compiles.html.

12. David Ignatius, "James Clapper Manages the Secret Empire," *The Washington Post*, October 23, 2013, http://www.washingtonpost.com/opinions/david-ignatius-james-clapper-manages-the-secret-empire/2013/10/23/361a0d16-3b62-11e3-a94f-b58017bfee6c_story.html.

13. Ibid.

14. FISA Amendments Act of 2008, Pub. L. No. 110-261. 122 Stat. 2436 (2002), 702a.

15. Exec. Order No. 12333, 46 FR 59941, 3 CFR, (1981), p. 200.

16. Charlie Savage, "Federal Prosecutors, in a Policy Shift, Cite Warrantless Wiretaps as Evidence," *The New York Times*, October 26, 2013, sec. U.S., http://www.nytimes.com/2013/10/27/us/federal-prosecutors-in-a-policy-shift-cite-warrantless-wiretaps-as-evidence.html; The government's opposition to the suit is at https://www.aclu.org/sites/default/files/assets/muhtorov_-_govt_response_to_motion_to_suppress.pdf.

17. James Bamford, "They Know Much More Than You Think," *The New York Review of Books*, August 15, 2013, http://www.nybooks.com/articles/archives/2013/aug/15/nsa-they-know-much-more-you-think.

18. Priest, "NSA Growth Fueled by Need to Target Terrorists."

19. "Prime Contractors Host Descriptions," *Business in a Minute with the NSA*, June 11, 2012, http://www.ncsi.com/biam/2012/hosts_industry.php.

20. Bamford, "They Know Much More Than You Think."

21. James Bamford, "NSA Snooping Was Only the Beginning. Meet the Spy Chief Leading Us Into Cyberwar," *WIRED*, June 12, 2013, http://www.wired.com/2013/06/general-keith-alexander-cyberwar/all.

22. Ibid.

23. Dana Priest, "NSA Growth Fueled by Need to Target Terrorists,".

24. Lichtblau and Schmidt, "Other Agencies Clamor for Data N.S.A. Compiles."

25. Ibid.

26. Ibid.

27. Ibid.

28. Bamford, "NSA Snooping Was Only the Beginning. Meet the Spy Chief Leading Us Into Cyberwar."

29. Ellen Nakashima and Joby Warrick, "For NSA Chief, Terrorist Threat Drives Passion to 'Collect It All,'" *The Washington Post*, July 14, 2013, http://www.washingtonpost.com/world/national-security/for-nsa-chief-terrorist-threat-drives-passion-to-collect-it-all/2013/07/14/3d26ef80-ea49-11e2-a301-ea5a8116d211_story.html.

30. Ibid.

31. Ibid.

32. Bamford, "NSA Snooping Was Only the Beginning. Meet the Spy Chief Leading Us Into Cyberwar."

33. "United States Cyber Command," *Wikipedia, the Free Encyclopedia*, accessed August 10, 2013, http://en.wikipedia.org/w/index.php?title=United_States_Cyber_Command&oldid=626085060.

34. Bamford, "NSA Snooping Was Only the Beginning. Meet the Spy Chief Leading Us Into Cyberwar."

35. Ibid. "Strangelovian" refers to the character, Dr. Strangelove, played by Peter Sellers in Stanley Kubrick's film of the same name.

36. Ibid.

37. Ibid.

38. *United States of America v. Thomas A.* Drake, July 15, 2011, United States District Court, District of Maryland. http://fas.org/sgp/jud/drake/071511-transcript.pdf.

39. Collaborative Government, "Leadership—Resilience—Flexibility—Communication: Insights from Gen. Keith B. Alexander," February 1, 2012, http://www.collaborativegov.org/2012/02/leadership-resilience-flexibility-communication-insights-from-gen-keith-b-alexander-uscybercom-nsa-css/#.VCXU1efPZhs.

40. "In Speech, Wyden Says Official Interpretations of Patriot Act Must Be Made Public," May 26, 2011, http://www.wyden.senate.gov/news/press-releases/in-speech-wyden-says-official-interpretations-of-patriot-act-must-be-made-public.

41. "Edward Snowden," *Wikipedia*, https://en.wikipedia.org/wiki/Edward_Snowden#Career, accessed August 1, 2015.

42. Mark Hosenball and Warren Strobel, "Snowden persuaded other NSA workers to give up passwords - sources", Reuters, November 7, 2013, http://www.reuters.com/article/2013/11/08/net-us-usa-security-snowden-idUSBRE9A703020131108, accessed August 1, 2015.

43. Peter Maass, "How Laura Poitras Helped Snowden Spill His Secrets," *The New York Times*, August 13, 2013, sec. Magazine, http://www.nytimes.com/2013/08/18/magazine/laura-poitras-snowden.html.

44. Eric Schmitt, "C.I.A. Warning on Snowden in '09 Said to Slip Through the Cracks," *The New York Times*, October 10, 2013, sec. U.S., http://www.nytimes.com/2013/10/11/us/cia-warning-on-snowden-in-09-said-to-slip-through-the-cracks.html.

45. Dion Nissenbaum, "Grand Jury Probes Firm That Cleared Snowden," *Wall Street Journal*, August 3, 2013, sec. US, http://online.wsj.com/news/articles/SB10001424127887323997004578644263900358822.

46. *United States of America v. Edward J. Snowden,* Criminal Complaint, Case No. 1:13 CR 265 (CMH), June 14, 2013, https://assets.documentcloud.org/documents/716888/u-s-vs-edward-j-snowden-criminal-complaint.pdf.

47. Ewen MacAskill, "Edward Snowden, NSA Files Source: 'If They Want to Get You, In Time They Will,'" Interview with Edward Snowden, June 10, 2013, *The Guardian*, http://www.theguardian.com/world/2013/jun/09/nsa-whistleblower-edward-snowden-why.

48. Glenn Greenwald, Ewen MacAskill, and Laura Poitras, "Edward Snowden: The Whistleblower behind the NSA Surveillance Revelations," *The Guardian*, June 9, 2013, sec. World News, http://www.theguardian.com/world/2013/jun/09/edward-snowden-nsa-whistleblower-surveillance.

49. Congressional Research Service, "Criminal Prohibitions on the Publication of Classified Defense Information," September 9, 2013, http://fas.org/sgp/crs/secrecy/R41404.pdf. The Congressional Research Service could not find any case where news media faced criminal prosecution for doing so.

50. James Risen and Eric Lichtblau, "Bush Lets U.S. Spy on Callers Without Courts," *The New York Times*, December 16, 2005, sec. Washington, http://www.nytimes.com/2005/12/16/politics/16program.html.

51. James Ball and Spencer Ackerman, "NSA Loophole Allows Warrantless Search for U.S. Citizens' E-mails and Phone Calls," *The Guardian*, August 9, 2013, sec. World News, http://www.theguardian.com/world/2013/aug/09/nsa-loophole-warrantless-searches-email-calls.

52. Barton Gellman, "NSA Broke Privacy Rules Thousands of Times per Year, Audit Finds," *The Washington Post*, August 15, 2013, http://www.washingtonpost.com/world/national-security/nsa-broke-privacy-rules-thousands-of-times-per-year-audit-finds/2013/08/15/3310e554-05ca-11e3-a07f-49ddc7417125_story.html.

53. Carol D. Leonnig, "Court: Ability to Police U.S. Spying Program Limited," *The Washington Post*, August 15, 2013, http://www.washingtonpost.com/politics/court-ability-to-police-us-spying-program-limited/2013/08/15/4a8c8c44-05cd-11e3-a07f-49ddc7417125_story.html.

54. Siobhan Gorman and Jennifer Valentino-DeVries, "New Details Show Broader NSA Surveillance Reach," *Wall Street Journal*, August 21, 2013, sec. US, http://online.wsj.com/news/articles/SB10001424127887324108204579022874091732470.

55. Charlie Savage and Scott Shane, "Secret Court Rebuked N.S.A. on Surveillance," *The New York Times,* August 21, 2013, http://www.nytimes.com/2013/08/22/us/2011-ruling-found-an-nsa-program-unconstitutional.html.

56. Dan Roberts, "NSA Analysts Deliberately Broke Rules to Spy on Americans, Agency Reveals," *The Guardian*, August 23, 2013, sec. World News, http://www.theguardian.com/world/2013/aug/23/nsa-analysts-broke-rules-spy.

57. Alison Smale, "Surveillance Revelations Shake U.S.-German Ties," *The New York Times*, August 25, 2013, sec. World / Europe, http://www.nytimes.com/2013/08/26/world/europe/surveillance-revelations-shake-us-german-ties.html.

58. Barton Gellman and Greg Miller, "'Black Budget' Summary Details U.S. Spy Network's Successes, Failures and Objectives," *The Washington Post*, August 29, 2013, http://www.washingtonpost.com/world/national-security/black-budget-summary-details-us-spy-networks-successes-failures-and-objectives/2013/08/29/7e57bb78-10ab-11e3-8cdd-bcdc09410972_story.html.

59. Jeff Larson, Nicole Perlroth, and Scott Shane, "Revealed: The NSA's Secret Campaign to Crack, Undermine Internet Security," *ProPublica*, accessed September 5, 2013, http://www.propublica.org/article/the-nsas-secret-campaign-to-crack-undermine-internet-encryption.

60. James Ball, "NSA Monitored Calls of 35 World Leaders after U.S. Official Handed over Contacts," *The Guardian*, October 24, 2013, sec. World News, http://www.theguardian.com/world/2013/oct/24/nsa-surveillance-world-leaders-calls.

61. Barton Gellman and Ashkan Soltani, "NSA Infiltrates Links to Yahoo, Google Data Centers Worldwide, Snowden Documents Say," *The Washington Post*, October 30, 2013, http://www.washingtonpost.com/world/national-security/nsa-infiltrates-links-to-yahoo-google-data-centers-worldwide-snowden-documents-say/2013/10/30/e51d661e-4166-11e3-8b74-d89d714ca4dd_story.html.

62. Ibid.

63. Ibid.

64. Barton Gellman, Todd Lindeman and Ashkan Soltani, "How the NSA Is Infiltrating Private Networks," *The Washington Post*, October 30, 2013, http://apps.washingtonpost.com/g/page/world/how-the-nsa-is-infiltrating-private-networks/542.

65. Barton Gellman and Ashkan Soltani, "NSA Tracking Cellphone Locations Worldwide, Snowden Documents Show," *The Washington Post*, December 4, 2013, http://www.washingtonpost.com/world/national-security/nsa-tracking-cellphone-locations-worldwide-snowden-documents-show/2013/12/04/5492873a-5cf2-11e3-bc56-c6ca94801fac_story.html?hpid=z3.

66. James Glanz, "United States Can Spy on Britons Despite Pact, N.S.A. Memo Says," *The New York Times*, November 20, 2013, sec. U.S., http://www.nytimes.com/2013/11/21/us/united-states-can-spy-on-britons-despite-pact-nsa-memo-says.html.

67. Ashkan Soltani, Andrea Peterson, and Barton Gellman, "NSA Uses Google Cookies to Pinpoint Targets for Hacking," *The Washington Post*, December 10, 2013, http://www.washingtonpost.com/blogs/the-switch/wp/2013/12/10/nsa-uses-google-cookies-to-pinpoint-targets-for-hacking/?hpid=z1.

68. "Statement by the President", The White House, June 7, 2013, https://www.whitehouse.gov/the-press-office/2013/06/07/statement-president.

69. Congressional Research Service, "NSA Surveillance Leaks: Background and Issues for Congress," September 4, 2013, http://fas.org/sgp/crs/intel/R43134.pdf, 10.

70. James Risen, "Bipartisan Backlash Grows Against Domestic Surveillance," *The New York Times*, July 17, 2013, sec. U.S. / Politics, http://www.nytimes.com/2013/07/18/us/politics/bipartisan-backlash-grows-against-domestic-surveillance.html.

71. "House Select Intelligence Committee Holds Hearing on Disclosure of National Security Agency Surveillance Programs," June 18, 2013, http://www.fas.org/irp/congress/2013_hr/disclosure.pdf.

72. "ODNI Statement on the Unauthorized Disclosure of NSA Cryptological Capabilities," *IC ON THE RECORD*, September 6, 2013, http://icontherecord.tumblr.com/post/60428572417/odni-statement-on-the-unauthorized-disclosure-of.

73. "Hearing of the House Permanent Select Committee on Intelligence on How Disclosed NSA Programs Protect Americans, and Why Disclosure Aids Our Adversaries," *IC ON THE RECORD*, June 18, 2013, http://icontherecord.tumblr.com/post/57812486681/heaing-of-the-house-permanent-select-committee-on.

74. "Bulk Collection of Telephony Metadata Under Section 215 of the USA Patriot Act," *Administration White Paper*, August 9, 2013, http://info.publicintelligence.net/DoJ-NSABulkCollection.pdf; National Security Agency, "The National Security Agency: Missions,

Authorities, Oversight, and Partnerships," August 9, 2013, http://www.nsa.gov/public_info/_files/speeches_testimonies/2013_08_09_the_nsa_story.pdf.

75. "NSA Lied about Scope of 4th Amendment Violations for Years," *Dirty Babylon*, August 22, 2013, http://dirtybabylon.com/2013/08/22/nsa-lied-about-scope-of-4th-amendment-violations.

76. Savage and Shane, "Secret Court Rebuked N.S.A. on Surveillance," See also "'Semiannual Assessment of Compliance with Procedures and Guidelines Issued Pursuant to Section 702 of the Foreign Intelligence Surveillance Act,'" Submitted by the Attorney General and the Director of National Intelligence: Reporting Period: June 1, 2012—November 30, 2012," Office of the Director of National Intelligence, August 2013, http://www.dni.gov/files/documents/Semiannual%20Assessment%20of%20Compliance%20with%20procedures%20and%20guidelines%20issued%20pursuant%20to%20Sect%20702%20of%20FISA.pdf.

77. Savage and Shane, "Secret Court Rebuked N.S.A. On Surveillance."

78. "Press Briefing: Mr. John DeLong, NSA Director of Compliance," *Office of the Director of National Intelligence: Public Affairs Office*, August 16, 2013, http://www.dni.gov/files/documents/DeLong_compliance%20briefing_Aug%2016%2013.pdf.

79. Ibid.

80. Gorman and Valentino-DeVries, "New Details Show Broader NSA Surveillance Reach."

81. Siobhan Gorman, Devlin Barrett, and Jennifer Valentino-DeVries, "Secret Court Faulted NSA for Collecting Domestic Data," *Wall Street Journal*, August 22, 2013, sec. US, http://online.wsj.com/news/articles/SB10001424127887323665504579027180087675564.

82. Ibid.

83. "Transcript of President Obama's Interview on 'New Day,'" *CNN*, August 23, 2013, http://www.cnn.com/2013/08/23/politics/barack-obama-new-day-interview-transcript/index.html.

84. Ibid.

85. Barack Obama, State of the Union address, February 12, 2013, https://www.whitehouse.gov/the-press-office/2013/02/12/remarks-president-state-union-address.

86. Josh Gerstein and Tim Mak, "White House: Obama 'Welcomes' Surveillance Debate," *Politico*, June 5, 2013, http://www.politico.com/story/2013/06/report-nsa-verizon-call-records-92315.html.

87. "Director James R. Clapper Interview with Andrew Mitchell, NBC News Chief Foreign Affairs Correspondent, Liberty Crossing, Tysons Corner, VA" *Office of the Director of National Intelligence,* June 8, 2013, http://www.dni.gov/index.php/newsroom/speeches-and-interviews/195-speeches-interviews-2013/874-director-james-r-clapper-interview-with-andrea-mitchell.

88. James R. Clapper to Dianne Feinstein, June 21, 2013, http://www.dni.gov/files/documents/2013-06-21%20DNI%20Ltr%20to%20Sen.%20Feinstein.pdf.

89. "Remarks by the President in a Press Conference" *The White House: Office of the Press Secretary,* August 9, 2013, http://fas.org/sgp/news/2013/08/wh080913.html.

90. Ibid.

91. Ibid.

92. "DNI Clapper Directs Annual Release of Information Related to Orders Issued Under National Security Authorities," *IC ON THE RECORD*, August 29, 2013, http://icontherecord.tumblr.com/post/59719173750/dni-clapper-directs-annual-release-of-information.

93. "ODNI Statement on the Unauthorized Disclosure of NSA Cryptological Capabilities."

94. Ignatius, "James Clapper Manages the Secret Empire."

95. Ibid.

96. Ibid.

97. Ibid.

98. "Remarks by President Obama in a Press Conference at the G20," The White House, September 6, 2013, http://www.whitehouse.gov/the-press-office/2013/09/06/remarks-president-obama-press-conference-g20.

99. Siobhan Gorman and Adam Entous, "Obama Unaware as U.S. Spied on World Leaders: Officials," Wall Street Journal, October 28, 2013, sec. Europe, http://www.wsj.com/articles/SB10001424052702304470504579162110180138036.

100. President Barack Obama, "President Obama Speaks to Fusion About NSA, Immigration, and Obamacare," Interview by Jim Avila on "AMERICA with Jorge Ramos," Fusion, October 28, 2013, http://wearefusion.tumblr.com/post/65384827480/transcript-president-obama-speaks-to-fusion-about.

101. "Statement by the Press Secretary on the Review Group on Intelligence and Communications Technology," *The White House*, August 27, 2013, http://www.whitehouse.gov/the-press-office/2013/08/27/statement-press-secretary-review-group-intelligence-and-communications-t.

102. McCarthy, "Obama Insists He Didn't Know about US Spying on Key Allies."

103. Mark Landler and Michael S. Schmidt, "Spying Known at Top Levels, Officials Say," *The New York Times*, October 29, 2013, sec. World, http://www.nytimes.com/2013/10/30/world/officials-say-white-house-knew-of-spying.html.

104. Spencer Ackerman, "House Forces Vote on Amendment That Would Limit NSA Bulk Surveillance," *The Guardian*, July 23, 2013, sec. World News, http://www.theguardian.com/world/2013/jul/23/house-amendment-nsa-bulk-surveillance.

105. Ibid.
106. Ibid.
107. James Ball and Spencer Ackerman, "NSA Loophole Allows Warrantless Search for U.S. Citizens' E-mails and Phone Calls."
108. "Wyden and Udall Letter to General Alexander on NSA's Section 702 Fact Sheet Inaccuracy," *Scribd*, June 24, 2013, http://www.scribd.com/doc/149791921/Wyden-and-Udall-Letter-to-General-Alexander-on-NSA-s-Section-702-Fact-Sheet-Inaccuracy.
109. Ellen Nakashima, "Lawmakers, Privacy Advocates Call for Reforms at NSA," *The Washington Post*, August 16, 2013, http://www.washingtonpost.com/world/national-security/lawmakers-privacy-advocates-call-for-reforms-at-nsa/2013/08/16/7cccb772-0692-11e3-a07f-49ddc7417125_story.html.
110. Charlie Savage, "N.S.A. Said to Have Paid E-Mail Providers Millions to Cover Costs From Court Ruling," *The New York Times*, August 23, 2013, sec. U.S., http://www.nytimes.com/2013/08/24/us/nsa-said-to-have-paid-e-mail-providers-millions-to-cover-costs-from-court-ruling.html.
111. Wallsten, "Lawmakers Say Obstacles Limited Oversight of NSA's Telephone Surveillance Program."
112. Ibid. Speaking at a House hearing on June 18, 2013, deputy attorney general James Cole told legislators "There's a great deal of minimization procedures that are involved here, particularly concerning any of the acquisition of information that deals or comes from U.S. persons."
113. Dustin Weaver, "Senators Skip Classified Briefing on NSA Snooping to Catch Flights Home," *The Hill*, June 15, 2013, http://thehill.com/homenews/senate/305765-senators-skip-classified-briefing-on-nsa-snooping-to-catch-flights-home.
114. Wallsten, "Lawmakers Say Obstacles Limited Oversight of NSA's Telephone Surveillance Program."
115. Charlie Savage and David E. Sanger, "Senate Panel Presses N.S.A. on Phone Logs," *The New York Times*, July 31, 2013, sec. U.S., http://www.nytimes.com/2013/08/01/us/nsa-surveillance.html.
116. Brian Fung, "Senators Lash out at NSA for Excessive Secrecy," *The Washington Post*, July 31, 2013, http://www.washingtonpost.com/blogs/the-switch/wp/2013/07/31/franken-to-introduce-nsa-transparency-bill.
117. Mark Landler and David E. Sanger, "Obama May Ban Spying on Heads of Allied States," *The New York Times*, October 28, 2013, sec. World / Europe, http://www.nytimes.com/2013/10/29/world/europe/obama-may-ban-spying-on-heads-of-allied-states.html.
118. Ibid.
119. David Ignatius, "James Clapper Manages the Secret Empire."
120. Holly Yeager, "House, Senate Intelligence Chairmen Voice Fresh Concerns about NSA Eavesdropping," *The Washington Post*, November 3, 2013, http://www.washingtonpost.com/politics/house-senate-intelligence-chairs-voice-fresh-concerns-about-nsa-eavesdropping/2013/11/03/cacd1e18-44b2-11e3-b6f8-3782ff6cb769_story.html?hpid=z3.
121. David Ignatius, "James Clapper Manages the Secret Empire."
122. Damian Paletta, "Five Ways Spying has Changed Since Snowden," *The Wall Street Journal*, June 1, 2015, sec. Global, http://blogs.wsj.com/washwire/2015/06/01/five-ways-spying-has-changed-since-snowden/.
123. "About EFF," *Electronic Frontier Foundation*, accessed September 28, 2014, https://www.eff.org/about.
124. Kenneth Roth, "Rethinking Surveillance," *NYRblog*, July 2, 2013, http://www.nybooks.com/blogs/nyrblog/2013/jul/02/electronic-surveillance-missing-laws.
125. Steven Aftergood, "NSA Surveillance and the Failure of Intelligence Oversight," *Federation of American Scientists*, July 1, 2013, http://fas.org/blogs/secrecy/2013/07/surv-oversight/; Major Dave Owen, "A Review of Intelligence Oversight Failure: NSA Programs that Affected Americans," in *Military Intelligence Professional Bulletin*, October—December 2012, http://www.fas.org/irp/agency/army/mipb/2012_04-owen.pdf.
126. Ibid.
127. Charlie Savage, "Nation Will Gain by Discussing Surveillance, Expert Tells Privacy Board," *The New York Times*, July 9, 2013, sec. U.S., http://www.nytimes.com/2013/07/10/us/nation-will-gain-by-discussing-surveillance-expert-tells-privacy-board.html.
128. James G. Carr, "A Better Secret Court," *The New York Times*, July 22, 2013, sec. Opinion, http://www.nytimes.com/2013/07/23/opinion/a-better-secret-court.html.
129. Landler and Sanger, "Obama May Ban Spying on Heads of Allied States."
130. Alison Smale and David E. Sanger, "Spying Scandal Alters U.S. Ties With Allies and Raises Talk of Policy Shift," *The New York Times*, November 11, 2013, sec. World, http://www.nytimes.com/2013/11/12/world/spying-scandal-alters-us-ties-with-allies-and-raises-talk-of-policy-shift.html.
131. Ibid.
132. Ibid.
133. Ibid.
134. Scott Shane, "No Morsel Too Minuscule for All-Consuming N.S.A.," *The New York Times*, November 2, 2013, sec. World, http://www.nytimes.com/2013/11/03/world/no-morsel-too-minuscule-for-all-consuming-nsa.html.
135. Rory Carroll, "NSA Director Keith Alexander Defends Surveillance Tactics in Speech to Hackers," *The Guardian*, July 31, 2013, sec. World News, http://www.theguardian.com/world/2013/jul/31/nsa-keith-alexander-black-hat-surveillance.
136. Bamford, "NSA Snooping Was Only the Beginning. Meet the Spy Chief Leading Us Into Cyberwar."
137. Ibid.

PART II STRUCTURE

The Concrete Expressions of Public Policy

The Constitution of the executive department of the proposed government claims next our attention. There is hardly any part of the system which could have been attended with greater difficulty in the arrangement of it than this; and there is perhaps none, which has been inveighed against with less candor, or criticized with less judgment.[i]

—Alexander Hamilton
The Federalist, No. 67

Structures are legislated delegations of authority and responsibility to designated public officials and organizations to take action on behalf of lawful policy and program objectives. These delegations identify specific means of taking action, such as expenditures of appropriated funds, issuance of rules and guidelines, awarding contracts and grants, setting user fees and charges, and creating various types of organizations. Governance scholar Lester M. Salamon has called these means the "tools of government."[ii] These structures are the principal form of leverage that policymakers have over public policy implementation and management.

Structures are described in

- the provisions and language of authorizing statutes;
- legislatively authorized and appropriated budgets;
- executive orders, regulations, and rules that have the force of law;
- decisions and directives by executives and managers within their lawful spheres of authority; and
- decisions, injunctions, and consent decrees of the courts having jurisdiction.

---

[i]Alexander Hamilton, "Federalist No. 67," *The Federalist Papers,* ed. C. Rossiter (New York, NY: New American Library, 1961).

[ii]Lester M. Salamon, *The Tools of Government: A Guide to the New Governance* (Oxford, UK: Oxford University Press, 2002).

As such, structures may be regarded as the concrete expressions of public policy. Delegated responsibilities and authorities of public managers may include

- creating additional administrative structures;
- establishing planning, decision-making, and communication processes;
- prescribing specific standards for the performance of functions and tasks; and
- allocating specific levels of personnel and budgetary resources to agency offices and activities together with rules and guidelines for their use.

These structures are the principal form of leverage that policymakers have over public policy implementation and management.

Structures may either enable or constrain the conduct and actions of public managers. Enabling structures permit or allow the exercise of managerial judgment. Constraining structures direct, require, or prohibit the exercise of managerial judgment. Both types of structures may emanate from sources of authority that are either external or internal to departments, bureaus, or agencies. A legislative directive to an executive branch agency is an external authorization of managerial judgment. Orders made by an elected executive, or directives issued by the head of a department or bureau, are internal authorizations of managerial judgment to subordinates by the issuing official. An example is a cabinet secretary's restructuring of reporting channels or job responsibilities of agency staff. Table II.1 shows how structures can, therefore, be classified according to

(1) whether they constrain or enable the exercise of managerial judgment, and

(2) whether their authorization is external or internal to the organization.

Enabling structures, shown in the first row of Table II.1, are formal delegations of authority that explicitly or implicitly allow discretion on the part of designated officials or organizations. Public managers' discretionary actions may create structures or infuse an existing structure with distinction and meaning (though these structures may not be wholly under the control of managerial actors). Enabling structures are communicated through provisions of authorizing statutes, executive orders, regulations, and rules.

Constraining structures, shown in the second row of Table II.1, are mandates, restrictions, conditions, and other boundary-defining measures. These constraints include specific rules and procedures such as mandatory decision-making or communication processes; standards and criteria for, and ways of organizing, the performance of jobs, functions, programs, and tasks; required reporting channels of authority or accountability; budgets; payment or reimbursement formulas; and rules governing evaluation, discipline, promotion, and termination of employees.

The view of structures as either enabling or constraining public managers is consistent with Elinor Ostrom's definition of "rules".[iii] She defines rules as "prescriptions commonly known and used by a set of participants to order repetitive, interdependent relationships" and to identify "which actions (or states of the world) are *required, prohibited,* or *permitted.*" Ostrom elaborates,

---

[iii]Elinor Ostrom, "An Agenda for the Study of Institutions," *Public Choice* 48, no. 1 (1986): 5.

| TABLE II.1 | **Examples of Enabling and Constraining Structures** |

	Source of Formal Authority in Relation to the Organization	
Type of Structure	**External**	**Internal**
Enabling: permit or allow exercise of managerial judgment	• Tenth Amendment to U.S. Constitution • Congressional creation of executive departments	• Forest Service rule regarding National Forest System Land Management Planning • Managers' delegations to subordinates for figuring out how to perform specific tasks
Constraining: direct, require, or prohibit managerial judgment	• Required use of performance incentives by legislation (e.g., Workforce Investment Act) • Required reporting lines of authority, detailed in legislation or external executive agency/ authority (e.g., process for Bush administration's Program Assessment Rating Tool)	• Job descriptions defined by managers • Details of performance incentives developed by managers and staff • Centers for Medicare & Medicaid Services regulations for physician reimbursement

Rules are the result of implicit or explicit efforts by a set of individuals to achieve order and predictability within defined situations by: (1) creating positions; (2) stating how participants enter or leave positions; (3) stating which actions participants in these positions are required, permitted, or forbidden to take; and (4) stating which outcome participants are required, permitted, or forbidden to affect.[iv]

Informal or shared understandings about relationships between actors or about ways of working are included in Ostrom's conception of a rule. In the three-dimensional framework used in this text, they are considered to be aspects of organizational culture (Part III).

PUBLIC MANAGEMENT'S PERFECT STORM: THE STRUCTURE DIMENSION

Structure figures prominently in the story of how Hurricane Katrina devastated New Orleans and surrounding areas in August 2005, especially structures related to command and communications.

The emergency management community had long anticipated the possibility that just such a severe hurricane would strike New Orleans with devastating consequences. In fact, only the year before, federal, state, and local officials had conducted an exercise, "Hurricane Pam," that simulated a Category 3 hurricane and its effects on New Orleans and predicted evacuation failures and other problems that occurred in Katrina's aftermath. But follow-up

---

[iv]Ibid.

on the Hurricane Pam exercise was weak, and when Katrina struck, the emergency procedures, plans, and prior agreements in place were ill-equipped to cope with an incident of this magnitude.

In the aftermath of Katrina, the U.S. Senate and the U.S. House of Representatives conducted detailed investigations and issued reports on the events leading up to and following the disaster.[v] Most of the 186 numbered findings in the Senate report address issues related to structure, and the overwhelming majority identified failures in those structures or in how they functioned. These include the following:

14. Confusion, ambiguity, and uncertainty characterized the perceptions of the Army Corps of Engineers, the local levee boards, and other agencies with jurisdiction over the levee system of their respective responsibilities, leading to failures to carry out comprehensive inspections, rigorously monitor system integrity, or undertake needed repairs (p. 590).

35. Although the Hurricane Pam exercise, among other things, put FEMA [Federal Emergency Management Agency] on notice that a storm of Katrina's magnitude could have catastrophic impact on New Orleans, Michael Brown and FEMA failed to do the necessary planning and preparations:

    a. to train or equip agency personnel for the likely needed operations;

    b. to adequately prearrange contracts to transport necessary commodities;

    c. to pre-position appropriate communications assets; or

    d. to consult with DOD [Department of Defense]) regarding back-up capability in the event a catastrophe materialized, among other deficiencies (p. 592).

69. The National Communications System failed to develop plans to support first-responder communications, assess the damage to the communications systems, and maintain awareness of the federal government's available communications assets. Local governments either had inadequate plans or were unable to rapidly repair damage to their first responder communications systems (p. 595).

83. The NRP [National Response Plan] does not adequately address the organizational structure and the assets needed for search and rescue in a large-scale, multi-environment catastrophe. Under the NRP, Emergency Support Function 9 (ESF9, Urban Search and Rescue) is focused on missions to rescue people in collapsed structures. ESF-9 gives the U.S. Coast Guard a support role for water rescue. However, the NRP does not provide a comprehensive structure for water and air rescues, which constituted a significant portion of the necessary search-and-rescue missions in the Katrina response (p. 596).

121. Early in the response, Mississippi recognized how severely Katrina had disrupted the state's infrastructure, and the resulting inability of many residents of south Mississippi to travel to the Points of Distribution to acquire life-saving supplies. The resulting "push" of supplies by the National Guard to residents was crucial to preventing additional hardship in south Mississippi (p. 599).

---

[v] U.S. Senate, *Hurricane Katrina: A Nation Still Unprepared: Special Report of the Committee on Homeland Security and Governmental Affairs* (Washington DC: Government Printing Office, 2006), http://www.gpoaccess.gov/serialset/creports/katrinanation.html; and U.S. House of Representatives, *A Failure of Initiative: Final Report of the Select Bipartisan Committee to Investigate the Preparation for and Response to Hurricane Katrina* (Washington, DC: Government Printing Office, 2006), http://www.gpoaccess.gov/katrinareport/fullreport.pdf.

145. While some active-duty and National Guard units are designed and structured to deploy rapidly as part of their military missions, the Department of Defense is not organized, funded, or structured to act as a first responder for all domestic catastrophic disasters (p. 601).

174. Due to lack of planning and preparation, much of FEMA's initial spending was reactive and rushed, resulting in costly purchase decisions and utilization of no-bid, sole-source contracts that put the government at increased risk of not getting the best price for goods and services (p. 604).

176. The NRP lacked clarity on a number of points, including the role and authorities of the Principal Federal Official and the allocation of responsibilities among multiple agencies under the Emergency Support Functions, which led to confusion in the response to Katrina. Plan ambiguities were not resolved or clarified in the months after the NRP was issued, either through additional operational planning or through training and exercises (p. 604).

These examples emphasize how structure—including the rule of law—shaped and constrained the activities of public officials in planning for and responding to Hurricane Katrina.

PART II OVERVIEW

Part II explores specific frameworks, theories, and concepts that illuminate the structure dimension of public management. These intellectual resources facilitate analysis of how structures shape the incentives, decisions, and actions of managers, frontline employees, and their agents. Public managers deal with such issues whether they operate within structures that are outside their power to change, or they have the authority to choose new structural arrangements or to change existing ones.

Part II of this book comprises four chapters:

- Chapter 4 discusses structures that emanate from the U.S. Constitution and from the constitutions and charters of state and local governments. It describes public management in a federal system of government with separation of powers as well as checks and balances at all levels.
- Chapter 5 is concerned with externally authorized structures that enable and constrain public managers and that as a whole constitute "the administrative state." It distinguishes between direct government and the primary alternatives for responding to market failures—government-sponsored enterprises, nonprofit organizations, and collaborations. The chapter describes in detail two prominent externally authorized constraining structures: budgets and public personnel systems.
- Chapter 6 considers the structural tools available to public managers to further enable and constrain the implementation of public policies. It describes the principal-agent model and the concept of transaction costs as fundamental analytical tools for decisions concerning these structures. The chapter describes a number of organizational structural aspects that a manager, through lawfully delegated authority, may be able to influence or change: job positions or tasks, street-level bureaucrats and local justice, budgetary choices, rules, contracting out, interdependence and collaboration, and management capacity.

- Chapter 7 focuses on a particular type of structure—rules and regulations and the organizations that create, administer, and enforce them. It describes rationales for regulation, regulatory actors and processes, and issues of enforceability and methods of enforcement.

This part of the book answers these questions:

1. How does the Constitution shape the responsibilities and the potential contributions of public officials in managerial roles?

2. How does politics influence what public managers do and why they do it?

3. In what ways can public managers improve their ability to do their jobs?

4. Why and with what consequences is there so much public regulation of private behavior and conduct?

4 Structure

James Madison's Legacies

INTRODUCTION

Public management in the United States is inextricably embedded in a system of governmental structures of constitutional origin. This scheme of governance was conceived primarily by James Madison, who drew examples from the state constitutions at the time. The essays of *The Federalist* justified four main elements of the system:

- a **separation of powers** among three branches of government: legislative, executive, and judicial;
- **checks and balances** designed to preclude any one branch from overpowering the others;
- **federalism**, a division and ordering of responsibilities between the federal government and the state governments, intended to preclude the central government from overpowering the states; and
- **"the people"** who, associating in various "factions" and electing legislators and other officers to represent them, preclude governments from overpowering their citizens.

In creating this complicated structure intended to ensure "limited government," Madison and the other Founders were influenced by Adam Smith, the Scottish moral philosopher and author of *An Inquiry into the Nature and Causes of the Wealth of Nations*.[1] Founders aimed to allocate political power in the most democratic way, resembling how Smith's scheme of free, albeit regulated, markets would allocate a nation's economic resources in the most efficient way. In both schemes, competition would promote liberty and justice. But, as both Smith and the Founders recognized, both schemes can fail if "the people" fail to conduct themselves in a "virtuous" manner, that is, without predatory or tyrannical intent or effect.

The implications of constitutional structures of governance for public management and public managers are the subject of this chapter.

CASE: PATIENT PROTECTION AND AFFORDABLE CARE ACT OF 2010: HOW MADISONIAN DEMOCRACY WORKS

On March 23, 2010, President Barack Obama signed into law the Patient Protection and Affordable Care Act of 2010 (the ACA). The ACA aimed to ensure access to essential health care services for millions of people who could previously see a doctor only in an emergency. This goal would be accomplished in two ways: (1) by helping eligible participants purchase private health insurance coverage for essential health care needs and (2) by extending state-administered Medicaid basic health coverage for low-income individuals who were previously ineligible for it.

The majority of Americans obtain their health insurance from private insurance companies and their health care from private providers. Many liberal and conservative health experts had long advocated reforming the health care system to make it more inclusive and more efficient.

- Liberals tended to favor a "single payer" approach to providing universal health insurance coverage. Two single-payer subsystems already exist in the United States: Medicare for older Americans and the Veterans Health Administration for retired military veterans. Why not extend the Medicare model to cover people of all ages?
- Conservatives tended to favor a system that relies on employers, insurance companies, and insurance exchanges or "marketplaces" to provide insurance coverage to anyone who wants it. The government's role would be limited to using a combination of taxes and subsidies to ensure that Americans who cannot afford to pay market prices for coverage can buy health insurance in the private market.

Neither of these approaches stood a chance of receiving congressional approval, however. Powerful interest groups with stakes in the status quo included pharmaceutical companies, insurance companies, state governors, and labor unions, to name only a few. The Obama administration sought to win stakeholder support for its aims by building on the current system rather than seeking to replace it. The administration wanted to get a bill passed, not start a prolonged debate.

Although the primary goal of the ACA was clear, its administration would be anything but straightforward. The challenge was to coordinate the countless operating parts of America's hybrid health care system. Further, while most of those affected by the ACA would probably be better off, a great many whose premiums increased might not. This reality was obscured by the rhetoric that accompanied efforts to gain congressional support for the ACA. "If you like your current plan, you can keep it," President Obama famously declared. As it turned out, for some people, he was wrong.

Madisonian Politics

Relying on the private health insurance industry to provide near-universal, affordable, high-quality, and nondiscriminatory coverage required the Obama administration and its supporters to use various carrots and sticks to get that industry to offer the desired menu of insurance plans and premiums. The administration's proposal required state governments, insurance companies, and health care providers to change their standard policies and practices. Such changes required, in turn, an exceedingly complex array of administrative tools: mandates, regulations and standards, matching grants and subsidies, opt-out provisions, penalties, and new institutions such as regulated **health insurance marketplaces**, also known as **health insurance exchanges.**

The administration's approach drew intense scrutiny by hundreds of lobbying groups, including powerful corporations, trade associations, and interest groups such as Pharmaceutical Research and Manufacturers of America, America's Health Insurance Plans, BlueCross/BlueShield, Planned Parenthood, the Service Employees National Union, the American Association for Retired Persons, and the U.S. Chamber of Commerce.[2] "About 1,750 businesses and organizations spent at least $1.2 billion in 2009 on lobbying teams to work on the health care overhaul and other issues."[3]

To become law, the final policy design would need the support of a supermajority (60 votes) of the Senate, a majority of the members of the House of Representatives, and, because of the inevitable legal challenges to many of the act's provisions, eventual approval by the U.S. Supreme Court. The main ideas in the act originated in conservative think tanks and policy proposals. However, Republicans were united in calling the proposed act tantamount to "socialized medicine" and declaring it unconstitutional. Administration negotiators had to strike numerous deals with lobbyists and lawmakers. With great difficulty, the congressional approval was obtained, albeit with no Republican support. The Supreme Court ultimately and narrowly upheld the act's most controversial provision, the **individual mandate** requiring all uninsured Americans (with some exceptions) to buy health insurance or pay a penalty (what the court majority deemed a legitimate "tax").

Among the most consequential features of the ACA is its reliance on federalism as a primary structure for expanding health insurance coverage.

- The act expanded (predominantly at federal expense) eligibility for the state-administered Medicaid program to all individuals whose incomes met federal eligibility criteria. The Act allowed states to opt out of the Medicaid expansion, although opt-out would mean the loss of all federal matching funds for the state's Medicaid program, a provision the Supreme Court would later declare unconstitutional (as discussed later in the chapter).
- The act authorized a new structure, health insurance exchanges, to be created and administered by the states alone or in partnership with the federal government. States could also opt out of participating in the health exchange program. If they did so, their residents could buy insurance through a federal health exchange, HealthCare.Gov.

Considerable state-to-state variation in how their residents obtained health insurance would inevitably arise from these ACA provisions, as many state governments opposed the ACA.

Medicaid Expansion

The Medicaid program, enacted in 1965, provides health insurance coverage to individuals and families with low incomes.[i] States are not required to participate in the program, but all do. The federal government

---

[i]Information on the Medicaid program is available at http://www.medicaid.gov/.

(Continued)

(Continued)

provides from 50 to nearly 75 percent of the cost of the program depending on the state's financial capacity. Although a condition of participation is that states agree to follow federal rules, states are allowed considerable discretion in how they cover medical services.[ii] The Secretary of Health and Human Services (HHS) may withhold Medicaid funds if a state fails to comply with federal rules, but that has never happened.

The ACA requires coverage by Medicaid of a minimum benefits package. This package includes 10 categories of benefits to nearly all people under age 65 at or below 138 percent of the federal poverty line. The federal government would cover the total costs of this coverage from 2014 through 2016, with the percentage declining to 90 percent thereafter.

As noted earlier, states that failed to expand their Medicaid programs in accordance with the terms required by the ACA risked losing all their Medicaid funding, not just the additional funding for the expanded coverage. States were thus confronted with both a carrot and a stick to induce them to accept the expanded program.

> **The Tenth Amendment states that all powers not enumerated as belonging to the federal government remain with the states and the people. Following ACA enactment, 25 states sued the federal government over the Medicaid expansion on constitutional grounds, claiming the Tenth Amendment had been violated.**

The Tenth Amendment states that all powers not enumerated as belonging to the federal government remain with the states and the people. Following ACA enactment, 25 states sued the federal government over the Medicaid expansion on constitutional grounds, claiming the Tenth Amendment had been violated.

They claimed the threat of withholding all of a state's federal Medicaid funding for noncompliance with the expansion exceeded the enumerated power of Congress, as previously interpreted by the court, to set conditions for receipt of federal funds. To be constitutional, conditions set by Congress must satisfy four factors. They must be (1) related to the general welfare, (2) stated unambiguously, (3) clearly related to the program's purpose, and (4) not otherwise unconstitutional.

In the court's decision on this case, Chief Justice John Roberts argued that the Medicaid expansion was, in effect, a new federal-state program, not an extension of the existing program, and, therefore was unconstitutionally coercive toward the states. This was the first time the court had ever reached such a decision concerning conditions set by Congress for federal matching of funds provided by the states. In his majority opinion for the court, Chief Justice Roberts stated,

> We have no need to fix a line . . . It is enough for today that wherever that line may be, this statute is surely beyond it. Congress may not simply "conscript state [agencies] into the national bureaucratic army," [a quote from an earlier Supreme Court decision] and that is what it is attempting to do with the Medicaid expansion.[4]

The Medicaid expansion program remained legal, however, because the constitutional violation was fully remedied by the court's ruling that the secretary of HHS may not withhold all or part of a

[ii]For more information about the Medicaid program's required and optional elements, *see* Kaiser Commission on Medicaid and the Uninsured, *Federal Core Requirements and State Options in Medicaid: Current Policies and Key Issues* (April 2011), available at http://www.kff.org/medicaid/8174.cfm.

state's matching funds for the original Medicaid program if a state does not implement the expansion. The effect of ruling's wording was to uphold the legality of the Medicaid expansion, which remained available to any state that affirmed its willingness to participate in the program.[5] The court had taken away the federal government's stick, but the rather succulent carrot of nearly total federal funding of the expansion remained.[iii]

The removal of the coercive stick of punishing states that did not expand Medicaid with withdrawal of total Medicaid financial support then interacted with the results of the midterm elections of 2010 to produce an extraordinary result: many states initially chose not to participate in the Medicaid expansion despite nearly total federal funding for the program (although a few later relented). Those midterm elections results reflected a conservative backlash against what conservatives called "Obamacare." The number of state governments entirely in Republican hands nearly doubled to a total of 24. As a consequence of that backlash and of lukewarm public support for the new ACA, more than half of the states initially decided not to participate in the lucrative Medicaid expansion even if significant percentages of their residents had no health insurance. More liberal states, in sharp contrast, warmly embraced Medicaid's expansion.

Health Insurance Exchanges

A second way in which the ACA has implications for federalism is in its provisions concerning reforms in private health insurance markets.

According to the "universal coverage" provision of the ACA, every individual, with certain exceptions, must purchase health insurance providing at least "minimum essential coverage" for themselves and their dependents or else pay a (then relatively small) penalty. A highly controversial provision, the "individual mandate" was upheld by the Supreme Court, which, as already noted, interpreted the "penalty" as a "tax" that is constitutionally permissible.[6]

Many then-existing insurance plans, including those provided by employers, already met the ACA's coverage test. The mandate was intended (originally by conservatives) to induce private insurance companies to provide adequate and affordable coverage to those families and individuals who had inadequate coverage or no coverage at all.[7] By guaranteeing a large customer base for insurance industry products, ACA supporters argued, the individual mandate would enable insurance companies to spread the risks of a policy holder's needing medical treatment over both healthy and medically needy individuals, thus bringing premiums into an affordable range.

But the mandate by itself was not thought to be enough to make adequate and affordable care available to low-income individuals and families and to small businesses. The mechanisms to bring that about were subsidies and tax credits to insurance companies. These subsidies would be administered through the state health insurance exchanges.

To sell plans through these exchanges, insurance companies would be required to offer affordable policies meeting coverage mandates. To qualify for the subsidized premiums, individuals would be required to purchase coverage through these exchanges. The exchanges also would enable the regulation of both insurance

---

[iii]The Supreme court's ruling implied that the court might eventually make similar rulings on other (numerous) joint federal-state programs, ranging from highway construction to elementary and secondary education. Dylan Scott, "Health Ruling Sets Up Potential Fallout for Federalism," June 29, 2012, http://www.governing.com/blogs/fedwatch/gov-supreme-court-ruling-potential-fallout-for-federalism.html.

(Continued)

(Continued)

company coverage and premiums and the eligibility of individuals to purchase subsidized coverage. Buyers and sellers could interact via a website that offered choices to customers who qualified for making a purchase.

The states were given the authority to establish these exchanges in accordance with the characteristics of their own insurance markets and their own political and policy priorities. Federal planning and implementation grants were available for the task. However, as already noted, states could opt out of creating such exchanges. Anticipating that eventuality, the ACA's designers authorized the federal government to establish and administer the state-level exchanges.

A third option existed: a "partnership exchange." Termed a "hybrid model" by policy experts, a state could choose to operate certain functions of a federally facilitated exchange. Thus, states were enabled "to assume primary responsibility for carrying out certain activities related to plan management, consumer assistance and outreach, or both."[8] The outcome might be a blending of federal and state policy and political priorities concerning the provision of health care coverage to small businesses and those with low incomes.[9]

The ACA's language could, however, be interpreted as authorizing subsidized premiums only to insurance plans sold through state-established exchanges. The Internal Revenue Service rejected that interpretation because it would deny subsidies to millions of people living in states that did not establish exchanges. The IRS decreed that the law's plain intent was to authorize subsidies for plans purchased through the federal exchange. This ruling initiated yet another legal battle over whether the law authorized federal tax credits for insurance purchased on the federal exchange. With two appellate courts making opposite rulings on the issue, in 2015 the Supreme Court ruled in *King v. Burwell* that tax credits for insurance purchased on the federal exchange had indeed been authorized by the ACA.[10]

SEPARATION OF POWERS

In *The Federalist No. 47*, James Madison offered a justification for "the particular structure of this government and the distribution of . . . power among its constituent parts."[11] The phrase "constituent parts" referred to the tripartite division of powers among the legislative, executive, and judicial branches of governments. He wanted to contest the claim by critics of the draft constitution, which required ratification by the states, that its blending of legislative, executive, and judicial powers—rather than maintaining their strict independence from one another—both offended "symmetry and beauty of form" and exposed some parts of government to domination by other parts. In *The Federalist No. 48*, Madison argued, "unless these departments [branches] be so far connected and blended as to give to each a constitutional control over the others, the degree of separation which the [separation of powers] maxim requires, as essential to a free government, can never in practice be duly maintained."

> . . . a separation of powers requires "checks and balances" to ensure the accountability of each department to the others . . .

The separation of powers was referred to by Madison in *The Federalist No. 47* as "this invaluable precept in the science of politics" and is associated with Montesquieu's argument in *The Spirit of Laws* in 1748 that there should be three departments of government, *trias politica*. But Madison argued that the doctrine was "presupposed": assumed, not justified.[12] Madison pointed to detailed justifications in the constitutions of several states. He took for granted that the separation of powers in all state constitutions justified its incorporation into the Founders' draft constitution. What is justified is the particular way in which the powers are separated in the draft constitution in order to produce the result to which the Founders aspired. The separation of powers was justified because it offered

> an indispensable means for locating responsibility and fixing accountability. An executive, unambiguously charged with executing a policy set by the "Law-makers," can be held liable for its performance or nonperformance. Let that clear line of distinction and responsibility be blurred, and liberty and the people's interest are alike in jeopardy.[13]

CHECKS AND BALANCES

The separation of powers is not, however, sufficient to protect against the tyranny of an overly powerful government. As Madison argued in *The Federalist No. 44,* a separation of powers requires "checks and balances" to ensure the accountability of each department to the others:

> What is to be the consequence, in case the Congress shall misconstrue this part [the necessary and proper clause] of the Constitution and exercise powers not warranted by its true meaning, I answer the same as if they should misconstrue or enlarge any other power vested in them . . . the success of the usurpation will depend on the executive and judiciary departments, which are to expound and give effect to the legislative acts; and in a last resort a remedy must be obtained from the people, who can by the elections of more faithful representatives, annul the acts of the usurpers.[14]

The elaborate system of checks and balances limits the encroachment of the branches upon each other.[i] Checks and balances, which are not labeled as such in the Constitution itself (though they are in *The Federalist*), have the effect not only of imposing structures on public managers but also of creating opportunities and challenges for managers practicing their craft within the confines of those structures. These explicit constitutional provisions may be referred to as **primary checks and balances** because they were given formal expression by the Founders. They are distinguished from **secondary checks and balances**, defined and discussed in the following.

Primary Checks and Balances

The most important of the primary checks and balances are listed in Box 4.1. The influence of these checks and balances on public management practice is illustrated in the examples that follow.

Constitutional scholar John Rohr has elaborated on how Congress delegates authority to—or imposes a duty on—subordinate officers, thereby providing them with independence from the president in specific situations defined by statute: "This accountability to Congress severs the hierarchical chain of command in the executive branch and exposes the subordinate to the full force of Congress's impressive powers to investigate the public administration and to subject it to the rigors of legislative oversight."[15] These delegations make explicit the fact that executive officers are not simply the president's appointees but are also officers of the law.

The following examples illustrate Rohr's argument.

---

[i]A complete list of constitutional checks and balances is available online at http://www.usconstitution.net/consttop_cnb.html. See also Rafael La Porta et al., "Judicial Checks and Balances," *Journal of Political Economy* 112, no. 2 (2004): 445–470; and James Madison, "Federalist No. 47," in *The Federalist Papers,* ed. C. Rossiter (New York, NY: New American Library, 1961), or any other edition of these seminal papers.

| Box 4.1 | **PRIMARY CHECKS AND BALANCES** |

- Legislative authority to make all laws governing the execution of powers vested in Congress, the government of the United States, or any department or officer thereof
- Legislative authority to provide advice and consent on certain executive branch appointments
- Legislative control of appropriations
- Requirement that both houses of Congress approve a statute
- Executive nomination of federal judges (subject to legislative advice and consent)
- Review of administrative actions by the judicial branch
- Presidential power to veto legislation passed by Congress and congressional power to override such vetoes
- Provision for legislative impeachment of the president and of federal judges
- First Amendment endorsement of freedom of the press
- Initiative, referendum, and recall provisions of state constitutions

Example: Supreme Court Ruling on Shoemaker v. United States (1893)

The case of *Shoemaker v. United States* (1893) illustrates the first two checks and balances listed in Box 4.1. The U.S. Supreme Court decision stated that Congress shares authority with the executive branch over the assignment of administrative responsibilities to executive branch offices: "It cannot be doubted, and it has frequently been the case, that Congress may increase the power and duties of an existing office without thereby rendering it necessary that the incumbent should be again nominated and appointed."

For the imposition of new duties on an officer to be valid under *Shoemaker,* two requirements must be met. First, the legislation must confer new duties on "*offices,* . . . [not] on any particular *officer.*" Second, the new duties must be "germane to the offices already held by" the affected officers.[16]

Under *Shoemaker,* for example, when it created the Department of Homeland Security in 2002, Congress had the authority to transfer the U.S. Coast Guard from the Treasury Department to the Homeland Security Department and modify the responsibilities of senior officials in both departments.

Example: Establishment of National Cancer Institute

The National Cancer Institute (NCI) was created during the presidency of Richard M. Nixon. The National Cancer Act of 1971 authorized a "war on cancer." Rather than leave it to the administration to decide how to organize this war, Congress decreed that the NCI should have substantial independence to carry out the mission. Congress promoted the NCI to bureau status within the Department of Health, Education, and Welfare (HEW), and its director was made a presidential appointee and authorized to coordinate the national cancer program. Furthermore, the director was authorized to submit his annual budget request directly to the president without prior review by the National Institutes of Health or the HEW.

The authorization created a "bypass budget," which is beyond the control of departmental management, an arrangement that exists to this day. The former National Cancer Advisory Council was promoted to the status of a presidentially appointed Cancer Advisory Board, and the President's Cancer Panel was created to oversee implementation and bring delays or barriers to the attention of the president. According to some experts, the early bypass budgets were merely wish lists, but, as budget resources became tighter over the years, it became more of a priority-setting management tool.

> **Federal judges have lifetime appointments, and their influence on the law and, thereby, on public management is enduring.**

Example: Senate Confirmation of Federal Judicial Nominees

Prominent among primary checks and balances is the role of the U.S. Senate in the confirmation of presidential nominees to the federal judiciary. Article II, Section 2, paragraph 2 of the Constitution states, "The President shall . . . nominate, and by and with the Advice and Consent of the Senate, shall appoint . . . Judges of the supreme Court . . . ." The Senate's "advice and consent" role was to be extended to all federal judicial appointments. Many state constitutions have a similar provision.

Inevitably, the process of filling federal judicial vacancies is intensely political. Federal judges have lifetime appointments, and their influence on the law and, thereby, on public management is enduring. Presidents and their political parties make every effort to ensure not only that judicial appointees are competent but also that they are likely to be sympathetic toward issues central to the values and ideas each party represents.

The process of judicial appointment begins with the submission of a nominee, usually after vetting with the legal profession and with key senators and constituencies, to the Senate. These nominations are referred to the Senate Committee on the Judiciary which, in turn, reviews the qualifications of the nominee and holds a hearing on the nomination. The committee then takes a vote of its members. On the basis of that vote, the committee then makes a recommendation concerning approval or disapproval to the full Senate, which conducts a debate on the nomination on the Senate floor. The debate ends when 60 Senators vote "yes" on ending it. The nominee is confirmed when a simple majority of the Senate votes "yes" in a floor vote.

When either party controls the presidency and both houses of Congress, the process of nomination and confirmation may be uneventful, though some presidential nominees have been rejected by their own party. But when political power is divided, and especially when the parties' political and ideological positions are polarized, nomination and confirmation may become bogged down in partisanship.

Such a polarized situation existed in 2013 following Barack Obama's reelection to the presidency. A relatively large number of vacancies existed on the federal bench, for many of which the president had made no nominations.[17] Republican criticism of the president was vitriolic. Part of the problem was that the chair of the Senate Judiciary Committee, Democrat Patrick Leahy of Vermont, scrupulously honored a Senate tradition, intended to ensure comity among senators over the long haul, not to process a nomination if either Senator from the nominee's home state opposed the nomination.[ii]

After months of partisan impasse, matters came to a head concerning three Obama administration nominations to fill vacancies on the United States Court of Appeals for the District of Columbia Circuit. This court is of extraordinary importance to public policy implementation because it is responsible, by statute and by jurisdiction

---

[ii]A consequence of this political dynamic, according to a Brookings Institution study was this: "Texas has almost 30 percent of the nominee-less vacancies—one dating from 2008, another from 2010, two from 2011, three from 2012, and one from 2013. Five of them meet the Judicial Conference's definition of a "judicial emergency," based on the vacancy's length and the court's workload. Two, both from 2011, are in a district with the third highest weighted caseload in the country, and the district with the 2008 vacancy has the ninth highest weighted caseload. (Split delegation state Pennsylvania has five of the nominee less vacancies, and Florida four.)"

granted by the Administrative Procedure Act, for reviewing the decisions and rulemaking of many federal independent agencies of the United States government. Some Republicans claimed that the court's workload was such that filling these vacancies was not essential.

In November 2013, Senate majority leader Nevada Democrat Harry Reid invoked what was commonly known as "the nuclear option" to break the impasse. Under existing Senate rules, 60 votes were required to confirm a nominee to federal judicial positions. With the support of his Democratic majority, Reid secured a change in the Senate's "filibuster rule" (because 60 votes were required to end a filibuster). Henceforth, only a simple majority was needed to confirm all federal judicial nominees except for Supreme Court nominees. This move gave the president sufficient votes in the Senate to ensure confirmation of his nominations to fill vacancies in district courts and in the courts of appeal. Two weeks later, an Obama nominee to the Washington, DC, Circuit was approved by the Senate. Approvals of other judicial nominees were to follow.

Senate minority leader Mitch McConnell, a Kentucky Republican, argued, "They did this for one reason: to advance an agenda that the American people do not want."[18] Other Republicans argued that use of the "nuclear option" put a deep chill on the legislative climate in the Senate, deepening partisan gridlock.[19] Republicans retaliated by blocking administration nominees to vacant ambassadorships, where the 60-vote rule was still in force.

As these examples show, primary checks and balances reach deeply into public management at all levels of government. They are both an actual and a potential restraint on managerial discretion. Thus, they are a factor in the balance of power among officials within the executive branch and can be altered in significant ways by legislatures and courts.

Secondary Checks and Balances

The much larger class of checks and balances at federal and state levels of government may be termed secondary checks and balances: they are not defined in a written constitution but instead are created by lawmakers pursuant to the exercise of constitutional authority. The original constitutional checks and balances are staples of all civics curricula, but secondary checks and balances are not usually identified as such. Sometimes they are defined in statutes. Sometimes they are not formally stated but, as with the Senate's deference to home state objections to judicial nominees, are widely acknowledged practices. Box 4.2 lists four categories of secondary checks and balances.

Box 4.2 **SECONDARY CHECKS AND BALANCES**

Between the branches of government

- Legislative authority to compel executive branch officials to testify under oath concerning their actions
- Judicial authority to issue and enforce consent decrees and injunctions
- Authoritative reports and recommendations of the Government Accountability Office, Congressional Budget Office, and state equivalents
- Foreign Intelligence Surveillance Act

- Legislative and legislatively authorized oversight and investigation
- "Sunset" laws mandating periodic reviews of rationales for public agencies

Within the branches of government

- Inspectors general
- U.S. Office of the Special Counsel
- Whistleblower and other public employee protections
- Separation of legislative authorization and appropriation processes
- Multitiered judiciary
- Overhead offices (personnel, budget, audit, general counsel)
- Professional advisory panels
- State laboratories

Outside the branches of government

- Administrative Procedure Act
- Freedom-of-information, government-in-the-sunshine acts; WTO disclosure rules
- Office of the IRS Taxpayer Advocate, ombudsmen
- Laws at all levels of government authorizing "citizen petitions"
- "Watchdog" groups organized under federal and state laws as nonprofit organizations

Distributions of power

- National Academy of Sciences/Institute of Medicine
- Federal False Claims Act
- Anonymous leaks of information
- Independent professionals (auditors, actuaries, statisticians, intelligence analysts, scientists)
- Negotiated and private standard setting and rulemaking.

Between the Branches of Government

The first category of secondary checks and balances adds to the original capabilities of each branch to check the others. It includes

- the activities of the Government Accountability Office and the Congressional Budget Office, both of which are agencies of Congress, and their equivalents in some states, to provide audits, analyses, research, and evaluations that often contain alternative perspectives to those of the executive branch on public policy and management issues and, therefore, provides a check on executive branch versions of issues and events;
- the authority of the courts to approve, monitor, and enforce consent decrees in lawsuits in which the government is a defendant; and
- the authority of legislatures to oversee, monitor, and investigate the activities of public officers and agencies and to authorize independent investigations for these purposes.

The following examples show how the branches check each other's authority. Congress uses its investigative arm to bring pressure to bear on public managers to implement particular kinds of analyses with the potential to influence legislative and managerial strategies. The courts use consent decrees to establish an ongoing oversight of executive agencies.

Example: Head Start Oversight

Head Start is a federal program that provides comprehensive early childhood education, health, nutrition, and parent involvement services to low-income children and their families.

A series of critical reports by the General Accounting Office (the predecessor of the Government Accountability Office) on the Head Start program illustrates how secondary checks and balances affect the relationships between branches of government. According to the GAO, "The body of research on current Head Start is insufficient to draw conclusions about the impact of the national program."[20] Republican legislators used the reports' findings during appropriations hearings in 1997 to challenge the effectiveness of Head Start.

As a consequence, Section 649(g) of the Head Start Act was amended (P.L. 105-285) to require the HHS to conduct a national analysis of the impact of Head Start. The legislation also charged the secretary to appoint an independent panel of experts to review and make recommendations on the design of a plan for research on the impact of Head Start within 1 year after the date of enactment of P.L. 105-285 and to advise the secretary regarding the progress of the research.

The Administration for Children and Families initiated the Head Start Impact Study (HSIS), which employed a rigorous, nationally representative, random assignment design. The study examined many outcomes across cognitive, social-emotional, health, and parenting practice domains. While some impacts of the program were evident during the preschool year, few effects were found into the early grade school years.[21] The absence of discernable impacts for the program has renewed calls from conservatives questioning the program.[22]

Example: Shakman Decrees

The Shakman decrees illustrate the review of judicial authority to issue and enforce consent decrees. In 1969, a group that included Michael Shakman, an independent candidate for delegate to the 1970 Illinois Constitutional Convention, filed suit against the Democratic Organization of Cook County. He argued that Chicago's long-standing system of political patronage used political loyalty to determine hiring, firing, promotion, and transfer decisions. This system denied independents like himself their legal and constitutional rights to seek and hold public office. The suit also alleged that public resources were spent on partisan political activity.

In 1972, several defendants, including the City of Chicago and its mayor, entered into a negotiated settlement, known as a **consent decree**, with the plaintiffs to resolve some of their claims. A consent decree commits the agency to remedial action and to improved monitoring and evaluation of agency operations and effectiveness. For the majority of city government positions, the 1972 consent decree specifically prohibited the city from "conditioning, basing or knowingly prejudicing or affecting any term or aspect of governmental employment with respect to one who is *at the time already a governmental employee,* upon or because of any political reason or factor." A subsequent consent decree was entered in 1983 that extended these prohibitions to the city's hiring practices as well. The U.S. District Court for the Northern District of Illinois has retained jurisdiction over the case. The court's powers included enforcement of the consent decrees.

In September 2001, the court held that the city had violated the decree almost 1,800 times over a period of nearly a decade. The court then instructed Shakman to file a rule showing why the city and its mayor should not be held in contempt of court for those violations. In response to the looming contempt proceedings, the mayor instructed the city's corporation counsel to attempt to vacate the long-standing decree, thereby disabling this check on patronage hiring.

On July 26, 2005, the plaintiffs in the Shakman lawsuit filed an application to hold the city and its mayor in civil contempt for violations of the court orders. On August 2, Judge Wayne R. Andersen appointed Noelle C. Brennan as the court's monitor in an effort to "ensure future compliance" with the Shakman decrees. As part of its appointment order, the court directed Brennan, along with her appointed legal counsel, to study Chicago's "existing employment practices, policies and procedures for non-political hiring, promotion, transfer, discipline and discharge." Further, the court ordered Brennan to propose a "mechanism for ensuring future employment actions [by the city] are in compliance with the Court's previous Orders." During 2006, federal criminal trials proceeded against several city officials accused of engaging in a vast and long-running conspiracy to reward political operatives with city jobs.

Finally, in 2014, the decree was lifted, with oversight of hiring processes transferred from the monitor to the City's Office of Inspector General:

> On June 16, 2014, Judge Sidney I. Schenkier of the U.S. District Court for the Northeastern District of Illinois entered a finding of substantial compliance with the *Shakman* Accord and therefore granted the joint motion of the *Shakman* plaintiffs and the City of Chicago to dismiss the City as a defendant from the case and terminate the Accord. The Monitor's Report on Substantial Compliance (filed May 21st, 2014), notes that, "The integrity of the City's hiring and employment practices is contingent upon an independent, vigorous, and effective compliance function. To date, the Office of the Inspector General has assumed the duties previously performed by the Monitor's office, and that office has the ability to report any future violations, should they occur, to the public."[23]

The City of Chicago was liberated from its Shakman shackles.

Within the Branches of Government

A second category of secondary checks and balances operates within the branches of government. Within the executive branch, it includes inspectors general, protections afforded to whistleblowers and other employee rights (including the right to sue employers), and offices that perform oversight functions such as budget review and execution, personnel administration, and internal audit. Within the judicial branch, it includes the multiple levels of review that oversee the decisions of trial courts. Within the legislative branch, it includes the separation of the authorization and the appropriations processes and a wide variety of rules that balance competing interests within representative institutions.

The first example shows that within the executive branch, employees have the power to check the authority of public managers by enlisting the assistance of the courts. The second example further illustrates this point but shows also that in certain instances—although not in this one—employees can claim First Amendment protection for certain communications with their superiors. To an important extent, the law, not managerial prerogative, governs employer-employee relations.

Example: United States Forest Service (USFS)

The Forest Service Employees for Environmental Ethics (FSEEE) was a self-organized group of pro-environmental employees of the USFS. They formed in 1989, arguing that the USFS was fighting too many fires, thereby endangering firefighters and harming the forest ecology.[iii] They filed a lawsuit against their employer requesting that the USFS study its policies concerning fire management, retardant use, and other matters.

The USFS responded, first noting that people were moving into fire-threatened areas, and the agency and its partners in the states are obligated to protect them and their property. Firefighting had become a big business for which there were many influential political stakeholders, including property owners and fire fighting agencies and their suppliers.[24]

In a related development, a longtime USFS biologist sued his superiors over whether their practice of sprucing up old logging roads without an environmental review was legal. The lawsuit alleged that the federal agency was reconstructing "roads to nowhere" in Alaska's Tongass National Forest without analyzing the potential effects on the environment. The biologist contended that the USFS was trying to encourage logging by circumventing the law, an allegation the federal agency denied.[25] On May 26, 2006, a federal judge ordered the USFS to stop working on two disputed logging roads in the southeast portion of the Tongass National Forest.[26]

Example: Citizen Speech and Employee Speech: What Is the Difference?

A case arising in the Los Angeles County district attorney's office illustrates secondary checks and balances affecting relationships within branches of government. Richard Ceballos had worked since 1989 in the Pomona branch as a deputy district attorney responsible for managing trial procedures. In February 2000, a defense attorney contacted Ceballos about a pending criminal case, saying there were inaccuracies in an affidavit used to obtain a critical search warrant. After examining the affidavit and visiting the location it described, Ceballos determined the affidavit did indeed contain serious misrepresentations. He recommended that the case be dismissed.

In a lawsuit filed against his employers, Ceballos claimed that as retaliation for disagreeing with his superiors, he was reassigned from his calendar deputy position to a trial deputy position, transferred to another courthouse, and denied a promotion. He argued that his superiors violated his First Amendment rights. The Supreme Court overturned the circuit court opinion in Ceballos's favor and ruled that Ceballos did not have "whistle-blower protection rights" under the First Amendment.[27]

The ruling turned on a distinction between "citizen speech" and "employee speech." If an employee's speech is found to be "citizen" speech, under the dichotomy the Court had established, these comments would be analyzed under a 1968 Supreme Court precedent that set up a balancing test for whether a public employee's speech is constitutionally protected. Courts weigh the employee's interest in commenting on matters of public concern against the employer's interests as a manager. The Supreme Court decision stated in part:

> In reaching its conclusion, the [Ninth Circuit] court looked to the First Amendment analysis set forth in *Pickering v. Board of Ed. of Township High School Dist. 205, Will Cty.,* 391 U.S. 563 (1968), and *Connick* [v. *Meyers,* 461 U.S. 138, 1983]. *Connick* instructs courts to begin by considering whether the expressions

---

[iii]See http://www.fseee.org/ for detailed information.

in question were made by the speaker "as a citizen upon matters of public concern." . . . . The Court of Appeals determined that Ceballos' memo, which recited what he thought to be governmental misconduct, was "inherently a matter of public concern." . . . . The court did not, however, consider whether the speech was made in Ceballos' capacity as a citizen. Rather, it relied on circuit precedent rejecting the idea that "a public employee's speech is deprived of First Amendment protection whenever those views are expressed, to government workers or others, pursuant to an employment responsibility. . . ."

We hold that when public employees make statements pursuant to their official duties, the employees are not speaking as citizens for First Amendment purposes, and the Constitution does not insulate their communications from employer discipline. . . . [Ceballos] did not speak as a citizen by writing a memo that addressed the proper disposition of a pending criminal case. When he went to work and performed the tasks he was paid to perform, Ceballos acted as a government employee. *The fact that his duties sometimes required him to speak or write does not mean his supervisors were prohibited from evaluating his performance* [emphasis added].[28]

Between the Public and Government

A third category of secondary checks and balances concerns the power of private citizens and groups with respect to the three branches of government. This category includes various transparency measures such as labor relations acts, freedom of information acts, administrative procedure acts, acts authorizing citizens' petitions, and "government in the sunshine" acts, some of which are written into state constitutions. Such measures provide citizens with opportunities to question the exercise of government authority. This category also includes not-for-profit watchdog groups. Many of these groups engage in virtually constant surveillance of public agency activity and actively engage in litigation on behalf of their constituencies.

Example: National Labor Relations Board (NLRB) Action

In June 2006, the NLRB (under the authority of the National Labor Relations Act) asserted jurisdiction over a private company that provided passenger and baggage screening services to the Kansas City International Airport. The NLRB took this action on behalf of company employees who wished to join a union. The decision countered a determination by Undersecretary James Loy of the Transportation Security Administration (TSA) that the NLRB lacked jurisdiction because the private employees were involved in protecting national security. Loy had previously denied union rights to the TSA's security screeners, which was within his statutory authority.

Secondary checks and balances may also operate outside the branches of government through the Administrative Procedure Act (APA) of the federal government and similar laws in every state government.[29] (The state acts apply to state agencies but not to agencies of local governments.[30]) In general, these acts are intended to ensure that administrative actions "embrace the basic democratic-constitutional values of openness for accountability; representativeness and public participation in policy formulation; reviewability for adherence to the rule of law; procedural due process for the fair treatment of individuals; and rationality when regulating private parties and other entities."[31]

Legal action by advocacy groups is another form of external secondary checks and balances. Advocacy groups regularly sue state and local departments and agencies that serve populations with specific needs—child protection, corrections, housing, education—or provide services in a nondiscriminatory manner—schools, police departments. The suits often allege that individuals served by these agencies are being denied their constitutional and statutory rights, usually because of mismanagement.

The suits often allege that individuals served by these agencies are being denied their constitutional and statutory rights, usually because of mismanagement.

These class actions have been termed **institutional reform** or **structural reform lawsuits** because the plaintiffs seek, among other things, far-reaching changes in agency management and operations.

Secondary checks and balances provide citizens with access to legal procedures that adjudicate their rights against the potentially arbitrary and capricious exercise of managerial authority.

Example: Children's Rights, Inc.

A suit filed in 1993 by Children's Rights, Inc. (among others), an organization that engages in extensive litigation on behalf of children (its website lists 18 lawsuits), alleged that the Milwaukee Department of Human Services conducted inadequate investigations of child abuse and neglect, failed to protect children vulnerable to abuse or neglect, failed to provide appropriate care and proper placements for children in their custody, and failed to create and implement appropriate plans to assure their proper care and appropriate placement. These failures violate children's rights under state and federal constitutions as well as under various statutes. Such lawsuits seek to compel public managers to respond to plaintiffs' allegations in court. Judges may decide that agencies and their managers must be closely monitored by outside experts or independent officers appointed by the court. Agencies may be under legally required surveillance for many years or even decades. Even though the state of Alabama had made significant improvements in child welfare services by 2005, a federal district judge declined to end court oversight arising from a suit filed in 1988 because the state had not proved that it could sustain its gains. And the historic *Wyatt v. Stickney* case mandating mental health facility reform, initiated in 1970, was finally terminated in 2003.

The Milwaukee lawsuit prompted the state to take over the management and operation of child welfare services from Milwaukee County and to institute extensive management reforms. Wisconsin state officials then claimed that court intervention was unnecessary. Nevertheless, the final settlement required defendants to meet specific percentage goals in closing cases in specific ways, meet specific percentage goals in providing specific support services to children and families in their custody, and meet specific standards in organizing and providing casework, such as creating special diagnostic/assessment centers for children over 12 years of age who need further assessment in order to determine the appropriate placement. Although noting that many of the required reforms had been completed, Children's Rights, Inc. was still actively monitoring the agency's management in 2014.[32]

In some cases, these kinds of suits can have beneficial consequences. Responsible officials—legislators, elected officials, and agency and overhead managers—may act to correct long-standing problems in agency organization and in relations with supervisory agencies and governors or mayors and their staffs. Officials must negotiate consent decrees with plaintiffs' representatives and the court. In other cases, however, the consequences may not be beneficial. This can occur when public managers have made responsible efforts to confront the issues raised by the lawsuit. The legal process can disrupt the orderly development of stable and effective management structures and routines and allow the intrusion of an adversarial process into the otherwise progressive and competent management and delivery of services.[33] And, as the following example shows, attempts to address one set of problems may raise altogether new problems.

Example: National Vaccine Injury Compensation Program (VICP)

The VICP provides an example of how citizens gain access to institutions empowered to address their concerns. Created in 1988, the VICP is administered by HHS and the Department of Justice (DOJ). The HHS component of the VICP is located in the Health Resources and Services Administration, Healthcare Systems Bureau, Division of Vaccine Injury Compensation. The DOJ component of the VICP is located in the Civil Division, Torts Branch, Office of Vaccine Litigation. This unit represents the secretary of HHS in legal proceedings before the U.S. Court of Federal Claims, also known as the "vaccine court."

The vaccine court decides which claims will be compensated and affords a no-fault alternative to civil lawsuits for parents who believe their children have been injured by a vaccine. In recent years, many claims have been filed alleging that vaccines cause autism in children. The Centers for Disease Control and Prevention and the American Academy of Pediatrics deny any scientific basis for such a causal relationship. According to legal scholar Stephen Sugarman,

> To win a VICP award, the claimant does not need to prove everything that is required to hold a vaccine maker liable in a product liability lawsuit. But a causal connection must be shown. If medical records show that a child had one of several listed [by HHS] adverse effects within a short period after vaccination, the VICP presumes that it was caused by the vaccine (although the government can seek to prove otherwise). An advisory committee helps to amend the list of adverse effects as the consensus view [within the scientific community] changes with the availability of new studies. If families claim that a vaccine caused an adverse effect that is not on the list [autism is not on the list], the burden of proof rests with them. . . . In the VICP context, proof of causation does not need to be shown to the extent of what some might call scientific certainty. Rather, it suffices to prove causation according to the civil-law standard of "the preponderance of the evidence," showing that causation is "more likely than not." Although proving a mere possibility won't suffice, proof "beyond a reasonable doubt" is not required.[34]

To resolve the large volume of autism claims more expeditiously, in 2002 the VICP announced that some test cases would examine the general causation question, putting aside the question of harm to any particular child. In its 2006 strategic plan, however, the VICP argued, "Relaxed standards for assessing causation of vaccine-related injury could jeopardize the public's trust of, and reliance upon, vaccines as the first line defense against serious infectious diseases. The relaxed standard may lead to more claims being compensated; and therefore, the public may think that vaccines are not safe."[35]

Distributions of Power

A fourth category of secondary checks and balances is the distribution of power and influence among individuals and entities created or allowed to exercise it. This category includes

- congressional chartering of the National Academy of Sciences (NAS) and the Institute of Medicine;
- the power inherent in the independent professional status of public employees such as actuaries, scientists, physicians, and statisticians;
- the Federal False Claims Act, which entitles employees of private firms under contract to the government who report deliberate waste of public funds to a share of any funds that are recovered through legal action;

- government's reliance on negotiated and private rulemaking and on self-regulation; and
- the power of individual employees to influence public debate about controversial policies by leaking privileged information, a long-standing practice included in what public administration scholar Rosemary O'Leary has termed "guerrilla government."[36]

The following examples show how influence can be exercised both formally and informally through nongovernmental entities that are able to take advantage of the separation of powers to create checks on managerial discretion by virtue of their influence on lawmakers, executives, and judges.

> Influence can be exercised both formally and informally through nongovernmental entities that are able to take advantage of the separation of powers to create checks on managerial discretion.

Example: The National Research Council (NRC)

The NRC is part of the National Academies, which include the NAS, National Academy of Engineering, and Institute of Medicine. They are private, non-profit institutions that provide science, technology, and health policy advice under a congressional charter. The act of incorporation for the NAS, signed by President Lincoln on March 3, 1863, established service to the nation as its dominant purpose. The NRC was organized by the NAS in 1916 to associate the broad community of science and technology with the academy's purposes of furthering knowledge and advising the federal government.

In 2005, the NRC weighed in on a controversial public policy issue, publishing "Guidelines for Human Embryonic Stem [hES] Cell Research."[37] The National Academies developed the guidelines on behalf of the scientific community and without government involvement. Of this project, the two cochairs wrote,

> As the study of hES cells accelerates worldwide, federal funding for this research area in the United States has been severely limited by ethical controversy. As a consequence, the normal leadership role of the U.S. National Institutes of Health in supporting health related research and providing the oversight that comes with federal funding has been absent. Investigation of hES cells is being funded increasingly by individual states and by private foundations in the absence of universal rules for conduct of the research. In most states, there are no regulations; in some, the research is illegal, either in whole or in part; and, in others, legislation has explicitly legalized research efforts and even provided public funding. Thus, the research is proceeding actively but under a confusing patchwork of regulations. This situation is particularly inappropriate for an area of investigation that, although offering great promise, raises ethical issues. In response to scientists' concerns about the lack of federal oversight, a committee of the National Research Council and the Institute of Medicine of the National Academies undertook to formulate guidelines for the appropriate conduct of hES cell research. The guidelines were released April 26, 2005, after eight months of deliberations, many meetings and a two-day public workshop.[38]

Example: Red Cross and Abu Ghraib

This example concerns the actions of the Red Cross following the Abu Ghraib scandal in Iraq. Physicians who cooperated with interrogations of prisoners at Abu Ghraib prison in Iraq were accused by the International Committee of the Red Cross and by members of the medical profession with violating the Geneva Conventions and widely accepted codes of ethics governing medical practice and with failure to report evidence of prisoner abuse.

These violations occurred when physicians provided information on the medical condition of individual prisoners to personnel engaged in interrogations to assist them in designing effective coercive methods. Physicians and psychiatrists were often on hand to monitor the use of these methods through one-way mirrors that concealed their presence.[39]

During the same period, lawyers in the judge advocate general's offices of the military services were vigorously contesting detainee interrogation policies they believed were in violation of applicable statutory and international laws and that jeopardized the lives of American military personnel.

FEDERALISM

The United States is a federal republic, a system of governance in which the authority to legislate and to administer and enforce the laws is distributed among the legislatures of a central government and of the governments of the several states. The goal of American federalism is to ensure that the federal government has sufficient power to act on behalf of national interests while preserving the powers of state governments and, ultimately, of the people to act on behalf of their own interests. The health insurance exchanges authorized by the Affordable Care Act represented both an essential element of the act and an arena for the contemporary meaning of "states rights" in a federal system.[40]

Unlike the Anti-Federalists (opponents of the Constitution's ratification who feared the potential erosion of the states' rights by a powerful national government), Madison dismissed the possibility of a dominant central government. Madison argued in *The Federalist No. 45* that,

> the number of individuals employed under the Constitution of the United States will be much smaller than the number employed under the particular States. There will consequently be less of personal influence on the side of the former than of the latter. The members of the legislative, executive, and judiciary departments of thirteen and more States, the justices of peace, officers of militia, ministerial officers of justice, with all the county, corporation, and town officers, for three millions and more of people, intermixed, and having particular acquaintance with every class and circle of people, must exceed, beyond all proportion, both in number and influence, those of every description who will be employed in the administration of the federal system.

On this point, Madison was prescient. Total full-time equivalent state and local employees in 2013 was just over 16 million. Total full-time equivalent federal government civilian employment was just over 2.5 million.[iv]

The Tenth Amendment clarifies the powers of the states: "The powers not delegated to the United States [the federal government] by the Constitution, nor prohibited by it to the States, are reserved to the States respectively, or to the people." In other words, if neither expressly delegated to the federal government nor denied to the states, power is assumed to belong to the states or to the people. Indeed, Madison believed that the greater threat to a balance of power between the federal government and the states would come from the states. The importance of the states and subunits of government was also noted by Thomas Jefferson:

> The way to have good and safe government is not to trust it all to one, but to divide it among the many, distributing to everyone exactly the functions he is competent to. Let the national government be entrusted with the defense of the nation, and its foreign and federal relations; the state governments with the civil rights, laws,

---

[iv]U.S. Census Bureau, 2013 Annual Survey of Public Employment and Payroll, released December 19, 2014. State employment figures from this table: http://factfinder.census.gov/faces/tableservices/jsf/pages/productview.xhtml?src=bkmk and federal employment figures from this table: http://factfinder.census.gov/faces/tableservices/jsf/pages/productview.xhtml?src=bkmk.

police, and administration of what concerns the state generally; the counties with the local concerns of the counties; and each ward direct the interests within itself. It is by dividing and subdividing these republics from the great national one down through all its subordinations until it ends in the administration of every man's farm by himself, by placing under everyone what his own eye may superintend, that all will be done for the best.[41]

With their reserved powers and governed by their own constitutions, states are often referred to as **laboratories of democracy.** That term was coined by U.S. Supreme Court Justice Louis Brandeis in *New State Ice Co. v. Liebmann* to describe how a "state may, if its citizens choose, serve as a laboratory; and try novel social and economic experiments without risk to the rest of the country." State-to-state variations in public programs and their management are certainly influenced by federal laws, resources, and policy priorities. But a great many factors shape these variations, ranging from differences in financial and other resources, demographics, structures of local governments, and politics; to less obvious factors such as voter turnout in midterm elections or processes of redrawing the boundaries of congressional redistricts following the decennial census.

A clear example of a state acting as a laboratory is a Massachusetts law, sponsored by a Republican governor, titled "An Act Providing Access to Affordable, Quality, and Accountable Health Care" passed in 2006, which is generally regarded as the model for the federal Patient Protection and Affordable Care Act of 2010.

The Affordable Care Act further illustrates the meaning of Madison's concept of "a compound republic." A federal statute, whose design reflects the profound influence of both primary and secondary checks and balances, achieves its purposes through conditional delegations of authority to state governments within limits established in constitutional law. The result is a health care system exhibiting wide variation across the states in ACA implementation.

Madisonian Governance in the States

The structures of state governments, too, have separation of powers, systems of checks and balances, and local governments structured and empowered by federal and state constitutions.[42] Yet as state government scholar G. Alan Tarr put it, "despite . . . superficial similarities, state governments are not merely miniature versions of the national government—or at least need not be."[43] State constitutional traditions and the particular characteristics of the rule of law in the states have evolved over time, vary widely, and may differ in significant ways from those of the federal government.

When first adopted, most state constitutions, while formally recognizing a separation of powers, were unconcerned with the balance of power among the three branches. Power was intentionally concentrated in legislatures. Popular dissatisfaction with corrupt legislatures grew in the nineteenth and early twentieth centuries. But power was not shifted to elected executives or to the courts. Instead power was shifted to the people, especially in the form of the direct election of state constitutional officers, such as attorneys general, secretaries of state, and treasurers. Many states amended their constitutions to incorporate forms of direct democracy and citizen empowerment, such as the initiative, the referendum, and the recall.

Most state governments also differ from the federal government in not having a unitary executive; many states have "weak" governors, and all have many state administrators who are elected rather than appointed by the governor. Another difference is the power state governors have over their budgets through the line-item veto, which the president of the United States does not have.

> **State constitutional traditions and the particular characteristics of the rule of law in the states have evolved over time, vary widely, and may differ in significant ways from those of the federal government.**

Example: The Executive Branch in Texas

The unique possibilities of the rule of law in the states are illustrated by the powers of the governor of Texas, which are surprisingly limited compared to states with structurally "strong governors." The plural executive in Texas limits the power of the governor by distributing power usually associated with a chief executive among many elected political leaders, including

- the attorney general,
- the comptroller of public accounts,
- the commissioner of the General Land Office,
- the commissioner of Agriculture,
- the Texas Railroad Commission, and
- the state Board of Education.

The only executive official appointed by the governor is the secretary of state. Other officials are elected independently and do not campaign for office as a unified slate. They do not have to answer to the governor, nor do they work together as a cabinet in the way that executive officials serve the president. Furthermore,

> this arrangement produces an executive branch whose officials jealously guard their jurisdiction, their power, and their prerogatives . . . . The Governor is often the nominal head of his or her party in the state, but this does not offset the institutional political base other executives possess. As a result, the executive branch lacks cohesion, with different executives and their agencies often pursuing different goals.[44]

As a candidate for president of the United States, George W. Bush was highly regarded for his inclusive approach to politics as governor of Texas. Texans knew that achieving policy priorities required working closely with other constitutional officers, the legislature, and interest groups.

Some states require extraordinary majorities to enact certain legislation, have procedural requirements for the legislative process, or impose substantive prohibitions on legislative action, none of which exist in the U.S. Constitution. One popular state constitutional provision, limiting the frequency and duration of legislative sessions, has a significant bearing on public management. A legislature not in session cannot exercise the same kind of oversight as one, such as the U.S. Congress, which is virtually always in session. Substitute provisions for control are adopted instead, such as the legislative veto and legislative appointment of officials performing executive functions.

Because constitutional and statutory structures are different across states and localities, the study of public management in a particular jurisdiction must be attentive to its unique institutional and political context.

Local Government: Closest to the People

The Constitution itself is silent on the structural relationship of local government to federalism. Even so, as quotes by Madison and Jefferson earlier in this chapter indicate, the Founders were fully aware of the importance of local government.

In the United States, local governments which govern cities, villages, counties, and towns are established and regulated by state law under the power reserved to states by the Tenth Amendment. Local governments' authority in relation to other units of local government and in relation to state government rests ultimately on state law. The procedures by which their governing bodies are elected and their administrative structures are organized rests on state law as well.[45] An 1868 decision by an Iowa state court subsequently adopted by the U.S. Supreme Court (now known as *Dillon's Rule*) states: "Municipal corporations [cities and towns] owe their origin to, and derive their powers and rights wholly from, the legislature. It breathes into them the breath of life, without which they cannot exist. As it [the legislature] creates, so may it destroy. If it may destroy, it may abridge and control."[v]

According to the U.S. Census Bureau, over 89,000 organizational units of state and local government were in place in 2012. Of these, almost 39,000 were "general purpose" organizations: counties, municipalities, and towns. The rest were "special purpose" organizations, including nearly 13,000 independent public school districts. Each unit of general purpose government is subdivided into offices and departments. Further, each of these subunits is subdivided into offices, bureaus, and agencies. Clearly, American state and local governments are vast, differentiated, and complex. So, too, are the unique challenges facing their public managers.

> American state and local governments are vast, differentiated, and complex. So, too, are the unique challenges facing their public managers.

States vary widely in the scope and types of authority granted to their units of local government. To avoid micromanagement by state legislatures, numerous municipalities have obtained **home rule charters** that grant local discretion over all matters not expressly precluded by state statutes or constitutions. Such matters may include public personnel policies and the administration of local property taxes.

In general, "the various levels of government . . . are tied together by a variety of factors: money, programs, political parties, and the play of interest groups among them."[46] As politics at the national level became increasingly polarized and stalemated, local governments began to be regarded as the new laboratories of democracy. "Cities have become the main source of fresh thinking about how to solve the world's problems—and mayors, more than their higher-ranking counterparts in public life, are the ones setting the course."[47]

Public interest groups may choose to move the locus of public debate to the setting most beneficial from their perspective. For example, they may shift lobbying efforts from Congress to state legislatures on matters such as expanding health coverage for the uninsured or controlling carbon emissions. Business interest groups may choose the federal government over the states as their regulators, for example, preferring national to state regulation of air quality and motor vehicle emissions standards. They may also choose to fight their battles in the courts rather than in legislatures, confronting public managers, as earlier examples in this chapter have shown, with litigation in addition to partisan legislative politics on the same issues.

Intergovernmental Relations

The division of powers among federal, state, and local governments is the basis of a field of study and practice within public administration and management known as **intergovernmental relations.** Intergovernmental relations are the operationalization of, and give effect to, federalism.

The Supreme Court has interpreted the commerce clause (Article I, Section 8, Clause 3) and general welfare clause (Article I, Section 8, Clause 1) of the Constitution to give the federal government substantial authority to compel and induce the states to implement laws enacted by Congress and rules issued pursuant to the implementation of federal policies. Federal laws and rules affect the choices and actions of organizations and

---

[v]*Clinton v. Cedar Rapids and the Missouri River Railroad*, 24 Iowa 455 (1868). The author of the opinion, John Forrest Dillon, was a justice of the Iowa Supreme Court who was later appointed to the federal bench by President Ulysses S. Grant.

individuals in all sectors of American society. Moreover, the Supreme Court is the final authority on the constitutionality of laws passed by the states.

The boundary between what is "federal" and what is "state" depends on the interpretation of "states' rights" by the Supreme Court. Moreover, the states have the ultimate power to determine what the Constitution is: two-thirds of the states may call for a convention to amend the Constitution, and three-fourths of the states approve of an amendment to the Constitution. That these possibilities may seem remote does not negate their importance to the constitutional scheme.

Federal, state, and local governments are linked by a variety of structural tools or instruments.[vi] These structures include mandates in the form of rules, regulations, or instructions that may be incorporated in the language of statutes, grants, or contracts that prescribe actions required by other levels of government. Directives accompanied by grants of financial support result in a combined carrot-and-stick relationship.

Another type of structure is devolution, where higher levels of government delegate to lower levels of government the authority to take various actions or exercise certain responsibilities. The granting of home rule charters by state legislatures is a form of devolution. Other examples include federal deregulation of an industry, as happened with the airline industry, or the substitution of broad-purpose grants for specific categorical grants, as was the case with the Community Development Block Grant program. The administration of a program may involve all three levels of government as well as agents—grantees, contractors, and subcontractors—within the private sector. Emergency management planning and response to a hurricane or natural disasters typically involve all levels of government and the nonprofit and for-profit sectors.

The logic of governance discussed later in this chapter links not only multiple levels within the federal or state governments but also levels of federal, state, and local governments and Native American tribes. Figure 4.1 shows the multiple levels of administration within the federal Head Start Program and how they are linked to multiple levels of local government administration of that program.

Intergovernmental relations may be both horizontal as well as vertical, as illustrated by the ACA. Departments and agencies of government at the same level cooperate and coordinate with each other through formal structures such as regional authorities, incident-related communication and coordination arrangements, and programs and projects sponsored by higher levels of government. The patterns of intergovernmental relationships resemble a matrix (or rectangular array) reflecting how the problems that policymakers address cannot be confined to a particular political jurisdiction.

Example: Children's Health Insurance Program (CHIP)

The federally authorized CHIP is a typical example of how the concept of federalism illuminates intergovernmental relations. The program first was enacted by Congress as in Title XXI of the Social Security Act in 1997 and has been reauthorized and extended since that time through other laws. The program is financed with federal and state funds and administered by states with flexibility on a number of policy and program dimensions.[48]

States may, for example, expand their Medicaid programs to provide additional coverage for children or create separate CHIP programs. CHIP provides a capped amount of funds to states on a matching basis. The Social Security

---

[vi]For overviews of federalism and intergovernmental relations, see Beryl A. Radin, "The Instruments of Intergovernmental Management," in *Handbook of Public Administration,* ed. B. Guy Peters and Jon Pierre (Thousand Oaks, CA: Sage, 2003), 607–618; Lester M. Salamon, ed., *The Tools of Government Action: A Guide to the New Governance* (Oxford, UK, and New York, NY: Oxford University Press, 2002); and Nicholas Henry, *Public Administration and Public Affairs,* 10th ed. (Upper Saddle River, NJ: Pearson Prentice-Hall, 2007), 349–392.

FIGURE 4.1   **Managerial Hierarchy: National, Regional, and Local Managerial Positions in the Head Start Program**

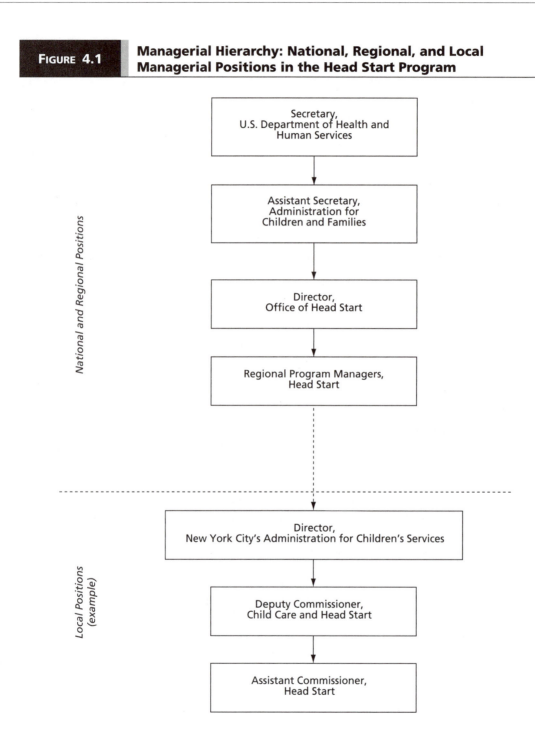

Act authorizes multiple waiver and demonstration authorities to allow states flexibility in operating Medicaid and CHIP programs. Each authority has a distinct purpose and distinct requirements. Each state, territory, and the District of Columbia has a coordinator for the CHIP program—a state-level managerial position required by federal law—who is responsible for the administration of the approved CHIP state plan. In Fiscal Year 2012, over 8 million children were covered by CHIP,[49] and a recent review of research on CHIP programs concluded,

> Taken together, the evidence is strong that improving coverage through CHIP and Medicaid has contributed to meaningful gains in access to care and the quality of care for low-income children. Further, studies that find an impact of CHIP and Medicaid on children's health show a positive impact, suggesting that the programs advance the end goal of coverage, better health.[50]

Example: Office of Management and Budget (OMB) Circulars

A number of OMB Circulars are directly concerned with state and local governments. These circulars are instructions or information issued by OMB to federal agencies, typically for 2 or more years.

For example, the purpose of OMB Circular A-102, Grants and Cooperative Agreements with State and Local Governments, is to establish "consistency and uniformity among Federal agencies in the management of grants and cooperative agreements with State, local, and federally-recognized Indian tribal governments." It is "issued under the authority of the Budget and Accounting Act of 1921, as amended; the Budget and Accounting Procedures Act of 1950, as amended; Reorganization Plan No. 2 of 1970; Executive Order 11541 and the Chief Financial Officers Act, 31 U.S.C. 503." Also included in the Circular are standards to ensure consistent implementation of sections 202, 203, and 204 of the Intergovernmental Cooperation Act of 1968, the Office of Federal Procurement Policy Act Amendments of 1983, and sections 6301-08, title 31, United States Code.

Intergovernmental relations are not confined to the structure dimension of public management. Habits of vertical or horizontal cooperation and coordination, or their opposite—secretiveness and refusal to share information or authority—may become institutionalized as cultural values. Within the constraints of structures and organizational cultures, individual managers may need to employ their craft to transcend their limitations: to promote good communication, maintain the transparency of relationships, and promote the goals of agencies, their policies, and programs, especially when under pressure from policymakers to demonstrate effectiveness or performance. The unifying element in how the thousands of units of American government relate to one another is, as public administration scholar Nicholas Henry notes, "based on broad rules of the game set by the Constitution and court decisions" and is a reflection of the rule of law.[51]

Checks and Balances in State and Local Governments

As *The Federalist* essays make clear, the Founders' design for the governance of the United States of America was informed by how the 13 states had designed and conducted their own schemes of constitutional governance. Though state constitutions of the 50 states vary, their governing frameworks resemble the federal government's framework. States have three branches of government, separated powers, systems of primary checks and balances, and political competition that sustain a constitutional balance of power. All states are similar to the federal government in having secondary checks and balances as well, but their specific manifestations are significantly different, reflecting differences in states' patterns of political competition. Following are examples of secondary checks and balances in state and local governments.

Example: Florida's Office of Program Policy Analysis and Government Accountability (OPPAGA)

The OPPAGA is an example of a check and balance between branches of government. According to its website, the OPPAGA "is an office of the Legislature. OPPAGA provides data, evaluative research, and objective analyses to assist legislative budget and policy deliberations. OPPAGA conducts research as directed by state law, the presiding officers, or the Joint Legislative Auditing Committee."[52] Many states have such legislature-affiliated offices designed to give lawmakers an independent, nonpartisan source of expert analysis of budget and program issues. The first was created by the State of California in 1941. The federal counterpart to these offices is the Congressional Budget Office.

Example: California Climate Action Team

Virtually all states have secondary checks and balances within branches of government. For example, the State of California's Climate Action Team (CAT), created by then-governor Arnold Schwarzenegger in 2005, "work[s] to coordinate statewide efforts to implement global warming emission reduction programs and the state's Climate Adaptation Strategy. The CAT members are state agency secretaries and the heads of agency, boards and departments, led by the Secretary of Cal/EPA."[53]

Example: The House Research Organization (HRO) for the Texas legislature

The HRO "is a nonpartisan independent department of the Texas House of Representatives. It provides impartial information on legislation and issues before the Texas Legislature. The HRO is governed by a broadly representative steering committee of 15 House members elected by the House membership to set policy for the organization, approve its budget, and ensure that its reports are objective."[54] The federal counterpart to such organizations is the Congressional Research Service.

Secondary checks and balances outside the branches of government are also evident in the states. Of particular note are those arising from the Progressive Era reform movement that persuaded many states to adopt laws authorizing **direct democracy** in the form of citizen petitions such as of **initiatives**, **referendums**, and **recall elections** (also mentioned in Chapter 2).[vii] According to provisions in many state laws and constitutions, citizens may place a legislative proposal on a ballot during a popular election or subject legislation enacted by a legislature to a popular vote. Recall petitions may subject elected officials to a popular vote before their terms in office are up on whether or not they should continue in office.

Example: Recall of California Governor Gray Davis

In 2003, California instituted a recall election for its governor, Gray Davis. For the gubernatorial recall to take place, the state required a citizen petition to have approximately 1.2 million signatures. In the end, the secretary of state

---

[vii]An overview is available on the website of the National Conference of State legislatures, http://www.ncsl.org/legislatures-elections/elections/initiative-referendum-and-recall-overview.aspx.

verified over 1.3 million signatures and the recall election took place.[55] Governor Gray Davis lost the election to Arnold Schwarzenegger. A similar popular effort to recall Wisconsin governor Scott Walker in 2012 failed.

Example: Massachusetts Growth Capital Corporation (MGCC)

"The Mission of the Massachusetts Growth Capital Corporation is to create and preserve jobs at small businesses, women and minority owned businesses, and to promote economic development in underserved, gateway municipalities and low and moderate income communities. MGCC provides a centralized resource at the state level that offers working capital, loan guarantees, and targeted technical assistance to solve specific financial and operational problems. MGCC will provide 50% of the cost of such assistance while the company being assisted will invest the other 50%."[56]

Example: Boiler Safety Standards in Alaska

Lawmakers in the State of Alaska created a regulatory framework "for the safe and proper construction, installation, repair, use, and operation of boilers and for the safe and proper construction, installation, and repair of unfired pressure vessels." The law states,

> The Department of Labor and Workforce Development may adopt the existing published codification of these definitions and regulations, known as the Boiler Construction Code of the American Society of Mechanical Engineers, and may adopt the amendments and interpretations made and published by that society. The Department of Labor and Workforce Development shall adopt amendments and interpretations to the code immediately upon their adoption by the American Society of Mechanical Engineers so that the definitions and regulations at all times follow generally accepted nationwide engineering standards.[57]

The State of Alaska has, in effect, delegated to a private entity, the American Society of Mechanical Engineers, the authority to establish and amend the standards governing boiler safety in the state. In cases such as this one, which legal scholar Chris Sagers has labeled "rubber stamp provisions," the state or local government's own legislative authority is in one way or another given away to a private group.[58]

AT THE APEX OF POWER: THE PEOPLE[59]

The Founders were wise enough to understand the vulnerability of their own handiwork. Madison likely would not be fazed by what many believe is America's drift in recent years toward plutocracy and wide inequalities in income and wealth. In addressing the many challenges to American democracy, from the power of wealth in politics to the gerrymandering of congressional district boundaries, he further would note that our constitutional scheme of governance has been associated with dramatic reductions in poverty and income inequality.

But Madison would probably insist that meeting democracy's challenges does not require structures different from those in the Constitution; it requires virtue among the people:

> Justice is the end of government. It is the end of civil society. It ever has been and ever will be pursued until it be obtained, or until liberty be lost in the pursuit. In a society under the forms of which the stronger faction can readily unite and oppress the weaker, anarchy may as truly be said to reign as in a state of nature, where the weaker individual is not secured against the violence of the stronger; and as, in the latter state, even the

stronger individuals are prompted, by the uncertainty of their condition, to submit to a government which may protect the weak as well as themselves; so, in the former state, will the more powerful factions or parties be gradually induced, by a like motive, *to wish for a government which will protect all parties, the weaker as well as the more powerful* (emphasis added).[60]

Alexander Hamilton concurred. Among his most famous utterance in *The Federalist* 70 is "Energy in the Executive is a leading character in the definition of good government." But, at the same time, administration must exhibit a "due dependence on the people [and] a due responsibility [in a republican sense]." In other words, the new nation must not tolerate the creation of European-style central institutions that the Founders saw as threatening liberty and property. The authority and legitimacy of American governing institutions and their outcomes are the faith placed in them by citizens, officials they elect, and judges who are elected or appointed by the people's representatives. Such faith requires a sense of responsibility on the part of all to the principles that protect all.

> The authority and legitimacy of American governing institutions and their outcomes is the faith placed in them by citizens, officials they elect, and judges who are elected or appointed by the people's representatives.

Sustaining that sense of responsibility of all to all is the continuing political duty of the people themselves. If he could observe contemporary American politics, Benjamin Franklin might say, as he did on the final day of the Constitutional Convention, that every member of our democracy should "doubt a little of his own infallibility." And Madison would surely remind us that if our structures fail, we (voters, candidates for office, and officeholders) must become no less than partisans and exemplars of virtue or else liberty and justice for all are at peril.

A LOGIC OF CONSTITUTIONAL GOVERNANCE

To clarify how public management relates to Madison's scheme of governance, with the people at its apex, it is useful to locate public management and public managers within a rule-of-law-based, multilevel **logic of governance.** This frame of reference depicts the mutual influences on managerial roles and practices and, through them, on government performance among

- the values and interests represented in civil society (the sovereign people),
- the preferences of the political branches (executive and legislative), and
- the role of legal institutions (federal judiciary, administrative law procedures).

Defining Governance

The term **governance** is defined here as a regime or system of laws, rules, judicial decisions, and administrative practices that constrain, direct, and enable the provision of publicly authorized and financed goods and services through formal and informal relationships with agents in the public and private sectors.[61] Although other definitions of governance—including other multilevel conceptualizations of governance—abound in the research literature, this particular definition links constitutional institutions with the processes of policymaking, public management, and service delivery operating within a given political, economic, and social environment.[viii]

[viii]For other definitions, see Laurence E. Lynn Jr., *Public Management: Old and New* (London, UK: Routledge, 2006); and Michael Hill and Peter Hupe, *Implementing Public Policy* (Thousand Oaks, CA: Sage, 2008).

Underlying this definition is recognition that governance involves the means for achieving direction, control, and coordination of individuals and organizations on behalf of public interests incorporated in public policies.[62] From the starting point of the rule of law defined by constitutional institutions, an analytic framework—a logic of governance—can be constructed to provide conceptual order to the complex system of checks and balances, federalism, and popular sovereignty that characterizes rule-of-law–based public administration and management in the United States.

Governance is the resultant of a dynamic process that can be expressed in a set of hierarchical interrelationships, depicted in Figure 4.2.

Viewing Governance in Three Dimensions

This multilevel (or nested) logic of governance is related conceptually to the three dimensions of public management depicted in Chapter 1. The logic of governance adds recognition of the legal and political environment within which public management is embedded. These relationships can be understood in terms of the following propositions:

- The structure dimension—formally authorized structures and processes—is shaped by the actions of public officials, including legislators, elected executives, public managers, field supervisors, and judges, operating at levels (b), (d), and (e) in the logic of governance and manifested at these levels as well as at the (c) level.

FIGURE 4.2 **A Constitutional Logic of Governance**

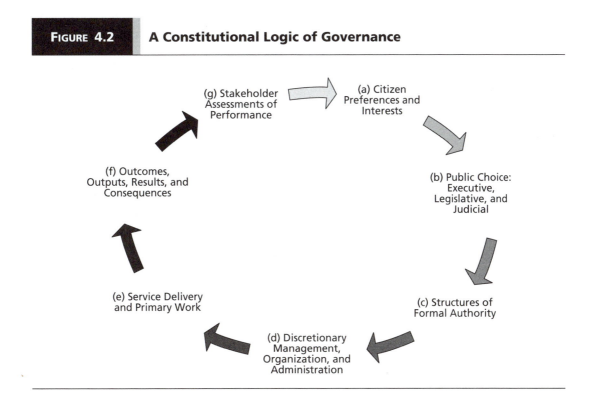

- The culture dimension—organizational cultures and the norms and standards governing organizational behavior and official conduct—is shaped by the exemplary actions and beliefs and values of public managers, supervisors, functional administrators (such as those in personnel and budget offices), and service providers operating at levels (d), (e), and (f) in the logic of governance.
- The craft dimension—managerial craftsmanship—like the culture dimension, comprises the actions of public managers and others with managerial and supervisory responsibilities at levels (d) and (e) in the logic of governance.

In other words, the actions and decisions taken at multiple levels of governance shape the actual institutions of governance and their interrelationships. In turn, the actions and decisions of policymakers, public managers, and service providers are shaped by those institutions. Though influence flows in multiple directions, a hierarchical, rule-of-law backbone structures the different levels of activity into a uniquely American system of governance.

KEY CONCEPTS

Separation of powers	Institutional/structural reform lawsuits
Checks and balances	Laboratories of democracy
Federalism	Home rule charters
"The people"	Intergovernmental relations
Health insurance marketplaces / Health insurance exchanges	Direct democracy
	Initiatives
Individual mandate	Referendums
Primary checks and balances	Recall elections
Secondary checks and balances	Logic of governance
Consent decree	Governance

CASE ANALYSIS: AUSTIN ENERGY

The structural issues discussed in this chapter, as well as the politics of bureaucratic structure, discussed in Chapter 5, are illustrated at the local level by the case of Austin Energy.

Austin Energy is an electric power utility that is owned by the citizens of the City of Austin, Texas (the state capital). It provides electric service to consumers in the city and surrounding areas of Travis and Williamson Counties. Created in 1895, when a hydroelectric power facility was constructed on the Colorado River,[63] Austin Energy is the eighth largest of over 2,000 community-owned electric utilities in the American Public Power Association (APPA). Among other things, the APPA advocates for these utilities' interests with public policymakers in Washington, DC.

A state or local community can establish a public utility to provide a service when its infrastructure costs cannot be adequately financed by private consumers and investors. Rules governing the public utility management reflect democratically determined community interests, not the financial interests of profit-seeking owners and investors. For example, a community-owned electric utility may be justified in rural areas where serving a widely dispersed population at affordable rates cannot be done profitably by the private sector.

The specific interests served by a public utility reflect the utility's political and economic context and structures of governance. One community may choose to emphasize environmental concerns while another may emphasize economic efficiency and low tax and electric rates. Yet another community might decide to privatize or deregulate the provision of electric service because economic factors no longer justify public ownership or control.

Who Should Govern Austin Energy?

The Austin City Council—10 elected members and an elected mayor—"sets our policies and strategic direction," states the Austin Energy website.[64] Austin has a council-manager form of government. So the council hires the city manager, who in turn hires Austin Energy's general manager. Although it is a city department, Austin Energy has more autonomy and a different salary scale than other city departments.

Revenue from Austin Energy's operations, on the order of $150 million in 2013, is returned to the City of Austin's general fund to help finance other services provided by the city. The electric power industry in Texas was deregulated by the Texas state legislature in 2002, replacing state rate setting with competitive pricing and distribution by electric power providers. However, Austin Energy was not required to deregulate.[65] Contrary to expectations, the price of electric power rose throughout most of Texas following deregulation. Austin's rates remained relatively low because "our electric rates reflect [citizen] priorities . . . Our customers also want electric rates to remain affordable and to provide help to customers who face financial difficulty."[66]

In February 2013, Austin mayor Lee Leffingwell and city council member William Spelman proposed the creation of an independent board of directors to oversee the operations of Austin Energy. In an article that appeared in the *Austin American-Statesman*, Leffingwell and Spelman explained their reasons for proposing the interposition of an "independent" board of directors between the city council and the public managers of Austin Energy.[67] They were not proposing the privatization of the utility, they insisted. Public ownership by the citizens of Austin would continue unchanged. Rather, they said, an independent board would add professional expertise to the oversight of an organization providing services in a competitive and highly complex industry. As they put it, "a professional board would emphasize efficiency and competitiveness. The city council emphasizes the customer's values and needs."

The creation of such a board had been recommended by the City of Austin's Electric Utility Commission. The commission is tasked by law to "Review and analyze all policies and procedures of the electric utility including the electric rate structure, fuel costs and charges, customer services, capital investments, new generation facilities, selection of types of fuel, budget, strategic planning, regulatory compliance, billing procedures, and the transfer of electric utility revenues from the utility fund to the general fund."[68] The commission advised the city council to "turn over management of Austin Energy to an independent board with expertise in the financial, legal, technical, and consumer-advocacy aspects of public power."[69]

Leffingwell and Spelman both had strong credentials and credibility in the community. Both had been reelected to office the previous year. The mayor was raised and educated in Austin, where his father had been a firefighter, and he had a degree in engineering from the University of Texas in Austin. Spelman earned a PhD in public policy from Harvard University's John F. Kennedy School of Government and was

(Continued)

(Continued)

a professor at the Lyndon B. Johnson School of Public Affairs at the University of Texas, where he taught courses in public management, applied statistics, and urban policy.

Austin Deliberates

In its first vote on the proposed independent board, the city council's support was virtually unanimous, and members set about drafting a detailed plan for its creation.

In 2013, the City of Austin was a liberal enclave in a deeply conservative state. A slogan coined to promote small business, "Keep Austin Weird," came to stand for Austin's generally laid-back culture, highlighted by its live music scene; the weekly Austin City Limits public television program; the annual South-by-Southwest music and arts festival; Whole Foods Markets, which was headquartered in Austin and promoted healthful foods; the movie *Slacker*, about Austinites who exhibited scant regard for the work ethic; all things University of Texas; and a world-class Formula One racetrack, which brought an international glitterati of racing fans to the City. A colorful variety of counter- and subcultures flourished in Austin, and most liberal political causes found warm support there, including energy conservation, green energy, and affordable energy for those in need. There was also a thriving, growing, and world-class information technology industry to the north and west of central Austin that was fueling growth in the area's upper-income neighborhoods.

Austin's community-oriented newspaper, the *Austin American-Statesman,* numerous civic groups and activists, and individual citizens weighed in on the Leffingwell-Spelman proposal and its endorsement by the city council. The *American-Statesman* termed the proposal "monumental" and, while never opposing it outright, pointed out that no crisis, emergency, or urgent need justified hasty action.

In the ensuing months, a number of issues emerged:

- One was philosophical, comparing the merits of democratic and corporate style management of the city's $1.5 billion asset, its largest. Leffingwell and Spelman argued that, "many of these decisions have a lot more to do with efficient operations than with customer values: hiring and firing the general manager; investing utility funds; deciding on purchased power agreements. . . . Realistically, the council needs to be able to make the final decision on issues like long-range planning and the debt that supports it. The council needs to be able to make the final decisions about electric rates, too, since they come out of the same taxpayers' pockets."[70] The skeptical *American-Statesman* argued, "Even with its flaws, Austin Energy's current governance has merit with strong accountability that allows the public to regularly register its approval or disapproval through city elections."[71]
- A second issue concerned the objective merits of the two forms of governance. Are independent boards associated with better management than city managers and city councils? Both sides cited as evidence nearby San Antonio's city-owned electric utility, which was overseen by an independent board.
- A third issue had to do with equity. Customers of Austin Energy who lived outside the City of Austin criticized the transfer of the utility's profits to the city's general fund that benefits Austin residents. A counterargument pointed out that customers living in Travis County used Austin roadways and benefited from a wide range of city-provided public services to those who work, shop, and play there.

- A fourth issue had to do with the political motivations of advocates for creating an independent board. The *American-Statesman* hinted darkly that the proposal was intended to forestall a move by the state legislature to deregulate Austin Energy as it had done for most of the Texas electric power market in 2002.
- A fifth issue concerned the necessity, or at least advisability, of allowing city residents to vote on the proposed independent board. The city's legal department ruled that Austin's Charter required a referendum on the proposal. A Democratic state senator from Austin who supported creation of an independent board asserted that no such vote was required and indicated that he had requested an opinion on the matter from the state's Republican attorney general.
- A final, possibly decisive, issue concerned the lame duck status of the sitting city council. Austinites for Geographic Representation had successfully promoted a change to the city's election system. This change took place in 2014 and would replace the former seven-member body that was elected citywide with 10 members who would each represent a specific district. Only the mayor would be elected citywide. Supporters argued that the new system would correct the bias of the old system toward west and north Austin where wealthier, more politically connected voters lived. Some felt that the decision to create an independent board to oversee Austin Energy, because of its far-reaching consequences, should be deferred until the new, more democratic electoral system was in place.

In the face of growing opposition, Leffingwell and Spelman doubled down, as Texans like to say. They were proud of Austin Energy, they declared. "The city's electric utility sells more megawatts of renewable energy than anyone in the country. Its rate structure encourages conservation and provides assistance to the poor. It's green. It's socially conscious."[72] But, they said, Austin Energy had been going broke:

> for two decades, the city has treated Austin Energy as a cash cow. The council didn't watch expenses and used it to pay for pet projects. We ignored the warning signs. Worse, city staffers who ought to have known better didn't sound the alarm until we'd lost $100 million.[73]

With the area and its economy growing rapidly and more than 20 other departments to oversee, Leffingwell and Spelman argued that the city council would not have time to manage a complex business; to ensure that Austin Energy continued to produce benefits for the community, professional management was needed. All relevant stakeholders could be represented on the board. The board's members would be selected by the city council, and its decisions would be subject to council review. There would be no loss of accountability to the community and its customers, they argued. With a hint of exasperation, they insisted, "under our proposal, the council retains discretionary authority over rates, debt issuance and reserves, and the right to review everything else. People who believe the board is making bad decisions can complain to the council and demand that we fix it (just like they do now)."[74]

Their argument was unpersuasive to the doubters, however. The contentious politics so muddled the issues that Mayor Leffingwell withdrew his support for the proposed board at a city council work session in May 2013. "In crafting its responsibilities, council members had effectively neutered the board and, Leffingwell was quoted as saying, 'muddled (the proposal) up into an almost unrecognizable mess.'"[75]

The proposal was dead, at least for the time being. As a fig leaf, a subcommittee of the council would be created to give more attention to issues concerning Austin Energy. On May 23, 2013, the Austin City Council voted to postpone indefinitely a vote on the proposal to create an independent board for Austin Energy.[76]

(Continued)

(Continued)

Discussion Questions

1. How would you describe the "logic of governance" for Austin Energy?

2. What checks and balances are evident in this Austin Energy case?

3. What are the strongest arguments for, and against, the creation of an independent board of directors for Austin Energy?

4. As an analyst, what kinds of additional information would you want to have in preparing to advise members of the Austin city council concerning the governance of Austin Energy?

5. In principle, are the interests of the citizens of greater Austin better served by a technically rational plan for meeting Austin's energy needs, subject to city council approval or by a Madisonian, that is, politically rational, process for the oversight of Austin Energy?

NOTES

1. This section draws on research reported in Laurence E. Lynn, Jr., "America's 'Broken Government': What Would James Madison Say?" *Administration & Society* 45 no. 5 (July 2013): 610–624.

2. Michael Beckel, "Number of Special Interests Vying to Influence Health Reform Legislation Swelled ss Debate Dragged On," Text, *Open-Secrets Blog*, March 19, 2010, http://www.opensecrets.org/news/2010/03/number-of-special-interest-groups-v.

3. Joe Eaton, M. B. Pell, and Aaron Mehta, "Lobbying Giants Cash in on Health Overhaul," *NPR.org*, March 26, 2010, http://www.npr.org/templates/story/story.php?storyId=125170643.

4. *National Federation of Independent Business v. Sebelius* 567 U.S. (2012), 132 S.Ct 2566, http://law2.umkc.edu/faculty/projects/ftrials/conlaw/NationalFederationvSebeliusspend.html.

5. Ibid.

6. *National Federation of Independent Business v. Sebelius* 567 U.S. (2012), 132 S.Ct 2566.

7. Alvin Tran, "FAQ: How will the Individual Mandate Work?" Kaiser Health News, January September 3, 2013, http://kaiserhealthnews.org/news/faq-on-individual-insurance-mandate-aca.

8. Department of Health and Human Services, Centers for Medicare & Medicaid Services, The Center for Consumer Information and Insurance Oversight, "Affordable Insurance Exchanges Guidance," January 3, 2013, https://www.cms.gov/CCIIO/Resources/Fact-Sheets-and-FAQs/Downloads/partnership-guidance-01-03-2013.pdf, 3.

9. Elizabeth Rigby and Jake Haselswerdt, "Hybrid Federalism, Partisan Politics, and Early Implementation of State Health Insurance Exchanges," *Publius* 43, no. 3 (Summer 2013): 368–391.

10. King v. Burwell 576 U.S. ____ (2015), http://www.supremecourt.gov/opinions/14pdf/14-114_qol1.pdf.

11. The source of all quotations from *The Federalist* Is *The Federalist*, Modern Library College Editions (softcover), (New York, NY: McGraw-Hill Humanities/Social Sciences/Languages, 1964).

12. Ibid.

13. "The Founders' Constitution," Volume 1, Chapter 10 (Chicago: The University of Chicago Press, 1987), http://press-pubs.uchicago.edu/founders/documents/v1ch10I.html.

14. James Madison, "Federalist No. 44" in *The Federalist Papers*, January 25, 1788, in "We Hold These Truths Quotes Database," http://www.westillholdthesetruths.org/quotes/category/separation-of-powers.

15. John A. Rohr, *Civil Servants and Their Constitutions* (Lawrence: University Press of Kansas, 2002), 101.

16. *Shoemaker v. United States*, 147 U.S. 282, 301 (1893).

17. Russell Wheeler, "Judicial Nominations and Confirmations: Fact and Fiction," *The Brookings Institution*, December 30, 2013, http://www.brookings.edu/blogs/fixgov/posts/2013/12/30-staffing-federal-judiciary-2013-no-breakthrough-year.

18. Tom McCarthy, "Senate Confirms Obama's Judicial Nominee under New Filibuster Rule," *The Guardian*, December 10, 2013, http://www .theguardian.com/world/2013/dec/10/senate-approves-court-nominee-filibuster-rule.

19. Burgess Everett, "How Going Nuclear Unclogged the Senate," *Politico*, August 22, 2014, http://www.politico.com/story/2014/08/ how-going-nuclear-unclogged-the-senate-110238.html

20. General Accounting Office, "Head Start: Research Provides Little Information on Impact of Current Program" (Washington, DC: GAO, 1997).

21. Mike Puma, Stephen Bell, Ronna Cook, Camilla Heid, Pam Broene, Frank Jenkins, Andrew Mashburn, and Jason Downer, *Third Grade Follow-up to the Head Start Impact Study: Final Report,* OPRE Report 2012-45 (Washington, DC: Office of Planning, Research and Evaluation, Administration for Children and Families, U.S. Department of Health and Human Services, 2012).

22. Michael G. Franc, "Head Start: Still Useless," *The National Review,* January 17, 2013, http://www.nationalreview.com/article/337924/ head-start-still-useless-michael-g-franc; Grover J. "Russ" Whitehurst," Can We Be Hard-Headed About Preschool? A Look at Head Start," *The Brookings Institution*, January 16, 2013, http://www.brookings.edu/research/papers/2013/01/16-preschool-whitehurst.

23. Office of the Inspector General, City of Chicago, "Hiring Oversight," accessed November 30, 2014, http://chicagoinspectorgeneral.org/ shakman-hiring-compliance.

24. George Lavender, Fighting "Fires is Big Business for Private Companies," Earth Island Journal, October 29, 2013, http://www.earthisland .org/journal/index.php/elist/eListRead/fighting_fires_is_big_business_for_private_companies.

25. Paula Dobbyn, "Biologist Files Suit Targeting Logging Roads," *Anchorage Daily News,* May 20, 2006, http://www.rainforestportal.org/ shared/reader/welcome.aspx?linkid=56549&keybold=Tongass%20logging%20lawsuit.

26. "Victories," *Forest Service Employees for Environmental Ethics*, accessed November 9, 2014, http://www.fseee.org/stay-informed/ victories#road.

27. *Garcetti v. Ceballos*, 547 U.S. 410 (2006), http://www.supremecourtus.gov/opinions/05pdf/ 04-473.pdf.

28. Ibid., 3–4.

29. "ABA Administrative Procedure Database Archive," *The Florida State University, College of Law*, accessed November 9, 2014, http://www .law.fsu.edu/library/admin.

30. David H. Rosenbloom, *Administrative Law for Public Managers* (Boulder, CO: Westview Press, 2003).

31. Ibid., 13.

32. "Class Actions," *Children's Rights*, accessed November 9, 2014, http://www.childrensrights.org/our-campaigns/class-actions.

33. Anthony M. Bertelli and Laurence E. Lynn, Jr., "A Precept of Managerial Responsibility: Securing Collective Justice in Institutional Reform Litigation." *Fordham Urban Law Journal*, 24, no. 1 (October 2001): 312–386.

34. Stephen D. Sugarman, "Cases in Vaccine Court—Legal Battles over Vaccines and Autism," *New England Journal of Medicine* 357, no. 13 (September 27, 2007): 1275–1277, http://content.nejm.org/cgi/content/full/357/13/1275.

35. "National Vaccine Injury Compensation Program," *U.S. Department of Health and Human Services, HRSA: Health Resources and Services Administration*, accessed November 9, 2014, http://www.hrsa.gov/vaccinecompensation/index.html.

36. Rosemary O'Leary, *The Ethics of Dissent: Managing Guerrilla Government* (Washington, DC: CQ Press, 2005).

37. Committee on Guidelines for Human Embryonic Stem Cell Research, National Research Council, *Guidelines for Human Embryonic Stem Cell Research* (Washington, DC: National Academies Press, 2005).

38. Jonathan D. Moreno and Richard O. Hynes, "Guidelines for Human Embryonic Stem Cell Research," *Nature Biotechnology 23*(2005): 793–794.

39. J. C. Nelson et al., "When Doctors Go to War," *New England Journal of Medicine 352*(April 2005): 1497–1499; Steven H. Miles, *Oath Betrayed: Torture, Medical Complicity, and the War on Terror* (New York, NY: Random House, 2006).

40. Rigby and Haselswerdt, "Hybrid Federalism."

41. Thomas Jefferson to Joseph C. Cabell, February 2, 1816, http://www.notable-quotes.com/j/jefferson_thomas_v.html.

42. "Checks and Balances," *Key 2 Liberty*, accessed November 9, 2014, http://www.key2liberty.com/checks01.php.

43. G. Alan Tarr, "Interpreting the Separation of Powers in State Constitutions," *NYU Annual Survey of American Law 59*(2003): 330.

44. The Texas Politics Project, "The Plural Executive," University of Texas at Austin, accessed May 7, 2015http://www.laits.utexas.edu/txp_ media/html/exec/print_exec.html#9.

45. "Local Government Law: An Overview," *Legal Information Institute, Cornell University Law School*, accessed November 9, 2014, http:// www.law.cornell.edu/wex/local_government_law.

46. David R. Berman, *Local Government and the States: Autonomy, Politics, and Policy* (Armonk, N.: M. E. Sharpe, 2003); 19.

47. Leon Neyfakh, "Rise of the Mayors: How a Once-Ceremonial Job Became a Powerful Force in American Politics," *BostonGlobe.com*, September 1, 2013, https://www.bostonglobe.com/ideas/2013/08/31/rise-mayors/Rnv8nJds6FP5ufnAQQMohM/story.html.

48. "Medicaid Program Description and Legislative History," The Social Security Administration, Office of Retirement and Disability Policy, Annual Statistical Supplement, 2011, accessed November 30, 2014, http://www.ssa.gov/policy/docs/statcomps/supplement/2011/

medicaid.html; "Children's Health Insurance Program Overview," Medicaid.gov, http://www.medicaid.gov/chip/chip-program-information.html.

49. Kaiser Family Foundation, "Total Number of Children Ever Enrolled in CHIP Annually," accessed November 30, 2014, http://kff.org/other/state-indicator/annual-chip-enrollment.

50. Julia Paradise, "The Impact of the Children's Health Insurance Program (CHIP): What Does the Research Tell Us?" *Kaiser Family Foundation*, July 17, 2014, http://kff.org/medicaid/issue-brief/the-impact-of-the-childrens-health-insurance-program-chip-what-does-the-research-tell-us/, accessed November 30, 2014.

51. Henry, *Public Administration and Public Affairs*, 10th ed. (Upper Saddle River, NJ: Pearson Prentice Hall, 2007), 350.

52. *OPPAGA: The Florida Legislature's Office of Program Policy Analysis & Government Accountability*, accessed November 9, 2014, http://www.oppaga.state.fl.us/shell.aspx?pagepath=about/about.htm.

53. *California Climate Change Portal*, accessed November 9, 2014, http://www.climatechange.ca.gov/.

54. *House Research Organization: Texas House of Representatives*, accessed May 7, 2015, http://www.hro.house.state.tx.us/pdf/focus/amend82.pdf.

55. Kevin Shelley, "Remarks by Secretary of State Kevin Shelley," Press Release KS03:053, July 23, 2003 (as prepared), http://admin.cdn.sos.ca.gov/press-releases/prior/2003/03_053.pdf.

56. "About Mass Growth Capital Corp," *Massachusetts Growth Capital Corporation*, accessed November 9, 2014, http://www.massgcc.com/about.

57. Findlaw search, AK Stat § 18.60.180 (2013), accessed May 7, 2015, http://lawcrawler.findlaw.com/LCsearch.html?restrict=pro&entry=AK+Stat+%C2%A7+18.60.180+%282013%29.

58. Chris Sagers, "Antitrust Immunity and Standard Setting Organizations: A Case Study in the Use of Liberal Models to Cope with Private Power," *Cardozo Law Review*, Vol. 23, pp. 1393-1427, 2004. Available at SSRN: http://ssrn.com/abstract=699642, 8.

59. This section is adapted from Lynn, "America's 'Broken Government.'"

60. James Madison, "Federalist No. 51" in *The Federalist Papers,* February 8, 1788, in "We Hold These Truths Quotes Database," http://westillholdthesetruths.org/quotes/219/justice-is-the-end-of-government.

61. Laurence E. Lynn Jr., Carolyn J. Heinrich, and Carolyn J. Hill, *Improving Governance: A New Logic for Empirical Research* (Washington, DC: Georgetown University Press, 2001). See also Laurence E. Lynn Jr., Carolyn J. Heinrich, and Carolyn J. Hill, "Studying Governance and Public Management: Challenges and Prospects," *Journal of Public Administration Research and Theory* 10, no. 2 (2000): 233–261.

62. Geoffrey Vickers, *The Art of Judgment: A Study of Policymaking* (New York, NY: Harper and Row, 1983); Lynn, Heinrich, and Hill, *Improving Governance*; Gary L. Wamsley, "The Agency Perspective: Public Administrators as Agential Leader," in Wamsley et al., *Refounding Public Administration* (Newbury Park, CA: Sage Publications, 1990).

63. Austin Energy, "Company Profile, accessed May 7, 2015, http://austinenergy.com/wps/portal/ae/about/company-profile.

64. Ibid.

65. Ibid.

66. Austin Energy, "Benefits of Public Power," accessed May 7, 201, http://austinenergy.com/wps/portal/ae/rates/benefits-of-public-power.

67. Lee Leffingwell and Bill Spelman, "Evolving Austin Energy Mission Sparks Need for Change," *Austin American-Statesman*, February 9, 2013, http://www.statesman.com/news/news/opinion/leffingwell-spelman-evolving-austin-energy-mission/nWKH9/.

68. AustinTexas.gov, "Electric Utility Commission," accessed May 17, 2015, http://www.austintexas.gov/euc.

69. Marty Toohey, "Austin Energy Should Be Run by an Independent Board, Advisory Commission Says," *Austin American-Statesman*, October 29, 2012, http://www.statesman.com/news/news/austin-energy-should-be-run-by-an-independent-boar/nSrLG/

70. Leffingwell and Spelman, "Evolving Austin Energy Mission"

71. Editorial Board, "City Council Should Build a Case Based on Facts for Changing Governance of Austin Energy," *Austin American-Statesman*, February 16, 2013, http://www.statesman.com/news/news/opinion/the-city-council-should-build-a-case-based-on-fact/nWQWP/.

72. Lee Leffingwell and Bill Spelman, "Independent Board Would Save Austin Energy," *Austin American-Statesman*, May 5, 2013, http://www.statesman.com/news/news/opinion/leffingwell-spelman-independent-board-would-save-a/nXfH7/

73. Ibid.

74. Ibid.

75. Marty Toohey, "Council Backpedals on Austin Energy Board," *Austin American-Statesman*, May 21, 2013, http://www.statesman.com/news/news/local/council-tables-austin-energy-board-vote-indefinite/nXyF8/.

76. Sarah Coppola, "Austin City Council Tables Austin Energy Decision, Supports X Games," *Austin American-Statesman*, May 23, 2013, http://www.mystatesman.com/news/news/local-govt-politics/austin-city-council-tables-austin-energy-decision-/nX2bw/.

5 | Structure

The Administrative State

INTRODUCTION

The executive branch organizations of federal, state, local, and special-purpose governments make up the U.S. administrative state. As described in the Part II Introduction, these administrative structures constitute delegations of authority and responsibility to designated officials and organizations to take action on behalf of lawful policy, program, and regulatory objectives.

This chapter is about administrative structures that legislatures create or authorize. Elected officials, acting in their policymaking role, decide not only the goals of public policies but also how those goals are to be achieved. Their decisions are rational from a political perspective, but they are seldom rational from a technical (or efficiency) perspective. Political scientist Terry Moe terms legislative decision-making processes "the politics of bureaucratic structure."[1] Discussed in this chapter, these processes further reflect the influence of James Madison on American governance.

The chapter explains how the politics of bureaucratic structure shape the American administrative state. It also explains how the structures established by these processes affect what public managers do and the results they achieve. The authority that is delegated to elected executives and their subordinates often allows them to create additional administrative structures necessary to accomplish public policy goals; Chapter 6 discusses the nature and significance of these additional administrative structures.

Beginning with a case involving the U.S. Bureau of Immigration and Customs Enforcement that illustrates many of the concepts, the chapter then describes

- the structures of direct government, that is, the production of public policy outcomes and outputs by government organizations and employees;
- the specialized structures associated with budgeting and financial management and with public personnel systems and human resource management; and

- the structures of indirect or third-party government, which includes organizations such as nonprofit and for-profit firms under contract to governments, as well as networks and partnerships among government and non-governmental entities that contribute to the production of public outputs and outcomes.

The chapter concludes with a case describing the successful reform of the juvenile justice system by organizations of the administrative state in Missouri.

CASE: IMMIGRATION AND CUSTOMS ENFORCEMENT

Congress established the U.S. Department of Homeland Security (DHS) in 2002. It incorporated 22 separate offices and agencies from across the federal government into a cabinet-level structure concerned with protecting the United States from threats to its security. This case describes specific implications from one aspect of this structural reorganization.

Pursuant to the Homeland Security Act of 2002, DHS created a new agency, Immigration and Customs Enforcement (ICE). ICE is a merger of the former Immigration and Naturalization Service from the Justice Department, and the U.S. Customs Service from the Treasury Department (minus their intelligence units). It is responsible for identifying and eliminating border, economic, transportation, and infrastructure security vulnerabilities. Its two primary components are Homeland Security Investigations (HSI) and Enforcement and Removal Operations (ERO).[i]

The following article, published by *Government Executive* magazine, describes how the creation of ICE enabled public managers to expand an investigation beyond what it otherwise would have covered under the prereform structural arrangements:

> Two years ago, investigators with the old Immigration and Naturalization Service in Albany, N.Y., began looking into reports that several Chinese restaurants in upstate New York were harboring illegal immigrants who were allegedly working in the kitchens. It hardly seemed an unusual case—the restaurant industry long has been known for its reliance on and exploitation of undocumented immigrant labor.

> Then the case took an unexpected turn. INS was abolished. The agency's investigators were partnered with Customs Service investigators in the bureaucratic equivalent of a shotgun marriage, one of many organizational twists that occurred when the Homeland Security Department was [formally] established in March 2003.

---

[i]DHS includes another new agency, the Bureau of Customs and Border Protection (CBP), responsible for regulating and facilitating international trade, collecting import duties, and enforcing U.S. regulations, including trade, customs, and immigration. At the time of DHS's creation and later, some experts advocated combining ICE and CBP in the interests of greater efficiency. Opponents claimed that such a combination would be so large that it would dominate state and local agencies that were also engaged in border protection. For a detailed structural analysis of such a merger, see U.S. Department of Homeland Security, Office of Inspector General, An *Assessment of the Proposal to Merge Customs and Border Protection with Immigration and Customs Enforcement*, OIG-06-04, November 2005.

The unholy union of immigration and customs investigators resulted in the Immigration and Customs Enforcement agency, known as ICE, which is part of Homeland Security's sprawling Border and Transportation Security bureau. In an agency where consensus can be hard to find, all parties seem to agree that the ICE merger was no love match. The divide ran deep, ranging from differences in cultures and investigation methods to training, databases, and contacts with state and local law enforcement organizations. Not surprisingly, the move into a new organization caused plenty of heartburn for everyone.

Nonetheless, the New York immigration investigation continued, but, like the new agency, with a twist. Jack McQuade, the resident agent in charge of the ICE office in Albany, says agents continued to pursue the case. But under orders from Peter Smith, the ICE agent in charge of the Buffalo regional office—which oversees the Albany office—the inquiry was expanded to include money-laundering.

McQuade, formerly a Customs agent, says it made sense to draw on the expertise of both agencies. "I told a [former] Customs agent, 'You're going to work an immigration case, but you're going to work it from a money-laundering perspective. We are going to go after these individuals' assets.' This would definitely not have occurred if this had remained strictly an immigration issue."

> **"'You're going to work an immigration case, but you're going to work it from a money-laundering perspective. We are going to go after these individuals' assets.' This would definitely not have occurred if this had remained strictly an immigration issue."**

The ICE agents conducted surveillance in New York City, where they discovered that restaurant owners upstate were operating a tour bus to pick up illegal immigrants in Chinatown, Brooklyn and Queens, and transport them to the Albany area. For months, investigators followed a trail that eventually led to a human smuggling ring holding at least several dozen illegal immigrants essentially enslaved as indentured servants and more than 40 illicit bank accounts. Along the way the Internal Revenue Service joined in, to pursue tax evasion charges, with investigators from the Labor Department, the U.S. attorney for the northern district of New York, the New York State Police and a number of local police departments.

Last November, ICE executed search warrants on several restaurants and homes, arrested ringleaders, and seized 11 vehicles and nearly $4 million in cash, real estate and other assets. The probe remains open as investigators continue to pore through cartons of seized documents.

"This is a perfect example showing how you can really hurt a criminal organization when you draw on expertise from both former Customs and former INS," says Smith. "The legacy immigration people knew exactly what to look for, what documents to get, what surveillance to do, what we needed to charge these people with, with regard to human trafficking. Then you come in with the legacy Customs powers. The legacy Customs people see that not only do we have a great immigration case, but we can now go after this group and their assets."

Adds McQuade: "This would not have happened had the decision not been made to work it from both angles. It's a good example of what you can do if you work together, and if you elicit the assistance of local police agencies."[2]

(Continued)

(Continued)

As separate entities, INS and the Customs Service likely would not have garnered the resources or followed the same investigation path. The issue might have fallen into the cracks between departments or might have become a source of conflict to be resolved at a higher administrative level. Structural reorganization enabled public managers to create a more comprehensive operation to occur in the field, with good results.

The division of responsibilities between CBP and ICE remained problematic, however. A 2005 report by the DHS Inspector General, written in response to a request from a congressional committee, reported, "The division between CBP and ICE is marked by a clear institutional barrier. Shortfalls in operational coordination and information sharing have fostered an environment of uncertainty and mistrust between CBP and ICE personnel."[3] Might further benefits from coordination of operations be gained by their merger?

The DHS Inspector General thought so. His 2005 report on the merger issues concluded, "The resulting consolidated border security agency with a single chain-of-command would be better positioned to coordinate mission, priorities, and resources to guarantee a comprehensive border security program."[4] By 2014, despite a heightened sense of urgency about border protection to limit terrorist threats, a merger of CBP and ICE had not occurred.

MADISONIAN POLITICS AND THE ADMINISTRATIVE STATE: THE POLITICS OF BUREAUCRATIC STRUCTURE

The Madisonian system of U.S. governance, with its separation of powers and checks and balances (described in Chapter 4) has direct implications for public management. These are starkly illustrated by Moe's explanation of the **politics of bureaucratic structure**.[5]

Moe conducts a thought experiment in which the political process has three principal actors: interest groups, politicians/policymakers, and bureaucrats. What kind of bureaucratic structure does each actor want? [6]

If an interest group were all-powerful, it would want politicians to delegate authority to bureaucrats subject to rules or constraints and to specific budgetary procedures. Interest groups want such constraints and limits to ensure the reliability of bureaucrats. Bureaucrats, on the other hand, want autonomy and freedom from burdensome rules because, as experts, they have ideas of their own about what to do to achieve public policy objectives. But bureaucrats realize the need to establish reputations for trustworthiness in order to minimize the constraints and limits imposed on them.

Knowing these things about lobbyists and bureaucrats, what would the politicians want? Realizing that their political power might be diminished in future election cycles, they want to use their current authority to reassure lobbyists whose political support they need that the structures they create are protected as much as possible from future power shifts. That is, they want to create a status quo that becomes entrenched.

Thus, a bureau's formal structure and, as will be shown later in this book, much of its "informal" structure—its institutionalized values—are the outcomes of political bargaining among the three self-interested groups of actors. When conflicting interests arise in these interactions, compromise becomes necessary. Bureaucratic structures will reflect these political compromises. Because the goal of compromising is political, considerations of efficiency and manageability may be of secondary importance.

Moe's thought experiment results in the following takeaways:

- Political choice is about policymakers' responding to interest groups.
- Interest groups compete with each other for design and control of bureaucratic structures. This creates two problems that must be addressed: uncertainty concerning the political future and the need to compromise.
- These two factors cause structural choices to deviate substantially from technical rationality, especially when political conflicts are intense.
- Bureaucrats in turn want to insulate themselves from political control and manipulation. This tendency is taken into account in striking the legislative bargain, resulting in a compromised array of limits and constraints on bureaucratic discretion.
- After the initial bargain is struck, subsequent politics is largely incremental, offering limited scope for administrative reform.

Paradoxically, then, rational political actors produce technically irrational public organizations:

> The driving force of political uncertainty causes the winning group to favor structural designs it would never favor on technical grounds alone: designs that place detailed formal restrictions on bureaucratic discretion, impose complex procedures for agency decision making, minimize opportunities for oversight, and otherwise insulate the agency from politics. The structures they create will deviate rather far from technical rationality.[7]

Moreover, efforts to create structures that limit the power of bureaucracy often have the opposite effect: they increase bureaucratic power.[8] The political bargaining over limits on bureaucratic discretion may give rise to limits that are vague or inconsistent, thus requiring discretionary judgments by bureaucrats to make them operational.

The structural politics within Congress itself further complicate the situation.[9] Intense bargaining often occurs within each chamber of Congress and between the House and Senate over committee assignments and subcommittee jurisdictions. Bureaucratic structures may be designed either to preserve or to deliberately alter these jurisdictions. Policymakers, then, are less concerned with general policy control and more concerned with particularized policy control over activities important to voters in their jurisdictions and to individuals and groups who finance their reelection campaigns. These tendencies have direct implications for public management.

Example: Charter School Reform in Texas

In June 2013, the Texas State Board of Education was made up of unpaid, part-time elected officials, who had the authority to approve applications for the creation of charter schools. The Texas Education Agency (TEA), a permanent administrative agency of Texas state government whose commissioner was appointed by the governor of Texas, had the authority to provide oversight of charter school operations in the state.

A proposal introduced by the chair of the Education Committee of the Texas state senate, who became a Republican candidate for governor in 2014, would have delegated the authority to both approve and oversee charter schools in a "new state entity." The bill would also authorize a significant expansion in the size of the charter school program, a high priority for Texas conservatives.[i]

---

[i]For background on charter school program in Texas see http://txedrev.org/wp-content/uploads/2014/06/Redd-et-al._An-Overview-on-Charter-Schools1.pdf.

At the time, the process of revoking a charter typically ended up in litigation that could take years—up to 12 years in one case—to resolve.[10] The state's Sunset Review Commission had recommended that lawmakers give the TEA clearer authority to revoke a charter quickly after 3 consecutive years of failure.

The Texas Charter Schools Association supported clearing up what it considered some of the gray areas in the law governing charter schools in order to make it easier to close schools that consistently failed either academically or financially. This interest group was concerned, however, that the Sunset Commission recommendation was too rigid, particularly for those charter schools that specialized in helping students at risk of dropping out of school. Their group argued that the TEA should have more leeway in decisions concerning charter revocation because some charter schools had assumed a more difficult mission. One school leader argued that automatic revocation of a charter might not allow for the TEA to take into consideration progress being made at his school.

As stakeholders in the public education system discussed the proposal, the head of the TEA, Michael Williams, positioned himself to be the "reliable agent" to which unified authority over charter schools should be delegated. He announced that the TEA was strengthening "its commitment to Texas charter schools" by improving coordination among the agency's different divisions and by creating a senior adviser position for charter school turnaround. He appointed to this position a long-time school turnaround specialist to lead the agency's improved charter school oversight, which Williams had initiated in response to legislative urging.

Democratic legislators, supported by the state's teachers' unions, opposed the extent of the expansion of charter schools. They advocated retention of a cap on the total number of charters in order to maintain some control over charter school quality. They also objected to rigid criteria for charter revocation, presumably drawing support from those charters struggling to deal with the most difficult students, whose parents typically voted Democratic.

In the end, compromises cleared the reform bill's passage by the Texas Senate in a near-unanimous bipartisan vote and its later enactment by the Texas House of Representatives.[11] A cap on the number of charters was maintained but set so that it would allow for some expansion of the program. Additional financial support for charter schools was authorized. The commissioner of education was given a role in the process of approving charters, although final approval authority remained with the state board of education.

An editorial in the *Austin American-Statesman* noted the importance of the politics of bureaucratic structure at work in deciding on charter school administration and expansion. "Competing interests and voices . . . helped shape a charter school expansion bill that didn't, as some conservatives wanted, eliminate all caps on charters schools and didn't, as some liberals called for, continue to limit charter school expansion. . . . The Legislature gave the Texas Education Agency greater authority to crack down on low-performing charters. Changes also shifted oversight of charter schools from the fractious and hyperpartisan State Board of Education to the Texas Education Agency."[12]

Similar accounts abound of agencies that are established and overseen by a legislative entity, whether by a state, a county board, or a city council. Following is an account, described by Moe, of the politics of bureaucratic structure at the federal level.

Example: The Federal Consumer Product Safety Commission (CPSC)[13]

The consumer protection movement had grown powerful in the late 1960, with advocates calling for a consumer product safety commission. The Nixon Administration was not enthusiastic but recognized the inevitable. The administration proposed an agency located within the Department of Health, Education, and Welfare while the Justice Department would provide enforcement. This arrangement would place the agency securely under presidential control.

In contrast, consumer advocates wanted an independent commission under their control and advocated structures that would ensure this. Consumer interests prevailed in several respects:

- An independent agency was created.
- Rulemaking could be initiated by petitions from outside parties (to which CPSC was obliged to respond within 120 days).
- Outside groups could propose standards that CPSC would consider.
- Private parties could go to court if the agency didn't enforce standards and could sue for damages when injured by products not meeting standards.
- Any injured party was granted standing.

Compromises with business groups were evident, however:

- A right to judicial review was created.
- The CPSC would henceforth have to rely on Justice Department for enforcement.
- A 3-year authorization was enacted.

When the agency was up for re-authorization in 1975, both business and consumer groups were unhappy. Though consumer groups' power had declined, they won new structural features that resulted in a stronger agency. These included greater CPSC independence in enforcement and removing the right of the White House to approve top agency staff. However, proposed rules had to be submitted to Congress 30 days prior to adoption so business and its allies could respond.

The CPSC continued to be politically controversial. Congress, the General Accounting Office (GAO; in 2004, the organization's name was legally changed to the Government Accountability Office), the Civil Service Commission, and the agency itself were dissatisfied. President Jimmy Carter wanted to abolish the CPSC in part because he had to answer for its poor performance but had no managerial control over it. When reauthorized for another 3 years in 1979, the commission chair would serve at the pleasure of the president. In 1981, with Reagan as president and a Republican-controlled Senate, another battle over structure took place. The CPSC rules were subject to congressional veto; the agency was instructed to give preference to voluntary standards; means of compliance were left up to businesses; and stringent criteria for issuance of standards were imposed.

For the ensuing 25 years, the CPSC was not particularly loved by anyone. Its initial appropriation (in constant dollars) and staffing levels shrank, and the quality of appointees to the CPSC declined. Moe argued that the CPSC never had a chance to perform well. Its structure was not intended to be an effective means of pursuing consumer protection but instead a means of engaging in political attack and defense.[14]

In 2008, however, following a series of product recalls and scandals involving the safety of children's toys, Congress used the CPSC in a purposeful way. The Consumer Product Safety Act was passed decisively by Congress under Democratic sponsorship, and Republican president George W. Bush signed the bill into law. This act imposed tough new standards and testing requirements on toy manufacturers, increased the CPSC's budget, and strengthened whistleblower protections of employees of manufacturers, private labelers, distributors, or retailers of consumer products. The act alienated the children's toy industry, which complained of its breadth and the extent of unintended, adverse effects on the toy business.[ii]

DIRECT GOVERNMENT CONTROL: THE BUREAUCRACY

What public administration professionals call "the administrative state," the general public calls "the **bureaucracy**." Though bureaucracy is often used as a synonym for inefficiency and unresponsiveness, the term is in fact an analytical description of the governments of advanced industrial democracies. Moreover it describes a way to organize production and delivery of products and services in virtually all large complex organizations, both public and private.

The emergence of modern American public bureaucracies acquired momentum during the Progressive Era, from the 1880s through the first decade of the twentieth century. The demands for public goods and services were growing as society was growing, diversifying, urbanizing, and industrializing. These demands included infrastructure, education, public health, regulation of a robust capitalist economy, and sufficient revenue to pay for it all. Concurrently, large public agencies such as the Departments of Labor and Commerce, regulatory agencies such as the Food and Drug Administration, and large business corporations such as the Ford Motor Company and United States Steel Company became major influences in American politics.

> Though bureaucracy is often used as a synonym for inefficiency and unresponsiveness, the term is in fact an analytical description of the governments of advanced industrial democracies.

The bureaucratic form of public governance that emerged at all levels of American government in the early twentieth century is called **direct government**: outputs and outcomes of public policies and programs—the services provided and their consequences for public welfare—are produced directly by public employees under the control of elected officials.[15] According to German sociologist Max Weber, it was inevitable that these new organizations were bureaucracies.[16] In the public sector, the political objective was to create organizations subject to control by the people's elected representatives who would act on behalf of the interests of their constituencies and stakeholders.

Where the rule of law prevails, Weber argued, the following principles are followed in governance and in business:

- Business is conducted on a continuous basis.
- There is a well-defined division of labor.
- Authority is hierarchical.
- Officials have neither an ownership interest in the organization's resources nor property rights in their positions.
- Business is conducted on the basis of written documents.[17]

These five principles are regarded as defining bureaucracy as distinct from more traditional forms of social organization. Although bureaucratic authority is hierarchical, the terms *hierarchy* and *bureaucracy* are not synonymous. Hierarchy is a necessary but not sufficient condition for bureaucracy: bureaucracies are by definition

---

[ii]In 2011, President Obama signed into law an amendment to the CPSA Improvement Act to categorically exclude off-road vehicles such as all-terrain vehicles and dirt bikes from the law's lead content provisions.

hierarchical, but other types of organizations can be hierarchical, too. Bureaucracy reflects the organization of power within societies and also the nature and complexity of the activities that citizens authorize through their elected representatives.

Weber also noted that the emergence and persistence of a stable system of bureaucracy depends on a stable source of income. For a public bureaucracy, this means a system of taxation. Without such income, Weber argued, bureaucracies tend to degenerate into plutocracies and administrative forms characteristic of patrimonies and feudal societies.

Bureaucracies have multiple, hierarchically ordered levels characterized by many layers, many structural parts, fragmentation, and coordination problems. This complexity is a major source of nonmarket failures, the **bureaucratic pathologies** discussed in Chapter 1, such as internalities and organizational goals focused on budget growth and information control. Public managers are embedded in these complex systems.

Public administration scholar Barry Bozeman points out that "according to some critics, bureaucracy is an inherently pathological organization form. So long as executive functions rely on hierarchical, highly controlled, authority-oriented organizational schemes, pathological behavior is the only possible result."[18, iii] Bozeman argues that four different types of theories explain bureaucratic failure:

- **goal ambiguity:** reflecting "one of the best-known maxims in the literature on public organizations and public management," this theory holds that bureaucrats will resist change and will focus on process or rule compliance and "minutiae" because they are faced with unclear goals;[19]
- **utility maximization:** this theory holds that individuals act in their own self-interest. Failures result when bureaucrats' interests are not aligned with those of the organization;
- **property rights** and **principal-agent problems:** these explanations focus on the misaligned incentives for bureaucrats to pursue organizational goals. This misalignment arises due to lack of profit motive in the property rights account and due to conflicts of interest and information asymmetries in the principal-agent model (discussed in Chapter 6); and
- **maladaptation:** this model holds that an organization's structure may not be appropriate for the environment in which it operates, leading to disconnect and bureaucratic failure.

Real-world bureaucracies, therefore, are challenging environments for public managers seeking to implement complex public policies.

Structures for Enabling and Constraining Managers

Delegations of authority and responsibility from legislatures create structures that define the scope of decisions and actions by public managers. **Enabling structures** allow the exercise of discretion. **Constraining structures** require or prohibit specific activities.

This section emphasizes delegations of authority that originate from actors such as legislatures and overhead bodies that are external to the implementing organization (thus, operating primarily at the "b" and "c" levels in the logic of governance described in Chapter 4). For example, a legislative directive to an executive branch agency

---

iiiPolitical scientist William Gormley identified "first-generation" pathologies of clientelism, incrementalism, arbitrariness, imperialism, and parochialism; and "second-generation" pathologies of bean-counting, proceduralism, avoidance, and defeatism. William T. Gormley, Jr., *Taming the Bureaucracy: Muscles, Prayers, and Other Strategies* (Princeton, NJ: Princeton University Press, 1989).

is an externally authorized structure. Enabling and constraining administrative authority are often accomplished in the same legislative provision. Indeed, public authority often takes the form of mandates—"the Secretary shall"—that command the exercise of authority for designated purposes or in prescribed ways.

Enabling structures are formal delegations of authority that explicitly or implicitly allow discretion by designated officials or organizations. Public managers' discretionary actions may either create structures or infuse an existing structure with distinction and meaning (though these structures may not be wholly determined by managerial actors).

A number of enabling structures are found in the Constitution, such as "the executive power shall be vested in a President of the United States of America." Amendments to the Constitution may also enable: The Tenth Amendment enables state governments in expressing "the powers not delegated to the United States by the Constitution, nor prohibited by it to the states, are reserved to the states respectively, or to the people." Enabling structures also can be found in provisions of authorizing statutes or executive orders, regulations, or rules. For example, the Homeland Security Act of 2002 states, "The Secretary is the head of the Department and shall have direction, authority, and control over it."

Constraining structures are found in congressional creation of federal departments and agencies, which determines the scope and content of missions, purposes, and programs; in statutorily mandated use of performance measurement and management systems; and in statutorily required requirements for reporting information and structures constituting the chain of command.

Examples of constraining structures from the U.S. Constitution include the statement "[The President] shall have power, by and with the advice and consent of the Senate, to make treaties, provided two thirds of the Senators present concur." The same Tenth Amendment, which is enabling to the states, is constraining to the federal government. Laws such as the Homeland Security Act constrain when they define jurisdiction: "Except as specifically provided by law with respect to entities transferred to the Department under this Act, primary responsibility for investigating and prosecuting acts of terrorism shall be vested not in the Department, but rather in Federal, State, and local law enforcement agencies with jurisdiction over the acts in question."

Legislative delegations of authority and overhead structures of the administrative state serve as externally authorized enabling and constraining structures on public organizations. While the following examples are drawn from federal agencies, similar processes and uses of language are followed at state and local levels.

Legislative Delegations of Authority

In their delegations of authority, legislatures both enable and constrain managerial discretion. Yet while the word *enable* appears in many statutory authorizations, the word *constrain* is almost never used. Instead the constraints and opportunities for discretion are expressed in terms such as *shall, shall ensure that, in accordance with, limited to, and as determined by.*

In establishing the Affordable Care Act (ACA), Congress enabled and constrained the role of the secretary of health and human services in leading the law's implementation:[iv]

- The following provision gives the secretary authority to enable states and their insurance exchanges to a particular task: create consumer protection entities:

[iv]Quotations in the following examples are from the text of the ACA. Emphases are added by the authors. The text of the ACA can be found at http://www.hhs.gov/healthcare/rights/law.

"The Secretary *shall award* grants to States *to enable* such States (or the Exchanges operating in such States) to establish, expand, or provide support for—(1) offices of health insurance consumer assistance; or (2) health insurance ombudsman programs."

- The following provision grants broad authority to the Secretary of Health & Human Services to impose constraints on insurance plan providers concerning their creating an internal claims and appeals process:

"[A] group health plan and a health insurance issuer offering group health coverage *shall provide* an internal claims and appeals process that initially incorporates the claims and appeals procedures (including urgent claims) set forth at section 2560.503–1 of title 29, Code of Federal Regulations, as published on November 21, 2000 (65 Fed. Reg. 70256), and shall update such process *in accordance with any standards established by the Secretary of Labor* for such plans and issuers."

- The following provision explicitly recognizes the need for expert judgment:

"The standards and associated operating rules adopted by the Secretary shall—(i) *to the extent feasible and appropriate,* enable determination of an individual's eligibility and financial responsibility for specific services prior to or at the point of care."

- The following provision gives authority to the appropriations committee to provide the Secretary of HHS with an unquantified, indefinite appropriation for carrying out a function, a term used for payments or services regarded as "entitlements":

"There is authorized to be appropriated to the Secretary for each fiscal year following the fiscal year described in paragraph (1), such sums as may be necessary to carry out this section."

- Even though legislative delegations of authority may sound quite broad, they constrain by defining the scope and content. The following provision of the nearly 1,000-page ACA contains cross references to six other provisions of that law:

"Coverage provided with respect to an individual described in section 1905(a)(4)(B) and covered under the State plan under section 1902(a)(10)(A) of the services described in section 1905(a)(4)(B) (relating to early and periodic screening, diagnostic, and treatment services defined in section 1905(r)) and provided in accordance with section 1902(a)(43), shall be deemed to satisfy the requirements of subparagraph (A)."

- The following provision imposes a task on state officials and, at the same time, indirectly confers regulatory authority on other standard-setting government entities:

"Subject to clause (ii), State health insurance commissioners *shall ensure* that health plans comply with the segregation requirements in this subsection through the segregation of plan funds *in accordance with* applicable provisions of generally accepted accounting requirements, circulars on funds management of the Office of Management and Budget, and guidance on accounting of the Government Accountability Office."

Statutory language may also grant qualified authority to subordinates of a higher level official. The ACA, for example, states, "The Centers for Medicare and Medicaid Services shall establish a process for determining the units and the allocated price for purposes of this section for those branded prescription drugs that are not separately payable or for which National Drug Codes are not reported." Left unsaid is whether and how the Secretary and the Director of CMS shall communicate concerning the execution of this task.

Filling the Gaps: Overhead Structures of the Administrative State

Legislative entities at all levels of government have created organizations to administer major government-wide functions and standards. The statutes governing these functions are major components of the legal framework for public management. A few of the many such statutes are

- the Administrative Procedure Act;
- Title 5 of the Code of Federal Regulations (CFR) governing personnel administration;
- relevant sections of the CFR governing the administration of an agency's programs;
- the Freedom of Information Act; and
- the Paperwork Reduction Act.

Authorizing statutes such as the ACA may deploy many federal overhead structures, as the following examples illustrate:

- Subject to clause (ii), State health insurance commissioners shall ensure that health plans comply with the segregation requirements in this subsection through the segregation of plan funds in accordance with applicable provisions of generally accepted accounting requirements, circulars on funds management of the Office of Management and Budget, and guidance on accounting of the Government Accountability Office.
- GENERAL.—The Director of the Office of Personnel Management . . . shall enter into contracts with health insurance issuers . . . without regard to section 5 of title 41, United States Code, or other statutes requiring competitive bidding, to offer at least 2 multi-State qualified health plans through each Exchange in each State. Such plans shall provide individual, or in the case of small employers, group coverage.

Taken together, the legislative delegations of authority and overhead structures of the administrative state are inscribed on a slate for public managers at all levels of government to refer to. As political scientist Herbert Kaufman has observed, "the slate is not clean."[20] Chalked onto the public manager's slate are thousands of pages of written directives and guidance, in statutes, government-wide guidelines and regulations, departmental and bureau regulations, opinions and judgments by courts, the views expressed by entities such as the GAO, and the reports of congressional committees or their counterparts in state and local governments.

> Chalked onto the public manager's slate are thousands of pages of written directives and guidance, in statutes, government-wide guidelines and regulations, departmental and bureau regulations, opinions and judgments by courts . . . .

The voluminous, specific, and often uncoordinated slates facing public managers explain why the *bureaucracy* is held to be rule-bound, rigid, and unresponsive by the public and even by the legislators who write the slate's content and the administrators who must live by them. At the same time, those overloaded slates are created to ensure what the citizens most want: official accountability to the rule of law. Chapter 6 builds on these ideas to consider how managers take on this responsibility using structural tools of their own to fulfill citizen expectations.

Similarly inscribed slates exist for every state and municipality. All governing laws, including constitutions and charters, rules, and codes are assembled and made accessible to the public as well as to the public officials who are empowered and governed by them.

FINANCIAL STRUCTURES: BUDGETS AND BUDGETING

Article I, section 9, clause 7 of the U.S. Constitution stipulates that "no money shall be drawn from the Treasury, but in Consequence of Appropriations made by Law; and a regular Statement and Account of the Receipts and Expenditures of all public Money shall be published from time to time." This and other clauses in the Constitution confer on Congress **the power of the purse**.[21] Similar powers are conferred on the legislative branches of state and local governments.

The exercise of the power of the purse results in the creation of public budgets that enable and constrain activities of the executive and regulatory government agencies. Public budgets specify how much and on what governmental entities are lawfully entitled to spend during the course of a fiscal year. They are created by a process that is both intensely political and technically arcane. The GAO's "Glossary of Terms Used in the Federal Budget Process" is almost 200 pages long, and the Office of Management and Budget's (OMB) guidelines for federal budget execution require 900 pages. Public budgeting is dominated by politicians and financial specialists. Public managers are thus pulled in two very different directions during the budget process.

Information on the processes, politics, and history of budgeting at federal, state, and local levels is vast. Many excellent resources provide rich detail on these aspects, including preparation of executive budgets, legislative authorization and appropriation procedures, budget execution, and financial and performance audits.[v] The following discussion reviews the historical background of contemporary budgeting processes; the process of budget creation, including some of the technical concepts and terms commonly used in budgeting; and types of budgets and how budget type affects policymaking and public management.

The Evolution of Contemporary Budgeting[22]

Just as the Founders had to confront the disadvantages of a weak government, evolving ideas about constitutional administration a century later coalesced around a particular idea: the need for strong elected executives. Frederick Cleveland argued, "We have purposely deprived ourselves of responsible executive leadership for fear we shall not be able to control it."[23]

The question was whether elected executives had the capacity to administer the rapidly expanding scope and reach of their governments. As was the case with government under the Articles of Confederation, public administration had no centralized authority to lead and coordinate governmental activities. Budgeting was done by Congress by processes that were rather ad hoc, and the president had little or no influence over why, how much, and for what Congress allocated resources to the executive branch. Public administrators had no need to appeal to the president for political support for their budgets.

---

[v]See, for example, Aaron Wildavsky, *The Politics of the Budgetary Process, 2nd edition* (Boston, MA: Little, Brown, 1974); Robert T. Golembiewski and Jack Rabin, eds., *Public Budgeting and Finance, Fourth Edition* (New York, NY: Marcel Dekker, 1997); Irene S. Rubin, *The Politics of Public Budget: Getting and Spending, Borrowing and Balancing* (Chatham, NJ: Chatham House, 1990); Robert L. Bland and Irene S. Rubin, *Budgeting: A Guide for Local Governments* (Washington, DC: International City/County Management Association, 1997); Allen Schick, *The Federal Budget: Politics, Policy, Process, Revised Edition* (Washington, DC: Brookings Institution, 2000); and the journal *Public Budgeting and Finance.*

The Budget and Accounting Act of 1921, a presidential initiative enacted by Congress, institutionalized the executive budget and for the first time put the president, by virtue of his role in budgeting, in a position of authority over the entire government, albeit under the watchful eye of Congress and the newly created GAO. The process of assembling, reviewing, and presenting the budget requests of federal departments and agencies to Congress would thereafter be supervised by a newly created Bureau of the Budget (now the OMB).

Traditional executive budgets were categorized in terms of inputs or **objects of expenditure**, that is, the types of goods and services purchased or paid for by budgeted funds: salaries and wages, capital outlays, utilities, and the like. The main purpose of this type of accounting was to enable audits of compliance with applicable budgetary laws. The categories (also called **line items**) could be subdivided into more specific objects, or they could be aggregated by program, activity, or agency.

In the decades following World War II, policymakers became increasingly interested in being able to account for the results or outputs of spending budgeted inputs. Beginning in 1960, Secretary of Defense Robert S. McNamara implemented a Planning-Programming-Budgeting System (PPBS). Rather than reviewing the department's budget solely in terms of inputs aggregated by the three military services, McNamara's PPBS enabled him to review the types of military capabilities for which funds were being budgeted: strategic nuclear forces, ground combat forces, and tactical air forces. President Lyndon Johnson was so impressed with McNamara's PPBS-based presentations of military budget issues that in August, 1965, he ordered all federal departments and agencies to adopt planning and budgeting systems similar to McNamara's.[24]

The idea that analytic approaches to policy planning and budgeting were useful to policymakers caught on, and public policy analysis and research are now staples of policy deliberations at all levels of government. In 1974, in an effort to match the executive branch's ability to present budget proposals in terms of the results to be achieved and their costs, Congress created a budget process to govern the formulation of budget legislation. At the same time it created the Congressional Budget Office (CBO) to support that process. In addition, the GAO and the Congressional Research Service (CRS) began strengthening their analytic capabilities.[25]

While many in and out of government were attracted to and motivated by the ideals of program budgeting, there was no political will to redesign the existing accounting system. The traditional input-oriented format for presenting the president's budget to Congress and for executing enacted budget legislation was preserved.

Though traditional object-of-expenditure accounting remains a foundation of federal budgeting, a steady evolution toward output-oriented policymaking is evident in federal planning and budgeting processes. The evidence "can be found in the president's annual budget submission, which includes a variety of analytical perspectives, in the documents produced by agencies in compliance with the Government Performance and Results Act (GPRA, discussed in Chapter 6), and in the reports of the CBO and GAO. This evidence is the cumulative result of efforts over the years to reform federal budget administration."[26]

The Budget Process

The current process of creating a budget for the federal government takes approximately 18 months.[vi] Under the supervision of the OMB, this process begins with the executive branch developing the president's annual budget

---

[vi]See "The Executive Budget Process: An Overview" published by the Congressional Research Service. GAO's Glossary of Terms Used in the Federal Budget Process, Appendix II. http://www.gao.gov/new.items/d05734sp.pdf.

request for federal departments and agencies. It submits this request to Congress, which reviews and appropriates funds. Then, the executive branch executes enacted appropriations and other budgetary legislation.

States and local governments follow similar processes.[vii,27] They involve development of an executive budget proposal by the jurisdictions' elected executive, review of the proposal and enactment of budgetary legislation by legislative entities, and administration of the lawfully enacted budget by the executive branch. Figure 5.1 is a flow chart of the budget process followed by the State of Idaho, for example. The City of Chicago publishes a calendar depicting the budgetary process on a month-by-month basis.[viii]

Budget Accounting

The federal government comprises many different organizational entities, each with its own mission or purpose. It serves many political constituencies, stakeholders, and interests. Financial information generated by federal entities must be able to serve multiple purposes.

A complex system of accounting underlies the U.S. federal budget process:

- Congress determines the basic **account classification** system for the federal budget: what funds are intended to pay for or accomplish.
- Congressional **appropriations**, the most basic form of **budget authority**, are made in terms of this classification system.
- These accounts contain the amounts that are available for **obligation** by federal government administrators.[ix]
- Obligations (or the authority to enter into obligations, such as contracts or the hiring of personnel) become actual outlays or **expenditures** as funds are disbursed from the U.S. Treasury according to the purposes to be served by the account.
- An appropriation account "typically encompasses a number of activities or projects and may be subject to restrictions or conditions applicable to only the account, the appropriation act, titles within an appropriation act, other appropriation acts, or the government as a whole."[28]
- An **apportionment** by the OMB "divides appropriated amounts available for obligation by specific periods (usually quarters), activities, projects, objects, or a combination thereof."
- An apportionment "may be further subdivided by an agency into **allotments, suballotments,** and **allocations**."[x] In the end, a law called the **purpose statute** states that "appropriations shall be applied only to the objects for which the appropriations were made."[29]
- Each appropriation account carries an 11-digit **classification code** assigned by the OMB. "These codes are used to store and access data in the budget database and run computer reports."[30] The codes permit analysis of data by agency (departments, independent agencies, and instrumentalities of the U.S. government);

[vii]A summary of the budget processes in the states is published by the National Association of State Budget Officers.

[viii]City of Chicago budget process, http://www.cityofchicago.org/city/en/depts/obm/provdrs/city_budg.html.

[ix]A distinction is made between *permanent programs*, prominently including all entitlements, and *discretionary programs*. The former are subject to a single process of authorization and appropriation; the latter are subject to a two-step process involving two distinct subprocesses for authorization and appropriation.

[x]Government Accountability Office, "A Glossary of Terms Used in the Federal Budget Process," 12. In apportioning any account, some funds may be reserved to provide for contingencies or to effect savings made possible pursuant to the Antideficiency Act.

FIGURE 5.1   **State of Idaho Budget Process**

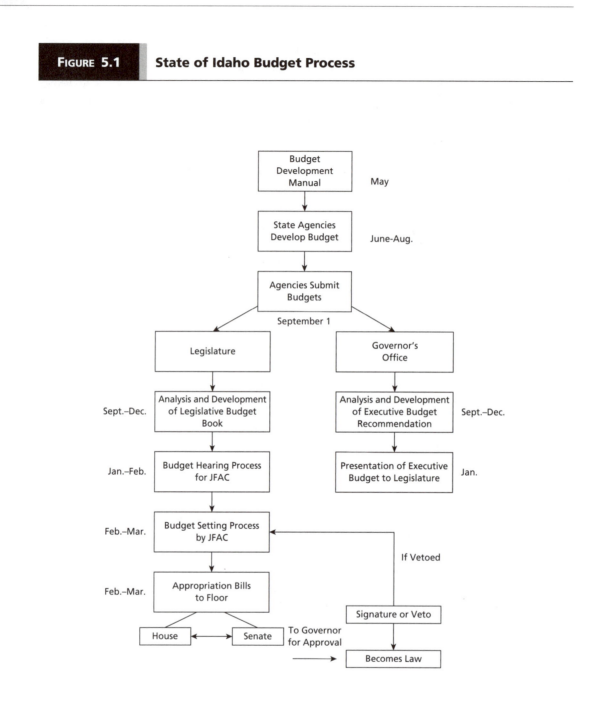

appropriation account; the timing of expenditures; type of fund (general, special, revolving, trust, etc.); and category (or subfunction) into which money in an account has been apportioned.

- The federal budget process produces a big-picture analysis of federal budget data based on the **functional classification system**. The GAO describes this system as "a way of grouping budgetary resources so that all budget authority and outlays of . . . federal entities and **tax expenditures** [revenue losses attributable to federal tax laws] can be presented according to national needs being addressed," such as national defense, international affairs, energy, and agriculture.[31]

- Functions are further divided into **subfunctions**; thus, "agriculture" has subfunctions such as "farm income stabilization" and "agricultural research and services." The functional and subfunctional totals are aggregates of functional budgetary allocations by all government agencies and organizations.

The picture that emerges is only a rough approximation of resources allocated to each need, though, because "each federal activity is placed in a single functional classification that best defines the activity's most important purpose even though many activities serve more than one purpose."[32] To determine how much is spent on achieving a particular policy result such as reduction of poverty or job creation, judgments are required: What kinds of government activity serve those goals? Which coded budget data are relevant? Often, no single objective answer to each question exists, and thus, different judgments will produce different answers regarding expenditures.

Congressional members and their staff members, auditors, and policy analysts can use the coded budget data for many different purposes and analyses. Congress and its committees seek to monitor federal spending and evaluate the need for budget increases or reductions. Auditors such as those in GAO will want to know if agencies are complying with budgetary statutes. Managers of federal entities need information on the benefits and costs of their programs. Policy analysts and program evaluators in agencies, think tanks, and academia want to know what government funds are accomplishing and seek to understand the effects of federal budgets on economic growth and equity, public debt, and social welfare and equity.[33]

Table 5.1 shows an excerpt of federal outlays across years by function and subfunction. Table 5.2 shows budget authority by function based on data from the president's 2015 budget.

PUBLIC PERSONNEL SYSTEMS: PROTECTION, PERFORMANCE, CONTROL

Public personnel systems that govern the hiring, compensation, training, promotion, disciplining, and termination of employees in public organizations are important structures constraining managerial flexibility in human resources administration.[xi] The federal civil service system and the personnel systems of states, cities, counties, and school districts are, as public administration scholar Patricia W. Ingraham observes,

---

[xi]Examples of sources with comprehensive discussions of personnel issues include: Sally Coleman Selden, *Human Capital: Tools and Strategies for the Public Sector* (Washington, DC: CQ Press, 2008); Donald F. Kettl, *The Politics of the Administrative Process* fifth ed. (Washington, DC: CQ Press, 2005), Part III: People in Government Organizations (pp. 231–314); and Katherine C. Naff, Norma M. Riccucci, and Siegrun Fox Freyss, *Personnel Management in Government: Politics and Process,* 7th ed. (Boca Raton, FL: CRC Press, 2013).

TABLE 5.1 Federal Outlays by Function and Subfunction (Excerpt)

Function and Subfunction	2012	2013	2014 estimate	2015 estimate	2016 estimate	2017 estimate	2018 estimate	2019 estimate
400 Transportation:								
401 Ground transportation	61,308	60,005	62,673	66,631	72,658	75,963	75,946	74,294
402 Air transportation	21,725	21,464	21,647	20,625	19,067	19,073	18,678	18,902
403 Water transportation	9,650	9,774	10,488	10,163	10,158	10,169	10,306	10,502
407 Other transportation	336	430	711	406	426	437	445	458
Total, Transportation	93,019	91,673	95,519	97,825	102,309	105,642	105,375	104,156
450 Community and Regional Development:								
451 Community development	8,769	7,814	12,040	9,775	12,557	13,516	9,001	5,498
452 Area and regional development	4,424	1,540	4,236	4,302	3,130	2,938	3,095	3,303
453 Disaster relief and insurance	11,939	22,982	17,029	14,788	10,068	7,944	6,051	5,396
Total, Community and Regional Development	25,132	32,336	33,305	28,865	25,755	24,398	18,147	14,197
500 Education, Training, Employment, and Social Services:								
501 Elementary, secondary, and vocational education	47,492	42,407	45,489	42,062	41,986	43,271	45,944	48,299
502 Higher education	12,113	-525	22,659	37,497	34,152	37,499	40,304	41,716
503 Research and general education aids	3,704	3,705	3,575	3,530	3,589	3,656	3,729	3,805
504 Training and employment	7,779	7,271	7,804	12,928	12,314	8,610	7,874	7,808
505 Other labor services	1,868	1,888	1,878	1,978	1,987	2,035	2,075	2,121
506 Social services	17,867	18,062	19,055	19,355	19,329	19,776	20,181	20,579
Total, Education, Training, Employment, and Social Services	90,823	72,808	100,460	117,350	113,357	114,847	120,107	124,328
550 Health:								
551 Health Care Services	308,160	321,849	412,526	475,325	512,505	541,440	559,628	589,019
552 Health research and training	34,502	32,881	33,523	31,903	32,090	32,119	32,700	33,931
554 Consumer and occupational health and safety	4,080	3,685	4,746	4,965	4,826	4,983	5,131	5,047

Function and Subfunction	2012	2013	2014 estimate	2015 estimate	2016 estimate	2017 estimate	2018 estimate	2019 estimate
Total, Health	346,742	358,315	450,795	512,193	549,421	578,542	597,459	627,997
570 Medicare:								
571 Medicare	471,793	497,826	519,027	532,324	574,888	581,436	594,983	654,127
600 Income Security:								
601 General retirement and disability insurance (excluding social security)	7,760	6,969	9,011	8,421	8,665	8,138	8,311	8,864
602 Federal employee retirement and disability	122,388	131,739	137,321	141,789	148,319	148,874	148,822	158,029
603 Unemployment compensation	93,771	70,729	63,983	51,038	45,447	46,060	47,107	48,491
604 Housing assistance	47,948	46,087	49,051	51,580	50,441	51,008	49,892	48,955
605 Food and nutrition assistance	106,871	109,706	108,397	106,883	106,438	105,673	105,489	105,635
609 Other income security	162,606	170,681	174,474	176,252	189,982	188,845	188,334	200,266
Total, Income Security	541,344	536,511	542,237	535,963	549,292	548,598	547,955	570,240
650 Social Security:								
651 Social security	773,290	813,551	857,319	903,196	952,022	1,007,997	1,067,597	1,131,060
(On-budget)	(140,387)	(56,009)	(26,204)	(32,388)	(35,274)	(38,811)	(42,391)	(46,076)
(Off-budget)	(632,903)	(757,542)	(831,115)	(870,808)	(916,748)	(969,186)	(1,025,206)	(1,084,984)
700 Veterans Benefits and Services:								
701 Income security for veterans	55,899	65,890	73,311	79,160	90,221	88,056	86,862	99,350
702 Veterans education, training, and rehabilitation	10,402	12,893	13,523	14,400	16,127	16,200	16,408	17,776
703 Hospital and medical care for veterans.	50,588	52,544	55,404	57,353	60,439	61,722	62,778	63,896
704 Veterans housing	1,413	1,328	2,096	332	433	523	1,225	1,297
705 Other veterans benefits and services	6,293	6,283	6,831	7,279	7,433	7,545	7,698	7,867
Total, Veterans Benefits and Services	124,595	138,938	151,165	158,524	174,653	174,046	174,971	190,186

Source: Excerpt from Table 3.2—"Outlays by Function and Subfunction: 1962–2019" in Office of Management and Budget, *Fiscal Year 2015: Historical Tables: Budget of the U.S. Government* (Washington, DC: U.S. Government Printing Office, 2014), p. 79, https://www.whitehouse.gov/sites/default/files/omb/budget/fy2015/assets/hist.pdf.

Note: In millions of dollars.

TABLE 5.2 Budget Authority by Function in the Adjusted Baseline

Function	2013 Actual	Estimate										
		2014	2015	2016	2017	2018	2019	2020	2021	2022	2023	2024
National Defense:												
Department of Defense–Military	585.2	586.9	589.5	593.1	607.3	621.8	636.3	651.9	667.1	736.0	754.0	772.3
Other	24.9	26.7	26.7	26.7	27.2	27.8	28.3	28.9	29.4	32.6	33.3	33.9
Total, National Defense	610.1	613.6	616.2	619.8	634.5	649.6	664.6	680.7	696.5	768.6	787.3	806.3
International Affairs	40.6	38.5	40.7	43.8	46.1	48.9	52.6	55.3	56.6	58.5	61.2	62.6
General Science, Space, and Technology	28.0	29.4	29.9	30.6	31.2	31.9	32.6	33.3	34.0	34.8	35.5	36.3
Energy	8.4	8.4	7.5	5.7	4.6	4.2	3.9	4.0	4.6	4.3	3.9	4.0
Natural Resources and Environment	41.0	37.0	38.0	39.0	40.6	41.7	42.7	44.2	45.2	46.3	47.7	48.6
Agriculture	27.4	24.8	18.0	24.4	27.9	26.7	20.3	20.6	20.5	20.3	20.7	20.8
Commerce and Housing Credit	−36.5	−62.9	−8.4	−5.0	−5.1	−6.2	−0.5	2.8	5.5	7.0	8.8	10.3
On-Budget	(−36.5)	(−63.2)	(−8.4)	(−5.3)	(−5.4)	(−6.5)	(−0.7)	(−2.5)	(−5.2)	(−6.7)	(−8.5)	(−10.0)
Off-Budget	(0.3)	(0.3)	(*)	(0.3)	(0.3)	(0.3)	(0.3)	(0.3)	(0.3)	(0.3)	(0.3)	(0.3)
Transportation	99.3	86.9	87.7	89.6	91.7	93.7	95.8	98.0	100.2	102.5	104.9	108.8
Community and Regional Development	51.1	17.9	13.0	12.7	12.8	13.7	14.0	14.2	14.7	15.0	15.3	15.5
Education, Training, Employment, and Social Services	71.2	91.3	96.4	107.3	112.4	116.7	120.1	122.6	125.2	128.4	130.5	132.1
Health	339.0	444.8	520.0	540.9	569.9	595.6	628.3	670.5	693.4	730.0	768.1	810.1
Medicare	507.8	525.1	535.4	586.6	603.2	624.3	689.7	742.3	798.8	888.6	923.9	957.4

| | | | | | | | Estimate | | | | | |
Function	2013 Actual	2014	2015	2016	2017	2018	2019	2020	2021	2022	2023	2024
Income Security	533.6	529.4	527.0	537.7	544.7	552.1	572.1	584.8	598.7	617.7	627.0	634.6
Social Security	816.5	860.8	905.4	956.1	1,012.7	1,073.3	1,137.8	1,206.1	1,274.8	1,348.8	1,427.7	1,511.8
On-Budget	(55.9)	(26.0)	(32.0)	(35.3)	(38.8)	(42.4)	(46.1)	(49.9)	(53.7)	(57.8)	(62.2)	(66.6)
Off-Budget	(760.6)	(834.8)	(873.4)	(920.8)	(973.9)	(1,030.9)	(1,091.7)	(1,156.2)	(1,221.1)	(1,291.0)	(1,365.5)	(1,445.3)
Veterans Benefits and Services	136.6	151.3	161.6	169.5	176.4	185.7	194.4	203.4	212.6	222.3	232.1	242.1
Administration of Justice	51.7	54.6	67.0	58.2	61.3	61.0	62.6	64.3	66.0	67.8	69.6	74.7
General Government	26.0	24.9	24.8	25.3	25.8	26.6	27.3	28.0	28.8	29.6	30.4	31.1
Net Interest	220.9	223.0	251.4	317.7	393.3	479.6	563.0	635.2	697.4	761.2	826.8	886.1
On-Budget	(326.5)	(323.3)	(347.6)	(410.6)	(485.3)	(571.2)	(654.3)	(725.4)	(787.8)	(847.8)	(911.1)	(967.9)
Off-Budget	(−105.7)	(−100.2)	(−96.2)	(−93.0)	(−92.0)	(−91.6)	(−91.2)	(−90.2)	(−90.4)	(−86.6)	(−84.3)	(−81.8)
Allowances		7.5	−30.1	−59.8	−54.6	−56.4	−57.3	−59.5	−62.5	−30.2	−31.4	−8.4
Undistributed Offsetting Receipts:												
Employer share, employee retirement (on-budget)	−65.2	−63.8	−66.2	−66.9	−70.3	−71.7	−73.5	−75.6	−77.8	−80.1	−82.4	−84.9
Employer share, employee retirement (off-budget)	−16.2	−15.7	−16.0	−16.7	−17.3	−17.9	−18.8	−19.6	−20.4	−21.3	−22.0	−22.7

(Continued)

TABLE 5.2 (Continued)

Function	2013 Actual	Estimate 2014	2015	2016	2017	2018	2019	2020	2021	2022	2023	2024
Rents and royalties on the Outer Continental Shelf	−8.9	−8.2	−8.2	−8.1	−7.5	−7.1	−7.3	−7.5	−7.8	−8.1	−8.4	−8.3
Sale of major assets	−2.6											
Other undistributed offsetting receipts		−0.7	−3.6	−10.6	−8.8	−6.2	−2.1	−0.3	−0.3	−0.2	−0.1	
Total Undistributed Offsetting Receipts	−92.8	−88.4	−94.0	−102.3	−103.8	−102.9	−101.7	−103.0	−106.3	−109.8	−113.0	−116.0
On-Budget	(−76.6)	(−72.7)	(−77.9)	(−85.6)	(−86.6)	(−85.0)	(−82.9)	(−83.4)	(−85.9)	(−88.5)	(−91.0)	(−93.3)
Off-Budget	(−16.2)	(−15.7)	(−16.0)	(−16.7)	(−17.3)	(−17.9)	(18.8)	(−19.6)	(−20.4)	(−21.3)	(−22.0)	(−22.7)
Total	**3,479.7**	**3,617.8**	**3,807.6**	**3,997.7**	**4,225.7**	**4,459.6**	**4,762.6**	**5,047.8**	**5,304.7**	**5,711.7**	**5,976.9**	**6,268.8**
On-Budget	(2,841.0)	(2,898.7)	(3,046.5)	(3.186.3)	(3,360.7)	(3,537.9)	(3,780.6)	(4,001.0)	(4,194.1)	(4,528.3)	(4,717.4)	(4,927.8)
Off-Budget	(638.8)	(719.1)	(761.1)	(811.4)	(865.0)	(921.7)	(982.0)	(1,046.8)	(1,110.6)	(1,183.4)	(1,259.5)	(1,341.0)
MEMORANDUM												
Discretionary budget authority:												
National Defense	600.4	606.0	608.1	611.6	626.4	641.3	656.3	672.3	688.3	760.4	779.1	797.9
International affairs	51.9	50.7	51.8	52.9	54.1	55.3	56.5	57.7	58.9	60.2	61.5	62.8
Domestic	484.0	470.7	444.1	441.9	452.2	463.0	476.0	487.8	499.5	547.5	561.4	575.5
Total, discretionary	1,136.3	1,127.4	1,104.0	1,106.4	1,132.7	1,159.6	1,188.7	1,217.7	1,246.7	1,368.1	1,401.9	1,436.2

Source: Table 25–10, "Budget Authority by Function in the Adusted Baseline," in Office of Management and Budget, *Fiscal Year 2015: Budget of the U.S. Government: Technical Budget Analyses* (Washington, DC: U.S. Government Printing Office, 2014), p. 391, https://www.whitehouse.gov/sites/default/files/omb/budget/fy2015/assets/technical_analyses.pdf.

Note: In billions of dollars.

often built upon both legal and bureaucratic rules and processes, [and] they are rather Byzantine [that is, nontransparent or confusing] structures and systems, involving many pages of rules and regulations, multiple processes for consultation and appeal (for employees), and substantial separation from political and other external authority.[34]

Personnel systems, together with the provisions of collective bargaining agreements with public employee unions, have been defined largely by their structural features rather than by their role in promoting good government. A standard complaint of public managers is that these systems prevent them from managing effectively. That has not always been the case.

As discussed in Chapter 2, throughout most of America's first century, public employees were chosen by elected officials according to political party affiliation and personal loyalty. Few rules governed their conduct in office, and government jobs were often exploited for personal gain or self-promotion. Following his election as president in 1828, the populist Andrew Jackson initiated a significant, whole-of-government public management reform, arguably the first effort at large-scale reform initiated by the federal executive branch.

> Personnel systems, together with the provisions of collective bargaining agreements with public employee unions, have been defined largely by their structural features rather than by their role in promoting good government.

Jackson's **spoils system** (to the victor belong the privileges of appointing officeholders) consisted of firing and hiring public officials with each change of the political party in power. This system replaced the elitist personnel practices of the Federalists who, more in the English style, preferred government by "gentlemen" of breeding and property. The spoils system dominated nineteenth-century selection and control of administrators (or "clerks," as they were then known), and the oversight of administration was exercised haphazardly by legislators, political parties, and the courts.

Protection: The Civil Service System

Following the Civil War, industrialization, urbanization, and immigration began to transform American society and to strengthen middle-class elites, who viewed spoils-ridden government as corrupt, incompetent, and an impediment to prosperity. In his famous 1887 academic essay, "The Study of Administration," political scientist and future president Woodrow Wilson memorably condemned the "poisonous atmosphere of city government, the crooked secrets of state administration, the confusion, sinecurism, and corruption ever and again discovered in the bureaux at Washington."[35] Promoted by academically oriented activists, the emerging administrative state reflected a number of currents in American thought: a progressive political agenda, the growing authority of science and of the idea of management, the professional development of administrative law, and a spirit of pragmatic empiricism.

The groundwork for change at the federal level was laid by the civil service reform movement, with the milestone Pendleton Civil Service Reform Act of 1883 (named after its legislative sponsor). This legislation created the U.S. Civil Service Commission and initiated the trend toward merit-based civil service protected from political reprisals by tenure in office.[36] Subsequent developments further strengthened and institutionalized the civil service system:

- The Classification Act of 1923 established a consistent system across the government for hiring and pay.
- The Hatch Act of 1939 ("An Act to Prevent Pernicious Political Activities") prohibited almost all executive branch employees from engaging in partisan political activity.

- The Classification Act of 1949 established the General Schedule (GS), for federal employees. It has 15 pay grades and ten steps within each grade.
- The Civil Service Reform Act of 1978 created the Senior Executive Service (SES) for executive branch civil servants. There were almost 8,000 SES positions in 2013, which could in principle be reallocated among agencies as needed to redistribute their incumbents' skills and experience.[37]

The federal civil service system includes "all appointive positions in the executive, judicial, and legislative branches of the Government of the United States, except positions in the uniformed services."[38] The federal civil service consists of three types of services:

- the **competitive service** in which the "individual must go through a competitive process (i.e. competitive examining) which is open to all applicants. This process may consist of a written test, an evaluation of the individual's education and experience, and/or an evaluation of other attributes necessary for successful performance in the position to be filled."[xii] Individuals in this group are civilian employees mainly in the executive branch, covered by the merit system;
- the **excepted service**, which includes most of the positions in the legislative branch and judicial branch. In addition, certain positions or entire organizations are in the excepted service by statute, for example, the Central Intelligence Agency, the Foreign Service, the Federal Bureau of Investigation, the U.S. Postal Service, and certain positions in the Department of Veterans Affairs and the Department of Defense; and
- the **Senior Executive Service** (SES) appointees to two types of positions: career reserved positions, which must be filled only by career appointees; and general positions, which may be filled by any appointee, whether career, noncareer, or limited (up to 3 years for "term" and up to 18 months for "emergency").

The civil service in the executive branch is administered by the Office of Personnel Management (OPM) in accordance with law found in Title 5 of the U.S. Code of Federal Regulations. The Civil Service Reform Act of 1978 requires the OPM to "hold managers and human resources officials accountable for efficient and effective human resources management in support of agency missions in accordance with Merit System Principles."[39] The enforcement function—holding officials accountable— is performed by three agencies:

- The Merit System Protection Board (MSPB), an independent, quasi-judicial agency of the executive branch. The "MSPB carries out its statutory responsibilities and authorities primarily by adjudicating individual employee appeals and by conducting merit systems studies. In addition, MSPB reviews the significant actions of the OPM to assess the degree to which those actions may affect merit."[40]
- The Office of Special Counsel (OSC) investigates allegations that an agency has committed a prohibited personnel practice. It may appeal to the MSPB to seek disciplinary or corrective action for a prohibited personnel practice it identifies.
- The Equal Employment Opportunity Commission (EEOC) makes the final administrative decision on claims that an agency has committed unlawful employment discrimination.

[xii]"Hiring Authorities: Background," U.S. Office of Personnel Management, accessed May 22, 2015, www.opm.gov.

The civil service system is enormously complex, with voluminous regulations governing its administration. As just one example, the GS system identifies hundreds of positions, classified on the basis of that position's complexity and degree of responsibility. Each grade includes scientific, engineering, accounting, medical, and other professions along with administrators, technicians, and clerical positions. Positions at the same grade across these professions are deemed to be of equal rank regardless of the complexity of the tasks, and they are paid within the same relatively narrow range. Navigating the civil service regulations in order to hire, pay, promote, or terminate public employees can be dauntingly difficult.

Not surprisingly, the civil service system has been a target of reformers who believe its complexity and inflexibility undermine the efficiency and effectiveness of governments. A 1983 report of the White House Science Council's Federal Laboratory Review Panel stated, "The inability of many Federal Laboratories—especially those under civil service constraints—to attract, retain, and motivate qualified scientists and engineers is alarming. The personnel problem is most serious at government-owned, government-operated laboratories (GOGO's) [and] . . . if not corrected will seriously threaten their vitality."[41] Citing a 1988 Office of Personnel Management publication, the 1993 *Creating a Government that Works Better and Costs Less* insisted that "anecdotal mistakes prompted additional rules. When the rules led to new inequities, even more rules were added. Over time . . . a maze of regulations and requirements was created, hamstringing managers . . . often impeding federal managers and employees from achieving their missions and from giving the public a high quality of service."[42]

To avoid the structural constraints imposed by personnel systems, public policymakers and managers have resorted to an increasing extent to the contracting out of public service delivery and of planning and management functions (discussed later in this chapter and in Chapter 6) and to reliance on part-time workers and independent contractors who are not governed by the full panoply of personnel rules or eligible for a full range of benefits.

By eroding the significance of the protection principle, these reforms pose a threat to the morale and commitment of public employees to the values of public service. What is gained in managerial flexibility may come at the cost of lower employee quality and dedication to agency missions. Opposition to these reforms is voiced by employees, unions, and legislators who favor employee rights and protection and who emphasize the need for constraining managerial discretion.

Reform of public personnel practices continues to be on agendas of legislators and public managers of governments at all levels.

Performance: Measuring and Paying for Results

As pressures for greater governmental efficiency and performance have mounted, the management of people has been more commonly referred to as **human resource management** or **human capital management**. These terms reflect a shift in emphasis from a rule-based approach of managing employees exemplified by civil service systems to an approach that "lets managers manage" by removing constraints on how they do their jobs. Reforms to personnel systems have introduced flexibility, managerial discretion, decentralization of authority over personnel matters, and performance-based pay.[43]

Performance-based pay, or **pay for performance**, reforms, refer to "a broad spectrum of compensation systems that can be clustered under two general categories: merit pay plans and variable pay plans, which include both individual and group incentive plans."[44] These systems are based on the idea that monetary incentives prompt greater employee effort and thus higher performance and productivity.

The effectiveness of performance-based pay systems has been a matter of some debate. Proponents argue that such systems are an improvement on tenure-based pay systems because they provide employees with explicit and meaningful incentives and feedback and ultimately improve organizational performance.[xiii] Yet pay for performance may only be effective when certain conditions are met relating to the structure of work, the culture of the organization, and the nature of the external environment,[xiv] for example, when the work task is well-defined and its successful performance is observable and easily measured and when employee motives are driven by absolute levels of income, not relative pay to others in the organization.

A review of performance-related pay research by public administration scholars James Perry and So Yun Jun concluded that "performance-related pay in the public sector consistently fails to deliver on its promise" for several reasons: performance-based pay system have failed to change employee motivations, in part because public employees are more service- than pay-oriented; context matters (such systems have had positive results in medical contexts but not in the regulatory and finance sectors); and the incentives are more effective at lower levels in an organization where job expectations are less ambiguous. For these and other reasons, legislatively imposed, one-size-fits-all performance-related pay systems may not achieve their promise because they fail to allow for the complexity of organizational, human, and contextual variability.[45]

Yet policymakers persist in their faith in performance-based pay for civil servants despite the absence of evidence that it leads to better performance.[46] Causal arguments that have enough validity to convince scholars of this may fail to move policymakers because such arguments do not readily translate into a convincing political argument. Government performance may have multiple, complex determinants, but rewarding measured performance is an easily grasped idea with popular appeal.[47]

Example: Pay for Performance in K-12 Teacher Salaries

The following excerpt from a Florida state law describes performance-based salary schedules for public school teachers in that state:

> By July 1, 2014, the district school board shall adopt a performance salary schedule that provides annual salary adjustments for instructional personnel and school administrators based upon performance determined under s. 1012.34. Employees hired on or after July 1, 2014, or employees who choose to move from the grandfathered salary schedule to the performance salary schedule, shall be compensated pursuant to the performance salary schedule once they have received the appropriate performance evaluation for this purpose.

[xiii]See, for example, Howard Risher, *Pay for Performance: A Guide for Federal Managers* (Washington, DC: IBM Center for the Business of Government, 2004); and George T. Milkovich and Alexandra K. Wigdor, ed., *Pay for Performance: Evaluating Performance Appraisal and Merit Pay* (Washington DC: National Research Council, 1991).

[xiv]See, for example, Iris Bohnet and Susan C. Eaton, "Does Performance Pay Perform? Conditions for Success in the Public Sector," in *For the People: Can We Fix Public Service?*, ed. John D. Donahue and Joseph S. Nye Jr. (Washington, DC: Brookings Institution Press, 2003): 238–254; and Milkovich and Wigdor, 1991.

a. Base salary. The base salary shall be established as follows:

(I) The base salary for instructional personnel or school administrators who opt into the performance salary schedule shall be the salary paid in the prior year, including adjustments only.

(II) Beginning July 1, 2014, instructional personnel or school administrators new to the district, returning to the district after a break in service without an authorized leave of absence, or appointed for the first time to a position in the district in the capacity of instructional personnel or school administrator shall be placed on the performance salary schedule.

b. Salary adjustments. Salary adjustments for highly effective or effective performance shall be established as follows:

(I) The annual salary adjustment under the performance salary schedule for an employee rated as highly effective must be greater than the highest annual salary adjustment available to an employee of the same classification through any other salary schedule adopted by the district.

(II) The annual salary adjustment under the performance salary schedule for an employee rated as effective must be equal to at least 50 percent and no more than 75 percent of the annual adjustment provided for a highly effective employee of the same classification.

(III) The performance salary schedule shall not provide an annual salary adjustment for an employee who receives a rating other than highly effective or effective for the year.[48]

Control: At-Will Employment

At the opposite end of the spectrum from civil service systems incorporating the protection principle are **at-will employment** contracts. In these systems, "an employer can terminate an employee at any time for any reason, except an illegal one, or for no reason without incurring legal liability. Likewise, an employee is free to leave a job at any time for any or no reason with no adverse legal consequences."[49]

At-will employment does not entitle an employer to violate laws protecting employees from discrimination unrelated to their ability to do their jobs. It does give employers far greater latitude and flexibility in making personnel decisions without being constrained by the exacting standards of fairness and due process followed in civil service systems. They may, for example, choose precise, measurable performance indicators of employee productivity or of the outputs and outcomes of an employee's organization on which to base rewards and punishments ranging from monetary bonuses to outright termination for below-standard performance.

The standard form of employer-employee relationship in the private sector, at-will employment contracts gained popularity in American state and local governments beginning in the 1990s among reformers advocating the replacement of tenure-and-seniority-based personnel systems featuring employment relationships that based hiring, compensation, promotion, and termination on employee or organizational performance.[50] At-will employment and pay-for-performance reforms have strong ideological appeal among voters and policymakers who have imbibed the belief, long popular in America (as noted in Chapter 1), that the corporate structures and practices were the gold standard for managing large, complex organizations.

> At-will employment and pay-for-performance reforms have strong ideological appeal among voters and policymakers who have imbibed the belief, long popular in America, that the corporate structures and practices were the gold standard for managing large, complex organizations.

The premise of at-will employment reforms is that they will increase the efficiency and productivity of public service delivery because public employees will have incentives to perform similar to those of workers in the for-profit sector. According to public administration scholars Jungin Kim and Edward Kellough,

> the expansion of at-will employment would make administrative sense if there was evidence that too few employees were terminated under traditional civil service systems or that the time needed to carry out terminations was seriously impeding organizational productivity. . . . there is no systematic empirical evidence, other than anecdotal stories, that either of these situations is true.[51]

The administration of at-will or performance-based systems can be problematic when measures of merit or performance are ambiguous or imprecise or when such measures do not cover all important aspects of the employee's work. Such circumstances can easily result in the kinds of political bargains and compromises described earlier in this chapter. The burden falls on public managers who must use their discretion and judgment to fill in the details of ambiguous legislation.

Example: At-Will Employment in the States

The State of Texas was the first to adopt a highly decentralized at-will employment system for public employees within the state.[52] Except when an explicit employment contract with a public entity exists, a public employee can be fired at any time for any legal reason.[53] A survey of personnel directors in the state found that while most of them thought at-will employment increased employee responsiveness to the objectives of public managers, it also made human resource administration more difficult and increased employee vulnerability to policies such as downsizing that had nothing to do with their job performance.[54]

Research on the consequences of at-will employment in states such as Georgia and Florida conclude that the benefits were probably not decisive and that adverse consequences also occurred. More recent research on the perceptions and attitudes of human resource professionals in states with at-will employment suggests that while commitment to such systems is favorable, views of its actual consequences, both positive and negative, vary widely and thus are generally inconclusive.

Statistical analysis of responses to a 2010 survey of 280 agency human resource managers in six states revealed that, while attitudes are mixed, agency managers are more likely to have positive attitudes toward at-will employment. Negative views were more likely among human resource managers who thought at-will employment could extend the reach of political patronage.[55]

Example: Bush Administration Personnel Reforms

At the federal level, the concept of at-will employment made its first appearance during the administration of President George W. Bush, which made determined efforts to replace the protection principle with systems combining performance with control.[56]

Through its **President's Management Agenda**, budget requests, and statements from OPM, the Bush Administration pushed for reform of SES pay and incentives. A system of six pay levels, infrequent bonuses, reputedly inflated performance ratings and salary caps on pay and bonuses was replaced in 2004 by provisions in the National Defense Authorization Act (PL 108-136) that replaced the pay levels with a single broad pay range, eliminated locality pay, raised the pay cap for all SES, and added a second higher cap for agencies that had a "certified performance appraisal system."[xv]

The National Defense Authorization Act (PL 108-136) also authorized the Department of Defense to develop a new personnel system, endorsing Secretary of Defense Donald Rumsfeld's argument that national security managers needed more control over how workers were paid, promoted, deployed, and disciplined to better fight the war on terror. The result was the National Security Personnel System (NSPS), which covered the more than 700,000 civilian employees of the Department of Defense (DoD). The final regulations governing administration of NSPS were published on November 1, 2005.[xvi] In January 2005, the Bush administration unveiled a new personnel system for the Department of Homeland Security (DHS), having obtained the authority to do so in the 2002 act creating DHS.[xvii] The system was intended to be a model for the rest of the federal government.

The NSPS featured a performance management system, including pay for performance and changes in procedures for staffing and workforce resizing; pay rates and systems; job classification; labor-management relations; and discipline, adverse actions, and employee appeals, although merit system principles and other features of the existing civil service system in some form would remain in force. According to one assessment, the NSPS would allow "more rigorous evaluation of employees by their managers, feedback on how to improve their performance and [use] employee job ratings to determine pay raises. Officials contend that the NSPS should increase accountability and make it more difficult for senior managers to avert their gaze when they see supervisors and employees who are not pulling their share of the load."[57]

Building on the DoD and DHS reforms, the Bush administration proposed the Working for America Act, which would have extended similar changes to the rest of the federal workforce. It emphasized performance management and, as the proposed act put it, "Results-Driven, Market-Based Compensation." The administration proposed to replace the 15 GS grades with broad pay bands and to set salaries according to occupation and local and national labor market rates, with job performance ratings influencing pay raises. It would have eliminated across-the-board pay increases that were unrelated to performance. Not all the Bush Administration's reform efforts gained traction. The courts threw out the key parts of the DoD and DHS system reforms primarily because they virtually eliminated employees' collective bargaining rights, thus preserving the protection principle. The Working for America Act was never enacted into law and has not revived in any form to date.

Public personnel systems and public budgeting processes are core components of direct government in the American system at federal, state, and local levels. These systems and processes are the quintessential bureaucratic structures: more often than not, they constrain rather than enable public managers.

[xv]L. Elaine Halchin, *Senior Executive System (SES) Pay for Performance System* (CRS Report No. RL33128) (Washington, DC: Congressional Research Service, 2007), 12. See also Maeve P. Carey, *The Senior Executive Service: Options and Background for Reform,* CRS Report No. R41801 (Washington, DC: Congressional Research Service, 2012).

[xvi]The regulations can be found at http://www.cpms.osd.mil/nsps/pdf/FinalNSPSFederalRegisterNotice.pdf. For an analysis of the process of designing the NSPS, see U.S. Governmental Accountability Office (GAO), *DOD's National Security Personnel System Faces Implementation Challenges* (GAO-05-730, July 2005).

[xvii]The Bush administration had been reluctant to create a new, sprawling bureaucracy. The price of overcoming this reluctance was congressional acquiescence in authorizing a personnel system for the department that, for the most part, was outside the traditional civil service framework. The text of the Homeland Security Act of 2002 is at http://news.findlaw.com/hdocs/docs/terrorism/hsa2002.pdf.

ALTERNATIVES TO DIRECT GOVERNMENT

In recent years, many public administration scholars have argued that direct government in advanced democracies is being supplemented or even replaced by collaborative arrangements among public and private organizations on behalf of achieving the goals of public policy.[58] The reason put forward for this trend is that traditional bureaucracies are no longer capable of meeting the complex managerial challenges presented by ambitious public policies.[59] The creativity, flexibility, and performance-orientation of the private sector are becoming, and should be, mobilized on behalf of societal goals.

A decision to turn over an existing function or activity to the private sector is termed **privatization**. If government provides funding for, but does not produce a good or service, the resulting use of a third party for the production is termed **contracting out** or **outsourcing**.[xviii] Governments may contract out the production of goods or services through arrangements with private sector entities, either for-profit or not-for-profit. Indeed, government contracts with private parties date back to the nineteenth century and have been relied on intermittently ever since. For example, in the late nineteenth century, a sophisticated awareness of the issues affecting public use of private charity had developed in the social work profession.[60]

> Civil society organizations, including those that are faith-based, and for-profit corporations have become agents, partners, and collaborators with public agencies because they have specialized skills, experience in particular localities, flexibility, and sense of mission that traditional government bureaucracy lacks.

Relationships between public and private sectors grew as government increased in size and in the reach of its responsibilities. Contracting out in social services began in earnest during the Kennedy and Johnson presidencies, in which there was not only a great expansion in the range of government supports for social services but also a strong emphasis on partnerships and cooperation with the private sector, especially the nonprofit sector. The trend toward financing privately provided services was given further impetus by the deinstitutionalization of state hospitals, state training schools, and public juvenile detention centers in favor of community-based counseling, training, and residential services. Civil society organizations, including those that are faith-based, and for-profit corporations have become agents, partners, and collaborators with public agencies because they have specialized skills, experience in particular localities, flexibility, and sense of mission that traditional government bureaucracy lacks.

The propensity for governments to contract out the production of goods and services has resulted in its own form of associated structures, referred to as **government by proxy**, **third party government**, **indirect government**, and the **hollow state**.[61] Research on tools of governance, third-party government, collaboration, and networks "has suffused the literature on both the study and practice of public administration."[62] H. Brinton Milward and Keith G. Provan describe the hollow state as

> any joint production situation where a governmental agency relies on others (firms, nonprofits, or other government agencies) to jointly deliver public services. Carried to extreme, it refers to a government that as

---

xviiiIn addition to the references cited in this section, see Steven J. Kelman, "Contracting," in *Beyond Privatizaion: The Tools of Government Action*, ed. Lester M. Salamon and Michael Lund (Washington DC: The Urban Institute Press, 1989), 282–318; Stephen Rathgeb Smith, "NGOs and Contracting," in *The Oxford Handbook of Public Management*, ed. E. Ferlie, L. E. Lynn, Jr., C. Pollitt (New York, NY, and Oxford, UK: Oxford University Press), 591–614; Jacques S. Gansler, *Moving Toward Market-Based Government: The Changing Role of Government as the Provider* (Arlington, VA: IBM Endowment for the Business of Government, 2003); Symposium on "Public Values in an Era of Privatization," *Harvard Law Review* 116, no. 5 (2003); John D. Donahue, *The Privatization Decision: Public Ends, Private Means* (New York, NY: Basic Books, 1989); and E. S. Savas, *Privatization and Public-Private Partnerships* (New York, NY: Chatham House, 2000).

a matter of public policy has chosen to contract out all its production capability to third parties, perhaps retaining only a systems integration function that is responsible for negotiating, monitoring, and evaluating contracts. . . . While hollowness varies from case to case, the central task of the hollow state does not—that is to arrange networks rather than to carry out the traditional task of government, which is to manage hierarchies.[63]

In an effort to determine the extent of the hollow state, public administration scholar Paul Light sought to measure the "true size of government" at the federal level, taking into account not only civil service, military, and postal service workers but also the number of contractors and grantees.[64] Light provides an interesting quantitative picture of the American administrative system, finding that between 1999 and 2005, the total number of federal contractor and grantee jobs grew by more than half, or 3.5 million jobs, to a total of 10.5 million jobs. This total was nearly four times the size of the federal civilian workforce, which remained stable during this period.[65]

Milward and Provan identified a number of problems with the hollowing out of the state:

- loss of managerial control over agents,
- loss of political control to organized contractor interests,
- substitution of self-interest for the public interest in service delivery,
- weakened or confused accountability to citizens and legislatures,
- lower service quality,
- creation of organizations dependent on public funds, and
- goal displacement in nonprofit sector.[66]

Yet views on hollowing out differ. Some are concerned that "extra-formal democracy"[xix] undermines traditional forms of democratic accountability.[67] Others argue that the debureaucratization of authority over publicly financed services enhances democratic legitimacy because it increases transparency, responsiveness, and citizen participation in setting priorities and evaluating results.[68] Still others view traditional direct government and the newer consociational structures and practices as complementary or that direct government is necessary for the newer structures to be effective and legitimate in the eyes of policymakers and citizens.[69]

Underlying these debates regarding the shift from direct to indirect government is the concept of **organizational form,** that is, whether an organization is public, private for-profit, private nonprofit, or a hybrid of these types of ownership. Organizational form is a fundamental structural characteristic that may determine particular types of preferences, activities, and incentives motivating managers, workers, and service providers. Nonprofits are private sector organizations that are prohibited by law from distributing surpluses of revenues over expenditures to any group of stakeholders (a characteristic feature of these nonprofit organizations known as the **nondistribution constraint**). Moreover, while government and business management share some similarities, they are also characterized by differences in what they do and how they do it, as discussed in Chapter 1.

The first section below discusses frameworks for considering when direct government is most appropriate. The following section discusses quasi-public organizations, which have the characteristics of both public and

---

[xix]See Chris Skelcher, "Fishing in Muddy Waters: Principals, Agents, and Democratic Governance in Europe." *Journal of Public Administration Research and Theory* 20, no. 6 (2010). For further discussion and illustration of this point, he explains, for example, that mechanisms of extra-formal democracy "supplement the more traditional process of periodic election and any constitutional provisions for citizens' initiatives or referenda on major proposals" (p. i164).

business organizations and, next, nonprofit organizations. Because organizational form can influence both the internal and external environments of managers who work in them, as well as managers in public sector organizations who interact with them, this section devotes considerable attention to the structural characteristic of the nonprofit organizational form.

When Is Direct Government Appropriate?

To determine whether direct government production is necessary or whether contracting out is the better choice, a first consideration is whether the activity is **inherently governmental**. OMB Circular A-76 describes an inherently governmental activity as

> an activity that is so intimately related to the public interest as to mandate performance by government personnel. These activities require the exercise of substantial discretion in applying government authority and/or in making decisions for the government. Inherently governmental activities normally fall into two categories: the exercise of sovereign government authority or the establishment of procedures and processes related to the oversight of monetary transactions or entitlements.

> An inherently governmental activity involves

> 1. Binding the United States to take or not to take some action by contract, policy, regulation, authorization, order, or otherwise;

> 2. Determining, protecting, and advancing economic, political, territorial, property, or other interests by military or diplomatic action, civil or criminal judicial proceedings, contract management, or otherwise; or

> 3. Significantly affecting the life, liberty, or property of private persons; or

> 4. Exerting ultimate control over the acquisition, use, or disposition of United States property (real or personal, tangible or intangible), including establishing policies or procedures for the collection, control, or disbursement of appropriated and other federal funds.[70]

Circular A-76 goes on to assert that "not every exercise of discretion is evidence that an activity is inherently governmental." An inherently governmental use of discretion

> commits the government to a course of action when two or more alternative courses of action exist and decision making is not already limited or guided by existing policies, procedures, directions, orders, and other guidance that (1) identify specified ranges of acceptable decisions or conduct and (2) subject the discretionary authority to final approval or regular oversight by agency officials.

On September 12, 2011, the Office of Federal Procurement Policy (OFPP) within the OMB issued its final policy letter on Performance of Inherently Governmental and Critical Functions. In addition to reiterating the Circular A-76 definition of "inherently governmental," it defined a critical function as one "that is necessary to the agency being able to effectively perform and maintain control of its mission and operations."[71] Examples of "inherently governmental" in the policy letter include

- the direct conduct of criminal investigation,
- the control of prosecutions and performance of adjudicatory functions (other than those relating to arbitration or other methods of alternative dispute resolution),
- the command of military forces, especially the leadership of military personnel who are performing a combat,
- combat support or combat service support role,
- the conduct of foreign relations and the determination of foreign policy,
- the selection or nonselection of individuals for federal government employment, including the interviewing of individuals for employment,
- participation as a voting member on any source selection board,
- determining prices to be fair and reasonable, and
- awarding contracts.

The OFPP Policy Letter provides a test of whether a task is an inherently governmental function. Tasks that are closely associated with inherently governmental functions are contractor duties that could expand to become inherently governmental functions.[72] The characteristics of inherently governmental activity just described are also evident in public administration scholar Christopher K. Leman's description of situations when direct government is appropriate:

- maintenance of some governmental capability is essential, such as in the case of the National Oceanographic and Atmospheric Administration and the National Aeronautics and Space Administration;
- the legitimate exercise of force is required, as in law enforcement functions and military operations;
- performance to a high standard cannot be left to chance, as in the case of airport security;
- considerations relating to equity in service provision and protection of civil rights predominate; and
- no effective private market exists or is likely to exist, which is often the case in rural or other underserved communities and locations.[73]

Whether direct government is appropriate may be largely a function of the law. The legal question is whether or not a private contractor may be considered a "state actor," that is, if there is a close nexus between the state and the challenged action that seemingly private behavior may be fairly treated as that of the state itself. This question, unfortunately, is a matter of opinion. Being heavily funded or heavily regulated by government are not necessarily criteria for determining whether service providers are state actors. But having a function considered "inherently governmental" would seem to be a reason to apply the state action doctrine.

Quangos and Government-Sponsored Enterprises

Half & Half

The quasi-autonomous nongovernmental organization, or **quango,** is a structural form that falls in the middle of the publicness spectrum, neither fully public nor fully private. This form is widespread in the United Kingdom, Ireland, and Australia, among other countries. Australia and Germany have relied on quangos regulated by government to control national and international air traffic, an activity regarded as inherently governmental in the United States.

Policymakers have specific reasons for preferring these types of organizations to direct government provision of services. In what public management scholar Sandra van Thiel terms "practitioner theory," she points to these reasons:[74] policymakers say that organizational arrangements that seem more like corporations (because of their financial motives) and less like public bureaucracies are apt to be more efficient and effective, closer to their customers, more flexible, more responsive, and less entangled in red tape.

Numerous such organizations exist at state and local levels of governments in the form of special districts. As explained by public administration scholars Thomas H. Stanton and Ronald C. Moe, "literally thousands of government authorities and enterprises, especially in areas of transportation, power production, and finance have been created, often as corporations." Stanton and Moe further point out that such organizations "are supposed to be financially self-sustaining from revenues that they derive from operations. Often state governments establish these organizations as a way to avoid state constitutional limitations on borrowing."[75]

Other U.S. quangos include the Internet Corporation for Assigned Names and Numbers, the National Center for Missing and Exploited Children, the National Democratic Institute, and its counterpart the International Republican Institute, the latter two of which promote democracy overseas.[76] **Government corporations** and **government-sponsored enterprises** (GSEs), as well, are examples of quangos. Government corporations at the federal level include the U.S. Postal Service, Amtrak, and the Tennessee Valley Authority.

Example: Federal National Mortgage Association (Fannie Mae)

GSEs are privately owned and operated federally chartered financial institutions that facilitate the flow of investment funds to specific economic sectors.[77] Examples include Fannie Mae, the Federal Home Loan Mortgage Corporation (Freddie Mac), the Federal Home Loan Bank System, and the Student Loan Marketing Association (Sallie Mae). Congress created GSEs to reduce the costs of borrowing for certain types of purposes such as housing and education.

The question of the public assumption of the financial risk associated with loans made by GSEs, especially by Fannie and Freddie, has been politically controversial in recent years. Regulatory oversight of Fannie and Freddie had been the responsibility of the Department of Housing and Urban Development, specifically, the Office of Federal Housing Enterprise Oversight, an entity whose operating funds were provided by the two corporations it regulated.

Following a series of accounting problems and reports questioning the extent to which these GSEs actually reduce the costs of borrowing for homeowners, calls for regulatory reform of Fannie and Freddie increased. In September 2008, during the U.S. subprime mortgage and financial crisis of 2007 to 2008, the Bush Administration ousted the chief executive officers of Fannie and Freddie and placed the organizations under public conservatorship with management control by the Federal Housing Finance Agency, a new federal regulator. Treasury Secretary Henry Paulson Jr. attributed the need for the move "primarily to the inherent conflict and flawed business model embedded in the GSE structure, and to the ongoing housing correction."[78]

The Bush Administration instituted other measures to help shore up the institutions, but many of the details affecting the future of Fannie and Freddie were left to future administrations. Paulson highlighted the political, policy, and structural issues raised by the decisions that would be faced:

> Because the GSEs are Congressionally-chartered, only Congress can address the inherent conflict of attempting to serve both shareholders and a public mission. The new Congress and the next Administration must decide what role government in general, and these entities in particular, should play in the housing market. There is a consensus today that these enterprises pose a systemic risk and they cannot continue in their current form. Government support needs to be either explicit or non-existent, and structured to resolve the conflict between public and private purposes. And policymakers must address the issue of systemic risk. I

recognize that there are strong differences of opinion over the role of government in supporting housing, but under any course policymakers choose, there are ways to structure these entities in order to address market stability in the transition and limit systemic risk and conflict of purposes for the long-term. We will make a grave error if we don't use this time out to permanently address the structural issues presented by the GSEs.[79]

By 2014, the conservatorship of Fannie and Freddie was still in place, and prospects were dim for congressional action on housing finance reform.[80]

Nonprofit Organizations

Nonprofit organizations can be viewed as a tool for organizing collective action, used instead of or in addition to direct government.[81] A number of rationales have been proposed to explain the formation and existence of the nonprofit organizational form. Many reference nonprofit organizations' role in responding to market failures (discussed in Chapter 1).

- Legal scholar Henry Hansmann developed a theory of nonprofits that explains why governments might prefer nonprofits to for-profits for producing human services. For-profit producers have incentives to increase profit by raising prices or cutting costs if the quality of a good or service is unknown or difficult to verify. Nonprofits have no such incentives, Hansmann argues, because of the nondistribution constraint, part of the legal framework that defines the nonprofit form. The nondistribution constraint prohibits managers or others associated with the organization from obtaining a share of revenues that exceed costs. In nonprofits, then,

  the discipline of the market is supplemented by the additional protection given the consumer by another, broader "contract," the organization's legal commitment to devote its entire earnings to the production of services. As a result of this institutional constraint, it is less imperative for the consumer either to shop around first or to enforce rigorously the contract he makes.[82]

- Economist Burton Weisbrod explained nonprofit formation using the theory of public goods. He argued that government and for-profit firms will underprovide collective goods because voters and investors may perceive no political or economic benefit in providing them or may free-ride on efforts of others to provide them.[83] Nonprofit organizations will be the organizational form that serves collective interests. Indeed, as is the case with education, medical care, nursing homes, and rehabilitation services, public and private provision may exist side by side, each sector providing somewhat different services.

- Economists Edward L. Glaeser and Andrei Shleifer focus on situations where high-powered incentives cannot sufficiently discourage inefficient provision or cutting corners on quality. They argue that the nonprofit organizational form "softens these incentives, and thus reassures [customers, donors, volunteers and employees] that quality will be higher."[84] The argument is that nonprofit status attracts entrepreneurs who have a sense of mission rather than a material orientation.

- Nonprofit scholar Lester Salamon argues that nonprofit organizations, not governments, respond to market failures and are the natural "first provider" of collective goods.[85] As with markets and governments, however, nonprofits, too, are vulnerable to particular kinds of failure:

- ○ **philanthropic insufficiency**, which occurs, partly due to free-rider problems, because nonprofits cannot attract enough resources to fully meet demands for what they provide;
- ○ **philanthropic particularism**, which occurs because nonprofits may choose to serve some needs or provide some services—for example, to those of a certain religion or ethnicity—but not others;
- ○ **philanthropic paternalism**, which occurs because nonprofit board members and donors may not reflect community values; and
- ○ **philanthropic amateurism**, which occurs because delivery of services by nonprofits may involve well-meaning but unskilled staff or service technologies that do not meet professional or scientific standards or best practices.

> **The nonprofit form provides a signal about the values and motives of nonprofit managers.**

Because they are unable on their own to overcome collective action problems, the public sector may step in to supplement nonprofit provision and co-opt nonprofit organizations into serving larger public purposes.

- • Nonprofit scholars Avner Ben-Ner and Theresa Van Hoomissen argue that a nonprofit organization will be formed only if a group of interested stakeholders (individuals or organizations) has the ability to exercise control over the organization. "Stakeholder control is a *sine qua non* for the existence of nonprofit organizations, because it avails the trust required for patronizing the organization, revealing demand to it, and making donations to it."[86]

Whatever the reason for the existence of nonprofits, both formal models and empirical evidence indicate that the nonprofit form provides a signal about the values and motives of nonprofit managers.[xx] Political economy scholar Susan Rose-Ackerman argues, however, that "organization form, per se, may not serve an important signaling function for patrons. It may only be an indication that certain kinds of entrepreneurs and managers find the nonprofit form desirable."[87]

Nonprofit scholar Dennis R. Young also suggests that screening of personalities and goals may underlie an entrepreneur's choice to organize as a for-profit or nonprofit. In particular, even though variation exists across for-profit and nonprofit organizations, he argues from case study evidence that "income seekers" and "independents" are drawn to the for-profit sector, while "believers," "conservers," "poets," "searchers," and "professionals" are more likely drawn to the nonprofit sector.[88]

As nonprofits are increasingly participants in third-party government, political scientists Steven Smith and Michael Lipksy argue that the administrative requirements of managing government contracts require professional skills and administrative expertise that some traditional nonprofit leaders may not have.[89] Professional managers of nonprofits that rely heavily on government contracts may have preferences that more closely mirror those of for-profit organizations than those of nonprofits with traditional community or public service roots.

Managerial preferences may be critical because monitoring and incentive problems may lead to difficulty in enforcing the nondistribution constraint. **Cross-subsidization**—using revenues from profitable activities such as art museum shops, to subsidize unprofitable activities such as art programs for low-income neighborhoods and

---

[xx]In addition to the references cited in this section, see Christoph Badelt, "Entrepreneurship in Nonprofit Organizations: Its Role in Theory and in the Real World Nonprofit Sector," in *The Study of the Nonprofit Enterprise: Theories and Approaches,* ed. Helmut Anheier and Avner Ben-Ner (New York, NY: Kluwer, 2003); and Dennis R. Young, "Entrepreneurs, Managers, and the Nonprofit Enterprise," in Anheier and Ben-Ner, *The Study of the Nonprofit Enterprise: Theories and Approaches,* 161–168.

groups—may occur and may be inconsistent with the intentions of donors who favor art acquisitions or consumers who favor low entry fees. Managers may be opportunistic and take advantage of the trust that donors and clients place in them.[90]

The nondistribution constraint means that nonprofits do not have strong incentives to minimize costs, which theory predicts would lead to excessively costly services to and overspending on perquisites, such as office amenities, leased vehicles, and expensive information technology or inflated salaries by nonprofit managers.[91] One review of the literature in human services, however, found no clear evidence that nonprofits were markedly different from for-profits in terms of cost minimization, concluding that "concerns about the operating inefficiency imposed upon the human services through their heavy reliance on nonprofit firms, while not entirely misplaced, are easily exaggerated."[92] In contrast to that view, another report indicates that confidence in the nonprofit sector is declining amid a belief that these organizations operate inefficiently.[93]

Such a decline in confidence, if real, should worry nonprofit managers and their boards. Public management scholars Laurence Lynn and Steven Smith describe the reliance on the legal roots of the nonprofit organizational form and the resulting vulnerability:

> The American nonprofit sector is a creature of the policies formalized in federal, state and local statutes and regulations regarding incorporation, exemption from corporate taxation and various regulations and the tax treatment of charitable donations. . . . As agents of public policy, nonprofit organizations are in principle accountable to legislatures, tax authorities, and various interest groups who comprise their stakeholders and they are thus vulnerable to the withdrawal of the privileges that substantially enable their existence.[94]

They argue that nonprofits must address these concerns through governance reforms and articulation of fiduciary norms.

Reinventing Government?

For those favoring a move from direct to indirect government and greater reliance on collaborative governance and public management, the fate of the Clinton Administration's **Reinventing Government** initiative is a cautionary tale. Vice President Al Gore argued, "The Federal Government is filled with good people trapped in bad systems: budget systems, personnel systems, procurement systems, financial management systems, information systems. When we blame the people and impose more controls we make the systems worse."[95] Reinventing traditional government was the initiative's goal.

One of the many tools for reinventing government was "performance partnerships," in which federal, state, and local governments and service providers jointly designed programs and measured program performance. The putative benefits included consolidated funding streams, devolved decision making, and reduced paperwork, with the implied reward of additional funding and other unspecified benefits financed by increased efficiency.[xxi]

The U.S. Environmental Protection Agency (EPA) responded by creating the National Environmental Performance Partnership System (NEPPS). The EPA and states developed "agreements [that] set out jointly-developed priorities and protection strategies and how EPA and the state will work together to address priority needs. States can choose to combine federal environmental program grant funds in Performance Partnership Grants (PPGs), which

---

[xxi]For more information on performance partnerships, see http://govinfo.library.unt.edu/npr/library/fedstat/2572.html.

allow states to direct resources where they are needed most or try innovative solutions to environmental problems."[96] A 2013 review of NEPPS implementation practices found:

> Overall, NEPPS is viewed as a valuable and beneficial process for advancing and strengthening the EPA-state partnership and deemed worthy of continued federal /state revitalization efforts. Senior leadership commitment (state and regional) is essential to break down internal barriers, help to identify cross-programmatic opportunities, and improve strategic planning/priority setting. However, it was also noted that allegiances to and protection of media programs at EPA and in the states are strong forces that make broadening the use and scope of NEPPS difficult.[97]

Federal grant money may induce agencies to join a formal partnership, but federal leverage over the politically motivated conduct of state and local management may not be strong enough to motivate significant change in public management.

More generally, political scientists Joel Aberbach and Bert Rockman argue that while some of the recommendations in "the Gore Report" were unarguably good ideas, their main thrust consisted of slogans and nostrums that could not withstand critical scrutiny. They note that "although many of the inefficiencies and restrictive rules [Gore] decried were legislatively mandated, [the report] largely ignored the need for legislative reforms, deemphasizing the role of Congress."[98] In general, slogans such as "partnering" and "networking" must be translated into operational concepts that are attractive both practically and politically. Potential collaborators must see a net benefit from participating in arrangements that increase their interdependence with other entities.

KEY CONCEPTS

Politics of bureaucratic structure
Bureaucracy
Direct government
Bureaucratic pathologies
Goal ambiguity
Utility maximization
Property rights and principal-agent
   problems
Maladaptation
Enabling structures
Constraining structures
The Office of Management and Budget
The Director of the Office of
   Personnel Management
The power of the purse
Objects of expenditure
Line items
Account classification
Appropriations
Budget authority
Obligation
Expenditures

Apportionment
Allotments
Suballotments
Allocations
Purpose statute
Classification code
Functional classification
   system
Tax expenditures
Subfunctions
Spoils system
Competitive Service
Excepted Service
Senior executive service
Human resource management
Human capital management
Performance-based pay
Pay for performance
At-will employment
President's management agenda
Privatization
Contracting out

Outsourcing
Government by proxy/third party government/
    indirect government/hollow state
Organizational form
Nondistribution constraint
Inherently governmental
Quango
Government corporations
Government-sponsored enterprises

Nonprofit organizations
Nondistribution constraint
Philanthropic insufficiency
Philanthropic particularism
Philanthropic paternalism
Philanthropic amateurism
Cross-subsidization
Reinventing government

CASE ANALYSIS: STATE OF MISSOURI'S REFORM OF ITS JUVENILE JUSTICE SYSTEM

Frederick C. Mosher, one of America's most respected public administration scholars, believed that the emergence of public management as a profession was a result of "a fundamental optimism that mankind could direct and control its environment and destiny for the better."[99]

Optimism can be hard to sustain when creating administrative structures that must meet the expectations of policymakers, stakeholders, and citizens. One of the most challenging domains of public policy in the American states is juvenile justice. Many juvenile justice systems are notorious for their inadequate facilities, poor treatment of youthful offenders, and incompetent management. A celebrated exception to the mediocre norm in juvenile justice administration is the State of Missouri.

Forty years ago, youth committed by the courts to the juvenile justice system were confined in large prison-like institutions and training schools, often far from home. State officials committed themselves to a broad program of reforms.[100] In Missouri, reform was led in part by "a bi-partisan Advisory Board whose members were judges, former legislators, civic leaders and concerned private citizens representing all regions of the state. The Board holds the system accountable, vitalizes it with new thinking, and partners with leadership to solve problems."[101]

The reformed system become known as "The Missouri Approach" to juvenile justice administration.[102] Importantly, the Division of Youth Services (DYS) in Missouri is located within the Department of Social Services (not the Department of Corrections, which oversees adult correctional centers). DYS is "charged with the care and treatment of delinquent youth committed to its custody by one of Missouri's 45 juvenile or family courts."[i]

The mechanism employed to changing juvenile justice practices in Missouri has been termed by experts "resolution": "the use of managerial authority and administrative directives to influence system change."[103] Missouri's system operates through state administrative structures and includes a number of structural reforms.

---

[i]"Who We Are," The Missouri Approach, accessed May 24, 2015, http://missouriapproach.org/approach.

(Continued)

(Continued)

Local jurisdictions throughout the state used a

"structured decision-making model that uses risk and needs assessments and a classification matrix: the Missouri Juvenile Offender Risk and Needs Assessment and Classification System. A major goal of the state in establishing this classification system is to promote statewide consistency in the classification and supervision of juvenile offenders. The three tools of the Missouri system are as follows:

- An actuarial risk assessment tool, completed before court adjudication, that classifies youth into three categories: high, moderate, or low probability of reoffending . . . .
- A classification matrix that recommends sanctions and service interventions appropriate to the youth's risk level and most serious adjudicated offense
- A needs assessment instrument that recommends services that will reduce the likelihood of a youth's reoffending by reducing risk factors linked to recidivism[104]

The Missouri approach is characterized by the following features:

- Programs for youth that are small, homelike (not institutional) and close to their homes;
- Group treatment models that focus on individualized case management and care;
- Fostering physical and emotional safety through supervision and building relationships, not through coercion;
- Supporting youths' future chances of success by providing academic learning, community service, and job skills training and opportunities;
- Involving the youths' families in consultation, therapy, and aftercare; and
- Following up after leaving the juvenile facility, through aftercare supervision, monitoring, and mentoring.[105]

An Annie E. Casey Foundation report on the Missouri program included information about costs in the program and also highlighted how comparing results of these kinds of programs across states can be difficult due to differing definitions (including the ages of juveniles themselves) and structures:

- Due to peculiarities in Missouri's budgeting process, the official budget for [DYS]—$63 million in 2008—substantially understates the actual cost of services by excluding fringe benefits of DYS employees and some central administrative costs. However, even a more realistic DYS budget estimated at $87 million—equivalent to $155 or each young person of juvenile age statewide—would still represent a cost to taxpayers that is lower than or comparable to the juvenile corrections costs in most states and substantially less than some.[106]
- For instance, Missouri's spending on youth corrections appears higher than that of Arizona and Indiana, but far lower than Maryland and Florida. Not including costs for juvenile probation, which is a state function in Maryland but not Missouri, Maryland's juvenile corrections agency spends more than $270 for every young person of juvenile age. Florida spends over $220 for every young person, not including costs for probation and detention, which are state-run in Florida but operated locally in Missouri.[107]
- [A key] factor in Missouri's modest juvenile justice costs are the salaries paid to DYS workers, which are lower than those of youth corrections workers in many states.[108]

Overall, the results of the Missouri approach have drawn national attention. "For every youth steered away from a life of crime, Missouri saves at least $3 million in victim costs and criminal justice expenses, in addition to any taxes the youth might pay during his or her lifetime . . . . Of the youth released from custody in 2010, 84 percent remained law-abiding one year after their release."[109]

Positive results of the program are not only gratifying to the state's public managers but are also politically attractive to policymakers and the citizens they represent. Replication by other states seems to be underway: "Missouri's statewide development of a continuum of graduated sanctions and services sets a very high standard for other states to follow."[110]

Discussion Questions

1. How are the politics of bureaucratic structure evident in Missouri's Division of Youth Services?

2. In what specific ways are managers in the Missouri Division of Youth Services enabled and constrained?

3. What direct government and indirect government entities are evident in this case?

4. As a management analyst, what additional information would you want to have in order to fully understand the politics of bureaucratic structure, direct and indirect government actors, and enabling and constraining structures that face managers in the Missouri Division of Youth Services?

NOTES

1. Terry Moe, "The Politics of Structural Choice: Toward a Theory of Public Bureaucracy," in *Organization Theory: From Chester Barnard to the Present and Beyond,* ed. Oliver E. Williamson (New York, NY: Oxford University Press, 1990), 116–153.
2. Katherine McIntire Peters, "Partners in Crimefighting," *Government Executive.com*, February 2, 2005, accessed August 6, 2014, http://www.govexec.com/excellence/management-matters/2005/02/partners-in-crimefighting/18482.
3. Department of Homeland Security, Office of Inspector General, "An Assessment of the Proposal to Merge Customs And Border Protection with Immigration and Customs Enforcement, *Office of Inspection and Special Reviews,* November 2005, 3.
4. Ibid., 8.
5. Moe, "The Politics of Structural Choice."
6. Moe, "The Politics of Structural Choice."
7. Moe, "The Politics of Structural Choice," 137.
8. James A. Morone, *The Democratic Wish: Popular Participation and the Limits of American Government* (New York: Basic Books, 1990).
9. Moe, "The Politics of Structural Choice."
10. Kate Alexander, "Lawmakers Say They Aim to Ensure Quality, Increase Access to Charter Schools," *Austin American-Statesman*, January 12, 2013, http://www.statesman.com/news/news/lawmakers-aim-to-ensure-quality-increase-access-to/nTtj6.
11. Liz Farmer, "Senate Passes Charter School Reform Bill After Compromises with Dems," *The Texas Observer*, April 11, 2013, http://www.texasobserver.org/senate-passes-charter-bill-after-compromises-with-dems/. Text of enacted legislation is at http://www.legis.state.tx.us/tlodocs/83R/billtext/pdf/SB00002F.pdf#navpanes=0.
12. Editorial Board, "Legislature Avoided Extremes in Reforming Public Education," *Austin American-Statesman*, May 29, 2013, http://www.mystatesman.com/news/news/opinion/legislature-avoided-extremes-in-reforming-public-e/nX6Dk.
13. Moe, "The Politics of Structural Choice."
14. Moe, "The Politics of Structural Choice."
15. Christopher K. Leman, "Direct Government" in *The Tools of Government: A Guide to the New Government,* Ed. Lester M. Salamon (Oxford, UK: Oxford University Press, 2002).
16. Laurence E. Lynn Jr., *Public Management: Old and New* (London, UK: Routledge, 2006).

17. Reinhard Bendix, *Max Weber: An Intellectual Portrait* (Berkeley: University of California Press, 1960), 424.

18. Barry Bozeman, *Bureaucracy and Red Tape* (Upper Saddle River, NJ: Prentice Hall, 2000), 21.

19. Ibid. 46–47.

20. Herbert Kaufman, "The Confines of Leadership," in *The Administrative Behavior of Federal Bureau Chiefs* (Washington, DC: Brookings Institution, 1981), 91–138

21. Government Accountability Office, "A Glossary of Terms Used in the Federal Budget Process," September 2005, http://www.gao.gov/new.items/d05734sp.pdf.

22. This section is adapted from Laurence E. Lynn, Jr., "The Study of Public Management in the United States: Management in the New World and a Reflection on Europe" in, *The Study of Public Management in Europe and the US: A Comparative Analysis of National Distinctiveness, ed. Walter J. Kickert* (London, UK: Routledge, 2008), 233–262.

23. Frederick A. Cleveland, "Popular Control of Government," *Political Science Quarterly 34* (1919): 252.

24. Laurence E. Lynn, Jr., "Reform of the Federal Government: Lessons for Change Agents" in *LBJ's Neglected Legacy: How Lyndon Johnson Reshaped Domestic Policy and Government,* ed. Robert H. Wilson, Norman J. Glickman, and Laurence E. Lynn, Jr. (Austin: University of Texas, 2015, 373–396).

25. James P. Pfiffner, "The American Tradition of Administrative Reform," in *The White House and the Blue House: Government Reform in the United States and Korea,* ed. Yong Hyo Cho and H. George Frederickson (Lanham, MD: University Press of America, 1998).

26. Wilson, Glickman, and Lynn, *LBJ's Neglected Legacy*

27. National Association of State Budget Officers, "Budget Processes in the States—Data on State Government Operations", (Washington, DC: NASBO), November 9, 2011, http://www.nasbo.org/publications-data/budget-processes-in-the-state.

28. Government Accountability Office, "A Glossary of Terms Used in the Federal Budget Process," 2.

29. 31 U.S.C. § 1301(a); Government Accountability Office, "A Glossary of Terms Used in the Federal Budget Process, 121.

30. Government Accountability Office, "A Glossary of Terms Used in the Federal Budget Process," 152.

31. Ibid., 124.

32. Ibid.

33. Government Accountability Office, "A Glossary of Terms Used in the Federal Budget Process," 121.

34. Patricia W. Ingraham, "Striving for Balance: Reforms in Human Resource Management," in *The Oxford Handbook of Public Management*, ed. Ewan Ferlie, Laurence E. Lynn, Jr., and Christopher Pollitt (Oxford, UK: Oxford University Press, 2005), 521–536.

35. Woodrow Wilson, "The Study of Administration," *in Classics of Public Administration,* 4th ed., ed. Jay M. Shafritz and Albert C. Hyde (Stamford, CT.: Wadsworth/Thomson Learning, 1997), 16.

36. Paul. P. Van Riper, *History of the United States Civil Service* (Evanston, IL.: Row, Peterson, 1958).

37. Pfiffner, "The American Tradition."

38. Title 5 U.S. Code, Part III, Subpart A, Chapter § 2101.

39. 5 U.S.C. § 1103(c)(2)(F).

40. U.S. Merit Systems Protection Board, "About MSPB," accessed May 16, 2015, http://www.mspb.gov/About/about.htm.

41. Committee on Alternative Futures for the Army Research Laboratory, *The Army Research Laboratory: Alternative Organizational and Management Options* (Washington, DC: National Academy Press, 1994), http://www.nap.edu/openbook.php?record_id=9030&page=162.

42. Al Gore, *From Red Tape to Results: Creating a Government that Works Better and Costs Less* (Washington DC: U.S. Government Printing Office, 1993), 20.

43. Curtis W. Copeland, *The Federal Workforce: Characteristics and Trends* (Washington, DC: Congressional Research Service, 2011).

44. George T. Milkovich and Alexandra K. Wigdor, ed., *Pay for Performance: Evaluating Performance Appraisal and Merit Pay* (Washington DC: National Research Council, 1991), 3.

45. James L. Perry, Trent Engbers, and So Yun Jun, "Back to the Future? Performance-Related Pay, Empirical Research, and the Perils of Persistence," *Public Administration Review* 69, no. 1 (2009): 39–51.

46. Ibid.

47. Laurence E. Lynn, Jr., "Public Administration Theory: 'Which Side Are You On?'," in *The State of Public Administration: Issues, Challenges, Opportunities,* ed. D. Menzel and H. White (Armonk, NY: M. E. Sharpe, 2010), 3–22.

48. The Florida Senate, CS/CS/SB 736: Education Personnel, 2011, http://www.flsenate.gov/Session/Bill/2011/0736/BillText/er/PDF.

49. "The At-Will Presumption and Exceptions to the Rule," National Conference of State Legislatures, accessed May 23, 2015, http://www.ncsl.org/research/labor-and-employment/at-will-employment-overview.aspx.

50. Jungin Kim and J. Edward Kellough, "At-Will Employment in the States: Examining the Perceptions of Agency Personnel Directors," *Review of Public Personnel Administration* 34 (2014): 218–236.

51. Ibid., 234n2.

52. Ibid., 222.

53. "Texas Labor and Employment Laws," *Lawyers.com*, accessed November 12, 2014, http://research.lawyers.com/texas/employment-law-in-texas.html.

54. J. D. Coggburn, "The Benefits of Human Resource Centralization: Insights From a Survey of Human Resource Directors in Decentralized States, *"Public Administration Review* 65 (2005): 424–435; Kim and Kellough, "At-Will Employment in the States."

55. Kim and Kellough, "At-Will Employment in the States," 220.

56. Laurence E. Lynn, Jr., "New Public Management Comes to America," Harris School Working Paper Series 08-04 (Chicago, IL: The University of Chicago, 2008), http://harris.uchicago.edu/sites/default/files/working-papers/wp_08_04.pdf.

57. Stephen Barr, "Concerns and Questions Increase as National Security Personnel System Nears," *The Washington Post*, July 26, 2005, http://www.washingtonpost.com/wp-dyn/content/article/2005/07/25/AR2005072501452.htm.

58. Laurence E. Lynn, Jr., "The Persistence of Hierarchy," in *The SAGE Handbook of Governance*, ed. Mark Bevir (Thousand Oaks, CA: Sage, 2010), 218–236.

59. Stephen Goldsmith, *Governing by Network: The New Shape of the Public Sector* (Washington, DC: The Brookings Institution, 2004).

60. Laurence E. Lynn, Jr., "Social Services and the State: The Public Appropriation of Private Charity," *Social Service Review* 76 (March 2002): 58–82.

61. H. Brinton Milward and Keith G. Provan, "The Hollow State: Private Provision of Public Services," in *Public Policy for Democracy*, ed. Helen Ingram and Steven Rathgeb Smith (Washington, DC: Brookings Institution, 1993); Donald F. Kettl, *Government by Proxy: (Mis?) Managing Federal Programs* (Washington, DC: CQ Press, 1988); Lester M. Salamon, "Rethinking Public Management: Third-Party Government and the Changing Forms of Government Action," *Public Policy* 29 (Summer 1981): 255–275.

62. Laurence E. Lynn, Jr., Carolyn J. Heinrich, and H. Brinton Milward, "A State of Agents? Sharpening the Debate and Evidence over the Extent and Impact of the Transformation of Governance," *Journal of Public Administration Research and Theory* (2009): i4.

63. H. Brinton Milward and Keith G. Provan, "Governing the Hollow State," *Journal of Public Administration Research and Theory* 10, no. 2 (2000): 359–379.

64. Paul C. Light, *The True Size of Government* (Washington, DC: Brookings Institution, 1999); Paul C. Light, "Fact Sheet on the New True Size of Government," Working Paper (Brookings Institution, 2003).

65. Light, "Fact Sheet," Table 1.

66. Milward and Provan, "The Hollow State."

67. Chris Skelcher, "Does Democracy Matter? A Transatlantic Research Design on Democratic Performance and Special Purpose Governments," *Journal of Public Administration Research and Theory* 17, no. 1 (2007): 77–94; David G. Frederickson and George H. Frederickson, *Measuring the Performance of the Hollow State* (Washington, DC: Georgetown University Press, 2006); Donald Kettl, *Transformation of Governance: Public Administration for Twenty-First Century America* (Baltimore, MD: The Johns Hopkins University Press, 2002); Gerry Stoker, "Governance as Theory: Five Propositions," *International Social Science Journal* 155 (March 1998): 17–28.

68. Lisa Bingham, Tina Nabatchi, and Rosemary O'Leary, "The New Governance: Practices and Processes for Stakeholder and Citizen Participation in the Work of Government," *Public Administration Review* 65, no. 5 (2005): 545–558; Linda deLeon and Peter deLeon, "The Democratic Ethos and Public Management," *Administration & Society* 34 (2002): 229–250.

69. H. George Frederickson and Kevin B. Smith, *The Public Administration Theory Primer* (Boulder, CO: Westview Press, 2003); Skelcher, "Does Democracy Matter?," 77–94

70. Executive Office of the President, Office of Management and Budget, "Circular No. A-76 (Revised)," A-2–A-3, May 29, 2003, https://www.whitehouse.gov/omb/circulars_a076_a76_incl_tech_correction.

71. Congressional Research Service, "Performance of Inherently Governmental Critical Functions: The Obama Administration's Final Policy Letter," October 5, 2011, https://www.hsdl.org/?view&did=719293.

72. Ibid.

73. Leman, "Direct Government."

74. Sandra Van Thiel, *Quangos: Trends, Causes and Consequences* (Burlington, VT.: Ashgate, 2001).

75. Thomas H. Stanton and Ronald C. Moe, "Government Corporations and Government Sponsored Enterprises," in *The Tools of Government: A Guide to the New Government*, ed. Lester M. Salamon (Oxford, UK: Oxford University Press, 2002), 80–116.

76. "Are Democracy Quangos Doomed?," *The American Interest*, April 1, 2012, http://www.the-american-interest.com/2012/04/01/are-democracy-quangos-doomed/.

77. Government Accountability Office, "A Glossary of Terms Used in the Federal Budget Process," 59.

78. U.S. Department of the Treasury Press Release, "Statement by Secretary Henry M. Paulson, Jr. on Treasury and Federal Housing Finance Agency Action to Protect Financial Markets and Taxpayers," September 7, 2008, http://www.treasury.gov/press-center/press-releases/Pages/hp1129.aspx.

79. Ibid.

80. Joe Light, "FHFA Won't Rule Out Ending Fannie, Freddie Oversight Without Congress," *The Wall Street Journal*, November 19, 2014, http://online.wsj.com/articles/senator-calls-for-fhfa-to-end-fannie-freddie-conservatorship-1416411254.

81. In addition to the references cited in this section, see Elizabeth T. Boris and C. Eugene Steuerle, eds., *Nonprofits and Government: Collaboration and Conflict* (Washington, DC: Urban Institute, 2006); Walter W. Powell and Richard Steinberg, Eds., *The Nonprofit Sector: A Research Handbook,* 2nd ed. (New Haven, CT: Yale University Press, 2006).

82. Henry B. Hansmann, "The Role of Nonprofit Enterprise," *Yale Law Journal* 89, no. 5 (1980): 835–901, 844.

83. Burton Weisbrod, Ed., *The Voluntary Nonprofit Sector* (Lexington, MA: D. C. Heath, 1977).

84. Edward L. Glaeser and Andrei Shleifer, "Not-for-Profit Entrepreneurs," *Journal of Public Economics* 81 (2001): 99–115, 100.

85. Lester M. Salamon, "Of Market Failure, Voluntary Failure, and Third-Party Government: Toward a Theory of Government-Nonprofit Relations in the Modern Welfare State," *Journal of Voluntary Action Research* 16, no. 1–2 (1987): 29–49.

86. Avner Ben-Ner and Theresa Van Hoomissen, "Nonprofit Organizations in the Mixed Economy: A Demand and Supply Analysis," *Annals of Public and Cooperative Economics* 62 (1991): 519–550, 544.

87. Susan Rose-Ackerman, "Altruism, Nonprofits, and Economic Theory," *Journal of Economic Literature* 34 (June 1996): 719.

88. Dennis R. Young, *If Not For Profit, For What? A Behavioral Theory of the Nonprofit Sector Based on Entrepreneurship* (Lexington, MA: D. C. Heath, 1983), 99.

89. Stephen Rathgeb Smith and Michael Lipsky, *Nonprofits for Hire: The Welfare State in the Age of Contracting* (Cambridge, MA: Harvard University Press 1993).

90. Richard Steinberg and Bradford H. Gray, "The Role of Nonprofit Enterprise' in 1992: Hansmann Revisited," *Nonprofit and Voluntary Sector Quarterly* 22, (Winter 1993): 297–316.

91. Henry B. Hansmann, "Economic Theories of Nonprofit Organization," in *The Nonprofit Sector: A Research Handbook,* ed. Walter W. Powell (New Haven, CT: Yale University Press, 1987), 27–42; Estelle James and Susan Rose-Ackerman, *The Nonprofit Enterprise in Market Economics* (New York. NY: Harwood Academic Publishers, 1986).

92. Henry B. Hansmann, "The Changing Roles of Public, Private, and Nonprofit Enterprise in Education, Health Care, and Other Human Services," in *Individual and Social Responsibility: Child Care, Education, Medical Care, and Long-Term Care In America,* ed. Victor R. Fuchs (Chicago, IL: University of Chicago Press, 1996), 249.

93. Paul C. Light, "Fact Sheet on the Continued Crisis in Charitable Confidence."

94. Laurence E. Lynn Jr. and Steven Rathgeb Smith, "The Performance Challenge in Nonprofit Organizations," Working Paper, February 17, 2007.

95. Al Gore, *From Red Tape to Results: Creating a Government that Works Better & Costs Less: Report of the National Performance Review* (Washington, DC.: Government Printing Office, 1993), 2.

96. U.S. Environmental Protection Agency, "National Environmental Performance Partnership System," last updated October, 7, 2014, http://www.epa.gov/ocir/nepps/index.htm.

97. Office of the Administrator, U.S. Environmental Protection Agency, "The National Environmental Performance Partnership System: A Review of Implementation Practices, (EPA 140-R-13-001, May 2013), http://www.epa.gov/ocir/nepps/pdf/review_NEPPS_implementation_practices_final_report_%202013.pdf.

98. Joel D. Aberbach and Bert A. Rockman, "Reinventing Government or Reinventing Politics? The American Experience," in *Politicians, Bureaucrats and Administrative Reform,* ed. B. Guy Peters and Jon Pierre (London, UK: Routledge, 2001): 24–34.

99. Frederick C. Mosher, "The American Setting," In *American Public Administration: Past, Present and Future*, ed. Frederick C. Mosher (University: The University of Alabama Press, 1975), 3.

100. Douglas N. Evans, "Pioneers of Youth Justice Reform: Achieving System Change Using Resolution, Reinvestment, and Realignment Strategies," *Research Evaluation Center,* July 2012, http://johnjayresearch.org/wp-content/uploads/2012/06/rec20123.pdf.

101. Missouri Department of Social Services, "The Missouri Approach—About Our History," 2010, http://missouriapproach.org/history.

102. Ibid.

103. Evans, "Pioneers of Youth Justice Reform," 1.

104. Mark W. Lipsey et al., "Improving the Effectiveness of Juvenile Justice Programs: A New Perspective on Evidence Based Practice," *Center for Juvenile Justice Reform* (December 2010): 44-46.

105. Richard A. Mendel, *The Missouri Model: Reinventing the Practice of Rehabilitating Youthful Offenders* (Baltimore, MD: Annie E. Casey Foundation, 2010), http://www.aecf.org/m/resourcedoc/aecf-MissouriModelFullreport-2010.pdf; "About the Missouri Approach," The Missouri Approach, accessed May 24, 2015, http://missouriapproach.org/approach.

106. Richard A. Mendel, *The Missouri Model: Reinventing the Practice of Rehabilitating Youthful Offenders* (Baltimore MD: The Annie E. Casey Foundation, 2010), http://www.aecf.org/m/resourcedoc/aecf-MissouriModelFullreport-2010.pdf, 11-12.

107. Ibid., 12.

108. Ibid., 12.

109. Douglas N. Evans, *Pioneers of Youth Justice Reform: Achieving System Change Using Resolution, Reinvestment, and Realignment Strategies* (New York, NY: John Jay College of Criminal Justice, City University of New York, 2012), 7

110. Mark W. Lipsey et al., "Improving the Effectiveness of Juvenile Justice Programs," 44.

6 STRUCTURE

TOOLS FOR PUBLIC MANAGERS

INTRODUCTION

The structures of the administrative state constrain public managers to act on behalf of lawful purposes but also enable them to direct, coordinate, and monitor the policies, programs, functions, and activities over which they have jurisdiction. Chapter 5 emphasized the externally authorized delegations of authority that frame duty and opportunity for public managers as they implement public policy. The result of these externally authorized structures is that the public manager's "slate is not clean."[1] Public managers have a duty to find the law, as emphasized in Chapter 2, in order to fully appreciate the many ways in which they are constrained and enabled. Thus, the staff members of departments and agencies must include specialists in the meaning and implementation of a vast collection of documents defining the rule of law for that agency.[i]

Their full slates notwithstanding, public managers may have considerable latitude to use their judgment in interpreting and implanting the policies for which they are responsible. Using the authority delegated to them in statutes and responding to opportunities inherent in managerial roles, public managers can be effective and politically influential, as discussed in Chapter 1. They have institutional, political, and personal interests that may not be congruent with their formal missions or the expectations of stakeholders. They also have access to their agency's resources and to expertise that might be employed toward their preferred ends. They are players in the politics of bureaucratic structure.

---

[i]THOMAS, a website maintained by the Library of Congress, provides detailed information on current legislative activity, legislative enactments, including appropriations acts, of recent Congresses, and a wealth of information on voting, sponsorship of legislation, and hearings.

Grants of authority enable public officials to impose significant constraints on other governmental or private entities.

Not incidentally, grants of authority enable public officials to impose significant constraints on other governmental or private entities. Delegations of authority from such public officials operate primarily at the "d" level in the logic of governance described in Chapter 4. For example, a cabinet secretary may restructure reporting lines or job responsibilities of agency staff. A public manager's imposition of constraints and responsibilities on others can be politically controversial and can invite lawsuits that subject managerial judgment to judicial review. Thus managers' effectiveness depends both on their skills and judgment and on the specific contexts and cultures in which they work. These craft and culture aspects of public management are the subjects of Chapters 8 through 11.

The current chapter explores the ways, means, and consequences of how managers use structures to further public policy implementation. The focus is on general management practice; highly specialized managerial functions are beyond the scope of the chapter. Examples of these specialized functions include management of human resources, financial accounting, auditing, program evaluation, and contract administration.

Following a case describing how one public manager used her delegated authority to restructure the U.S. Department of State, the chapter then describes two general frameworks (principal-agent analysis and transaction cost analysis) that can be used for many analytical challenges that managers face. Next, the chapter discusses the settings in which public management takes place, namely, organizations—the departments, agencies, bureaus, and offices of federal, state, and local governments—using perspectives from organizational theory. The chapter emphasizes how managers can make strategic use of structural tools to create and enhance their organization's overall capacity to manage effectively in accordance with the rule of law. These tools include agency-level rule-making, the employment of agents using grants and contracts, and less hierarchical ways of sharing authority over policy implementation with organizations within and outside of government. The chapter concludes with a case that explores the public management issues associated with the highly consequential rollout of the Patient Protection and Affordable Care Act of 2010 (ACA).

CASE: REORGANIZING U.S. FOREIGN ASSISTANCE PROGRAMS

Public managers often use internal reorganization to accomplish the political objective of centralizing or decentralizing authority and influence within their organizations. As secretary of state in the George W. Bush administration, Condoleezza Rice often reorganized subordinate agencies to increase her control over policymaking and implementation.

In February 2006, Rice reorganized the administration of foreign aid programs under her jurisdiction.[2] She created a new Office of Foreign Assistance (OFA) to coordinate the State Department's foreign aid activities. Senior aides described the "reorganization [as] necessary because, for example, when Rice asked how much money was being spent on democracy-related programs, it was not 'easy to get that answer'" due to the many different aid programs created over the years.[3] Rice appointed Randall Tobias, a former Global AIDS coordinator, as director of the OFA.

At the same time, Rice put Tobias in charge of the U.S. Agency for International Development (USAID) in a move aimed to consolidate her control over foreign assistance priorities. USAID is "an independent federal government agency that receives overall foreign policy guidance from the Secretary of State."[4] Yet the Tobias appointment reduced USAID's actual independence. Many AID employees complained that the professionalism of the agency was being compromised to serve an ideological agenda; Rice's appointee was a well-known opponent of U.S. assistance for birth control programs.

Several months later, the House Foreign Operations Appropriations Subcommittee held hearings in response to congressional concerns over the State Department's internal restructuring of foreign aid programs. Tobias described the challenges he had begun to address: "a planning and budgeting process that is fragmented among numerous departments and agencies; duplication of programs; poor accountability; and the lack of linkage between strategic objectives and implementation."[5]

Whether the reorganization would eventually be seen as visionary or simply a rearranging of the boxes on organization charts at the State Department would not be known until long after Rice and her colleagues left Washington. Rice speculated that realizing the benefits of her restructuring would take "a generation."[6]

But because of the political sensitivity of foreign aid programs, judgments about the effectiveness of the reorganization were made much earlier. In 2008, the Carnegie Endowment for International Peace published a report by a former senior official of USAID that contained the following conclusions: *Bet Judge*

- The new system confuses strategic decisions, which should be made in Washington, with tactical ones better suited to context-knowledgeable field officers. Reforms also require that any change made to a foreign assistance project receive approval from the newly created Director of Foreign Assistance (DFA) position, creating huge potential for gridlock.
- In the quest for greater strategic control, the reorganization actually diminishes Washington's ability to evaluate the objectives and successes of foreign assistance projects. Detailed narratives which provided rationale for programs under the old system have been replaced by a complex, numbered grid system that lacks critical information, making a serious assessment of projects in Washington difficult.
- The reorganization was led by "core country teams," the members of which, in many instances, had only a passing knowledge of the country they were to plan for. The implementation process also failed to involve many key stakeholders, including ambassadors, USAID missions, and congressional leaders.
- The reorganization was instituted due in large part to the Secretary's inability to answer congressional inquiries regarding U.S. spending on democracy promotion. The new system places an exaggerated emphasis on the ultimately futile attempt to instantly report on U.S. foreign assistance expenditures and detail the outcomes of an $11 billion program.[i,7]

Another independent evaluation was focused less on political issues than on issues of measurement and process:

> The new reforms emphasized centralized planning . . . set of common indicators for all sectors of foreign assistance activity, and an increased emphasis on monitoring.

(Continued)

(Continued)

The new guidance and requirements determined shortly after F [agency symbol for OFA] was created strengthened the focus on accountability . . . reporting on processes and outputs to external audiences including the White House and Congress. Although some effort has been made to include outcome indicators, F's original list of over 600 standard indicators . . . were primarily output indicators. These are reported . . . through a comprehensive and cumbersome database called the Unified Foreign Assistance Coordination and Tracking System (FACTS).

F had emphasized budgeting and monitoring and had ignored evaluation. In 2008, F created an evaluation unit and defined the F role as coordinating, facilitating, and advocating for:

- policy, guidance, and standards for foreign assistance;
- cross-cutting and multi-agency evaluations;
- technical assistance (advice and support) to program staff;
- analysis of evaluation data including gaps and priorities;
- documentation and dissemination.[8]

Rice's restructuring of foreign assistance administration and the aftermath of this process exemplify how political rationality and technical rationality intersect in public policy implementation. While the nature and purposes of the reorganization can be set forth in the language of technical rationality, as Tobias testified before the House committee, the political motivations were almost certainly a factor as well.

The dual role of Tobias was a deft, if controversial, move to enhance the secretary's authority to redirect foreign aid programs in support of the Bush administration's foreign policy objectives. By 2014, the leader in charge of USAID and the Office of Foreign Assistance Resources (the former OFA) was no longer the same individual. The DFA was no longer a deputy undersecretary of state but, instead, reported to one.

In the meantime, USAID reestablished its independence and brought back a function it had abandoned in 2006, creating a bureau of policy, planning, and learning. The bureau focuses on "policy and strategy, ensures policy coherence and coordination, informs external audiences about Agency direction, ensures development perspectives are actively considered in foreign and national security policy formulation, and reinvigorates USAID's leadership within the development community."[9]

CONFRONTING PUBLIC MANAGEMENT'S CHALLENGES: ANALYTICAL TOOLS

Public managers have many sources of guidance and insights concerning how to balance political and technical rationality in achieving good results: their own experience, knowledge, and common sense; the expertise within their organizations; the lore of best practices; consultancies; and professional literatures. In addition to these resources, achieving success requires the personal ability to meet the analytical demands of public management. The discussion to follow sets forth some analytical tools that enable critical analysis of the challenges of implementing public policy.

Two intellectual tools that have proven especially useful for analysis of public management's distinctive challenges are derived from the application of economic concepts and models to problems of public policy implementation. Both the principal-agent model and transaction cost theory can frame analysis of structural arrangements for accomplishing an organization's work. Many such structures may be imposed by policymakers, but public managers, especially at senior levels, generally have the latitude to make at least some of these choices.

The Chain of Command: Principals and Agents

Significant insights into the challenges of public management in an administrative hierarchy can be derived from what political economists call the **principal-agent problem**.[ii] The basic characteristics of principal-agent relationships are

- a hierarchical superior (the principal) aims to achieve a particular result or outcome but must rely on another party (the agent) for implementation, and
- both principal and agent are assumed to be rational and to act in ways consistent with their own best interests.

The relationship is further characterized by at least two types of **information asymmetries,** or differences in the information they have, about the preferences, actions, and achievements of the agent:

- **Adverse selection** refers to differences in preferences, beliefs, or knowledge on the part of principal and agent that are present *ex ante* or prior to entering into an agreement.
- **Moral hazard** refers to the actions an agent takes *ex post,* after entering into the contract agreement.[10]

The principal's goal is to design a contractual relationship with incentives that induce the agent to pursue the principal's objectives even in the presence of these information asymmetries. In other words, the principal wants to design incentives and monitoring that "[prompt] the agent to behave as the principal herself would under whatever conditions might prevail."[11] Such concerns are often present in "organizational analysis, whether the substance has to do with decentralization, division of labor, formal rules, structure, communication, or ownership vs. control: all are reflections of efforts to control the productive efforts of organization members."[12]

> The principal's goal is to design a contractual relationship with incentives that induce the agent to pursue the principal's objectives even in the presence of these information asymmetries.

Principal-agent problems are often present in organizations with frontline service providers, because they have relatively high levels of discretion and autonomy from organizational authority (increasing the risk of moral hazard), and because their interests and preferences differ from those of managers (adverse selection). The efforts of social workers and police officers, for example, are difficult for managers to observe and evaluate, and these working professionals may have different values than their managers in carrying out their responsibilities.

Regardless of the specific setting, principal-agent problems exist because the principal and agent cannot fully describe and agree in advance on the actions to be taken in every conceivable situation. Although structures such

---

[ii]In addition to the references cited in this section, see Kenneth Arrow, "The Economics of Agency," in *Principals and Agents,* ed. John Pratt and Richard Zeckhauser (Boston, MA: Harvard Business School Press, 1985).

as rules, agreements, regulations, or contracts may be defined and imposed *ex ante* to govern the behavior of agents, it simply is not possible to know the preferences of the agent or to conceive of every problematic situation that might arise on which agreement in advance would be needed.

Ex ante agreements also do not ensure full compliance because of the moral hazard problem; even with a specification covering a particular contingency, the principal may not be able to tell whether the agent abides by its terms: Did the social worker really make every effort desired by management to encourage a client to find work? Performance measurement and management attempt, as the reorganization of foreign assistance illustrates, to reduce information asymmetries between principals and agents.

Yet the managerial challenge of aligning interests remains. Ideally, it will be in the agent's interest to pursue the outcomes that the principal desires and to make the desired level of effort, with as few structural constraints as possible. The culture and craft aspects of public management may be effective in aligning interests and ensuring compliance in principal-agent relationships.

Transaction Costs

The **transaction costs** associated with exchanges and interactions between actors are another concept that managers can use to analyze formal and informal contractual relationships.[13] Transaction cost analysis has been used to examine the making of economic policy, antitrust rules, local governments' decisions on whether to contract with an agent to produce or provide goods or services to other public or private sector entities, and the relative efficiency of private versus public vision of, for example, mental health services.[iii] The general point is that it may be cheaper and easier to organize transactions one way rather than another.

With the transaction as the unit of analysis, transaction cost theory holds that in any exchange, costs—of money, time, or opportunity—are incurred to gain information, bargain, monitor, and enforce agreements between actors. An analysis based on transaction cost theory focuses on three main characteristics of the transaction:

- frequency (how often the transaction take place);
- uncertainty (the predictability of the production process and other factors affecting either party to the transaction over the time period of the transaction); and
- asset specificity (the degree to which assets, both physical and human, are uniquely suited to a particular transaction and cannot be easily converted to other uses).

Asset specificity is important because specialized investments in facilities, equipment, or specialized skills may be difficult to convert to other uses. Investing in a specialized facility may create a dependency on continued support because that facility can perform no other kind of work; the principal and the agent may become locked in to a continued relationship.

[iii]For economic policy, see Avinash Dixit, *The Making of Economic Policy: A Transaction Cost Politics Perspective* (Cambridge, MA: MIT Press, 1996); antitrust rules, Paul L. Joskow, "Transaction Cost Economics, Antitrust Rules, and Remedies," *Journal of Law, Economics, and Organization* 18, no. 1 (2002): 95–116; contracting out, Trevor L. Brown and Matthew Potoski, "Transaction Costs and Institutional Explanations for Government Service Production Decisions," *Journal of Public Administration Research and Theory* 13, no. 4 (2003): 441–468; and contracting out mental health services, Anne M. Libby and Neal T. Wallace, "Effects of Contracting and Local Markets on Costs of Public Mental Health Services in California," *Psychiatric Services* 49 (1998): 1067–1071.

Transaction cost analysis uses information about the frequency, uncertainty, and asset specificity of transactions to identify structures—typically, markets or hierarchies—that are consistent with achieving the lowest transaction costs. Transactions that are infrequent, have low uncertainty and have low asset specificity tend to incur lower transaction costs and are best conducted through markets, while transactions that are frequent, uncertain, and have high asset specificity tend to be more costly, and these costs might be minimized by conducting the transaction in-house, rather than in the market:

- The acquisition of standard office computers for a particular government office would tend to have low transaction costs because their purchase occurs relatively rarely, the technology or the time needed to produce and deliver them is fairly predictable, and neither the computers nor the resources used to produce them are uniquely suited for that particular transaction or ultimate office destination. Therefore, the preferred way to provide computers for an office would be through the market.
- In contrast, the design of a complex new weapon system to meet specialized military requirements, because it is a onetime undertaking that is fraught with uncertainty and requires unique capabilities, might be better conducted by an in-house research and development organization rather than by a contractor.

Ensuring that both parties' expectations are satisfied—achieving what is termed **reciprocity**—can be viewed through the lens of transaction costs. Taking into account the key components of transaction costs is fundamental to reasonably guaranteeing that all parties are satisfied with the results of the contract exchange. For example, a no-questions-asked product return policy will be costly for a producer or seller but may attract customers who want assurances that they will be satisfied with their purchase.

Principal-agent analysis and transaction cost analysis are not the only theories or analytic tools available to public managers as they consider the management challenges they face. Further, the potential applications of these two analytic tools extend far beyond those issues faced by individual managers to include institutional relationships as well. Still, these two approaches are particularly relevant to public managers addressing issues and problems internal to their organizations.

ORGANIZATIONAL STRUCTURE

Public management takes place in organizations: departments, agencies, bureaus, and offices of federal, state, and local governments. Cases and examples throughout the book exemplify these types of organizations, such as the U.S. Department of Health and Human Services and its subordinate entity the Centers for Medicare and Medicaid Services; the Office of the Director of National Intelligence and the National Security Agency; the State of Missouri's Division of Youth Services; and the City of Austin's publicly owned electric utility, Austin Energy.

Structured by political processes, these organizations are where public policies are implemented by managers within the structures of authority established in law by policymakers. Managers in these organizations are under pressure to be efficient and effective, even though technical rationality was not the primary factor in their development.

Organizational theorists have considered how and why organizations are internally structured in order to accomplish their missions. The following are some examples:

- Administration scholars Derek S. Pugh and colleagues define and operationalize the dimensions of organization structure as specialization, standardization, formalization, centralization, and configuration.[14]
- Organization theorist Richard Scott focuses on those elements "defining the division of labor—structural differentiation, including occupational and role specialization, departmentalization, and multidivisional forms—and those relating to coordination and control of work—formalization, hierarchy, centralization, and various structures for facilitating lateral information flows."[15]
- Organization scholar James D. Thompson points out, "major components of a complex organization . . . are further segmented, or departmentalized, and connections are established within and between departments," leading to "internal differentiation and patterning of relationships."[16]

These definitions of organization structure, not surprisingly, clearly belong to the structure dimension of public management. Identifying these aspects and understanding their implications for managerial choice and organizational performance will be an important part of managerial analysis. For example, the next section concerns the specification and relationships of positions and job tasks. Subsections will also consider other important structural features that managers may influence: budgeting, contracting out, and management of networks, for example.

Public management teaching, research, and practice cut across many scientific disciplines and specialized fields of study. Throughout this section, theories, models, and frameworks are drawn from economics, political economy, political science, and organization theory that have proven especially useful in public policy and management analysis.

Positions and Tasks

One major constraining structure is that of the job positions, tasks, and reporting relationships in an organization. Job positions and their relationship to each other are often conveyed in an organization chart, which represents the formal and usually hierarchical structure of work in an organization. Figure 6.1 shows the organization chart of the Sheriff's Office in Catawba County, North Carolina.

Positions in an organization can be classified as either line or staff positions. **Line positions**—narcotics investigators, night-shift road patrol officers, detention officers—deliver services or are otherwise directly involved in implementation or production of the organization's output. **Staff positions,** such as the business managers or administrative assistants, provide administrative support for the line positions but are not directly involved in the implementation of the organization's programs or policies, in this case, ensuring safety. Public administration scholars Patricia W. Ingraham and Amy Kneedler Donahue focus on the importance of having adequate staff positions to perform an organization's overhead functions: financial management, human resources management, information technology management, and capital management.[17] They argue that these "[administrative functions] support all of the other managerial work of government more directly related to running programs."[18] Assuring such functional capability, they believe, is a necessary condition for managing and achieving effective policy implementation.

Public administration scholar Paul C. Light has documented the trend within federal agencies toward the "thickening government," the number of managerial positions between the frontline positions providing services and the top management position.[19] Using information from the *Federal Yellow Book* directory, Light reports that federal managerial position titles and layers grew in number from 17 managerial titles in 1960, including secretary, undersecretary, assistant secretary, and deputy assistant secretary, to 64 in 2004, adding positions of principal associate deputy secretary, principal assistant deputy undersecretary, and chief of staff to the assistant secretary.[20] The breadth of the hierarchy has also grown, from 451 senior executives in 1960 to 2,592 in 2004. (These positions

FIGURE 6.1

Catawba County, NC, Sheriff's Office Organization, Fiscal Year 2014 to 2015

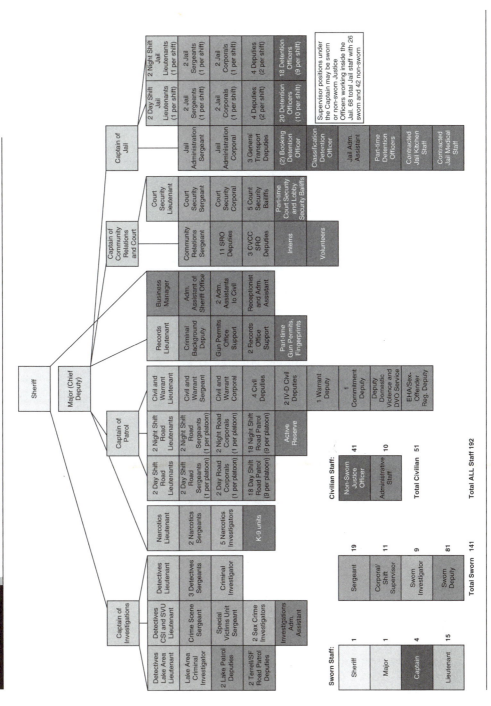

Source: http://www.catawbacountync.gov/sheriff/SHFOrgChart.pdf.

include political appointees as well as career staff.) In Light's view, four explanations account for the thickening trends: "(1) an ever-expanding federal agenda, (2) the use of promotions in lieu of pay increases as a reward for senior career executives, (3) the effort to control the federal bureaucracy through ever denser networks of political appointees, and (4) the creation of new titles such as the chief information officer and inspector general by Congress."[21]

Certain positions by definition have power over others. In the Catawba County Sheriff's Office, the organization chart indicates that the two night shift road lieutenants have power over the two night shift road sergeants but not over the community relations sergeant. Positions in and of themselves impart power, as Scott explains, because

> differences in power are built into the design of the technologies or into the definition of relations among positions, and these power differences are normatively justified. . . . Those with structural power do not need to mobilize resources in order to have their interests taken into account. It is automatically assumed that they are "entitled" to be represented in any matter affecting their interests. By contrast, interests that are not structured have to become mobilized if they are to be heard.[22]

Positions therefore are structural features that directly affect working relationships within the organization.

An organization is said to be **tightly coupled** if its organization chart provides a reasonably accurate depiction of its interdependence of relationships—that is, the positions are highly interdependent, and their formal structures determine or closely correspond with how work actually gets done in the organization. If, on the other hand, the organization chart does not provide an accurate depiction of how work is actually accomplished—that is, the positions have low interdependence and the formal structure and actual activity are not closely linked—the organization is said to be **loosely coupled.** (Public schools are the quintessential loosely coupled organizations.) In loosely coupled organizations, formal structure primarily serves as the "myth and ceremony" rather than the hard reality of organizational life (further discussed in Chapter 9).[23]

The social sciences offer a number of theories and heuristics that can provide insight into structuring jobs, positions, and tasks.

Multitask Principal-Agent Problems

When multiple tasks must be completed, a manager (as principal) must decide on job design (how the tasks will be grouped into job positions for the agent). These situations are extensions of the moral hazard problem. Economists Bengt Holmstrom and Paul Milgrom point out that in multitask situations,

> incentives for tasks can be provided in two ways: either the task itself can be rewarded or the marginal opportunity cost for the task can be lowered by removing or reducing the incentives on competing tasks. Constraints are substitutes for performance incentives and are extensively used when it is hard to assess the performance of the agent.[24]

The implication for managers is that tasks that are easier to observe and measure should be assigned to different jobs than those tasks that are more difficult to measure. In this way, constraints—structures through job position definition—may be effective for directing the work of agents toward managerial or organizational goals, even when performance is not measured.

Another model implication is that if an agent's work requires many different tasks but performance on some is more easily measured than on others, strong incentives should not be provided for the more easily measured tasks. If strong incentives are present, agents will devote less effort to job tasks where performance is difficult to measure.[25]

For example, casework in a welfare-to-work office involves assessing clients' needs at intake, assigning clients to education or work activities, monitoring clients in these activities, developing job contacts, and other activities. Managers may find it easier to assess the number of job contacts that a caseworker has developed but more difficult to assess the caseworker's success in assessing clients' needs. A caseworker whose job definition includes the full range of casework tasks would be more likely to devote attention to developing job contacts than to focusing on clients' needs at intake. A multitask principal-agent perspective would lead the manager to either offer weak incentives for any specific task for caseworkers responsible for the full range of activities or to have some caseworkers specialize in developing job contacts and placements.[26]

> **If an agent's work requires many different tasks but performance on some is more easily measured than on others, strong incentives should not be provided for the more easily measured tasks.**

Common Agency (Multiple Principals) Problems

When an agent has two or more principals, each principal will offer specific incentives so the agent's activities align with the principal's interests.[27] These situations involve both adverse selection and moral hazard. In theory, this situation can lead to an efficient aggregation of the principals' varying interests. But an agent may have interests of his or her own that differ from those of one or all principals.

For example, a manager may hire an employee to serve as a financial coordinator for a department. Seeking to cut costs, the manager may share the position with another department within the same broad organizational unit. While the financial coordinator job functions may be similar or even identical for the two departments, a common agency problem arises. Each principal will have preferences about how the agent spends his or her time and how he or she handles particular tasks, and their preferences may differ. The financial coordinator may be able to take advantage of the resulting uncertainty as to who is the boss and create greater autonomy for himself or herself. The situation is similar when two organizations receive financial support and direction from more than one external organization.[iv]

Advisory Tasks, Operating Tasks, and Uncertainty Absorption

Political scientist Thomas H. Hammond argues that a bureaucratic structure "influences which options are to be compared, in what sequence, and by whom. Thus, *a particular organizational structure is, in effect, the organization's agenda* [emphasis in orginal]."[28] He concludes that "it is impossible to design a 'neutral' structure, that is, a structure that does not influence the choices that are made via the structure."[29] Structure always influences outcomes.

Hammond's analytic model addresses two types of tasks: the flow of advice upward through the organization (**advisory tasks**) and the resolution of operational conflicts (**operating tasks**). Hammond develops several propositions for advisory tasks, including the following:

- "The organizational structure can influence what options the [agency head] has available for choice, and thus can influence what choices the director makes."
- "Different structures may convert the same raw data into different kinds of official organizational beliefs."[30]

[iv]For a fuller discussion of common agency problems, see Anthony M. Bertelli and Laurence E. Lynn Jr., "Policy Making in the Parallelogram of Forces: Common Agency and Human Services," *Policy Studies Journal* 32 (August 2004): 297–315.

Hammond argues that operating tasks are fundamental to decision making in bureaucracies:

> When there are conflicts among field officials doing some work, a low-level supervisor will often settle the dispute on the spot so the work can proceed. The director may never even discover that some informal "policy" has thereby been adopted or, perhaps even worse, that some "official" policy is being contravened. . . .
>
> The organizational structure will determine which of these conflicts rise to the director for resolution and which do not. What the director knows about his organization, and thus what kinds of issues he has influence over, will be a function of the structure. If we think of structures as agendas affecting who makes what choices from among what options, these agendas may be even more important for operating tasks than for advisory tasks because they will keep high-level officials *from being involved at all* in some kinds of issues.[31]

Uncertainty absorption occurs when the recommendations that staff develop based on a body of evidence are communicated to hierarchical superiors, but the evidence itself is not communicated. Managers may have difficulty judging the validity, consistency, or correctness of the recommendations they receive. A perennial example of uncertainty absorption is the president's daily brief (PDB), a daily intelligence report for which the director of national intelligence is responsible. In the PDB, statements or claims—not detailed evidence—tend to be reported, and the claims depend in turn upon the coordination of intelligence across a number of sources, which usually means they incorporate compromises and gloss over doubts or disagreements.

Findings from the investigation of the space shuttle *Columbia* accident illustrate insights from this model. The accident report suggested that NASA administrator Sean O'Keefe did not know about concerns at lower levels of the organization regarding the dangers to the orbiter while it was in flight. One implication of Hammond's analysis is that a structure could have been created that would have pushed the NASA engineers' anxieties up to higher levels, perhaps all the way to O'Keefe, in a timely fashion. The causes of the *Columbia* accident were almost certainly multidimensional, not only structural. Yet Hammond's framework provides a specific explanation for understanding the role that structure might have played in this situation.

Routine

Sociologist Charles B. Perrow focuses on positions and tasks in an organization as well. He argues that work processes (or technologies) may be divided into two dimensions: the *frequency* with which exceptional situations arise and the degree to which these exceptions are *analyzable*, that is, whether rational investigation and intervention can address and correct them.[32]

- At one end of the range are **routine technologies**, characterized by few exceptions that are easily analyzable, such as administrative support jobs that require checking completed forms or making copies.
- At the other end of the range are **non-routine technologies**, characterized by many exceptions that are difficult to analyze, such as research and development activities.

Between these two ends are technologies with combinations of the two characteristics:

- **craft technologies** with few exceptions but difficult to analyze, such as budget analysis; and
- **engineering technologies** with many exceptions relatively easy to analyze, such as auditing review.

Perrow argues that the type of task technology has implications for management and supervision of activities.

- Routine tasks can be managed with more rules and less coordination and communication.
- Less-routine tasks must be managed with fewer rules, a greater amount of communication and coordination, and therefore, greater decentralization of authority.

Example: An Attempt to Change the Administrative Technology of Criminal Prosecution

Prosecution of crimes is an administrative technology that might be considered non-routine, with processes that are not easily standardized. Criminal prosecutions tend to be decentralized, with local prosecutors deciding on the strategies for each case. In 2003, when John D. Ashcroft was the U.S. attorney general, he sought to change the basic technology of prosecutions by directing federal prosecutors to seek the most serious provable charges in almost all cases and thus to reduce the amount of plea-bargaining.[33]

This directive was intended to impose routine into prosecutions, subject to standards from the central office. Exceptions to the policy would require approval from higher levels in the Justice Department. Critics charged that Ashcroft was taking away discretion from local prosecutors. A *New York Times* story described the likely behavioral responses to the new policy:

> Almost no one expects strict enforcement of the directive. Instead, if history is any guide, local prosecutors will retain substantial flexibility but will exercise it quietly and early, before, rather than after, charges are filed . . .
>
> Allowing prosecutors to decide on which crimes are "readily provable" also gives them great discretion. And several prosecutors said they doubted that officials in Washington would have a way to enforce the policy in far-flung districts.[34]

Ashcroft's reform sought to change fundamentally the administrative technology of criminal prosecutions by imposing a constraining structure on local prosecutors. Yet in one sense, this directive could not change the fundamental nature of the prosecutorial task or the amount of discretion involved, because discretion was merely shifted to an earlier stage in the process.

Observability of Outputs and Outcomes

In his popular monograph, *Bureaucracy: What Government Agencies Do and Why They Do It,* political scientist James Q. Wilson identifies four types of work in public organizations, defined as different aspects of two factors: outputs—the nature of the day-to-day work, or the operational activities of the organization—and outcomes—the nature of the impact of this work on individuals and society:

- In **production organizations**, outputs and outcomes are easily observed and relatively easily measured. Public managers can, within the constraints of their political contexts, more readily pursue the goal of efficient operations. Wilson cites the Internal Revenue Service (IRS) and the Social Security Administration (SSA) as production organizations.
- In **procedural organizations**, outputs are observable by managers, but outcomes may be far less observable or measurable. Here, Wilson cites human service organizations, such as mental health agencies, where treatments

can be observed, but impacts on patients or clients may be difficult to identify. In procedural organizations, public managers tend to focus on measuring work activity rather than outcome achievement.

- In **craft organizations**, operational activities are difficult to observe, but the outcomes are more readily observable. Wilson points to investigative agencies whose operations may be less standardized and are conducted in the field, such as those that regulate mines, slaughterhouses, and assembly lines. Public managers in these organizations may allow considerable discretion to employees in the field and seek to earn their trust.

- In **coping organizations**, neither operational activities nor their impacts are observable. Wilson sees police departments and public schools, especially in urban areas, as coping organizations. Here the public managers may face chronic conflict with operational personnel and external stakeholders, and their jobs are often regarded as impossible, a phenomenon discussed further in Chapter 12.

This section has focused on how particular positions, tasks, and technologies are organized to carry out the work of an organization. Managers who either are operating within already-defined structures with particular positions or types of tasks, or have control over how to define those positions, need to be aware of the various implications for how work is done and how it can (or cannot) be managed effectively. While adequate staffing of major administrative functions is undoubtedly important, so, too, is the capability of line operations and, in particular, the capabilities of those on the front lines of service provision.

On the Front Lines: Discretion and Local Justice

Street-level bureaucrats are the people who implement policies or deliver services at the front lines, where public employees and their agents directly engage citizens.[35] They are local prosecutors, teachers, welfare caseworkers, prison guards, police officers, forest rangers, customs officials, and agricultural extension agents.

> **Street-level bureaucrats are local prosecutors, teachers, welfare caseworkers, prison guards, police officers, forest rangers, customs officials, and agricultural extension agents.**

Their work can be controversial because it directly affects people's well-being. The competence and judgment of front line workers literally may have life and death significance. Many such workers, moreover, perform labor-intensive services. Modern technology, such as radar guns for police to catch speeders and digitized systems for tracking welfare cases, may help them be more productive. But, as individuals, their positions and tasks are indispensable to the implementation of public policies.[v]

Awareness of the position of street-level bureaucrats and how they perform their jobs is important for public managers because the priorities of managers and street-level bureaucrats may differ. Political scientist Michael Lipsky, who coined the term *street-level bureaucrats*, argues that managers tend to be oriented toward high-level organizational and policy goals, while frontline workers tend to be client oriented; managers want cooperation with higher level objectives and accountability (on which the manager's own

---

[v]In addition to the sources cited in this section, see Evelyn Z. Brodkin, "Inside the Welfare Contract: Discretion and Accountability in State Welfare Administration," *Social Service Review* 71, no. 1 (1997): 1–33; Marcia K. Meyers and Susan Vorsanger, "Street-Level Bureaucrats and the Implementation of Public Policy," in *Handbook of Public Administration,* ed. B. Guy Peters and Jon Pierre (Thousand Oaks, CA: Sage, 2003) 245–255; Norma M. Riccucci, *How Management Matters: Street-Level Bureaucrats and Welfare Reform* (Washington, DC: Georgetown University Press, 2005); and Steven Rathgeb Smith, "Street-Level Bureaucracy and Public Policy," Peters and Pierre, 354–365.

success may depend), while frontline workers want support, resources, and freedom from undue interference.[36] Each depends on the other, but tensions are inevitable, and breakdowns in relationships are common.

Attorney General Ashcroft's unsuccessful efforts to minimize prosecutorial plea-bargaining by U.S. attorneys in the field during the George W. Bush Administration were a direct managerial attempt to limit local prosecutors' discretion, described earlier. Ashcroft believed that "defendants shouldn't receive different sentences depending on which assistant prosecutor they happen to get."[37] As noted, the attempted reform merely shifted the locus of prosecutorial discretion to other steps in the process of criminal prosecution:

> If a defendant actually sold five kilograms of cocaine but is found for sentencing purposes to have sold only four, his sentencing range will be 8 to 10 years instead of 10 to 12. This reduction can be accomplished if the prosecutor stipulates, as part of a plea agreement, to less cocaine than he could prove, or if the judge finds that, despite evidence of five kilos, only four have been proven. . . . . The length of the average federal drug sentence has been declining since the early 1990s, largely as a result of choices made by both prosecutors and judges during plea bargaining and sentencing. And sentence manipulation is not confined to drug cases.[38]

In the logic of the principal-agent model, a frontline agent engaged in multiple, complex tasks may be able to evade a principal's directive that does not take account of task complexity.

Example: Agricultural Inspection and the Customs and Border Protection Agency

Agricultural inspection officers are street-level bureaucrats.[vi] Before they became part of the Customs and Border Protection (CBP) agency of the U.S. Department of Homeland Security (DHS), these officers were part of the Plant Protection and Quarantine Agency in the Agriculture Department. Their job is to implement the Plant Protection Act, which is designed to keep pests and illegal or diseased plants from entering the United States. The act empowers this agency to impose civil penalties on violators of the law if, first, the person "made a negative declaration (oral or written) to the primary inspector," that is, lied about trying to bring in illegal plants, and, second, "if the primary declaration was negative, the person must have been given an opportunity to amend that declaration," that is, given a chance to tell the truth.[39]

Prior to the structural reform that created the CBP, an officer from either Immigration and Naturalization Service (INS) or U.S. Customs (USC) obtained the initial declaration. If that officer was suspicious, the person would be sent to a second inspector, an agriculture officer, for a more thorough review. If appropriate, the second officer would administer the second criterion, asking for an amended declaration. A civil penalty could be imposed on someone trying to smuggle illegal plants into the country only if both officers, in sequence, did their jobs.

With the creation of DHS, terrorism deterrence became the chief mission of border protection. The primary inspector from INS or USC now asks a person "in general terms" what he or she is bringing into the country; if the response raises suspicion, the primary inspector may pursue the second criterion and may search the vehicle, instead of automatically bringing in an agricultural officer. Because primary inspectors now have discretion over whether to refer someone to a secondary inspector, some vehicles are released without further referral to an agricultural officer. The result, according to one agricultural inspection officer, is that protecting agriculture has a lower

---

[vi]This example is based on information in Max Leimgruber, "Agricultural Inspections on the California-Mexico Border: The Impacts of Public Policy," *Public Administration & Management: An Interactive Journal* 8, no. 3 (2003): 215–224.

priority than it did before the structural reorganization of DHS, and smugglers know this.[40] This example points to the influence of structural arrangements on discretion and the locus of control, the importance of discretion, the potential disconnect between the interests of street-level bureaucrats and their hierarchical superiors, and the challenges of managing in organizations that include street-level bureaucrat positions.

Street-level bureaucrats' judgments are indispensable to quality service and to individualized justice that can reflect the unique aspects of each situation or individual. Human services clients expect that the workers serving them have discretion and the power to address their particular problems. The values, motives, and incentives facing frontline workers are likely to shape their judgments. One implication is that street-level bureaucrats who work for private sector organizations (for-profit or nonprofit)—a growing trend in social services—may exercise judgment in ways fundamentally different from employees of public organizations.[vii] Managing in organizations involving street-level bureaucrats, no matter which sector employs them, is likely to involve structure as well as aspects of organizational culture and managerial craft, discussed in Chapters 8 through 11.

The organization and provision of services by frontline workers and first responders have broad ramifications for social justice. Field-level workers in public bureaucracies have the power to allocate scarce resources among program beneficiaries. Their decisions may introduce inequities or biases, what Jon Elster called **local justice**. These judgments may or may not be subject to checks and balances such as class action lawsuits alleging violations of constitutional and statutory rights. Constituencies may be unduly subsidized or protected or, alternatively, they may be overregulated or penalized.

Budgets: Is Bigger Always Better?

As noted in Chapter 5, budgets are constraining structures that convey priorities of budget makers in the form of resource constraints and rules for their use. Political scientist Aaron Wildavsky described a budget as "a series of goals with price tags attached."[41]

While budgets provide prominent constraints for public managers and their agencies, the characteristics of many budget processes mean that budgets can also be enabling structures. That is, managers may be able to play a role in defining and shaping their budgets and hence their programmatic priorities.

But when it comes to their budgets, what do public managers want? Questions concerning whether and how public managers have control over their budgets are raised in the theories of economist William A. Niskanen and political scientist Patrick Dunleavy.

Employing a rational choice perspective, Niskanen argues that self-interested public agency officials are focused on increasing their own power and prestige.[42] He argues that the path to greater power is through larger budgets. This **budget-maximizing bureaucrat** model has been the primary rational choice view of public managers. It is consistent with stereotypes of self-serving, inefficient bureaucrats whose budgets are always inadequate for good performance. From a structural perspective, the model's implication is that policymakers and public managers influence a primary structure under which governments and their agents operate: their budgets.[viii]

[vii]See, for example, Janice Johnson Dias and Steven Maynard-Moody, "For-Profit Welfare: Contracts, Conflicts, and the Performance Paradox," *Journal of Public Administration Research and Theory* 17, no. 2 (2007): 189–211.

[viii]For a critical appraisal of this theory, see Andre Blais and Stephane Dion, eds., *The Budget-Maximizing Bureaucrat: Appraisals and Evidence* (Pittsburgh, PA: University of Pittsburgh Press, 1991).

In contrast to Niskanen's monolithic view, Dunleavy's model of the **bureau-shaping bureaucrat** holds that public officials do not have a uniform interest in maximizing their budgets.[43] Individuals will only pursue goals that have a net payoff greater than the payoff from doing something else. Because of the collective action problems that exist within agencies, if the effort costs to an individual official of securing a larger budget are greater than the expected value of that larger budget to the official, then the individual has an incentive to free-ride on the efforts of other officials by letting them work for budget increases.

Rather than seeking larger budgets, senior officials are more likely to pursue work-related benefits that preserve or enhance their standing or their future opportunities. Dunleavy argues that they want satisfying work, a congenial work environment, and a balance of intrinsic (personal) and extrinsic (economic) rewards that include status, prestige, patronage, and influence. The consequence is that "rational officials want to work in small, elite, collegial bureaus close to political power centers. They do not want to head up heavily staffed, large budget but routine, conflictual, and low-status agencies."[44]

> Public managers are drawn to bureau-shaping strategies that include structural aspects such as major internal reorganizations, transformation of internal work practices, competition with other bureaus, contracting out, and load-shedding.

An implication of this model is that public managers are drawn to bureau-shaping strategies that include structural aspects such as major internal reorganizations, transformation of internal work practices, competition with other bureaus, contracting out (provision by government but production by the private sector or other governmental entities, discussed later in this chapter), and load-shedding (encouraging provision and production by the private sector).

Laurence E. Lynn, Jr. also argues that public managers' motives are more complex than budget maximization. Managers seek discretion and control within a given budget and "regularly seek to demonstrate to sponsors the existence of unmet needs, deficiencies in the quality of output, inadequate enforcement, insufficient outreach, and the like."[45] In state and local agencies, in contrast, "it is not unusual for officials to seek reputations for maintaining control over spending, eliminating waste, fraud, and abuse from budgets and for achieving gains in efficiency that save money."[46]

Rules

A **rule** in the public administration context is "an agency statement of general or particular applicability and future effect designed to implement, interpret, or prescribe law or policy or describing the organization, procedure, or practice requirements of an agency."[ix] Examples include rules from the Affordable Care Act (see the discussion questions at the end of this chapter) and regulation of greenhouse gases (see Chapter 2).[x] Rulemaking is a major responsibility of public management, supplementing legislative statutes. It provides detailed guidance regarding the implementation of lawfully authorized policies and programs. All federal rulemaking is governed by the Administrative Procedure Act of 1946, although other statutes affect the rulemaking of specific agencies such as the EPA.

[ix]5 U.S.C. § 551(4) in Congressional Research Service, "A Brief Overview of Rulemaking and Judicial Review, January 4, 2011, 1, http://www.wise-intern.org/orientation/documents/CRSrulemakingCB.pdf. For a nonlegal discussion of federal rulemaking, see CRS Report RL32240, *The Federal Rulemaking Process: An Overview*, by Curtis W. Copeland.

[x]Federal rules and related documents can be found at www.federalregister.gov.

Rulemaking takes place in two types of federal agencies: regulatory agencies and programmatic agencies. Chapter 7 discusses rulemaking by regulatory agencies, a vast and highly specialized function of the American administrative state. These agencies include the Federal Communications Commission and the Federal Election Commission, which are administratively independent of the executive branch. The aim is impartial regulatory processes.

The discussion in this section is concerned with rulemaking that takes place in programmatic or line departments and agencies such as the Department of Health and Human Services (HHS). Within HHS, rulemaking is conducted by line agencies, such as the Centers for Medicare and Medicaid Services (CMS) and by the Food and Drug Administration (FDA). These organizations function with a substantial degree of independence from the political chain of command. The difference emphasized here is that rulemaking in a nonregulatory department or agency is inevitably influenced by the policy politics associated with the missions it is mandated and empowered to carry out. Rulemaking is subject to judicial review, as described in Chapters 2 and 7.

Appreciation of the specialized effort needed to translate legislative mandates into government operations and their outputs and outcomes will enhance the effectiveness of public management and citizens' understanding of how their governments work within the rule of law. By far the most commonly used rulemaking process is **informal rulemaking**, also known as notice-and-comment, or Section 553, rulemaking (a reference to the APA provision that authorizes it).[xi] According to the CRS, "agencies are required to provide the public with adequate notice of a proposed rule followed by a meaningful opportunity to comment on the rule's content."[47]

A detailed record of federal rulemaking is maintained in the Unified Agenda of Federal Regulatory and Deregulatory Actions, which is published by the Regulatory Information Service Center (RISC), a component of the U.S. General Services Administration (GSA), for the Office of Management and Budget's (OMB) Office of Information and Regulatory Affairs (OIRA). The Unified Agenda lists information in the following categories:

- "active" actions, including rules in the prerule stage (e.g., advance notices of proposed rulemaking that are expected to be issued in the next 12 months);
- proposed rule stage (i.e., notices of proposed rulemaking that are expected to be issued in the next 12 months or for which the closing date of the comment period is the next step); and
- final rule stage (i.e., final rules or other final actions that are expected to be issued in the next 12 months);
- "completed" actions (i.e., final rules or rules that have been withdrawn since the last edition of the Unified Agenda); and
- "long-term" actions (i.e., items under development that agencies do not expect to take action on in the next 12 months).[xii]

[xi]Comprehensive and detailed information on the rulemaking process, as discussed in Chapter 7, has been prepared by the Federal Register.

[xii]Congressional Research Service, "Upcoming Rules Pursuant to the Patient Protection and Affordable Care Act: The Spring 2014 Unified Agenda, June 30, 2014, http://fas.org/sgp/crs/misc/R43622.pdf. Unified Agenda at http://www.reginfo.gov/public/do/eAgendaMain. Section 1311 of PL 111-148 is an 11-page section of the ACA. Rule issued under its authority is now in 45 CFR 155 and 156.

For example, as a result of a rulemaking process, the U.S. Department of Agriculture's Forest Service issued a rule concerning National Forest System Land Management Planning:

> In this final rule, guidelines are described as "information and guidance for project and activity decision-making." Guidelines will not contain final decisions approving activities and uses. A Responsible Official has the discretion to act within the range of guidelines, as well as the latitude to depart from guidelines when circumstances warrant it. In the latter case, the Responsible Official should document the rationale for taking such exception to guidelines.[48]

This language constitutes a clear delegation to field-level managers of authority to use their discretion in deciding how rigorously to adhere to agency-provided guidelines.

Example: NHTSA, General Motors, and Recalls of Faulty Ignition Switches

The exercise of discretion by agency regulators can be perilous. In the spring of 2014, the General Motors Corporation (GM) came under intense criticism that failing to delay recalls of faulty ignition switches had caused fatal accidents. Considerable finger pointing identified not only GM's management but also regulators at the National Highway Traffic Safety Administration (NHTSA), an agency of the U.S. Department of Transportation.[49] Were regulators insufficiently aggressive in investigating reports of faulty switches that they began receiving as early as 2007? Did GM managers fail to provide sufficient information to NHTSA to enable an appropriate regulatory response?

Placed on the defensive, NHTSA officials insisted that the agency's overall record of investigating consumer complaints concerning vehicle safety and initiating recalls was excellent. According to NHTSA statements: "Each potential defect investigation is unique and dependent on the data gathered in each case. NHTSA uses a number of tools and techniques to gather and analyze data and look for trends that warrant a vehicle safety investigation, and possibly a recall."[50] The secretary of transportation, under pressure from legislators, initiated a review of how well regulators within the department were doing their jobs.

The controversies surrounding the ignition switch problem revealed the extent to which regulatory judgments, at the front line and elsewhere, are affected by competing priorities, preconceptions, faulty intuition, and ambiguous and incomplete information, all with public safety, agency reputation, and citizens' trust in government at stake.

Engaging Third Parties in Public Policy Implementation

As discussed in Chapter 5, public policymakers and public administrators have created a wide variety of alternatives to direct government. Among the most widespread is the employment of third parties (agents) to perform tasks that would otherwise be performed by public employees. Terms for this type of activity include **contracting-out, outsourcing, devolution,** and **privatization.** This section discusses the kinds of mechanisms used by government principals with third-party agents.

Contracts

Contracts are a ubiquitous enabling and constraining structure. A **contract** is a compact or agreement between actors with mutual interests that "encourage[s] the sort of actions each is to take, any payments that might flow from one to another, the rules and procedures they will use to decide matters in the future, and the behavior that each might expect from the others."[51] A successful contract is one that ensures full reciprocity between the contracting parties in the sense that each receives exactly what it expects to receive.

All of government involves contracts in the sense that agreements and understandings (formal or informal, explicit or implicit) have been reached between parties at many levels of government, involving interorganizational and intraorganizational relationships, that effort will be exchanged for rewards. They exist between

- citizens and elected officials,
- between elected officials and appointed officials and agency permanent staff,
- between managers and frontline workers in public organizations, and
- between public organizations and contractors in the public or private sectors.

In each of these relationships, the contractor is voluntarily under contract to meet the expectations of a superior or collaborator.

The discussion in this section concerns formal contractual relationships. Such contracts may be classified as either complete or incomplete:

- A **complete contract** covers all conceivable circumstances of interest to both parties, taking account of every relevant situation, incorporating uncertainty, and spelling out the actions the implementer will take.
- An **incomplete contract** does not (usually because it cannot) anticipate all conceivable circumstances that might arise. A solution to this problem is the relational contract. It frames a relationship without formalizing all aspects of it, perhaps supplemented by implicit contracts that express shared expectations and depend on trust for their reliable execution.

The Make-or-Buy Decision

Deciding whether to keep production of goods or services in-house or to contract it out is referred to as the **make-or-buy decision**. *In-house* in the current context means production by government agencies or organizations. As noted in Chapter 5, in some instances, mandates to contract out may be given by authorities external to the organization. These mandates could be expressed in laws, regulation, or other guidance from policymakers.

In other instances, the decision to contract out lies with an individual manager within the organization. When a public manager is making a decision about whether and how to contract out, understanding the benefits, costs, and trade-offs of the decision requires careful analysis. If contracting out is decided upon, the terms of the contract must be determined or negotiated, managed, and the contractor's performance must be monitored.

Direct government production may be optimal when the characteristics of the good or service are inherently governmental, as discussed in Chapter 5. When contracting out is possible, then the desirability of doing so can be analyzed using a number of different analytical approaches.

Transaction costs. Public management scholars Trevor L. Brown and Matthew Potoski consider local governments' decisions to make or buy more than 60 types of services such as data processing, treatment for drug and alcohol dependence, running correctional facilities, and sewage collection and treatment.[52] They propose the following hypotheses drawing on transaction cost theory, principal-agent theory, and institutional theory. Using data from the International City/County Management Association, the researchers find support for each of these hypotheses:

- Governments will produce a service in-house if it is characterized by high asset specificity (though high fixed costs may lead to contracting out for services that are highly asset specific). Producing in-house would protect the government from exploitation by opportunistic monopoly providers.
- Competitive markets for services lead to lower transaction costs and lower inefficiencies because of the information about quality, quantity, and price revealed through the bidding process. When markets for services are competitive, governments tend to contract out more.
- When governments do contract out services that are highly asset specific, that produce outcomes that are difficult to measure, or that exist in noncompetitive markets, they will more likely contract with other governments or use joint contracting. In joint contracting, a government "contracts with an external vendor while retaining a portion of the service production in-house or contracts simultaneously with several vendors for the same service."[53]

Competitive markets. Availability of several potential suppliers who compete on the basis of price as well as quality is often essential to successful contracting relationships. When competition is absent, public and private sector entities may become dependent on each other, and government becomes vulnerable to manipulation and exploitation by the monopolist contractor.

The supply of body armor for troops in Iraq is one case in which a limited number of suppliers caused difficulties. The Pentagon was widely criticized for failing to provide adequate body armor to the troops in Iraq. A design challenge was to keep the armor as light as possible, but the private contractors who were producing vests with innovative new materials were part of "a cottage industry of small armor makers with limited production capacity. In addition, each company must independently come up with its own design for the plates, which then undergo military testing."[54] Because the military services are often unable to secure the rights to use the designs from these small contractors, successful designs cannot be contracted out to other manufacturers. This example shows how the lack of competition hindered the large-scale production of this needed equipment and the exposure of the military for relying on a few small-scale suppliers.

Incomplete contracts. When uncertainty makes it impossible to write contracts that cover all possible contingencies, incomplete contracts (specifically employment contracts) can be more efficient. In an employment contract, an employee agrees to accept the supervision and guidance of an employer when performing the types of activities over which the employer has jurisdiction. The employer accepts the responsibility of ensuring that stakeholders are satisfied with the results. Employment contracts can afford greater flexibility in defining and controlling work and ensuring that reciprocity is achieved.

Economists Oliver S. D. Hart, Andrei Shleifer, and Robert W. Vishny focus on quality issues in incomplete contracts. They consider a private sector supplier's incentives to implement cost-reducing or quality-enhancing innovations that were not addressed in the initial contract between government and the supplier.[55] Because these innovations were not foreseen or specified in the contract *ex ante,* this is an example of an incomplete contract.

The authors develop a formal model to show the trade-offs of the make-or-buy decision. Key assumptions and implications of the model include the following:

- The government derives a benefit of observable but unverifiable quality from the produced good.
- The private sector producer will implement innovations during the contract period that will reduce its costs but will wait until contract renegotiation to bargain over innovations that can increase quality because these kinds of innovations will raise the producer's costs during the contract term.
- Under these circumstances, results from the model indicate that costs are always lower when governments contract out instead of producing in-house, even though "the private contractor's incentive to engage in cost reduction is typically *too* strong since he ignores the adverse impact on quality."[xiii]
- Quality may be higher or lower in private production compared with in-house government production.

Reflecting on the implications of their model for different types of services, the authors conclude that

> the case for in-house provision is very strong in such services as the conduct of foreign policy and mainte-
> nance of police and armed forces, but can also be made reasonably persuasively for prisons. In contrast, the
> case for privatization is strong in such activities as garbage collection and weapons production, but can also
> be made reasonably persuasively for schools. In some other services, such as provision of health care, an
> analysis of the efficiency of alternative arrangements . . . requires a much more detailed model of competi-
> tion, contracts, and regulation.[56]

The issues considered by Hart, Schleifer, and Vishny arise often in practice. For example, quality problems have been observed in the Medicare program, which outsources many of its enforcement activities to private contractors who often overlook or ignore quality issues. Medicare reimburses costs according to procedure, test, physician encounter, or length of stay; virtually no consideration is given to the quality of care provided. An in-depth investigation of the Medicare program by *The Washington Post* found

> a pervasive problem that costs the federal insurance program billions of dollars a year while rewarding doc-
> tors, hospitals and health plans for bad medicine. In Medicare's upside-down reimbursement system, hospi-
> tals and doctors who order unnecessary tests, provide poor care or even injure patients often receive higher
> payments than those who provide efficient, high-quality medicine.[57]

The Hart, Shleifer, and Vishny model did not distinguish between for-profit and nonprofit suppliers for its private sector actor (see discussion of nonprofit organizations in Chapter 5). To illustrate the structural impli-cations for public management of different organizational forms, health policy scholar Karen Eggleston and

---

[xiii]Oliver Hart, Andrei Shleifer, and Robert W. Vishny, "The Proper Scope of Government: Theory and an Application to Prisons," *Quarterly Journal of Economics* (November 1997): 1129. In a related paper, Timothy Besley and Maitreesh Ghatak also use an incomplete contracting framework but allow for consideration that private sector producers be value-driven. Their model is sufficiently general to include a special case of profit-maximizing producers, but the model focuses on asset specificity and hold-up problems, and the primary applications of inter-est are the relationships between governments and nongovernmental organizations in developing countries in deciding on inputs and financ-ing for public projects. See "Government versus Private Ownership of Public Goods," *Quarterly Journal of Economics* 116, no. 4 (November 2001): 1443–1472.

economist Richard Zeckhauser developed a model that shows how it can be technically (if not necessarily politically) rational for government to take advantage of the strengths and weaknesses of different ownership forms in the health care market.[58]

All three ownership forms—public, private for-profit (investor owned), and private nonprofit—provide health care through hospitals. Government plays a role in distributing access to health care through its tax and expenditure policies, although health care has limited public goods characteristics. Certain kinds of health care services, such as immunizations, do provide community benefits, however (discussed in Chapter 1). Health care delivery has no contractible uncertainties, such as the extent and nature of quality improvement and the emphasis on cost control, meaning that contracts for health care are necessarily incomplete. Cost control, moreover, may come at the expense of service quality.

Eggelston and Zeckhauser's model builds on the incomplete contracts framework and assumes it is not possible to fully specify and contract for treatment costs, innovations, or quality of care above some minimum. Furthermore, the model assumes that the three different ownership forms are equally productive, meaning that they can treat a given condition equally effectively and have equal preferences between cost (or efficiency) and quality. While oversimplified, these assumptions provide a baseline for examining the different incentives across the three sectors.

- In the case of a government-owned facility, Eggleston and Zeckhauser find that the provider would deliver the minimum acceptable quantity and quality of care unless payments could be renegotiated from time to time and the provider could count on sharing in the benefits of cost control and quality improvement, although the share may be low because of government compensation constraints. Here, incentives exist to pursue innovations that increase patient benefits.
- In an investor-owned facility, the owner has property rights over the benefits of cost reduction and has a strong incentive to pursue cost controls. These controls may be pursued even at the expense of treatment quality unless the provider can renegotiate the reimbursement rates to cover the costs of quality-enhancing innovation. Still, the result may not be high levels of innovation. "Even with identical preferences, public and private providers will make different investment choices because they have different claims on the returns from those investments."[59] If aggressive cost control has adverse side effects on the quality of patient care, the implication is that government ownership is preferred.

  > Whether in-house provision is preferable to contracting out to a for-profit provider will depend on several issues: the characteristics of the health services in question, the ability to specify desired quality and treatment intensity in the contract, and the availability of complementary purchasing strategies (such as allowing patient choice of provider to motivate investment in quality enhancement).[60]

- In the case of nonprofits, the providers have incentives to maximize their surplus and redirect it into perks or into mission-related activity. For this reason, nonprofits may be more motivated by altruism toward patients (which may or may not be desirable) and less motivated by cost control possibilities unless the organization is operating in a competitive environment. Among nonprofit providers, quality may actually be overemphasized, resulting in expenditures on state-of-the-art equipment or patient amenities that are not socially optimal.

Eggleston and Zeckhauser also discuss structural features of contracts for health care. For example, a pre-paid capitation agreement has different implications than a fee-for-service contract, which entails higher costs, especially in the case of for-profit providers. If quality is multidimensional, providers have an incentive to emphasize those dimensions that patients are likely to notice. When patients are heterogeneous, incentives are present for patient selection or cream skimming. Payers may use risk adjustment to weaken these incentives. If the budget constraint is soft—that is, if providers are likely to be bailed out of financial difficulties—then budgets are likely to grow.

Eggleston and Zeckhauser's analysis is one example of how the structure dimension— specifically, ownership type and contractual terms—provides insight into the comparative advantage of different sectors in supplying health care.

Once a decision has been made to contract out—to buy—public managers must deal with further structural issues likely to arise within their scope of authority—oversight of the design, management, and implementation of the contract. Public management scholar Richard Elmore has observed, "Managing indirect relations—on either end—requires an understanding of differences in incentive structures and modes of operation among different types of organizations and also of the mechanisms of influence other than direct controls. Indirect management requires a range of skills far wider than those necessary for more conventional superior-subordinate relationships."[61] Meeting the challenges of managing contracts may be (or perhaps can only be) met with structural solutions, although, as indicated, the craft and culture dimensions may also be necessary for effective results.

> A manager enabled to exercise the make-or-buy decision may need to revisit that decision over time if principal-agent problems arise or intensify.

Contracts are often designed to to address potential information asymmetries and divergent interests between principals (the government) and agents (the contractor). Transaction cost characteristics of the relationships (asset specificity, uncertainty, and frequency) may affect how contracts are specified and managed.[xiv] A manager enabled to exercise the make-or-buy decision may need to revisit that decision over time if principal-agent problems arise or intensify.

Example: Coast Guard Outsourcing

In 2002 the U.S. Coast Guard had outsourced the development and acquisition processes for replacing its aging fleet of patrol boats and other systems to two venerable defense contractors: Lockheed Martin and Northrop Grumman. This acquisition was part of what the Coast Guard called its Deepwater program, a 25-year, $24 billion effort to upgrade and replace many of the service's ships, aircraft, and systems. Responsibility for all development and acquisition activities had been given to an entity called Integrated Coast Guard Systems (ICGS), which was comanaged by the two companies.[62]

[xiv]In addition to the references cited in this section, see Robert D. Behn and Peter A. Kant, "Strategies for Avoiding the Pitfalls of Performance Contracting," *Public Productivity and Management Review* 22, no. 4 (1999): 470–489; Trevor L. Brown and Matthew Potoski, "Managing Contract Performance: A Transaction Costs Approach," *Journal of Policy Analysis and Management* 22, no. 2 (2003): 275–297; Trevor L. Brown, Matthew Potoski, and David M. Van Slyke, "Managing Public Service Contracts: Aligning Values, Institutions, and Markets," *Public Administration Review* (May/June 2006): 323–331; National State Auditors Association, "Contracting for Services: A National State Auditors Association Best Practices Document," June 2003, http://www.nasact.org/onlineresources/downloads/BP/06_03-Contracting_Best_ Practices.pdf.

Over time, the Coast Guard's management of its contract with ICGS drew intense scrutiny from Congress and from the government's own management analysts. The chief complaint was that the Coast Guard had, in effect, assigned management responsibilities that might reasonably have been regarded as "inherently governmental" to the private sector, thus weakening its capacity to exercise proper oversight of a major acquisition program. The first products of this arrangement, eight redesigned patrol boats, malfunctioned badly. According to a report by the CBS News program *60 Minutes*, "the $24 billion project has turned into a fiasco that has set new standards for incompetence, and triggered a Justice Department investigation."[63]

The denouement came when Coast Guard Commander Thad Allen told reporters, "I just signed a decision memorandum approving the termination of the current FRC-B acquisition with Integrated Coast Guard Systems, and we are reassigning that to the Coast Guard Office of Acquisition." The FRC-B was a Fast Response Cutter that the Coast Guard believed was needed, and soon, to replace its aging 110-foot patrol boats.[64]

The rationale for this decision to make program management from then on, not buy it, was twofold. First, Coast Guard leaders claimed that the organization now had management capacity, personnel, and support contracts that it had lacked a few years earlier. Second, Coast Guard leaders now acknowledged, "We are the patrol-boat experts pretty much worldwide. We really understand this market. We've already researched what's out there."[65]

Who Bears the Risk?

Crucial to understanding the dynamics of contracting is exposure of either or both parties to the risk that their expectations will not be met due to factors that are beyond their control. If expectations are not met, then the question of compensation arises: Who bears the costs of disappointed expectations? Contracting parties typically do not want to bear any costly risks; they are risk averse. If risks are inherent in the situation simply because it is impossible to spell out in advance all possible contingencies, then a contracting party will make every effort to shift the risk onto the other party, minimizing its own exposure.

With a **cost-plus-fixed-fee contract**, in which the contractor agent receives reimbursement for all costs plus a fee or profit, the contractor assumes none of the risks that costs will be higher than expected. If risks are quantifiable, then it may be possible for the contractor to take out insurance against them because their costs can be accurately estimated. A seller of a product may offer such insurance in the form of a service agreement or a warranty so that the buyer bears no costly risk. Or the buyer may purchase insurance against risks that are beyond either party's control.

The issue of risk underlies contracting for outputs or outcomes, where concern focuses on measurability as well as on risk sharing:

- For activities such as issuing drivers' licenses, contracting for outputs or for outcomes may be identical.
- For activities such as welfare-to-work casework, however, the issues involved with contracting for outputs or outcomes may diverge considerably. It may be difficult to attribute an improvement in recipients' ultimate well-being to a program output (such as number of hours of job training completed). Causal relationships between program and outcome are difficult to establish because many other personal, organizational, and environmental factors might have led to the outcome (see discussion on causality in Chapter 1).
- Agents therefore prefer to contract for outputs rather than for outcomes, because outputs are more predictable and in the agent's control. If agents must contract for outcomes, they want to minimize their exposure to risk if outcomes do not occur because of factors beyond their control (see discussion on performance measurement in Chapter 12).

Consider a policy whose goal is to achieve favorable outcomes for a particular clientele such as the profoundly disabled. The policy goal of improved functioning can be considered the desired outcome. In one scenario, a **fee-for-service contract** might establish a fee schedule for contractor-produced outputs thought to be related to a favorable outcome. Yet from the contractor's or agent's point of view, the best arrangement is a cost-plus contract that reimburses whatever costs are incurred in producing the outputs: the contractor is paid whether or not any useful outputs or outcomes are produced. In this arrangement, the contractor bears no risk if outputs or outcomes are not achieved: all risks are borne by the principal (the government) if the program does not work as intended or hoped.

In another scenario, a performance contract might establish a fee schedule for contractor-produced outcomes. The fee might be a flat rate based on a calculated average cost of achieving these kinds of outcomes or a rate that represents what the government is willing to pay or thinks the outcome is worth. Because the contractor is not paid more if costs exceed the agreed-upon rate, and is not paid at all if outcomes are not achieved, regardless how much time, effort, and money the contractor spent trying to produce the outcome, the contractor bears full risk while the government bears no risk at all, except criticism for choosing a method of implementation that produces no results.

Whether contracts are imposed on managers as constraining structures, or are available to managers through enabling structures, an appreciation of the structure dimension of public management necessarily must include understanding the incentives and various issues that arise with contracts. The hollow state, decentralized service delivery, and the multifaceted issues and actors involved in a particular public policy arena raise the need for structures that can coordinate service provision across a number of actors and providers. The definition and management of those structures are of increasing interest in public management and are examined in the next section.[xv]

Identifying and Managing Interdependence

The discussion of alternatives to direct government in Chapter 5 cited research suggesting the existence of a trend toward the debureaucratization of authority over the provision of publicly financed goods and services. While the extent of this transformation of governance is debatable, it is unquestionably the case that public managers, as well as lawmakers, are using their delegated authority to employ an expanding variety of tools to achieve the goals of public policy. These tools include, in addition to contractual arrangements with public and private organizations, various consociational structures that identify or create, then take advantage of, interdependence among otherwise autonomous entities.[xvi]

[xv]See, for example, the dedicated issues of *Journal of Public Administration Research and Theory* 20 (January 2010), *Public Administration Review* (December 2006), and *International Journal of Public Management* 10, no. 1 (2007).

[xvi]In addition to the references cited in this section, see also Robert Agranoff and M. McGuire, *Collaborative Public Management: New Strategies for Local Governments* (Washington, DC: Georgetown University Press, 2003); Eugene Bardach, *Getting Agencies to Work Together: The Practice and Theory of Managerial Craftsmanship* (Washington, DC: Brookings Institution, 1998); Stephen Goldsmith and William D. Eggers, *Governing by Network: The New Shape of the Public Sector* (Washington, DC: Brookings Institution Press, 2004); Erik-Hans Klijn, "Networks and Inter-organizational Management: Challenging, Steering, Evaluation, and the Role of Public Actors in Public Management," in *The Oxford Handbook of Public Management*, ed. Ewan Ferlie, Laurence E. Lynn, Jr., and Christopher Pollitt (Oxford, UK: Oxford University Press, 2005), 257–281; Laurence E. Lynn, Jr., "Policy Achievement as a Collective Good: A Strategic Perspective on Managing Social Programs," in *Public Management: The State of the Art*, ed. Barry Bozeman (San Francisco, CA: Jossey-Bass, 1993), 108-133; Jodi R. Sandfort, "The Structural Impediments to Front-line Human Service Collaboration: Examining Welfare Reform at the Front-lines," *Social Service Review* 73, (Number 3, 1999): 314–339.

Network governance, for example, is a way of achieving coordination of largely autonomous actors without either markets or hierarchies.[66] Networks include arrangements that promote voluntary self-enforcement and cooperation even when self-interest might call for defection, noncooperation, or opportunism. Public management scholar Laurence J. O'Toole, Jr. has defined networks as "structures of interdependence, involving multiple organizations or parts thereof, where one unit is not merely the formal subordinate of the others in some hierarchical arrangement," where "the institutional glue congealing networked ties may include authority bonds, exchange relations, and coalitions based on common interest, all within a single multiunit structure."[67]

Example: Creating and Governing Networks and Collaborative Partnerships

The Family and Community Trust (FACT) in the State of Missouri is a complex partnership of networks of organizations providing services to children and families. The following description is from FACT's website:

In November of 1993 an Executive Order (93-43) was signed that established The Family Investment Trust (FIT) to promote collaboration and innovation in service delivery for Missouri's children and families. It called for change in the way services were delivered, where services were delivered and mandated that local decision-making be utilized in the process. These changes were to drive a new and different relationship between state government and communities. This model approach was then known as Caring Communities.

FIT was setup as a private/public board that included the leaders of state departments as well as community leaders from the corporate and civic arenas to guide the general direction and engage communities in the work of Caring Communities.

In 2001 this work was reaffirmed by Executive Order (01-07) but renamed the organization to The Family and Community Trust (FACT) to better emphasize the role of communities in the work.

Twenty-one Caring Community organizations were established around the state to implement this innovative approach with six core result areas as their focus. Those Core Results are Parents Working, Children Safe, Children Ready to Enter School, Children & Families Healthy, Children & Youth Succeeding in School and Youth Ready to Enter the Work Force.

FACT is now a non-profit corporation with nineteen members drawn from the top leadership in state government and the private sector. It governs the work of the twenty community partnerships across the state. The board's mission is to promote and support effective public/private partnerships and community involvement to develop innovative solutions for improving the lives of Missouri's children and families. Funding to support this work comes from the state legislature through the Department of Social Services and is a combination of general revenue and matching federal dollars.

There are currently twenty Community Partnerships across Missouri. These non-profit organizations work in concert with local, state and federal partners to implement effective community strategies to meet local needs.[68]

Why would autonomous organizations form or join a network or a collaboration[xvii] that makes them dependent on other organizations?[69]

- It may be mandated by legislation.
- It may be the preferred strategy of public managers pursuing goals such as continuity of care, wrap-around services, and holistic treatments.
- It may advance an autonomous organization's own mission by enlarging its access to resources, information, and expertise.

The governance and management of collaborative effort is quite different from those of market/exchange relationships and of traditional hierarchical arrangements. Collaborative governance may take the form of implicit, open-ended agreements among autonomous units. Such an arrangement may facilitate achieving the reciprocity of exchange or of partnerships that involve explicit elements of sharing and cooperation. Yet despite the best of intentions, collaborations may encounter difficulties:

- Participants may vary in the level of effort they devote to the collaboration, potentially reducing the effectiveness of the entire enterprise.
- Collaboration may require higher productivity for some providers than for others, such as those assigned particularly difficult clients or ambiguous tasks.
- Collaboration might call for reassignment of tasks among organizations or for retraining workers in ways that provoke resistance.
- Collaboration might require team decision making rather than hierarchical decision making, such as when management of a troubled child might require consensus among an interagency team of specialists with differing values. Team decision making would restrict unilateral agency discretion to place a child in a residential home or reunite the child to a high-risk family.[70]

> **Relying solely on informal coordination to organize network or collaborative members is unrealistic. Voluntary arrangements may need to be actively managed.**

How can individual and organizational commitment, creativity, learning, adaptability to change, and willing subordination of narrow organizational interests to a larger public interest be elicited from actors who have the option of withholding or withdrawing from their participation and support? What kinds of behaviors and mechanisms sustain their existence when organizational interactions are primarily voluntary rather than structured by the formal authority of laws and directives? Relying solely on informal coordination to organize network or collaborative members is unrealistic. Voluntary arrangements may need to be actively managed.

Public administration scholars Robert Agranoff and Michael McGuire declare "not all is peace and harmony" in managing networks engaged in public action.[71] Issues that must be confronted include

- the influence of differences in power,
- the need for mechanisms of control and accountability, and
- the value of synergies and creativity.

[xvii]The term *collaboration* as used here refers to cooperation, joint action, and coordination among legally autonomous public and private agencies, that is, among entities that do not report to each other.

Goal conflicts and other challenges were observed by public administration scholars Keith Provan and Brinton Milward in their study of a mental health service provider network.[72] Coordination among network actors is costly, both in terms of transaction costs and in terms of dependency on other organizations, which restricts flexibility. Numerous conflicts among goals and notions of effectiveness are likely. Provan and Milward point to the importance of "network administrative organizations" (NAOs)—a structural feature—to govern coordination, goal selection, and the monitoring of efficiency and effectiveness. But the challenges to governance are intense because each action or decision may not be in the best interests of every party involved in the network—communities, organizations, clients/customers. Thus, trade-offs are needed, and if organizations see the trade-offs as contrary to their interests, the network will fall apart or come to be dominated by the most powerful members.

When problems of coordination do occur in networks or collaborations, one solution is to establish a governing authority with responsibility for monitoring and arbitrating disputes over resource allocation, similar to the NAO in the Provan and Milward study. This authority might be a government agency or an executive appointed by networked agencies. To ensure fair allocation, the authority must be able to monitor performance, which itself is a cost of collaboration. The higher the perceived benefit, all other things equal, the more likely it is that an autonomous agency will collaborate. Public management scholars Bin Chen and Elizabeth A. Graddy analyzed the effectiveness of nonprofit lead-organization networks engaged in children and family services. The found that networks and partnerships that responded primarily to funders' requirements exhibited enhanced perceptions of interorganizational relationships, and organizational learning but not client outcomes. Chen and Graddy also found that learning was most supported when network partners shared motivation and vision, cautioning, "partners of convenience do not produce successful partnerships."[73]

Management of networks can involve culture and craft as well as the structure dimension of public management. For example, public administration scholars Ann Marie Thompson and James L. Perry point to five aspects of any collaborative process: governance, administration, organizational autonomy, mutuality, and norms.[74] They argue that active management of these aspects is necessary in order for a collaboration to be effective, that is, to address the challenges involved in managing multiple network participants and coordinating service provision. Managing collaborations and designing governance mechanisms to promote their effective performance require, among other things, attention to

- the motives behind each participant's involvement in the collaboration or network,
- the organizational structures and operating technologies of each participant in the network,
- the types of resource exchanges involved, and
- the degree of discretion for participants in each organization.[75]

The success of some collaborations and partnerships notwithstanding, information asymmetries and conflicts of interest, poorly defined technologies, and ambiguous performance standards tend to be the rule rather than the exception in public service collaborations because of their political origin. That there is any coordination or cooperation at all may be better explained by long-established position relationships and shared norms than by the rational, calculated conduct of participants.

Creating and Maintaining Management Capacity

Having adequate capability to manage an organization's core functions is not in itself sufficient to ensure the kind of performance that sustains political support and the public's trust. In addition, the decisions managers make about the deployment of these resources are the real point of public management. Effective use of the four core management systems discussed earlier in this chapter depends on four levers to make them work:

- the character [quality] of a government's management systems;
- the level and nature of leadership emphasis;
- the degree of integration and alignment across its management systems; and
- a commitment to results.[76]

Elements of the core management systems interact with other structural features of the levers (the character of the systems, the degree of integration/alignment, and a managing-for-results emphasis), as well as with craft aspects (leadership emphasis). In this view, managing the structures of organizations has direct consequences for the capacity for effective management.

In Chapter 12, performance measurement and management is discussed from the three dimensions of structure, culture, and craft. In the current section, performance initiatives at the national and state levels are discussed in the context of improving the capacity of public managers.

The Government Performance and Results Act

The **Government Performance and Results Act** (GPRA) was enacted in 1993 largely on the initiative of conservative Republicans and signed into law by President Bill Clinton. The law has become a framework for public management in the federal government and a catalyst for America's expanding practice of performance management at all levels of government. The act requires each federal agency, in cooperation with Congress and in coordination with the budget process, to formulate forward-looking performance plans and to conduct performance evaluations using agreed-upon performance measures.

The GPRA's intended effect is to strengthen the government's capacity for effective implementation of public policies enacted by Congress. Public administration scholar John Rohr sees the GPRA as an example of traditional legislative preeminence within the American separation of powers: "By law it requires nothing less than close cooperation between executive branch agencies and congressional subcommittees, first in developing goals and plans and then in evaluating performance measured against these same goals and plans."[77] The Government Accountability Office (GAO), which was tasked with monitoring GPRA's implementation, was not pleased after a decade of executive branch effort, viewing with concern the less-than-wholehearted use of performance information in government-wide or agency management.[78]

The effects of Congress's decision to enact and implement GPRA resulted mainly in the proliferation of products on paper: the output of a seemingly far-reaching technocratic effort, with copious documentation, to create plans, performance standards and targets, the measures by which to assess their attainment, and their links to the budget.[79] These paper products were generated in response to GPRA's process requirements. Many evaluations of the reforms focus on the technical adequacy of these paper products and of the processes underlying them. Little interest was shown in whether or not public policy planning and implementation, as measured by actual results, had occurred.

The GPRA's success depended on creating a professionalized bureaucracy able to make detailed objectives, plans, and measurements in consultation with legislative committees. Its effects were undermined by the distrust of recent federal administrations in the kind of professionalized administration and complex administrative machinery required by GPRA and its engagement with Congress.

The net result was that improvements in the government's management capacity were slow and incremental at best. In frustrated response, Congress enacted the **Government Performance and Results Modernization Act in 2010**. The federal government's website Performance.Gov describes the importance and purpose of the act as follows:

> The Act modernizes the federal government's performance management framework, retaining and amplifying some aspects of the [GPRA] while also addressing some of its weaknesses. . . . The GPRA Modernization Act established important changes to existing requirements that move toward a more useful approach to performance planning and reporting.
>
> The GPRA Modernization Act serves as a foundation for helping agencies to focus on their highest priorities and creating a culture where data and empirical evidence plays a greater role in policy, budget, and management decisions. The purposes of the GPRA Modernization Act were to:
>
> - Modernize and refine the requirements established by GPRA in order to produce more frequent, relevant data which can then inform decision makers and agency operations;
> - Codify and strengthen existing resources for performance management, including the Chief Operating Officer (COO), Performance Improvement Officers (PIOs) within the federal agencies and the interagency Performance Improvement Council (PIC);
> - Apply the latest technologies and lessons learned from nearly two decades of GPRA implementation;
> - Lead to more effective management of government agencies at a reduced cost.[80]

The Senate Committee report on the Modernization Act directs the OMB to require

> - [a government-wide] plan to establish performance goals for each crosscutting federal government priority goal;
> - OMB identify the various agencies, organizations, program activities, regulations, tax expenditures, policies and other activities that contribute to each federal government performance goal;
> - a lead government official be assigned for each federal government performance goal;
> - OMB establish common federal government performance indicators to measure and assess progress across agencies toward shared goals; and
> - OMB identifies government and cross-agency management challenges and plans to address such challenges.[81]

The GAO monitors federal agencies' responses to GPRA mandates. The results have continued to be disappointing. In 2014, GAO reported that:

> agencies' reported use of performance information, as measured by GAO's use of performance information index, generally did not improve between 2007 and 2013. The index was derived from a set of survey questions in the 2007 and 2013 surveys that reflected the extent to which managers reported that their agencies used performance information for various management activities and decision making. GAO's analysis of the average index score among managers at each agency found that most agencies showed no statistically significant change in use during this period. . . . only two agencies [the Office of Personnel Management and the Department of Labor] experienced a statistically significant improvement in the use of performance information. During the same time period, four agencies experienced a statistically significant decline in the use of performance information.[82]

GAO also reported that increased use of performance information is associated with its long-espoused agenda for public management improvement: "(1) aligning agency-wide goals, objectives, and measures; (2) improving the usefulness of performance information; (3) developing agency capacity to use performance information; (4) demonstrating management commitment; and (5) communicating performance information frequently and effectively."[83]

In recent years, serious breakdowns in managerial effectiveness in agencies such as the Department of Veterans Affairs, the U.S. Secret Service, the Centers for Medicare and Medicaid Services, and the Centers for Disease Control and Prevention reveal the extraordinary difficulty of changing the balance between political rationality and the technical rationality favored by the GAO. An unsatisfactory status quo will likely continue unless an agency enjoys unusually strong and sustained executive leadership or the agency's continued existence is threatened by Congress or the administration and it must change to eliminate the threat.

Performance Management in State and Local Governments

The news about public sector performance management may be somewhat better in state and local governments. In 2008, 11 public-interest associations, such as the National Governors Association and the National Financial Officers Association, created The National Performance Management Advisory Commission to promote performance management in state and local governments. In 2010, the Commission published its final report, *A Performance Management Framework for State and Local Government: From Measurement and Reporting to Management and Improving.* It constituted "a message from the elected and appointed government leaders who served as members on the commission."[84]

The report defines performance management in the public sector as "an ongoing, systematic approach to improving results through evidence-based decision making, continuous organizational learning, and a focus on accountability for performance. Performance management is integrated into all aspects of an organization's management and policy-making processes, transforming an organization's practices so it is focused on achieving improved results for the public."[85] It identified seven fundamental performance management principles (Box 8.1).[86]

Box 6.1   **SEVEN PRINCIPLES OF PERFORMANCE MANAGEMENT**

1. A results focus permeates strategies, processes, the organizational culture, and decisions.

2. Information, measures, goals, priorities, and activities are relevant to the priorities and well-being of the government and the community.

3. Information related to performance, decisions, regulations, and processes is transparent--easy to access, use, and understand.

4. Goals, programs, activities, and resources are aligned with priorities and desired results.

5. Decisions and processes are driven by timely, accurate, and meaningful data.

6. Practices are sustainable over time and across organizational changes.

7. Performance management transforms the organization, its management, and the policy-making processes.

Source: Government Finance Officers Association.

The report's appendices provide many examples of performance management initiatives at both state and local levels. These demonstrate how America's federalism constitutes, as noted in Chapter 4, a set of laboratories for testing the effectiveness of various structures and tools of public management. The results from the state and local laboratories may help public managers understand how elusive objectives such as relevance, transparency, pertinence, alignment, and sustainability can be achieved in America's Madisonian political system.

KEY CONCEPTS

Principal-agent problem
Information asymmetries
Adverse selection
Moral hazard
Transaction costs
Reciprocity
Line positions
Staff positions
Tightly coupled
Loosely coupled
Advisory tasks
Operating tasks
Uncertainty absorption
Routine technologies
Non-routine technologies
Craft technologies
Engineering technologies
Production organizations
Procedural organizations
Craft organizations
Coping organizations

Street-level bureaucrats
Local justice
Budget-maximizing bureaucrats
Bureau-shaping bureaucrats
Rule
Informal rulemaking
Contracting-out
Outsourcing
Devolution
Privatization
Contract
Complete contract
Incomplete contract
Make-or-buy decision
Cost-plus-fixed-fee contract
Fee-for-service contract
Government Performance and Results Act/
    Government Performance and
    Results Modernization Act

CASE ANALYSIS: MANAGING THE ROLLOUT OF HEALTHCARE.GOV

As has been noted, the ACA passed with no Republican support. Once it became law, its ideological opponents coalesced into what became known as the Tea Party movement. Its goal was to disrupt the ACA's implementation and, even better, secure the law's repeal. Buoyed by the act's lukewarm reception by the public as revealed in public opinion polls, the midterm elections in November 2010 had profound consequences for the immediate future of the ACA.

The Democratic Party lost control of the House of Representatives and saw its majority in the Senate reduced to below the number

> Buoyed by the act's lukewarm reception by the public as revealed in public opinion polls, the midterm elections in November 2010 had profound consequences for the immediate future of the ACA.

(Continued)

(Continued)

needed to end filibusters. Republicans gained control of both houses of many more state legislatures. As a result, many of the more conservative states chose not to establish their own insurance exchanges or to participate in the Medicaid expansion. Conflicts over the idea of universal coverage and the role of government in meeting health care needs devolved to state governments.[i] In the end, opponents argued, the ACA would make millions more Americans dependent on a government entitlement, enlarging the "welfare state" and the ability of bureaucracies to control the lives of individuals and families.

President Obama promised a successful launch of HealthCare.gov. But its spectacularly unsuccessful rollout on October 1, 2013, was a first indication that the exquisitely complex challenges of ACA implementation had been underestimated or mismanaged. Many other indications were to follow.

Mismanagement

Investigative reporting by journalists and testimony in committee hearings by the Republican-controlled House in 2013 and 2014 revealed that Obama Administration officials had chosen a number of managerial strategies that, in hindsight, appear questionable:

- CMS was given responsibility for implementing the act's complex provisions although it had little experience with the extraordinary software engineering required for operating the federal insurance exchange.
- No single official was made responsible for the act's implementation or for the creation and testing of the website.
- Issuance of important rules and guidelines governing the act's implementation were delayed by the White House until after the 2012 elections in order, it appears, to avoid inciting further political conflict and opposition. As depicted in Chapter 3, devils are in the details of administration, and senior officials wanted no inconvenient devils to become public. But preannounced deadlines for completing tasks meant that rules and guidelines remained unchanged. Sticking to these deadlines seems to have exacerbated conflicts between private contractors and the government and between CMS and the White House.
- A major consequence of the administration's management approach was that testing of the various components of the HealthCare.gov website was delayed, and adequate testing was never conducted before the rollout. It was reported that government officials and contractors proceeded with the rollout despite a botched crucial test days earlier. They ran a simulation, unsuccessfully, in which a few hundred people tried to log onto the website at the same time. The failure proved an early warning of the bumpy road to come. Officials went forward with the launch, and the website locked up almost immediately when 2,000 users tried to sign up.
- The president himself made a number of promises and commitments that experts on the act's key provisions knew, correctly as it turned out, probably or certainly could not be kept. Among the most consequential were (1) his declaration that those who liked their current insurance plans could keep them, "period;" (2) on the opening day of HealthCare.gov, choosing a health insurance plan would be as easy as choosing a travel itinerary on Expedia or purchasing a product on Amazon.com;

---

[i]In the longer term, according to one expert, the exchange provisions threatened "to fundamentally reshape the balance of state and federal authority in insurance regulation. This change will not be for the better." Congress would have the authority to regulate insurance provision "in a way that could destroy the distinction between what is national and what is local." Steven D. Shwinn, "The Framers' Federalism and the Affordable Care Act," *Connecticut Law Review* 44, no. 4 (2012): 1071–1097.

(3) those whose insurance plans were cancelled by insurers because they failed to comply with the act's minimum-benefits requirements would be given an additional year of coverage under their existing plans; and (4) the website would be "fixed," defined as working smoothly for the vast majority of users, by November 30, 2013.

- Channels of communication between the lead contractor for creating the website, CMS managers of the website's construction, senior HHS officials, and senior White House aides were unclear and uncoordinated, which led to considerable internal tension, uncertainty, and conflict and thus endangered the ACA's implementation.

Mismanagement's Harvest of Woes

As implementation dragged on, unfortunate consequences, some of them foreseen, began to pile up. Consumers, providers, insurers, and regulators began changing their behavior in response to the new realities and uncertainties that were emerging:

- Insurance companies were quick to cancel existing plans that would fail to meet federal standards for insurance plans in effect after January 1, 2014. As the number of cancellations climbed into seven figures, the president was accused of misleading the American people about their ability to keep their plans if they liked them.
- To appease critics, the president abruptly announced that substandard policies could remain in effect for an additional year, that is, until January 1, 2015. This announcement produced an immediate protest from insurers who believed they could not undo the cancellations and from state insurance regulators who believed that they could not fail to enforce the law's requirements as written.
- The initial premiums for plans offered through insurance exchanges were significantly higher than expected for many consumers. Consumers began complaining that they were being forced to pay for one-size-fits-all coverage that they neither needed nor wanted, such as maternity benefits for women beyond child-bearing age.
- A related issue, only belatedly realized, was that companies were dramatically increasing deductibles and copayments in order to hold down premiums. Thus, although monthly premiums might be affordable, out-of-pocket costs for actual services for many consumers were not.[87]
- Many insurance companies were anxious to meet the standards for affordability and adequacy of their plans as required by the ACA. They began cutting higher cost, often higher-quality providers from their networks, leaving customers without access to their doctors or facing higher copays and deductibles for using now out-of-network providers. Critics claimed that another Obama promise—if you like your doctor, you can keep your doctor—had also been broken.
- Some health care providers, anticipating reductions in reimbursement rates by insurers, refused to accept insurance plans that patients had purchased on the insurance exchanges. Some consumers who had changed their plans because of the ACA subsidies thus could not keep their doctors.
- In a sluggish economy, employers who had been providing health insurance plans to their workers and who anticipated a reduction in the number of workers opting-out of company-provided plans accelerated ongoing efforts to steer them to plans requiring higher deductibles and increasing copayments for their family members.[88]

(Continued)

(Continued)

With the health care marketplace in turmoil following the missed deadline for a functioning federal health insurance exchange website, the president and his advisers decided to set a new deadline for themselves: HealthCare.gov would "work smoothly for the vast majority of users"—generally regarded to mean that eight out of 10 users would be successful—by November 30, 2013. Again, there were widespread doubts within the information technology community that the new deadline was realistic.

As that deadline drew near, the White House began taking measures to discourage a crush of customers with pent-up frustration from overwhelming HealthCare.gov, fearing that it might still be too fragile to handle the traffic.[89] The administration also began defining its measure of success as 50,000 users would be able to use the website simultaneously, far below what had been forecast as the peak demand the website should be prepared for (250,000 users simultaneously). Republican critics claimed that the goalposts had been moved—again.

As it turned out, the functioning of the website's consumer interface was much improved at the November 30 deadline. Though there were bugs, the Obama administration could credibly claim that the website had been "fixed" and that further improvements would be made in due course. But health reform remained vulnerable to unanticipated changes in the behavior of those affected by the ACA and to its implacable critics. But the White House had never made it clear that there would be both winners and losers because of the ACA. Tens of millions would ultimately have better, more affordable health insurance. However, some Americans would indeed have to pay more for health care because of added coverage that was required, and some would find their doctors no longer in an insurer's network. The argument that winners greatly outnumbered losers was ineffective against the claim that promises had been broken.

As an Election Year Began . . .

On December 19, just days before the December 23 deadline for consumers to sign up for coverage as required by the individual mandate, the Obama administration abruptly announced new rules of the game: millions of consumers whose individual insurance policies had been canceled could buy bare-bones plans or even avoid entirely a requirement that most Americans have health coverage.[90] Without these changes, the administration feared that the number of Americans without health insurance might actually rise rather than fall because of the ACA's implementation problems.

Caught by surprise, the insurance industry, which had been working hard to increase enrollments and enlarge risk pools so that premiums could be controlled, reacted with dismay.[91] Congressional critics asserted that the president was illegally usurping authority that belonged to Congress because the administration repeatedly changed the rules concerning ACA implementation.[ii]

By the summer of 2014, only a few months before the November midterm elections, the chickens began coming home to roost for the Obama administration:

- Public opinion polls revealed that 53 percent of Americans disapproved of Obamacare, and only 41 percent liked it.[92]
- The GAO published its first report on implementation of the ACA, citing ineffective planning and lax oversight by CMS:

[ii]For an analysis of administration actions during ACA implementation, see Congressional Research Service, *Implementing the Affordable Care Act: Delays, Extensions, and Other Actions Taken by the Administration*, 2014, http://fas.org/sgp/crs/misc/R43474.pdf.

To be expedient, CMS issued task orders to develop the federally facilitated marketplace (FFM) federal data services hub (data hub) systems when key technical requirements were unknown, including the number and composition of states to be supported and, importantly, the number of potential enrollees. CMS used cost-reimbursement contracts, which created additional risk because CMS was required to pay the contractor's allowable costs regardless of whether the system was completed. CMS program staff also adopted an incremental information technology development approach that was new to CMS. Furthermore, CMS did not develop a required acquisition strategy to identify risks and document mitigation strategies and did not use available information, such as quality insurance plans, to monitor performance and inform oversight.[93]

- Even though the CBO projected that 12 million additional people would have health care coverage by the end of 2014, only an additional seven million would be covered by the end of 2015, leaving a total of 55 million people without health insurance.[94] Because of various **The challenge of competent administration and high performance was enormous, even unprecedented.** exemptions, however, 90 percent of these uninsured would not be required to pay the penalty for being uninsured.[95] In a decade, 11 percent of U.S. residents may have no health insurance, significantly less than would have been the case without the ACA but far from the universal coverage that was its goal.[96]

Why Did It Happen This Way?

Its undoubted successes notwithstanding, significant and lasting damage had been done to the reputation for competence and honesty of the president and his administration and to public trust in government. The president's second term had lost political momentum, and a question in the minds of many inside and outside of government persisted: Why did the launch of the president's most significant policy initiative go so badly? The challenge of competent administration and high performance was enormous, even unprecedented. But was the administration's performance the best that could have been expected from government and its managers?

A counterfactual analysis of Affordable Care Act design and implementation might reveal some useful lessons into policy design and implementation in a Madisonian democracy:

- Would the outcome have been the same if the goals of health care reform were more modest? Many advisers and health experts urged this approach.
- Would the outcome have been different if the Act's likely implementation challenges had been identified *ex ante* and vetted with key officials and industry professionals in health and information technology?
- Would the outcome have been different if the implementation involved a more efficient structure and process for implementing the new law that relied on experienced managers of complex institutional reforms?
- Would the outcome have been different if the president's advisory system had been designed to provide him, on a routine basis, with bad news in a timely manner about health care reform?

(Continued)

(Continued)

Further insight into these possibilities can be gleaned from correspondence between administration advisers more than 3 years before the rollout. On May 11, 2010, David Cutler, an Massachusetts Institute of Technology economist and an adviser to the Obama election campaign, sent a four-page, single-spaced memo to the White House Director of the Domestic Policy Council, fellow economist Larry Summers. The memo's subject was "Urgent Need for Changes in Health Reform Implementation." Cutler said, "I am concerned that the personnel and processes you have in place are not up to the task, and that health reform will be unsuccessful as a result." He claimed that his views were "widely shared."[97]

Cutler made many points and made them forcefully. For example, of placing CMS in charge of implementation, he wrote, "The agency is demoralized, the best people have left, IT services are antiquated, and there are fewer employees than in 1981 despite a much larger burden." Instead, he argued, a new structure should be created to implement the reform, one led by people "who know how to manage health care or other complex operations." Individuals assuming key responsibilities, he said, naming names, lacked the specific technical, operational, and collaborative skills and the experience needed for designing and implementing the act's complex provisions in cooperation with insurers, providers, and other key stakeholders. Specifically,

> You need to bring in people who share the President's vision and who know how to manage health care or other complex operations [starting with] a strong team at the White House. That team needs to lay out the milestone goals for the next 5 to 10 years, coordinate across various agencies, and communicate with the public.

Cutler appended to his memo an organization chart for the kind of implementation process he was recommending.

White House officials rejected Cutler's approach and decided to continue, in Cutler's words, "piling new responsibilities onto a broken system." Perhaps the main reason was political: relying on aides and officials who had succeeded in getting the ACA enacted by Congress and on existing agencies and personnel must have seemed, given virulent opposition by Republicans, politically safer than creating new structures managed by more technically skilled but less politically experienced outsiders. CMS, after all, had been in charge of implementing the Bush administration's reform of the Medicare program, which added coverage of prescription drugs. That judgment proved costly.

In another irony, Cutler's idea of putting experienced experts in charge was embraced following the failed rollout of HealthCare.gov.[98] Jeffrey Zients, an experienced and successful private sector IT consultant (he had also been Obama's chief performance officer and would later become his chief economics aide), was put in charge of fixing the website. He chose to create a team of technically qualified software engineers, headed by an individual on leave from Google, which operated in an isolated location in nearby Maryland. The team saw to it that at least the consumer experience at the front door of Obamacare was improved to the point that the White House could claim it had met its deadline for the fix. When Zients left to assume his new responsibilities, an executive from Microsoft was brought in to take his place.

Major but less visible problems with the website—accommodating small business firms, ensuring the smooth, accurate, secure transmission of consumer data to insurers—were put off until later. Hard political and managerial choices were at last being made.

The reality of the ACA implementation through its first year was that the encounter between a comprehensive and exceedingly complex public policy, and America's Madisonian scheme of republican governance had left deep scars. Jobs were lost, reputations were injured, and the public was made skeptical albeit uninformed about the whole idea of universal health coverage.

Yet by April 2014, President Obama's chief of staff, Denis McDonough, and other top White House advisers were still focusing on questions other than skilled management and implementation. They claimed to have focused on the wrong things in preparing for the HealthCare.gov rollout: "The big questions at the time, among policy people and the press, [were]: Were you going to be able to put these marketplaces together? Were they going to have competition? Were the premiums going to be affordable?"[99]

Discussion Questions

1. Analyze the HealthCare.gov rollout process in terms of its political rationality and technical rationality.

2. Consider each of the counterfactual situations posed. Assume that all other aspects are held constant except for the alternative specified:

   a. What, if any, details of the case would you expect to change as a result of the alternative condition?

   b. Do you expect the outcome would have changed? On the basis of your analysis, to what extent was the alternative factor a causal mechanism in producing the outcome that actually occurred?

3. Consider the make-or-buy question in the context of HealthCare.gov. Should the design, rollout, and implementation of HealthCare.gov have been contracted out or kept in-house? Use these frameworks described in the chapter to analyze this question:

   a. Inherently governmental activities

   b. Complete/incomplete contracts

   c. Principal-agent

   d. Transaction costs

4. *Ex post* analysis is often easier than *ex ante analysis* (hindsight is better than foresight). Consider the timeline and rollout of HealthCare.gov. Using your analysis from the previous three questions, would it have been possible in 2011 to anticipate the problems the rollout would encounter? What are the one or two *key* management changes you would recommend if you could do it all over again? Support your argument.

5. This question gives practice in finding the law: What rulemaking activity was involved in the HealthCare .gov rollout?

   → Go to the Federal Register at www.federalregister.gov

   → Type in the search terms "affordable care act" and "healthcare.gov" (How many records are located?)

(Continued)

(Continued)

- → Sort from oldest to newest
- → Select a particular type (Notice, Proposed Rule, Rule) (How many records of each type are listed?)

    a. Read at least one document of each type.

    b. Considerable expertise is needed to create and to understand the implications of the language in these documents. Public managers face the challenge of balancing deference to the experts and taking the time to master the details themselves. Drawing on your understanding of the complex dynamics of Madisonian politics and of the need for delegated authority that is both constrained and enabled, answer the following questions and provide reasons for your answers:

        i. As a citizen, how do you think public managers should strike this balance?

        ii. How much detailed and technical information do you believe citizens should have available to them, that is, what does *transparency* mean in the implementation of complex public policies?

        iii. How much should the president and the White House staff be involved in the design and approval of complex regulations?

NOTES

1. Herbert Kaufman, "The Confines of Leadership," in *The Administrative Behavior of Federal Bureau Chiefs* (Washington, DC: Brookings Institution, 1981), 91.
2. Robb Todd, "Rice Seeks To Transform Diplomacy," *CBS News*, January 20, 2006, http://www.cbsnews.com/news/rice-seeks-to-transform-diplomacy.
3. Ibid.
4. Foreignassistance.gov, U.S. Agency for International Development, accessed May 21, 2015, http://www.foreignassistance.gov/web/Agency_USAID.aspx.
5. CRS Report for Congress, "Restructuring U.S. Foreign Aid: The Role of the Director for Foreign Assistance," June 16, 2006, CRS-2, http://fas.org/sgp/crs/row/RL33491.pdf.
6. "Secretary of State Condoleezza Rice," U.S. Department of State Archive, Information released online from January 20, 2001 to January 1, 2009, http://2001-2009.state.gov/secretary.
7. Gerald Hyman, "Assessing Secretary of State Rice's Reform of U.S. Foreign Assistance," *Carnegie Endowment for International Peace*, February 11, 2008.
8. Richard Blue, Cynthia Clapp-Wineek, and Holly Benner. *Beyond Success Stories: Monitoring & Evaluation for Foreign Assistance Results. Evaluator Views of Current Practice and Recommendations for Change*, 2009, http://www.usaid.gov/sites/default/files/documents/1868/060909_beyond_success_stories.pdf.
9. "Bureau for Policy, Planning and Learning," *USAID*, last updated July 24, 2014, http://www.usaid.gov/who-we-are/organization/bureaus/bureau-policy-planning-and-learning.
10. Avinash Dixit, "Incentives and Organizations in the Public Sector: An Interpretive Review," *Journal of Human Resources* 37, no. 4 (2002): 696–727; Aidan R. Vining and David L. Weimer, "Economic Perspectives on Public Organizations," in, ed. E. Ferlic, L E. Lynn, Jr., and C. Pollitt, *The Oxford Handbook of Public Management* (New York, NY and Oxford, UK: Oxford University Pres), 209–233; and Terry Moe, "The New Economics of Organization," *American Journal of Political Science* 28, no. 4 (1984): 739–777.
11. Moe, "The New Economics of Organization," 757.
12. Ibid., 755.

13. Oliver Williamson, "The Economics of Organization," *American Journal of Sociology 87*(1981): 548–577; Oliver Williamson, *The Mechanisms of Governance* (New York, NY: Oxford University Press, 1996).

14. Derek S. Pugh et al., "Dimensions of Organization Structure," *Administrative Science Quarterly* 13, no. 1 (1968): 65–105.

15. W. Richard Scott, *Organizations: Rational, Natural, and Open Systems* (Upper Saddle River, NJ: Prentice Hall, 1998), 227.

16. James D. Thompson, *Organizations in Action: Social Science Bases of Administrative Theory* (New York, NY: McGraw-Hill, 1967), 51.

17. Patricia W. Ingraham, Philip G. Joyce, and Amy Kneedler Donahue, *Government Performance: Why Management Matters* (Baltimore, MD: Johns Hopkins University Press, 2003).

18. Patricia W. Ingraham and Amy Kneedler Donahue, "Dissecting the Black Box Revisited: Characterizing Government Management Capacity," in *Governance and Performance: New Perspectives,* ed. Carolyn J. Heinrich and Laurence E. Lynn Jr. (Washington, DC: Georgetown University Press, 2000), 292–318.

19. Paul C. Light, *Thickening Government: Federal Hierarchy and the Diffusion of Accountability* (Washington, DC: Brookings Institution, 1995); Paul C. Light, "Fact Sheet on the Continued Thickening of Government" (Brookings Institution, July 23, 2004).

20. Light, "Fact Sheet."

21. Ibid.

22. Scott, *Organizations*, 311.

23. John W. Meyer and Brian Rowan, "Institutionalized Organizations: Formal Structure as Myth and Ceremony," *American Journal of Sociology* 83, (1977): 340–363.

24. Bengt Holmstrom and Paul Milgrom, "Multitask Principal-Agent Analyses: Incentive Contracts, Asset Ownership, and Job Design," *Journal of Law, Economics, and Organization* 7, Special Issue (1991): 24–52, 27.

25. Ibid., 26.

26. Carolyn J. Hill, "Casework Job Design and Client Outcomes in Welfare-to-Work Programs," *Journal of Public Administration Research and Theory* 16, no. 2 (2006): 263–288.

27. B. Douglas Bernheim and Michael D. Whinston, "Common Agency," *Econometrica* 54, no. 4 (July 1986): 923–942.

28. Thomas H. Hammond, "Agenda Control, Organizational Structure, and Bureaucratic Politics," *American Journal of Political Science* 30, no. 2 (1986): 379–420, 382.

29. Ibid., 416.

30. Ibid., 393, 400.

31. Ibid., 400, 402.

32. Charles Perrow, "A Framework for the Comparative Analysis of Organizations," *American Sociological Review* 32, no. 2 (1967): 194–208. Also see Hal G. Rainey, *Understanding and Managing Public Organizations* (San Francisco, A: Jossey-Bass, 2003), 192–193.

33. John Ashcroft, "Memo Regarding Policy on Charging Criminal Defendants," U.S. Department of Justice, September 22, 2003, http://www.justice.gov/archive/opa/pr/2003/September/03_ag_516.htm.

34. Adam Liptak and Eric Lichtblau, "New Plea Bargain Limits Could Swamp Courts, Experts Say," *The New York Times*, September 24, 2003, sec. U.S., http://www.nytimes.com/2003/09/24/us/new-plea-bargain-limits-could-swamp-courts-experts-say.html.Liptak and Lichtblau.

35. Michael Lipsky, *Street-Level Bureaucracy* (New York, NY: Russell Sage Foundation, 1980).

36. Ibid.

37. Adam Liptak and Eric Lichtblau, "New Plea Bargain Limits Could Swamp Courts, Experts Say," *The New York Times*, September 24, 2003, sec. U.S., http://www.nytimes.com/2003/09/24/us/new-plea-bargain-limits-could-swamp-courts-experts-say.html.Liptak and Lichtblau.

38. Frank O. Bowman III, "When Sentences Don't Make Sense," *The Washington Post,* August 15, 2003, http://www.prisontalk.com/forums/showthread.php?t=2387.

39. Max Leimgruber, "Agricultural Inspections on the California-Mexico Border: The Impacts of Public Policy," *Public Administration & Management: An Interactive Journal* 8, no. 3 (2003): 215–224, 219.

40. Ibid.

41. Aaron Wildavsky, *The Politics of the Budgetary Process, 2nd edition* (Boston, MA: Little, Brown, 1974), 4.

42. William A. Niskanen, Jr., *Bureaucracy and Representative Government* (New York, NY: Aldine-Atherton, 1971).

43. Patrick Dunleavy, "The Bureau-Shaping Model," Chapter 7 in *Democracy, Bureaucracy and Public Choice* (Englewood Cliffs, NJ: Prentice-Hall, 1992), 174–209.

44. Ibid., 202.

45. Ibid., 64.

46. Ibid., 65.

47. Congressional Research Service, "A Brief Overview of Rulemaking and Judicial Review, January 4, 2011, http://www.wise-intern.org/orientation/documents/CRSrulemakingCB.pdf.

48. Department of Agriculture, Forest Service, "Final Rule on National Forest System Land Management Planning," 36 CFR Part 219, RIN 0596-AB86, http://www.fs.fed.us/emc/nfma/includes/rule%20.pdf, January 5, 2005.

49. Bill Vlasic and Christopher Jensen, "Something Went 'Very Wrong' at G.M., Chief Says," *The New York Times*, March 17, 2014, http://www.nytimes.com/2014/03/18/business/gm-chief-barra-releases-video-on-recalls.html.; Joseph B. White and Jeff Bennett, "Did Regulator Drop the Ball in GM Recall?," *Wall Street Journal*, March 25, 2014, sec. Business, http://online.wsj.com/news/articles/SB10001424052702303949704579461680682611294?mod=WSJ_hp_LEFTTopStories&mg=reno64-wsj.

50. Statement Of The Honorable David Friedman Acting Administrator, National Highway Traffic Safety Administration Before The Committee On Energy And Commerce Subcommittee On Oversight and Investigations U.S. House Of Representatives, Hearing on The GM Ignition Switch Recall: Why Did It Take So Long? April 1, 2014.

51. Paul Milgrom and John Roberts, "Bounded Rationality and Private Information," in *Economics Organization & Management* (Englewood Cliffs, NJ: Prentice Hall, 1992): 127.

52. Trevor L. Brown and Matthew Potoski, "Transaction Costs and Institutional Explanations for Government Service Production Decisions," *Journal of Public Administration Research and Theory* 13, no. 4 (2003): 441–468.

53. Ibid., 444.

54. Michael Moss, "U.S. Struggling to Get Soldiers Updated Armor," *The New York Times*, August 14, 2005, sec. International/Middle East, http://www.nytimes.com/2005/08/14/international/middleeast/14armor.html.

55. Oliver Hart, Andrei Shleifer, and Robert W. Vishny, "The Proper Scope of Government: Theory and an Application to Prisons," *Quarterly Journal of Economics* (November 1997): 1127–61.

56. Ibid., 1159.

57. Gilbert M. Gaul, "Bad Practices Net Hospitals More Money," *The Washington Post*, July 24, 2005, sec. Nation, http://www.washingtonpost.com/wp-dyn/content/article/2005/07/23/AR2005072300382.html.

58. Karen Eggleston and Richard Zeckhauser, "Government Contracting for Health Care," in *Market-Based Governance: Supply Side, Demand Side, Upside, Downside*, ed. John D. Donahue and Joseph S. Nye Jr. (Washington, DC: Brookings Institution, 2002).

59. Ibid., 42.

60. Ibid., 44.

61. Richard F. Elmore, "Graduate Education in Public Management: Working the Seams of Government," *Journal of Policy Analysis and Management* 6, no. 1 (Autumn 1986): 74.

62. Trevor L. Brown, Matthew Potoski, and David M. Van Slyke, *Complex Contracting Government Purchasing in the Wake of the U.S. Coast Guard's Deepwater Program*, (New York, NY: Cambridge University Press, 2013).

63. "The Troubled Waters of 'Deepwater,'" *CBS News: 60 Minutes*, updated August 14, 2007, http://www.cbsnews.com/news/the-troubled-waters-of-deepwater/.

64. Patricia Kime and Christopher P. Cavas, "U.S. Coast Guard Takes Control of Patrol Boat Program: Ends Contract with Lockheed Martin, Northrop Grumman," *defensenews.com*, March 15, 2007, http://defensenews.com/story.php?F=2624965&C=navwar.

65. Ibid.

66. Walter W. Powell, "Neither Market Nor Hierarchy: Network Forms of Organization," *Research in Organizational Behavior 12* (1990): 295–336.

67. Laurence J. O'Toole, "Treating Networks Seriously: Practical and Research-Based Agendas in Public Administration," *Public Administration Review 57*(1997): 45–52, 45.

68. "History," MOFACT, accessed May 21, 2015, http://mofact.org/history.

69. Adapted from Carolyn J. Hill and Laurence E. Lynn, Jr. "Producing Human Services: Why Do Agencies Collaborate?" *Public Management Review* 5, no. 1 (2003): 63–81.

70. Carolyn J. Hill and Laurence E. Lynn, Jr. "Producing Human Services: Why Do Agencies Collaborate?", *Public Management Review* 5, no. 1 (2003): pp. 63–81.

71. Robert I. Agranoff and Michael McGuire, "Big Questions in Public Network Management Research," *Journal of Public Administration Research and Theory* 11 (2001): 295–326.

72. Keith G. Provan and H. Brinton Milward, "Do Networks Really Work? A Framework for Evaluating Public Sector Organization Networks," *Public Administration Review* 61 (2001): 414–423.

73. Bin Chen and Elizabeth A. Graddy, "The Effectiveness of Nonprofit Lead-Organization Networks for Social Service Delivery," *Nonprofit Management & Leadership* 20, no. 4 (Summer 2010): 405–422. Quote is from p. 419.

74. Ann Marie Thompson and James L. Perry, "Collaboration Processes: Inside the Black Box," *Public Administration Review* 66, no. 1 (2006): 20–32.

75.   Carolyn J. Hill and Laurence E. Lynn, Jr., "Producing Human Services: Why Do Agencies Collaborate?," *Public Management Review* 5, no. 1, (2003): 63–81; Marcia K. Meyers, "Organizational Factors in the Integration of Services for Children," *Social Service Review* 67, no. 4 (1993): 547–575.

76.   Ingraham and Donahue, "Dissecting the Black Box Revisited: Characterizing Government Management Capacity"; Ingraham, Joyce, and Donahue, *Government Performance.*

77.   John Rohr, *To Run A Constitution: The Legitimacy of the Administrative State* (Lawrence: University Press of Kansas, 1986).

78.   Government Accountability Office, "Results-Oriented Government: GPRA Has Established a Solid Foundation for Achieving Greater Results," GAO-04-594T, 2004.

79.   Office of Management and Budget, *Government-Wide Performance Plan, Budget of the United States Government, Fiscal Year 1999* (Washington, DC: U.S. Government Printing Office, 1998).

80.   "What Is the GPRA Modernization Act of 2010 and Why Is it Important?" Performance.Gov, http://www.performance.gov/faq, accessed May 21, 2015.

81.   "Report of the Committee on Homeland Security and Governmental Affairs to Accompany H.R. 2142, GPRA Modernization Act of 2010," December 16, 2010, http://www.gpo.gov/fdsys/pkg/CRPT-111srpt372/pdf/CRPT-111srpt372.pdf.

82.   Ibid.

83.   Ibid.

84.   Government Finance Officers Association, "National Performance Management Advisory Commission Releases Framework for State and Local Governments," *Government Finance Review,* June 2010, http://www.gfoa.org/sites/default/files/GFR_JUN_10_47.pdf.

85.   National Performance Management Advisory Commission, *A Performance Management Framework for State and Local Government: From Measurement and Reporting to Management and Improving* (Chicago, IL: National Performance Management Advisory Commission), http://www.nasbo.org/sites/default/files/APerformanceManagementFramework.pdf.

86.   Government Finance Officers Association, "National Performance Management Advisory Commission."

87.   Leslie Scism and Timothy W. Martin, "High Deductibles Fuel New Worries of Health-Law Sticker Shock," *Wall Street Journal*, December 9, 2013, sec. US, http://online.wsj.com/news/articles/SB10001424052702303330204579246211560398876?mod=WSJ_hpp_LEFT TopStories.

88.   Theo Francis, "Companies Prepare to Pass More Health Costs to Workers," *Wall Street Journal*, November 25, 2013, sec. US, http://online.wsj.com/news/articles/SB10001424052702304607104579212351200702342?mod=WSJ_hpp_LEFTTopStories.

89.   Michael D. Shear and Robert Pear, "A Plea to Avoid Crush of Users at Health Site," *The New York Times*, November 26, 2013, sec. U.S./Politics, http://www.nytimes.com/2013/11/27/us/politics/white-house-urges-caution-on-health-site.html.

90.   Amy Goldstein, "Obama Administration Relaxes Rules of Health-Care Law Four Days Before Deadline," *The Washington Post*, December 19, 2013, http://www.washingtonpost.com/national/health-science/obama-administration-relaxes-rules-of-health-care-law-four-days-before-deadline/2013/12/19/81bc3132-690b-11e3-8b5b-a77187b716a3_story.html?hpid=z1.

91.   Ibid.

92.   "Section 8: Health Care, Marijuana, Common Core, Other Domestic Issues," *Pew Research Center for the People and the Press*, June 26, 2014, http://www.people-press.org/2014/06/26/section-8-health-care-marijuana-common-core-other-domestic-issues.

93.   Government Accountability Office, "HEALTHCARE.GOV: Ineffective Planning and Oversight Practices Underscore the Need for Improved Contract Management," GAO-14-694, July 2014, http://www.gao.gov/assets/670/665179.pdf.

94.   Congressional Budget Office, Insurance Coverage Provisions of the Affordable Care Act—CBO's April 2014 Baseline, http://www.cbo.gov/sites/default/files/cbofiles/attachments/43900-2014-04-ACAtables2.pdf.

95.   Stephanie Armour, "Fewer Uninsured Face Fines as Health Law's Exemptions Swell," *Wall Street Journal*, August 7, 2014, sec. US, http://online.wsj.com/articles/fewer-uninsured-face-fines-as-health-laws-exemptions-swell-1407378602?mod=WSJ_hpp_MIDDLENexttoW hatsNewsThird.

96.   Jeffrey Young, "Why Obamacare May Have Trouble Signing Up As Many Uninsured Next Year," *Huffington Post*, August 14, 2014, http://www.huffingtonpost.com/2014/08/14/obamacare-uninsured-rate-2014-sign-ups_n_5676458.html.

97.   Ezra Klein, "The Memo That Could Have Saved Obamacare," *The Washington Post*, November 4, 2013, http://www.washingtonpost.com/blogs/wonkblog/wp/2013/11/04/the-memo-that-could-have-saved-obamacare.

98.   Sheryl Gay Stolberg and Michael D. Shear, "Inside the Race to Rescue a Health Care Site, and Obama," *The New York Times*, November 30, 2013, sec. U.S./Politics, http://www.nytimes.com/2013/12/01/us/politics/inside-the-race-to-rescue-a-health-site-and-obama.html.

99.   Michael D. Shear, "Health Goal Met, White House Reviews Missteps," *The New York Times*, April 9, 2014, http://www.nytimes.com/2014/04/10/us/politics/health-goal-met-white-house-reviews-missteps.html.

7 Structure

Rules and Regulations

INTRODUCTION

In a republic governed by the rule of law, regulation is an essential means for establishing and enforcing the "rules of the game": the institutions governing the behavior and conduct of individuals, organizations, and other social entities. Under the authority of statutes, regulators define the precise terms of the social contract between citizens and their governments. As such, regulation is about securing the liberty and justice for all necessary to sustaining domestic tranquility and social stability. Regulation is concerned with conduct by individuals and organizations that affects the lives or livelihoods of others. The actual and potential reach of regulation is vast because it could conceivably cover any conduct with social implications.

You cannot, for example, physically or emotionally abuse your children. You cannot manufacture and sell products—foods, drugs, automobiles, baby cribs—that might harm or injure others. You cannot do things in ways that are dangerous or disruptive to others, such as causing air pollution by burning fossil fuels or driving under the influence of alcohol. You cannot withhold information that others might need to ensure their own well-being; required information includes the content of labels on cigarettes, processed foods, pharmaceuticals, and the details of your income. The more advanced and diverse a society, the more the rules and the competence with which they are established and enforced matter.[i]

> **Regulation is concerned with conduct by individuals and organizations that affects the lives or livelihoods of others. The actual and potential reach of regulation is vast because it could conceivably cover any conduct with social implications.**

---

[i] On its website, the Food and Drug Administration has a long list of product categories it regulates. It also notes, "Often frustrating and confusing for consumers is determining the appropriate regulatory agency to contact." Other agencies engaged in related types of regulation include the Federal Trade Commission, the Department of the Treasury's Alcohol and Tobacco Tax and Trade Bureau, the Consumer Product Safety Commission, the Drug Enforcement Administration, the Food Safety and Inspection Service, the Environmental Protection Agency, and the Animal and Plant Health Inspection Service.

Because the rules that govern us can affect individual liberty and property rights, it is important to be clear about why and how regulations are written and enforced and why regulatory processes can ignite intense political controversy. Often, constitutional issues are at the heart of political conflicts; examples include reproductive rights, pornography, voting rights, and other civil and states' rights issues. The economic, political, and social effects of regulation are pervasive and, in many cases, they have life or death consequences (such as rules governing the use of force by police or the dispensing of controlled substances).

The life of every American, from birth to death,[ii] is affected by regulation: the rules, guidelines, and standards promulgated both by governments at all levels and by private sector regulators acting with the explicit or implicit sanction of lawmakers. In common parlance, regulation encompasses the processes of making rules, setting standards, licensing professionals, certifying compliance with rules and standards, issuing permits, approving applications, conducting hearings and appeals, and issuing guidelines, procedures, and directives.

Fundamental facts about regulation as a managed administrative process include these:

- Regulation is the operationalization, through definition and elaboration, of policy statements written into public law. It is distinct from laws enacted by legislative entities and from judicial rulings clarifying and interpreting those laws (discussed in Chapters 2 and 5).
- Regulation is an administrative responsibility delegated to organizations. These organizations include independent regulatory agencies, boards and commissions with broad policy-making responsibilities, and special purpose authorities created by federal, state, and local legislatures and courts of law. As such, it further enables and constrains the responsibilities, duties, and rights of organizations and individuals in furtherance of legislated policy goals.[iii]
- Regulation may take the form of

  o definitions and instructions promulgated by governments,
  o contractual obligations that bind parties to an agreement (for example, provisions of contracts between insurers and their policyholders),
  o self-regulation by an industry through, for example, a trade association, or
  o behavioral regulation such as codes of personal conduct.

- Regulation that occurs during public policy implementation by executive departments and agencies is discussed in Chapter 6. The current chapter is concerned with regulation by independent regulatory agencies such as the Federal Communications Commission (FCC) and by regulatory agencies such as the Food and Drug Administration within the Department of Health and Human Services. Although not autonomous, these organizations are expected to function independently of political supervision by their parent agencies.[iv]

[ii]Regulation's influence actually begins before birth, governing reproductive health services and neonatal care. Regulation also continues after death, governing the disposition of a deceased individual's property and other assets.

[iii]For comprehensive analyses of regulatory governance, see David Levi-Faur, "Regulation and Regulatory Governance" in *Handbook of the Politics of Regulation,* ed. David Levi-Faur (Northampton, MA: Edward Elgar, 2011); Congressional Research Service, "A Brief Overview of Rulemaking and Judicial Review," January 4, 2011; Congressional Research Service, "Independence of Federal Financial Regulators," February 24, 2014.

[iv]In a sense, the type of regulation discussed in Chapter 6 is a means to accomplish the goals of public policies. The regulation covered in this chapter is, itself, the public policy goal.

This chapter is organized as follows: An opening case explores how the enabling and constraining structures of financial system regulation might have contributed to the occurrence and aftermath of the major financial crisis that began in 2008: Had there been too much regulation of the financial services industry or too little? Reviewed next are the main theories of the emergence and expansion of an American "regulatory state" and the politics associated with regulatory policymaking. The broad landscape of the American regulatory state and how it operates is then described, including the agencies, the tasks, and the processes involved in **rulemaking**, the term for the most common type of regulatory process. The challenges and methods of regulatory enforcement are reviewed. The chapter concludes with a case exploring the regulatory issues involved in high-volume hydraulic fracturing (HVHF, or **fracking**), a process to extract oil and natural gas from shale rock deposits.

CASE: THE FINANCIAL CRISIS OF 2008

Most post mortems of the 2008 financial crisis in American financial markets that spawned the Great Recession in America and globally have concluded that a great many factors— a perfect storm—contributed to its occurrence. These factors prominently included financial institutions behaving badly; failures of policymaking in Congress, the Federal Reserve system, and the executive branch; and a roster of failures in the housing finance sector leading to the residential housing bubble that was bound to burst—and did. The factor drawing the most focused attention, however, was the structural lever that policymakers would inevitably reach for in responding to the crisis: government regulation of the financial industry.

Reasons

> **The factor drawing the most focused attention, however, was the structural lever that policymakers would inevitably reach for in responding to the crisis: government regulation of the financial industry.**

Modern financial system regulation originated with the creation of the Federal Reserve System, America's central bank, created during the Progressive Era following years of financial crises. Over the next century, as financial institutions and practices adapted to domestic and global economic change, so did the regulatory framework that governed them. The regulation of the financial services sector of the American economy became exceedingly complex. In 2008, regulation was the responsibility of eight federal regulatory agencies:

- the U.S. Securities and Exchange Commission (SEC),
- the Financial Industry Regulatory Authority (FINRA),
- the Commodity Futures Trading Commission (CFTC),
- the Federal Reserve System,
- the Federal Deposit Insurance Corporation (FDIC),
- the Office of the Comptroller of the Currency (OCC),
- the National Credit Union Administration (NCUA), and
- the Office of Thrift Supervision (OTS).

As if that weren't enough, American financial services institutions are also regulated by the states.[i] In sharp contrast, two regulatory agencies provide oversight of the financial services industry in Great Britain. Prior to 2013, the United Kingdom, like most industrialized countries, had only one.

Investigations and scholarly research were soon underway, seeking to identify the reasons for the crisis and ways to prevent similar crises in the future. Two government-sponsored investigations were launched, each of which culminated in an authoritative report:

- U.S. Senate Permanent Subcommittee on Investigations, Committee on Homeland Security and Governmental Affairs, *Wall Street and the Financial Crisis: Anatomy of a Financial Collapse* (2011).[1]
- Financial Crisis Inquiry Commission (FCIC). *The Financial Crisis Inquiry Report: Final Report of the National Commission on the Causes of the Financial and Economic Crisis in the United States* (2011).[2]

Although these reports identified multiple factors contributing to the financial system meltdown, attention inevitably focused on the role played by regulation—or the lack of it:

- Was the regulatory system poorly managed?
- Was the regulatory framework poorly designed?
- Were there factors other than regulation contributing to what happened in both domestic and global financial markets?

This case explores evidence in the two official reports that bears on these questions.

Was Regulation Poorly Managed?

A widely quoted finding of the FCIC pointed to individuals, including regulators, who made bad choices: "this financial crisis was avoidable. The crisis was the result of human action and inaction."[ii] The report stated,

---

[i]The Federal Financial Institutions Examination Council (FFIEC) was "established on March 10, 1979, pursuant to title X of the Financial Institutions Regulatory and Interest Rate Control Act of 1978 (FIRA), Public Law 95-630 . . . . [I]t is a formal interagency body empowered to prescribe uniform principles, standards, and report forms for the federal examination of financial institutions . . . and to make recommendations to promote uniformity in the supervision of financial institutions. To encourage the application of uniform examination principles and standards by the state and federal supervisory authorities, the Council established . . . an advisory State Liaison Committee composed of five representatives of state supervisory agencies. In accordance with the Financial Services Regulatory Relief Act of 2006, a representative state regulator was added as a voting member of the Council in October 2006." http://www.ffiec.gov/about.htm.

[ii]"The Financial Crisis Inquiry Report: Final Report of the National Commission on the Causes of the Financial and Economic Crisis in the United States," *The Financial Crisis Inquiry Commission*, January 2011, xvii. Neither the FCIC report nor the Senate subcommittee report reflected the unanimous findings a bipartisan membership. The texts of both reports offered a perspective similar to Senate Democrats' (then in the majority) views of the George W. Bush administration's stance on regulation: Republicans did not wish to engage in rigorous oversight of the financial services industry. They preferred deregulation and did not believe it was an important contributor to the Great Recession.

(Continued)

(Continued)

> [W]e do not accept the view that regulators lacked the power to protect the financial system. They had ample power in many arenas and they chose not to use it. To give just three examples
>
> - The Securities and Exchange Commission could have required more capital and halted risky practices at the big investment banks. It did not.
> - The Federal Reserve Bank of New York and other regulators could have clamped down on Citigroup's excesses in the run-up to the crisis. They did not.
> - Policymakers and regulators could have stopped the runaway mortgage securitization train. They did not.
>
> In case after case after case, regulators continued to rate the institutions they oversaw as safe and sound even in the face of mounting troubles, often downgrading them just before their collapse. And where regulators lacked authority, they could have sought it. Too often, they lacked the political will—in a political and ideological environment that constrained it—as well as the fortitude to critically challenge the institutions and the entire system they were entrusted to oversee.[3]

The FCIC Report further stated that "there was pervasive permissiveness; little meaningful action was taken to quell the threats in a timely manner. The prime example is the Federal Reserve's pivotal failure to stem the flow of toxic mortgages."[4] Furthermore,

> [W]e conclude the government was ill prepared for the crisis, and its inconsistent response added to the uncertainty and panic in the financial markets . . . [K]ey policy makers—the Treasury Department, the Federal Reserve Board, and the Federal Reserve Bank of New York—who were best positioned to watch over our markets were ill prepared for the events of 2007 and 2008.[5]

The Senate report strongly implied that regulators failed to use the regulatory authority delegated to them. The report was based on four case studies, which the Senate report described as follows:

> The case studies are Washington Mutual Bank, the largest bank failure in U.S. history; the federal Office of Thrift Supervision which oversaw Washington Mutual's demise; Moody's and Standard & Poor's, the country's two largest credit rating agencies; and Goldman Sachs and Deutsche Bank, two leaders in the design, marketing, and sale of mortgage related securities.

Based on the case studies, the Senate report identified four causal factors for the crisis:

1. lenders introduced new levels of risk into the U.S. financial system,

2. credit rating agencies labeled the new financial instruments "safe,"

3. federal banking regulators failed to intervene and insist on safe lending practices and risk management, and

4. investment banks spread the risk through creating structure investment products based on the unsafe loans.[6]

While these factors are all interconnected, according to the report, the choices of federal banking regulators—their failure to intervene—were obviously pivotal, allowing risk levels to rise further and the continued spreading of the rising risk throughout the financial system.

Public administration scholar Richard Green elaborated on the avoidability theme in an article published in 2012. He argued that public administrators were among those who could and should have foreseen and prevented the financial crisis, but they "failed miserably."[7]

Was Regulation Poorly Designed?

The regulators who were charged with behaving badly were enabled to make choices and simultaneously constrained in the choices they could make by the statutory framework of financial system regulation and the premises on which its design was based. In other words, structures were also an underlying cause of the financial crisis.

The politics of bureaucratic structure were clearly a factor in the design of the regulatory system. According to the FCIC report,

> To create checks and balances and keep any agency from becoming arbitrary or inflexible, senior policy makers pushed to keep multiple regulators. In 1994, Greenspan testified against proposals to consolidate bank regulation: "The current structure provides banks with a method . . . of shifting their regulator, an effective test that provides a limit on the arbitrary position or excessively rigid posture of any one regulator. The pressure of a potential loss of institutions has inhibited excessive regulation and acted as a countervailing force to the bias of a regulatory agency to overregulate." Further, some regulators, including the OTS and Office of the Comptroller of the Currency (OCC), were funded largely by assessments from the institutions they regulated. As a result, the larger the number of institutions that chose these regulators, the greater their budget[8]. . . .

> The Fed supervised financial holding companies as a whole, looking only for risks that cut across the various subsidiaries owned by the holding company. To avoid duplicating other regulators' work, the Fed was required to rely "to the fullest extent possible" on examinations and reports of those agencies regarding subsidiaries of the holding company, including banks, securities firms, and insurance companies. The expressed intent of Fed-Lite was to eliminate excessive or duplicative regulation. However, Fed Chairman Ben Bernanke told the FCIC that Fed-Lite "made it difficult for any single regulator to reliably see the whole picture of activities and risks of large, complex banking institutions."[9]

According to the FCIC report,

> More and more, regulators looked to financial institutions to police themselves—"deregulation" was the label. Former Fed chairman Alan Greenspan put it this way: "The market-stabilizing

(Continued)

(Continued)

> private regulatory forces should gradually displace many cumbersome, increasingly ineffective government structures. . . . And if problems outstripped the market's ability to right itself, the Federal Reserve would take on the responsibility to restore financial stability.[10]

The FCIC report identifies some of the specific structural problems, including this one:

> During the 1990s, various federal agencies had taken increasing notice of abusive subprime lending practices. But the regulatory system was not well equipped to respond consistently— and on a national basis—to protect borrowers. State regulators, as well as either the Fed or the FDIC, supervised the mortgage practices of state banks. The OCC supervised the national banks. The OTS or state regulators were responsible for the thrifts. Some state regulators also licensed mortgage brokers, a growing portion of the market, but did not supervise them.

> Despite this diffusion of authority, one entity was unquestionably authorized by Congress to write strong and consistent rules regulating mortgages for all types of lenders: the Federal Reserve, through the Truth in Lending Act of 1968. In 1969, the Fed adopted Regulation Z for the purpose of implementing the act. But while Regulation Z applied to all lenders, its enforcement was divided among America's many financial regulators.[11]

The FCIC report gives an example of how the diffusion of enforcement authority affected regulator decision making. Both the Fed and the Federal Trade Commission (FTC) have the legal authority to regulate non-bank entities such as subprime mortgage lenders. According to its report, "Fed officials had been debating whether they—in addition to the FTC—should enforce rules for nonbank lenders. But they worried about whether the Fed would be stepping on congressional prerogatives by assuming enforcement responsibilities that legislation had delegated to the FTC."[12] Thus, pleas to the Fed for help in regulating the burgeoning subprime loan market went unheeded.

The constraining structures that regulators inhabited, and the premises on which they were based, narrowed the range of choices they would regard as legitimate under the rule of law.

Something More?

Blame for the crisis was distributed more broadly than toward the regulatory system and its administrators, however:

- Policymakers in both Congress and the executive branch came under fire from critics. A member of the Federal Reserve System's board of governors, for example, said in May 2012,

> Neither the statutory framework for, nor supervisory oversight of, the financial system adapted to take account of the new risks posed by the broader trend [in financial services]. On the contrary, regulatory change for the 30 years preceding the crisis was largely a deregulatory program, designed at least in part to address the erosion of banks' franchise value caused by the rapid growth of credit intermediation through capital markets.[13]

- According to the FCIC report,

    Fannie and Freddie [the Federal National Mortgage Association and the Federal Home Loan Mortgage Association, government-sponsored enterprises promoting home ownership had become] crucial to the housing market, but their dual missions—promoting mortgage lending while maximizing returns to shareholders—were problematic. Former Fannie CEO Daniel Mudd told the FCIC that "the GSE structure required the companies to maintain a fine balance between financial goals and what we call the mission goals . . . . [T]he root cause of the GSEs' troubles lies with their business model.[14]

- Also, according to the FCIC report,

    the financial industry itself played a key role in weakening regulatory constraints on institutions, markets, and products. It did not surprise the Commission that an industry of such wealth and power would exert pressure on policy makers and regulators. From 1999 to 2008 the financial sector expended $2.7 billion in reported federal lobbying expenses; individuals and political action committees in the sector made more than $1 billion in campaign contributions. What troubled us was the extent to which the nation was deprived of the necessary strength and independence of the oversight necessary to safeguard financial stability.[15]

Perverse incentives within the private sector also contributed to the crisis. The FCIC concluded that **"dramatic failures of corporate governance and risk management at many systemically important financial institutions were a key cause of this crisis."** Further, **"We conclude the failures of credit rating agencies were essential cogs in the wheel of financial destruction** [emphasis in original]."[16]

The FCIC stated,

Stock options became a popular form of compensation, allowing employees to buy the company's stock in the future at some predetermined price, and thus to reap rewards when the stock price was higher than that predetermined price. In fact, the option would have no value if the stock price was below that price. Encouraging the awarding of stock options was 1993 legislation making compensation in excess of $1 million taxable to the corporation unless performance-based. Stock options had potentially unlimited upside, while the downside was simply to receive nothing if the stock didn't rise to the predetermined price. The same applied to plans that tied pay to return on equity: they meant that executives could win more than they could lose. These pay structures had the unintended consequence of creating incentives to increase both risk and leverage, which could lead to larger jumps in a company's stock price. . . . The dangers of the new pay structures were clear, but senior executives believed they were powerless to change it.[17]

(Continued)

(Continued)

The FCIC's indictment of the private sector was broad:

> Lending standards collapsed, and there was a significant failure of accountability and responsibility throughout each level of the lending system. This included borrowers, mortgage brokers, appraisers, originators, securitizers, credit rating agencies, and investors, and ranged from corporate boardrooms to individuals. Loans were often premised on ever-rising home prices and were made regardless of ability to pay.[18]

Regulation Evolves

Even before the verdicts were in from the two official reports, a Democratic-controlled Congress inaugurated the next stage in financial system regulation. In July 2010, Congress passed the Dodd-Frank Wall Street Reform and Consumer Protection Act, widely regarded as the most significant reform of financial system regulation since the Great Depression of the 1930s. Its general thrust was to strengthen regulation, including the creation of a new regulatory agency, the Consumer Financial Protection Bureau (CFPB), in ways that would ensure its unpopularity with the financial services industry and, therefore, continuing political controversy.

Only time will tell whether or not financial stability will be increased by making a structurally complex regulatory infrastructure even more so. It will be up to the public managers within the redesigned regulatory system to bend a politically rational structural arrangement toward technically rational financial system outcomes.

WHY REGULATE?

A major transformation of public governance at all levels in the United States began, as noted in Chapter 6, during the Progressive Era. Prior to the Progressive Era, according to regulatory historians Marc T. Law and Sukkoo Kim, "regulation was local and judicial because Americans distrusted centralized powers of government. The common law of nuisance and *salus populi* (people's welfare) tradition provided the main principles of regulation. Local courts and militia enforced these rules."[19]

From the 1880s until World War I, American governance evolved from rule by political parties, legislatures, and courts to government by an administrative state. It comprised agencies staffed by qualified public servants with expertise in carrying out an expanding array of responsibilities delegated to them by legislatures. Among these responsibilities was the regulation of a widening expanse of economic, political, and social activities and complex, often very large and politically powerful, private sector organizations. Regulating the complex activities of a rapidly modernizing society, however, outgrew the capacities of amateur legislators and local officials to address the technical issues that were emerging.

> Regulating the complex activities of a rapidly modernizing society, however, outgrew the capacities of amateur legislators and local officials to address the technical issues that were emerging.

From the Progressive Era onward, lawmakers delegated the writing of the "rules of the game" to experts, professional regulators in public agencies comprising what is commonly referred to as the **regulatory state**. But their rulemakings were subject to challenge by individuals and organizations affected by them, which initiated judicial review and interpretive rulemaking by the courts.

Now, "We live in the golden era of regulation," according to David Levi-Faur, a leading scholar of regulation.[20] He said this before the U.S. Congress passed both the Dodd-Frank Wall Street Reform and Consumer Protection Act and the Affordable Care Act in 2010. As noted in the opening case, Dodd-Frank created a major new regulatory agency, the CFPB. A Congressional Research Service (CRS) report estimates that Dodd-Frank required or permitted over 300 rulemaking provisions by 11 regulatory agencies.[21] A single rulemaking may produce hundreds of pages of regulatory language.

Scholars from the fields of law, economics, political science, and history have put forward a variety of theories to explain why public regulation of private conduct is necessary and why the American administrative state has emerged in the form that it has. According to legal scholar Stephen P. Croley, the point of departure for these explanations is a theory of politics known as **pluralism**.[22] Terry Moe's theory of the politics of bureaucratic structure, discussed in earlier chapters of this book, is an illustration of pluralism's dynamics. Private sector interest groups form to pursue their own interests in the political process. "Legislative and administrative decisions thus reflect the balance of interest-group competition."[23] Other specific theories are discussed next.

Public Choice Theory. Theorists in economics and political science argue that the pluralist doctrine is inadequate to account for the regulatory state.

> [Public choice theory] treats legislative, regulatory, and electoral institutions as [constituting] an economy in which the relevant actors—including ordinary citizens, legislators, agencies, and organized interest groups most affected by regulatory policies—exchange regulatory "goods," which are "demanded" and "supplied" according to the same basic principles governing the demand and supply of ordinary economic goods. [24]

The outcomes of the regulatory marketplace, public choice theorists point out, reflect the private interests of groups that have disproportionate power in the political process: industries, companies, unions, wealthy entrepreneurs, high status professions, and the like. This occurs at the expense of the regulatory interests of consumers, employees, disadvantaged groups, and advocates for public interests such as environmental quality and energy conservation. "Individual citizens have little or no occasion for registering their regulatory interests, including their interests against regulatory policies that bring them no benefits."[25]

Neopluralist Theory. In opposition to public choice theory is another argument, also originating in the discipline of economics. Neopluralist theories of regulation posit that interest groups—policy scholars might call them **advocacy coalitions**—will organize themselves so as to be able to assemble sufficient financial and political resources to influence policymakers to adopt regulations whose benefits outweigh the resource costs incurred by the groups to achieve them. Groups that are successful in winning favorable regulatory action, then, are those that are politically efficient, mobilizing support from voters, donors, activists, and allied professional groups sufficient to secure their goals. A wider array of interests than public choice theories allow for is influential in policymaking. It remains the case, however, that poorer, less widely popular interests—those who advocate for groups considered "undeserving" of public assistance—will not fare well in the political process.

Public Interest Theory. A somewhat more optimistic explanation for regulatory outcomes that reflect the broad public interest is that of public interest theory. According to Croley's account of this perspective,

[R]egulatory outcomes ameliorate market failures and vindicate the citizenry's interests not routinely, but sometimes, and much more commonly than other scholars of regulation acknowledge: Regulation may not always further the citizenry's general interests, but [some] major regulatory initiatives are inexplicable without incorporating some variation of the old public interest theory.[26]

Public interest theory, according to Croley, features three types of participants:

- citizens at large, who recognize the general benefits of regulatory activity in areas such as environmental protection, consumer protection, workplace safety, and food and drug safety;
- special interest groups with an ongoing interest in favorable regulation; and,
- a new factor: the regulators themselves.

Regulators have self-interests in the maintenance of political support for what they do and in their agencies' reputations for competence. Because of their expertise and commitment to the mission of their agency, regulators may also be more likely to value the achievement of the public interests served by their organization. These aspects of reputation public service values are aspects of organizational culture, discussed in Chapters 8 and 9. Regulatory outcomes depend on political competition among citizens, interest groups, and regulators. They also depend on what Croley calls **regulatory slack:** citizens' trust in and deference to the expertise, experience, and actions of regulators. This slack can be highly variable across time, policy issues, and jurisdictions.

Civic Republicanism. As arguably the most idealistic theory of the regulatory state, civic republicanism posits that regulatory action reflects shared values among those with a stake in regulatory outcomes, arrived at through dialogue and deliberation. Regulation, in other words, reflects broad civic consensus forged over time.[27] The theory assumes that participants' preferences for regulatory action are not fixed but are shaped by the process of deliberation itself. Furthermore, it assumes that participants value the very phenomenon of consensus and are willing to compromise in order to achieve it. Argues Croley,

> Strong claims about the inevitability of regulatory failure due to regulated parties' privileged access to regulatory decisionmakers are untenable in the light of the decisionmaking procedures regulators employ, the broader legal environment in which regulatory decisions are made, and the available evidence about the types of parties that participate in regulatory decisionmaking.[28]

Croley's analysis of the literature on regulation identifies what he regards as unanswered questions:

- With respect to informal agency decision-making processes: How much regulating do agencies accomplish through informal orders, and which interests have significant influence on informal agency decisions? What is the significance of agency-initiated communication with interest groups during the rulemaking process?
- Concerning rulemaking: Are public interest groups' and small businesses' views given extra weight during rulemaking or other decisionmaking processes? Are negotiated rules responsive to a broader set of regulatory interests relative to ordinary rules? Do participants in rulemaking often revise their own regulatory goals in light of information supplied by other parties?

- Concerning adjudication: How independent are [administrative law judges (ALJs)] from their own agencies? Do narrow interest groups usually get what they want as a final result of the formal adjudication process? How often do they appeal ALJs' decisions, for example, and with what effect?
- Concerning advisory committees: What weight do agencies give to advisory-committee recommendations about regulatory policy issues? Does wide-ranging interest representation on an advisory committee mean that agency decisions really reflect wide-ranging interests?
- Concerning communication with the White House: What effect do [Office of Informational and Regulatory Affairs (OIRA)] contacts with outside groups have on White House evaluation of major rules? Are White House contacts with groups concerned about the substance of a pending rule largely exercises in public relations, or does the identity of those who meet with OIRA staff reveal something about which interests have influence? [29]

HOW DOES FEDERAL REGULATION HAPPEN?

As noted in the introduction, this chapter is primarily about public agencies and officials that are expected to act independently of partisan political direction, within the legal framework that governs their work. While regulatory agencies exist in both the public and private sectors, all are implicitly governed by the same procedures and norms of independence and fairness.

Where Regulators Work

No analytically constructed classification of federal independent regulatory agencies exists because no such classification of all government agencies exists. Legislative entities at all levels can create public organizations with characteristics derived from the politics of bureaucratic structure and call them whatever they deem appropriate. Thus, an organization created to be an "independent" regulator of industries, activities, or individuals may be named an "agency," a "bureau," a "commission," a "board," or an "administration" no matter what its actual structure and tasks. (Where regulators work in state and local governments is discussed later in the chapter.)

> An organization created to be an "independent" regulator of industries, activities, or individuals may be named an "agency," a "bureau," a "commission," a "board," or an "administration" no matter what its actual structure and tasks.

Independent regulatory agencies, at the federal level, are agencies created by an act of Congress that are independent of executive departments. Though they are considered part of the executive branch, these agencies are created to promulgate and enforce rules free of political supervision by elected or appointed public executives. According to the U.S. Code, 44 USC § 3502,

> the term "independent regulatory agency" means the Board of Governors of the Federal Reserve System, the Commodity Futures Trading Commission, the Consumer Product Safety Commission, the Federal Communications Commission, the Federal Deposit Insurance Corporation, the Federal Energy Regulatory Commission, the Federal Housing Finance Agency, the Federal Maritime Commission, the Federal Trade Commission, the Interstate Commerce Commission, the Mine Enforcement Safety and Health Review Commission, the National Labor Relations Board, the Nuclear Regulatory Commission,

the Occupational Safety and Health Review Commission, the Postal Regulatory Commission, the Securities and Exchange Commission, the Bureau of Consumer Financial Protection, the Office of Financial Research, Office of the Comptroller of the Currency, and any other similar agency designated by statute as a Federal independent regulatory agency or commission.[30]

Definitions of *independence* and detailed discussions of the structural similarities and differences among independent regulatory agencies can be found in the *Sourcebook of United States Executive Agencies* published by the Administrative Conference of the United States.[v]

Far less wellknown than public regulators are private (mainly nonprofit) regulatory corporations, many with authority delegated by statute, that engage in what is commonly termed **self-regulation**. Examples of such corporations, which reveal the complex interrelationships between the public and private sectors, include the following:

- The Public Company Accounting Oversight Board (PCAOB)—According to its website,

  The PCAOB is a nonprofit corporation established by Congress to oversee the audits of public companies in order to protect the interests of investors and further the public interest in the preparation of informative, accurate and independent audit reports. The PCAOB also oversees the audits of broker-dealers, including compliance reports filed pursuant to federal securities laws, to promote investor protection.[31]

- The Internet Corporation for Assigned Names and Numbers (ICANN)—According to its website, "We bring together individuals, industry, non-commercial and government representatives to discuss, debate and develop policies about the technical coordination of the Internet's Domain Name System."[32]

- The Municipal Securities Rulemaking Board (MSRB)—According to its website, "The MSRB is a self-regulatory organization created under the Securities Acts Amendments of 1975. It is also incorporated as a Virginia non-stock corporation." Its mission is "to protect investors, municipal entities and the public interest by promoting a fair and efficient municipal market, regulating firms that engage in municipal securities and advisory activities, and promoting market transparency."[33]

- The National Futures Association (NFA)—According to its website, NFA is a nonprofit organization:

  National Futures Association (NFA) is the self-regulatory organization for the U.S. derivatives industry, including on-exchange traded futures, retail off-exchange foreign currency (forex) and OTC derivatives (swaps). NFA has developed and enforced rules, provided programs and offered services that safeguard market integrity, protect investors and help our Members meet their regulatory responsibilities and has done so for more than 30 years.[34]

- The Financial Industry Regulatory Authority, Inc. (FINRA)—According to its website,

  FINRA is dedicated to investor protection and market integrity through effective and efficient regulation of the securities industry. FINRA is not part of the government. We're an independent, not-for-profit

---

[v]David E. Lewis and Jennifer L. Selin, *Sourcebook of United States Executive Agencies* (Administrative Conference of the United States: Office of the Chairman, 2013), http://www.acus.gov/publication/sourcebook-united-states-executive-agencies. According to its website, the ACUS "is committed to promoting improved government procedures including fair and effective dispute resolution and wide public participation and efficiency in the rulemaking process by leveraging interactive technologies and encouraging open communication with the public."

organization authorized by Congress to protect America's investors by making sure the securities industry operates fairly and honestly.[vi]

- The Board of Certification, Inc. (BOC)—According to its website, the BOC "was incorporated in 1989 to provide a certification program for entry-level Athletic Trainers (ATs). The BOC establishes and regularly reviews both the standards for the practice of athletic training and the continuing education requirements for BOC Certified ATs. The BOC has the only accredited certification program for ATs in the US."[35]

What Regulators Do

Regulators perform numerous functions requiring specialized technical expertise and advanced training. Because their work has profound consequences for industries, organizations, individuals, and communities, their writ is typically more precisely enabled and constrained than the policy-implementation activities of cabinet-level executive agencies.

There is a distinct law-enforcement flavor to the regulator's job, which can include investigations or audits of regulated organizations or activities, the imposition of financial penalties on violators, and issuing orders requiring violators to take specific remedial measures.

The generic tasks associated with regulation have been described by LexisNexis, a consultancy specializing in certain types of regulatory activity:

They must keep track of constant changes in the law. They must process and communicate those changes to thousands of individual agents, as well as to the companies they monitor. And they must be able to make every piece of regulatory information—including hearings, inquiries, and letters—available for examination on the public record at any time. [36]

A comprehensive description of what regulators do is provided by the Federal Communications Commission (FCC). An independent regulatory agency, the FCC regulates interstate and international communications by radio, television, wire, satellite, and cable. According to its website, the FCC

is the United States' primary authority for communications law, regulation and technological innovation. In its work facing economic opportunities and challenges associated with rapidly evolving advances in global communications, the agency capitalizes on its competencies in:

- Promoting competition, innovation and investment in broadband services and facilities
- Supporting the nation's economy by ensuring an appropriate competitive framework for the unfolding of the communications revolution
- Encouraging the highest and best use of spectrum domestically and internationally
- Revising media regulations so that new technologies flourish alongside diversity and localism
- Providing leadership in strengthening the defense of the nation's communications infrastructure.

[vi]"About FINRA," Financial Industry Regulatory Authority, http://www.finra.org/AboutFINRA/. A 2014 *Wall Street Journal* investigation found that information on many regulatory red flags on dubious practices of individual stockbrokers had been reported to FINRA but were not made available to state government regulators, prompting calls for greater transparency on the part of FINRA. (Jean Eaglesham and Rob Barry, "Wall Street's Watchdog Doesn't Disclose All Regulatory Red Flags," *Wall Street Journal*, December 27, 2014, sec. Markets, http://www.wsj.com/articles/wall-streets-watchdog-doesnt-disclose-all-regulatory-red-flags-1419645494?mod=WSJ_hp_LEFTTopStories.)

... Bureau and office staff members regularly share expertise to cooperatively fulfill responsibilities such as the following:

- Developing and implementing regulatory programs
- Processing applications for licenses and other filings
- Encouraging the development of innovative services
- Conducting investigations and analyzing complaints
- Public safety and homeland security
- Consumer information and education.[37]

At the state level, businesses that provide utilities such as electricity or telecommunications are regulated by state commissions. The commissions hold public hearings for proposed services, hear complaints about services, and in general seek to provide consumer protection. For example, these commissions

- Administer lifeline policies that provide low-cost telecommunications and energy rates for needy families
- Are responsible for keeping rates under control
- Encourage competition, technological advances, and fiscal responsibility among providers
- Ensure customer satisfaction in urban and rural areas
- A few regulate water, waste, grain, manufactured housing, real estate, and motor carriers.[38]

Regulators are hardly isolated from the distinctive challenges of public management discussed in Chapter 1. According to a 2013 report by *The Wall Street Journal*, a staff regulator at the U.S. Food and Drug Administration (FDA), citing published scientific research findings, argued that a popular class of blood-pressure drugs was linked to a higher risk of cancer. FDA senior management, citing FDA's own studies that included results reported by the manufacturers, labeled the regulator's claim "a diversion." The issue raised by the acerbic debate within FDA was whether the agency placed a high enough priority on ensuring the safety of long-marketed drugs as compared to new drugs. Of the dispute, one respected outside expert said, "My impression is there isn't a relationship between ARBs and cancer, but there could be one with a low frequency. It's not something easily detectable."[39]

How Federal Regulations Are Produced

Because regulations have "the force of law,"[40] and because of its pervasive consequences for economic and social well-being, regulation is governed by—what else?—rules that both proscribe and prescribe how rulemaking, the procedural manifestation of regulation, is to be done.[vii]

What Is "Rulemaking"?

The meaning of the term *rules* as an administrative structure was discussed in Chapter 6. In administrative law, the term *rulemaking* refers to the processes by which executive and regulatory agencies promulgate regulations

---

[vii]The U.S. Office of Information and Regulatory Affairs (OIRA), a unit of the Office of Management and Budget (OMB), is a comprehensive source of information on all aspects of federal rulemaking: http://www.reginfo.gov. Also see Maeve P. Carey, *The Federal Rulemaking Process: A Overview*, CRS Report No. RL32240 (Washington, DC: Congressional Research Service, 2013) http://fas.org/sgp/crs/misc/RL32240.pdf.

in accordance with authority delegated to them by statutes. Rulemaking processes are generally designed to ensure that

- the public is informed of proposed rules before they take effect;
- the public can comment on the proposed rules and provide additional data to the agency;
- the public can access the rule making record and analyze the data and analysis behind a proposed rule;
- the agency analyzes and responds to the public's comments;
- the agency creates a permanent record of its analysis and the process; and
- the agency's actions can be reviewed by a judge or others to ensure that the correct process was followed.[41]

"Notice-and-Comment" Rulemaking

Although an agency may choose, or be directed by statute, to use various methods of rulemaking, the most common is **notice-and-comment rulemaking,** whose procedural requirements, officially termed **informal rulemaking**, are spelled out in § 553 of the Administrative Procedure Act (APA). This section is shown in its entirety in Box 7.1.

Box 7.1   **RULEMAKING UNDER § 553. OF THE ADMINISTRATIVE PROCEDURE ACT**

(a) This section applies, according to the provisions thereof, except to the extent that there is involved—

(1) a military or foreign affairs function of the United States; or

(2) a matter relating to agency management or personnel or to public property, loans, grants, benefits, or contracts.

(b) General notice of proposed rule making shall be published in the Federal Register, unless persons subject thereto are named and either personally served or otherwise have actual notice thereof in accordance with law. The notice shall include—

(1) a statement of the time, place, and nature of public rule making proceedings;

(2) reference to the legal authority under which the rule is proposed; and

(3) either the terms or substance of the proposed rule or a description of the subjects and issues involved.

Except when notice or hearing is required by statute, this subsection does not apply—

(A) to interpretative rules, general statements of policy, or rules of agency organization, procedure, or practice; or

(B) when the agency for good cause finds (and incorporates the finding and a brief statement of reasons therefore in the rules issued) that notice and public procedure thereon are impracticable, unnecessary, or contrary to the public interest.

(Continued)

(Continued)

(c) After notice required by this section, the agency shall give interested persons an opportunity to participate in the rule making through submission of written data, views, or arguments with or without opportunity for oral presentation. After consideration of the relevant matter presented, the agency shall incorporate in the rules adopted a concise general statement of their basis and purpose. When rules are required by statute to be made on the record after opportunity for an agency hearing, sections 556 and 557 of this title apply instead of this subsection.

(d) The required publication or service of a substantive rule shall be made not less than 30 days before its effective date, except—

(1) a substantive rule which grants or recognizes an exemption or relieves a restriction;

(2) interpretative rules and statements of policy; or

(3) as otherwise provided by the agency for good cause found and published with the rule.

(e) Each agency shall give an interested person the right to petition for the issuance, amendment, or repeal of a rule.

The agency reviews public comments, prepares a final rule, and submits "significant" rules to OIRA for review.[viii] The final rule is published in the *Federal Register* and the U.S. Code of Federal Regulations (CFR) is amended to reflect the rule.[ix]

Depending on the type of rule and its circumstances, it may be implemented immediately, within 30 days, within 60 days, or later. The Small Business Regulatory Enforcement Fairness Act of 1996 requires that final rules be submitted to Congress for final review. **Major rules** cannot be implemented until Congress finishes its review (within 60 days), although it may take action to delay implementation further. Major rules are defined by the act as those estimated to have an effect on the economy of $100 million or greater, that will result in a "major increase in costs or prices for consumers, individual industries, Federal, State, or local government agencies, or geographic regions," or that will result in "significant adverse effects on competition, employment, investment, productivity, innovation, or on the ability of United States-based enterprises to compete with foreign-based enterprises in domestic and export markets." (§ 804.)

> **Parties who believe they will be harmed by new rule, which often include state governors and affected industries and firms, may sue the agency in federal courts to challenge the rule's constitutional or statutory legality.**

That is hardly the end of the process, however. Parties who believe they will be harmed by new rule, which often include state governors and affected industries and firms, may sue the agency in federal court to challenge the rule's constitutional or statutory legality.

[viii]Under certain circumstances the agency may issue an interim final rule, or a direct final rule. For further information on these special types of final rules, see OMB's Reg Map, or the Federal Register's guide: https://www.federalregister.gov/uploads/2011/01/the_rulemaking_process.pdf.

[ix]The CFR can be found at http://www.gpo.gov/fdsys/browse/collectionCfr.action?collectionCode=CFR.

5

Indeed, the threat of a suit may be made during the comment period. The judicial rulings that result from litigation may turn on interpretations of specific constitutional and statutory provisions, such as states' rights, the separation of powers, or the permissible limits of statutory authority or they may be based on a court's judgment as to whether the promulgating agency's purposes and reasons for the regulations merit judicial deference.[x]

An agency may choose to engage in notice-and-comment rulemaking even when it is not specifically required or permitted by legislation; the legislative language prompting its use may be that the agency or official "shall require" (see Chapter 5). These **non-legislative rules** do not have the force of law, however.[42]

In order to promote greater understanding of the rulemaking process, the OIRA has created what it calls the Reg Map.[xi] The Reg Map is a large, colorful, and detailed graphic overview of the nine-step informal rulemaking process:

- Step 1: Initiating Events
- Step 2: Determination Whether a Rule Is Needed
- Step 3: Preparation of Proposed Rule
- Step 4: OMB Review of Proposed Rule
- Step 5: Publication of Proposed Rule
- Step 6: Public Comments
- Step 7: Preparation of Final Rule, Interim Final Rule, or Direct Final Rule
- Step 8: OMB Review of Final Rule, Interim Final Rule, or Direct Final Rule
- Step 9: Publication of the Final Rule, Interim Final Rule, or Direct Final Rule

Figure 7.1 depicts Step 3 of the Reg Map, illustrating the level of detail involved in each step of the rulemaking process.

According to OIRA website,

> The Reg Map is based on general requirements. In some cases, more stringent or less stringent requirements are imposed by statutory provisions that are agency specific or subject matter specific. Also, in some cases more stringent requirements are imposed by agency policy. In a typical case, a rulemaking action would proceed from step one through step nine with a proposed rule and a final rule. However, if a rulemaking action is exempt from the proposed rulemaking procedures under the Administrative Procedure Act provisions (explained under step three) or under other statutory authority, an agency may:
>
> - promulgate a final rule omitting steps three through six, or
> - promulgate an interim final rule omitting steps three through six, but providing a comment period and a final rule after step nine.
>
> Also, if an agency determines that a rule likely would not generate adverse comment, the agency may promulgate a direct final rule, omitting steps three through six, but with a duty to withdraw the rule if the agency receives adverse comments within the period specified by the agency.[xii]

---

[x]Judicial deference may be based on the quality of the scientific analysis the agency has used in justifying its regulations. Maeve P. Carey, *Cost-Benefit and Other Analysis Requirements in the Rulemaking Process*, CRS Report No. R41974 (Washington, DC: Congressional Research Service, 2014), http://fas.org/sgp/crs/misc/R41974.pdf.

[xi]See U.S. Office of Information and Regulatory Affairs, "Reg Map," http://www.reginfo.gov/public/reginfo/Regmap/index.jsp.

[xii]"Using the Reg Map," Office of Information and Regulatory Affairs, http://www.reginfo.gov/public/reginfo/Regmap/regmap_using.jsp.

| Figure 7.1 | Reg Map Step 3: Preparation of the Proposed Rule |

Step Three

Preparation of Proposed Rule

Proposed Rule

A notice of proposed rulemaking proposes to add, change, or delete regulatory text and contains a request for public comments.

Administrative Procedure Act Provisions

Under the Administrative Procedure Act provisions at 5 U.S.C. 553, rules may be established only after proposed rulemaking procedures (steps three through six) have been followed, unless an exemption applies. The following are exempted:

- Rules concerning military or foreign affairs functions
- Rules concerning agency management or personnel
- Rules concerning public property, loans, grants, benefits, or contracts
- Interpretive rules
- General statements of policy
- Rules of agency organization, procedure, or practice
- Nonsignificant rules for which the agency determines that public input is not warranted
- Rules published on an emergency basis

Note: Even if an exemption applies under the Administrative Procedure Act provisions, other statutory authority or agency policy may require that proposed rulemaking procedures be followed.

**Optional Supplementary Procedures
to Help Prepare a Proposed Rule**

Advance Notice of Proposed Rulemaking

An advance notice of proposed rulemaking requests information needed for developing a proposed rule.

Negotiated Rulemaking

Negotiated rulemaking is a mechanism under the Negotiated Rulemaking Act (5 U.S.C. 561-570) for bringing together representatives of an agency and the various interests to negotiate the text of a proposed rule.

Source: U.S. Office of Information and Regulatory Affairs, "Reg Map: Step 3," http://www.reginfo.gov/public/reginfo/Regmap/regmap3.jsp.

Example: Regulation of Food Additives

The FDA regulates food additives. According to its website,

> any substance that is reasonably expected to become a component of food is a food additive that is subject to premarket approval by FDA, unless the substance is generally recognized as safe (GRAS) among experts qualified by scientific training and experience to evaluate its safety under the conditions of its intended use, or meets one of the other exclusions from the food additive definition in section 201(s) of the Federal Food, Drug, and Cosmetic Act (FFDCA). Any food additive that is intended to have a technical effect in the food is deemed unsafe unless it either conforms to the terms of a regulation prescribing its use or to an exemption for investigational use. Otherwise, in accordance with section 409 of the Act, the substance is deemed an unsafe food additive. Any food that contains an unsafe food additive is adulterated under section 402(a) (2) (C) of the FFDCA. [43]

Figure 7.2 depicts the decision tree created by FDA to "help in determining the regulatory status of a food ingredient. It is the responsibility of the manufacturer of any food to ensure that all ingredients used are of food-grade purity and comply with specifications and limitations in all applicable authorizations. The overall regulatory status of a food is affected by the regulatory status of each individual food ingredient."

The graphic depiction of the regulatory decision tree might make the process seem straightforward, but, as with so many areas of regulation, the process can be fraught with controversy. An investigative report published by *The Washington Post* in August 2014 noted that an "explosion of new food additives" due to the growing popularity of processed foods had been accompanied by an "easing of [regulatory] oversight requirements" by the FDA.[44]

According to the report, due to staff shortages and industry complaints, a "voluntary certification system" whereby manufacturers determined if additives were GRAS had replaced the more rigorous process of FDA determination of food additive safety. As a consequence, "in hundreds of cases, the FDA doesn't even know of the existence of new additives."

FDA officials had apparently hoped that greater reliance on voluntary compliance would reduce industry underreporting of additives. There seemed to be general agreement on all sides that additives were escaping detection but little agreement on whether consumers were at greater risk of unsafe additives or, if so, how the system might be fixed. Unlike automobile parts which, if not fixed, might cause serious injury and death, the dangers of food additives seem to be a less compelling cause for public alarm.

Regulation by State and Local Governments

While federal regulatory agencies often attract intense media and political attention, a broad and pervasive range of regulatory activities, many of them locally controversial, is undertaken by state, local, and special purpose governments.[xiii]

Regulation by the States

Online lists of state regulatory agencies by policy area range from "aging and elderly services" to "workers compensation."[45] Other agencies in state government (including secretaries of state, attorneys general, human services, and departments of commerce) regulate businesses, professional licensing, charities, and elections.

[xiii]"One central site that lists webpages controlled and managed by state and local government agencies is http://www.statelocalgov.net/.

Figure 7.2	**Food Additives Regulation Decision Tree**

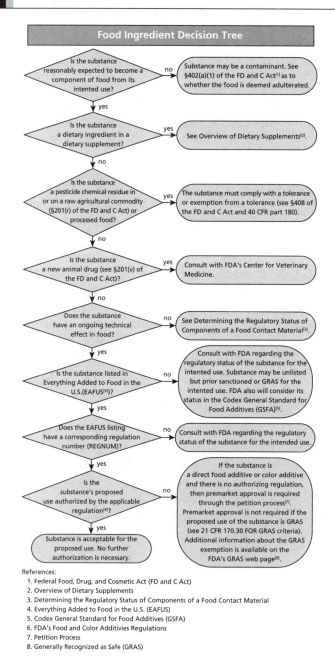

References:
1. Federal Food, Drug, and Cosmetic Act (FD and C Act)
2. Overview of Dietary Supplements
3. Determining the Regulatory Status of Components of a Food Contact Material
4. Everything Added to Food in the U.S. (EAFUS)
5. Codex General Standard for Food Additives (GSFA)
6. FDA's Food and Color Additives Regulations
7. Petition Process
8. Generally Recognized as Safe (GRAS)

Source: U.S. Food and Drug Administration, http://www.fda.gov/Food/IngredientsPackagingLabeling/FoodAdditivesIngredients/ucm228269.htm.

States now compile the body of state regulations (analogous to the federal CFR) and make it available online.[xiv] The Library of Congress has a guide for each state that provides access to the laws and regulations, as well as statutes and judicial opinions.[46]

Wide variation exists in the existence, nature, and scope of state and local regulatory structures and processes. A study of the effects of one type of regulation, occupational licensing, noted that

- partially licensed occupations include librarians, respiratory therapists, dieticians, and nutritionists;
- fully licensed occupations include lawyers, dentists, and cosmetologists; and
- fully unlicensed occupations include economists, computer programmers, and glaziers.[47]

The essential character of state and local regulatory activities, therefore, is best illustrated by the following examples:

- The State of Colorado's Department of Regulatory Agencies (DORA) is "dedicated to preserving the integrity of the marketplace and is committed to promoting a fair and competitive business environment in Colorado. Consumer protection is our mission."[48] Beginning in 1877, Colorado successively instituted regulation of banks, the insurance industry, public utilities, securities markets, the real estate industry, credit unions, and civil rights. Regulatory entities created along the way included the boards of medical and dental examiners, boards of nursing, accountancy, and optometric examiners. DORA now serves as the umbrella agency for these and other entities, including those for architects, engineers, land surveyors, nursing aides, bail bond organizations, barbers and cosmetologists, outfitters, addiction counselors, passenger tramway safety examiners, and many other professionals, specialists, and types of businesses.
- The National Pesticide Information Center provides a guide to state agencies concerned with pesticide regulation and control.[49] Each state has one agency that works cooperatively with the U.S. Environmental Protection Agency (EPA) to enforce federal pesticide regulations and respond to potential complaints. The center's website provides links to these agencies. Subjects of pesticide regulations include:

  o Certification/licensing for pesticide applicators, consultants, businesses;
  o Investigation of pesticide incidents, including spills and misapplications;
  o Pesticide product registration in each state; and
  o Pesticide labeling.

The politics of regulation at state and local levels of government can be no less contentious and controversial than those at the federal level, sometimes even drawing national attention.

The Health Resources and Services Administration (HRSA) of the U.S. Department of Health and Human Services (HHS) funds the National Resource Center for Health and Safety in Child Care and Early Education (NRC) whose mission is

> [t]o improve the quality of child care and early education programs by supporting child care providers and early educators, families, health professionals, early childhood comprehensive systems, state child care regulatory agencies, state and local health departments, and policy makers in their efforts to identify and promote healthy and safe child care and early education programs.[50]

[xiv]Two examples are "Administrative Rulemaking: A Procedural Guide," *Office of the Attorney General–State of Nevada*, 2014, http://ag.nv.gov/uploadedFiles/agnvgov/Content/Publications/RulemakingManualComplete.pdf, and "Administrative Rulemaking," *Minnesota House of Representatives*, August 2001, http://www.house.leg.state.mn.us/hrd/pubs/admrule.pdf.

The center's website includes a link to each state's licensing and regulation information. It also features resource pages directed toward different stakeholders: caregivers/teachers, parents/guardians, regulators, child care health consultants, early childhood systems leaders, and home visitors. Its materials developed for caregivers address handwashing, playground safety, diapering procedures, and inclusion of children with special needs. Its materials developed for parents address topics including biting, child care provider qualifications, supervision requirements, immunizations, and physical activity. Its materials developed for regulators and policymakers address topics such as medication administration/delegation policies, appropriate staff-to-child ratios, emergency preparedness, preventing the spread of contagious illnesses, and first aid training requirements.

- In Virginia, the licensing of child care providers is the responsibility of the Department of Social Services. As in other states, different licensing standards apply to child care centers and to family child care homes. According to the Child Care Aware website, in 2013 Virginia ranked near the top (#4) out of 50 states plus the District of Columbia and the Department of Defense (which operates its own centers) in terms of licensing and oversight of child care centers. But it ranked last in terms of licensing and oversight of family child care homes. According to an investigative report in *The Washington Post* published in September 2014, "In Virginia, a hot-dog cart, a nail salon and a pet shop require more licensing and regulation than some of the places that care for our tiniest, most vulnerable humans."[51] In an interview with *The Washington Post,* Bill Bolling, former lieutenant governor, observed, "In general, there is a reluctance in Virginia to impose excessive regulatory burdens on anyone.... You need to be able to justify it with a compelling argument."[52] Virginia lawmakers had not found an argument sufficiently compelling to regulate what many regarded as babysitters.
- Certain types of state regulation, some of them pursuant to federal regulatory mandates, raise constitutional questions. For example, the issue of whether therapy and advice were "conduct" and thus legally subject to regulation or "free speech" (protected by the First Amendment) was raised in several cases:
  - A state regulation that prohibited licensed medical providers from using talk therapy to try to change a minor's sexual orientation.[53]
  - A state ruled that a diabetic blogger must cease offering dietary advice to fellow diabetics through his website because such advice amounted to "nutritional assessing and counseling" subject to state licensing requirements.[54]

A U.S. Court of Appeals ruled talk therapy to be conduct, not speech. Another U.S. Court of Appeals ruled that the blogger's advice (like that of any advice columnist) was free speech.

Regulation by Local Governments

Cities, townships, counties, and other forms of local government in the United States make decisions about and regulate parks, property use, and other issues. Localities also include thousands of **special purpose districts**. These districts pertain to a particular geographic area and are formed to govern, provide, produce, or regulate goods or services such as schools, highways, mass transit, fire protection, or water supply. While they cannot make laws, they can establish regulations that have the force of law.

Example: Liquor Licensing in Boston

Regulation is a lively and controversial political issue in local government. Data-Smart City Solutions, an organization working to catalyze adoption of data projects on the local government level, engaged in a project called "Regulatory Reform for the 21st Century City."[55] Among the numerous examples of city-level regulatory reform on its website was one called "Innovative Permitting in Boston."[56]

In 2014, Massachusetts state legislators began "considering a law that would allow municipalities to control the liquor licensing process." At the time, "the state determine[d] the number of liquor licenses a municipality [could] offer based on a formula linked to population." In Boston, a statutory cap had long been in place, "which resulted in escalating liquor license costs as well as the migration of licenses to rich downtown areas from outlying neighborhoods in need of economic activity." The case study pointed out that "the process for gaining approval can be arduous. In many cases, federal, state, or local governments do not regularly update regulations to ensure they remain relevant . . . which can result in antiquated regulations that add unnecessary hurdles to the process." The City of Boston organized a series of workshops in which all stakeholders in the city's liquor-licensing process contributed to the creation of a better understanding of how licensing could be more flexible and dynamic.

ENFORCEABILITY AND ENFORCEMENT

If their statutory purposes are to be achieved, regulations must be enforced. As is true of the promulgation of regulations, the diversity of the objects of regulation—from banks and hospitals to municipal drinking water and home building to industrial pesticide use and food additives—makes it difficult to encapsulate regulatory enforcement in a one-size-fits-all analytic or legal framework. It also makes it difficult to convey the flavor of regulatory enforcement in practice with generalizations. The pervasive importance of how regulatory enforcement actually affects the lives of everyone living in or visiting the United States justifies some effort to convey what it involves.

Accordingly, enforcement is depicted in this section primarily through examples of enforcement processes, methods, and outcomes. Enforcement administered by the EPA or the California Department of Pesticide Regulation will not be identical to enforcement by the Department of Labor or the Texas Department of Transportation. However, the degree of procedural complexity and the kinds of judgments needed to use the procedures to achieve policy goals is assuredly similar across the diverse array of regulatory agencies at all levels of government. A deeper understanding of individual regulatory arenas requires more specialized study.

> Monitoring might take the form of inspections, audits, measurement, patrols, mandated reporting, documentation, or other methods for determining compliance with rules and standards.

Enforcement: The Basics

Enforcement requires the monitoring of regulated actions or behavior to detect possible violations. Depending on the nature of regulated behavior or action, monitoring might take the form of inspections, audits, measurement, patrols, mandated reporting, documentation, or other methods for determining compliance with rules and standards.

The effectiveness of enforcement depends on a number of factors:

- the regulation's enforceability, that is, the ease and cost of detecting violations;
- the deterrent effect of prospective or actual penalties or punishments imposed on violators;

- the quality of regulatory management, that is, the adequacy of the skills and resources devoted to monitoring regulated activity and holding violators accountable for noncompliance; and, finally,
- the quality of regulatory governance, that is, the extent to which the regulators themselves are monitored and held accountable for their performance in meeting the goals of regulation.

Effective enforcement involves confronting a number of issues, such as those listed below:

- To what extent should regulators either coerce and punish, on the one hand, or persuade and negotiate with, on the other, possible or actual violators?
- To what extent should enforcement be rule-and-compliance oriented, on the one hand, or goal- and results-oriented, on the other?
- How should the likely short-run economic costs of regulations borne by industries, firms, and individuals as well as on regions and society as a whole be weighed against the more uncertain and longer term benefits they are intended to produce?

Enforcement in Practice

The EPA, one of the world's most active and important line agencies with significant standard-setting and regulatory enforcement responsibilities, provides on its website a comprehensive overview of what is involved in regulatory enforcement. The following summary is adapted from that overview.[57]

The EPA has two types of enforcement programs:

- **civil enforcement** that protects human health and the environment by taking legal action to bring polluters into compliance with the law, and
- **criminal enforcement** that investigates and assists in the criminal prosecution of deliberate or egregious violations of environmental laws or regulations and any associated violation of the U.S. criminal code.

The two types of enforcement programs differ in terms of legal standard, burden of proof, results, types of enforcement actions, and types of enforcement results:

- Legal standard

  "Environmental civil liability is strict: it arises simply through the existence of the environmental violation," perhaps caused by an accident or mistake, regardless what the responsible party knew about the matter. "Environmental criminal liability is triggered through some level of intent," that is, conscious and informed action brought about the violation.

- Burden of proof

  "The preponderance of the evidence," which means that the proposition is more likely to be true than not true, is the standard of proof in a civil action. "Beyond a reasonable doubt," a stricter standard, is the standard of proof in a criminal action.

- Types of enforcement actions

    Civil administrative actions do not involve judicial court processes. "An administrative action by EPA or a state agency may be in the form of a notice of violation or a Superfund notice letter, or an order . . . directing an individual, a business, or other entity to take action to come into compliance, or to clean up a site." **Civil judicial actions** are formal lawsuits against persons or entities that have failed to comply with statutory or regulatory requirements or with an administrative order, or who owe EPA response costs for cleaning up a Superfund site. "**Criminal actions** are usually reserved for the most serious violations, those that are willful, or knowingly committed. A court conviction can result in fines or imprisonment."

- Types of enforcement results

    "If a civil defendant is found liable or agrees to a consent decree, the result is usually a monetary fine (designed to recover the economic benefit of noncompliance and to account for the severity of the violation), injunctive relief (the actions required to correct the violation such as installing pollution control equipment), or additional actions taken to improve the environment." "If a criminal defendant is convicted or pleads guilty, the result can be a criminal fine (for example, a fine paid to the U.S. Treasury), restitution (for example, reimbursing the government for the cost of cleanup or response, paying for the harm caused by the violation such as paying for medical testing for people exposed to asbestos), or imprisonment."

An overview of what is involved in regulatory enforcement can be found on the websites of many federal, state, and local regulatory agencies. The specific features of agency enforcement will vary depending on the type of conduct, technology, or outcome being regulated, of course, but they can be instructive concerning how different jurisdictions have chosen to administer regulatory law.[xv]

On Being Regulated

What is it like to be regulated? Anecdotal evidence abounds about how particular industries, companies, and individuals are affected by rules that constrain their conduct or impose costs on them. A systematic perspective on regulation from a business perspective is depicted in the following excerpt from a law firm's website on the regulation of banks titled "Dealing with Increased Risk of Regulatory Enforcement Action":

> Each federal banking agency has policies and procedures applicable to the initiation of an enforcement action. While the agencies may take a different approach as to whether an enforcement action should be instituted or the degree of severity of an enforcement action, the agencies all use similar enforcement tools. Consequently, this article focuses on one agency, the OCC, and its enforcement tools. However, the descriptions generally will apply to enforcement actions by other federal agencies.
>
> There are two broad categories of enforcement actions: informal and formal. There are two major distinctions between informal and formal actions. First, the OCC does not make public informal actions but is required to publish documents issued in formal enforcement actions. In the current banking environment, where public confidence has been decimated by the credit crisis, this can be significant. The media will

---

[xv]For example, see the website of the California Department of Pesticide Regulation at: http://www.cdpr.ca.gov/docs/mill/actions/enfact.htm.

report on the formal enforcement action; usually, such reporting results in headlines that may cast the bank in a much worse light than is warranted by the bank's condition. Second, the OCC may file an action in federal court to enforce a formal enforcement action. There are no such enforcement procedures for an informal enforcement action. The OCC bases its decision as to whether to institute an enforcement action (formal or informal) on bank examination findings. The OCC has identified certain red flags that, if present in a bank, may lead to an enforcement action:

- Rapid growth and aggressive growth strategies
- Deterioration in the economy
- Management oversight deficiencies
- Inappropriate limits on OCC access to bank staff and documents
- Risk management deficiencies
- Significant off-balance-sheet exposure
- Asset securitization
- Derivatives
- Asset quality deterioration
- Significant allowance for loan and lease losses (ALLL) and asset adjustment issues
- Strained liquidity
- Insider abuse and fraud.[xvi]

Example: FDA's Risk Evaluation and Mitigation Strategy requirement

It is one thing to understand the risk of violating rules that are reasonably clear or where enforcement is predictable. It is quite another thing to deal with rules that are neither clear nor enforced in a predictable way.

For example, the Food and Drug Administration Amendments Act of 2007 gave FDA the authority to require a Risk Evaluation and Mitigation Strategy (REMS) from manufacturers of drugs to ensure that the benefits of a drug or biological product outweigh its risks.[58]

The Inspector General of HHS reviewed the implementation of the REMS program and, in 2013, reported these findings:

> FDA approved 199 REMS between 2008 and 2011, 99 of which were still required in 2012. Nearly half of sponsor assessments for the 49 REMS we reviewed did not include all information requested in FDA assessment plans, and 10 were not submitted to FDA within required timeframes. FDA determined that 7 of the 49 REMS we reviewed met all of their goals. However, FDA has not identified reliable methods to assess the effectiveness of REMS. Finally, FDA's assessment review times exceeded its goal of 60 days for all but one sponsor assessment, which reduces sponsors' time to make suggested changes before submitting subsequent assessments.[59]

[xvi]Frank C. Bonaventure Jr., "Dealing with Increased Risk of Regulatory Enforcement Actions," *Bank Accounting and Finance,* November 2009, © CCH Incorporated, a Wolters Kluwer company. http://www.ober.com/publications/19-dealing-increased-risk-regulatory-enforcement-actions. Another law firm posted on its website advice to financial services firm regarding "disclosure requirements." Eben P. Colby, Thomas A DeCapo, and Kenneth E. Burdon, "Disclosure and Collateral Consequences of Enforcement Actions for Regulated Financial Services Firms," October 2, 2014, http://www.skadden.com/insights/disclosure-and-collateral-consequences-enforcement-actions-regulated-financial-services-firms.

From the perspective of professional pharmacists, it is not surprising that the REMS program is highly problematic. The director of federal regulatory affairs for the American Society of Health-System Pharmacists, Christopher J. Topoleski, argued that "current REMS programs are negatively affecting the already limited time that pharmacists have to care for and ensure the safety of their patients."[60] This can occur because each REMS is different and lengthy, "crammed with various communication, intervention, registration, or verification elements" that must be navigated.[61] Furthermore, prescriptions for some drugs under the REMS program can be filled only at particular pharmacies. This can be confusing and time-consuming for patients. For example, some drugs require the patient to be tested in a laboratory before receiving a refill. An outpatient pharmacy might not be on the REMS program and not have the drug, whereas a hospital "inpatient pharmacy might have the drug, because drug reimbursement is bundled into Diagnosis-Related Group (DRG)[xvii] payments—meaning that hospitals have easier access to REMS drugs on an inpatient basis."[62] In order for the patient to receive the refill under this scenario, the patient would have to be admitted to the hospital for testing (and refill of the prescription). Patients face increased costs as a result, argues Topoleski.

The REMS program exemplifies the kind of confusion that can arise when regulations created for different purposes produce inconsistencies in their impact and enforcement. Those whose conduct is regulated, and citizens affected by that regulated conduct, may encounter situations that seem to defy common sense and may be poorly understood by regulators themselves, which compounds the frustration.

Judicial Review of Rulemaking

With few exceptions, agency regulatory actions are subject to judicial review, especially if constitutional issues are raised.[63] The Administrative Procedure Act states

> The reviewing court shall . . . hold unlawful and set aside agency action, findings, and conclusions found to be —
>
> (A) arbitrary, capricious, an abuse of discretion, or otherwise not in accordance with law;
>
> (B) contrary to constitutional right, power, privilege, or immunity;
>
> (C) in excess of statutory jurisdiction, authority, or limitations, or short of statutory right;
>
> (D) without observance of procedure required by law;
>
> (E) unsupported by substantial evidence in a case subject to sections 556 and 557 of this title or otherwise reviewed on the record of an agency hearing provided by statute; or
>
> (F) unwarranted by the facts to the extent that the facts are subject to trial de novo by the reviewing court.
>
> In making the foregoing determinations, the court shall review the whole record or those parts of it cited by a party, and due account shall be taken of the rule of prejudicial error.[64]

[xvii]A Diagnosis-Related Group (DRG) is a statistical system of classifying any inpatient stay into groups for the purposes of payment. The DRG classification system divides possible diagnoses into more than 20 major body systems and subdivides them into almost 500 groups for the purpose of Medicare reimbursement, American Health Lawyers Association, "Health Law Wiki," https://www.healthlawyers.org/hlresources/Health%20Law%20Wiki/Diagnosis-related%20group%20%28DRG%29.aspx.

A reviewing court must determine whether the evidence indicates that the agency lacks the authority to take regulatory action under review. Courts grant varying levels of deference to agency justifications for their actions. (See the discussion of the concept of deference in Chapter 2. Further discussion of the significance of judicial review is in Chapter 12.)

THE POLITICS OF REGULATION

Political scientist James Q. Wilson argued that there can be no general political theory of regulation.[65] But, as the survey of explanations for the regulatory state earlier in this chapter makes clear, establishing the rules of the game is, itself, a high-stakes game from any theoretical or practical perspective.

As already emphasized, rules matter greatly to society as a whole, to industries and political jurisdictions, and to particular individuals, professions, and businesses. The same rulemaking, moreover, may provide benefits to some individuals and businesses but impose costs on others. Citizens, professions, and businesses may experience administrative rules as restrictions on their freedom or invasions of their civil and property rights.[66] Businesses may experience such rules as restricting their freedom to be competitive in the marketplace.

Regulatory politics reflects those experiences and is also affected by ideology. Those who believe that the less regulation the better for economic growth and prosperity are apt to be skeptical of rulemaking in principle. Those who believe in positive government as necessary to ensure public safety and social equity and stability are likely to favor rulemaking in principle. It follows that the nature and extent of political partisanship as reflected in party politics are significant factors in the extent and character of rulemaking.

> **The nature and extent of political partisanship as reflected in party politics are significant factors in the extent and character of rulemaking.**

The partisan "blame game" that accompanied the government's efforts to confront the 2008 to 2009 financial crisis illustrates these points:

- On one side: Liberal Democrats were responsible for the inadequately regulated lending practices in the housing market.
  - On another side: Conservative Republicans were responsible for inadequate regulation of banks and other financial institutions.

- On one side: Liberals favor tough rules and strict enforcement.
  - On another side: Conservatives favor flexible or negotiated rules and voluntary compliance.

- On one side: During the administration of President George W. Bush, crises in markets and the business sector were blamed on inept, poorly enforced regulation.
  - On another side: During the administration of Barack Obama, the same kinds of crises were blamed on regulatory overreach.

Public awareness of regulation is greatest in those instances when

(1) rules are the subject of litigation, especially when their lawfulness is finally determined by the U.S. Supreme Court;

(2) during crises, such as the BP oil spill in the Gulf of Mexico, that raise questions as to whether rules were violated, poorly enforced, or inadequate; and

(3) the livelihoods and well-being of industries, communities, and large groups of individuals are adversely affected.

Regulatory processes themselves have politically influential constituencies. For example, the National Association for Regulatory Administration (NARA) has as its mission "to bring the highest quality of comprehensive, evidence-based professional development services within reach of every human care regulatory agency and every individual who is, or who aspires to become, a professional human care regulator."[67] NARA states that is "provides leadership and forums for broad public consideration of [protection of children and vulnerable adults in out-of-home care] in an era of downsizing, regulatory reform, [and] privatization." It considers its "partners" to include "providers, consumers and their families, regulators, advocates, concerned citizens, business and religious communities, policy-makers, universities, researchers, and allied professionals from the academic, technical and treatment disciplines."[68]

Another organization committed to effective rulemaking is the Administrative Conference of the United States. According to its website, it is

> an independent federal agency dedicated to improving the administrative process through consensus-driven applied research, providing nonpartisan expert advice and recommendations for improvement of federal agency procedures. . . . [It is] committed to promoting improved government procedures including fair and effective dispute resolution and wide public participation and efficiency in the rulemaking process by leveraging interactive technologies and encouraging open communication with the public. In addition the Administrative Conference's mandate includes fostering improvements to the regulatory process by reducing unnecessary litigation, and improving the use of science and the effectiveness of applicable laws.[69]

Specific regulatory tools can become politically controversial. For example, those favoring consumer protection want businesses to comply with rules protecting consumers and want companies to pay for the damages they cause as confirmed by independent third parties. Those opposing overregulation of business, especially small business, believe such confirmations to be unnecessary and unduly costly. The same phenomenon holds true for regulations governing workplace and product safety.

An illustration of regulatory politics is provided by the CFPB, an agency created amidst much controversy in the aftermath of the 2008 to 2009 financial crisis. Its primary responsibility is regulating consumer protection with regard to financial products and services in the United States. The CFPB made the list for the Heritage Foundation's "10 Worst Regulations of 2012." The Heritage Foundation, a conservative think tank and vigilant critic of government overreach, said this about the CFPB in that year:

> In July, the [CFPB] released its proposal for a more "consumer friendly" mortgage process, with a stated goal of simplifying home loans. The rules run an astonishing 1,099 pages. In August, the bureau proposed more than 560 pages of rules for mortgage servicing, which includes the collection of mortgage payments, maintenance of escrow accounts, and loan modifications and foreclosures. Many of the provisions would micromanage the timing, (expanded) content, and format of various disclosures. All of this, of course, will—simply—reduce consumer mortgage lending options and increase costs.[70]

The politics of regulation is, as illustrated by the Heritage Foundation's assessment of CFPB activities, often ideological. In a similar vein, in 2013 *The Wall Street Journal* commented on additional requirements of the Affordable Care Act:

> Starting this month, companies must record nearly every transaction with doctors—from sales reps bearing pizza to compensation for expert advice on research—to comply with the so-called Sunshine Act provision of the U.S. health-care overhaul. The companies must report data on individual doctors and how much they received to a federal health agency, which will post it on a searchable, public website beginning September 2014.[71]

Fueled by advocacy, self-interest, ideology, bureaucratic politics, professional opinion, and the sheer complexity of regulatory issues, the politics of regulation is inevitably fraught with partisanship and uncertainty. Despite that, America's regulatory state is both durable and of increasing significance in American society.

KEY CONCEPTS

Regulation	Informal rulemaking
Rulemaking	Major rules
Fracking	Non-legislative rules
Regulatory state	Special purpose districts
Pluralism	Enforcement
Advocacy coalitions	Civil enforcement
Regulatory slack	Criminal enforcement
Independent regulatory agencies	Civil penalties
Self-regulation	Injunctive relief
Notice-and-comment rulemaking	

CASE ANALYSIS: FRACKING REGULATION

In December 2014, the administration of Andrew Cuomo, the Governor of New York, announced that it would ban the use of hydraulic fracturing, popularly termed *fracking*, in the extraction of natural gas from the state's shale oil deposits. New York was reportedly the first state with significant shale oil resources to do so.[72] The reason, according to the state's health commissioner, was the potential public health risk, perhaps not yet fully known, associated with the water contamination and air pollution caused by the process.[i]

In pursuing a total ban on fracking, the state was bucking a national trend widely termed "the shale revolution." Over a six-year period, the increase in production of energy from shale had nearly doubled U.S. oil and natural gas production and dramatically increased the nation's energy self-sufficiency.[73]

---

[i]The Department of Health simultaneously released an 84-page "health review" of high volume hydraulic fracturing: "A Public Health Review of High Volume Hydraulic Fracturing for Shale Gas Development," *New York State Department of Public Health,* December 2014, http://www.health.ny.gov/press/reports/docs/high_volume_hydraulic_fracturing.pdf.

Fracking was regarded by its advocates in New York State as a key to the economic revival of depressed communities along New York's border with Pennsylvania, a state where fracking was a major economic development tool, exploiting shale deposits the two states shared. But the governor's core liberal constituencies actively opposed fracking based largely on environmentally related public health arguments. Because of this opposition, New York State courts had already ruled that local communities could ban fracking using their legal authority over local land use. Many had done so, including those encompassing more than half of the state's shale oil deposits.[ii] Further, according to the New York Sierra Club, administrative actions by the state had created what it called "a de facto moratorium . . . for new drilling of natural gas wells in New York State using hydrofracking technology."[74]

In supporting a ban on fracking, Governor Cuomo insisted that the decision was not political but, rather, one dictated by the judgment of experts objectively weighing the facts:

> "I am not a scientist," he said. "I'm not an environmental expert. I'm not a health expert. I'm a lawyer. I'm not a doctor. I'm not an environmentalist. I'm not a scientist. So let's bring the emotion down, and let's ask the qualified experts what their opinion is."[75]

A month before Cuomo announced his administration's decision, the governor of Maryland, Martin O'Malley, also a Democrat, and his administration reached the opposite conclusion: regulation would reduce the risks of fracking to an acceptable level, and the process would not be banned there.[76] Nationwide, opponents of fracking hoped that the action to ban fracking by the State of New York would embolden other states to act in a similar manner.

What Is Fracking?

High-volume hydraulic fracturing (HVHF), or fracking, comprises various techniques for high-pressure injection through drilled wells of large amounts of water mixed with sand and various chemicals deep into underground shale formations containing trapped oil and natural gas, enabling the release and extraction of commercially valuable quantities of energy resources.[iii]

Shale containing oil and natural gas is likely to be located in rural areas,[77] and residents of economically depressed surrounding communities may welcome energy companies that will create jobs and income using the fracking process. But an expanding body of scientific research has revealed potentially significant public health and other risks associated with fracking. The New York State Health Review, published in 2014, summarized these risks as follows:

[ii]State and local government use of their regulatory authority can be complex, as illustrated by the state environmental review's reference to the 1997 New York City Watershed Memorandum of Agreement (MOA): "The MOA is a landmark agreement that recognizes both the importance of preserving high-quality drinking water and the economic health and vitality of communities located within the watershed. It is a legally binding 145 page contract, with 1500 pages of attachments, between NYC, the State, EPA, nearly 80 local governments in the watershed and environmental groups." http://www.health.ny.gov/press/reports/docs/high_volume_hydraulic_fracturing.pdf.

[iii]A U.S. Department of Energy-sponsored primer on HVHF is located at http://energy.gov/sites/prod/files/2013/03/f0/ShaleGasPrimer_Online_4-2009.pdf.

(Continued)

(Continued)

- *Air impacts* that could affect *respiratory health* due to increased levels of particulate matter, diesel exhaust, or volatile organic chemicals.
- *Climate change impacts* due to methane and other volatile organic chemical releases to the atmosphere.
- *Drinking water impacts* from underground migration of methane and/or fracking chemicals associated with faulty well construction.
- Surface spills potentially resulting in *soil and water contamination.*
- *Surface-water contamination* resulting from inadequate wastewater treatment.
- *Earthquakes* induced during fracturing.
- *Community impacts* associated with boom-town economic effects such as increased vehicle traffic, road damage, noise, odor complaints, increased demand for housing and medical care, and stress.[78]

Based on such claims, environmentalists, public health professionals, and many community residents began mobilizing politically at local and state levels on behalf of the regulation or outright banning of fracking.

Legal Issues in the Regulation of Fracking

Which level of government should regulate fracking operations? State and local governments had already been engaged in regulation of fracking. Some view this as the most appropriate regulatory approach. They argue that the benefits and costs of fracking are mostly local and vary widely across the jurisdictions in which it takes place. Others contend, however, that the environmental consequences of large-scale fracking are likely to become national problems beyond the scope of any single state's regulatory authority. For this reason, federal regulation is more appropriate than a patchwork of state-by-state regulation to balance the social benefits and costs of this technology.[79]

According to an overview of U.S. state-level fracking regulations by ALS, an international analytical testing services company, state regulation of fracking operations

typically focus[es] on site design, drilling procedures, well design and specifications, regulatory oversight/monitoring, and handling of materials and wastes. . . . Four components of fracking operations are generally addressed in states' regulations. These are 1) pre-drilling, 2) groundwater and surface water impact, 3) liquid wastes and fluids, and 4) solid wastes.[80]

States that have regulated fracking include Colorado, North Dakota, Ohio, Pennsylvania, Texas, West Virginia, and Wyoming. In the states, according to a CRS overview,

hydraulic fracturing tort litigation[iv] has raised questions about causation; whether hydraulic fracturing is an abnormally dangerous activity; and whether hydraulic fracturing may constitute

---

[iv]"Tort litigation" refers to lawsuits brought by individuals who claim they have been injured or harmed in some way by the actions of another individual or organization.

a subsurface trespass to land.[v] Also, several municipalities have attempted to ban hydraulic fracturing through zoning restrictions and other local laws, creating potential conflicts with oil and gas industry regulation at the state level.[81]

At the federal level, several environmental statutes bear on the regulation of fracking by both the federal and state governments. At the time the State of New York banned fracking, however, a comprehensive federal regulatory approach to fracking had not been developed. The difficulties of doing so are readily apparent in the CRS's review of the potential legal basis for a federal regulatory approach:

An amendment to the Safe Drinking Water Act (SDWA) passed as a part of the Energy Policy Act of 2005 (EPAct 2005) clarified that the Underground Injection Control (UIC) requirements found in the SDWA do not apply to hydraulic fracturing, although the exclusion does not extend to the use of diesel fuel in hydraulic fracturing operations. The underground injection of wastewater generated during oil and gas production (including hydraulic fracturing) does require a UIC permit under the SDWA, as do injections for enhanced oil and gas recovery operations. Under the Clean Water Act (CWA), parties seeking to discharge produced water may have to apply for a permit under the National Pollutant Discharge Elimination System. Under the Clean Air Act (CAA), the Environmental Protection Agency (EPA) has issued new rules covering emissions of volatile organic compounds from hydraulic fracturing operations.

Provisions of the Resource Conservation and Recovery Act (RCRA) exempt drilling fluids, produced waters, and other wastes associated with the exploration, development, or production of crude oil, natural gas, or geothermal energy from regulation as hazardous wastes under Subtitle C of RCRA. However, these wastes are subject to other federal laws (such as the SDWA and the CWA), as well as to state requirements. Facility owners and operators and other potentially responsible parties could potentially face liability under the Comprehensive Environmental Response, Compensation, and Liability Act (CERCLA) for cleanup costs, natural resource damages, and the costs of federal public health studies, if hydraulic fracturing results in the release of hazardous substances at or under the surface in a manner that may endanger public health or the environment.

The National Environmental Policy Act (NEPA) requires federal agencies to consider the environmental impacts of proposed federal actions before proceeding with them. An agency would be obligated to consider the impacts of an action that involves hydraulic fracturing if that action takes place on federal lands or when there is otherwise a sufficient federal nexus to hydraulic fracturing.

Under the Emergency Planning and Community Right-to-Know Act (EPCRA), owners or operators of facilities where certain hazardous hydraulic fracturing chemicals are present above certain thresholds may have to comply with emergency planning requirements; emergency release notification obligations; and hazardous chemical storage reporting requirements.

[v]Fracking wells may be drilled horizontally beneath productive farmlands that overlay the shale deposits.

(Continued)

(Continued)

In August 2011, environmental groups petitioned EPA to promulgate rules under the Toxic Substances Control Act (TSCA) for chemical substances and mixtures used in oil and gas exploration or production.[82]

Whatever a technically rational federal strategy for regulation of fracking might look like, the actual design would emerge from the same political processes that have already complicated the prospects for comprehensive action by the EPA.

What New York Can Learn from Pennsylvania

Writing the regulations is one thing. Choosing and implementing an appropriate enforcement philosophy is quite another. As New York State was designing its regulatory approach, many experts argued that New York might learn valuable lessons from the State of Pennsylvania's experience with fracking regulation.

> Whatever a technically rational federal strategy for regulation of fracking might look like, the actual design would emerge from the same political processes that have already complicated the prospects for comprehensive action by the EPA.

A report published by Pennsylvania's auditor general in July 2014 documented a number of shortcomings in the state's efforts to regulate fracking operations.[83] In August 2014, *The Ithaca Journal*, an e-newspaper, asked two state experts for their views on what New York might learn from the Pennsylvania auditor general's report with respect to a number of issues associated with regulating fracking.

A significant insight from the newspaper's reporting was the importance of the enforcement philosophy adopted by Pennsylvania's Department of Environmental Conservation (DEC). Fracking rules required DEC to issue administrative orders to companies compelling them to clean contaminated water supplies created by fracking processes. DEC regulators were, according to the auditor general's report, inconsistent in the issuance of these orders.

The Pennsylvania regulators argued that, in the light of a shortage of financial and human resources devoted to regulatory enforcement, they needed flexibility in setting enforcement priorities. As a consequence, they decided that resources needed to prepare and issue administrative orders when water contamination was, in their view, insignificant or when companies indicated cleanup was already underway would be better devoted to more immediate needs, such as oversight of drilling well construction and cementing. One New York critic characterized DEC's philosophy as "let's warn them first, and if they comply we don't have to do anything like an administrative order."[84]

Critics of the DEC's enforcement philosophy argued that issuing administrative orders created a public record that made the need for and effectiveness of the regulatory process more transparent. Said one, "We don't really know, in Pennsylvania, how many cases of well-water contamination ever occurred. How do you do a cost-benefit analysis if you don't know what the true costs were?"[85]

DEC's critics also argued that regulators did not respond clearly and in a timely way to complaints, and that complaint tracking was ineffective, again because of resource problems: information processing capacity was inadequate. For the same reason, many legally required oil and gas drilling well inspections were not being conducted, and DEC "did not use a manifest system for tracking fracking well waste from the well site to disposal," using instead "a disjointed process that includes self-reporting by well operators and comes with no assurances that waste was properly disposed."[86] Said one New York State expert, "If you're going to go through the effort of writing really tough regulations, follow up and make sure that they are carried out by competent inspection and they're enforced, end of story Ibid.[87]

Discussion Questions

1. States and communities will vary in their designs of fracking regulations and their regulatory enforcement philosophies. Two responses to this inevitable variability are possible, summarized below. Construct an argument that supports each of these positions. What facts, evidence, and theoretical supports are particularly useful for your argument? What additional information do you need?

Position A: State and local variation in regulatory design and enforcement enables more flexible technical and political responses to issues at the local level: closest to the people. This is good public policy. The citizens of New York, Pennsylvania, and Maryland will be better served if fracking regulation is the responsibility of lawmakers responsible to them. A one-size-fits-all federal mandating of tough regulatory designs and enforcement requirements would be difficult to enforce because of the inevitable local variation in implementation and the difficulties of coordinating responses to this variation.

Position B: Patchwork regulation of fracking operations is likely to be ineffective in addressing the national implications of fracking technology and shale energy industry growth. The economic health of the industry and the benefits of greater energy independence, not to mention furthering liberty and justice for all, regardless of where you live, will be furthered by a uniform, better coordinated, and more predictable federal regulatory framework.

NOTES

1. "Wall Street and The Financial Crisis: Anatomy of a Financial Collapse," *Majority and Minority Staff Report: Permanent Subcommittee on Investigations-United States Senate,* April 13, 2011, http://www.hsgac.senate.gov//imo/media/doc/Financial_Crisis/FinancialCrisisReport.pdf?attempt=2.

2. "The Financial Crisis Inquiry Report: Final Report of the National Commission on the Causes of the Financial and Economic Crisis in the United States" *The Financial Crisis Inquiry Commission*, January 2011. http://www.gpo.gov/fdsys/pkg/gpo-fcic/pdf/gpo-fcic.pdf.

3. Ibid., xviii.

4. Ibid., xvi.

5. Ibid., xxi.

6. "Wall Street and the Financial Crisis," *Permanent Subcommittee on Investigations,* 12.

7. Richard T. Green, "Plutocracy, Bureaucracy, and The End of Public Trust," *Administration & Society* 44 (2012): 109–143. Material in this section is adapted from Laurence E. Lynn, Jr., "Rick Green Has Seen the Enemy: Guess Who?" *Administration & Society* 44 (2012): 754–765.

8. "The Financial Crisis Inquiry Report," *The Financial Crisis Inquiry Commission*, 54.

9. Ibid., 55.

10. Ibid., 28.

11. Ibid., 75–76.

12. Ibid., 76.

13. Daniel K. Tarullo: Member, Board of Governors of the Federal Reserve System, "Regulatory Reform Since the Financial Crisis: to the Council on Foreign Relations, May 2, 2012, http://www.federalreserve.gov/newsevents/speech/tarullo20120502a.pdf.

14. "The Financial Crisis Inquiry Report," *The Financial Crisis Inquiry Commission*, 41.

15. Ibid., xvii.

16. Ibid., xviii.

17. Ibid., 63.

18. Ibid., 125.

19. Marc T. Law and Sukkoo Kim, "The Rise of the American Regulatory State: A View from the Progressive Era," in *The Handbook on the Politics of Regulation,* ed. David Levi-Faur (Northampton, MA: Edward Elgar, 2011), 113.

20. David Levi-Faur, "Regulation & Regulatory Governance," in David Levi-Faur, ed., *Handbook on The Politics Of Regulation* (Northampton, MA: Edward Elgar, 2011), 3.

21. Curtis W. Copeland, *Rulemaking Requirements and Authorities in the Dodd-Frank Wall Street Reform and Consumer Protection Act,* CRS Report No. R41472 (Washington, DC: Congressional Research Service, November 3, 2010).

22. Steven P. Croley, "Theories of Regulation: Incorporating the Administrative Process," 98 *Colum. L. Rev.* (1998): 1–168, http://ssrn.com/abstract=11407.

23. Ibid., 33.

24. Ibid., 34.

25. Ibid., 37.

26. Ibid., 66.

27. Ibid., 77.

28. Ibid., 167.

29. Ibid., 164–165.

30. 44 U.S.C. § 3502, http://www.law.cornell.edu/uscode/text/44/3502.

31. "PCAOB Oversees: The Auditors of Companies to Protect Investors," Public Company Accounting Oversight Board, http://pcaobus.org/Pages/default.aspx.

32. "Discover ICANN," ICANN, https://www.icann.org/search/#!/?searchText=Discover%20ICANN.

33. "About MSRB," Municipal Securities Rulemaking Board, accessed May 19, 2015, http://www.msrb.org/About-MSRB.aspx.

34. "Who We Are," National Futures Association, accessed May 19, 2015, http://www.nfa.futures.org/NFA-about-nfa/index.HTML.

35. "About Us: What is the BOC?," Board of Certification for the Athletic Trainer, accessed May 19, 2015, http://www.bocatc.org/about-us.

36. "Regulatory & Administrative," LexisNexis, accessed May 19, 2015, http://www.lexisnexis.com/en-us/search.page?q=Regulatory%20%26%20Administrative.

37. "What We Do," Federal Communications Commission, accessed May 19, 2015, http://www.fcc.gov/what-we-do.

38. "State Regulatory Boards and Offices," State and Local Government on the Net, accessed May 19, 2015, http://www.statelocalgov.net/50states-regulatory.cfm.

39. Thomas M. Burton, "Dispute Flares inside FDA over Safety of Popular Blood-Pressure Drugs," *Wall Street Journal,* May 31, 2013, sec. Business, http://www.wsj.com/articles/SB10001424127887324682204578515172395384146.

40. "Administrative Law Research Guide," University of New Hampshire School of Law, Accessed August 1, 2015, http://library.law.unh.edu/AdminLaw.

41. "Formal Rulemaking-Administrative Agency Rulemaking-Administrative Law," US Legal, accessed May 19, 2015, http://administrativelaw.uslegal.com/administrative-agency-rulemaking/formal-rulemaking.

42. Congressional Research Service, "Rulemaking Requirements and Authorities in the Dodd-Frank Wall Street Reform and Consumer Protection Act," November 3, 2010, http://www.law.umaryland.edu/marshall/crsreports/crsdocuments/R41472_11032010.pdf.

43. "Determining the Regulatory Status of a Food Ingredient," U.S. Food and Drug Administration, last updated, December 12, 2014, http://www.fda.gov/Food/IngredientsPackagingLabeling/FoodAdditivesIngredients/ucm228269.htm.

44. Kimberly Kindy, "Food Additives on the Rise as FDA Scrutiny Wanes," *The Washington Post,* August 17, 2014, http://www.washingtonpost.com/national/food-additives-on-the-rise-as-fda-scrutiny-wanes/2014/08/17/828e9bf8-1cb2-11e4-ab7b-696c295ddfd1_story.html?hpid=z2.

45. "State Regulatory Agencies," All Things Political, accessed May 19, 2015, http://www.allthingspolitical.org/Agency/state_regulatory_agencies.htm.

46. "Guide to Law Online: U.S. States and Territories," Library of Congress, accessed May 19, 2015, http://www.loc.gov/law/help/guide/states.php.

47. Morris M. Kleiner, *Licensing Occupations: Ensuring Quality or Restricting Competition?* (Kalamazoo, MI: W.E. Upjohn Institute for Employment Research, 2006).

48. "Department of Regulatory Agencies," Colorado.gov, accessed May 19, 2015, http://cdn.colorado.gov/cs/Satellite?c=Page&childpagename=DORA%2FDORALayout&cid=1249686120221&pagename=CBONWrapper.

49. "State Pesticide Regulatory Agencies," National Pesticide Information Center, accessed May 19, 2015, http://npic.orst.edu/reg/state_agencies.html.

50. The NRC Mission," National Resource Center for Health and Safety in Child Care and Early Education, accessed May 23, 2015, http://nrckids.org/index.cfm/about-us.

51. Petula Dvorak, "Virginia's Inadequate Child-Care Regulations Put Its Most Vulnerable Residents at Risk," *The Washington Post*, September 2, 2014, http://www.washingtonpost.com/local/virginias-inadequate-child-care-regulations-put-its-most-vulnerable-residents-at-risk/2014/09/01/acece8dc-31f2-11e4-9e92-0899b306bbea_story.html.

52. David S. Fallis and Amy Brittain, "In Virginia, Thousands of Day-Care Providers Receive No Oversight," *The Washington Post*, August 30, 2014, http://www.washingtonpost.com/sf/investigative/2014/08/30/in-virginia-thousands-of-day-care-providers-receive-no-oversight/.

53. David L. Hudson, Jr. "1st Amendment at Issue in Ban on Gay Conversion Therapy for Minors," *ABA Journal*, January 1, 2014, http://www.abajournal.com/magazine/article/1st_amendment_at_issue_in_ban_on_gay-conversion_therapy_for_minors/. For U.S. Ninth Circuit Court of Appeals decision and related case activity, see http://www.ca9.uscourts.gov/content/view.php?pk_id=0000000635.

54. Cooksey vs. Futrell et al.: "Caveman Blogger Fights for Free Speech and Internet Freedom," Institute for Justice, http://www.ij.org/paleo speech, accessed May 22, 2015. The Appeals Court opinion can be found here: http://www.ij.org/images/pdf_folder/first_amendment/paleo/paleo-4th-opinion.pdf.

55. "Regulation," *Data-Smart City Solutions*, accessed May 19, 2015, http://datasmart.ash.harvard.edu/regulation.

56. Jessica Huey, "Innovating Permitting in Boston," Data-Smart City Solutions, July 10, 2014, http://datasmart.ash.harvard.edu/news/article/innovating-permitting-in-boston-490.

57. "Enforcement Basic Information," Environmental Protection Agency, last updated April 30, 2015, http://www2.epa.gov/enforcement/enforcement-basic-information.

58. "Approved Risk Evaluation and Mitigation Strategies (REMS)," U.S. Food and Drug Administration, last updated April 30, 2015, http://www.fda.gov/drugs/drugsafety/postmarketdrugsafetyinformationforpatientsandproviders/ucm111350.htm.

59. "FDA Lacks Comprehensive Data to Determine Whether Risk Evaluation and Mitigation Strategies Improve Drug Safety," Department of Health and Human Services: Office of Inspector General, February 12, 2013, https://oig.hhs.gov/oei/reports/oei-04-11-00510.asp.

60. Stephen Barlas, "Pharmacists, Deluged with Requirements, Pressure FDA to Standardize REMS Programs," *Pharmacy and Therapeutics* 39, no.1 (2014): 12–13. http://www.ncbi.nlm.nih.gov/pmc/articles/PMC3956378/.

61. Ibid.

62. Ibid.

63. Vanessa K. Burrows and Todd Garvey, *A Brief Overview of Rulemaking and Judicial Review*, CRS Report No. R41546 (Washington, DC: Congressional Research Service, 2011). Also see Carey, "The Federal Rulemaking Process: An Overview."

64. Administrative Procedure Act, 5 U.S.C. § 706, 2 (1946), *Legal Information Institute*, http://www.law.cornell.edu/uscode/text/5/706.

65. James Q. Wilson, "The Politics of Regulation," in *The Politics of Regulation,* ed. James Q. Wilson (New York, NY: Basic Books, 1980), 357, 393; Croley, "Theories of Regulation," 166.

66. Donald P. Moynihan and Pamela Herd, "Red Tape and Democracy: How Rules Affect Citizenship Rights," *American Review of Public Administration* 40, no. 6 (2010): 654–670.

67. "Mission Statement," National Association for Regulatory Administration, accessed April 8, 2015, http://www.naralicensing.org/about_NARA. Reprinted with permission from National Association for Regulatory Administration.

68. Ibid.

69. "About the Administrative Conference of the United States," Administrative Conference of the United States, accessed May 19, 2015, http://www.acus.gov/about-administrative-conference-united-states-acus.

70. Diane Katz and James L. Gattuso, "The 10 Worst Regulations of 2012," The Heritage Foundation, December 27, 2012, http://www.heritage.org/research/reports/2012/12/the-10-worst-regulations-of-2012.

71. Peter Loftus, "Doctors Face New Scrutiny over Gifts," *Wall Street Journal*, August 22, 2013, sec. Business, http://www.wsj.com/articles/SB10001424127887323455104579014812178937016.

72. Thomas Kaplan, "Citing Health Risks, Cuomo Bans Fracking in New York State," *The New York Times*, December 17, 2014, http://www.nytimes.com/2014/12/18/nyregion/cuomo-to-ban-fracking-in-new-york-state-citing-health-risks.html.

73. Joe Nocera, "Shale and the Falling Price of Oil," *The New York Times*, December 22, 2014, http://www.nytimes.com/2014/12/23/opinion/joe-nocera-shale-and-the-falling-price-of-oil.html.

74. Susan Lawrence, "Conservation Update," *Sierra Club Hudson/Mohawk Group* 48(1) (Winter 2014).

75. Kaplan, "Citing Health Risks, Cuomo Bans Fracking in New York State."

76. Chris Mooney, "These Two States Had the Same Basic Information about Fracking. They Made Very Different Decisions," *The Washington Post*, December 22, 2014, http://www.washingtonpost.com/blogs/wonkblog/wp/2014/12/22/these-two-states-had-the-same-basic-information-about-fracking-they-made-very-different-decisions/. The State of Maryland's report on fracking, "Potential Public Health Impacts of Natural Gas Development and Production in the Marcellus Shale of Western Maryland," can be accessed at http://www.mde.state.md.us/programs/Land/mining/marcellus/Documents/Final_Distribution_Draft_11.25.14.pdf.

77. "Modern Shale Gas Development in the United States: A Primer," *U.S. Department of Energy*, April 2009, ES-2, http://energy.gov/sites/prod/files/2013/03/f0/ShaleGasPrimer_Online_4-2009.pdf.

78. "A Public Health Review of High Volume Hydraulic Fracturing for Shale Gas Development," *New York State Department of Public Health*, December 2014, http://www.health.ny.gov/press/reports/docs/high_volume_hydraulic_fracturing.pdf.

79. "Should the Federal Government Regulate Fracking?," *Wall Street Journal*, April 14, 2013, sec. Journal Reports: Energy, http://www.wsj.com/articles/SB10001424127887323495104578314302738867078.

80. "Fracking Regulations by State," ALS Global, accessed May 19, 2015, http://www.alsglobal.com/en/Our-Services/Life-Sciences/Environmental/Capabilities/North-America-Capabilities/USA/Oil-and-Gasoline-Testing/Oil-and-Gas-Production-and-Midstream-Support/Fracking-Regulations-by-State.

81. Adam Vann, Brandon J. Murrill, and Mary Tiemann, *Hydraulic Fracturing: Selected Legal Issues* CRS Report No. R43152 (Washington, DC: Congressional Research Service, 2014), http://fas.org/sgp/crs/misc/R43152.pdf.

82. Ibid.

83. Jon Hurdle, "Pennsylvania's Auditor General Faults Oversight of Natural Gas Industry," *The New York Times*, July 23, 2014, http://www.nytimes.com/2014/07/24/us/pennsylvanias-auditor-general-faults-oversight-of-natural-gas-industry.html.

84. Andrew Casler, "What N.Y. Can Learn from Pa.'s Fracking Problems," *Ithaca Journal*, August 11, 2014, http://www.ithacajournal.com/story/news/local/2014/08/08/pa-fracking-failures-teach-newyork/13795841/.

85. Ibid.

86. Ibid.

87. Ibid.

88. Ibid.

PART III | CULTURE

Norms, Values, and Institutions

> *Commitments and the cultures they form can be as elusive as they are important. . . . The commitments that drive the work of a public program might not be included in a legislative mandate or even a mission statement. They are, instead, intricately entwined with the day-to-day work of implementing a public program. . . . The commitments that take hold might not be pretty, but they most likely provide confidence and sometimes merely comfort for participants implementing controversial, poorly funded, or politically unpopular programs. Commitments exist because people act upon them and make decisions based upon them. It is through commitments that participants understand what they are doing and why they are doing it.[i]*

> —Anne M. Khademian
> *Working with Culture: The Way the*
> *Job Gets Done in Public Programs*

Public managers do their work within the structures of formal authority described in Part II. Within the formal organization, however, there exists the informal organization comprising the uncodified norms of conduct, the values, and the rituals and ceremonies that reflect and reveal the meanings an organization's people give to their work beyond the formal, codified requirements of their tasks. These informal systems of meaning have come to be referred to as the *organization's culture.*[ii]

---

[i]Anne M. Khademian, *Working with Culture: How the Job Gets Done in Public Programs* (Washington, DC: CQ Press, 2002), 5.

[ii]A synonym for the term *culture* in this context is *ethos*, comprising the customs, sentiments, character, and disposition by which a group of individual employees come to constitute a whole that is greater than the sum of its parts.

> **Culture means the norms, values, and standards of conduct that provide meaning, purpose, and motivation to individuals working within an organizational unit.**

Culture encompasses shared, normative understandings about what the organization's work should be and how it should be accomplished. Organizational culture is a manifestation of the values, ethical precepts, and motivations of individual participants in the organization: frontline employees, professionals, and managers. Because these cultural aspects are likely to have developed over time, they may be as real or factual to individual employees as the formal structures of authority that govern their conduct.

The entrenched, informal aspects of an organization are likely, therefore, to enable or constrain a manager just as much as formal structural aspects do. To the extent that informal and formal aspects are inflexible, managers are creatures of their organizational environments, as discussed in Chapter 1. To the extent that informal and formal are malleable, however, managers may act as creators in aligning formal and informal organizations in the achievement of public policy goals, adjusting each to the other.

In this text, culture means the norms, values, and standards of conduct that provide meaning, purpose, and motivation to individuals working within an organizational unit. As emphasized by political scientist Anne Khademian's quote above, the culture dimension is fundamental to an organization's capacity to carry out its lawful responsibilities.

PUBLIC MANAGEMENT'S PERFECT STORM: THE CULTURE DIMENSION

At least in part, the lack of coordination among local, state, and federal agencies that might have contributed to a joint rescue effort during Hurricane Katrina can be traced to organizational cultures and institutional histories that emphasized turf protection and short-term organizational interests at the expense of addressing the immediate needs of citizens and communities in storm-ravaged areas. The lack of coordination and communication regarding responsibility for the levees mentioned in the Part II introduction can likely be traced to just such turf protection and short-term interests, which added up to a dysfunctional government response to the emergency.

Although organizational cultures compounded structural (and craft) failures before and after Katrina, positive responses by employees in public, nonprofit, and for-profit organizations, stemming partly from their strong organizational cultures, helped alleviate the highly visible suffering of the storm's victims and prevented further loss of life. For example, intergovernmental cooperation resulted in a relatively smooth and successful evacuation by vehicle in accordance with the "Contraflow" plan of more than 1 million people.[iii] The U.S. Coast Guard, an independent agency within the U.S. Department of Homeland Security (DHS), quickly deployed resources as they were needed during and after the storm, rescuing more than 30,000 people. The Coast Guard's response was a reflection of its culture. According to one scholar,

> the Coast Guard instills in its members a powerful organizational culture and gives them much latitude for independent decision making. . . . In granting on-scene initiative, Coast Guard leadership allows subordinates to alter the particular plan for their specific operation based on their local knowledge, but this must be done without violating the overarching and generally unchanged 'commander's intent.' . . . The

---

[iii]Martha Derthick, "Where Federalism Didn't Fail," *Public Administration Review,* 67 Issue Supplement (2007): 36-47.

sort of decentralized teamwork that the Coast Guard expects 'works through the common understanding of how individual incidents or situations are normally handled.'[iv,v]

The Senate report described other examples of how organizational culture influenced response to the storm and its aftermath:[vi]

87. The individuals working on behalf of federal, state, and local agencies to rescue victims worked in chaotic situations often at great risk to themselves. Yet search-and-rescue resources, including boats and helicopters, were insufficient despite the accelerated deployment through the first week of the landfall. [p. 596]

122. The federal government's medical response suffered from a lack of planning, coordination, and cooperation, particularly between the U.S. Department of Health and Human Services (HHS) and the Department of Homeland Security. [p. 599]

134. The NOPD [New Orleans Police Department] was overwhelmed by Katrina. Under extraordinarily difficult circumstances, most of its officers performed their duties. [p. 600]

148. On the whole, the performance of the individual Coast Guard personnel, sailors, soldiers, airmen, and Marines—active, Guard, and Reserve—was in keeping with the high professional standards of the United States military, and these men and women are proud of their service to help the victims of this natural disaster. [p. 601]

Many of these examples show how organizational culture interacted with structure in shaping the preparation for and response to Katrina. In some cases, culture impeded the effective use of structures. In others, organizational cultures were instrumental in overcoming structural constraints, enabling more effective responses, and reflecting initiative by individuals exercising responsible professional judgment.

PART III OVERVIEW

Part III explores specific frameworks, theories, and concepts that illuminate the culture dimension of public management. Interactions with other dimensions are explored as well. Part III comprises two chapters:

* Chapter 8 discusses the individual building blocks of culture in public organizations. These include the ethics, values, and motives that individuals bring with them to their jobs. It includes as well the ways that

---

[iv]U.S. Coast Guard, *America's Maritime Guardian: U.S. Coast Guard Publication 1* (2002), 53, cited by Steven Horwitz, "Making Hurricane Response More Effective: Lessons From the Private Sector and the Coast Guard during Katrina," in *The Political Economy of Hurricane Katrina and Community Rebound,* ed. Emily Chamlee Wright and Virgil Henry Storr (Cheltenham, UK: Edward Elgar), 60.

[v]Steven Horwitz, "Making Hurricane Response More Effective: Lessons From the Private Sector and the Coast Guard during Katrina," in *The Political Economy of Hurricane Katrina and Community Rebound,* ed. Emily Chamlee Wright and Virgil Henry Storr (Cheltenham, UK: Edward Elgar), 59–60.

[vi]U.S. Senate, *Hurricane Katrina: A Nation Still Unprepared: Special Report of the Committee on Homeland Security and Governmental Affairs* (Washington, DC: Government Printing Office, 2006), http://www.gpoaccess.gov/serialset/creports/katrinanation.html.

organizational contexts shape these individual aspects. The ways in which professions shape values and norms are discussed.

- Chapter 9 discusses the institutionalized values of an organization commonly known as organizational culture. Unique cultures in different types of public organizations are emphasized, particularly those that have a bearing on increasing trust and confidence in government as discussed in the Part I introduction. Characteristics for framing this discussion include culture in loosely coupled or tightly coupled organizations and in high-reliability organizations. The influence of culture in organizational learning is emphasized, as are the possibilities for public managers to prompt change in organizational cultures.

This part of the book provides answers to four questions:

1. **What is organizational culture?**

2. **What theories, frameworks, and heuristics can be used to gain analytical traction on understanding it?**

3. **How is an organization's culture created and sustained?**

4. **What are the implications of organizational cultures for how organizations implement public policies and reflect the public interest?**

8 CULTURE

The Building Blocks

INTRODUCTION

The shared understandings that form an organization's culture are developed over time, through repeated interactions among organizational members. Although organizational culture is an organizational level construct, its elemental features derive from both individual- and group-level characteristics. Thus, an understanding of culture grows from analysis at both the individual and the organizational levels.

The history of public administration and management places a special emphasis on the responsibility to constitutional principles of individuals in public service. Recent theories and empirical research point to the potential importance of the motives of individuals who serve in public organizations. These and other individual characteristics are likely to be an important part of the informal organization in which public managers do their work.

The ethics, values, motives, and capacity for professional judgments of individuals in public organizations are significant factors in public management for at least two reasons. First, these factors may influence the decisions and behaviors of individuals in the organization over whom the manager has control. Second, these factors will influence the decisions and behaviors of managers themselves. Both of these considerations are reflected in the culture of the organization. And both potentially influence managers' ability or inability to exercise their craft.

The chapter's opening case considers (a) the ethical dilemmas that arise for health care workers who visit patients in their homes and (b) the influence of professional training in how these frontline workers perform. Next, the historical foundations of a concern with the bases of individual action are reviewed. Subsequent sections discuss, in turn, the ethics, values, and motives of public employees. The roles of professionals in an organization and in ensuring accountability and the public interest and the law are discussed next. The end-of-chapter case considers how systems for compensating public employee may be viewed in the light of the individuals who constitute the building blocks of organizational culture.

CASE: HOME VISITING IN EARLY HEAD START

Early Head Start (EHS) is a federally funded program, authorized by the Head Start Act in 1994, and implemented by grants to local agencies in communities throughout the United States. Program design and oversight is conducted by the Office of Head Start (OHS) in the Administration for Children and Families (ACF) in the U.S. Department of Health and Human Services (DHHS). EHS, which serves infants and toddlers up to age 3 as well as pregnant women, has the following goals:

- To provide safe and developmentally enriching caregiving which promotes the physical, cognitive, social, and emotional development of infants and toddlers, and prepares them for future growth and development;

- To support parents, both mothers and fathers, in their role as primary caregivers and teachers of their children, and families in meeting personal goals and achieving self-sufficiency across a wide variety of domains;

- To mobilize communities to provide the resources and environment necessary to ensure a comprehensive, integrated array of services and support for families;

- To ensure the provision of high quality responsive services to family through the development of trained, and caring staff.[1]

Program services may be offered in centers, through home visits, through home-based care, or through some combination of these options. This case focuses on the home visiting option. Other home visiting models for infants and young children are offered in programs such as Nurse-Family Partnership, Parents as Teachers, or Healthy Families America. Many localities offer home visiting programs that provide health care or mental health care for adults, as well.

Home Visitor Job Responsibilities and Qualifications

OHS sets guidelines that apply to all grantees regarding the EHS home visiting component. Under this option, an EHS home visitor comes to the home each week. Twice per month, participants in this option gather as a group.

OHS also sets guidelines that apply to all grantees regarding EHS home visitor qualifications and job responsibilities. The qualifications are described in Section 1304.52(e) of the Head Start Program Performance Standards:

(e) Home visitor qualifications. Home visitors must have knowledge and experience in child development and early childhood education; the principles of child health, safety, and nutrition; adult learning principles; and family dynamics. They must be skilled in communicating with and motivating people. In addition, they must have knowledge of community resources and the skills to link families with appropriate agencies and services.[2]

The position posting for an EHS home visitor, shown in Figure 8.1, describes the scope as well as the details of a home visitor's job.

FIGURE 8.1	Early Head Start Home Visitor Job Posting in Lane County

Early Head Start Home Visitor

Position Purpose

Primary case manager for EHS families enrolled in the home-base option. To provide in-home instruction as well as a group socialization experience to parents and children (infants/toddlers) which will enhance the parents' ability to fill the role of primary nurturer of their child. Maintain on-going contact with families and work with all other components (health, nutrition, family services, mental health, special services, parent education and resource/referral) to integrate services into the family setting. Must meet requirements per Federal Head Start Performance Standards and any local, state and or agency policies and procedures.

Essential Job Responsibilities: Performance Indicators

Home Visits (50%)

1. Create and maintain respectful partnerships with families.

2. Drive to family home and deliver health, educational, nutritional and child growth and development information to parents via weekly meetings.

3. Coordinate with parents to ensure that prenatal, well-child exams, immunizations, health screenings, and nutrition assessments are complete and necessary follow up occurs.

4. Complete family partnership agreements, developmental screenings and all other required assessments with families in a timely manner.

5. Assist and support families in locating resources and scheduling appointments with community resources that best meets their needs.

6. Provide support in parent and child activities that encourages developmentally appropriate activities for the changing needs of infants and toddlers.

Classroom Time (15%)

1. Meet the needs of all children including those at risk, those with special needs, those who are gifted, and those who are culturally diverse.

2. Integrate all Head Start components into classroom time.

3. Develop and utilize lesson plans which reflect both mandated elements and parental and cultural influences, and which promote the social emotional, physical, and cognitive development of Head start children.

(Continued)

| **Figure 8.1** | **(Continued)** |

4. Individualize one-to-one and group activities to reflect the unique needs and strengths of all children in the classroom.

5. Provide an atmosphere that promotes and reinforces parental involvement in the classroom.

6. Work with appropriate agencies and other resources to develop Individual Family Service Plans (IFSP).

7. Coordinate special needs staff in the classroom and develop a collaborative approach that benefits all children and meets the needs specified in the IFSP.

Planning, Preparation and Documentation (25%)

1. Review each child's goals and write comprehensive individual plans designed to promote current learning and attend to nutritional, health, and social issues.

2. Develop and utilize teaching methods and materials for use in the classroom and home.

3. Maintain accurate written/electronic records including: health information, assessments, IFSP documentation, screening instruments, anecdotal observations, and other required forms.

Parent Meetings and Coordination (5%)

1. Plan and facilitate group meetings which provide education and information on current Head start policy and curriculum development.

2. Coordinate parent volunteer schedule, assuring adequate involvement and an appropriate adult to child ratio.

3. Communicate frequently with other staff and parents; serve as liaison among medical and social services in the community; act as advocate for Head start families.

Staff Trainings/Meetings and Misc. (5%)

1. Meet regularly with consultants and community collaborators to assure quality services.

2. Attend meetings, Staffings, trainings, and professional development activities as appropriate.

3. Perform other duties as requested.

All communications are potentially sensitive and are subject to Head Start's policy on confidentiality.

Minimum Requirements:

• Must have knowledge and at least one year experience in child development and early childhood education, adult learning and family dynamics including knowledge of community resources and skill to link families with appropriate agencies and services. Infant Toddler CDA and/or a combination of knowledge and experience that cover the areas listed above is required. An Associate Degree in ECE or higher is preferred.

- Must have flexible schedule to accommodate family needs, may include some evening or weekend hours.
- Excellent written and verbal communication skills. Bilingual English/Spanish skills highly desirable.
- Intermediate to advanced computer skills, internet and e-mail.
- Must have a valid Oregon Driver's License and proof of insurance and must provide own vehicle for home visits.
- Within 30 days of employment must be Pediatric CPR and First Aid certified and have a current Food Handlers Card.
- Health Appraisal Questionnaire is required at hire and will be updated annually.
- At time of hire must be currently enrolled in Child Care Division-Central Background Registry and must renew every two years.

Knowledge, Skills and Abilities:

- Frequent significant decision and problem solving abilities.
- Ability to work as a team member collaborating with parents and community resources.
- Ability to supervise and monitor children at all times to ensure a safe environment. This includes the physical ability to monitor and move quickly in order to respond to children who are very active and may need restraint or redirection in order to insure their safety or the safety of others.
- Ability to respond appropriately to an emergency or a crisis situation.
- Frequent driving for home visits sometimes in outlying areas.
- Regular kneeling, bending and sitting on the floor to attend to child's needs.
- Occasional lifting up to 50 pounds.

Position Information

- Full Year Position
- Supervised by EHS Manager.

Source: Head Start of Lane County, Oregon.

In 2010, at least 71 percent of EHA home visitors had a Child Development Associate credential (CDA); 45 percent had at least a bachelor's degree.[3] The Center for Law and Social Policy estimated the national annual salary of home visitors in 2010 as $28,944.[4]

Ethical and Professional Issues in Home Visiting

In the course of their work, home visitors may confront ethical dilemmas and other boundary issues[i] with the families in the program. The challenges in these situations may be particularly acute for frontline employees because of the service location in the client's home and the very nature of the program. Figure 8.2 is a briefing memo that illustrates these challenges:

[i]"The concern about appropriate boundaries is, at least in part, a concern about the effects of the power differential between client and professional. It is primarily a concern about boundary violations." C. Dietz and D. Thompson, "Rethinking Boundaries: Ethical Dilemmas in the Social Worker-Client Relationship," *Journal of Progressive Human Services* 15, no. 2 (2004): 2.

FIGURE 8.2	**Boundaries in Home Visiting**

Heidi Roibal,
BS August, 2013

NMAIMH competencies addressed

Law, Regulations, & Agency Policy

- Ethical practice and agency policy Thinking
- Analyzing information Reflection
- Professional/personai development

Imagine a home visit with the following scenarios:

1. As you sit down with a family you have been working with for 3 months, the mother tells you she is out of diapers and needs to run to the store. She asks you if you could watch her infant "for a few minutes."

2. You are living in a small town and are the major professional support person for many of the families that you see. You frequently run into the families in the community. Many families have access to your personal phone numbers and home address. How do you set and maintain professional boundaries?

3. During a scheduled visit, you notice a parent with a black eye. What do you say to the parent? What are some considerations for your discussion?

4. A family that you have been working with for a year invites you to their child's first birthday party. How do you respond?

"Professional boundaries," in home visiting can be described as the distinct *awareness* of the differences between a professional relationship and a friendship. Our internal awareness may be called into action on a daily basis. One distinction we can make is that a professional relationship involves legal and ethical paperwork such as assessments and reports and these responsibilities are not typically a part of a friendship. Reflective supervision can help develop home visitors' ability to recognize and discuss ethical dilemmas such as professional boundaries, which may trigger an emotional response and challenge our ability to honor these boundaries.

When we put into practice our capacity to understand our emotional responses to ethical dilemmas, we engage our internal ability to reflect and examine our thoughts, feelings and internal processes while striving to keep an open mind, stay curious and take in the perspectives of others. Ethical dilemmas require a plan of action to protect professional boundaries and to protect the family and the home visitor. Role-playing the scenarios described above during a staff meeting can provide everyone the time to reflect; time to stop and think about what *is* happening, what *has* happened and what *could* happen next. Regular staff meetings can help facilitate discussions about best practices to support professional boundaries for all involved: the home visitor, the family and the infant.

Reviewing how home visitors establish boundaries with families early in the professional relationship and clear discussions with parents about boundaries at the first visit will help clarify your role as that of a professional. Parents will appreciate knowing that home visitors provide information and support in a professional role and it's important to set clear boundaries everyone understands. As one experienced home visitor remarked, "I let the family know that I am there as a professional and I will not be able to accept family party invitations, Facebook friend invites or other invites because of our Code of Ethics and agency policies. I know that the family understands this and it prevents any misunderstandings or hurt feelings."

Professional boundary discussions may also include clarifying and if necessary, reviewing/updating program policies and procedures about the use of cell phones and social media and how these technologies impact our work as home visitors. As emerging technologies develop, honoring boundaries can take on a new look as we work towards being responsive to families while maintaining boundaries in a world where instant messaging, texting and social media prevail as modes of communication.

Combining our understanding of program policies, along with our own personal values, beliefs and emotions can be helpful as we navigate through these territories. Home visiting involves legal and ethical responsibilities to our program, our families and ourselves. By using reflection to identify priorities, discuss concerns and formulate a plan of action for different situations, we can be confident of navigating both professional and personal boundaries as they arise.

Talking Points for Supervisors:

- What boundaries challenge your home visitors most?
- If one of your home visitors is working with a family that challenges professional boundaries, what do you need to assist them?
- What are some cultural considerations to think about?
- What is the home visitor's primary role with this family?

References/Additional Resources

Heffron, Mary Claire, Murch, Trudi. (2010) Reflective Supervision and Leadership In Infant and Early Childhood Programs. Washington, DC: Zero to Three.
Luna County Parents as Teachers Home Visiting Program.

Source: Reprinted with permission from the New Mexico Children, Youth and Families Division Home Visiting Program.

The individual home visitor's own values, ethics, and professional training provide support for navigating these challenges. Ongoing professional development and support from supervisors that recognizes these dilemmas is also fundamental. The EHS National Resource Center[5] provides materials for the home visiting option, including

- a video and transcript on "Connecting with Families" that addresses the boundary and ethical issues a home visitor may encounter; and
- a "Home Visitor's Handbook" and "Home-Based Supervisor's Manual" including videos and resources.

The publication "Head Start and Early Head Start Relationship-Based Competencies for Staff and Supervisors Who Work with Their Families" also provides insight into the ethical, boundary, and cultural issues that arise in the home visiting program:

Supervisors of family services staff and home visitors do important work in HS/EHS programs. They enhance the organizational climate and culture and develop staff knowledge and skills. . . . Research shows that reflective supervision supports individuals in establishing and maintaining healthy relationships with families. . . . Many of the families at HS/EHS have experienced severe hardship. Reflective supervision can help staff gain new insights and knowledge when dealing with complicated relationships and challenging family circumstances.[6]

For the relationship-based competency of "positive, goal-oriented relationships," one of the skills listed for frontline staff is "makes ethical decisions that maintain professional boundaries and family confidentiality," and a corresponding one for supervisors is "demonstrates the ability to support and model ethical practice when interacting with staff and families." For the relationship-based competency of "foundations for professional growth," a skill listed for supervisors is "demonstrates the ability to support and model ethical practice when interacting with staff and families."[7]

This case illustrates how frontline workers' ethics, motives, values, and professional training can substantially affect the experience of participants in public programs, constituting what amounts to systems of local justice discussed in Chapter 6. Awareness of these aspects, and fostering a culture that supports implementation consistent with the program's mission, is not a routine task for program managers.

THE BUILDING BLOCKS OF CULTURE: HISTORICAL PERSPECTIVE

Informal norms expressed through individual values have long been a concern in public administration. In the field's scholarship, the earliest concerns were about professional rather than agency or organizational values.[i] In particular, the focus has been on values that motivate and ensure the legitimacy of "unelected bureaucrats" in the public's mind. Because bureaucrats may have job protection under a merit-based personnel system and may be resistant to formal accountability, Americans have been suspicious of the antidemocratic values that they regard as endemic to bureaucratic "big government."

As discussed in Chapter 2, advocates of "the new public administration" believed that public officials imbued with a sense of responsibility to democratic institutions would counteract the potential risks of unelected bureaucrats. Woodrow Wilson argued in 1887 that Americans need not fear professional administration of public affairs if they can rely on public administrators to exhibit responsible conduct—accountability to citizens and their representatives.[8] The theme of a sense of responsibility as the foundational public service value ran continuously through public administration literature during the ensuing 6 decades.

Anticipating the later emergence of the concept of "informal organization," in 1927 John Dickinson argued that defining a rule for everything public officials must do is impossible. Some entity other than the law must be used to control discretion. That entity is "political responsibility of government to the governed."[9] In 1936, John Gaus argued that responsibility is an evolving concept and multidimensional: not only political and constitutional but also professional, which ensures an **inner check** on official conduct.[10]

---

[i]In addition to the references cited in this section, see Herbert Kaufman, *The Forest Ranger: A Study in Administrative Behavior* (Washington, DC: Resources for the Future, 1960); Philip Selznick, *Leadership in Administration* (Evanston, IL: Row, Peterson, 1957); Dwight Waldo, *The Administrative State* (Somerset, NJ: Ronald Press, 1949).

The notion of an inner check created tensions concerning how to reconcile administrative discretion with responsibility to democratic values.[11] This tension was manifest in the 1940 debate between political scientists Herman Finer and Carl Friedrich over the sources of administrative responsibility.

- Finer argued that responsible administration in a democracy can be ensured only through external control: "The servants of the public are not to decide their own course; they are to be responsible to the elected representatives of the public, and these are to determine the course of action of the public servants to the most minute degree that is technically feasible."[12]
- Friedrich took a dim view of the ability of courts and legislatures to control administration.[13] In his view, any movement toward democratic responsibility requires that officials have the right orientation toward their work. The checks on abuse of administrative discretion are expertise and professionalism: the administrators' preferences and values, in particular their fidelity to democratic accountability.

The appropriateness of intrinsic motivation and self-control by public managers, a recurring issue since the Friedrich-Finer debate, is reflected in later discussions of administrative values. For example,

- John Rohr said, "Administrators should use their discretionary power in order to maintain the constitutional balance of powers in support of individual rights."[14]
- Robert B. Denhardt urged that public managers commit themselves to "values that relate to the concept of freedom, justice, and the public interest."[15]
- H. George Frederickson argued that public managers "must resist, thwart, or refuse to implement policy that runs counter to the founding documents or to American regime values."[16]

A long theme within the field of public administration and management, holds that, as creatures of America's constitutional scheme of governance and as a matter of principle, public mangers must create a belief on the part of the public that their work is legitimate and that they can be trusted to do it effectively.

ETHICS

Ethics are "rules of conduct and behavior . . . which relate to questions of right or wrong, good and evil."[17] Public employees at all levels, including public managers in their roles as both creatures and creators, encounter a range of situations that present ethical dilemmas. These may range from the seemingly inconsequential (can a U.S. postal carrier accept a $10 gift card from one of the families on her daily route?) to the obviously consequential (can the director of a procurement office demand a $20,000 personal payment from a contractor in return for awarding a contract to that entity?). This section discusses the types of guidelines and offices involved in supporting ethical action by civil servants, as well as resolving ethical dilemmas for individuals.

> As creatures of America's constitutional scheme of governance and as a matter of principle, public mangers must create a belief on the part of the public that their work is legitimate and that they can be trusted to do it effectively.

Ethics Guidelines for Civil Servants

Guidance on ethical action for civil servants at the federal, state, and local levels is available through special offices or committees in the executive, legislative, and judicial branches.

At the federal level, the Office of Government Ethics (OGE), an executive branch agency, "oversees the executive branch ethics program and works with a community of ethics practitioners made up of over 5,000 ethics officials in more than 130 agencies to implement that program."[18] A Designated Agency Ethics Officer (DAEO) in each agency works with the OGE on these and other issues. The "Standards of Ethical Conduct for Employees of the Executive Branch" are the final regulations issued by OGE codified in 5 C.F.R. Part 2635, as amended at 76 FR 38547, July 1, 2011). The Standards begin with a statement on the obligation of public service, followed by 14 general principles. OGE makes these 14 principles available in posters, brochures, wallet cards, and other products for federal employees (Box 8.1).

Box 8.1

EXCERPTS FROM § 2635.101 BASIC OBLIGATION OF PUBLIC SERVICE

(a) *Public service is a public trust.* Each employee has a responsibility to the United States Government and its citizens to place loyalty to the Constitution, laws and ethical principles above private gain. To ensure that every citizen can have complete confidence in the integrity of the Federal Government, each employee shall respect and adhere to the principles of ethical conduct set forth in this section, as well as the implementing standards contained in this part and in supplemental agency regulations.

(b) *General principles.* The following general principles apply to every employee and may form the basis for the standards contained in this part. Where a situation is not covered by the standards set forth in this part, employees shall apply the principles set forth in this section in determining whether their conduct is proper.

   (1) Public service is a public trust, requiring employees to place loyalty to the Constitution, the laws and ethical principles above private gain.

   (2) Employees shall not hold financial interests that conflict with the conscientious performance of duty.

   (3) Employees shall not engage in financial transactions using nonpublic Government information or allow the improper use of such information to further any private interest.

   (4) An employee shall not, except as permitted by subpart B of this part, solicit or accept any gift or other item of monetary value from any person or entity seeking official action from, doing business with, or conducting activities regulated by the employee's agency, or whose interests may be substantially affected by the performance or nonperformance of the employee's duties.

   (5) Employees shall put forth honest effort in the performance of their duties.

   (6) Employees shall not knowingly make unauthorized commitments or promises of any kind purporting to bind the Government.

   (7) Employees shall not use public office for private gain.

   (8) Employees shall act impartially and not give preferential treatment to any private organization or individual.

   (9) Employees shall protect and conserve Federal property and shall not use it for other than authorized activities.

(10) Employees shall not engage in outside employment or activities, including seeking or negotiating for employment, that conflict with official Government duties and responsibilities.

(11) Employees shall disclose waste, fraud, abuse, and corruption to appropriate authorities.

(12) Employees shall satisfy in good faith their obligations as citizens, including all just financial obligations, especially those—such as Federal, State, or local taxes—that are imposed by law.

(13) Employees shall adhere to all laws and regulations that provide equal opportunity for all Americans regardless of race, color, religion, sex, national origin, age, or handicap.

(14) Employees shall endeavor to avoid any actions creating the appearance that they are violating the law or the ethical standards set forth in this part. Whether particular circumstances create an appearance that the law or these standards have been violated shall be determined from the perspective of a reasonable person with knowledge of the relevant facts.

(c) *Related statutes.* In addition to the standards of ethical conduct set forth in this part, there are conflict of interest statutes that prohibit certain conduct. Criminal conflict of interest statutes of general applicability to all employees, 18 U.S.C. 201, 203, 205, 208, and 209, are summarized in the appropriate subparts of this part and must be taken into consideration in determining whether conduct is proper. Citations to other generally applicable statutes relating to employee conduct are set forth in subpart I and employees are further cautioned that there may be additional statutory and regulatory restrictions applicable to them generally or as employees of their specific agencies. Because an employee is considered to be on notice of the requirements of any statute, an employee should not rely upon any description or synopsis of a statutory restriction, but should refer to the statute itself and obtain the advice of an agency ethics official as needed.[19]

Source: United States Office of Government Ethics.

The Standards go on to detail guidelines for federal employees in situations concerning gifts from outside sources, gifts between employees, conflicting financial interests, impartiality in performing official duties, seeking other employment, misuse of position, and outside activities.

Individual federal agencies provide further support for their employees. For example, the Standards of Conduct Office within the Department of Defense (DoD) Counsel's Office provides online links to DoD guidance on topics such as "Holiday Guidance for Department of Defense Personnel" and "Participation in Military Balls Sponsored by Non-Federal Entities and Fundraising."[20] Also posted on this site is the "Encyclopedia of Ethical Failure," a 168-page (and growing) description of cases where DoD personnel "intentionally or unwittingly violated the standards of conduct. Some cases are humorous, some sad, and all are real. Some will anger you as a Federal employee and some will anger you as an American taxpayer."[21] A *Foreign Policy* magazine article titled "The Military Has Catalogued Its Ethical Failures, and They're Kind of Awesome," described the appeal of the Encyclopedia for ethics training: "Forget the stuffy, bureaucratic-ese of most government publications . . . The *Encyclopedia* is all written in a breezy, informal style meant to attract attention to all the wrongdoing even as it repeatedly details all the U.S. code violations and governmental regulations in question."[22]

At the state level, ethics education, support, and enforcement is provided through entities concerned with the executive branch in each state. For example, Kentucky's Executive Branch Ethics Commission lists its function and mission as

to promote the ethical conduct of elected officials, officers and other employees in the executive branch of state government. The Commission seeks to fulfill its mission through:

- administering a program of training and education on the code of ethics;
- providing guidance to state employees concerning their ethical conduct;
- enforcing the provisions of the code of ethics;
- interpreting the code of ethics through the issuance of advisory opinions;
- registering executive agency lobbyists; and
- recommending legislation to the General Assembly.

The office of the Commission reviews and houses records for public inspection including

- statements of financial disclosure required of elected officials, candidates and certain state employees;
- executive agency lobbyists registration statements;
- gift disclosure statements; and
- the day to day public record of the Commission.

The Commission's staff provides state employees, executive agency lobbyists and the public with information, guidance and training aimed at promoting ethical conduct of executive branch employees.[23]

Example: Gift Limits for Executive Branch Officials in Virginia

Following the high-profile case of bribery brought against his predecessor, Virginia governor Terence R. McAuliffe signed an executive order in January 2014 that set limits on gifts to Virginia executive branch employees:

Part I–Importance of the Initiative

Every citizen of the Commonwealth is entitled to have complete confidence and the highest degree of trust in Virginia's government. It is the intent of this Executive Order (the "Order") to ensure that Virginians are governed and represented with integrity. This Order is initiated to establish an ethical framework for state Executive Branch officers and employees with regard to gifts that will enhance the public's trust in the actions of such officers and employees by addressing the receipt of gifts that may result in, or create an appearance of, impropriety.

Part III–Personnel Directive – Prohibited Conduct

No officer or employee of the state Executive Branch or an immediate family member of such officer or employee shall (i.) solicit anything of value, or (ii.) accept, directly or indirectly, any gift from any lobbyist or from any principal or employee or agent of a principal, as the terms "lobbyist" and "principal" are defined in § 2.2-419 of the Commonwealth's lobbying laws, § 2.2-418 et seq. of the Code of Virginia, or (iii.) accept directly or indirectly, any gift valued at over $100, from any one source, singularly or in the aggregate over the course of any given calendar year. An officer or employee may receive or may be reimbursed for any legitimate travel and related expenses incurred while engaging in an activity that serves a legitimate public purpose. The receipt of anything of value with a value of $25 or less does not count toward the $100 cumulative total set forth in this paragraph.[24]

Example: Ethics Offices in Local Government

City and county ethics office and commissions perform similar functions at the local level. An example is the Board of Ethics for the City of Sioux Falls, SD:

> The proper operation of a republic requires that public officers and employees be honest, impartial, and responsible to the people; that governmental decisions and policy be made in the proper channels of the governmental structure; that public office not be used for personal gain; and that the public have confidence in the integrity of its government. The purpose of the Board of Ethics is to promote these beliefs through enforcement of the ethical standards set forth in the ordinances and charter provisions of the City of Sioux Falls.[25]

Ethics and Individual Action

Public administration scholars Herbert A. Simon, Victor A. Thompson, and Donald W. Smithburg assert that "administrators and employees . . . have considerable freedom to decide matters on the basis of their own ethical promptings."[26] Public administration scholar H. George Frederickson argues that because public administrators operate within particular contexts defined by rules, budgets, and enabling legislation, they practice **bounded ethics**, "generally accept[ing] the agency's purposes and policies, and practic[ing] ethics within those bounds."[27]

Whistleblowing or the leaking of information may reflect what employees regard as ethical behavior because they are revealing misconduct within their organizations. As discussed in Chapter 2, legal protections are in place to shield **whistleblowers** (those who observe and report an incident of illegal or wasteful activity involving their agency) from reprisals for their revelations, although enforcement of such protections by the Justice Department is not always zealous.

Procedural and legal requirements such as those administered by the OGE provide structural safeguards for ethical behavioral. Managers further can encourage an ethical climate by clearly specifying ethical standards (for an example, see Box 8.2), providing training, and conveying clear rules and expectations about appropriate behaviors and consequences of wrongdoing.[ii]

Public management scholar Christopher Pollitt has observed, however, that simply posting a code of ethics is insufficient for ensuring ethical behavior because "the existence and vigorous use of disciplinary procedures are likely to be a much more important curb on their activities than codes of ethics."[29]

[ii]See also the Organisation for Economic Co-operation and Development (OECD) report cited in Pollitt, *The Essential Public Manager;* OECD, *Principles for Managing Ethics in the Public Service,* PUMA Policy Brief no. 4, May 1998.

Box 8.2	**AMERICAN SOCIETY FOR PUBLIC ADMINISTRATION'S CODE OF ETHICS**[28]

The American Society for Public Administration (ASPA) advances the science, art, and practice of public administration. The Society affirms its responsibility to develop the spirit of responsible professionalism within its membership and to increase awareness and commitment to ethical principles and standards among all those who work in public service in all sectors. To this end, we, the members of the Society, commit ourselves to uphold the following principles

1. **Advance the Public Interest**. Promote the interests of the public and put service to the public above service to oneself.

2. **Uphold the Constitution and the Law.** Respect and support government constitutions and laws, while seeking to improve laws and policies to promote the public good.

3. **Promote democratic participation.** Inform the public and encourage active engagement in governance. Be open, transparent and responsive, and respect and assist all persons in their dealings with public organizations.

4. **Strengthen social equity.** Treat all persons with fairness, justice, and equality and respect individual differences, rights, and freedoms. Promote affirmative action and other initiatives to reduce unfairness, injustice, and inequality in society.

5. **Fully Inform and Advise.** Provide accurate, honest, comprehensive, and timely information and advice to elected and appointed officials and governing board members, and to staff members in your organization.

6. **Demonstrate personal integrity.** Adhere to the highest standards of conduct to inspire public confidence and trust in public service.

7. **Promote Ethical Organizations:** Strive to attain the highest standards of ethics, stewardship, and public service in organizations that serve the public.

8. **Advance Professional Excellence:** Strengthen personal capabilities to act competently and ethically and encourage the professional development of others.

Source: Reprinted with permission by the American Society for Public Administration (ASPA) www.aspanet.org.

Example: Ethics Violations by Director of Phoenix
Department of Veterans Affairs' Health Care System

In the summer of 2014, the Veterans Administration came under fire for delayed care for veterans (see case analysis at end of Chapter 9). At the center of the many of the charges was Sharon Helman, director of the Phoenix Department of Veterans Affairs (VA) Health Care System. A member of the Senior Executive Service, Helman was fired by the VA. An administrative judge for the Merit Systems Protection Board upheld Helman's firing, not for mismanaging the wait-lists for veterans seeking health care or for other direct management failures, but instead for ethical lapses that the agency was able to prove. In particular, Helman was found to have accepted gifts of airline tickets, a Disneyland vacation, and Beyoncé concert tickets from the vice president of a consulting group whose clients were contractors or potential contractors with the VA. The decision by Chief Administrative Judge Stephen C. Mish read, in part,

> as an SES Director of a sizable health care system with a large budget, one must be scrupulous to avoid even the appearance of a conflict of interest and to correctly report the things of monetary value one receives from others.

> Sincerely forgetting about one of the plane rides purchased for her might be understandable in some circumstances, but the notion she actually forgot them all strains credulity. Moreover, accepting gifts such as tickets to a popular performer's concert from a person who represents companies seeking to do business with the agency was, more probably than not, not an accident or mistake. I conclude the appellant's offenses are serious and more likely than not, intentional.

> I find she was on notice that not accurately completing the Office of Government Ethics Form 278 was actionable misconduct, because the form advised next to the signature box that by signing she was certifying that the statements she made on the form were true, correct and accurate to the best of her knowledge. The form also states in the following section that another official must certify that the appellant's answers avoid even the appearance of a conflict of interest.

> I conclude the appellant has little rehabilitative potential. She has steadfastly denied any wrongdoing in the course of this appeal and attempted to deflect attention from her own actions by pointing to political considerations and complaining the agency has been looking in to her private life. While it is likely that the political spectacle which followed the revelations about how the agency was conducting its business is what led the agency to apply scrutiny to her, taking a close look was not unwarranted under the circumstances. Moreover, even if it was somehow inappropriate for the agency to scrutinize the appellant in the manner it did, when the agency did look, it found serious financial improprieties on her part. They are not to be simply ignored. Her failure to take responsibility for any of the sustained misconduct does not support a finding of rehabilitative potential.[30]

VALUES

The drawing of rigorous distinctions between concepts such as ethics, values, and morals is a preoccupation of philosophers and theologians, even lawyers, and views differ on such distinctions. In very general terms, however, ethics are thought of as rules of personal conduct that distinguish between right and wrong. Values, in contrast, are beliefs that are the basis of personal judgments about what is true, just, virtuous, or appropriate. In public administration, values are reflected in beliefs about what is in the public interest, how to promote social justice, or what serves the greater good. From that perspective, morals might be thought of as a comprehensive system of values such as that derived from religion or ideology.

Individual Values

Individual participants in organizations hold intrinsic **values,** or "complex and broad-based assessment[s] of an object or set of objects . . . characterized by both cognitive and emotive elements, arrived at after some deliberation."[31] Dwight Waldo emphasized the role of values in democratic administration: "There is no realm of 'factual' decisions from which values are excluded. To decide is to choose between alternatives; to choose between alternatives is to introduce values." [32]

There is no realm of 'factual' decisions from which values are excluded. To decide is to choose between alternatives; to choose between alternatives is to introduce values.

Even public administrators' decisions regarding efficiency, which were often regarded as a technical matter, Waldo argued, were often value laden.

Values are one factor (though not the only one) in **local justice.** As noted in Chapter 6, Jon Elster has defined this concept in the context of frontline workers' decisions regarding the allocation of scarce resources such as college admissions, kidney transplants, military service, or immigration. For example, staff in welfare-to-work offices can exercise discretion and steer clients to particular activities such as basic education or job training. Within their scope of discretion, judges may require or allow participation in rehabilitation. In determining whom to treat and how, norms of thoroughness and compassion may guide a physician's decision instead of the economic incentives governing medical practice. Such decisions reflect local justice and are influenced by a number of factors including structures, politics, incentives, public opinion, and information.[33] They also reflect values and the professional norms developed through education and training (discussed in a later section of this chapter).

Example: Expressions of Religious Faith by Public Employees

Religious beliefs may be a source of spiritual or moral values for some individuals. These values may influence individual decisions or frameworks; religious beliefs may be visibly displayed through dress or other symbols. The U.S. Equal Employment Opportunity Commission describes the implications of Title VII of the Civil Rights Act of 1964 in its publication "Religious Garb and Grooming in the Workplace: Rights and Responsibilities." The guide includes a number of questions and answers, along with illustrative vignettes. One section directly concerns public employees:

> **11. Do government agencies whose employees work with the public have to make exceptions to uniform policies or otherwise allow religious dress and grooming practices if doing so would not cause an undue hardship?**
>
> Yes. Government agency employers, like private employers, must generally allow exceptions to dress and grooming codes as a religious accommodation, although there may be limited situations in which the need for uniformity of appearance is so important that modifying the dress or grooming code would pose an undue hardship. Therefore, it is advisable in all instances for employers to make a case-by-case determination of any needed religious exceptions.

EXAMPLE 12

Public Employee

Elizabeth, a librarian at a public library, wears a cross as part of her Catholic religious beliefs. In addition, after church services she attends on Ash Wednesday each year, Elizabeth arrives at work with a black ash mark on her forehead in the shape of a cross, which she leaves on until it wears off. Her new supervisor directs her not to wear the cross in the future while on duty, and to wash off the ash mark before reporting to work. Because Elizabeth's duties require her to interact with the public as a government employee, the supervisor fears that her cross and ash mark could be mistaken as government endorsement of religion in violation of the Establishment Clause of the First Amendment to the U.S. Constitution. He cites the need to avoid any appearance of religious favoritism by government employees interacting with the public, and emphasizes that librarians must be viewed as impartial with respect to any information requests from library patrons. However, because the librarian's cross and ash mark are clearly personal in this situation, they would not cause a perception of government endorsement of religion. Accordingly, accommodating Elizabeth's religious practice is not an undue hardship under Title VII.

EXAMPLE 13

Public Employee

Gloria, a newly hired municipal bus driver, was terminated when she advised her supervisor during new-employee orientation that due to the tenets of her faith (Apostolic Pentecostal), she needs to wear a skirt rather than the pants required by the transit agency dress code. Absent evidence that the type of skirt Gloria must wear would pose an actual safety hazard, no undue hardship would have been posed by allowing this dress code exception, and Gloria's termination would violate Title VII.[34]

Public Values

Public management scholar Barry Bozeman defines **public values** as providing "normative consensus about (a) the rights, benefits, and prerogatives to which citizens should (and should not) be entitled; (b) the obligations of citizens to society, the state, and one another; and (c) the principles on which governments and policies should be based."[35] Public management scholars Torben Beck Jørgensen and Barry Bozeman argue that public values are not solely reflected by government organizations but are associated with political authority.[36] This idea complements Bozeman's work on "degrees of publicness," discussed in Chapter 1, which locates public and private sector organizations along a continuum of authority from economic to political.[37]

To identify unique public values, Jørgensen and Bozeman examined more than 230 research articles published in public administration journals from 1990 to 2003.[38] They identified 72 unique public values (Table 8.1).

Example: Changing Values to Stop Racial Profiling

Racial profiling by local police departments is an example of the value categories "behaviors of public employees toward citizens" and "relationship between public administration and citizens" in the Jørgensen and Bozeman framework. The example below describes a case of racial profiling during traffic stops by New Jersey state troopers, reflecting a culture of racial bias in the organization. As a result of the particular incident described, the courts placed the New Jersey State Police under a consent decree that required federal supervision of their operations.

TABLE 8.1	**Values Found in Recent Public Administration Literature**

Value Category	Value Set
Public sector's contribution to society	• Common good (public interest, social cohesion) • Altruism (human dignity) • Sustainability (voice of the future) • Regime dignity (regime stability)
Transformation of interests to decisions	• Majority rule (democracy, will of the people, collective choice) • User democracy (local governance, citizen involvement) • Protection of minorities (protection of individual rights)
Relationship between public administrators and politicians	• Political loyalty (accountability, responsiveness)
Relationship between public administrators and their environment	• Openness-secrecy (responsiveness, listening to public opinion) • Advocacy-neutrality (compromise, balancing of interests) • Competitiveness-cooperativeness (stakeholder or shareholder value)
Intraorganizational aspects of public administration	• Robustness (adaptability, stability, reliability, timeliness) • Innovation (enthusiasm, risk-readiness) • Productivity (effectiveness, parsimony, business-like approach) • Self-development of employees (good working environment)
Behavior of public-sector employees	• Accountability (professionalism, honesty, moral standards, ethical consciousness, integrity)
Relationship between public administration and the citizens	• Legality (protection of rights of the individual, equal treatment, rule of law, justice) • Equity (reasonableness, fairness, professionalism) • Dialogue (responsiveness, user democracy, citizen involvement, citizen's self-development) • User orientation (timeliness, friendliness)

Source: Adapted from Torben Beck Jørgensen and Barry Bozeman, "Public Values: An Inventory," *Administration & Society* 39, no. 3 (2007): table 1, 360–361. © SAGE Publications, Inc.

This formal legal process was apparently successful in changing the culture of the state police, bringing about changes in values.

On the night of April 23, 1998, state troopers stopped three Black teenagers and one Hispanic teenager in a rented van on the New Jersey Turnpike. Claiming that the van backed toward them, the troopers opened fire, wounding basketball players heading south for a series of games. In defense of the troopers' actions, the state police superintendent characterized minority groups as being largely responsible for drug trafficking. His statements revealed a culture of racial bias within his organization. He was fired.

Attorney General Peter Verniero admitted that citizens were stopped and searched on the New Jersey Turnpike based on the color of their skin. Sued by the federal government, the State of New Jersey entered into a consent decree with the Justice Department in December 1999. As part of this decree, an independent monitor was assigned to review and analyze implementation of the numerous remedial provisions.

To gather data, video cameras were installed in the front of the patrol cars to tape troopers as they engaged drivers. In accepting a plea bargain in another lawsuit concerning the shooting of minority motorists in 2001, two troopers acknowledged that the state police taught racial profiling, that supervisors encouraged it, and that they and others tried to cover up racial profiling by providing false stop data. Two months later, the New Jersey Supreme Court, noting "widespread abuse of our existing laws," outlawed "consent searches" where no reasonable suspicion exists. Because of a culture that tolerated racial profiling, detailed interventions by higher levels of government and by the courts restricted the discretion of law enforcement officers. In September 2009, a U.S. federal court judge dissolved the consent decree, with ongoing monitoring to continue by the state attorney general's office. At the time, State Superintendent of Police Rick Fuentes observed,

> The court-ordered lifting of the federal consent decree represents a watershed moment for all of the more than four thousand members of the New Jersey State Police who have worked tirelessly to gain and maintain the public's trust and confidence through transparency, sound managerial oversight and holding fast to the best practices of police professionalism and reform.[39]

Ingrained values among New Jersey State Police seem to have undergone a major transformation during the consent decree period. At the end of 2014, racial tensions were high between police and local communities elsewhere in the country: Ferguson, Missouri; Cleveland, Ohio, New York City. Public values of police, among other frontline employees, remain an issue of enduring interest and controversy.

MOTIVES

Individuals' values and ethics in turn influence motives, though they do not necessarily dictate **motives**—"psychological constructs used to answer the question '*why* did she/he/they want to do that?'"[40] For example, the fundamental motive underlying rational choice theories and frameworks such as the principal-agent model and transaction cost theory (see Chapter 6) is self-interest: Individuals act in ways that, without necessarily violating their values or codes of ethics, further their own interests.[iii]

At the opposite end of the spectrum, stewardship theory asserts that individuals are motivated not by self-interest but by a desire to serve the collective so that their interest are aligned with, or even subordinated to, the organization and its leaders.[41] Although potentially useful for understanding the motives of public sector employees, the theory has been tested almost exclusively in private sector organizations.[iv]

One example that seems consistent with stewardship theory (but does not invoke it explicitly) is John D. DiIulio Jr.'s case study of the Federal Bureau of Prisons (BOP). He argues that rational choice models do not

---

[iii]For further information on assumptions of rational choice theory and its variants, see Chapter 2, "The Nature of Rational Choice Theory," in Donald P. Green and Ian Shapiro, *Pathologies of Rational Choice Theory: A Critique of Applications in Political Science* (New Haven, CT: Yale University Press, 1994), 13–32.

[iv]Principal-agent theory and stewardship theory were used to examine the government-nonprofit contracting relationship in David M. Van Slyke, "Agents or Stewards: Using Theory to Understand the Government-Nonprofit Social Service Contracting Relationship," *Journal of Public Administration Research and Theory* 17, no. 2 (2007): 157–187.

sufficiently characterize the motives of many participants in public organizations. Instead, DiIulio suggests an alternative model of "principled agents" "who do not shirk, subvert, or steal on the job even when the pecuniary and other tangible incentives to refrain from these behaviors are weak or nonexistent."[42] DiIulio develops this model based on observations of the behaviors and motives of BOP guards and managers:

> Rational choice theorists of bureaucracy underestimate the propensity of people to redefine their self-interest in terms of the preferences of leaders they respect, the wellbeing of co-workers they care about, and the survival and reputation of organizations they labor for. It may well be true that under most conditions, most bureaucrats, especially within government, follow narrow definitions of self-interest. But that is neither the whole story nor the most important part of the story of what public servants . . . do on a day-to-day basis. Even in the bowels of government agencies, there is more self-sacrifice, and less self-interest, than rational choice theory allows.[43]

In their theory of **public service motivation** (PSM), James L. Perry and Lois Recascino Wise propose a related framework for understanding motivation of employees in public organizations.[44] Drawing on work by Anthony Downs, Luther Gulick, Frederick Mosher, H. George Frederickson, and others, Perry and Wise argue that a unique PSM has three bases:

- *Rational motives* reflect an individual's personal interest or commitment to a particular program, desire to participate in the policy process (which can be exciting and personally fulfilling), and use of his or her public service position for advocacy for a favored position or group.
- *Norm-based motives* reflect an individual's interest in social equity, a sense of loyalty or duty to government itself, and a desire to serve the public interest.
- *Affective motives* reflect specific convictions about the particular program an individual works in. They may also reflect a "patriotism of benevolence"—a construct described by Frederickson and David K. Hart meaning "an extensive love of all people within our political boundaries and the imperative that they must be protected in all of the basic rights granted to them by the enabling documents."[45]

Empirical studies of the PSM framework have found some support for it. Studies suggest that PSM is positively related to organizational commitment; that whistleblowers exhibit higher levels of PSM than "inactive observers" (those who observe but do not report illegal activity); that PSM is positively associated with higher levels of job satisfaction, performance, and intention to remain in public service; that PSM is positively related to employees viewing their jobs as important and, in turn, to work effort; and that PSM is positively related to interpersonal citizenship ("helping behavior directed at coworkers") in public organizations.[46]

Not all studies have found positive effects of PSM, however. These inconsistent findings may be the result of a mediating influence: Bradley E. Wright and Sanjay K. Pandey find that the relationship between PSM and job satisfaction is "mediated by the extent to which the employee perceives that his or her values are congruent with those of the public sector organization."[47]

In their assessment of a wide range of PSM research, public management scholars Barry Bozeman and Xuhong Su note that burgeoning interest in the field has resulted in a lack of conceptual clarity or intended area of application.[48] Sometimes the concept is used in a way implying altruism, or service motivation, or prosocial motives;

it is also unresolved whether the concept is meant to apply uniquely to public organizations. Bozeman and Su suggest that development of PSM theory could be helped by validating it in laboratory studies and research that distinguishes between its environmental context and dispositional components.

Awareness of the motives of employees (to the extent they are observable) may be important for public sector managers in situations such as managing change or in personnel recruitment and selection.[v]

PROFESSIONS AND PROFESSIONAL TRAINING

Through their education and training, individuals may develop strong identification with **professional values and norms** that can transcend the cultures or norms of specific organizational contexts. These values and norms shape behavior and decisions. They also shape the professional's analytical reasoning processes:

- Lawyers tend to use "analogical reasoning and formal, inductive logic applied to the essential facts of a case."
- Medical doctors tend to employ "a highly compressed version of the formal logic of deductive science in which facts are examined in the light of pre-formed hypotheses as to what they might mean."
- Business and public administrators tend to reason in ways that are "experiential and associative, involving pattern recognition and intuition."[49]
- Policy analysts combine the analytically rigorous reasoning processes of law or medicine with the more experiential reasoning processes of business or public administrators. (One of the goals of this book is to encourage analysis and argument by public managers that incorporate theory, analytic frameworks, *and* experience.)

Structure, Culture, and Professionals

Trained and credentialed professions may influence the cultures of organizations directly through decisions that affect structure and service technology. As organizational sociologist W. Richard Scott observes,

> More so than other types of collective actors, the professions exercise control by defining social reality—by devising ontological frameworks, proposing distinctions, creating typifications, and fabricating principles or guidelines for action. They define the nature of many problems—from physical illness to economic degrees— monopolizing diagnostic techniques as well as treatment regimes. They underwrite the legitimacy of providers as well as practices.[50]

Changes in organizational priorities, structures, and cultures may occur a result of professionals' involvement:

- Political scientist James Q. Wilson contrasts the role of professionals in the U.S. Forest Service and the U.S. National Park Service. In the Forest Service, forestry professionals defined the work of the organization to be the "scientific management of forests in order to produce a sustained yield of timber and other natural resources." But the Park Service never encouraged an analogous professional "park ranger."[51] The result is

---

[v]In addition to the references cited in this section, see Marissa Golden, *What Motivates Bureaucrats? Politics and Administration During the Reagan Years* (New York, NY: Columbia University Press, 2000); H. George Frederickson, *The Spirit of Public Administration* (San Francisco, CA: Jossey-Bass, 1997); James L. Perry and Annie Hondeghem, eds., *Motivation in Public Management: The Call of Public Service* (Oxford, UK: Oxford University Press, 2008).

that the main focus of Park Service rangers tends to be on the protection and management of visitors, not on the physical aspects of the parks.

- The increased presence in social service organizations of managers with MBA degrees has resulted in tensions as their emphasis on the bottom line clashes with the more traditional social service values of line staff.
- Policy analysts won "a place at the decision table"[52] beginning in the 1960s and 1970s for their contributions of evidence-based, rigorous analysis.[53] Economist Alice Rivlin observed that "analysts have probably done more to reveal how difficult the problems and choices are than to make the decisions easier,"[54] shifting both the way work is done and organizational culture.
- In a study of policy analysts at the Department of Energy, political scientist Martha Feldman concluded that although the reports and information the policy analysts produced had little direct effect on decision making, their activities "affect[ed] the definition of problems and the composition of participants in the problem-solving process" and therefore their work was an important, if indirect, part of the decision-making process.[55]
- Political scientists Marc Allen Eisner and Kenneth J. Meier analyzed an initiative by an assistant attorney general in the Department of Justice to increase the staff of PhD economists and assign them more central roles in the selection of antitrust cases. Previously, this process had been dominated by legal staff.[56] Eisner and Meier were interested in whether this change would affect the types of antitrust cases—price-fixing, mergers, or monopoly—the agency pursued. They found,

> the economists' professional norms and values (as embodied in the dominant school of economic thought) came to play a central role in the definition of antitrust policy. The interplay of bureaucratic evolution and critical shifts in the economics discipline provided the basis for change in antitrust.[57]

Illustrating the central role that economists came to play, mandatory training in economics and industrial organization was conducted, and cases were pursued only if an economic analysis supported them.

The Role of Professionals in Ensuring Accountability

Professional norms and standards serve as guidance for responsible behavior (an "inner check") for individuals in public organizations. Unique and identifiable norms are developed through professional training and the shared experiences of professionals such as attorneys, doctors, scientists, researchers, teachers, police officers, firefighters, forest rangers, and social service workers, among others. James Q. Wilson describes how professional norms influence individual behavior:

Professional norms and standards serve as guidance for responsible behavior (an "inner check") for individuals in public organizations.

In bureaucracy, professionals are those employees who receive some significant portion of their incentives from organized groups of fellow practitioners located outside the agency . . . Because the behavior of a professional is not entirely shaped by organizational incentives, the way such a person defines his or her task may reflect more the standards of the external reference group than the preferences of the internal management.[58]

In their book *Working, Shirking, and Sabotage,* political scientists John Brehm and Scott Gates identified the role of professional norms and professionalism in ensuring responsible behavior. They sought to understand whether and why frontline bureaucrats

- *work* (comply with the wishes of their hierarchical superiors to perform assigned tasks),
- *shirk* (devote their effort to other tasks), or
- *sabotage* (actively undermine the work they are supposed to do).

Brehm and Gates base their study on modeling and on empirical analysis of social workers and police officers. They argue, "To the extent that professionalism provides a signal to supervisors about a bureaucrat's true type, then professionalism and functional preferences help to solve a significant part of the agency problem."[59] This fact, Brehm and Gates argue, points to the importance of the hiring process in selecting employees from the outset who will act responsibly and in ways consistent with the organization's preferences.

Public administration scholars Barbara S. Romzek and Melvin J. Dubnick emphasized the importance of the professions in one dimension of their accountability framework (discussed in Chapter 2). Central to this dimension is deference to expertise within an organization, built on the acknowledgment that professional accountability can be assumed or ensured through these externally influenced norms.[60]

Professional judgment, and thus reliance on professional accountability, may be affected by recent performance measurement reforms, public administration scholar Beryl Radin argues. Problems can arise when reforms remove discretion, at the core of professional accountability, especially when there is "a conflict between quality norms defined by a professional group and the fiscal agenda of the organization."[61] At the same time, professional accountability may be particularly important in situations where programs and services previously provided directly by public organizations have been outsourced.[62]

The presence of professionals in an organization is not a panacea for accountability problems, however. Economist Susan Rose-Ackerman observes, "An organizational designer must find the mixture of behavioral rules and discretion which assures that officials will be both competent and motivated." The balance between rules and discretion can favor the professionalism of public officials, especially if appropriate behavior or actions are uncertain. Among the pitfalls of this approach, though, is that

> strong professional norms may themselves conflict with agency goals, and the similar background and training of officials may lead them to band together to suppress criticism of their colleagues or, in extreme cases, to further collusive attempts to undermine agency purposes.[63]

The organizational designer may instead choose to emphasize rules that prescribe behavior, overcoming principal-agent problems but risking organizational rigidity and stifled professional motivation.

Under these conditions, Rose-Ackerman argues, pay-for-performance systems could be appropriate. The efficacy of such incentives would depend on the ability of officials to make clear connections between financial rewards and individual performance:

> Even seemingly quite straightforward cases may contain pitfalls which make the design of a workable economic incentive system difficult. . . . The design of a workable scheme of economic incentives depends on the measurability of output, on who can observe this output, and on the risk aversion of officials.[64]

If officials are risk averse and want to avoid any possibility their pay will be affected by factors beyond their control, and if the relationship between behavior and performance is poorly understood as it often is in public sector work, then reliance on professionalism may be superior to economic incentives.

CASE ANALYSIS: PAY IN PUBLIC ORGANIZATIONS

This case considers the role that culture might play in the implementation of structural reforms that link pay to performance for employees of public organizations. As discussed in Chapter 5, pay-for-performance systems are based on the idea that monetary incentives will promote greater employee effort, greater productivity, and higher performance. The suitability of pay for performance likely depends in large part on structural elements of the job: how specific tasks or accomplishments are rewarded.

But the culture dimension almost certainly matters as well. Two conceptual tools for gaining traction on the culture aspects are the gift exchange and the public service bargain.

Pay as Gift Exchange

Economist George A. Akerlof developed the idea of employee compensation as a **gift exchange:** the exchange of labor for wages is based partially on norms of behavior that are determined by the employment relationship itself.[65] He argues that employees develop sentiments for their fellow employees and for the organization for which they work.

As part of these sentiments, norms of behavior develop based on a comparison of one's own situation with others in the organization. Norms of "fairness" and fair treatment arise from these comparisons, with the resulting norms being relative, not absolute.

Basing his claims on empirical evidence and formal modeling, Akerlof shows that the optimal labor contract may not set wages at the minimum level acceptable to the employee. The idea is that just as part of worker effort is a gift, so, too are a part of wages.

In public organizations, employees may be motivated by public service values. On top of this, norms of fair treatment have evolved over time as part of the traditional pay systems (often protection through the civil service system, described in Chapter 5). Together, these aspects of public service values and traditional pay system norms constitute a traditional, and entrenched, gift exchange in public organizations.

Pay-for-performance systems introduce arrangements where labor contracts define market-determined wages for individuals of different capabilities and skills. Measured performance determines wage increases. Such pay-for-performance reforms may mute or threaten the traditional gift exchange and may undermine the relevance of public service values to work in public organizations.

Pay as a Public Service Bargain

Christopher Hood's description of **public service bargains**, or "reciprocal exchange relationships between public servants and other actors in a political system"[66] is related to Akerlof 's gift exchange idea.

Hood argues that public sector reforms often involve essential changes in the nature of a public service bargain. Various provisions of the merit systems at federal, state, and local levels have traditionally characterized the public service bargain for public sector employees. Pay for performance represents a fundamentally different kind of relationship between public employees and other actors.

In particular, Hood is concerned with the greater use of the **thermostatic control model** of a public service bargain. In these mechanisms, heads of government units are given outputs to achieve and latitude in choosing ways to achieve them. Output measurements are obtained, and rewards or sanctions are meted out accordingly: rewards if desired output is exceeded, sanctions or penalties if output falls short of desired output. The No Child Left Behind Act is an example of a thermostatic control mechanism.

The public service bargain implied by such reforms, can be characterized in this way:

> Public managers accept career risk and personal blame in exchange for some decision autonomy and—in most versions—pay and perks at a managerial level, while politicians undertake to steer managers only by transparent and achievable preset objectives in exchange for avoidance of formal blame for operational failures.[67]

In other words, the public service bargain for these reforms involves

- policymakers giving up on assigning impossible jobs to agencies and then holding them responsible when these jobs are not done well;
- policymakers also giving up the practice of controlling executive agencies by controlling what they do or what they spend rather than what they accomplish; and
- public employees agreeing to devote their creative efforts and energies toward accomplishing the highest outputs achievable with the resources appropriated to them.

Is Performance Pay Reform Worth the Price?

Viewed through the lens of either the gift exchange or the public service bargain, pay for performance in public sector organizations represents more than just a structural shift for public employees.

Public management scholar Donald Moynihan has cautioned that these kinds of reforms may stamp out benefits from public service motivation in two ways:

(1) through a selection effect, by attracting and retaining those with primarily extrinsic motivations; and

(2) through an incentive effect, by crowding out intrinsic motivations.[68]

Two examples of the clashes between contract incentives and frontline work motivations can be found in the job training and welfare-to-work literatures:

(Continued)

(Continued)

- In their retrospective of performance management and incentives, Carolyn Heinrich and Gerald Marshke describe research findings from the Job Training Partnership Act (JTPA) sites:

  . . . the hiring of caseworkers in Corpus Christi, Texas, who exhibited strong preferences for serving the disadvantaged, in line with a stated goal of JTPA to help those most in need, likely lowered service costs (i.e., wage costs) in Corpus Christi. Alternatively, an emphasis on client labor market outcomes in a Chicago area agency that was exceptional in its attention to and concern for meeting the federal performance standards appeared to temper these public-service motivations . . . .

  With performance expectations strongly reinforced by administrators and in performance-based contracts, caseworkers' client intake and service assignment decisions were more likely to be made with attention to their effects on meeting performance targets and less so with concern for who would benefit most from the services (the other basic goal of the JTPA legislation).[69]

- The implementation of contract incentives in a for-profit welfare-to-work office was analyzed by Janice Johnson Dias and Steven Maynard-Moody:

  To achieve low-cost rapid job placement, management sought to curtail staff attention to clients' needs, but those efforts were never fully successful. Staff continually revolted, and this led to a chaotic and hostile environment, not efficiency. This clash between cost-cutting managers and service-oriented street-level worker was predictable, almost inevitable. Frontline staff were hired for their devotion to client-centered service—they were social workers by either training and/or orientation—yet at WorkOpts they were being asked to forgo their training and ethics for an economic model that they maintain did not benefit them or their clients.[70]

It remains to be seen whether public service values as a motivating factor influence the successful implementation of performance pay systems (including the response of employees to the specific incentives that are introduced, such as tying promotions and pay raises to student test scores). It also remains to be seen whether the organizational cultures of different public organizations can accommodate and adapt to the changing public service bargains and gift exchanges represented by pay for performance.

Discussion Questions

Chapter 5 included an excerpt from a 2014 Florida law that instituted teacher pay for performance in the state's public schools. Similar reforms have been implemented or discussed in other jurisdictions.

1. What are the possible values and motives of individuals who choose to become K-12 public school teachers?

2. What kinds of professional training do K-12 public school teachers receive?

3. What role do teachers' unions play in in the determination of how and what teachers are paid?

4. Consider the concepts of gift exchange and the public service bargain in traditional teacher compensation systems with their emphasis on credentials and seniority.

   a. How would you characterize the way these concepts might be reflected in traditional systems of teacher pay?

   b. How would you characterize how these concepts might be reflected in or incorporated into pay-for-performance systems?

5. When pay-for-performance systems are implemented for K-12 teachers:

   a. do you anticipate selection effects or incentive effects like those described by Donald Moynihan? Locate empirical evidence from research that can inform your analysis.

   b. do you anticipate responses analogous to those described in the case in job training and welfare-to-work offices? Or, based on your analyses of the previous questions, do you anticipate different responses? Locate empirical evidence from research that can inform your analysis.

NOTES

1. "About Early Head Start," Early Head Start National Resource Center, last updated September 30, 2014, https://eclkc.ohs.acf .hhs.gov/hslc/tta-system/ehsnrc/about-ehs.

2. "§ 1304.52 Human resources management," Head Start, accessed May 7, 2015, http://eclkc.ohs.acf.hhs.gov/hslc/standards/ hspps/1304/1304.52%20Human%20resources%20management..htm.

3. "Supporting Our Youngest Children: Early Head Start Programs in 2010," CLASP, March 2012, http://www.clasp.org/resources-and-publications/ publication-1/EHS-Trend-Analysis-Final.pdf.

4. Ibid.

5. "Home-based Program Option," Early Head Start National Research Center, last updated March 31, 2015, http://eclkc.ohs.acf .hhs.gov/hslc/tta-system/ehsnrc/poi/home-based/home.html.

6. "Head Start and Early Head Start Relationship-based Competencies for Staff and Supervisors Who Work with Families," The National Center on Parent, Family, and Community Engagement, June 6, 2012, https://eclkc.ohs.acf.hhs.gov/hslc/tta-system/family/foundations/ ohs-rbc.pdf, 3

7. Ibid. 5, 13.

8. Woodrow Wilson, "The Study of Administration," *Political Science Quarterly* 2 (1887): 216.

9. John Dickinson, *Administrative Justice and the Supremacy of Law in the United States* (New York, NY: Russell and Russell, 1927), 277.

10. John M. Gaus, "The Responsibility of Public Administration," in *The Frontiers of Public Administration,* ed. John M. Gaus, Leonard D. White, and Marshall E. Dimock (Chicago, IL: University of Chicago Press, 1936), 26–44, 40; Anthony M. Bertelli and Laurence E. Lynn Jr., *Madison's Managers: Public Administration and the Constitution* (Baltimore, MD: Johns Hopkins University Press, 2006).

11. Bertelli and Lynn, *Madison's Managers.*

12. Herman Finer, "Administrative Responsibility in Democratic Government," *Public Administration Review* 1, (1940): 336.

13. Carl J. Friedrich, "Public Policy and the Nature of Administrative Responsibility," in *Public Policy: A Yearbook of the Graduate School of Public Administration, Harvard University, 1940,* ed. Carl Friedrich and Edward Mason (Cambridge, MA: Harvard University Press, 1940), 3–24.

14. John A. Rohr, *To Run a Constitution: The Legitimacy of the Administrative State* (Lawrence: University Press of Kansas, 1986), 181.

15. Robert B. Denhardt, *The Pursuit of Significance: Strategies for Managerial Success in Public Organization*s (Belmont, CA: Wadsworth, 1993), 20.

16. H. George Frederickson, *The Spirit of Public Administration* (San Francisco, CA: Jossey-Bass, 1997), 229.

17. Christopher Pollitt, *The Essential Public Manager* (Maidenhead, UK: Open University Press, 2003), 133.

18. "Mission & Responsibilities," United States Office of Government Ethics, access date January 7, 2015, http://www.oge.gov/About/Mission-and-Responsibilities/Mission—Responsibilities.

19. "Standards of Ethical Conduct for Employees of the Executive Branch," 5 C.F.R. Part 2635, United States Office of Government Ethics, August 7, 1992, http://www.oge.gov/Laws-and-Regulations/Employee-Standards-of-Conduct/Employee-Standards-of-Conduct.

20. "Standards of Conduct Office," Department of Defense, last updated May 30, 2014, http://www.dod.mil/dodgc/defense_ethics.

21. Standards of Conduct Office, Office of General Counsel, Department of Defense, "Encyclopedia of Ethical Failure," updated October 2014, p. 3.

22. Gordon Lubold, "The Military Has Cataloged Its Ethical Failures, and They're Kind of Awesome," *Foreign Policy*, January 30, 2014, http://foreignpolicy.com/2014/01/30/the-military-has-cataloged-its-ethical-failures-and-theyre-kind-of-awesome.

23. "Authority," Executive Branch Ethics Commission: Commonwealth of Kentucky, accessed January 7, 2015, http://ethics.ky.gov/Pages/default.aspx.

24. "Governor McAuliffe Signs Executive Order Establishing Gift Limit for Administration Officials and Executive Branch Ethics Commission," press release, Virginia.Gov, January 11, 2014, https://governor.virginia.gov/newsroom/newsarticle?articleId=2562.

25. "Board of Ethics," City of Sioux Falls, accessed January 7, 2015, http://www.siouxfalls.org/mayor/boards-commissions/board-ethics.aspx.

26. Herbert A. Simon, Victor A. Thompson, and Donald W. Smithburg, *Public Administration* (New Brunswick, NJ: Transaction, 1991), 539.

27. Frederickson, *The Spirit of Public Administration*, 171.

28. "Code of Ethics (revised March 2013)," American Society for Public Administration, http://www.aspanet.org/public/ASPA/About_ASPA/Code_of_Ethics/ASPA/Resources/Code_of_Ethics/Code_of_Ethics1.aspx?hkey=222cd7a5-3997-425a-8a12-5284f81046a8.

29. Pollitt, *The Essential Public Manager*, 147.

30. Sharon Helman v. Department of Veterans Affairs, DE-0707-15-0091-J-1, United States of America Merit Systems Protection Board: Denver Field Office, December 22, 2014, http://www.mspb.gov/netsearch/viewdocs.aspx?docnumber=1122129&version=1126602&application=ACROBAT, pages 58, 59, 60, 61.

31. Barry Bozeman, *Public Values and Public Interest: Counterbalancing Economic Individualism* (Washington, DC: Georgetown University Press, 2007), 117.

32. Dwight Waldo, "Development of Theory of Democratic Administration," *American Political Science Review* 46, no. 1 (1952): 81–103, 97.

33. Jon Elster, *Local Justice* (New York, NY: Russell Sage Foundation, 1992), 143.

34. "Religious Garb and Grooming in the Workplace: Rights and Responsibilities: sec.11," U.S. Equal Employment Opportunity Commission, accessed January 7, 2015, http://www1.eeoc.gov//eeoc/publications/qa_religious_garb_grooming.cfm?renderforprint=1#_ftn11.

35. Bozeman, *Public Values and Public Interest*, 13.

36. Torben Beck Jørgensen and Barry Bozeman, "Public Values: An Inventory," *Administration & Society* 39, no. 3 (2007): 354–381.

37. Barry Bozeman, *All Organizations are Public: Bridging Public and Private Organizational Theories* (San Francisco, CA: Jossey-Bass, 1987).

38. Jørgensen and Bozeman, "Public Values: An Inventory," 354–381.

39. "State Police Racial Profiling Consent Decree Dissolved: Federal Judge Acts on Joint Petition by State and U.S. Justice Department," press release, Office of the Attorney General: The State of New Jersey, September 21, 2009, http://www.nj.gov/oag/newsreleases09/pr20090921a.html.

40. Pollitt, *The Essential Public Manager*, 133.

41. James H. David, F. David Schoorman, and Lex Donaldson, "Toward a Stewardship Theory of Management," *Academy of Management Review* 22, no. 1 (1997): 37.

42. John D. DiIulio Jr., "Principled Agents: The Cultural Bases of Behavior in a Federal Government Bureaucracy," *Journal of Public Administration Research and Theory* 4, no. 3 (1994): 277–318, 282.

43. Ibid., 316.

44. James L. Perry and Lois Recascino Wise, "The Motivational Bases of Public Service," *Public Administration Review* 50, no. 3 (1990): 368.

45. H. George Frederickson and David K. Hart, "The Public Service and the Patriotism of Benevolence," *Public Administration Review* 45 (September/October 1985): 547–553, 549.

46. Philip E. Crewson, "Public-Service Motivation: Building Empirical Evidence of Incidence and Effect," *Journal of Public Administration Research and Theory* 7, no. 4 (1997): 499–518; Gene A. Brewer and Sally Coleman Selden, "Whistle Blowers in the Federal Civil Service: New Evidence of the Public Service Ethic," *Journal of Public Administration Research and Theory* 8, no. 3 (1998): 413–439; Katherine C. Naff and John Crum, "Working for America: Does Public Service Motivation Make a Difference?" *Review of Public Personnel Administration* 19, no. 4 (1999): 5–16; Bradley E. Wright, "Public Service Motivation: Does Mission Matter?" *Public Administration Review* 67, no. 1 (2007): 54–64; Sanjay K. Pandey, Bradley E. Wright, and Donald P. Moynihan, "Public Service Motivation and Interpersonal Citizenship Behavior in Public Organizations: Testing a Preliminary Model," *International Public Management Journal* 11, no. 1 (2008): 89–108.

47. Bradley E. Wright and Sanjay K. Pandey, "Public Service Motivation and the Assumption of Person-Organization Fit: Testing the Mediating Effect of Value Congruence," *Administration & Society* 40, no. 5 (2008): 502–521.

48. Barry Bozeman and Xuhong Su, "Public Service Motivation Concepts and Theory: A Critique," *Journal of Public Administration and Theory*, July 22 2014, http://onlinelibrary.wiley.com/enhanced/doi/10.1111/puar.12248.

49. Laurence E. Lynn Jr., *Teaching and Learning with Cases* (Chappaqua, NY: Seven Bridges Press, 1999), 7, 9, 11.

50. W. Richard Scott. *Organizations: Rational, Natural and Open Systems*, 4th ed. (Upper Saddle River, NJ.: Prentice Hall, 1998), 211.

51. Wilson, *Bureaucracy*, 64–65.

52. Alice Rivlin, *Systematic Thinking for Social Action* (Washington, DC: Brookings Institution, 1971), 4.

53. Laurence E. Lynn Jr., "A Place at the Table: Policy Analysis, Its Postpositive Critics, and the Future of Practice," *Journal of Policy Analysis and Management* 18, no. 3 (1999): 411–424.

54. Rivlin, *Systematic Thinking for Social Action*, 5.

55. Martha S. Feldman, *Order without Design: Information Production and Policy Making* (Stanford, CA: Stanford University Press, 1989).

56. Marc Allen Eisner and Kenneth J. Meier, "Presidential Control Versus Bureaucratic Power: Explaining the Reagan Revolution in Antitrust," *American Journal of Political Science* 34, no. 1 (1990): 269–287.

57. Ibid., 283.

58. James Q. Wilson, *Bureaucracy: What Government Agencies Do and Why They Do It* (New York, NY: Basic Books, 1989), 60.

59. John Brehm and Scott Gates, *Working, Shirking, and Sabotage: Bureaucratic Response to a Democratic Public* (Ann Arbor: University of Michigan Press, 1999), 202.

60. Barbara S. Romzek and Melvin J. Dubnick, "Accountability in the Public Sector: Lessons from the Challenger Tragedy," Public Administration Review 47, no. 3 (May/June 1987)

61. Beryl A. Radin, *Challenging the Performance Movement: Accountability, Complexity, and Democratic Values* (Washington DC: Georgetown University Press, 2006), 238.

62. Donald F. Kettl, *The Transformation of Governance: Public Administration for Twenty-First Century America* (Baltimore, MD: Johns Hopkins University Press, 2002); Barbara S. Romzek, "Where the Buck Stops: Accountability in Reformed Public Organizations," in *Transforming Government: Lessons from the Reinvention Laboratories*, ed. Patricia W. Ingraham, James R. Thompson, and Ronald P. Sanders (San Francisco, CA: Jossey-Bass, 1998), 193–219; Laurence E. Lynn, Jr., *Public Management: Old and New* (New York, NY: Routledge, 2006). See also Stephen Page, "The Web of Managerial Accountability: The Impact of Reinventing Government," *Administration & Society* 38, no. 2 (May 2006): 166–197.

63. Susan Rose-Ackerman, "Reforming Public Bureaucracy through Economic Incentives?" *Journal of Law, Economics and Organization* 2, no. 1 (1986): 131, 132.

64. Ibid., 131, 133.

65. George A. Akerlof, "Contracts as Partial Gift Exchange," *Quarterly Journal of Economics* 97, no. 4 (November 1982): 543–569.

66. Christopher Hood, "Control, Bargains, and Cheating: The Politics of Public-Service Reform," *Journal of Public Administration Research and Theory* 12, no. 3 (2002): 309–332, 310.

67. Ibid., 310.

68. Donald P. Moynihan, "The Normative Model in Decline? Public Service Motivation in the Age of Governance," in *Motivation in Public Management: The Call of Public Service,* eds. James L. Perry and Annie Hondeghem (Oxford, UK: Oxford University Press: 2008), 248.

69. Carolyn J. Heinrich and Gerald Marshke, "Incentives and Their Dynamics in Public Sector Performance Management Systems," *Journal of Policy Analysis and Management* 29, no. 1 (2010): 191.

70. Janice Johnson Dias and Steven Maynard-Moody, "For-Profit Welfare: Contracts, Conflicts, and the Performance Paradox," *Journal of Public Administration Research and Theory* 17 (2007): 207-208.

9 Culture

Institutionalized Values

INTRODUCTION

Institutionalized values, or organizational cultures, constitute the shared norms, values, and understandings that provide meaning, purpose, and motivation to individuals in their roles as employees of an organizational unit. Organizational cultures are the shared experiences resulting from both low- and high-profile successes and failures, patterns of conduct, and self-regulating practices in an organization. Whether they are explicit or implicit, organizational cultures shape the ingrained views and habitual behaviors of workers at all levels of the organization—field-level workers, middle managers, and senior career officials.

The culture dimension is fundamental to an organization's capacity to carry out its lawful responsibilities. Culture can infuse employees with beliefs and values that enhance the organization's reputation for reliability and competent service, integrity, and performance, or it can produce a set of dysfunctional and unproductive responses that harm the organization's reputation.

Organizational cultures may have significant negative or positive implications for organizational effectiveness. Further, organizational cultures may have significant negative or positive implications for structural strategies and managerial ambition and entrepreneurship.

This chapter begins with a case describing how institutionalized values mattered in the space shuttle *Columbia* disaster. Next, organizational culture is defined as institutionalized values, and this understanding is placed in historical perspective. The section discusses aspects of how culture supports or impedes rules and routines in an organization: through mission, through special roles in loosely coupled organizations and high-reliability organizations, through learning and innovating organizations, and through establishing reputation and trust. The next section addresses the central role of culture in any reform efforts. The end-of-chapter case considers reports of the "corrosive culture" at the Veterans Health Administration as well as efforts to change that culture.

> Culture can infuse employees with beliefs and values that enhance the organization's reputation for reliability and competent service, integrity, and performance, or it can produce a set of dysfunctional and unproductive responses that harm the organization's reputation.

CASE: THE SPACE
SHUTTLE *COLUMBIA* ACCIDENT

On February 1, 2003, the National Aeronautics and Space Administration (NASA) space shuttle *Columbia* disintegrated while returning to earth after a 16-day scientific mission, known within NASA as STS-107, killing its seven crew members. On the day of the accident, NASA administrator Sean O'Keefe appointed a 12-member Columbia Accident Investigation Board (CAIB) board to investigate it. The CAIB was chaired by retired admiral Harold Gehman, an experienced investigator and military commander.

Less than 7 months later, the CAIB issued a report containing a detailed analysis of the *Columbia* accident's causes, along with 29 recommendations for ensuring the space shuttle program's safe return to flight.[i] As will be discussed in Chapter 12, the CAIB's analysis demonstrates how multiple dimensions of public management contribute to understanding the *Columbia* accident. The CAIB's report was notable, among other reasons, for its emphasis on the organizational culture of NASA that contributed to the *Columbia* accident. This emphasis is illustrated with this CAIB report excerpt:

> The human space flight culture within NASA originated in the Cold War environment. The space agency itself was created in 1958 as a response to the Soviet launch of Sputnik, the first artificial Earth satellite. In 1961, President John F. Kennedy charged the new space agency with the task of reaching the moon before the end of the decade, and asked Congress and the American people to commit the immense resources for doing so, even though at the time NASA had only accumulated 15 minutes of human space flight experience. With its efforts linked to U.S.-Soviet competition for global leadership, there was a sense in the NASA workforce that the agency was engaged in a historic struggle central to the nation's agenda.

> The Apollo era created at NASA an exceptional "can-do" culture marked by tenacity in the face of seemingly impossible challenges. This culture valued the interaction among research and testing, hands-on engineering experience, and a dependence on the exceptional quality of its workforce and leadership that provided in-house technical capability to oversee the work of contractors. The culture also accepted risk and failure as inevitable aspects of operating in space, even as it held as its highest value attention to detail in order to lower the chances of failure.

> The dramatic Apollo 11 lunar landing in July 1969 fixed NASA's achievements in the national consciousness, and in history. However, the numerous accolades in the wake of the moon landing also helped reinforce the NASA staff's faith in their organizational culture. Apollo successes created the powerful image of the space agency as a "perfect place," as "the best organization that human

---

[i]Press releases related to the CAIB's activities are available *at* http://govinfo.library.unt.edu/caib/news/press_releases/default.html. The full CAIB report as well as other information related to the *Columbia* are available on the NASA website, http://www.nasa.gov/columbia/home/index.html.

(Continued)

(Continued)

beings could create to accomplish selected goals." . . . During Apollo, NASA was in many respects a highly successful organization capable of achieving seemingly impossible feats. The continuing image of NASA as a "perfect place" in the years after Apollo left NASA employees unable to recognize that NASA never had been, and still was not, perfect, nor was it as symbolically important in the continuing Cold War struggle as it had been for its first decade of existence. NASA personnel maintained a vision of their agency that was rooted in the glories of an earlier time, even as the world, and thus the context within which the space agency operated, changed around them.

As a result, NASA's human space flight culture never fully adapted to the Space Shuttle Program, with its goal of routine access to space rather than further exploration beyond low-Earth orbit. The Apollo-era organizational culture came to be in tension with the more bureaucratic space agency of the 1970s, whose focus turned from designing new spacecraft at any expense to repetitively flying a reusable vehicle on an ever-tightening budget. This trend toward bureaucracy and the associated increased reliance on contracting necessitated more effective communications and more extensive safety oversight processes than had been in place during the Apollo era, but the Rogers Commission found that such features were lacking.

In the aftermath of the Challenger accident, these contradictory forces prompted a resistance to externally imposed changes and an attempt to maintain the internal belief that NASA was still a "perfect place," alone in its ability to execute a program of human space flight. Within NASA centers, as Human Space Flight Program managers strove to maintain their view of the organization, they lost their ability to accept criticism, leading them to reject the recommendations of many boards and blue-ribbon panels, the Rogers Commission among them.

External criticism and doubt, rather than spurring NASA to change for the better, instead reinforced the will to "impose the party line vision on the environment, not to reconsider it," according to one authority on organizational behavior. This in turn led to "flawed decision making, self-deception, introversion and a diminished curiosity about the world outside the perfect place." . . . The NASA human space flight culture the Board found during its investigation manifested many of these characteristics, in particular a self-confidence about NASA possessing unique knowledge about how to safely launch people into space . . . the Board views this cultural resistance as a fundamental impediment to NASA's effective organizational performance.[1]

As the CAIB emphasized, at least part of NASA's early successes were associated with its "can-do" organizational culture, showing how the informal aspects of organizations can prove to be a source of stability, motivation, and reliability. Such stable cultures can provide continuity and an insulating buffer in the face of ill-conceived or politically motivated attempts to impose change that might go undetected by existing structures for oversight and approval. Yet resistance to change may have a downside, as it may present obstacles to implementing necessary structural changes such as oversight reforms and the realignment of agency priorities.

In the *Columbia* case, institutionalized values were reflected by shuttle program managers who subordinated safety to maintenance of flight schedules and budgets, by the reluctance of NASA employees to speak up forcefully in opposition to those values, and by the acceptance of risks to flight safety from debris strikes as normal and acceptable.

WHAT ARE INSTITUTIONALIZED VALUES?

Institutionalized values provide a unifying source of meaning and purpose to organizational participants. **Institutionalization** is the process by which the members of an organization "acquire values that go beyond the technical requirements of organizational tasks" or "the emergence of orderly, stable, socially integrating patterns out of unstable, loosely organized, or narrowly technical activities."[2] James G. March and Johan P. Olsen define **institutions** as "the beliefs, paradigms, codes, cultures, and knowledge that support rules and routines."[3] They argue that organizational participants seek to act in ways consistent with their institutional environment.[4]

Institutionalized values may also be viewed as **organizational culture**. An extensive literature on organizational culture, much of it concerned with the private sector, has sought to define the term and capture its role in an organization.[i] Definitions tend to emphasize the informal, shared, and functional aspects of organizational life:

- "the tribal aspect of contemporary organizations"[5]
- "the way we do things around here"[6]
- "persistent, patterned way of thinking about the central tasks of and human relationships within an organization." [7]
- "a pattern of shared basic assumptions that the group learned as it solved its problems of external adaptation and internal integration, that has worked well enough to be considered valid and, therefore, to be taught to new members as the correct way to perceive, think, and feel in relation to those problems." [8]
- "(1) substance, which consists of shared systems of beliefs, values, and norms, and (2) forms, which are observable ways that members of a culture express cultural ideas."[9]

Organizations are unlikely to have just a single overarching culture. Instead, multiple cultures or subcultures are often present. Different bases for these subcultures include

- occupations in the organization;
- informal groups in the organization (friends and coalitions);
- formal groups in the organization (technology and work flows, departments, line and staff distinctions, and hierarchical differences); and
- managerial cultures or demographic groups that transcend organizational boundaries.[10]

> **Organizations are unlikely to have just a single overarching culture. Instead, multiple cultures or subcultures are often present.**

---

[i]For comprehensive treatments of organizational culture, see Linda Smircich, "Concepts of Culture and Organizational Analysis," *Administrative Science Quarterly* 28 (1983): 339–358; Harrison M. Trice and Janice M. Beyer, *The Cultures of Work Organizations* (Englewood Cliffs, NJ: Prentice Hall, 1993); Edgar H. Schein, *Organizational Culture and Leadership,* 2nd ed. (San Francisco, CA: Jossey-Bass, 1992); J. Steven Ott, *The Organizational Culture Perspective* (Chicago, IL: Dorsey Press, 1989). See Ott's Chapter 3 appendix for many different definitions of organizational culture found in the literature.

Example: Blending Multiple Cultures at the Department of Homeland Security

In January 2007 the Culture Task Force (CTF) of the Department of Homeland Security (DHS) Advisory Council issued its report with recommendations for "creating and sustaining an energetic, dedicated, and empowering mission-focused organization." Its fourth recommendation addressed the issue of multiple cultures in the department:

> The CTF believes that given the diversity, history and strong culture of many of its component organizations, there can be no hierarchically imposed "single culture" within the Department. We do, however, believe that an overarching and blended culture can be developed that is based on threads of common values, goals, and focus of mission among DHS Headquarters and its component organizations. The CTF recommends that the Secretary appoint a senior career/general schedule homeland security employee reporting to the Secretary to assist/support the Secretary in the continuous development and sustainment of the overarching/blended culture within the Department. With the support and direction of the Secretary and supported by staff from all DHS components, this leader will help develop the Secretary's overarching cultural vision and the strategic goals required to create the desired diverse but mission focused Homeland Security culture. This individual will also provide staff support for monitoring, testing, and supporting the continuous improvement of that culture with ultimate emphasis upon the readiness and the esprit de corps of the "troops in the field."[11]

The potential problem of merging multiple cultures had been identified years earlier, when the department was formed.[ii] The problems were echoed in a 2014 press report on DHS staff turnover. It pointed to culture, among other factors, for the challenges the agency continues to face:

> In small and not-so-small ways, some unique to DHS and others not, the department can be an infuriating, exhausting place to work, numerous former and current officials say. The frustrations reflect the fundamental wiring of the department, which was created by plucking 22 autonomous agencies from across the government and welding them into one.
>
> Today, employees describe a stifling bureaucracy made up of agencies with clashing employee cultures and overtaxed by high-pressure responsibilities and relentless congressional carping.[12]

Unfortunately, foreseeing the potential problems with combining multiple cultures when DHS was formed, along with the efforts of the Culture Task Force, have not been enough to overcome the culture problems in DHS.

HISTORICAL PERSPECTIVE

The publication in 1938 of Chester I. Barnard's *The Functions of the Executive* established an organizational context for considering how the values and ingrained norms of workers influence organizational behavior.[13] In their report on the famous Hawthorne studies of worker motivation at a manufacturing plant, Fritz Roethlisberger and William J. Dickson described how the informal norms of workers, the "informal organization," could frustrate the achievement of management's goals.[14]

[ii]See, for example, Louis Jacobsen, "Merging Cultures of Homeland Security Agencies Will be a Big Challenge," *Government Executive*, June 13, 2002, http://www.govexec.com/management/2002/06/merging-cultures-of-homeland-security-agencies-will-be-big-challenge/11842/; Michael Scardaville, "Principles the Department of Homeland Security Must Follow for an Effective Transition," February 28, 2003, http://www.heritage.org/research/reports/2003/02/principles-the-department-of-homeland-security.

Herbert A. Simon incorporated the notion of an informal organization in tension with the formal structure into public administration doctrine. In *Administrative Behavior: A Study of Decision-Making Processes in Administrative Organizations,* Simon defines **informal organization** as "interpersonal relationships in the organization that affect decisions within it but either are omitted from the formal [organization chart] or are not consistent with that scheme." Formal and informal organizations are interrelated, Simon argued. Because it cannot govern behavior in detail, the formal organization requires an informal organization to supplement it. The function of the formal organization, in turn, is to prevent the informal organization from becoming dysfunctional and to encourage "attitudes of cooperation within the formal structure."[15]

Beginning in the 1950s, the term *organizational culture* began to appear regularly in academic journals such as *Administrative Science Quarterly* and *Public Administration Review.* One concern was how individuals with particular civic values, such as those who recognized "no patterned authority," could be socialized into the acceptance of bureaucratic values. In his 1968 study of an antipoverty agency in southern Appalachia, Robert Denhardt argued that socialization was "an essential element of organizational maintenance."[16] With respect to deference to authority, Denhardt found that organizational culture can overcome the influence of the local area's civic culture, while integrating local values into the work of the organization.

The concept of organizational culture matured as a subject of academic investigation in the 1980s. Organizational culture scholar Edgar Schein sees the origins of the field in social psychological studies of group norms and organizational climate.[17] But, in their 1985 survey article "Organizational Culture," William Ouchi and Alan Wilkins argue that "though anthropology and cognitive psychology have made significant contributions to this new field, the study of organizational culture may be seen as a return to some of the most basic concerns about the nature of organizations and the appropriate methods for analyzing them" by sociologists.[18] In Ouchi and Wilkins's view, the academic study of culture was eclipsing the study of formal structure, organizational environments, and bureaucracy.

The concept of culture moved beyond the academic realm with publication of widely read books such as Thomas Peters and Robert Waterman's *In Search of Excellence* and Terrence Deal and Allan Kennedy's *Corporate Cultures: The Rites and Rituals of Corporate Life.*[19] With the publication of the first edition of *Organizational Culture and Leadership* in 1985, Schein gave definitive intellectual shape to the concept and linked it to roots of leadership training studies from the 1940s.

The fields of business and public administration began incorporating organizational culture into their analytic toolkits as they confronted organizational competitiveness, performance, and adaptability to change. Efforts to understand reasons for performance differences led to interest in organizational culture:

> What has really thrust the concept into the forefront is the recent emphasis on trying to explain why U.S. companies do not perform as well as some of their counterpart companies in other societies, notably Japan. In observing the differences, it has been noted that national culture is not a sufficient explanation. One needs concepts that permit one to differentiate between organizations within a society, especially in relation to different levels of effectiveness, and, for this purpose, organizational culture has served well.[20]

CULTURE AS SUPPORT (OR IMPEDIMENT) FOR RULES AND ROUTINES

As noted earlier, March and Olsen defined an institution as "the beliefs, paradigms, codes, cultures, and knowledge that support rules and routines."[21] This "support" may manifest in positive ways that advance the organization's goals. Or it may manifest in negative ways that run counter to the organization's goals. Thus, the symbiosis

Thus, the symbiosis between the formal and informal organization—between structure and culture—that Herbert Simon described introduces both opportunities and challenges for public managers.

between the formal and informal organization—between structure and culture—that Herbert Simon described introduces both opportunities and challenges for public managers.

The interactions between culture and structure are numerous and complex. Public administration scholar Carolyn Ban's study of U.S. federal agencies highlighted the mediating effect of organizational culture. Even when faced with similar structural constraints, managers' responses ranged from adhering strictly to the constraints to finding ways to work around them through informal channels.[22] Ban attributed these strategy differences in part to differences in organizational cultures.

Ban's insight was investigated further by public management scholars Sanjay K. Pandey, David H. Coursey, and Donald P. Moynihan, who sought to test whether culture mediates the relationship between red tape (a structural constraint) and organizational effectiveness.[23] The authors found that

> Two organizations with the same level of red tape might see their effectiveness suffer, but the organization with a culture more attuned to coping with and working around red tape is likely to experience smaller performance declines. The implication is that in public organizations in which the reduction of red tape is often, at best, difficult to achieve, fostering cultures that promote adaptive responses to red tape may mitigate the negative aspects of burdensome rules and procedures.[24]

The following discussion focuses on five areas where the formal and informal organization interact: organizational mission, work and culture in loosely coupled organizations, work and culture in high-reliability organizations, organizational learning, and organizational reputation and trust. In many of these cases, managerial craft also plays an important role. Thus, aspects of structure, culture, and their interactions may present managers with the "givens" of their internal environments and place them in roles as creatures who respond to and operate within these constraints. Or these aspects may present opportunities for managers to act as creators to shape structure, culture, and perhaps their interactions.

Organizational Mission

By shaping shared values and norms, a sense of mission can motivate employees and frame their understanding of their work in the organization.[25] Public administration scholar John Bryson distinguishes an organizational **mission**, which "clarifies an organization's purpose, or *why* it should be doing what it does" from organizational **vision**, which "clarifies *what* the organization should look like and *how* it should behave."[26]

Example: Organizational Visions and Missions for the Department of Homeland Security and its Units

The DHS website distinguishes between vision and mission. It states: "The vision of homeland security is to ensure a homeland that is safe, secure, and resilient against terrorism and other hazards."[27] It also lists its five core missions:

1. Prevent terrorism and enhancing security

2. Secure and manage our borders

3. Enforce and administer our immigration laws

4. Safeguard and secure cyberspace

5. Ensure resilience to disasters.[28]

Organizations within DHS each have distinct visions and missions as well. For example, the vision of the U.S. Secret Service is "to uphold the tradition of excellence in its investigative and protective mission through a dedicated, highly-trained, diverse, partner-oriented workforce that employs progressive technology and promotes professionalism."[29] Its mission is

> to ensure the security of our President, our Vice President, their families, the White House, the Vice President's Residence, national and visiting world leaders, former Presidents, and events of national significance. The Secret Service also protects the integrity of our currency and investigates crimes against our national financial system committed by criminals around the world and in cyberspace.[30]

A mission statement may be considered a structural aspect of organization life that drives the organization's work. Yet managers may try to influence the organization's mission and ultimately its culture. Political scientist James Q. Wilson argues that managers should actively focus on shaping an organization's mission, instead of leaving culture to be formed by "the chance operation of predispositions, professional norms, interest-group pressures, or situational imperatives."[31] Wilson acknowledges the difficulty of shaping mission, with the following constraints on the manager:

- multiple goals,
- numerous legal and political structural constraints, and
- limited opportunities to rewrite the mission statement (which typically occurs when an organization is first formed).

An empirical analysis of mission statements in public schools, however, found that "missions are fluid, open to interpretation, multilayered, and contested."[32] This finding suggests that managers may in some settings be in a position to influence missions and to influence the organization's culture.

Loosely Coupled Organizations

In **loosely coupled organizations** (such as public schools) the formal organizational structure tends not to reflect the actual activities of its participants (see Chapter 6).[33] Instead, structures such as organization charts may shape organizational culture by providing **myth and ceremony**. John Meyer and Brian Rowan illustrate the central role that culture, through myth and ceremony, plays in this kind of organization:

> Activities are performed beyond the purview of managers. In particular, organizations actively encourage professionalism, and activities are delegated to professionals.

> Goals are made ambiguous or vacuous, and categorical ends are substituted for technical ends. Hospitals treat, not cure patients. Schools produce students, not learning. In fact, data on technical performance are eliminated or rendered invisible. Hospitals try to ignore information on cure rates, public services avoid data about effectiveness, and schools deemphasize measures of achievement.

> Integration is avoided, program implementation is neglected, and inspection and evaluation are ceremonialized.

> Human relations are made very important. The organization cannot formally coordinate activities because its formal rules, if applied, would generate inconsistencies. Therefore individuals are left to work out technical interdependencies informally. The ability to coordinate things in violation of the rules—that is, to get along with other people—is highly valued.[34]

Management scholar William G. Ouchi underscores the importance of employee selection and socialization processes. **Clans** are organizations that use these processes to ensure accountability and control in the absence of market or bureaucratic controls, particularly important in the case of loosely coupled organizations:

> If it is not possible to measure either behavior or outputs and it is therefore not possible to "rationally" evaluate the work of the organization, what alternative is there but to carefully select workers so that you can be assured of having an able and committed set of people, and then engaging in rituals and ceremonies which serve the purpose of rewarding those who display the underlying attitudes and values which are likely to lead to organizational success, thus reminding everyone of what they are supposed to be trying to achieve, even if they can't tell whether or not they are achieving it?[35]

Example: Clan-like Organizations

In their analysis of accountability frameworks for special education classrooms, Patrick Wolf and Brian Hassel include a discussion of accountability relationships in William Ouchi's clan-like—or what they call "community"— organizations. *Principled agents* (a term introduced by John DiIulio and discussed in Chapter 8) are mentioned by Wolf and Hassel and are central to the clan-like organizations they observed.

> With principled agents delivering services to the organization's clients, community-based agencies often do not overly concern themselves with *ex post* accountability instruments. Their leaders instead tend to rely on their own constant readings of whether the community is thriving and, if not, what might be done to improve its condition. Operators and clients who have performed particularly well in the view of the leader might receive praise during a community gathering or have their roles within the organization enhanced in some way. Operators and clients who have performed poorly in the view of the leader might receive a private admonition, role reduction, or, in extreme cases, banishment from the community.[36]

Myths, ceremonies, norms, and values work together with the formal structure to define and shape the organization's work.

High-Reliability Organizations

Generating nuclear power, controlling air traffic, or ensuring airport security are examples of activities in which mistakes or operating failures would have disastrous consequences. Organizations in which these activities are conducted are known as **high-reliability organizations** (HROs).[iii] Opening its report on recent lapses in the Secret Service, for example, The United States Secret Service Protective Mission Panel stated, "The paramount mission of the United States Secret Service—protecting the president and other high-ranking national officials—allows no tolerance for error. A single miscue, or even a split-second delay, could have disastrous consequences for the Nation and the world."[37]

Political scientist Todd R. LaPorte and colleagues have developed a conceptual logic for analyzing HROs. This logic takes into account organizational culture as well as formal structures. It highlights the interdependencies involved with organizational communication and decision-making processes among senior officials.

[iii]In addition to the references cited in this section, see Charles Perrow, *Normal Accidents: Living with High Risk Technologies* (New York, NY: Basic Books, 1984); Karl E. Weick, "Organizational Culture as a Source of High Reliability," *California Management Review* 29, no. 2 (1987): 112–127; Todd R. LaPorte and Paula M. Consolini, "Working in Practice but Not in Theory: Theoretical Challenges of High-Reliability Organizations," *Journal of Public Administration Research and Theory* 1, no. 1 (1991): 19–47.

LaPorte and colleagues find that HROs have a strong norm of "mission accomplishment," integrated with a "safety culture" or "culture of reliability." Mission accomplishment generally refers to error-free operation while the safety culture guides action when unforeseen circumstances arise. Such circumstances may not be covered by detailed standard operating procedures (SOPs), but the safety culture guides professional action and decision making nonetheless.

> **LaPorte and colleagues find that HROs have a strong norm of "mission accomplishment," integrated with a "safety culture" or "culture of reliability."**

Because formal rules and incentives are insufficient to cover all contingencies, operating effectiveness "requires a more fully engaged person responding to the norms of individual and group relations that grow out of the particular demands and rewards of the hazardous systems involved."[38] LaPorte and colleagues identify common norms:

- operator "élan," characterized by competitiveness and a "prideful wariness";
- an expectation of autonomy and responsibility; and
- tensions between those who develop the complex systems involved (the engineers) and those who operate them.

Together, these norms constitute the "dominant workways and attitudes about appropriate behaviour at the operating levels" that "give a sense of the strength of the affective nature of HRO operations and provide the basis for the expressive authority and identitive compliance norms that enable the close cooperation necessary" in these organizations.[39]

Example: Teams and Culture in a High-Reliability Organization

A National Academies report examined the human factors associated with the air traffic control system—a high-reliability organization. In the following excerpt, the report emphasizes the importance of teams in the organizational culture of air traffic control. It highlights potential structural breakdowns as well as remedies, the role of teamwork and its incorporation into the culture for responding to breakdowns that inevitably occur, and the importance of visible and continuing support from managers to foster these processes.

> Teamwork, reflected in verbal communication among controllers and their supervisors and between controllers and flight crews, is likely to be a critical component of air traffic control for the foreseeable future. As in other technological endeavors, a high percentage of operational errors involves breakdowns in communications, coordination, and group decision making. Crew resource management training has proved to be effective in improving team coordination in flight crews and is being mandated on a worldwide basis. Similar training for air traffic controllers and their supervisors and trainers has the potential to provide similar enhancement of teamwork. This potential will only be realized if the necessary commitment by and support from FAA management becomes evident.
>
> The automation of components of the air traffic system may influence team interactions and can, in some circumstances, have a negative effect on teamwork and the ability of controllers to maintain situation awareness. The panel has identified a number of approaches to improving team coordination and communication in the air traffic control system:
>
> 1. Making team issues a part of the organizational culture of the air traffic system by defining the nature of team coordination as part of the organization's task description. It is important to include evaluation of team as well as individual skills as part of performance assessment.

2. Focusing on team as well as individual factors in the investigation of operational errors in the air traffic control system.

3. Make team training a centrally funded program required at all air traffic control facilities.[40]

The report suggested six additional approaches that could support team coordination. Perhaps because failure is so visible in high-reliability settings such as air traffic control or nuclear power, the cultures that sustain the continued high functioning of these organizations by definition shape their accountability relationships as well. These cultures emphasize discretion and autonomy, implying an emphasis on professional accountability as described in Barbara Romzek and Melvin Dubnik's accountability framework (see Chapter 2).

Understanding the role that culture plays in HROs provides a useful device for analyzing reliability not only for "error adverse" organizations such as nuclear power plants but also for a broader class of "error tolerant" organizations that are performing "impossible jobs"[41] (see Chapter 12). Can child protection agencies, which are typically plagued with management problems, ever become high-reliability organizations?

Learning and Innovating Organizations

Managerial efforts to promote a learning organization aim to dissolve interpersonal, organizational, and cultural barriers to the generation and consideration of fresh ideas.

Organizational culture may affect, and be affected by, whether and how the organization learns, adapts, and innovates. Two related concepts—organizational learning and the learning organization—have attracted considerable attention from scholars, especially those in business administration.[iv] Many definitions and emphases of **organizational learning** are found in the literature; they reflect cultural, cognitive, and behavioral aspects of learning and focus on changes in cognition, in potential behavior, or in actual behavior.[42] Some accounts focus on individual learning as a step toward organizational learning, while others examine change at the organizational level. In one view, "Although organizational learning occurs through individuals, it would be a mistake to conclude that organizational learning is nothing but the cumulative result of their members' learning."[43] Managerial efforts to promote a learning organization aim to dissolve interpersonal, organizational, and cultural barriers to the generation and consideration of fresh ideas.

Organizational Learning

One definition of organizational learning, offered by Chris Argyris and Donald A. Schön is "the detection and correction of error." They distinguish **single-loop learning** in which "individuals respond to error by modifying strategies and assumptions within constant organizational norms" from **double-loop learning** in which "response to detected error takes the form of joint inquiry into organizational norms themselves, so as to resolve their inconsistency and make the new norms more effectively realizable."[44]

Institutional scholars Barbara Levitt and James G. March describe organizational learning as "encoding inferences from history into routines that guide behavior" where **routines** are

> the forms, rules, procedures, conventions, strategies, and technologies around which organizations are constructed and through which they operate . . . [plus] the structure of beliefs, frameworks, paradigms, codes, cultures, and knowledge that buttress, elaborate, and contradict the formal routines.[45]

[iv]In addition to the references cited in this section, see James G. March, *Organization Science,* Special Issue: Organizational Learning: Papers in Honor of (and by) James G. March (1991): 71–87.

Management scholar Eric Tsang notes that the literature on organizational learning is sharply divided into normative and prescriptive studies that focus on how organizations *should* learn and the analytical and empirical studies that focus on how organization actually *do* learn.[46] An example of a normative study is organizational behavior scholar Swee Goh's identification of the strategic architecture of a learning organization.[47] All organizations can learn, he argues, if they develop five core building blocks:

Building blocks of org. learning

- clarity and support for mission and vision,
- shared leadership and involvement,
- a culture that encourages experimentation,
- ability to transfer knowledge across organizational boundaries, and
- teamwork and cooperation.

The foundations for this architecture, Goh says, must consist of an effective organizational design and appropriate employee skills and competencies to execute that design.

By Goh's standards, organizational learning would seem to require that the organization have a technically rational design. Furthermore, it must be able to engage external and internal constituencies on its own terms. This condition presumes considerable autonomy for agency managers and considerable stability or longevity for officials associated with the effort. These conditions are rare in a governance regime with political competition and turnover associated with regular elections.

An example of the analytical and empirical approach to organizational learning is Baiyin Yang, Karen Watkins, and Victoria Marsick's model that incorporates three structural elements and four human elements:

Structural Elements of Organizational Learning

- Connecting the organization to its environment
- Establishing systems to capture and share learning
- Providing strategic leadership for learning

Human Elements of Organizational Learning

- Creating continuous learning opportunities
- Promoting inquiry and dialogue
- Encouraging collaboration and team learning
- Empowering people toward a collective vision[48]

The authors argue that relationships among these elements lead to gains in organizational knowledge and improvements in organizational performance.

The concept of organizational learning has not penetrated American public management thinking, because the prerequisites for the concept often do not fit public organization contexts. An exception is research by public management scholar Julianne Mahler. She argues from case evidence that "learning by agency actors depends not only on the collection and retrieval of output data and other kinds of information, [but] it also depends on the culture of beliefs, norms, and professional identities that provides the context of meaning for this information."[49] Other research has examined learning in the context of performance management and crisis management and response.[50]

The concept of organizational learning is not universally popular even on its home ground in the private sector. "There are severe limitations to organizational learning as an instrument of intelligence," argue Levitt and March. "The same processes that yield experiential wisdom produce superstitious learning, competency traps, and erroneous inferences" stemming partly from "inadequacies of human cognitive habits, partly from features of organizations, partly from the characteristics of the structure of experience."[51]

Learning is an appealing paradigm, however. Managers can promote it at an organizational level, for example, by institutionalizing planning and evaluation practices, advisory groups, and in-house analytic processes and personnel.[v]

Innovation

Learning organizations may be more likely to produce **innovations**—creative solutions to familiar problems. Over the past half century, creative problem solving (CPS) has become the subject of a considerable research literature, consultancies, and management development and training activities.

An example of an innovation is providing a device to domestic violence victims under court-ordered protection that enables them to send a signal to police if threatened by an abuser. Another example is the "installation" of speed bumps that are optical illusions created by two-dimensional panels and painted areas. These can be installed at a fraction of the cost of actual speed bumps.

Managers might consider specific techniques to stimulate creativity and innovation. One technique is **mind mapping,** in which participants are urged to identify and visually suggest possible associations among facts, ideas, claims, and other elements of a problem situation until new patterns and relationships emerge that might be the basis of creative solutions.[vi] A well-known CPS process originating with the work of Alex Osborn and Sidney J. Parnes involves several stages of fact-finding, idea generation, and solution identification.[vii] The model deliberative process described in Chapter 1 itself might be used as the basis for creativity exercises involving multidimensional reframing of problem situations.

Learning organizations and **innovative organizations** are closely related. Public management scholar Robert Behn argues that to create an innovative public organization, two conditions must be fulfilled: "[Public managers] must convince frontline workers that the leadership supports [frontline workers]; and, they must ensure that frontline workers understand the big picture."[52] Behn's approach is based on what he terms an "implicit contract" with frontline workers that involves a "gift exchange" (see the end-of-chapter case study in Chapter 8): "You produce for us, we'll look after you." Behn's ten hints are summarized in Box 9.1.[53]

---

[v]In James L. Perry, ed. *Handbook of Public Administration* (San Francisco, CA: Jossey-Bass, 1996), see Sandra J. Hale, "Achieving High Performance in Public Organizations," a highly prescriptive piece with a section on "Learning" (136–150), described as the most important value of a high performance organization. Its elements include innovation, risk taking, training and the right tools, communication, and work measurement. In the same source, Douglas C. Eade, a consultant with 25 years of experience with more than 300 public and nonprofit organizations, writes in another prescriptive piece, "Leading and Managing Strategic Change" (499–510), that personal mastery is an important discipline in a learning organization, its spiritual foundation.

[vi]Study Guides and Strategies, http://www.studygs.net/mapping.

[vii]Creativity Manual, http://www.ideastream.com/create.

9.1

TEN HINTS FOR INVOLVING FRONTLINE WORKERS IN CREATING INNOVATIVE ORGANIZATIONS

CONDITION 1: Frontline Workers Know that Leadership Is on Their Side

Hint 1: Be immediately responsive to requests for improved working conditions (or when they ask for a new photocopier, produce it).

Hint 2: Support mistakes (or sit next to the first honest innovator who is called before a legislative committee).

CONDITION 2: Frontline Workers Understand the Big Picture

Hint 3: Create an explicit mission and related performance measures (or give people a real reason to be innovative).

Hint 4: Broaden job categories (or don't let each individual do only one narrow task).

Hint 5: Move people around (or don't let workers think they need learn only one job for life).

Hint 6: Reward teams, not individuals (or find ways to beat the formal performance-appraisal and promotion systems).

Hint 7: Make the hierarchy as unimportant as possible (or at least walk around without an entourage).

Hint 8: Break down functional units (or don't let the procurement guys tell everyone "no").

Hint 9: Give everyone all the information they need to do the job (or don't let the overhead units hoard the critical data).

Hint 10: Tell everyone what innovations are working (or have frontline workers report their successes to their colleagues).

Sources: Robert D. Behn, "Creating an Innovative Organization: Ten Hints for Involving Frontline Workers," *State and Local Government Review* 27, no. 3 (1995), www.govleaders.org/behn_innovation.htm. © SAGE Publications, Inc.

In the final analysis, cautions Behn, "creating an innovative public agency is itself a task of innovation. Each innovative organization will be different. . . . There is no recipe for replicating an innovation."[54]

Reputation and Trust

An organization's reputation provides a signal about its typical views or actions. Reputations develop over time and through repeated interactions with external actors. Internal and external actors depend on organizational reputations to help them anticipate organizational behavior in the future and to interpret organizational responses and products.[viii]

Because "reputation . . . allows predictability in an uncertain world," political actors may take reputation into account when designing bureaucratic structures.[55]

Internal and external actors depend on organizational reputations to help them anticipate organizational behavior in the future and to interpret organizational responses and products.[viii]

Example: Reputation's Role in Oversight Recommendations

Treasury Department officials in the George W. Bush administration wanted to shift oversight of the Federal National Mortgage Association (Fannie Mae) away from the Department of Housing and Urban Development (HUD). HUD had a reputation within Treasury for practicing lax oversight. Treasury wanted to bring oversight of Fannie Mae in-house, where Treasury itself would have greater control. Congress, however, resisted the proposal. Concerned legislators seemed to trust HUD oversight more than what they anticipated from Treasury. This classical political conflict, which stalled regulatory reform, may have contributed to the 2008 financial crisis which led to the federal government's takeover of Fannie and Freddie (discussed in Chapter 5).

As part of his study of the Food and Drug Administration, *Reputation and Power: Organizational Image and Pharmaceutical Regulation at the FDA,* political scientist Daniel Carpenter describes four dimensions of reputation:

- *performative* (did the agency get it right?),
- *technical* (does the agency have the know-how and methods to get it right?),
- *procedural* (does the FDA follow accepted procedures suggested by law and science?), and
- *moral* (does the agency show compassion to those affected by its decisions? Is it captured or inappropriately influenced?). [emphasis added][56]

Carpenter concludes in his study that FDA's strong reputation for "competence and vigilance" has been a fundamental source of its power, but that in recent years both its reputation and power have waned.

In the world of policymaking (and in the world of public management, as this text argues), a reputation for **neutral competence** can be valuable.[57] It connotes the ability to use "appropriate methods for assessing problems and predicting the consequences of policy alternatives as well as neutrality in choosing and arguing for the social values that provide a basis for comparison of the alternatives."[58] The Government Accountability Office (GAO) and the Congressional Budget Office (CBO) are legislative branch organizations that have reputations for contributing "skillful, neutral, and nonpartisan analysis to the public discourse on policy issues."[59] Resources for the Future, the RAND Corporation, and MDRC are examples of independent organizations with such reputations.

Neutral competence reflects the skills and reputation of organizational members as well as the structure of the organization itself. In part because of the professionals employed by them, independent organizations such as the CBO can more easily establish a reputation for neutral competence than, for example, the office of the Assistant Secretary for Planning and Evaluation (ASPE) in the Department of Health and Human Services (HHS), even though within HHS, ASPE may be viewed as having greater neutral competence than analysts in the program bureaus of the department.

[viii]David M. Kreps uses concepts from economic theory, such as transaction costs, focal points, information asymmetries, and contracts, to explain corporate culture. See David M. Kreps, "Corporate Culture and Economic Theory," in *Perspectives on Positive Political Economy,* ed. James E. Alt and Kenneth A. Shepsle (Cambridge, MA: Cambridge University Press, 1990), 90–143.

Example: Neutral Competence at the Congressional Budget Office

The reputation for neutral competence at the CBO was a function both of its goals (a structural feature) and of the support and emphasis on those goals by CBO directors. In his study of CBO's history, public administration scholar Philip G. Joyce emphasized

> the importance of leadership in creating and maintaining an organization that remains true to its mission. Returning to the goals articulated for the CBO in its initial organizational meeting—respected, nonpartisan, independent, and communicative—review of evidence appears to indicate that it has been a spectacular success on all these fronts. This did not just happen. It resulted from conscious choices, particularly on the part of CBO's directors, to keep it that way. It is a tribute to the organizational culture of CBO—created by Alice Rivlin, affirmed by Rudy Penner, and emphasized in a generally consistent fashion by subsequent directors.[60]

The presence of trust underlies the dependence on neutral competence and other positive reputations. The presence of distrust will, of course, have the opposite effect. **Trust** is a "firm belief in the reliability, truth, ability, or strength of someone or something."[61] Trust forms the basis for cooperation and repeated interactions over time.[62] Trust facilitates interactions when

- actors are vulnerable to the opportunistic actions of others,
- when a situation poses risks of unpredictable action, and
- when stable expectations about the behavior of other actors can be developed.[63]

Yet whether these characteristics are antecedents to trust, or whether trust enables these characteristics to develop, is a matter of some debate.

Trust between organizations and their principals, especially in the context of service provider agreements, is of considerable interest as public managers operate in their external environments—for example, in promoting cooperation among providers and other actors in mental health networks, in interlocal networks of service providers, and on environmental issues.[64] Because organizations in a network are likely to exhibit different cultures (and subcultures), additional uncertainty is introduced into these relationships[65] (see discussion of interdependence in Chapter 6).

Reform is taken up in the next section, focusing on the ways in which culture plays a role in organizational reform efforts—whether the reform goals address structure or culture itself.

REFORM

Parts I and II provide a number of examples of structural reforms, often intended to address an accountability problem or to respond to developing events. Sometimes, these reforms or reorganizations have intended or unintended implications for organizational culture. In other cases, cultural change itself may be the goal. In such cases, reform is often accomplished through structural reorganizations. These changes may be externally authorized or internally authorized.

Chapter 12 argues that public management reform efforts often involve all three dimensions of public management: structures, organizational culture, and managerial craftsmanship. But because structural reforms often target or demand cultural change, the current chapter focuses on the intersection of these two dimensions.

The very process by which reform or change takes place illustrates interactions between structure and culture. For example, the structures of deliberation and decision making—whether a strategic or policy planning process is transparent, whether policy decisions are reached systematically or in an ad hoc manner, whether deliberation is confined to a few or allows broad participation—interact with organizational cultures. These processes can be used to define roles for organizational participants and empower them. For example, participants may be given access to forums and opportunities to influence important organizational actions. Legislators like to create specific offices to further constituent interests to ensure that those interests have a place at the decision-making table. Role-defined behaviors become a basis for the formation of cultures. Including policy analysis and program evaluation officials in organizational budget making, for example, enhances the status and influence of these specialized skills in the wider organizational culture.

Insight into the interaction between the structures of deliberation and organization subcultures was provided by Michael Cohen, James March, and Johan Olsen in their **garbage can model** of organizational choice.[66] In many organizations, participation in the processes of deliberation and decision making may be fluid and participants are opportunistic. Those whose concerns are with putting problems on the agenda vie with those who are determined to "sell" preferred solutions. All participants bring their personal ambitions, motivations, and reputations to the table. The outcome of the deliberation might or might not be related to its original purpose, much less to technical or even political rationality. The outcome will depend on the mix of "stuff" (garbage) that participants dump into the process (the can). Managers can structure deliberation to minimize diversions from original purposes.

When the Focus Is Structural Change

Structural changes—introduction of new formal delegations of authority or revision of existing ones—by authorities external or internal to the organization may interact with culture in complex ways. A full discussion of the theories, mechanisms, and development of this literature is beyond the scope of this book.[ix] The goal here is to provide an example of three types:

- where culture affects the implementation of new structures or mediates the effects of those new structures on outputs or outcomes;
- where structural changes affect culture; and
- where both types of effects seem to be operating simultaneously.

Culture Influences Success of Structural Change

The U.S. Department of Energy was created in 1977. When responsibilities in areas as disparate as nuclear weapons and energy conservation were brought together under the new department's umbrella, organizational cultures unique to each program clashed, affecting the success of the reorganization and the performance of the department.[x]

[ix]For detailed accounts, see, for example, W. Richard Scott, "Unpacking Institutional Arguments," in *The New Institutionalism in Organizational Analysis,* ed. Walter W. Powell and Paul J. DiMaggio (Chicago, IL: University of Chicago Press, 1991); and W. Richard Scott, *Organizations: Rational, Natural, and Open Systems,* 4th ed. (Upper Saddle River, NJ: Prentice Hall, 1998).

[x]For further information on the creation of the Department of Energy and clashes of cultures, see Federation of American Scientists, http://www.fas.org/sgp/library/pfiab/root.html.

History seemed to repeat itself when the DHS was formed. As described earlier in this chapter, culture clashes and turf wars erupted as 22 organizations, including the Federal Emergency Management Agency, the Coast Guard, and the Secret Service were brought under one organizational tent.

The opening case in Chapter 5 described combining the former Immigration and Naturalization Service (INS) and the Customs Service to create the new Immigration and Customs Enforcement (ICE) bureau in DHS. A GAO report indicated that "the integration of INS and Customs investigators into a single investigative program has involved the blending of two vastly different workforces, each with its own culture, policies, procedures, and mission priorities." That blending resulted in "no love match." Because of the different cultures within ICE, managers faced "a greater challenge in creating a unified bureau."[67] Although they introduced challenges, the new structural arrangements were not completely crippled by the cultural clashes between the two former agencies; in at least one instance, the structural reorganization led to a more successful kind of operation.

Jane E. Fountain's book, *Building the Virtual State* offers another example of culture influencing the implementation of structural changes.[68] Fountain focuses on technology adoption by public organizations. Examples include the use of websites, internal agency networks, or cross-agency networks or systems. Fountain argues that the enactment of such "objective" technologies (the actual physical technology of hardware or software) is not a linear, rational process and is not identical across organizations. Instead, the technology enactment process is indeterminate due to the cultural, political, cognitive, and legal environments in which organizations operate.

> **The technology enactment process is indeterminate due to the cultural, political, cognitive, and legal environments in which organizations operate.**

The intention to use alternative dispute resolution (ADR) in the Environmental Protection Agency (EPA) is another illustration of culture influencing the implementation of structural changes and their intended effects. In 2000, the EPA announced its intention to increase the use of ADR, a structural mechanism already in use, to resolve disputes involving the agency. In their analysis of past use of ADR, Rosemary O'Leary and Susan Summers Raines found that the EPA's organizational culture was not supportive of ADR and was likely to impede its expanded use. Lack of support was reflected in managers' comments, such as the "EPA sees itself as the most important party to the negotiation," and "The EPA has a strong tradition of being cautious, particularly in policy development. Issues must go up and down a chain of command."[69] Such comments indicate that it would be no small task to overcome the entrenched views of EPA employees to promote greater use of ADRs.

Structural Change Influences Culture

As an organization adjusts to new ways of organizing work or new accountability requirements, its new structures may influence culture. In the mid-1970s the Social Security Administration (SSA) began administering the Supplemental Security Income (SSI) program. In the early 1980s, it was tasked with performing reviews of eligibility for recipients of disability insurance. The implementation of these programs was characterized by many errors in SSI payment processing and in disability eligibility determination. Martha Derthick found that the agency's culture suffered as a result:

> In both instances [SSA] was left with responsibility for a fragmented, decentralized program over which it had lost its customary share of policy control. To the extent that uniform policies and practices were sacrificed (to the states in SSI, to the courts in the disability review), so was the essential character of the SSA as a national agency. Relations with employees and state agents were impaired as a consequence of their having been assigned demoralizing tasks.

Finally, the agency suffered a loss of prestige and self-confidence. Historically, it had had an exceptional degree of pride. It was the Marine Corps of the domestic civil service—elite and invincible.... SSI and the disability review therefore came as rude shocks, both from the evidence that the agency was not as good as it thought it was (however good nonetheless) and from the brutal criticism by Congress, press, and the courts. Whether or not pride was lost, a sense of invulnerability certainly was. After 1974, the agency wore a wounded air.[70]

Nonprofit social service organizations that provide services under contract provide another example of how structural change can affect organizational cultures. The increased "marketization" of nonprofits has led to a kind of business professionalization and emphasis on the values reflected by those professionals, introducing interests beyond those of the nonprofit's mission: "Rather than focus on responding to the organization's founding commitments, executives now grapple with organizational survival and professional career advancement."[71]

Bidirectional Effects of Structure and Culture

Culture may affect the implementation and effectiveness of structural change, and structural change may affect culture. For example, Barbara S. Romzek and Jocelyn M. Johnston found that the organizational cultures of the Area Agencies on Aging (AAAs), nonprofits that provided contracted case management services for Medicaid in Kansas, exhibited direct influence on implementation. Although the relationships between the AAAs (the agent) and the state departments of Social and Rehabilitation Services and Aging (the principals) were aided by a shared "culture of service," "these shared values have not offset other tensions created by the differences in administrative culture and policy role."

In addition, the structural changes influenced culture in the AAAs, reflecting the challenges they faced in implementing the policy. Because the contract essentially called for the AAAs to "expand their role beyond advocacy to encompass service delivery," their cultures were affected by structural changes such as more reliance on field offices, a different mix of professionals, and different divisions of labor.[72]

Another example of interactions and feedback loops among structure and culture is the series of reforms intended to make NASA more efficient and responsive to changed circumstances. The cultural changes that resulted from these reforms may have increased the likelihood of *Challenger* and *Columbia* accidents:

> Reliance on outside contractors has left personnel at NASA centers like the Goddard Space Flight Center in Greenbelt, MD, and the Marshall Space Flight Center in Huntsville, AL, with little hands-on expertise . . .
>
> Scientists said that the agency's original sense of mission and can-do spirit had largely given way to a civil-service culture, with a maze of bureaucratic rules, overlaid by a risk-averse approach that permeated NASA after the Challenger explosion in 1986. As a result, these experts said, it was difficult to attract ambitious young talent.[73]

The examples in this section illustrate the interactions between structural change and culture. The interactions are likely to be complex and perhaps unpredictable or indeterminate. What seems clear is that structural change seldom consists of only a technical or rational implementation process. Managers may exercise their craft and influence structural changes (to the extent possible) so they are more congruent with their organizational cultures. Or, managers may attempt to influence cultures following a structural change. The possibilities for managerial craft are discussed further in Chapters 10 and 11 and a three-dimensional approach to reform in Chapter 12.

When the Focus Is Cultural Change   *Prob.*

When managers are able to influence the cultures of their organizations, they are exercising their roles as creators. Doing so is unlikely to be straightforward, quick, or easy. Rather, it requires concerted and sustained efforts. Political scientist Anne Khademian observes, "Political scientists, sociologists, and anthropologists alike acknowledge the power of culture in determining organizational behavior but believe that culture is highly resistant to the change efforts of leaders."[74]

The political context is one reason for this resistance in public organizations. Many police departments and public schools, for example, exhibit cultures that are resistant to determined efforts to change them.

Example: The Need for Cultural Change at DOE Weapons Laboratories

President Bill Clinton asked a special investigative panel of the President's Foreign Intelligence Advisory Board to examine issues of security in the Department of Energy's laboratories that design nuclear weapons. The panel reported that structural reforms proposed by energy secretary Bill Richardson were necessary but not sufficient to address the lax attitudes toward security in the labs. Instead, the panel concluded, fundamental changes in culture and employee attitudes and behaviors were essential:

> The Department of Energy is incapable of reforming itself—bureaucratically and culturally—in a lasting way, even under an activist Secretary.

> The panel has found that DOE and the weapons laboratories have a deeply rooted culture of low regard for and, at times, hostility to security issues, which has continually frustrated the efforts of its internal and external critics, notably the GAO and the House Energy and Commerce Committee. Therefore, a reshuffling of offices and lines of accountability may be a necessary step toward meaningful reform, but it almost certainly will not be sufficient.

> Even if every aspect of the ongoing structural reforms is fully implemented, the most powerful guarantor of security at the nation's weapons laboratories will not be laws, regulations, or management charts. It will be the attitudes and behavior of the men and women who are responsible for the operation of the labs each day. These will not change overnight, and they are likely to change only in a different cultural environment—one that values security as a vital and integral part of day-to-day activities and believes it can coexist with great science.[75]

But even resistant cultures may be susceptible to change under fortuitous leadership and the right combination of circumstances:

- In *The Functions of the Executive,* Barnard argued that a primary task of the organization's leader is to create and shape a culture that can unify the employees and improve organizational performance.[76]
- Schein distinguishes leaders from managers based on their propensities to be creators or creatures: "Leaders create and change cultures, while managers and administrators live within them."[77]
- DiIulio emphasizes the importance of the leadership role of managers in affecting culture: "It is organizational leaders who either set or do not set in motion the organizational socialization processes that transcend principal-agent problems by nurturing a culture of principled agents."[78]

Another way that managers may influence culture is through what Khademian calls broad, "relentless" attention to internal roots of culture and their link to organizational commitments, as well as to external political principals and stakeholders.[79] She argues that structures and task requirements create frameworks for **organizational commitments**, a term adopted from Philip Selznick's work and defined as the "common understandings held by people working together in an organization or program" that form the "roots" of organizational culture. In turn, these commitments define how the work of the agency is done.

Cultural change is only possible when a manager works with the roots of an organization's culture and its commitments . . .

Khademian acknowledges the difficulties that managers face in changing culture. She emphasizes that a manager or leader of an organization cannot simply change culture by fiat.[80] Cultural change is only possible when a manager works with the roots of an organization's culture and its commitments, argues Khademian. She provides guidance for identifying **roots of culture** in public organizations by examining three primary areas:

- tasks,
- resources and personnel, and
- the organization's external environment.

Analyzing the roots of culture might, for example, focus on specifics in each of these primary areas such as

- identifying the language used to describe how work is done, how customers or clientele are referred to;
- understanding the educational backgrounds and work experiences of employees; and
- how political superiors and stakeholders are described; and identifying the formal structures of authority.[81]

Example: Information Technology (IT) Modernization at the Internal Revenue Service (IRS)

Khademian's framework can be used to analyze the experiences of the IRS with implementing IT modernization. Barry Bozeman studied this process and writes that IRS culture is characterized by risk aversion, insularity, and mistrustfulness. All have led to some spectacular organizational failures in IRS IT modernization.[82]

The IRS is charged with processing an enormous volume of different kinds of tax returns, dealing with a wide variety of filing formats, and adapting to changes in tax laws every year. IRS employees are mostly "lifers" who have been through turbulence and survived. In addition, tensions are evident between headquarters and field staff. The external environment of the IRS is strongly top down, with the organization subject to a high level of involvement in its affairs by the Office of Management and Budget, the GAO, Congress, and even the National Academy of Sciences. These roots of culture result in the following IRS employee commitments:

- to getting the job done without complaining,
- to suppressing dissent,
- to hiding or suppressing bad news, and
- to protecting turf and boundaries.

Bozeman reports that IT modernization is occurring at the IRS, but it is focused on incremental and manageable projects, not on fundamental restructuring of agency-wide systems. This picture suggests that the IRS as an institution is changing very slowly, if at all, because no one has been able to change the roots of its culture.

Making explicit links to an employee's public service motivation (discussed in Chapter 8) may be another way of tapping into cultural roots and commitments of public organizations. Managers may practice "values management" by focusing on different levels:

- the individual worker,
- the job,
- the workplace,
- the organization, and
- the society.[83]

Public administration scholars Laurie E. Paarlberg, James Perry, and Annie Hondeghem argue that attention to these different levels extends the strategies for harnessing public service motivation "beyond the formal human resource management system to look at social systems of leadership, culture, and interpersonal relationships that shape people and their attitudes and behaviors."[84] They glean specific tactics from the literature that managers can use at each of the five levels of analysis:

- *At the individual level:* "provide formal and informal opportunities for newcomers to learn about organizational values and expectations for employee behavior that reflect public service values."
- *At the job level:* "interpret broad public service missions in terms of clear and meaningful work expectations."
- *At the workplace level:* "create and maintain incentives that align organizational mission and employee predispositions."
- *At the organization level:* "articulate and symbolize organization mission and vision in ways that connect with employees' zone of existing public service values."
- *At the society level:* "advocate for and provide opportunities for pre-service experiences."[85]

Though not invoking public service motivation, John DiIulio echoed the themes of Paarlberg and colleagues in his study of the Bureau of Prisons and related work:

> the importance of leadership in government has less to do with cultivating outside constituency groups, fine-tuning pay scales, or refereeing intra- or inter-bureaucratic battles, and more to do with establishing social and moral reward systems that make it possible for government agencies to tap the creativity, sense of duty, and public-spiritedness of their workers.[86]

Example: Local Police Department Reorganization

The interdependence of the structure and culture dimensions is commonly observed in state and local public management. After less than 3 weeks on the job, Bryan, Texas, police chief Tyrone Morrow announced a reorganization of his department. Three former divisions concerned with patrol, investigations, and administration were combined into two: operations and operations support. The stated purpose was to change a culture in which investigators considered themselves "a step above" patrol officers into one in which the priority would be "boots on the ground" patrolling Bryan's neighborhoods. "We're not going to have egos and people who don't want to play in the sandbox with the others," Morrow said. "We're going to support our field operations to facilitate our primary mission, which is crime control."[87] Accompanying the reorganization was a plan for promotions and reassignments that would place Morrow's personnel choices in strategic administrative positions, presumably to reinforce the intent of the reorganization. Concurrently, the former chief of investigations announced his retirement, removing an impediment to cultural change.

A manager who seeks to change the culture of his or her organization—whether by redefining the mission or by attention to the culture's building blocks, roots, and organizational commitments—faces a difficult task. Indeed, Trice and Beyer offer a list of "mistaken assumptions" about culture that a naïve manager might make:

- that [managers] can unilaterally decide what the culture of their firm should and will be,
- that a single homogenous culture can be easily created,
- that having such a culture is largely positive and functional, and
- that culture arises from what managers say rather than what they do.[88]

Given structural constraints (emanating from formal authority both internal and external to the organization), and ingrained and perhaps resistant values and motives of organizational members, changing the fundamental culture of an organization undoubtedly takes time and concerted, relentless effort. Yet managerial influence over culture is possible and can have important consequences for how an organization and its employees go about their work.

Example: Managers' Efforts to Instill a New Culture of Caution and Dissent

The December 2007 National Intelligence Estimate (NIE) revealed new assessments regarding the nuclear threat from Iran, but it also acknowledged some uncertainty regarding the analysis. That such an NIE could be written was due in large part to the craft of the director of National Intelligence, Mike McConnell, and his deputies, Thomas Fingar and Donald M. Kerr, particularly their efforts to change the culture that surrounded the development of the NIEs. These efforts included "greater transparency about the sources of intelligence," used in the NIE, "challeng[ing] existing assumptions when new information does not fit," and allowing qualifications to the analysis. They "jettisoned a requirement that each conclusion in an NIE reflect a consensus view of the intelligence community," resulting in NIEs that conveyed differences of opinion.[89]

KEY CONCEPTS

Institutionalized values
Institutionalization
Institutions
Organizational culture
Informal organization
Mission
Vision
Loosely coupled organizations
Myth and ceremony
Clans
High-reliability organizations
Organizational learning
Single-loop learning

Double-loop learning
Routines
Innovations
-- Mind mapping
⌐ Learning organizations
Innovative organization
Reputation
Neutral competence
Trust
— Garbage can model
Organizational commitments
Roots of culture (tasks, resources and personnel,
    external environment)

CASE ANALYSIS: "CORROSIVE CULTURE" IN THE VETERANS HEALTH ADMINISTRATION

In the spring of 2014, news stories started to appear about two sets of books—two wait lists—in the Phoenix Veterans Affairs Health System (PVAHS). April 27 headlines read

- "A Fatal Wait: Veterans Languish and Die on a VA Hospital's Secret List" (CNN)[90]
- "Official Inquiries Begin for Phoenix VA Hospital with Alleged 'Secret Waiting List'" (The Washington Post)[91]

The official wait lists reported to the VA office in Washington corresponded with what the agency wanted to hear, while the actual "secret" waitlists reflected reality on the ground. Employee performance contracts were in part based on meeting a performance goal of a 14-day wait time.

The dual wait list revelations were the result of a whistleblower's actions. Dr. Sam Foote had been an internist at the PVAHS until his retirement in December 2013. He had contacted congressional offices, news sources, and the VA Office of Inspector General (OIG) with his concerns.[92]

Throughout the summer, a continuing stream of revelations and official reports detailed staff gaming of wait lists not only at the Phoenix VA hospital but also at other sites around the country:

- Investigations were undertaken by the VA OIG, the White House, the FBI, and the Office of Special Counsel.
- On May 30, Eric Shinseki, the Secretary of Veterans Affairs, resigned; President Obama appointed Sloan Gibson as Acting Secretary.
- Legislation overhauling the VA health system was passed and signed into law on August 7: The Veterans Access, Choice, and Accountability Act of 2014.

One of the investigations was conducted by Rob Nabors, the White House Deputy Chief of Staff. On June 27, 2014, the White House released a summary of that report (see Figure 9.1) in which Nabors describes a "corrosive culture" at the VA. Each major point in the summary included a brief background, observations, and recommendations.

As it released the summary, the White House described reforms the VA had already implemented:

- Initiating reforms to improve access to care: Over the last month, VA has completed outreach to 135,000 Veterans across the country, scheduled approximately 182,000 additional appointments, trained approximately 10,000 schedulers, and allocated $393 million to accelerate care. Additionally, VA has taken specific actions at some of the most challenged VA facilities, including: hiring more support staff to help get veterans off wait lists and into clinics, deploying more mobile medical units for veterans awaiting care, and expanding access to care to local communities. VA is also utilizing high-performing facilities to help those that need improvement.

- Increasing transparency: At the direction of the Acting Secretary, the Veterans Health Administration (VHA) has begun to post twice-monthly updates to the access data at VA.gov/health to enhance transparency and provide the most immediate information to veterans and the public on veterans' access to quality healthcare.

- Protecting whistleblowers: Acting Secretary Gibson has expressed his strongest support for the rights and protections of whistleblowers, and has made clear that problems raised should be taken seriously and fully investigated. Following a letter to the President from the VA Office of Special Counsel regarding VA whistleblowers, VA directed a comprehensive review of all aspects of the Office of Medical Inspector's operation, to be completed within 14 days. This review is underway.[93]

Discussion Questions

1. What are the roots of culture and the organizational commitments in the VA health system?

2. What dimensions of structure are important for understanding the work of the VA health system? How do the structure and culture dimensions interact?

3. What public service values, ethics, and motives are evident among VA health system employees?

4. Is it possible to change the culture of the VA health system?

   a. If the reforms Nabors suggests are implemented, what would be the effects on culture?

   b. Review the Veterans Access, Choice, and Accountability Act of 2014. Identify structural changes that would influence culture or would be influenced by culture.

   c. Do you recommend any additional reforms? What are they, and why do you recommend them?

FIGURE 9.1	Summary of VA Wait Time Analysis by White House Deputy Chief of Staff Rob Nabors

June 27, 2014

ISSUES IMPACTING ACCESS TO TIMELY CARE AT VA MEDICAL FACILITIES

There is a strong sentiment among many Veterans and stakeholders that in general VA provides high quality health care "once you get in the door" and that the current system needs to be fixed, not abandoned or weakened. The vast majority of VA employees are dedicated, hardworking, and committed to the Veterans they serve. VA doctors, nurses, and staff could choose to work at other facilities, often for greater compensation. They choose to work at the VA because they believe in this Nation's promise to its Veterans, and they work each day to realize that promise and deliver the quality care Veterans have earned and deserve. However, I also believe that it is clear that there are significant and chronic systemic failures that must be addressed by the leadership at VA.

- The 14-day scheduling standard is arbitrary, ill-defined, and misunderstood. The manner in which this unrealistic goal was developed and deployed has caused confusion in reporting and, in some cases, may have incentivized inappropriate actions. It is a poor indicator of either patient satisfaction or quality of care and should be replaced with a more insightful measure.
- The Veterans Health Administration (VHA) needs to be restructured and reformed. It currently acts with little transparency or accountability with regard to its management of the VA medical structure. The VHA Leadership structure is marked by a lack of responsiveness and an inability to effectively manage or communicate to employees or Veterans.
- A corrosive culture has led to personnel problems across the Department that are seriously impacting morale and, by extension, the timeliness of health care. The problems inherent within an agency with an extensive field structure are exacerbated by poor management and communication structures, distrust between some VA employees and management, a history of retaliation toward employees raising issues, and a lack of accountability across all grade levels.
- The Department's failures have generated a high level of oversight. The Department must be more agile and responsive in addressing legitimate oversight inquiries.
- The technology underlying the basic scheduling system used by VA medical facilities is cumbersome and outdated. However, with regard to increasing access to care, the software underlying the scheduling system is secondary to the need for additional resources to actually schedule – doctors, nurses, and other health professionals; physical space; and appropriately trained administrative support personnel.
- Many of the resource issues VA faces are endemic to the health care field (for example, shortages of certain types of specialists, an aging patient base, or geographical shortages around the country) or to the Federal government (for example, slowness in the hiring process or an inability to compete with private sector wages). However, VA has also demonstrated an inability to clearly articulate budgetary needs and to tie budgetary needs to specific outcomes.
- VA needs to better plan and invest now for anticipated changes in the demographics of the veterans. This includes geographical changes, an increased number of female veterans, a surge in mental health needs, an increase in the special needs of younger veterans returning from Iraq and Afghanistan, and specific needs associated with a growing number of older veterans.

(Continued)

(Continued)

Assessment: Issues Impacting Access to Timely Care at VA Medical Facilities

The 14-day scheduling standard is arbitrary, ill-defined, and misunderstood. The manner in which this unrealistic goal was developed and deployed has caused confusion in reporting and, in some cases, may have incentivized inappropriate actions. It is a poor indicator of either patient satisfaction or quality of care and should be replaced with a more insightful measure.

Background:

In 1995, the Veterans Health Administration (VHA) set a 30-day goal for scheduling primary and specialty care medical appointments. In 2011, VHA shortened that goal to 14 days. VHA includes these performance measures in the performance contracts for Veterans Integrated Service Network (VISN) and VA Medical Center (VAMC) directors. VA also includes these measures in its budget submissions and performance reports to Congress. Also from FY2005 to FY2012, the number of appointments scheduled through VHA has increased approximately 19 percent from 5.3 million to 6.3 million.

Recognizing the inherent issues associated with the 14-day scheduling goal, VA has removed it from employee performance contracts.

Observations:

- The 14-day standard creates an unrealistic comparison between VHA and the private sector. Directly comparable data is not available for the private sector, primarily because experts seem to believe that time-to-appointment is only one component of overall patient satisfaction. Further, anecdotal evidence suggests that wait times for appointments are often times equal to, if not longer, in private facilities.

- The performance goal is complicated to compute and to understand because of vagaries around which "date" is being entered. For new patients, wait times are measured from the "create date" or the date on which an appointment is made. For existing patients, the wait times are measured from the "desired date" or the date on which the patient or health care provider wants the patient to be seen. Because the "desired date" is manually entered by a scheduler, it is more susceptible to manipulation. The "create date" is computer-generated date.

- The 14-day standard was included as a measure in employee performance contracts. This may have created an incentive for employees to try to reduce a number over which they personally had very little direct control. In 2010, William Schoenhard, Deputy Under Secretary for Health for Operations and Management, authored a memo detailing a number of "gaming strategies" used to artificially make wait times look lower. Schoenhard noted, "[workarounds may mask the symptoms of poor access and, although they may aid in meeting performance measures, they do not serve our Veterans. They may prevent the real work of improving our processes and design of systems."

Solutions:

- The Department plans to establish a panel of health care experts and industry leaders to catalogue best practices for measuring timely delivery of health care to Veterans and make recommendations to the new Under Secretary for Health.

- Certain performance measures, like wait time data, should be used as management tools to help identify proper deployment of resources but not as a measure of whether high- quality health care has been delivered in an appropriate fashion.

VHA needs to be restructured and reformed. It currently acts with little transparency or accountability with regard to its management of the VA medical structure. In its most modest form, this insularity has impeded innovation and change. In its more extreme manifestations, it has impeded appropriate management, supervision, and oversight. The VHA leadership structure often is unresponsiveness and unable to effectively manage or communicate to employees or Veterans.

Background:

VHA is America's largest integrated health care system with over 1,700 sites of care, serving 8.76 million Veterans each year. In addition, VHA is the Nation's largest provider of graduate medical education and a major contributor to medical research. In 2013, VA obligated approximately $150 billion. Approximately 98 percent of total funding went directly to Veterans in the form of monthly payments of benefits or for direct services, such as medical care. The existence of such a vast and geographically widespread field structure makes communication to and from the VA Central Office all the more critical.

Observations:

- VHA delivers quality care, but is resistant to reforms and change. Many recommendations or directives from VA Central Office or from oversight entities are minimized, slowly implemented, or ignored.
- The VHA field structure is not accountable or transparent to Veterans, the Secretary, or the Department as a whole. For example, performance data from the field is often slow to be reported and sometimes openly contested by VAMCs through the press in direct contravention of facts and established procedures.
- The VHA leadership team is not prepared to deliver effective day-to-day management or crisis management. Instead, VHA is marked by an inherent lack of responsiveness and a belief many issues raised by the public, the VA Leadership, or oversight entities are exaggerated, unimportant, or "will pass."

Solutions:

- VA needs increased transparency into the way VHA operates. VHA needs a better structure and more accountability in how to manage the field structure.
- VA Central Office needs to be much more hands on with the VHA field structure.
- The reforms needed at VHA are not political - they are structural and operational. VHA requires significant leadership and management restructuring that:

  - One, allows for increased, consistent flow of information from the VA Central Office to the regional and local field structure; and

  - Two, allows for unobstructed flow of information from the field structure to regional and National management and leadership.

(Continued)

(Continued)

A corrosive culture has led to personnel problems across the Department that are seriously impacting morale and, by extension, the timeliness of health care. The problems inherent within an agency with an extensive field structure are exacerbated by poor management and communication structures, a corrosive culture of distrust between some VA employees and management, a history of retaliation toward employees raising issues, and a lack of accountability.

Observations:

- The vast majority of VA employees are dedicated, hardworking, and committed to the Veterans they serve. VA doctors, nurses, and staff could choose to work at other facilities, often for greater compensation. They choose to work at the VA because they believe in this Nation's promise to its Veterans, and they work each day to realize that promise and deliver the quality care Veterans have earned and deserve.
- There is a culture across much of the Department that encourages discontent and backlash against employees. Whistleblower complaints suggest poor management and reflect a palpable level of frustration at the local, regional, and National levels. As an example, approximately one-fourth of all whistleblower cases OSC is currently reviewing across the Federal government come from the Department of Veterans Affairs.
- There is a tendency to transfer problems rather than solve problems. This is in part due to the difficulty of hiring and firing in the Federal government.
- There is culture that tends to minimize problems or refuse to acknowledge problems all together.

Solutions:

- The Department should strengthen management and reporting structures at the VA Central Office and throughout the VHA field structure as referenced above.
- The Department must take swift and appropriate accountability actions. There must be recognition of how true accountability works.
- The tone at the top should encourage employees to speak up about problems, but also to think of and be a part of solutions.

The Department's failures have generated a high level of oversight. The Department must be more agile and responsive in transparently addressing all legitimate oversight requirements.

Background:

There is an incredible amount of oversight on the Department's activities. The IG, OSC, GAO, and several Congressional committees have conducted investigations and reviews into the Department's provision of timely care to Veterans. Over the last 4 1/2 years, VA has provided responses to over 104,000 Congressional inquiries. Over the last 2 1/2 years, VA has responded to over 7,500 requests for policy-related information. And, in the first 6 months of this fiscal year alone, the Department has participated in 33 hearings and 213 briefings for Congress. In the last five weeks, VA has sent over 100 letters to Members of Congress and delivered over 10,000 pages of documents. Twenty-one VA witnesses have provided hours of testimony at 11 hearings. In addition, VA has conducted daily outreach and information exchange between local VA facilities and local Congressional offices. VA has endeavored to be receptive to recommendations and responsive to requests for information - but could still do more.

Observations:

- There have been a number of problems identified and recommendations made by the IG, GAO, OSC, Congress, and others. VA has not followed through on sufficiently addressing those problems or implementing those recommendations.
- The IG is currently conducting investigations at 77 VA facilities. Since at least 2005, GAO and the IG have been identifying concerns regarding scheduling practices and data reliability.
- As of June 23, the OSC had over 50 pending cases, all of which allege threats to patient health or safety. Of those, OSC has referred 29 cases to the VA for investigation. This represents over a quarter of all cases referred by OSC for investigation government-wide. Additionally, 5 U.S.C. § 2302(c) requires agencies to ensure that employees are informed of the rights and remedies available to them under the Whistleblower Protection Act and related laws. OSC has a whistleblower certification program to provide agencies with a process for meeting this requirement. VA is not certified.

Solutions:

- VA should more proactively engage with its various oversight bodies.
- VA should track oversight reports and recommendations. The Department should release quarterly metrics on recommendations made by oversight bodies and VA's response.
- The Secretary should separately meet with the IG, OSC, and the Comptroller General on a quarterly basis. The General Counsel should separately meet with representatives of the IG, OSC, and GAO on a monthly basis.
- The Department should review its process for responding to OSC whistleblower cases (underway), and should designate an official to assess the conclusions and the proposed corrective actions in OSC reports.
- VA should also complete OSC's whistleblower certification program.

The technology underlying the basic scheduling system used by VA medical facilities is cumbersome and outdated. Lack of certain functionalities cause scheduling delays and, in some cases, reporting inaccuracies. However, with regard to increasing access to care, the software underlying the scheduling system is secondary to the need for additional resource to actually schedule - doctors, nurses, and other health professionals; physical space; and appropriately trained administrative support personnel.

Background:

VA began using the VistA electronic health records system in 1985. VistA is the single integrated health information system used throughout VHA in all of its health care settings. VistA is open source and has been used in a number of civilian hospitals.

(Continued)

(Continued)

The VA's VistA system has not changed in any appreciable way since 1985. This system predates the widespread use of the internet. From an engineering or work order management perspective, VistA has many flaws. But, it is state of the art in terms of providing an integrated health record that captures all documentation associated with a patient and it enables the collaboration of the delivery of that care. A 2011 survey by the American Academy of Family Physicians and a similar 2012 Medscape poll found that VistA was better than a large majority of health IT solutions, including those offered by market leaders McKesson and Epic.

VA plans to overhaul the outdated scheduling system and bring an innovative scheduling product into the electronic health record system. VA hopes to award a contract for the new patientscheduling system by the end of this fiscal year and have the system in place in fiscal 2015.

Observations:

- Dated scheduling systems and practices are causing significant problems for the Department of Veterans Affairs' ability to deliver timely access to quality health care. But neither the systems – nor the schedulers - are the source of extended wait times for Veterans seeking care.
- Many of the resource issues VA face are endemic to the health care field (for example, shortages of certain types of specialists or geographical shortages around the country) or to the Federal government (for example, slowness in the hiring process or an inability to compete with private sector wages). However, VA has also demonstrated an inability to clearly articulate budgetary needs and to tie budgetary needs to specific outcomes.

Solutions:

- Immediate problems with scheduling systems and practices can and are being addressed. The Department will procure new technology and will train frontline personnel on a stronger, modem system.
- VA needs additional resources to ensure adequate and appropriate health care for our Nation's Veterans. Those resources include:

  o Primary Care Physicians
  o Specialty Care Physicians
  o Administrators and Support Staff
  o Space (parking, examination, and surge space)

- VA needs to start planning and investing now for anticipated changes in the demographics of the Veterans. This includes geographical changes, an increased number of female Veterans, a surge in mental health needs, an increase in the special needs of younger Veterans returning from Iraq and Afghanistan, and specific needs associated with older Veterans.
- In the short term, VHA is working to increase the use of contract care. However, VHA must proceed with this carefully as proper oversight of the quality and timeliness of contract care is essential.

Source: https://www.whitehouse.gov/sites/default/files/docs/va_review.pdf.

NOTES

1. *Report of the Columbia Accident Investigation Board,* vol. 1 (Washington, DC: National Aeronautics and Space Administration, 2003), 101–102, https://www.nasa.gov/columbia/caib/html/VOL1.html.

2. Jean-Claude Thoenig, "Institutional Theories and Public Institutions: Traditions and Appropriateness," in *Handbook of Public Administration,* ed. B. Guy Peters and Jon Pierre (London, UK: Sage, 2003), 129; Philip Selznick, *TVA and the Grass Roots,* quoted in Jane E. Fountain, *Building the Virtual State: Information Technology and Institutional Change* (Washington, DC: Brookings Institution Press, 2001), 92.

3. James March and Johan Olsen, *Rediscovering Institutions* (New York, NY: Free Press, 1989), 22.

4. Ibid.

5. Lee G. Bolman and Terrence E. Deal, *Reframing Organizations* (San Francisco, CA: Jossey-Bass, 1991), 270.

6. Terrence E. Deal and Allan A. Kennedy, *Corporate Cultures: The Rites and Rituals of Corporate Life* (London, UK: Penguin, 1982).

7. James Q. Wilson, *Bureaucracy: What Government Agencies Do and Why They Do It* (New York, NY: Basic Books, 1991), 91.

8. Edgar Schein, *Organizational Culture and Leadership* (San Francisco, CA: John Wiley & Sons, 2010), 12.

9. Harrison M. Trice and Janice M. Beyer, *The Cultures of Work Organizations* (Englewood Cliffs, NJ: Prentice Hall, 1993), 32.

10. Ibid.

11. Homeland Security Advisory Council, "Report of the Culture Task Force," January 2007, http://www.dhs. gov/xlibrary/assets/hsac-culture-010107.pdf.

12. Jerry Markon, Ellen Nakashima, and Alice Crites, "Top-Level Turnover Makes It Harder for DHS to Stay on Top of Evolving Threats," *The Washington Post,* September 21, 2014, http://www.washingtonpost.com/politics/top-level-turnover-makes-it-harder-for-dhs-to-stay-on-top-of-evolving-threats/2014/09/21/ca7919a6-39d7-11e4-9c9f-ebb47272e40e_story.html.

13. Chester Irving Barnard, *The Functions of the Executive* (Cambridge, MA: Harvard University Press, 1938).

14. Fritz J. Roethlisberger and William J. Dickson, *Management and the Worker* (Cambridge, MA: Harvard University Press, 1939), cited by William G. Ouchi and Alan L. Wilkins, in "Organizational Culture," *Annual Review of Sociology* 11, (1985): 457–483.

15. Herbert A. Simon, *Administrative Behavior: A Study of Decision-Making Processes in Administrative Organization,* 3rd ed. (New York, NY: Free Press, 1976), 148-149.

16. Robert B. Denhardt, "Bureaucratic Socialization and Organizational Accommodation," *Administrative Science Quarterly* 13, no. 3 (1968): 441–450, 449.

17. Edgar Schein, "Organizational Culture," Working Paper #2088-88 (Cambridge, MA: MIT Sloan School of Management, December 1988)

18. Ouchi and Wilkins, "Organizational Culture," 457–483.

19. Thomas J. Peters and Robert H. Waterman, *In Search of Excellence: Lessons from America's Best-Run Companies* (New York, NY: Harper and Row, 1982); Deal and Kennedy, *Corporate Cultures;* Schein, *Organizational Culture and Leadership.*

20. Edgar Schein, "Organizational Culture," Working Paper, 3.

21. James March and Johan Olsen, *Rediscovering Institutions* (New York, NY: Free Press, 1989), 22.

22. Carolyn Ban, *How Do Public Managers Manage? Bureaucratic Constraints, Organizational Culture, and the Potential for Reform* (San Francisco, CA: Jossey-Bass, 1995).

23. Sanjay K. Pandey, David H. Coursey, and Donald P. Moynihan, "Organizational Effectiveness and Bureaucratic Red Tape," *Public Performance and Management Review* 30, no. 3 (2007): 398–425.

24. Ibid., 416.

25. Janet A. Weiss, "Public Management and Psychology," in *The State of Public Management,* ed. Donald Kettl and Brint Milward (Baltimore, MD: Johns Hopkins University Press, 1996).

26. John M. Bryson, *Strategic Planning for Public and Nonprofit Organizations,* 4th ed. (San Francisco, CA: Jossey-Bass, 2011), p. 127.

27. "Our Mission," Department of Homeland Security, December 17, 2012, http://www.dhs.gov/our-mission.

28. Ibid.

29. "Vision Statement," United States Secret Service, accessed January 7, 2015, http://www.secretservice.gov/mission.shtml.

30. Ibid.

31. James Q. Wilson, *Bureaucracy: What Government Agencies Do and Why They Do It* (New York, NY: Basic Books, 1989), 95.

32. Janet A. Weiss and Sandy Kristin Piderit, "The Value of Mission Statements in Public Agencies," *Journal of Public Administration Research and Theory* 9, no. 2 (1999): 193–223, 221.

33. Karl E. Weick, "Educational Organizations as Loosely Coupled Systems," *Administrative Science Quarterly* 21, no. 1 (1976): 1–19.

34. John W. Meyer and Brian Rowan, "Institutional Organizations: Formal Structure as Myth and Ceremony," *American Journal of Sociology* 83, (1977): 357.

35. William G. Ouchi, "A Conceptual Framework for the Design of Organizational Control Mechanisms," *Management Science* 25, no. 9 (1979): 833–848, 844.

36. Patrick J. Wolf and Brian C. Hassel, "Effectiveness and Accountability, Part 1: The Compliance Model," in *Rethinking Special Education for a New Century*, ed. Chester E. Finn Jr., Andrew J. Rotherham, and Charles R. Hokanson Jr. (Washington, DC: Thomas B. Fordham Foundation, 2001), 58, http://www.ppionline.org/documents/ SpecialEd_ch03.pdf.

37. Joseph Hagin et al., "Executive Summary to Report from the United States Secret Service Protective Mission Panel to the Secretary of Homeland Security," *United States Secret Service Mission Panel (USSSPMP)*, 2014, http://www.dhs.gov/sites/default/files/publications/14_1218_usss_pmp.pdf.

38. Todd R. LaPorte, "High-Reliability Organizations: Unlikely, Demanding and At Risk," *Journal of Contingencies and Crisis Management* 4, no. 2 (1996): 64.

39. Ibid., 65.

40. Christopher D. Wickens et al., *Flight to the Future: Human Factors in Air Traffic Control* (Washington, DC: National Academies Press, 1997), 150.

41. Todd R. LaPorte and H. George Frederickson, "Airport Security, High Reliability, and the Problem of Rationality," *Public Administration Review* 62, no. 1 (2002): 33–43.

42. Eric W. K. Tsang, "Organizational Learning and the Learning Organization: A Dichotomy between Descriptive and Prescriptive Research," *Human Relations* 50, no. 1 (1997): 73–89; see also C. Marlene Fiol and Marjorie A. Lyles, "Organizational Learning," *Academy of Management Review* 10, no. 4 (1985): 803–813.

43. B. Hedberg, "How Organizations Learn and Unlearn," in *Handbook of Organizational Design*, ed. Paul C. Nystrom and William H. Starbuck (London, UK: Oxford University Press, 1981), 6.

44. Chris Argyris and Donald A. Schön, *Organizational Learning: A Theory of Action Perspective* (Reading, MA: Addison-Wesley), 2, 29.

45. Barbara Levitt and James G. March, "Organizational Learning," *Annual Review of Sociology* 14, (1988): 320.

46. Tsang, "Organizational Learning and the Learning Organization.

47. Swee C. Goh, "Toward a Learning Organization: The Strategic Building Blocks," *SAM Advanced Management Journal* 63, no. 2 (1998): 15–22.

48. Baiyin Yang, Karen E. Watkins, and Victoria J. Marsick, "The Construct of the Learning Organization: Dimensions, Measurement, and Validation," *Human Resource Development Quarterly* 15, (2004): 31–55.

49. Julianne Mahler, "Influences of Organizational Culture on Learning in Public Agencies," *Journal of Public Administration Research and Theory* 7, no. 4 (1997): 519–540, 521.

50. Jostein Askim, Åge Johnsen, and Knut-Andreas Christophersen, "Factors Behind Organizational Learning from Benchmarking: Experiences from Norwegian Municipal Benchmarking Networks," *Journal of Public Administration Research and Theory* 18, no. 2 (2008): 297–320; Donald P. Moynihan, "Goal-Based Learning and the Future of Performance Management," *Public Administration Review* 65, no. 2 (2005): 203–216; Thomas A. Birkland, *Lessons of Disaster: Policy Change after Catastrophic Events* (Washington, DC: Georgetown University Press, 2006); Donald P. Moynihan, "Learning under Uncertainty: Networks in Crisis Management," *Public Administration Review* 68, no. 2 (2008): 350–361.

51. Levitt and March, "Organizational Learning," 335.

52. Robert D. Behn, "Creating an Innovative Organization: Ten Hints for Involving Frontline Workers," *State and Local Government Review* 27, no. 3 (1995), www.govleaders.org/behn_innovation.htm.

53. Ibid.

54. Ibid.

55. Terry M. Moe, "The Politics of Structural Choice: Toward a Theory of Public Bureaucracy," in *Organization Theory: From Chester Barnard to the Present and Beyond* (New York, NY: Oxford University Press, 1990), 134.

56. Daniel Carpenter, *Reputation and Power: Organizational Image and Pharmaceutical Regulation at the FDA* (Princeton, NJ: Princeton University Press, 2010), pp. 46-47.

57. Hugh Heclo, "OMB and the Presidency–The Problem of 'Neutral Competence," *Public Interest*, 38 (Winter 1975): 80–99.

58. David L. Weimer, "Institutionalizing Neutrally Competent Policy Analysis: Resources for Promoting Objectivity and Balance in Consolidating Democracies," *Policy Studies Journal* 33, no. 2 (2005): 132.

59. Ibid.,138.; See also Philip G. Joyce, *The Congressional Budget Office: Honest Numbers, Power, and Policymaking* (Washington, DC: Georgetown University Press, 2011).

60. Philip Joyce, *The Congressional Budget Office*, 212.

61. Oxford Dictionaries, s.v. "trust," accessed December 31, 2014, http://www.oxforddictionaries.com/us/definition/american_english/trust.

62. Russell Hardin, *Collective Action* (Baltimore, MD: Johns Hopkins University Press, 1982); Robert Axelrod, *The Evolution of Cooperation* (New York, NY: Basic Books, 1984).

63. Jurian Edelenbos and Erik-Hans Klijn, "Trust in Complex Decision-Making Networks: A Theoretical and Empirical Exploration," *Administration & Society* 39, no. 1 (2007): 25–50.

64. Ibid.; Erik-Hans Klijn, "Networks and Inter-organizational Management: Challenging, Steering, Evaluation, and the Role of Public Actors in Public Management," in *The Oxford Handbook of Public Management,* eds. Ewan Ferlie, Laurence E. Lynn Jr., and Christopher Pollitt (Oxford, UK: Oxford University Press, 2007), 257–281.

65. Joop Koppenjan and Erik-Hans Klijn, *Managing Uncertainties in Networks: A Network Approach to Problem Solving and Decision Making* (New York, NY: Routledge, 2004).

66. Michael D. Cohen, James G. March, and Johan P. Olsen, "A Garbage Can Model of Organizational Choice," *Administrative Science Quarterly* 17, no. 1 (March 1972): 1–25.

67. Government Accountability Office, "Department of Homeland Security: Addressing Management Challenges that Face Immigration Enforcement Agencies" (GAO-05-664T), Testimony of Richard M. Stana, Director, Homeland Security and Justice Issues, May 5, 2005, 5, 8.

68. Jane E. Fountain, *Building the Virtual State: Information Technology and Institutional Change* (Washington DC: Brookings Institution Press, 2001).

69. Rosemary O'Leary and Susan Summers Raines, "Lessons Learned from Two Decades of Alternative Dispute Resolution Programs and Processes at the U.S. Environmental Protection Agency," *Public Administration Review* 61, no. 6 (2001): 682–692, 687.

70. Martha Derthick, *Agency Under Stress: The Social Security Administration in American Government* (Washington, DC: Brookings Institution 1990), 47.

71. Steven Rathgeb Smith and Michael Lipsky, *Nonprofits for Hire: The Welfare State in the Age of Contracting* (Cambridge, MA: Harvard University Press, 1993), 95. See also Lester M. Salamon, "The Marketization of Welfare: Changing Nonprofit and For-Profit Roles in the American Welfare State," *Social Service Review* 67, no. 1 (1993): 16–39.

72. Barbara S. Romzek and Jocelyn M. Johnston, "Reforming Medicaid through Contracting: The Nexus of Implementation and Organizational Culture," *Journal of Public Administration Research and Theory* 9, no. 1 (1999): 107–139, 136, 135.

73. James Glanz, "Loss of the Shuttle: Bureaucrats Stifled Spirit of Adventure, NASA's Critics Say," *The New York Times,* February 18, 2003.

74. Anne M. Khademian, *Working with Culture: The Way the Job Gets Done in Public Programs* (Washington, DC: CQ Press, 2002), 24.

75. The White House/President's Intelligence Advisory Board, "Science at Its Best, Security at Its Worst: A Report on the Security Problems at the U.S. Department of Energy," June 1999, http://www.fas.org/sgp/library/pfiab.

76. Chester I. Barnard, *The Functions of the Executive* (Cambridge, MA: Harvard University Press, 1938).

77. Schein, "Organizational Culture," Working Paper, 5.

78. John D. DiIulio Jr, "Principled Agents: The Cultural Bases of Behavior in a Federal Government Bureaucracy," *Journal of Public Administration Research and Theory* 4, no. 3 (1994): 314.

79. Khademian, *Working with Culture*

80. Ibid., 3.

81. Ibid., see Box 5.1, page 119, for a full set of guidelines.

82. Barry Bozeman, *Government Management of Information Mega-Technology: Lessons from the Internal Revenue Service's Tax Systems Modernization* (Washington, DC: IBM Center for the Business of Government, 2002).

83. Laurie E. Paarlberg, James L. Perry, and Annie Hondeghem, "From Theory to Practice: Strategies for Applying Public Service Motivation," in *Motivation in Public Management: The Call of Public Service,* ed. James L. Perry and Annie Hondeghem (London, UK: Oxford University Press, 2008).

84. Paarlberg, Perry, and Hondeghem, "From Theory to Practice" (Working Paper Version), 3.

85. Ibid., 6, 11, 15, 19, 23.

86. DiIulio Jr., "Principled Agents," 315.

87. April Avison, "Changes Starting at Bryan PD," *The Eagle,* Bryan-College Station, Texas, September 29, 2007, Sec. A.

88. Trice and Beyer, *The Cultures of Work Organizations*, 356.

89. Joby Warrick and Walter Pincus, "Lessons of Iraq Aided Intelligence on Iran: Officials Cite New Caution and a Surge in Spying," *The Washington Post,* December 5, 2007, Sec. A.

90. Scott Bronstein and Drew Griffin, "A Fatal Wait: Veterans Languish and Die on a VA Hospital's Secret List," *CNN*, April 23, 2014, http://www.cnn.com/2014/04/23/health/veterans-dying-health-care-delays.

91. Josh Hicks, "Official Inquiries Begin for Phoenix VA hospital with Alleged 'Secret Waiting List,'" *The Washington Post*, April 27, 2014, http://www.washingtonpost.com/blogs/federal-eye/wp/2014/04/27/official-inquiries-begin-for-phoenix-va-hospital-with-alleged-secret-waiting-list.

92. Sam Foote, "Why I Blew the Whistle on the VA," *The New York Times*, May 23, 2014, http://www.nytimes.com/2014/05/24/opinion/why-i-blew-the-whistle-on-the-va.html.

93. The White House, "Readout of the President's Meeting with Acting Veterans Affairs Secretary Sloan Gibson and Rob Nabors," June 27, 2014, https://www.whitehouse.gov/the-press-office/2014/06/27/readout-president-s-meeting-acting-veterans-affairs-secretary-sloan-gi-0.

PART IV CRAFT

Public Managers as Creators

Although the confines of leadership are indeed binding, they are not necessarily paralyzing. . . . Even leaders who recognize the limits on what they can accomplish during their terms of office are inclined, especially if they are the spirited, driving persons the system tends to select, to use all their powers for whatever effect they can have. . . . To toil at making a small difference, then, is not inevitably an exercise in futility. . . . Pragmatists confronted by constraints do what they can within the constraints.[i]

—Herbert Kauffman
The Administrative Behavior of Federal Bureau Chiefs

Given an identical set of circumstances—political environments, organizational structures and cultures, unfolding situations, policy conflicts—will any two individuals do exactly the same thing and go about assessing and acting on the situation in the same way? Will they draw on the same information? Will they pursue the same goals? Will they react in the same way when confronted with the unexpected? Will they make the same decisions? Will they place the same emphasis on communicating with colleagues and superiors? Analyzing how a particular manager navigates a situation shines the light on managerial craft.

As a dimension of public management, craft comprises the decisions and actions by which public managers, as individuals in their own right, influence the achievement of public policy outcomes.

As has been emphasized in earlier chapters, how public managers define and pursue their responsibilities is often constrained by structures and processes of formal authority and by institutionalized standards, norms, and values. But public managers are not merely role players constrained to follow scripts written by legislators, elected executives, budget officers, or departmental lawyers. These same structures enable them to be creators, that is, to exercise their own judgment, in implementing public policies.

---

[i]Herbert Kaufman, *The Administrative Behavior of Federal Bureau Chiefs* (Washington, DC: Brookings Institution, 1981), 136.

Craft comprises the decisions and actions by which public managers, as individuals in their own right, influence the achievement of public policy outcomes.

Thus, the identities of the individuals are who are exercising managerial responsibilities are likely to matter, perhaps even to matter decisively. Likely to matter too are what their own motives and values are, what they know, how they learn, and the skills they possess relevant to the specific nature of their responsibilities. Their characters, personalities, and competence will in turn affect how their superiors, peers, and subordinates exercise their own responsibilities and the energy and commitment with which they meet them.

EVOLUTION OF THE CRAFT PERSPECTIVE

The earliest conceptualizations of the public manager's job were prescriptive, emphasizing the democratically responsible exercise of administrative authority by public administrators who were obedient to statutory and judicial guidance. As mentioned in Chapter 1, the most complete and best-known answer to the question, "What do public managers do?" was Luther Gulick's famous POSDCORB, which stands for planning, organizing, staffing, directing, coordinating, reporting, and budgeting.[ii] Public managers were conceived as performing the basic functions of management within the framework of legal authority: managerial craft was neither possible nor desirable. Little consideration was given to the "nature of the craft," that is, of managerial skill.[iii]

Chester Barnard's *The Functions of the Executive* in 1938 laid the groundwork for new perspectives on responsibilities of managers. Barnard "defined administrative responsibility as primarily a moral question or, more specifically, as the resolution of competing and conflicting codes—legal, technical, personal, professional, and organizational—in the reaching of individual decisions."[iv] Barnard influenced John Millett, whose 1954 book, *Management in the Public Service,* is an early exemplar of the craft perspective:

> The challenge to any administrator is to overcome obstacles, to understand and master problems, to use imagination and insight in devising new goals of public service. No able administrator can be content to be simply a good caretaker. He seeks rather to review the ends of organized effort and to advance the goals of administrative endeavor toward better public service.[v]

More recently, behavioral approaches to public management have tended to emphasize a concern for choices, decisions, and outcomes; for the political skill needed to perform effectively in specific managerial positions; and for the psychological and emotional demands of managing in the public sector. By emphasizing the strategic political role of public managers within given political and institutional settings, these newer conceptions are concerned with the immediate, pragmatic concerns of managers at executive levels of government organizations more than with the broader role of management in the constitutional scheme of governance. These approaches

[ii]Luther Gulick, "Notes on the Theory of Organization," in *Papers on the Science of Administration*, ed. Luther Gulick and Lyndall F. Urwick (New York, NY: Institute of Public Administration, Columbia University, 1937), 1–46.

[iii]Roscoe C. Martin, "Paul H. Appleby and His Administrative World," in *Public Administration and Democracy: Essays in Honor of Paul H. Appleby*, ed. Roscoe C. Martin (Syracuse, NY: Syracuse University Press, 1965), 8.

[iv]Frederick C. Mosher, *Democracy and the Public Service* (New York, NY: Oxford University Press, 1968), 210. Discussion in this section draws on Lynn, "Public Management."

[v]John D. Millett, *Management in the Public Service: The Quest for Effective Performance* (New York, NY: McGraw-Hill, 1954), 401.

place lower priority on managers' efforts to develop and sustain institutional capacity, mold organizational cultures, and adhere to durable democratic values—that is, on public management as an institution.

Literature on the craft perspective tends to be based on the study and analysis of particular cases of managerial experience.[vi] In his foundational article comparing public and private management, political scientist Graham T. Allison noted, "The effort to develop public management as a field of knowledge should start from problems faced by practicing public managers."[vii] Such studies focus on what managers actually do in specific settings. Critics view this approach as an "ongoing effort to create a new 'myth' for public management . . . . By emphasizing a political and activist orientation—heroes and entrepreneurs became the stock and trade of its case studies" at the expense of institutions.[viii] Examples of this genre include Kenneth Ashworth's *Caught Between the Dog and the Fireplug, or How to Survive in Public Service,* Steven Cohen and William Eimicke's *The Effective Public Manager,* Philip Heymann's *The Politics of Public Management,* Robert Reich's *Public Management in a Democratic Society,* Behn's *Leadership Counts,* and Mark Moore's *Creating Public Value.[ix]*

Anxious to inspire public officials with the conviction that "management counts" and with an entrepreneurial, proactive spirit, the craft literature has turned heavily to prescription. The best of this literature—for example, Norma Riccucci's *Unsung Heroes,* Paul Light's *Sustaining Innovation,* and Eugene Bardach's *Getting Agencies to Work Together*—represents an appreciation of the existential challenges of public management at all levels of government and in the nonprofit sector and an attempt to deduce best or smart practices from closely analyzed cases.[x] Other contributions, such as Cohen and Eimicke's *The New Effective Public Manager* and Richard Haass's *The Bureaucratic Entrepreneur,* are explicitly didactic and feature numerous prescriptions and principles based on the experiences and reflections of effective practitioners, including the authors themselves.[xi]

Many craft-oriented public management scholars tend to disregard or downplay the structure and culture dimensions of public management or to take them as given. They concern themselves with the temperamental and psychological capacities of managers to confront multiple pressures in given situations. This approach leads to a preoccupation with the traits and personalities of managers. Successful managers are characterized as enterprising or entrepreneurial, inclined to take risks, purposeful, imaginative and intuitive, and disposed to act rather than reflect. For example, Moore argues:

[vi]A more extensive review of this literature is in Laurence E. Lynn Jr., *Public Management as Art, Science and Profession* (Chatham, NJ: Chatham House, 1996), 65–86.

[vii]Graham T. Allison Jr., "Public and Private Management: Are They Fundamentally Alike in All Unimportant Respects?" *Proceedings for the Public Management Research Conference,* OPM Document 127-53-1 (Washington, DC: Office of Personal Management, November 19–20, 1979), 38.

[viii]J. Patrick Dobel, Review of Erwin C. Hargrove and John C. Glidewell, *Impossible Jobs* (Lawrence: University Press of Kansas, 1990), in *Journal of Policy Analysis and Management* 11, no. 1 (1992): 144–147.

[ix]Kenneth H. Ashworth, *Caught Between the Dog and the Fireplug, or How to Survive in Public Service* (Washington, DC: Georgetown University Press, 2001); Steven Cohen and William Eimicke, *The Effective Public Manager: Achieving Success in a Changing Government* (San Francisco, CA: Jossey-Bass, 2002); Philip Heymann, *The Politics of Public Management* (New Haven, CT: Yale University Press, 1987); Robert Reich, *Public Management in a Democratic Society* (Englewood Cliffs, NJ: Prentice Hall, 1990); Robert D. Behn, *Leadership Counts: Lessons for Public Managers from the Massachusetts Welfare, Training, and Employment Program* (Cambridge, MA: Harvard University Press, 1991); and Mark H. Moore, *Creating Public Value: Strategic Management in Government* (Cambridge, MA: Harvard University Press, 1995).

[x]Norma Riccucci, *Unsung Heroes: Federal Execucrats Making a Difference* (Washington, DC: Georgetown University Press, 1995); Paul Light, *Sustaining Innovation: Creating Nonprofit and Government Organizations that Innovate Naturally* (San Francisco, CA: Jossey-Bass, 1998); Eugene Bardach, *Getting Agencies to Work Together* (Washington, DC: Brookings Institution, 1998).

[xi]Cohen and Eimicke, *The Effective Public Manager;* Richard N. Haass, *The Bureaucratic Entrepreneur: How to Be Effective in Any Unruly Organization* (Washington, DC: Brookings Institution, 1999).

Cool, inner concentration, in the end, can and should guide the calculations of those who would lead public organizations. It describes the 'managerial temperament' that is appropriate for those who would lead organizations that work for a divided and uncertain society. . . . Ideas and techniques . . . can be no substitute for good character and experience. But, with luck, they might help to extend the limits of one's character and experience.[xii]

Other craft-oriented public management experts emphasize simple, generic processes— such as establishing and reiterating clear goals, managing by "walking around"[xiii] or by "groping along"[xiv]—or adhering to unexceptional principles such as developing and focusing on a narrow agenda or paying attention to people. Behn observes, "Most management concepts are simple, and, to have any impact these simple management ideas must be expressible in some pithy phrase."[xv] But their simplicity can be deceptive. After citing five unimpeachable principles for achieving influence as a manager—such as look for opportunities to act, be careful—Haass asserts, "Being effective is that simple—and that complicated."[xvi]

Such oversimplifications should not discredit the importance of managerial craft as a fundamental dimension of public management. The behavioral and intellectual challenges that any good manager must take into account can be a significant factor in government performance. What Barnard termed "non-logical" aspects of managerial behavior affect whether a manager's reactions are timely, whether perceptions are intuitive, and, ultimately, whether judgment is sound.

PUBLIC MANAGEMENT'S PERFECT STORM: THE CRAFT DIMENSION

The introductions to Parts II and III highlight the structure and craft dimensions reflected in the Senate's report on the Katrina response.[xvii] The report also details a number of examples of managerial craft at all levels. As was the case with structure, many findings focused on managerial failures to exercise craft responsibly and effectively:

25. Governor [Kathleen] Blanco and Mayor [Ray] Nagin failed to meet expectations set forth in the National Response Plan to coordinate state and local resources "to address the full spectrum of actions" needed to prepare for and respond to Hurricane Katrina. Funding shortages and inadequacies in long-term planning doomed Louisiana's preparations for Katrina. [p. 591]

34. Secretary [Michael] Chertoff appointed a field commander, [FEMA director] Michael Brown, who was hostile to the federal government's agreed-upon response plan and therefore was unlikely to perform effectively in accordance with

[xii]Mark H. Moore, *Creating Public Value: Strategic Management in Government* (Cambridge, MA: Harvard University Press, 1995).

[xiii]Tom Peters and Robert H. Waterman, *In Search of Excellence: Lessons from America's Best Run Companies* (New York, NY: HarperCollins, 1982).

[xiv]Robert D. Behn, "Management by Groping Along," *Journal of Policy Analysis and Management* 8 (1988).

[xv]Ibid., 651.

[xvi]Richard N. Haass, *The Power to Persuade: How to be Effective in Government, the Public Sector, or Any Unruly Organization* (New York, NY: Houghton, Mifflin, 1994), 230.

[xvii]U.S. Senate, *Hurricane Katrina: A Nation Still Unprepared: Special Report of the Committee on Homeland Security and Governmental Affairs* (Washington, DC: Government Printing Office, 2006), http://www.gpoaccess.gov/serialset/creports/katrinanation.html.

its principles. Some of Secretary Chertoff's top advisors were aware of these issues but Secretary Chertoff has indicated that he was not. Secretary Chertoff should have known of these problems and, as a result, should have appointed someone other than Brown as Principal Federal Official. [p. 592]

53. Michael Brown, FEMA's director, was insubordinate, unqualified, and counterproductive, in that he:

    a. sent a single employee, without operational expertise or equipment and from the New England region to New Orleans before landfall;
    b. circumvented his chain of command and failed to communicate critical information to the Secretary;
    c. failed to deliver on commitments made to Louisiana's leaders for buses;
    d. traveled to Baton Rouge with FEMA public-affairs and congressional-relations employees and a personal aide, and no operational experts;
    e. failed to organize FEMA's or other federal efforts in any meaningful way; and
    f. failed to adequately carry out responsibilities as FEMA's lead official in the Gulf before landfall and when he was appointed as the Principal Federal Official after landfall. [p. 593]

155. During this initial period after landfall, a number of military commanders within the services were proactive, identifying, alerting, and positioning assets for potential response, prior to receiving requests from FEMA or specific orders. Many of these preparations proved essential to the overall response; however, they reflected the individual initiative of various commanders rather than a pre-planned, coordinated response as is necessary for a disaster of this magnitude. [p. 602]

177. Although DHS was charged with administering the plan and leading the response under it, DHS officials made decisions that appeared to be at odds with the NRP, failed to fulfill certain responsibilities under the NRP on a timely basis, and failed to make effective use of certain authorities under the NRP. [p. 604]

186. Where and when personnel with experience and training on NIMS ICS [National Incident Management System Incident Command System] were in control with an adequate number of trained support personnel, coupled with the discipline to adhere to the doctrine of NIMS ICS, it made a positive difference in the quality and success of implementing an incident command structure, establishing a unified command, and the response. [p. 605]

Every public management story, whether the rollout of the Affordable Care Act's insurance exchanges, the surveillance of Americans' communications by the National Security Agency, the successful reform of Missouri's juvenile justice system, or the managerial responses to Hurricane Katrina, contains accounts of how individuals did, or didn't do, their jobs. Managerial craft may not be the whole story, but it is always part of the story.

PART IV OVERVIEW

Part IV explores specific frameworks, theories, and concepts that illuminate the craft dimension of public management, facilitating the analyses of a public manager's individual contributions. Craft aspects that are largely operational in nature, such as working with the media, interacting with interest groups, promoting teamwork, and working with political superiors and peers are not covered here.[xviii]

Part IV comprises two chapters:

- Chapter 10 addresses managerial styles. It discusses how personality traits, types, or temperaments affect a manager's approach to a situation. The chapter describes leadership as an aspect of craft, drawing conceptual frameworks for its analysis from both theory-based and practice-based literatures.
- Chapter 11 discusses a number of heuristics that can be used by managers to sharpen their craft in areas of decision making, learning, and strategizing. These heuristics also provide the tools for sharpening the analysis of craft to discern the contribution of craft, as distinct from structure and culture, in a given situation.

This part of the book provides answers to two questions:

1. **What qualities or characteristics of individuals affect how they carry out managerial responsibilities in government?**

2. **In what ways might public managers improve their craft and be more effective in serving public interests?**

[xviii]Kenneth H. Ashworth, *Caught Between the Dog and the Fireplug, or How to Survive in Public Service* (Washington, DC: Georgetown University Press, 2001); Steven Cohen and William Eimicke, *The Effective Public Manager: Achieving Success in a Changing Government* (San Francisco, CA: Jossey-Bass, 2002); Philip Heymann, *The Politics of Public Management* (New Haven, CT: Yale University Press, 1987); Robert Reich, *Public Management in a Democratic Society* (Englewood Cliffs, NJ: Prentice Hall, 1990); Robert D. Behn, *Leadership Counts: Lessons for Public Managers from the Massachusetts Welfare, Training, and Employment Program* (Cambridge, MA: Harvard University Press, 1991); and Mark H. Moore, *Creating Public Value: Strategic Management in Government* (Cambridge, MA: Harvard University Press, 1995).

10 | Craft
Managerial Styles

INTRODUCTION

Because explicit or implicit delegations of authority to public managers are inevitable, the exercise of managerial craft is almost always a necessary contribution to public policy implementation. As emphasized in Part II, structures enable and often mandate the exercise of managerial craft. These situations occur when

- an enacting coalition explicitly delegates authority to executive agencies and their managers to specify details of a policy or administrative process or content;
- a mandate is ambiguous (intentionally or unintentionally) and managers must figure out what decisions to make and what actions to take so implementation can proceed; and
- fulfilling legislative or administrative objectives requires judgment in applying rules and standards to particular situations.

Empirical analyses reveal frequent instances of how managers affect the character, quality, and availability of public services.[1] The efficacy of managerial craftsmanship is not robust, however, and scholars disagree over its importance. For example, in her study of the implementation of the federal Temporary Assistance for Needy Families program, public management scholar Norma M. Riccucci showed that the influence of management on the behaviors and actions of frontline service workers was negligible.[2] Their activities were influenced much more by professional norms, work customs, and occupational cultures than by managerial directives. In her studies of the same kinds of programs, however, public management scholar Evelyn Z. Brodkin reached virtually the opposite conclusion, that managerial directives affect the fairness and effectiveness of these programs by constraining how service workers interact with clients.[3]

Making good choices concerning strategies and tools can enable public managers to make a difference on a worthwhile, and occasionally even noteworthy, scale. Gordon Chase, a former public manager in New York City and the Commonwealth of Massachusetts whose honesty, integrity, and leadership were an inspiration to many, observed,

> No single combination of education, experience, personality, and talent will make the same person a great commissioner of welfare for New York City and a smashing water and sewer director in Seattle. Each state, city, county, and township has a unique set of political, social, and economic challenges to which an aspiring public manager must adapt. But . . . there are predictable problems, dilemmas, conflicts, and confrontations that are sure to occur at some point, to some degree, in every public manager's life . . . . Stay honest, be smart, and care—the public will be the better for it.[4]

The men and women who manage government agencies, programs, and activities make a difference. Often it is a positive difference but not always. The absence of managerial creativity, sound judgment, or strategic thinking may contribute to policy failures or to an organization's reputation for incompetence. By ignoring or poorly organizing and supervising an agency's tasks, the public manager can undermine the agency's effectiveness. By failing to capitalize on opportunities for significant improvements in operations, political and public support continues to erode.

A public manager is exercising managerial craft when he or she

- actively influences the design of structures by participating in the drafting of legislation, executive orders, and regulations;

Effective management results from a good fit between the particular demands of a management position and the particular characteristics of the manager in that position.

- discovers and implements innovative ways to overcome or mitigate constraints;
- reorients organizational cultures by exemplifying and rewarding goal-oriented behavior; or
- interprets and evaluates, resolves conflicts, defines priorities, or represents his or her organization in different forums.

Individuals in managerial roles differ in their temperaments and therefore in how they practice their craft, perhaps as a delegator or a micromanager. But individuals of different temperaments and skill sets can be effective managers, not necessarily equally so in the same roles. Effective management results from a good fit between the particular demands of a management position and the particular characteristics of the manager in that position.

This chapter begins with a comparison of the craft of two cabinet secretaries during the George W. Bush administration. Next, temperament and personality as foundations of craft are considered. The fit between personality and the requirements of the job or situation is of special interest here. Then, leadership theories and heuristics are discussed. The end-of-chapter case provides insight into the temperament and leadership of an executive director of a food bank in Chicago.

CASE: A TALE OF TWO CABINET SECRETARIES

Samuel W. Bodman and John D. Ashcroft both served as senior federal-level cabinet officials in the administration of President George W. Bush, yet they present sharp contrasts in managerial craftsmanship. Bodman assumed major responsibilities and, although many of his views were controversial, he was generally regarded as a successful manager. Ashcroft, in contrast, engendered considerable controversy, and assessments of his effectiveness as a manager are decidedly mixed.

SAMUEL BODMAN, SECRETARY OF ENERGY

Bodman was confirmed by the Senate as the secretary of energy on January 31, 2005. He had previously served in the George W. Bush administration as the deputy secretary of both the Commerce Department and the Treasury Department. Before his public service, Bodman headed Cabot Corporation, a global specialty chemicals and materials company. He also had held positions in the financial services industry as a venture capitalist and as a faculty member at the Massachusetts Institute of Technology, where he earned a PhD in chemical engineering. He has been described as "the most qualified secretary [of energy] we've ever had."[5]

Bodman began his tenure at the Department of Energy (DOE) by "devour[ing] several fat three-ring briefing binders describing the $24 billion behemoth he was about to manage."[6] Within months, he effectively used a "corporate-style structure." His appointees to senior positions, reflecting his belief that the Capitol was where the money is, were praised as "not big ideologues," but as people "very interested and willing to work with both sides of the aisle on the Hill."[7] He held weekly staff meetings of more than 20 top officials so they might communicate with each other about their activities and become familiar with the department as a whole.

On April 11, 2006, Bodman sent a memorandum to DOE employees and contractors, indicating his inclination to manage through establishing and enforcing specific, market-oriented goals:

> all DOE Federal and contractor personnel have the right—and the responsibility—to identify and report concerns associated with safety, quality, environment, health, security, or management of DOE operations without fear of reprisal. . . . In turn, DOE Federal and contractor managers are expected to respond respectfully to these concerns in a prompt and effective manner to ensure efficient operation of programs under their jurisdiction.[8]

A profile of Bodman in the journal *Science* described him as self-effacing but relishing a challenge and "an engineer, not a scientist."[9] Among the challenges he chose to define for himself were reversing cuts in DOE's budget for basic science and increasing White House support for applied energy initiatives. His success in meeting both challenges and in creating the new position of science adviser to the secretary led to his characterization as a "hero of science." He was praised by independent experts as having "his values in the right location."

(Continued)

(Continued)

Yet Bodman also courted controversy. He dismissed DOE's science advisory board, saying he preferred to receive advice from "those on the payroll," including officials at DOE's far-flung laboratories. He spoke little of energy conservation and used a limousine and SUVs for his entourage, at the same time emphasizing the promise of nuclear energy. Many saw his new energy initiatives as too small relative to the problem of achieving energy independence.

Bodman's rationalist strategy stemmed from a handful of policy convictions and a pragmatic weighing of his challenges and opportunities. His approach tended to reflect the problem-oriented style of an engineer—factual and analytical—and the kind of engaging extraversion associated with those who enjoy the social demands of managerial roles.

JOHN ASHCROFT, ATTORNEY GENERAL

Ashcroft, a lawyer and former U.S. senator from Missouri, had served as attorney general from February 2001 through February 2005, during George W. Bush's first term. Following the 9/11 terrorist attacks, Ashcroft became the principal advocate for the controversial USA Patriot Act, which, as noted in Chapter 3, expanded the federal government's powers to combat terrorist threats. An editorial in the Austin, Texas, *American-Statesman* argued, "the Patriot Act would be far less controversial if Ashcroft were not so furtive about when, how, how often and for what it is used."[10] The editorial described Ashcroft as "a public official with a penchant for secrecy" who "barely gives Congress the time of day and is even less forthcoming with the press and the public."

In an interview with *U.S. News & World Report,* Ashcroft noted that his job was nothing less than changing the Justice Department from an agency that prosecutes offenders to one that prevents the most dangerous offenses: terrorism and related acts.[11] "In order to move an institution and its mentality," he said, "sometimes you have to draw very clear lines." Ashcroft defended what many commentators saw as his harsh rhetoric by saying that he needed to let the American people know exactly how he was handling things. For Ashcroft, the public management challenge was regarded by many as a matter of shifting the institutionalized values of the Justice Department.

Among his policy priorities, Ashcroft forcefully insisted on uniformity of law enforcement across all the U.S. attorney offices, as illustrated in the examples in Chapter 6. No one told Ashcroft to choose this strategy; he just believed it was the right thing to do even though a predecessor had tried the strategy without success and even though it was intensely controversial within the Justice Department and state law enforcement communities.

Ashcroft's view of his job was "not to micromanage but to offer big-picture, results-oriented leadership—what he likes to call 'noble inspiration.'"[12] Critics within the department said that he was isolated from the staff attorneys, that he got information by phone and e-mail rather than through personal contact, and that decision making was opaque.

Ashcroft approached his responsibilities in a manner consistent with his devoutly evangelical religious faith, displaying unshakable commitment to principle and the personal aloofness of an inner-directed individual. His strategy, although similar to those of other officials engaged in homeland security, was articulated and pursued with fervor and little patience with inside-the-Beltway political processes.

CONTRASTING CRAFT

Certainly Bodman and Ashcroft led departments constrained and enabled to differing degrees, and operated in different political environments with different constituencies. While firm conclusions concerning their effectiveness require deeper investigation, it is clear that the managerial craft of both men made a difference, at the very least an incremental one, in their departments. And both Bodman and Ashcroft shared a common characteristic of decisiveness, both faced many difficult decisions, and neither shrank from the challenge.

This case took the approach of examining the craft of two persons in similar kinds of jobs. Analyses of managerial craft can also produce insights by

- examining the craftsmanship of two or more different individuals in the same position (at different times); this approach "holds the position constant" and varies the manager in the job in an effort to identify contributions of managerial craft.
- examining the craftsmanship of a single individual in two or more different positions (at different times). This approach "holds the individual constant" and varies the job or position that the person holds in an effort to identify the contributions of managerial craft.

Both these approaches can only approximate the true counterfactual; they cannot constitute it. The external and internal environments, the enabling and constraining structures, and the organizational cultures a manager faces at any particular point in time will always be at least somewhat different than in another time or position. Still, these strategies can help gain a foothold for managerial analysis of the contribution of craft.

Another example of "holding the position constant" is a study of the managerial craft of two secretaries of defense, Robert S. McNamara and Melvin S. Laird:

> McNamara sought to use control over the force structure and associated budget allocations, together with careful analysis of military requirements, to influence military capabilities. In contrast, Laird preferred to exert his influence through establishing budget ceilings, issuing general policy guidance, and intervening selectively in shaping weapons proposals, leaving the analysis of military requirements to the services and detailed budgetary allocations to the comptrollers. Their management approaches mattered far less to the results each achieved than their personal efforts to influence specific decisions.
>
> In the end, both . . . succeeded in exercising limited influence over weapons design, procurement, and performance through becoming involved . . . in individual weapons projects. . . . A management system . . . can create or enlarge opportunities to manage, but the Secretary must then take the time to manage. The system is not the solution.[13]

A manager's craft is shaped by his or her own unique experiences, knowledge, perspectives, ideas, preferences, and proclivities. Even so, the exercise of managerial craftsmanship will vary across organizational and policy contexts. The consequences will vary as well. This all means that a public manager may practice effective or ineffective craft at different points in a work process or at different stages of a career: one may perform well under a particular set of circumstances and poorly in others.

Their management approaches mattered far less to the results each achieved than their personal efforts to influence specific decisions.

HOW TEMPERAMENT AND PERSONALITY AFFECT CRAFT

Individuals differ in how they think and learn, how they deliberate and make decisions, how they solve problems, and how they lead. These differences are affected by individuals' emotions, values and attitudes, and preferences for information processing and analysis. Some characterizations are normative; they prescribe how managers *should* think and act to be effective, and they tend to idealize particular types or styles of management. Others are experiential or empirical; they depict how managers *do* think and act based on observation, and they tend to identify the strengths and weaknesses of different styles or types of management in given situations.

The study of temperament and personality contributes empirical insight into an individual's managerial craft. The fact that individual **temperament** exists has long been recognized, "dat[ing] at least from the ancient Greek idea that a person's typical mood and behavior result from the balance of four humors in the body: blood, black bile, yellow bile, and phlegm."[14] Contemporary understandings of temperament include "individual differences in affect, activity, attention, and self-regulation"; they reflect biological and emotional bases of temperament but acknowledge experiential influences as well.[15] The domain of **personality** includes traits, characteristic adaptations to specific environments, and personal narratives.[16] While distinct research streams have addressed temperament and personality, more recently the two streams have converged in their concern with **traits**: "relatively stable patterns of behavior, motivation, emotion, and cognition."[17]

Acknowledging the individual contribution to public management craft carries a number of implications: individuals gravitate toward problems, tasks, and situations that allow them to exploit their strengths, and they instinctively avoid situations that might create undue stress or that put them in a bad light. Later in the chapter, findings from a study by political scientists Jameson W. Doig and Erwin C. Hargrove are discussed that indicate even widely acknowledged successful managers have failed or made mistakes at some point. Effective public managers know the strengths and weaknesses of their own deliberation and decision-making processes and are able to evaluate the strengths and weaknesses of how individuals of different types deliberate and make decisions, using these insights to manage more effectively.

A reasonable presumption, for example, is that people are more comfortable with colleagues whose personalities or temperaments are similar to their own than they are with colleagues whose temperaments are sharply different from theirs. Destructive conflict often develops between individuals of different types. A corollary, however, is that a manager, especially one with strong preferences, may benefit from having diverse types on a management team, as different preferences complement one another in addressing complex challenges.

For example, in her book *Team of Rivals,* historian Doris Kearns Goodwin describes how President Abraham Lincoln surrounded himself with cabinet leaders whose views often ran counter to his own.[18] Lincoln fostered these diverse views, which Kearns Goodwin argues was crucial to his success. The book and the concept caught the attention of Barack Obama, who wanted to put together his own team of rivals following his election to president in 2008. At the time, Valerie Jarrett, an adviser and family friend who would later serve as senior advisor to the president during his two terms, was quoted as saying,

> This is an essential part of his management style, one he's embracing throughout his transition . . . He enjoys hearing perspectives that are different from his own. He embraces the rigor of a back-and-forth on an issue, where everyone speaks openly.[19]

Yet the essential management style did not seem to last. Following reelection to a second term in November 2012, Obama turned to loyalists—a "band of brothers" instead of a "team of rivals."[20] He wouldn't be the first president to take this approach in his second term. "But it leaves Obama vulnerable to criticism, including from his supporters, that he is burrowing deeper into an insular inner circle rather than reaching out for new people and their ideas."[21] Some pointed to Jarrett among others as part of the insular core:

> So, was the Team of Rivals ever a real thing? Or was it a mythology created by Obama and a willing media? . . . the president's key inner core—David Axelrod, Dan Pfeiffer and Valerie Jarrett to name three— was always at the center of every decision and, in many ways, superseded the people he put in the Cabinet.[22]

Temperament and personality play a role in how individuals relate to the others, to learning, and to seeking information. Two separate but related approaches provide further insight into understanding personality: the five-factor model of personality and the Myers-Briggs Type Indicator.

The Five-Factor Model of Personality

Over the last few decades, research in psychology has converged on an understanding of five fundamental dimensions of personality: extraversion (E), agreeableness (A), conscientiousness (C), neuroticism (N) (or its inverse, emotional stability), and openness to experience (O).[23] Referred to as the **five-factor model** (FFM), "the Big Five," or by the acronyms CANOE or OCEAN, these dimensions of personality have been validated empirically by separate teams of researchers using different instruments. Broad agreement exists on the existence and general stability of these dimensions and on the belief that personality traits can be viewed in a hierarchical way, with these dimensions at the top of the hierarchy.

Yet researchers disagree on the precise definitions of the Big Five, with further disagreement on the components of each.[24] The search for measurement and definition of subtraits continues. Subtraits (or "facets") identified by one set of researchers have been operationalized in the Revised NEO Personality Inventory (NEO-PI-R):

- Conscientiousness: competence, order, dutifulness, achievement striving, self-discipline, deliberation;
- Agreeableness: trust, straightforwardness, altruism, compliance, modesty, tender-mindedness;
- Neuroticism: anxiety, angry hostility, depression, self-consciousness, impulsiveness, vulnerability;
- Openness to Experience: fantasy, aesthetics, feelings, actions, ideas, values;
- Extraversion: warmth, gregariousness, assertiveness, activity, excitement seeking, positive emotions.[25]

One group of researchers used the NEO-PI-R to describe the personalities of U.S. presidents, to classify them into eight types (such as dominators, philosophes, maintainers; examples are LBJ, Jefferson, and McKinley, respectively) and correlate them with previous studies of "greatness."[26] The authors summarized their findings with respect to personality subtraits and greatness in the following way:

> The traits associated with Neuroticism were not found to be useful correlates of historical greatness. Being anxious, depressed, angry and hostile, or self-conscious is not associated with poor presidential standing. Historically great presidents can be well adjusted or neurotic.

> Great presidents score higher than less successful peers on Openness to Experience, Assertiveness, Activity, Positive Emotions, Openness to Aesthetics, Feelings, Actions, Ideas and Values, Tender Mindedness, Competence, Self-Discipline, and Achievement Striving. Two of these traits, Assertiveness and Achievement Striving, were the most powerful predictors of greatness. Factor scores for conscientiousness also emerged as a predictor of historical greatness . . . Historically great presidents were low on Straightforwardness, Vulnerability, and somewhat on Order. Overall, our results suggest that Big Five personality dimensions and their facets, as measured by the NEO PI-R, are useful in the prediction of presidential greatness.[27]

> The appeal of the FFM lies both in its empirical validation as well as in its resonance with commonly understood aspects of personality.

The appeal of the FFM lies both in its empirical validation as well as in its resonance with commonly understood aspects of personality.[28] While the FFM seems to represent the received wisdom about core aspects of personality among scholars, its use in public management research and practice has been limited. An exception is a recent study of the five factors to explain job satisfaction and organizational citizenship behaviors in a sample of city and county public managers.[29] At the federal level, the Office of Personnel Management (OPM) offers a "Leadership Profiler" assessment based on the FFM. OPM indicates the assessment is "applicable to all levels of leadership in the Federal Government, including team leads, supervisors, managers, and executives" and that "developmental feedback also provides information on how the participant's personality impacts performance as a Federal leader, as defined by the 28 leadership competencies associated with OPM's Executive Core Qualifications (ECQs)."[30]

While empirical evidence linking the FFM to public employee or organization performance is lacking, recent research from the private sector shows support for some elements of the theory. For example, a study examined the relationship of personality (using the FFM constructs) and leadership to organizational performance, using a sample of chief executive officers and top management teams (TMT) in 96 credit unions in the United States.[31] The study found a robust, positive relationship between mean conscientiousness of the TMT and financial performance of the credit union: "teams that on average plan more of their work, exert greater effort, and are more persistent in doing their work are more likely to arrive at superior strategic decisions and are more successful in implementing the established strategy or tactics."[32] Indirect, positive relationships of the CEO's emotional stability and openness to experience to organizational performance were also found, with the indirect effects operating through "transformational leadership" (a concept discussed later in this chapter).

Apart from the study of presidents, using the FFM to understand personalities and temperaments of public leaders or employees has not been common either in the popular press or academic research. Insight into personality or temperament of a public figure might be gained, however, by drawing on the FFM (with the appropriate cautions regarding accuracy and available information). An instructor of a psychology class, for example, suggested the following questions as an assignment for her students to understand the personality of entertainer Johnny Carson by reading a detailed obituary:

> What can we say about Johnny Carson's disposition? Was he neurotic or emotionally stable? Extraverted or introverted? Open or conventional? Agreeable or disagreeable? Conscientious or aimless?
>
> In other words, based on the evidence presented in the [obituary], where would a personality psychologist place Carson on each of the five dimensions of the FFM? On which facets would he be particularly high or low?
>
> What does the life of Johnny Carson illustrate about the stability and change of human personality? What stayed the same and what changed about him over the course of his life?[33]

A similar line of questioning might be used to understand a public manager's personality. Doing so could provide insight into his or her craftsmanship.

Myers-Briggs Type Indicator (MBTI)

While the reach of the FFM in public and nonprofit sector organizations seems relatively limited, the opposite can be said of the Myers-Briggs Type Indicator (MBTI) instrument.[34] Based on responses to a lengthy questionnaire, the MBTI reports on individuals' preferred ways of apprehending the world—how they perceive reality—and of reacting to issues that arise in their perceived world—how they make judgments or decisions. It is associated with applications of Carl Jung's theory of psychological types.[i]

The MBTI instrument is widely used in executive training and counseling. It is pervasive in public sector organizations at all levels, as well as in nonprofit organizations:[35]

> About 200 federal agencies pay for Myers-Briggs as part of their training programs. The military . . . has been one
> of the test's longest and most avid users. "There's a story that goes around that says if you've risen to the rank of
> major in the Army, you've taken the MBTI at least once . . . It's widely used within the State Department, the
> Department of Veterans Affairs, the CIA and nearly every federal department you could name."[36]

The four dimensions of MBTI are listed below:

- *Sensing (S) or Intuition (N)*: Individuals perceive or become aware of the world about them either by becoming aware of things directly through sensory experience or by relying on subconscious processes to construct what the individual regards as the real world.
- *Thinking (T) or Feeling (F)*: Individuals judge or reach conclusions about perceived reality either by using logical, analytical processes to produce conclusions or by reaching conclusions by bestowing on things a personal, subjective value.
- *Extraversion (E) or Introversion (I)*: Individuals differ in their relative interest in their "outer" and "inner" worlds: some are more engaging and transparent in their learning and deciding, while others are oriented mainly to private processing of reality.
- *Judging (J) or Perceiving (P)*: Some individuals prefer the process of evaluating, reaching conclusions, and deciding, even if they do not have all the information that might be desirable or available; others prefer widening their grasp of reality.

Individuals' temperaments are manifestations of these four preferences, which they have come to rely on over the course of their lives as the basis for intentional behavior. Sixteen possible personality types arise from combinations of the four preferences. Each type is associated with a particular pattern of behavior in given situations. The MBTI purports to be nonjudgmental concerning whether a particular type, style, or preference is inherently good or bad. In the United States, 55 percent to 60 percent of all people are extraverts, and roughly 60 percent prefer sensing and judgment to intuition and perception. Moreover, although all types appear in managerial samples, most managers are both Ts and Js, reflecting logical or rational decision making.[37] When the other traits are added, the resulting typical managerial types tend to fall into four groups:

- *ISTJ* (introverted, sensing, thinking, and judging) managers are practical, orderly, matter-of-fact, logical, realistic, and dependable. They make up their minds as to what should be accomplished and work toward it steadily, regardless of distractions or controversies.
- *ENTJ* (extraverted, intuitive, thinking, and judging) managers are frank, decisive, and leaders in activities. They like to draw others out, asking questions, engaging in discussion and debate. They are usually good at team-oriented planning and public testimony.

---

[i]This section is adapted from Laurence E. Lynn Jr., *Managing Public Policy* (Boston, MA: Little, Brown, 1987), 116–119

- *INTJ* (introverted, intuitive, thinking, and judging) managers are original and determined, especially when their own interests and beliefs are engaged. They may be less inclined to deliberate, compromise, or promote teamwork.
- *ESTJ* (extraverted, sensing, thinking, and judging) managers are practical and realistic, down-to-earth, with a natural instinct for organization and administration. They will probe for the facts, for what their teams know, and will be impatient with abstractions and speculation.

An *ESTP* may perform far less successfully than an *INTJ* in situations requiring conceptual mastery and intellectual concentration. An *INTP* placed in a position that calls for establishing rapport with diverse constituencies and quick, intuitive reactions is likely to do less well than an *ENTJ*. The nature of the fit between personalities and circumstances is of considerable significance in explaining the variations in managerial performance observed in the public sector. An individual of average abilities may perform better in a position for which he or she is well suited than a highly talented individual in the wrong job.

An instructive example of the application of the general idea of managerial type is Yves Gagnon's study of experienced public officials' decision making about adoption of new technologies.[38] Respondents answered 79 survey questions concerning who they were, what they did, and what happened as a result. The sample had approximately equal numbers of each basic type, and the managers differed from each other along some dimensions predicted by theory. Specifically, their self-identified characteristics and behaviors placed them along a continuum from "administrator/trustee" to "entrepreneur/promoter." The managers who tended to behave in an entrepreneurial way paid less attention to "social consideration," which might be interpreted as organizational culture. The entrepreneurial types seemed to want to press ahead forcefully and override the culture. The administrative/managerial types, in contrast, paid attention to social considerations while introducing new technologies.

Social consideration was positively associated with the success of new technology projects. The success in this particular type of organizational change tended to be associated with managers who adopted deliberate, culturally sensitive, longer-term plans. In short, in enacting new technologies, the individual public manager must establish contact with institutionalized values; the more successful change agents were those who instinctively do so, that is, those whose preferences incline them toward considering the social implications of technology.

While use of the MBTI is extensive, consistent evidence of its validity and reliability has been lacking.[39] Yet, parts of it may reflect the "Big Five" factors,[40] and it can provide a heuristic for many to understand variation across individuals in their responses to particular situations and how these might be reflected in their effectiveness.

Managerial Pegs in Situational Holes

Despite the wide varieties of behaviors exhibited by individuals of differing temperaments, the implication in much of the prescriptive, best-practices literature on public management is that, within the constraints imposed by formal authority and organizational cultures, the effectiveness of public managers is proportional to the quality or appropriateness of their personality, skills, and motivations. In this view, there is such a thing as a managerial personality, or character, or temperament, or persona that enables those who possess it to outperform those who don't no matter what the context in which they are working.[ii] Certain types of people, in this view, will always do better than others, no matter what the challenge.

This impression is reinforced by writers who claim to have identified the correlates of business, military, and political success, and by the popularity of well-known leaders as motivational speakers, such as Rudolph Giuliani, former New York City mayor and hero of 9/11; Jack Welch, former CEO of General Electric Corporation; and Gen. Norman Schwarzkopf, the commander of the 1991 expulsion of Iraq from Kuwait. These individuals often write about "how I did it and how you can do it, too."

To investigate this idea of the ideal manager, political scientists Jameson W. Doig, Erwin C. Hargrove, and an interdisciplinary team of colleagues studied the accomplishments of a dozen individuals "whose careers at managerial levels were linked to innovative ideas and to efforts to carry these ideas into effect, often attended by some risk to their organizations and to their own careers," individuals widely considered to be effective leaders. Although all had achieved conspicuous success at some point in their lives, the puzzle was that all had also experienced reversals, failures, or mixed results that, for some of them, outweighed the successes. Doig and Hargrove reached two conclusions:

- "Achievement is favored by a good match of individual skill and the organizational task attempted."
- "The favorable match of skill to task must be reinforced by favorable historical conditions if there is to be significant achievement."[41]

In other words, success is as much contextual as it is personal. Individuals who have succeeded in one endeavor are not guaranteed success in all endeavors.

Laurence E. Lynn Jr. reached a similar conclusion in his study of five federal government managers appointed by President Ronald Reagan.[42] He concluded that a public manager's strategies to change agency operations were more important to success than their personalities and skill sets. Managers may be personable and skilled but may doom their change efforts by misreading the political context. Constraints on managerial discretion also matter. Well-liked and respected managers may achieve little in a given position if they choose the wrong strategies or if they prove unable, perhaps through no defect in their personal characteristics and skills, to overcome obstacles to success.

An experienced public manager understands that what is best for one situation may not be best for another.

> **Success is as much contextual as it is personal. Individuals who have succeeded in one endeavor are not guaranteed success in all endeavors.**

LEADERSHIP

Americans take pride in having a government of laws, not of men, but they also yearn for what is widely termed *leadership*. They want people in positions of responsibility who motivate and inspire others, transform situations, overcome obstacles, and show the way, intellectually and by personal example, toward better futures that honor the nation's values.

[ii]For an interesting analysis, see J. A. Chatman, D. F. Caldwell, and C. A. O'Reilly, "Managerial Personality and Performance: A Semi-Idiographic Approach," *Journal of Research in Personality* 33 (1999): 514–545.

But, according to findings from the 2012 National Leadership Index, compiled by the Center for Public Leadership at Harvard University's Kennedy School of Government, 69 percent of Americans believe the country faces a "leadership crisis."[43] Across 13 sectors identified by the Center, the greatest confidence was expressed in leadership in the military, and the least in Congress, with leadership in nonprofits and charities, local government, state governments, and the executive branch in between.

Following a series of high-profile security breaches, the Secret Service was the subject of an independent review in 2014. Leadership problems were highlighted:

> Of the many concerns the Panel encountered, the question of leadership is, in our view, the most important. The Panel found an organization starved for leadership that rewards innovation and excellence and demands accountability. From agents to officers to supervisors, we heard a common desire: More resources would help, but what we really need is leadership.[44]

The yearning for leadership has elicited a large literature on the topic, much of it offering prescriptions for inspirational leadership.[iii] Yet, despite a substantial mainstream leadership literature, "a distinctive public-sector leadership literature focusing on the significant constraints and unique environments of public sector leaders" has not emerged,[45] with some important exceptions. Notable among these exceptions are treatises such as *On Leadership* by John W. Gardner (one-time secretary of the Department of Health, Education and Welfare), *On Becoming a Leader* by Warren G. Bennis, and *Leadership* by former New York City mayor Rudolph Giuliani (with Ken Kurson).[46]

Also in the realm of public affairs, James MacGregor Burns's *Leadership* popularized the distinction between **transformational leadership** and **transactional leadership**.[47] He defined transformational leadership as transcendent change of an organization or a people and transactional leadership as effective interactions between leaders and followers (or those in subordinate roles).

Many writers hold that leadership is different, and far rarer, than management. According to a popular maxim, "managers are people who do things right and leaders are people who do the right things."[48] In this view, leadership has a moral dimension: vision, exemplary conduct, and principled commitment are viewed as transcending expediency, partisanship, and self-interest. Public administration scholar Jonathan R. Tompkins put it this way:

> Government is often thought to be too political, too bureaucratic, and too procedures oriented to allow for [the pursuit of excellence. But] achieving higher levels of agency functioning is entirely possible for public managers who possess the will and determination to exercise leadership on behalf of the public good . . . . Because government truly matters, public servants bear a moral obligation to help their agencies carry out their missions as effectively as possible.[49]

Other students of leadership argue that the public manager must both lead and manage. Richard Haass, an experienced public manager, insists, "There is and can be no distinction between leadership and management if you are to be effective. Direction without means is feckless, and means without direction is aimless. The two—leadership and management—are inseparable."[50] Public management scholar Robert Behn argues that leadership

---

[iii]Amazon.com lists thousands of books dealing with leadership. Two classic academic studies are Bernard M. Bass, *Bass & Stogdill's Handbook of Leadership* (New York, NY: Free Press, 1990); and Edgar H. Schein, *Organizational Culture and Leadership*, 3rd ed. (San Francisco, CA: Jossey-Bass, 2004).

by public managers "can contribute to the working of [the American system of governance] by compensating for some of the failures of the legislature, the judiciary, and their elected chief executive."[51]

In the view of some scholars and practitioners, the role of leadership in public management is constrained by the fact that public officials are, above all, responsible to constitutional principles and institutions. In this view, public sector leadership should be provided not by administrators but by legislative leaders, elected executives, and those appointed to executive positions in the departments, commissions, and agencies that implement public policies. Reflecting this view, scholars and practitioners commonly speak of public servants and public service. Scholars such as Robert Greenleaf and Larry Terry have formulated concepts such as **servant-leadership** and the leader as conservator of constitutional principles and organizational capabilities.[52]

Leadership in Theory

Public management scholars Janet V. Denhardt and Kelly B. Campbell provide a concise overview of public sector leadership theories, distinguishing among approaches that emphasize

- the traits or attributes of individuals in a position to lead;
- situations or specific contexts and settings in which leaders and followers interact;
- organizational transformation based on vision and entrepreneurial initiative by executives; and
- the realization of ethical and moral values in relationships between leaders and their followers.[iv]

Keying off these four basic types of theories, Denhardt and Campbell discuss corresponding learning objectives and sample teaching approaches for understanding these approaches to leadership. An alternative way to understand leadership theories is by their normative or positive bent in describing generic functions of leadership.

Normative Approaches

In his comprehensive assessment of the administrative leadership literature, Montgomery Van Wart concludes that its strength "has been its hearty normative discussions about the proper roles of administrators in a democratic system. . . . The field has had remarkably few empirical studies that are not largely descriptive and has overly emphasized leadership as an executive function" rather than as a desirable characteristic of management and supervision across a wide variety of functions and roles.[53]

The essentially normative approach of Philip Selznick illustrates Van Wart's point. Selznick observed in his classic 1957 study, *Leadership in Administration,* "what leaders do is hardly self-evident. And it is likely that much failure of leadership results from an inadequate understanding of its true nature and tasks." Selznick, a sociologist, provides a generic normative account of the tasks of leadership in large, complex organizations:

- defining institutional mission and role;
- infusing institutional purpose into the organization's social structure;
- defending institutional values and distinctive identity; and
- maintaining an appropriate balance of power among the organizations' various interest groups.

[iv]Janet V. Denhardt and Kelly B. Campbell, "Leadership Education in Public Administration: Finding the Fit Between Purpose and Approach," *Journal of Public Affairs Education* 11, (2005): 169–179. For additional discussion, see Peter Northouse, *Leadership Theory and Practice,* 4th ed. (Thousand Oaks, CA: Sage, 2006).

In summary, "The executive becomes a statesman as he makes the transition from administrative management to institutional leadership." Selznick continues: "Authority and communication must be broadly understood to take account of the social psychology of obedience, perception and co-operation."[54]

More recent examples of normative leadership theory include the following public administration scholars:

- Robert W. Terry views leadership as a skill embodying authenticity, ethics, and spirituality. In this view, "authentic leadership" is genuine and trustworthy because it is based on reflective thought by the leader and a leader-initiated search for common ground among participants.[v]
- John Bryson and Barbara Crosby view leadership as promoting positive change under circumstances where power is widely dispersed (or "shared") and political regimes are weak.[55] The role of leadership, therefore, is to create opportunities for mutual gain through reframing problems. This reframing can enable individuals to perceive, and then act on, their common interests by forming constituencies of conscience and vision. Effective public leadership is both omnidirectional—concerned with individuals, organizations, and political and legal institutions—and integrative—concerned with synthesizing ideas and interests until the reality of purposefully shared power is attained.

Positive Approaches

Positive approaches to leadership theory offer a contrasting view from the normative approaches just described. An example of an inductive approach is Montgomery Van Wart's *Dynamics of Leadership in Public Service*. In this work, Van Wart integrates the many aspects of public sector leadership—five major elements and seventy subelements—into a "leadership action cycle," which is premised on 17 specific assumptions. The last of these assumptions illustrates the spirit of his approach:

> Leader effectiveness is not a unidimensional concept any more than is leadership itself. It can emphasize technical performance, follower development, organizational alignment, and a public-service and ethical focus, among others. It can balance a number of these perspectives. The proper proportion is a value, not a technical judgment.[56]

An example of a positive approach to leadership that is developed deductively is political scientist Gary Miller's theory of leadership.[57] Miller sketches two strategies for managing an organization:

- **Optimal contracts**, which align the incentives of employees with organizational goals through budget allocations (remuneration, rewards, and similar mechanisms)
- Leadership, which involves inspiring employees' voluntary and creative cooperation with organizational interests

With this framework, Miller's reasoning proceeds as follows:

1. Designing optimal incentives is analytically, not to mention practically, impossible. No system of incentives can entirely eliminate noncooperative behavior. No system of formal authority or incentives can prevent organizational pathologies and inefficiencies. In other words, no system can prevent organizations from failing to accomplish their goals.

---

[v]See, for example, Robert W. Terry, *Authentic Leadership: Courage in Action* (San Francisco, CA: Jossey-Bass, 1993).

2. Miller regards the use of repeated game theory as appropriate for analyzing managerial strategies because it posits continuing interactions among self-interested organizational participants. In light of point (1), applying repeated game theory yields indeterminate outcomes or multiple equilibriums.

3. A manager's role is to select one of these equilibriums and persuade people to cooperate in its achievement. In so doing, the manager guides participants to transcend short term self-interest. "Leadership" is the act of selecting and inspiring cooperation with a particular equilibrium.

4. The manager induces a cooperative equilibrium with **myths and expectations**: Activities that convey meaning and inspire loyalty.

5. The task of organizational leadership is to create mutually reinforcing expectations concerning the benefits of cooperative behavior and teamwork on behalf of shared objectives.

An example of a "myth and expectation" that supports a cooperative equilibrium is the concept of a *gift exchange* described in Chapter 8.[58] A manager may offer the gift of above-market incomes in the expectation of an employee's reciprocal gift of cooperative effort when called upon. The manager initiates job-enhancing opportunities and wins extraordinary cooperation as a result. This gift exchange can be construed as both "rational behavior" and "normative or conventional behavior," in other words, as both economic and socialized behavior.

Forty-five years before Miller's publication, Donald Stone, then an official in the Bureau of the Budget and one of public administration's important leaders, offered an observation that anticipated Miller's final point. Stone argued that the public executive's "success . . . will be, in important measure, determined by his success in developing a body of commonly shared ideas."[59]

> The public executive's "success . . . will be, in important measure, determined by his success in developing a body of commonly shared ideas."

Example: Using Managerial Craft to Change Culture at the Illinois Department on Aging (IDOA)

Public managers may seek to change organizational cultures by using their personalities and skills to inspire behaviors that support the organization's goals. An important function of organizational leadership is to motivate cooperation with organizational purposes through a combination of inducements such as various forms of personal recognition and effective communication of the value to the organization of cooperative behavior. As described in the following example, a new director's personal style of deliberation and decision making and his knowledge of the agency were instrumental for building trust, minimizing internal conflicts, and inducing cooperation around politically necessary goals, illustrating Miller's leadership theory.

The IDOA is responsible for carrying out the mandates of the federal Older Americans Act of 1965 through the department's Community Care Program (CCR) and Case Coordination Units (CCUs).[vi] When Victor L. Wirth assumed the position of IDOA director in 1990, the state of Illinois and its agencies were under severe fiscal stress, the agency's culture emphasized risk aversion and compliance, and relationships among the department, the CCUs, service providers, and aging advocacy groups were hostile. In only a year on the job—he resigned for personal reasons in 1991—Wirth, by the testimony of all relevant stakeholders, successfully

---

[vi]This account is adapted from Barbara Koremenos and Laurence E. Lynn Jr., "Leadership of a State Agency: An Analysis Using Game Theory," in *The State of Public Management*, ed. Donald F. Kettl and Brinton Milward (Baltimore, MD: Johns Hopkins University Press, 1996), 213–240.

refocused his department's operations on client service, induced cooperative relationships with providers, and complied with the governor's budget directives.

Wirth had the advantage of prior experience in IDOA in a number of positions. Observers credit his success as director to maintaining open communications with agency employees and including them in decision making. The theme of these efforts was the need to support street-level workers in providing services to older persons. At the same time, he reduced paperwork by 60 to 70 percent by accepting the recommendations of a task force dominated by the CCUs, which had the effect of reducing the emphasis on complying with rules and protocols. According to Wirth, the task force "helped tremendously in drawing the group together because it is the first time the department had ever really come to the CCUs and said, 'Would you be our partners?'"[vii] He also made structural changes such as combining advisory committees and appointing outside rather than inside chairpersons for these committees.

Barbara Koremenos and Laurence Lynn employed game theory reasoning to analyze the dynamics of the transformation Wirth brought about at IDOA:

> Wirth's problem was noncooperation originating at the top of the agency and institutionalized primarily at the division manager level, from where it was transmitted downward to the field. At lower levels, Wirth had ideological allies whom he could easily mobilize to squeeze the division managers into line. This is not a universal principle of public management, however. In a social service agency where noncooperation originates at lower levels . . . a better strategy . . . might be the opposite of Wirth's: to recruit middle management to monitor the field and deliver rewards and sanctions sufficient to overcome resistance to change. What works, therefore, will depend on the internal dynamics of the agency.[viii]

Wirth's intuition—that leadership could transform the culture of his formerly hunkered-down agency—proved to be highly effective in the particular context in which he found himself. As Koremenos and Lynn point out, in different contexts, and with managers of other types, a different strategy might well succeed and Wirth and his strategy might have failed.

Leadership in Practice

At least three different perspectives on leadership as an essential element of public affairs practice can be identified:

- To **leadership believers**, including authors such as Giuliani of inspirational books on leadership, the importance of leadership in public life and the need for behavioral skills such as self-awareness, team building, conflict resolution, and effective written and oral communication are self-evident articles of faith.
- To **leadership skeptics**, including many empirical social scientists concerned with government performance, (1) "leadership" has never been shown to have *a priori* theoretical content; leaders are individuals our culture celebrates after the fact, and leadership tends to be in the eye of the beholder; (2) so-called principles of leadership are vacuous proverbs that are either so general as to be useless or are easily invalidated by examples of leaders who clearly violated them.

[vii]Barbara Koremenos and Laurence E. Lynn Jr., "Leadership of a State Agency: An Analysis Using Game Theory," in *The State of Public Management,* ed. Donald F. Kettl and Brinton Milward (Baltimore, MD: Johns Hopkins University Press, 1996), 232.

[viii]Ibid., 235.

- To **leadership pragmatists,** such as Doig and Hargrove, an emphasis on leadership must not be viewed as a panacea or be restricted to a generic behavioral model. Its meaning must be grounded in research. They tend to view leadership as

    o emerging from specific contexts. Instances or episodes of leadership that can be identified only after the fact are the product of a good fit or match between the skills and attributes of an individual in a leader role and the specific demands of that role in a given time and place. An individual may be regarded as a leader during one phase of his or her life but not during other phases, when the situational fit was less propitious.

    o elicited by the need for disruptive change in a status quo—it is and ought to be relatively uncommon because disruptive change is often not an appropriate strategy.

    o lacking a lowest common denominator or sufficient condition. Individuals with many different skill sets can and have been leaders.

    o one of several factors that are important to the performance of governance. Other factors are policy designs, organizations, resources, management, and public service values. Indeed, a leader must recognize that many factors contribute to organizational performance, and that many of them are not under the leader's control.

In the public sector, the context of leadership is almost always organizations in specific political contexts. The possibilities for active leadership, especially when it involves organizational transformation, can either be influenced by or thwarted by the structure and culture dimensions of public management. Based on the work of Doig and Hargrove, three important aspects of managerial craft crucial to successful leadership in these contingent and uncertain circumstances can be identified:

(1) a capacity to engage in systematic analysis of the possibilities for change;

(2) an ability to see new possibilities offered by the evolving historical situation and communicate such possibilities to the organizational and political environment; and

(3) the manager's desire to "make a difference" and to commit his or her energies and personal reputation toward transformative goals.

KEY CONCEPTS

Temperament	Transactional leadership
Personality	Servant leadership
Traits	Optimal contracts
Five-factor model	Myth and expectations
(FFM or Big Five)	Leadership believers
Leadership	Leadership skeptics
Transformative leadership	Leadership pragmatists

CASE ANALYSIS: KATE MAEHR AND THE GREATER CHICAGO FOOD DEPOSITORY

The following *Chicago Tribune* profile provides insight into the temperament and leadership style of Kate Maehr, the executive director of the Greater Chicago Food Depository. Earlier in her career, Maehr was recognized by Crain's Chicago Business as one of its "40 under 40" leaders to watch. She is a 2005 graduate of the Leadership Greater Chicago class.

Every September, Kate Maehr raises awareness for the 47 million Americans who receive food stamps by walking in their shoes.

She spends $35 on groceries for herself for a week, which is about the average benefit for participants in the federal program. . . . She buys a lot of rice, bread, oatmeal and beans because she can't afford many of the staples of her normal diet: fresh fruits and vegetables and proteins like salmon. Also, she doesn't go out to lunch with colleagues or enjoy a pizza with her husband and two boys. . . .

"By Wednesday or Thursday, I'm crabby," Maehr said.

But the exercise keeps her grounded and reminds her why her work as chief executive officer of the Greater Chicago Food Depository is so important.

As head of one of the nation's largest food banks, Maehr, 46, is on the front lines of the fight against hunger in Chicago and Cook County. Her organization helps feed 142,000 people each week. . . .

The foodbank distributes more food today than it did when Maehr took over the nonprofit organization in 2006.

Despite that grim statistic, Maehr remains optimistic—some might say hopelessly idealistic—that government and the private sector can work together to end hunger not only in Chicago but across the United States.

"I'm sure people roll their eyes behind my back," she said. "But we'll never get there if we don't plan for it. We will be doomed if we don't try, if we don't aspire to a world without hunger."

Her ambition has transformed an organization that was primarily a logistics company since it opened in 1979. Today the Greater Chicago Food Depository has a sprawling $30 million warehouse near Midway Airport with a fleet of trucks that runs like clockwork, a commercial kitchen that prepares hot meals for low-income children and a never-ending army of volunteers packing food. The food bank gets about $80 million a year in cash, in-kind contributions and grants, according to its income tax returns.

But for Maehr, providing food to hungry people is only half the battle. She has steered the organization to advocacy, pressing elected officials to protect and strengthen the federal food stamp program, known as the Supplemental Nutrition Assistance Program or SNAP, the school breakfast program at Chicago Public Schools and other key social safety nets.

"Our advocacy is not advocacy for us," said Maehr, who has earned national recognition for her work. "Our job is to advocate for hungry people and the food they need to lead healthy, productive lives."

Maehr is a relentless anti-hunger advocate. Her policy work takes her to Washington two or three times a year and to Springfield three or four times. She regularly visits with newspaper editorial boards and writes op-ed pieces. More recently, she turned to Twitter and other social media to spread her message. . . .

"You see the really tough choices people make when they are struggling with food insecurity," Maehr said. "They have so few resources and yet have to spend so much time shopping. It's really humbling." . . .

Management's participation in the SNAP Challenge is one way Maehr builds *esprit de corps* at the food bank's headquarters at the 268,000-square-foot warehouse, which opened in 2004.

On a day in December, Maehr is excited to meet the new graduates of the food bank's culinary school. Since 1998, the organization has offered a free 14-week training program that prepares unemployed or underemployed adults to find jobs in the food-service industry.

For the graduation ceremony, the food bank invited Chicago chef Mindy Segal, owner of restaurant Hot Chocolate, to be the guest speaker. Segal has hired interns from the training program.

Maehr walked into the conference room where the graduates were waiting before the ceremony, her easy smile so big it could melt a walk-in freezer. She introduced Segal to the graduates, and as she often does, Maehr told a story.

"I had a chance to meet (Segal) for the first time this summer. We were eating in her restaurant. We were talking about her partnership (with the culinary program)."

Maehr turned to Segal and said, "You were talking, and you got all choked up. She's all tough, and she starts crying, and she's like, 'I'm all in.'"

Maehr continued, "I have thought about that so much this past year. What does it mean to be 'all in'?"

Segal interjected with tears in her eyes, "It means you cry."

Maehr has also been known to shed a few tears at work. At new-employee orientation, Maehr talks about the history of food banking, how it got started in Phoenix in 1967. "And every single time, she's in tears," Howe said. "It's amazing."

Patrick Mulhern, the food depository's board chairman, likes that Maehr is an emotional leader. "You want someone whose heart is in it," he said. . . .

"This is not a happy cause," Mulhern said. "She handles it with incredible optimism. I don't know that I've met anybody that is a better fit for what they do. This is her calling."

(Continued)

(Continued)

The youngest of three children, Maehr was exposed to politics and social justice issues at an early age. Her father was a professor at the University of Illinois at Urbana-Champaign, where he researched motivation and achievement in education and much of his work focused on inner-city schools.

Her mother, a kindergarten teacher, was politically active. She volunteered for the George McGovern presidential campaign in 1972 and would tote Maehr on voter-canvassing drives. Maehr said she proudly hangs in her Oak Park home a McGovern campaign poster that her mom gave her. McGovern, with Sen. Bob Dole, led national efforts to combat hunger.

When she was 5, her father took a sabbatical and moved the family to Iran. At the time, some Illinois professors were doing research in Iran related to education, modernization and other subjects.

The experience was so different from her comfortable childhood in Urbana that Maehr has vivid memories of her yearlong stay there.

"I can still remember seeing children in the streets who had virtually no clothes and were helping their mothers wash dishes in the streets," Maehr said. "You see the incredible poverty. That certainly had an impact on me and helped me understand the wider world in a way that I wouldn't have if I had lived in Urbana the whole time."

In high school, Maehr joined an anti-nuclear weapons group and volunteered for Paul Simon's U.S. Senate campaign. Her interest in public service led her to Macalester College, a small, private liberal arts institution in St. Paul, Minn., where "service to society" is part of its mission.

Although she majored in English literature and art history, Maehr said her time at Macalester helped her understand "that what I really wanted to do was to be of service to my community." She also started dating Sam Pickering, an English major, and they would later marry.

Her first job was at a nonprofit literary group in St. Paul where she edited poetry and short fiction. She also started handling administrative tasks, such as writing grant proposals.

Maehr left after five years to pursue a graduate degree in public policy at the University of Wisconsin. In her last semester, she took a course in urban poverty and food systems. Armed with a master's degree, she thought she would move to Washington and work for a nonprofit or the Department of Agriculture.

While she was planning her future, she applied for a fundraising job at the Chicago food bank. Anne Goodman, the food bank's director of development at the time, called her, and they spoke for 40 minutes.

"She didn't have the qualifications that were dead-on for the position I was filling," said Goodman, president and CEO of the Greater Cleveland Food Bank. "But she could see clear to the issue, and I felt like she could learn whatever she needed to learn. You can't teach someone to be sharp, and you can't teach someone to be interested. And Kate had those things in spades."

Goodman left the food bank in 1999, and Maehr replaced her as director of development. In 2001, under the leadership of then-executive director Michael Mulqueen, a former Marine, the food bank launched the largest fundraising effort in its history, a campaign to raise $30 million for a bigger warehouse to meet the growing need.

The organization met its goal in about four years during the choppy economic conditions after 9/11.

"To me, it's not about raising money," said Maehr, who was promoted to CEO when Mulqueen retired in 2006. "It's about connecting people with the need and with the opportunity to be a part of the solution." . . .

In its fiscal year ended in June, the Chicago food bank distributed 66 million pounds of food, a 63 percent increase from 40.4 million pounds distributed in fiscal 2007 during Maehr's first year as CEO.

Maehr is proud that fresh fruit and vegetables make up a third of what the food bank distributes, up from a quarter when she started. The fact that she couldn't afford much produce while taking the SNAP Challenge influenced the organization's top aim in its five-year strategic plan implemented in 2010: increase access to healthy food.

A copy of the strategic plan hangs on the wall above Maehr's desk, a constant reminder of the food bank's daunting goal. Striving to end hunger has always been a part of the organization's mission, but Maehr brought a new vision to achieving its aim. As Maehr sees it, taking big steps like expanding access to fresh fruit can't be done by a food bank alone. Political action needs to be taken, which has meant the food depository needed to find its political voice, using advocacy and education as a tool.

For Maehr, political advocacy was a natural extension of the organization because the people who rely on food stamps and the children who get school breakfasts are often the same people the food bank feeds.

Being an advocate also comes naturally to Maehr. She has an easy rapport with people and can connect with them on an emotional level.

But some members of the board of directors were not sure the food bank should be championing causes. Mulhern, for one, had his doubts.

"You can spend a lot of time and money on an issue and be outspent," he said. "It can be a black hole."

Maehr and her staff spent a lot of time educating the board about SNAP and other safety-net programs, and directors came around to her strategic vision.

"SNAP is not well-portrayed," Mulhern said. "You hear all about the abuse and fraud, but it's one of the most successful programs the federal government has ever had."

He pauses for a moment, reflecting on what he had just said. "I never thought I would say that."

The food bank organizes bus trips to Springfield for food pantry leaders to talk to legislators. The organization sends out "advocacy alert" emails to supporters.

(Continued)

(Continued)

After an alert went out in December 2012 about potential cuts to SNAP, one of the food bank's large donors responded in an email that he didn't believe government should be involved in feeding hungry people.

Maehr personally replied to the donor, politely disagreeing with him and explaining why. They exchanged a few more emails on the subject. A few months later, the donor and his granddaughter came to the food bank to volunteer. He brought with him newspaper clippings about the food stamp program.

"I just love that he's thought about it so much," Maehr said.

For her, the donor represents the best of the food bank.

"There are all sorts of people who support this mission," she said. "We don't vote the same, and we don't have the same perspective on the size or role of government. But the thing we agree upon is that people should not go hungry. If we can start there as a common point, we can actually all work together and come up with solutions."[60]

Discussion Questions

Use the model deliberative process described in Chapter 1 to develop your answers to the following questions:

1. Based on the details in this profile, how would you describe Kate Maehr's personality, or temperament?

    a. Use both the Five Factor Model and the Myers-Briggs dimensions to inform your analysis.

    b. What additional information, or types of information, would you like to have to gain further insight into Maehr's temperament?

    c. What is the "fit" between Maehr's personality and her responsibilities as the Greater Chicago Food Depository executive director? Use Doig and Hargrove's two general conclusions to frame your analysis.

    d. Based on your analysis, describe the characteristics of a managerial position that likely would *not* be a good fit with Maehr's personality.

2. Analyze Maehr's leadership:

    a. Use the normative theories mentioned in this chapter, or others, to frame your analysis.

    b. Use the positive theories described in this chapter, or others, to frame your analysis.

    c. What do the different heuristics and theories add to your ability to specify key characteristics of Maehr's leadership? What further information do you need to enrich your analysis?

3. Identify another leader in a managerial position similar to Maehr's. With available information, compare and contrast their personalities and leadership styles.

4. Identify the distinctive challenges of public management described in Chapter 1 that you think Maehr might face in this position. Describe how you might expect her to respond.

NOTES

1. Carolyn J. Hill and Laurence E. Lynn Jr., "Is Hierarchical Governance in Decline?" *Journal of Public Administration Research and Theory* 15 (2005): 173–195.

2. Norma M. Riccucci, *How Management Matters: Street-Level Bureaucrats and Welfare Reform* (Washington, DC: Georgetown University Press, 2005).

3. Evelyn Z. Brodkin, *The False Promise of Administrative Reform: Implementing Quality Control in Welfare* (Philadelphia, PA: Temple University Press, 1987).

4. Gordon Chase and Elizabeth C. Reveal, *How to Manage in the Public Sector* (New York, NY: Random House, 1983), 20, 178, 179.

5. Eli Kintisch, "With Energy to Spare, an Engineer Makes the Case for Basic Research," *Science* (March 10, 2006): 1369–70.

6. Ibid., 1369.

7. Justin Blum, "Officials Earn High Marks on the Hill," *The Washington Post,* August 9, 2005, Sec. A., http://www.washingtonpost.com/wp-dyn/content/article/2005/08/08/AR2005080801226.html.

8. Steven Chu, "Memorandum for all Federal and Contractor Employees-Subject: Employee Concerns Statement," October 5, 2012, http://energy.gov/sites/prod/files/Employee%20Concerns%20Program%20Statement%20October%202012.pdf.

9. Kintisch, "With Energy to Spare," 1369.

10. "Ashcroft's Style of Secretness Harmful to American Justice," *Austin American-Statesman,* January 24, 2004, A14.

11. Chitra Ragavan, "Ashcroft's Way," *U.S. News and World Report,* January 26, 2004, http://chitraragavan.com/usnews/ashcroft.pdf.

12. Ibid., 36.

13. Laurence E. Lynn, Jr. and Richard I. Smith, "Can the Secretary of Defense Make a Difference?" *International Security* 7, no.1 (1982): 67-68.

14. Rebecca L. Shiner and Colin G. DeYoung, "The Structure of Temperament and Personality Traits: A Developmental Perspective" in *The Oxford Handbook for Developmental Psychology, Volume 2: Self and Other,* ed. Philip David Zelazo (Oxford, UK: Oxford University Press, 2013), 115.

15. Ibid.

16. Ibid.

17. Shiner and DeYoung, "The Structure of Temperament and Personality," 115. Also see Bryan Caplan, "Stigler-Becker Versus Myers-Briggs: Why Preference-Based Explanations Are Scientifically Meaningful and Empirically Important," *Journal of Economic Behavior & Organization* 50 (2003): 391–405.

18. Doris Kearns Goodwin, *Team of Rivals: The Political Genius of Abraham Lincoln* (New York, NY: Simon & Schuster, 2005).

19. Christi Parsons, "Obama Hopes to Appoint a 'Team of Rivals,'" *Chicago Tribune,* November 15, 2008, http://articles.chicagotribune.com/2008-11-15/news/0811140501_1_clinton-and-obama-lincoln-presidency-sen-hillary-clinton.

20. Scott Wilson, "Obama Turns to like-Minded Allies, Advisers to Fill out His Second-Term Cabinet," *The Washington Post,* January 10, 2013, http://www.washingtonpost.com/politics/obama-turns-to-like-minded-allies-advisers-to-fill-out-his-second-term-cabinet/2013/01/10/3c8eeaa0-5b38-11e2-9fa9-5fbdc9530eb9_story.html.

21. Ibid.

22. Chris Cillizza, "How Chuck Hagel's Dismissal Is Another Nail in the Coffin of the 'Team of Rivals' Theory," *The Washington Post,* November 24, 2014, http://www.washingtonpost.com/blogs/the-fix/wp/2014/11/24/how-chuck-hagels-dismissal-is-another-nail-in-the-coffin-of-the-team-of-rivals-theory.

23. John M. Digman, "Personality Structure: Emergence of the Five-Factor Model," *Annual Review of Psychology* 41 (1990): 417–440; Robert R. McCrae and Oliver P. John, "An Introduction to the Five-Factor Model and Its Applications," *Journal of Personality* 60, no. 2 (1992): 175–215; Paul T. Costa, Jr. and Robert R. McCrae, "Domains and Facets: Hierarchical Personality Assessment Using the Revised NEO Personality Inventory," *Journal of Personality Assessment* 64, no. 1 (1995): 21–50.

24. McCrae and John, "An Introduction to the Five-Factor Model," 175–215; Costa, Jr. and McCrae, "Domains and Facets," 21–50.

25. Paul T. Costa, Jr. and Robert R. McCrae, *Revised NEP Personality Inventory (NEO-PI-R) and NEP Five-Factor Inventory (NEP-FFI): Professional Manual* (Odessa, FL: Psychological Assessment Resources, Inc., 1992).

26. Steven Rubenzer, Thomas Faschingbaur, Deniz Ones, "Assessing the U.S. Presidents Using the Revised NEO Personality Inventory" *Assessment* 7, no. 4 (2000): 403–419.

27. Ibid., 417.

28. McCrae and John, "An Introduction to the Five-Factor Model," 188–189.

29. Christopher A. Cooper et al., "Taking Personality Seriously: The Five-Factor Model and Public Management," *The American Review of Public Administration* 43, no. 4 (2013): 397–415.

30. "Assessment & Evaluation: Leadership Assessments," *U.S. Office of Personnel Management,* accessed December 23, 2014, http://www.opm.gov/services-for-agencies/assessment-evaluation/leadership-assessments.

31. Amy Colbert, Murray Barrick, and Bret Bradley, "Personality and Leadership Composition in Top Management Teams: Implications For Organizational Effectiveness," *Personnel Psychology* 67, no.2 (2014): 351–387.

32. Ibid., 377.

33. Marianne Miserandino, "Heeeere's Johnny: A Case Study in the Five Factor Model of Personality," *Teaching of Psychology* 34, no. 7 (2007): 38.

34. Isabel Briggs Myers and Peter B. Myers, *Gifts Differing: Understanding Personality Type* (Mountain View, CA: Davis-Black, 1980).

35. Cooper et al., "Taking Personality Seriously, 397-415.

36. Lillian Cunningham, "Myers-Briggs: Does It Pay to Know Your Type?," *The Washington Post*, December 14, 2012, http://www .washingtonpost.com/national/on-leadership/myers-briggs-does-it-pay-to-know-your-type/2012/12/14/eaed51ae-3fcc-11e2-bca3-aadc9b7e29c5_story.html.

37. William L. Gardner and Mark J. Martinko, "Using the Myers-Briggs Type Indicator to Study Managers: A Literature Review and Research Agenda," *Journal of Management* 22, (1996): 59.

38. Yves-C. Gagnon, "The Behavior of Public Managers in Adopting New Technologies," *Public Performance and Management Review* 24, (2001): 337–350; Cunningham, "Myers-Briggs."

39. Danile Druckman and Robert A. Bjork, eds., *In the Mind's Eye: Enhancing Human Performance* (Washington, DC: National Academy Press, 1991), 96-101; But see Robert M. Capraro and Mary Margaret Capraro, "Myers-Briggs Type Indicator Score Reliability Across Studies: A Meta-Analytic Reliability Generalization Study," *Educational and Psychological Measurement* 62 (2002): 590.

40. Paul T. Costa, Jr. and Robert R. McCrae, "Reinterpreting the Myers-Briggs Type Indicator From the Perspective of the Five-Factor Model of Personality," *Journal of Personality* 57, no. 1 (1989): 17–40.

41. Jameson W. Doig and Erwin C. Hargrove, *Leadership and Innovation: A Biographical Perspective on Entrepreneurs in Government* (Baltimore, MD: Johns Hopkins University Press, 1987), 7–8, 14.

42. Laurence E. Lynn Jr., "The Reagan Administration and the Renitent Bureaucracy," in *The Reagan Presidency and the Governing of America,* ed. Lester M. Salomon and Michael S. Lund (Washington, DC: Urban Institute Press, 1985), 339–370.

43. S. A. Rosenthal, "National Leadership Index 2012: A National Study of Confidence in Leadership," *Center for Public Leadership, Harvard Kennedy School,* 2012, http://www.centerforpublicleadership.org/images/pdf/NLI/cpl_nli_2012.pdf.

44. Joseph Hagin et al., "Executive Summary to Report from the United States Secret Service Protective Mission Panel to the Secretary of Homeland Security," *United States Secret Service Mission Panel (USSSPMP),* 2014, 3.

45. Montgomery Van Wart, "Public-Sector Leadership Theory: An Assessment," *Public Administration Review* 63, (2003): 224.

46. John W. Gardner, *On Leadership* (New York, NY: Free Press, 1993); Warren G. Bennis, *On Becoming a Leader,* rev. ed. (Cambridge, MA: Perseus, 2003); Rudolph W. Giuliani, *Leadership* (New York, NY: Miramax Books, 2002).

47. James MacGregor Burns, *Leadership* (New York, NY: Harper Perennial, 1982).

48. Warren Bennis and Burt Nanus, *Leaders: The Strategies for Taking Charge* (New York, NY: Harper and Row, 1985), 21.

49. Jonathan R. Tompkins, *Organization Theory and Public Management* (Belmont, CA: Thomson Wadsworth, 2005), 400.

50. Richard Haass, *The Bureaucratic Entrepreneur: How To Be Effective in Any Unruly Organization* (Washington DC: Brookings Institution Press, 1999), 81.

51. Robert D. Behn, "What Right Do Public Managers Have to Lead?" *Public Administration Review* 58 (1998): 209.

52. "Robert K. Greenleaf, *The Servant as Leader* (The Greenleaf Center for Servant Leadership, 2008). Also see Robert K. Greenleaf, *Servant Leadership: A Journey into the Nature of Legitimate Power and Greatness* (Mahwah, NJ: Paulist Press, 2002); Larry D. Terry, "Leadership in the Administrative State: The Concept of Administrative Conservatorship," *Public Administration Review* 21, no. 4 (1990): 395–412.

53. Van Wart, "Public-Sector Leadership Theory," 224, 225.

54. Philip Selznick, *Leadership in Administration: A Sociological Interpretation* (Berkeley: University of California Press, 1984), 4, 22, 31.

55. John M. Bryson and Barbara C. Crosby, *Leadership for the Common Good: Tackling Public Problems in a Shared-Power World* (San Francisco, CA: Jossey-Bass, 1992).

56. Montgomery Van Wart, *Dynamics of Leadership in Public Service: Theory and Practice* (Armonk, NY: M. E. Sharpe, 2005), xix.

57. Gary J. Miller, "Managerial Dilemmas: Political Leadership in Hierarchies," in *The Limits of Rationality,* ed. Karen Schweers Cook and Margaret Levi (Chicago, IL: University of Chicago, 1990), 324–357.

58. George A. Akerlof, "Labor Contracts as Partial Gift Exchange," *Quarterly Journal of Economics* 97, (1982): 543–569.

59. Donald C. Stone, "Notes on the Governmental Executive: His Role and His Methods," *Public Administration Review* 5 (1945): 210–225.

60. Ameet Sachdev, "Executive Profile: Kate Maehr," *Chicago Tribune*, February 3, 2014, http://articles.chicagotribune.com/2014-02-03/site/ct-kate-maehr-executive-profile-biz-0203-20140203_1_food-bank-kate-maehr-federal-food-stamp-program.

11 CRAFT

Managerial Heuristics

INTRODUCTION

That the exercise of managerial craft—in effective or ineffective ways—is inevitable is an overarching theme of this book. Opportunities for craftsmanship occur both when managers are enabled as well as when they are constrained; when they are creators as well as creatures. Another ongoing theme is that public managers can best confront the distinctive challenges they face when they think systematically and analytically about the origins or causes of the problems and opportunities they face:

- They must formulate and weigh alternative solutions in terms of their likely consequences for public policy outcomes.
- They must articulate reasons for the strategies and actions that they believe are appropriate in given situations.
- They must diagnose and respond to unfolding events and analyze past situations.

Thinking and acting in three dimensions, with the guiding principle of the rule of law, provides an overarching framework for practicing analytical public management. This chapter discusses theories, ideas, and heuristics that managers may use to consciously examine their processes for systematic analysis of the challenges and opportunities before them. These same theories, ideas, and heuristics can be used by outside observers to understand and analyze the decisions, strategies, and actions of public managers in a variety of roles.

The opening case, about Michelle Rhee, chancellor of Washington, DC, public schools from 2007 to 2010, illustrates the use of chapter's concepts. Next, strategies and pitfalls of deliberation and decision making are reviewed. Then, the styles and strategies for learning about their internal and external environments are discussed. Following a description of managerial strategies and approaches, the end-of-chapter case further illustrates the concepts of decision-making processes, learning style, and strategic thinking of Paul Vallas during his terms as leader of public schools in three large cities.

CASE: MICHELLE RHEE
AND DC PUBLIC SCHOOL REFORM

In June 2007, Mayor Adrian Fenty appointed Michelle Rhee as chancellor of the Washington, DC, public school system. In her late 30s at the time, Rhee immediately instituted reforms and continued to do so throughout her term. She implemented policy changes and initiatives, often controversial, intended to transform the system and improve conditions and outcomes for students. The eyes of DC students and parents, and of education policymakers across the country, were on Rhee and her reforms over the next 3 years.[i]

The Status Quo

When Rhee arrived in DC, its schools were "by almost any measure—test scores, attendance, safety—among the worst in the country."[1] There was broad acknowledgement that the system was broken, but there were no clear strategies for fixing it.

The DC schools had fallen far since the 1960s, when they were considered some of the best Black public schools in the country. "Washington thrived because it could rely on a class of educators—in this case, African Americans—who were mostly kept out of other professions."[2] Nonetheless, a confluence of social forces and events led many middle-class African Americans to leave DC in the 1960s and 1970s.

In the early 1970s, Marion Barry was elected to the DC school board and the city council; in 1979 he was elected the city's mayor. "Barry quickly grasped that the school system could do more than just facilitate his own rise. . . . A new political base was emerging, populated by teachers and led by Barry."[3] He saw the schools as a source of patronage and "a place where blacks [could] get better jobs, higher salaries, and more benefits."[4] An *Atlantic* profile of Rhee by Clay Risen argued that Barry's legacy in this respect resulted "a generation later [in] a system that was overstaffed, inefficient, and resistant to change, even as it got worse at its primary role of educating students."[5]

At the time of Rhee's arrival in June 2010, there was no question that the DC schools faced enormous challenges. A *Washington Post* article titled "Can D.C. Schools be Fixed?" described systemic problems and specific examples of the challenges: physical plant disrepair and safety issues, inefficient and dysfunctional personnel and administrative systems, attacks and violence in schools, bloated administrative budgets, low spending on instruction and teachers. One observer described the issues as "mindboggling."[6]

School districts in many large cities face challenges meeting the needs of the students they serve, many of whom come from low-income families and face additional challenges in their homes and communities. Even given these challenges, DC schools seemed to be doing a particularly bad job.[7]

The Reforms

In April 2007, a "historic transfer of power" took place when the DC City Council, anxious to dilute the influence of entrenched interests, voted to cede control of the DC schools to the new, reform-minded mayor.[8]

---

[i]In addition to the sources cited in this case, other profiles and stories on Rhee's tenure in DC include, for example, "The Education of Michelle Rhee," *Frontline*, January 8, 2013, http://www.pbs.org/wgbh/pages/frontline/education-of-michelle-rhee/; and "School Reformer: The Tenure of Michelle Rhee" *Education Week*, October 8, 2010, http://www.edweek.org/ew/articles/2010/10/15/08_michelle_rhee_timeline.h30.html.

Mayor Fenty sought this control and the associated responsibility for improving the schools, following similar processes in New York City, Chicago, and other large cities. Fenty convinced Rhee to take the job as the first chancellor of DC public schools, pledging his full support for her reform efforts. At the time of Rhee's appointment, Fenty commented, "This system needs radical change; it really needs a shake-up. . . . We did not want to pick someone to tinker around the edges."[9]

An interactive timeline available on *the Washington Post* website shows Rhee's initiatives, gains, and setbacks beginning with her arrival as chancellor in DC.[10] Selected headlines from the timeline convey the scope and pace of Rhee's efforts:

"A Tough Tone for Tenure" (July 1, 2007)

"Rhee Gains Power to Fire Some Employees" (October 12, 2007)

"Rhee Moves to Close Schools" (November 28, 2007)

"Kids Head to School on Weekends" (January 20, 2008)

"An Ambitious Agenda" (February 22, 2008)

"Rhee Trims District Staff" (March 7, 2008)

"Rhee Offers Teacher Buyouts" (April 10, 2008)

"Rhee Signs Controversial Agreement" (April 28, 2008)

"Rhee Fires Principals—Including her Children's" (May 5, 2008)

"A School Overhaul" (May 15, 2008)

"Rhee Unveils Plan for Mass Firings" (July 3, 2008)

"One Year In, D.C. Schools Show Strong Gains" (July 9, 2008)

"For Best Teachers, Rhee Proposes $130,000 a Year" (July 23, 2008)

"Union: Pay Package a Non-Starter" (August 7, 2008)

"District Pays Students for Performance" (August 21, 2008)

"Rhee Fires Shot at Union" (October 2, 2008)

"A Five Year Plan to Turn Around Schools" (November 18, 2008)

"Growing Celebrity Stirs Controversy" (December 1, 2008)

"Rhee Wants to Shutter Elementary Schools" (February 6, 2009)

"Rhee: Teachers to be Evaluated on Student Progress" (March 11, 2009)

"Rhee Admits to Pushing Change Too Fast" (March 13, 2009)

The *Post's* Rhee timeline feature ended in spring 2009, but Rhee's initiatives and controversy did not. Headlines from the education policy publication *Education Week* outline the major turns:

(Continued)

(Continued)

"D.C. Chancellor Warns of Cuts after Hiring Hundreds of Teachers" (September 22, 2009)

"Foundations Would Help Fund D.C. Teachers' Contract" (April 20, 2010)

"D.C. Teachers Ratify Contract with Pay for Performance" (June 7, 2010)

"New D.C. Evaluation Process Targets Hundreds for Firing" (August 10, 2010)

"Rhee Reflects on her Stormy Tenure in D.C." (September 22, 2010)

"Rhee Resigns, Urging D.C.: 'Keep the Reforms Going'" (October 13, 2010)

As the policy proposals and structural changes rolled out during her term as chancellor, Rhee herself was as much a central part of the story as the reforms she sought and implemented.

The Reformer

Rhee was a nontraditional choice for leading DC's public school system. She had never been a district super-intendent, had only a few years of teaching experience (as an elementary school teacher in Baltimore), was raised in Ohio as the daughter of Korean immigrants, and would be the first head of DC schools in 40 years who was not African-American.[11]

Rhee earned her undergraduate degree from Cornell and a master in public policy degree from Harvard's Kennedy School of Government. In 1997, Rhee founded the New Teacher Project, a nonprofit organization that helped school systems identify, recruit, and train new teachers and developed training programs for individuals trained in other areas who sought to become teachers. It was the idea of Wendy Kopp, leader of Teach for America, who had sought out Rhee to head up the new organization.[12] Rhee had been head of the New Teacher Project for 10 years when Fenty recruited her to lead DC schools.

As chancellor, Rhee was irreverent, brash, and driven. In his *Atlantic* profile of Rhee, Risen observed that Rhee "pepper[s] her sentences with words like crappy and awesome," that she "comes across as passionate and talented, armed with a casual, biting wit," and that she "does not suffer fools, gladly or otherwise."[13] A front-page *Washington Post* assessment, written by Bill Turque 2 years into Rhee's term, described her as bringing "passion, urgency, and a conviction" to the job.[14] Another profile of Rhee—written by Amanda Ripley and published in *Time* magazine as a cover story with a controversial photo showing Rhee with a broom in a classroom—described accompanying the chancellor on visits to DC schools: "she walked into the first classroom she could find and stood to the side, frowning like a specter. . . . Within 2 minutes, she had seen enough, and she stalked out to the next classroom."[15] Ripley observed that Rhee was "far nicer to students than to most adults. In many private encounters with officials, bureaucrats and even fundraisers . . . she doesn't smile or nod or do any of the things most people do to put others at ease . . . [she] walk[s] out of small meetings held for her benefit without a word of explanation."[16]

As the timelines of media stories demonstrate, Rhee's reforms were rolling out at a fast pace. Those who supported the reforms referred to Rhee and her staff as "Rhee-volutionaries"; to those who were less enamored of the reform efforts, the same staff were "Rhee-bots."[17] Among some groups, there was a sense that Rhee was "run[ning] roughshod over the community—that she [was] less a chancellor than a dictator."[18] Others pointed to the effectiveness of Rhee's personal touch. The PTA president at the public elementary school that Rhee's own children attended observed, "Her office will announce something to be done, like close a school. Everybody hates that. But when she goes and talks to the parents, many of them do a 180."[19]

Rhee was tireless in her efforts to reform DC schools, working early morning til late at night. When she wasn't in meetings or at public forums (and sometimes even when she was), she was communicating by Blackberry or cell phone or working on her computer(s).[20] She directly answered emails, including those from students, parents, and community members. The *Atlantic* profile reported that Rhee had responded to over 95,000 emails in a single year.[21]

A hallmark of Rhee's reforms was that she wanted to hold teachers and schools accountable for student learning despite the difficulties children faced in their neighborhoods and homes. She emphasized the need for "personal responsibility" on the part of teachers.[22] In his profile of Rhee, Risen observed, "this sort of moral certitude is exactly what turns off many veteran teachers . . . [Rhee] seems to be asking for superhuman efforts. . . . Making missionary zeal a job requirement is a tough way to build morale, not to mention support, among the teachers who have to confront the D.C. ghetto every day."[23] Rhee's "rising celebrity" and nationwide exposure "alienated key constituencies at home. Teachers seethed as she told anecdotes painting them as incompetent, lazy or hostile to change."[24]

Turque's front-page *Post* article described some of the "hard lessons" that Rhee had encountered and noted some of the adjustments she seemed to be making. She had started meeting with "hundreds of teachers and listen[ing] to their concerns in small, after-hours groups," and acknowledged in a March 2009 "contrite" letter to teachers that she "might have pushed too many changes on them at once."[25] Rhee emphasized that "her message hasn't changed, only that she's worked to communicate more directly so that her views aren't 'warped and diluted' by the media or central bureaucracy."[26]

Data and policy analysis were key elements of Rhee's learning, strategy, and efforts to hold teachers and schools accountable. Her proclivity for data-informed management may have been driven by her professional training at the Kennedy School, as well as by her experiences with Teach for America. In DC, she held weekly SchoolStat meetings with staff to "pore over data on everything from student performance to facilities' work orders."[27]

Rhee saw herself "not as a politician but as a technocrat; a decider, not a negotiator."[28] At the beginning of Rhee's term as chancellor, Rhee "operated as if only one power center counted: the mayor's office," given the structural reforms the City Council had approved.[29] Turque observed, "Council members chafed at the lack of regard she displayed, saying that her appearances were infrequent and that she often left questions half-answered . . . the chancellor and her young senior staff conveyed an 'us against them' attitude about transparency and communication."[30]

During her tenure as chancellor, Rhee "lost none of her zeal. But those who know her well say she's found that converting conviction into sustainable change requires more patience, indulgence and attentiveness to politics than may come naturally to her."[31]

(Continued)

(Continued)

Moving On

Rhee campaigned for Fenty during his reelection campaign in 2010. When he failed to win a second term, speculation swirled concerning whether the incumbent, Vincent Gray, would keep Rhee in the chancellor post. On October 13, Rhee resigned, saying,

> Today, Mayor Fenty, [City Council] Chairman Gray and I have reached the mutual decision that I will leave my post as Chancellor of the D.C. Public School System. This is not a decision we made lightly. But it is one that I believe is essential to allow Chairman Gray to pursue our shared goal of uniting this city behind the school reforms that are making a difference in the lives of our children. In short, we have agreed—together—that the best way to keep the reforms going is for this reformer to step aside.[ii]

Gray appointed Rhee's deputy, Kaya Henderson, as interim chancellor until June 11, 2011, when the city council approved her appointment as chancellor.

DECISION MAKING

Public managers engage in many different kinds of activity. They read reports, supervise and respond to staff members and their needs and concerns, conduct and participate in meetings, visit field offices, attend conferences, make speeches and presentations, give press conferences, and testify before legislative committees. Although the particular mix of activities varies—by the nature of the policies and programs being managed, by the manager's hierarchical position and responsibilities, by the institutionalized norms of the manager's organization—all public managers must allocate their time and attention across diverse activities. Public managers must deliberate and make decisions. Careful deliberation and sound decision making are foundations of analytical public management.

As described in Chapter 6, decision making is in part an organizationally structured activity, a matter of procedures and protocols and due process, prescribed by law and institutionalized values or established by public managers themselves. Viewed through the lens of the craft dimension, decision making is a personal activity, influenced, as discussed in Chapter 10, by an individual public manager's cognitive and emotional capacities and inclinations.

A **decision** is "a conclusion or resolution reached after consideration."[32] **Deliberation** is the process of consideration. Each day may be consumed with meeting, talking, listening, questioning, reading, reflecting, and observing. These are steps in the learning and deliberation processes that culminate in decision making. Once decisions are made, deliberation is transformed into organizational purpose and achievement.

[ii]"Resignation Statement of Michelle Rhee," District of Columbia Public Schools Press Release, October 13, 2010, http://dcps.dc.gov/DCPS/About+DCPS/Press+Releases+and+Announcements/Press+Releases/Resignation+Statement+of+Michelle+Rhee.

Specific decisions on issues of policy, program, and organization, however, may be infrequent, and deliberation may be spontaneous, unstructured, and ongoing. Deciding need not be a discrete event, nor does it necessarily follow an explicit process; rather, a decision may evolve over time through a series of deliberations and tentative steps. Moreover, a decision to maintain the status quo (to "do nothing") is as much a decision as one to take a specific action to

> A decision to maintain the status quo (to "do nothing") is as much a decision as one to take a specific action to change the status quo...

change the status quo, as Michelle Rhee aggressively did. Decisiveness appropriate to the context is a fundamental component of a public manager's skill set.

Through deliberation and decision-making processes, public managers may formulate strategies, confront obstacles, solve problems, and develop arguments in support of their preferences and actions. These processes are likely to be influenced by unconscious psychological and emotional factors and the inclination to appear reasonable and act logically in the light of the facts. The fit between the manager and the circumstances of a particular managerial role may or may not produce the craftsmanship needed for fully effective performance. Simon wrote, "Of all the knowledge, attitudes, and values stored in a human memory, only a very small fraction are evoked in a given concrete situation."[33] Placing different kinds of people in a given role is likely to lead to different kinds of role behavior: As noted earlier in the book, whether a social worker is a mother, of the same race or age as a client, formerly on welfare herself, professionally educated, or an ideological liberal or conservative may well have a bearing on how she responds to the individuals she serves.

Managers as Rational Actors

A popular theory of choice holds that individuals—citizens, policymakers, public managers, street-level bureaucrats—are intendedly **rational**; that is, they pursue their goals and interests in ways that are efficient in the use of scarce resources of time, attention, and money to maximize goal attainment. All other things being equal, rational individuals weigh the costs and benefits of alternative ways of pursuing their goals and make decisions that are consistent in the light of that analysis. Proponents of this view argue that a great deal of human behavior is intendedly rational. This is especially true in the world of public affairs, where the pressures to be both efficient and effective in pursuing public policy objectives with the taxpayers' money are naturally strong, where punishment for careless and preventable waste may be severe, and where judicial rulings defer to managers who offer reasonable justifications for their actions.

In a managerial context, the demands of rationality are not unrealistic or academic. Instead, real-world rationality has a common sense motivation and interpretation. It "has something to do with thinking, reason, and reasoning processes. An action seems rational if it is agreeable to reason: if it is not absurd, preposterous, extravagant, or foolish, but rather intelligent, sensible, self-conscious, deliberate, and calculated."[34] Or, as public administration scholar John M. Pfiffner has put it, the managerial decision maker "saves face by supporting his decision with reasons which possess face validity" (a caution that brings to mind the need for managers to support their decisions with solid arguments, as emphasized in the model deliberative process described in Chapter 1). Looked at this way, says Pfiffner, rationality as logical, common sense reasoning and persuasive argument is even more demanding than narrower scientific or engineering notions of rationality in that "it takes into consideration a greater variety of data."[35] These data include the kinds of intuitive, anecdotal, and experiential information that are accumulated during human learning processes.

Rationality has explicit motivations within the U.S. constitutional scheme. In political contests between the executive and the legislature, the transparent reasonableness of a political strategy confers an advantage on its proponents.[36] When decision making in either branch lacks transparency, justified suspicions arise that the process that produced the decision is not to be trusted. With the maturing of administrative law, the demonstrable rationality of managerial decisions has become an important criterion for judicial determinations concerning whether or not deference to administrative judgment is warranted.

Example: A Reasonable Argument for an Endangered Species Listing

On May 14, 2008, Secretary of the Interior Dirk Kempthorne announced that the polar bear had been listed as a "threatened species," that is, likely to become endangered in the foreseeable future, as defined by the Endangered Species Act. He explained the logic of his decision in a statement announcing it and included graphic images based on satellite photography of the shrinking of the Arctic ice cap, which provides habitat for polar bears. The secretary's concise logic, for which he relied on the knowledge and expertise of the department's scientists, provided a transparent justification for a decision that has face validity—it is apparently reasonable:

> In taking these actions, I accept the recommendations of the Assistant Secretary for Fish and Wildlife and Parks, Lyle Laverty, and the Director of the U.S. Fish and Wildlife Service, Dale Hall. I also relied upon scientific analysis from the Director of the U.S. Geological Survey, Dr. Mark Myers, and his team of scientists. . . . Today's decision is based on three findings. First, sea ice is vital to polar bear survival. Second, the polar bear's sea-ice habitat has dramatically melted in recent decades. Third, computer models suggest sea ice is likely to further recede in the future. Because polar bears are vulnerable to this loss of habitat, they are, in my judgment, likely to become endangered in the foreseeable future—in this case 45 years. . . . Although the population of bears has grown from a low of about 12,000 in the late 1960s to approximately 25,000 today, our scientists advise me that computer modeling projects a significant population decline by the year 2050. This, in my judgment, makes the polar bear a threatened species. . . . I have also accepted these professionals' best scientific and legal judgments that the loss of sea ice, *not* oil and gas development or subsistence activities, are the reason the polar bear is threatened.[37]

Alternatives to Rationality

It is, however, intuitively obvious that individuals, including public managers, are not always or often enough rational or reasonable in their information processing. Social and behavioral scientists have identified numerous ways in which individuals depart systematically from the strict assumptions of rationality in information processing and problem solving.[i] A rational explanation for a decision might conceal underlying nonrational motivations. Public managers should be aware of these frequently encountered possibilities for at least three reasons:

- to increase self-awareness of their own deliberation and decision-making processes;
- to sharpen their ability to evaluate the arguments of those who advise or attempt to influence them; and
- to sharpen their ability to critique and react to criticisms by their external constituencies, stakeholders, and service recipients—an important step in constructing arguments to support their decisions.

The following discussion of departures from strict rationality includes situations commonly encountered in public affairs.

---

[i]In addition to the references cited in this section, see Daniel A. Kahneman, *Thinking Fast and Slow* (New York, NY: Farrar, Straus and Giroux, 2011).

Bounded Rationality

Herbert Simon's concept of **bounded rationality** acknowledges that individuals are typically limited in how well they solve complex problems—in how much effort they make to search for, store, retrieve, and analyze information. They resort to various shortcuts that reduce stress and increase their confidence in the choices they make, relying, perhaps, on conventional wisdom, rules of thumb, cues from those thought to be expert or well informed, or principles of appropriateness, duty, or loyalty.[ii]

Because there is a kind of rationality in resorting to shortcuts that ease the practical, cognitive, and emotional burdens of decision making, such simplified choice making is not considered simply irrational. If individuals depart from strict rationality—that is, identifying all alternatives, collecting all relevant information, weighing all uncertainties—they do so for rational reasons: Search and analysis costs are too high to justify an exhaustive analysis. A good decision is one that is *good enough,* one in which the decision maker has confidence. Expending significant additional resources of time and effort that could improve the quality of decisions by only a little is hardly reasonable. Instead of "optimizing," decision makers may prefer **satisficing**, or settling for an adequate solution to a problem given the costs of doing more.

Bounded rationality may be just as unreasonable, however. Policymakers and public managers also reduce the stresses and uncertainties of decision making by ruling out choices that violate long-held assumptions and beliefs that might well be wrong or have become outdated. Intelligence analysts who had become convinced that Saddam Hussein's Iraq had weapons of mass destruction ignored conflicting evidence provided by defectors, many of whom said the weapons had been destroyed and production halted. The response to the threat posed by al Qaeda prior to the September 11, 2001 attacks may have lacked urgency because many policymakers at the time assumed that states such as China, Russia, Iran, Libya, and Iraq posed more significant threats to U.S. interests and security than did threats from stateless terror groups.

> Instead of "optimizing," decision makers may prefer "satisficing," or settling for an adequate solution to a problem given the costs of doing more.

Policymaking and management concerning health policy confront the issue of bounded rationality in a fundamental way. Proponents of consumer-driven health care argue that the nation's health care system would be more efficient if everyone shopped more carefully and considered a wider range of choices in the light of evidence concerning the costs and benefits of alternative insurance plans, providers, treatments, medications, and hospitals. But consumers of medical care, especially if they are ill, may feel incompetent to make choices on matters in which they are not experts and may be inclined, perhaps out of fear of making a bad choice, to trust their physician's recommendations, to accept the advice of family members or others who have had similar ailments, or to trust what they might have read or heard in various media.

In the end, then, health care choices may be more emotional than strictly rational. Even physicians, out of habit or inertia or reliance on their own intuition and experience, may fail to accept evidence concerning what appears to be best practices, in whether to use minimal or invasive treatments, when to be cautious rather than acting quickly, and what medications to use. Forcing citizens to confront a wider array of choices and to appraise large amounts of specialized information may lead not to more efficient consumption of health care but to an even greater reliance on unreliable sources of advice. More choices and more demands on information processing may lead to confusion and stress.[iii]

[ii]See Herbert A. Simon, "Rationality as Process and as Process of Thought," *American Economic Review* 68 (1978): 1–16; and John Conlisk, "Why Bounded Rationality?" *Journal of Economic Literature* 34 (1998): 669–700.

[iii]For additional discussion of choice overload, see Barry Schwartz, *The Paradox of Choice: Why More Is Less* (New York, NY: Ecco, Harper Collins, 2005).

Prospect Theory

Psychologists Amos Tversky and Daniel Kahneman reject the version of rational choice theory known as expected utility theory, which makes strong assumptions concerning decision quality, because it does not provide a plausible account of how many decisions are actually made.[38] According to Kahneman and Tversky, individuals are irrational but not randomly so. They are irrational in systematic ways.

Kahneman and Tversky's fundamental claim, termed **prospect theory,** is that decisions depend on the way that the prospective consequences of decisions, or prospects, are framed, that is, presented or described. Prospects may be viewed as positive or negative deviations from a neutral reference point or starting point, which is often the status quo. Above such a point—when prospects involve possible gains—individuals tend to be risk averse. They tend to prefer a sure gain to the risky prospect of a much larger gain or else losing what they have. Below such a point—when prospects involve possible losses—individuals tend to take more risks, preferring the risky prospect of no losses, but possibly a much larger loss, to the sure prospect of a specific loss.

Evidence that the way prospects are framed changes the decisions people make violates a fundamental postulate of expected utility theory: the invariance of decisions to the particular ways in which choices are presented or described. This behavior would not occur if decision makers systematically saw through the presentation to the underlying values at stake; for example, if they aggregated concurrent prospects of gains and losses or if they reduced such prospects to a common unit of assessment. But quite often they do not do these things because it requires more cognitive skill than they typically possess and is more costly in time and effort.

These **framing effects** can be especially poignant in decision making on medical treatment. Describing a patient's chances in terms of likelihood of living instead of the risk of dying will affect a patient's decisions on treatment.[39] In one study, 44 percent of patients chose a specific course of therapy when risks were presented as the reduced chances of dying, but only 18 percent did so when outcomes were expressed as increased chances of living.[40] Other factors that have been shown to influence choices include the amount of data; the vividness of the presentation (real versus abstract); whether outcomes are expressed as numbers, graphs, or narratives; whether harms are presented as absolute risks or relative risks; and the use of lay language versus medical terminology.[41]

Example: Framing Prospects for the Iraq War

The idea that decision makers may take more risks if prospects are framed as avoiding losses found its way into the debate over President George W. Bush's controversial 2007 decision to surge troop levels in Iraq. In the following excerpt, Princeton University economist and *The New York Times* columnist Paul Krugman makes the argument that the Bush administration was framing the surge prospects in terms of the increased possibility of additional lives saved rather than the reduced possibility of continuing loss of life. The administration wanted the public to see the issue that way, too, and stay at the Iraq table rather than turning away. The result of the surge was a substantial increase in "lives saved," that is, a substantial reduction in "lives lost" relative to the reference point: the presurge casualty levels.

> The only real question about the planned "surge" in Iraq—which is better described as a Vietnam-style escalation—is whether its proponents are cynical or delusional.
>
> Senator Joseph Biden, chairman of the Senate Foreign Relations Committee, thinks they're cynical. He recently told the *The Washington Post* that administration officials are simply running out the clock, so that the next president will be "the guy landing helicopters inside the Green Zone, taking people off the roof."

Daniel Kahneman, who won the Nobel Memorial Prize in Economic Science for his research on irrationality in decision-making, thinks they're delusional. Mr. Kahneman and Jonathan Renshon recently argued in *Foreign Policy* magazine that the administration's unwillingness to face reality in Iraq reflects a basic human aversion to cutting one's losses—the same instinct that makes gamblers stay at the table, hoping to break even.[42]

Cognitive Dissonance

In 1957, psychologist Leon Festinger developed the concept of **cognitive dissonance.**[43] Cognitive dissonance is a state that individuals reach when they have a conflict of cognitions, defined as mental acquisitions of knowledge through thought, experience, or the senses. A person in a state of cognitive dissonance will tend to seek consonance.

Example: Cognitive Dissonance at NASA

The idea that cognitive dissonance is often arbitrarily resolved was reflected in a *New York Times* report on the National Aeronautics and Space Administration (NASA)'s launching the space shuttle *Discovery* following the shuttle *Columbia* accident. The dissonance—maintaining flight schedules requires taking risks, but taking risks might lead to another accident—was resolved by ignoring, or accepting, the risks. The *Times* reported that the chair of the *Columbia* Accident Investigation Board, Harold Gehman, believed that NASA had

> significantly reduced the overall risk that falling foam will lead to disaster again . . . even though a NASA panel that monitored the agency's progress in meeting those goals found that it had fallen short in three areas, including the prevention of all launching debris and the ability to repair damage in space. "I'm sure that this next flight will be safer than the previous ones," Admiral Gehman said. But he added, "By any measure of 'safe,' this is not safe."[44]

Festinger proposed that cognitive dissonance is a psychological tension similar to hunger and thirst, and that people seek to resolve this tension as a matter of urgency. There are various ways to achieve this. One way is to promptly reevaluate all prior beliefs. But this process is expensive. Changing a cognition entails some discomfort: individuals undergoing this process have to reflect and admit to themselves that they have been wrong or that their knowledge is no longer relevant. Therefore, rather than adapt to a new cognition, they may eliminate the conflict by denying its validity. A common term for this is "being in denial." Or they might take the further step of refusing to recognize the validity of all dissonant cognitions, systematically screening them out, perhaps by never listening to a particular adviser or reading a particular publication or source.

Obviously a person feels better when not suffering from cognitive dissonance. But the price of cognitive comfort achieved by refusing to acknowledge conflicting realities may be the consequences of the bad decisions that result. For example, one cognition may be that terrorist threats are sponsored by states such as Iraq (under Saddam Hussein), Syria, and Iran. Another is that a serious breach of security has been caused by an apparently independent, non-state-sponsored entity such as al Qaeda. Consonance may be obtained by insisting that the activities of terrorist cells and networks are in reality sustained by state sponsors, who then become the targets of threats, sanctions, or invasion, even if evidence for this argument is weak.

Groupthink

Based on his study of public policy fiascos—including President Truman's decision to escalate the war against North Korea despite the very real threat of Chinese intervention, and President Kennedy's invasion of Cuba at the Bay of Pigs despite evidence that it would not provoke an uprising against Fidel Castro—Irving Janis coined the term **groupthink,** which "refers to a deterioration of mental efficiency, reality testing, and moral judgment that results from in-group pressures."[iv] The term often surfaces in discussions of public policy and management decisions that have not turned out well.[45]

Two well-known examples of groupthink occurred at NASA: the decision to launch the *Challenger* space shuttle, which exploded shortly after launch, killing the crew; and management reactions to the damage to the *Columbia* space shuttle that eventually caused its destruction on re entry, also killing the crew. In both instances, an inner circle of decision makers—those who decided whether to launch—screened out people and evidence that contradicted the view on which they had reached concurrence and their consensus seemed to be invulnerable to any kind of dissent or analysis of alternative views. Deliberations leading to the decision to attack and occupy Iraq in 2003 are often regarded as having been affected by groupthink. Secretary of State Colin L. Powell, who frequently dissented from the White House consensus, found himself excluded from high-level meetings on matters directly affecting his department and the conduct of foreign policy presumably because he was disruptive of group consensus.

Example: Groupthink at the CIA

The term *groupthink* has become a popular explanation for all kinds of public policy decisions that become widely perceived as failures. It is even used to characterize entire organizations, as in the following case for the Central Intelligence Agency (CIA). An example in Chapter 9 describes an effort to transform the culture of the National Intelligence Estimate to allow for dissent and qualifications in the analysis. "Group think grinds top-secret papers into intellectual pulp," said Angelo Codevilla, a former senior staff member of the Senate intelligence committee. "Our intelligence community thinks in herds: Stay close. Don't get out ahead. Don't be thought of as crazy," he said. "There is a tremendous lack of diversity of mind. The most typical phrase in an intelligence estimate is 'We believe' the corporate belief, the official view, calibrated to satisfy—not 'I think.'"[46]

Groupthink has a number of symptoms, including the propensity of members of the group to overestimate the importance and morality of the group, the tendency to offer rationalizations rather than reasons for members' preferred solutions, self-imposed censorship and subtle pressures to ward off threats to group solidarity, and preserving the illusion of unanimity. Groups especially vulnerable to groupthink are those that are cohesive, screened from outside scrutiny, and led by leaders who enforce conformity. The purpose is to reduce the stresses and uncertainties of decision making. The psychological props and ploys that individuals employ in stressful circumstances are reinforced by the concurrence-seeking behavior of the group.

[iv]Irving L. Janis, *Victims of Groupthink* (Boston, MA: Houghton Mifflin, 1972), 9. For further discussion, see Gregory Moorhead and Richard Ference, "Group Decision Fiascoes Continue: Space Shuttle Challenger and a Revised Groupthink Framework," *Human Relations* 4 (1991): 539–550; J. K. Esser, "Alive and Well after 25 Years: A Review of Groupthink Research," *Organizational Behavior and Human Decision Processes* 73 (1998): 116–141.

Victims of groupthink fail to analyze relevant alternatives, are biased in assembling and assessing evidence, seek little outside help or advice, fail to reexamine premature agreements or preferences, and neglect implementation problems and contingency plans. They seek unanimity and conformity and actively discourage threats to achieving them. Pressures to conform are likely to lead to an implicit bargaining in which dissidents are coerced into silence, perhaps under the implied threat of expulsion from the group.

Other Psychological Biases

Psychologists have confirmed the existence of a wide variety of **psychological biases** in decision making.[47] Among them are several important to the craftsmanship of public managers.

- *Hindsight bias.* After an event happens, people tend to claim they knew all along that it would happen. Psychologists have confirmed this tendency with experimental evidence. In other words, after the fact, people assign a higher probability to the event than they did before it happened, a form of retrospective overconfidence. "Liberals' assertion that they 'knew all along' that the war in Iraq would go badly are guilty of the hindsight bias," according to psychologist Hal Arkes.[48]

Example: Hindsight Bias on No Child Left Behind

In mid-2007, President George W. Bush urged Congress to reauthorize the No Child Left Behind Act, a signature achievement of his administration. The legislation required public schools to show progress in the test scores of all groups of students. Unexpected opposition arose from officials formerly associated with creating and administering the act, who might have been exhibiting hindsight bias.

> Bush might have expected that Eugene W. Hickok, a relative of the legendary frontier lawman Wild Bill Hickok and the original sheriff of No Child Left Behind, would support his drive for renewal. As the No. 2 Education Department official in Bush's first term, Hickok wrangled states and schools into compliance with the law so forcefully that foes called him "Wild Gene."
>
> But Hickok, who is now urging Congress to revamp the initiative, said in a recent interview that he always harbored serious doubts about the federal government's expanding reach into the classroom.
>
> "I had these second thoughts in the back of my mind the whole time," said Hickok, a former deputy education secretary. "I believe it was a necessary step at the time, but now that it has been in place for a while, it's important to step back and see if there are other ways to solve the problem."[49]

- *Immunity to repeated warnings of danger.* Neuroscientists postulate that people gradually become immune to repeated warnings of danger or threat, thus attenuating their vigilance.[50] A related psychological phenomenon, also confirmed by experimental evidence, is called "inattentional blindness" by psychologist Brian Scholl, who argues that "attending to things is not without cost, so you can't attend to everything."[51] Therefore, repeated warnings to be on the lookout for unattended backpacks might displace your attention from other clues, such as inappropriate clothing or behavior, and gradually become ineffective as well.
- *Seeking positive features for favored candidates, negative features for rejected candidates.* Psychologist Eldar Shafir argues on the basis of experimental evidence that when people are asked to choose whom to accept

for a role or assignment, they tend to look for positive features in the candidates.[52] When asked whom to reject, they look for negative features as a basis for rejection. This insight is a justification for political candidates running negative campaign ads about their opponents. The mudslinging tends to provide a reason to reject some candidates and increase the attractiveness of the candidates who may have no conspicuous negative qualities—and perhaps no conspicuous positive qualities either.

- *Conflicting recollections of the same events.* Former National Security Council staff member Richard Clarke and former National Security Adviser Condoleezza Rice had different memories of her reactions to his warnings concerning the dangers posed by al Qaeda prior to the September 11 attacks. The issue may not be who is telling the truth, but a reflection of common memory errors. Memories tend to fade over time, especially of specific details of an experience. Details are often attributed to the wrong source, and recollections of past attitudes are based on current attitudes.[53] Memory shifts from recounting the past to reconstructing a version of it based on general knowledge and beliefs.

- *Compromised objectivity.* Decision makers honestly may not realize how easily and often their objectivity is compromised by, for example, receiving remuneration or honoraria even if there are no strings attached. People who recognize that others may engage in self-deception or biased thinking may not accept that they themselves are at risk. But, according to psychologist Daniel Gilbert, "research shows that while people underestimate the influence of self-interest on their own judgments and decisions, they overestimate its influence on others. . . . People act in their own interests, but . . . their interests include ideals of fairness, prudence and generosity." Gilbert's lesson: "Because the brain cannot see itself fooling itself, the only reliable method for avoiding bias is to avoid the situations that produce it," such as potentially compromising compensation or honoraria.[54] Avoiding even the appearance of a conflict of interest is psychologically sound. This point provides another perspective on ethics guidelines described in Chapter 8.

- *Causal attributions.* Experiments have shown that individuals are inclined to view their own statements and actions as caused by someone else's statements and actions, whereas the possible causes of others' statements and actions are overlooked. Partisan conflicts therefore are usually initiated by the other side. Further, according to Gilbert, "hitting back," and hitting back harder than one was hit in the first place, tend to be regarded as justifiable because the initiator is at fault, not the retaliator.[55]

The foregoing enumeration is not a complete account of psychological biases affecting perception, deliberation, and decision making. Other factors, described in the decision-making literature, that can impede problem solving and decision making include

- defensive avoidance (procrastination or failure to address the task caused by a sense of hopelessness, perhaps due to cognitive dissonance);
- hypervigilance (a tendency to overreact in given situations or to invent problems);
- cognitive bolstering (overemphasis on facts or opinions that support one's inclinations);
- escalation of commitment (a high initial investment in an individual, contract, or course of action that leads to even greater commitments regardless of performance);
- stereotyping, projection, and halo error (biased perceptions of individuals that distort accurate evaluation of their capacities or performance); and
- social loafing or free riding (a tendency to make less effort when working as part of a group than when working alone).

Even those processes of deliberation and decision making thought to be reasonably constructive can be distorted. For example, **brainstorming** is widely regarded as a way to elicit good ideas. According to psychologist Paul B. Paulus, however, "There are so many things people do in management because they think it's good, but there's no evidence for it. Teamwork is a good example. Brainstorming is another."[56] It is too seldom acknowledged, he argues, that group brainstorming enables all kinds of self-serving or intimidating behavior by participants, the triumph of bad ideas over good ones, the displacement of blame, confirmation of obvious or lowest-common-denominator ideas, and punishment of those who appear uncooperative.

At the level of the organization, these distortions can be consequential. Michael Cohen, James March, and Johan Olsen point out that an organization is a structure made up of diverse "streams": choices looking for problems, issues and feelings looking for situations in which they might be expressed, solutions looking for problems to which they might be the answer, and decision makers looking for work.[57] Ordinary forums for deliberation and decision making provide opportunities for these various streams to come together. As described in Chapter 9, these forums become **garbage cans** into which participants dump their particular issues, concerns, and objectives, and a wide variety of decisions can emerge from the mix. The process that results may be anything but reasonable in a conventional sense, and decision makers may be hard-pressed to construct reasonable arguments and justifications after the fact. The difficulties are compounded when participation is fluid, individual styles and personalities differ, problems are ambiguous, and technologies are unclear.

Craftsmanship and Reasonableness

The previous section illuminates difficulties for policymakers and public managers in attempting to be "reasonable." With so many possibilities for unreasonableness to distort deliberation and decision making, public managers must be prepared to prevent them or to minimize their adverse effects.

Methods for overcoming groupthink, for example, were suggested by Janis:

- The group convener withholds judgment until a full airing of members' views has taken place.
- A preselected individual is assigned the role of devil's advocate: This person challenges any suggestion presented, which encourages other participants to justify their ideas and to point out flaws in others' thinking and reduces the stigma associated with being the first to dissent.
- Anonymous or private feedback is supported; negative or dissenting views can be offered with no individual being seen to do so. This technique preserves the social solidarity of the group, as each member has plausible deniability that he or she disrupted group cohesion.
- Members are divided into subgroups to consider particularly vexing issues, discussing any differences in their views and recommendations.
- The group draws on outside experts.

More reasonable management can result from privileging arguments supported by reasons, evidence, and qualifications. It can result as well by setting the example and by creating processes like those just enumerated that reward reasonable deliberation.

A more fundamental type of intervention is termed **double-loop learning** by psychologists Chris Argyris and Donald Schön because it requires examining not only the reasonableness of arguments but also what is out of sight: the values, attitudes, and assumptions that lie behind and motivate

> **More reasonable management can result from privileging arguments supported by reasons, evidence, and qualifications.**

such arguments.[v] Managerial emphasis on introspective deliberation may over time promote the emergence of the kind of learning organization discussed in Chapter 9.

HOW PUBLIC MANAGERS CAN LEARN

Few public managers assume their responsibilities in full possession of all they need to know to do their jobs well.[vi] Even familiarity with the formal structures and processes and with the institutionalized values of their organizations (as might be acquired in subordinate positions) will not fully prepare an incoming public manager for the specific contexts of higher-level or more wide-ranging responsibilities.

Chapter 10 provided insights into how a manager's temperament or type affects the kinds of information and analysis he or she prefers during deliberation and decision making. In a given situation, some managers may appear to be learn quickly and others may seem to have a relatively flat learning curve; some search for facts; others assemble ideas and seek vision. The following sections consider general sources of ideas, information, and analysis that managers of any type might draw upon.

Paradigms and Ideologies

Public managers may have settled beliefs about how the world works and about the causes and appropriate remedies for problems. Their decisions may be guided by these taken-for-granted beliefs and presumptions about the issues they face.

The term **paradigm** generally refers to assumptions, concepts, values, and practices that constitute a specific way of viewing reality for the group or community that shares them. Paradigms provide a framework for decision making and action. A "bureaucratic paradigm," for example, is a way of thinking that views hierarchical organizations governed by statutes, rules, and formal procedures—traditional departments, commissions, and bureaus—as the preferred means for implementing public policies. As another example, "The New Paradigm" during President George W. Bush's administration "rest[ed] on a reading of the Constitution that few legal scholars share—namely, that the President, as Commander-in-Chief, has the authority to disregard virtually all previously known legal boundaries, if national security demands it."[58]

The terms paradigm and **ideology** have related meanings. A paradigm is a "shared view containing a number of assumptions," while an ideology is "an internally coherent set of ideas designed to persuade people of a particular worldview."[59]

Individuals from outside the organization who assume a managerial position may encounter a prevailing paradigm, ideology, or mindset and, either consciously or unconsciously, incorporate it into or embrace it as their own world view without sufficient reflection. (Such a phenomenon was said to have been labeled "going native" by John Ehrlichman, an adviser to President Nixon, who complained that politically appointed cabinet officials became advocates for their departments' views and values rather than for the views of the president.)

Managerial learning may be guided, consciously or unconsciously, by ideologies or other closed systems of thought. The manager's preferred system of thought may be based on abstract principles or on sensory experience,

---

[v]Chris Argyris and Donald A. Schön, *Organizational Learning: A Theory of Action Perspective* (Reading, MA: Addison-Wesley, 1978). See also Chris Argyris, *Overcoming Organizational Defenses: Facilitating Organizational Learning* (Boston, MA: Allyn and Bacon, 1990).

[vi]For an interesting discussion, see Stephen Fineman, "Emotion and Managerial Learning," *Management Learning* 28 (1997): 13–25. Note the existence of a journal devoted to managerial learning.

on logical deduction or empathy and emotion. Some scholars have argued that management itself, that is, the belief that good management is essential to good government, is an ideology or paradigm. Henry Mintzberg talks about a managerialist ideology based on several premises or assumptions: Particular activities can be isolated, both from one another and from direct authority; performance can be fully and properly evaluated by objective measures; and activities can be entrusted to autonomous professional managers held responsible for performance.[60] A fourth element might be added to that kind of managerialist ideology: If the above assumptions are not fulfilled by a program or policy, then the government should not be doing it. This view turns on its head the familiar proposition that government does what the private sector cannot or will not do, discussed in Chapter 1.

In her book *Challenging the Performance Movement: Accountability, Complexity, and Democratic Values,* Beryl Radin identifies what she regards as the mind-set, or ideology, underlying advocacy of performance measurement and management. Such advocacy, she argues, is based on the following assumptions:

- Goals can be defined clearly and set firmly as the basis for the performance measurement process.
- Goals are specific and the responsibility of definable actors.
- Outcomes can be specified independently of inputs, processes, and outputs.
- Outcomes can be quantified and measured.
- Outcomes are controllable and susceptible to external timing.
- Data are available, clear, and accurate.
- Results of the performance measurement can be delivered to an actor with authority to respond to the results.[61]

In other words, public managers attempting to institute performance measurement and management believe that such an effort will succeed, yet this belief is often unsubstantiated. Radin argues that they do not institute such systems on the basis of evidence, obtained through careful analysis, and that the circumstances necessary for success are seldom in fact present.

A distinction is often drawn between those public officials who are regarded as pragmatic and those who are regarded as ideologues (or, if you are an ideologue, as principled leaders or idealists). For example, a belief that public budget deficits and rising levels of national indebtedness seriously weaken our economy is often invoked on behalf of actions to put caps on government indebtedness and to impose across-the-board limits on government spending increases, no matter what the possible adverse consequences might be. This ideology is widely labeled "austerity" or "small government." The across-the-board spending cuts imposed on certain categories of federal spending in 2013, known as "the sequester," were imposed by Congress in the name of austerity even if it meant cuts in national defense and other arguably essential government programs.

Another popular ideology is based on the belief that direct democracy, that is, citizen participation in all matters affecting them, ought to guide the conduct of public management in order to counter the influence of large corporations and other well-funded special interests. The "Occupy movements" that emerged beginning in 2011 reflected this ideological orientation. Public administration scholars Peter and Linda deLeon urge that public managers adopt as a core value the promotion of what they call the **democratic ethos** at all stages and at all levels of policymaking and management.[62] Their assumption is that citizens only need empowering to become fully proficient at enacting their own and society's best interests. Moreover, the democratic ethos view asserts that this principle of empowerment should be extended to the employees of public agencies; they, too, should be consulted at every stage and level of policymaking and implementation. This consultation should be authentic, the deLeons insist, not a cynical attempt to make citizens believe they have an influence they do not in fact have.

Best Practices

Best practices or **leading practices** refer to those processes, strategies, and techniques that contribute to the success of a manager, an activity, a program, or an organization. To some scholars and practitioners, the term is synonymous with the craft perspective. Such practices are heavily oriented toward managerial behavior rather than toward structural or institutional/cultural considerations.

A common method for identifying best practices is to study in detail the practices of managers and organizations that are widely considered to be successful, discover potential cause-and-effect relationships revealed by the case studies, and

(1) establish the practices that seemed to account for success or effectiveness as well as their consequences in given contexts as an ideal against which to compare one's own practices and accomplishments, or

(2) distill general principles of effective managerial practice that seem to apply in a wide range of contexts.[63]

The concept of a best practice has roots in the scientific management movement that was inspired by the research of Frederick W. Taylor early in the twentieth century. "Among the various methods and implements used in each element of each trade," Taylor said, "there is always one method and one implement which is quicker and better than any of the rest," a perspective that came to be known as the "one best way."[64] The identification of best practices in public management, however, has depended less on scientific analysis of operational data—Taylor is famous for his time-and-motion studies of factory workers—than on the close analysis of specific cases, on inferences drawn from experiential information, and on the codification of richly textured folk wisdom.

> The identification of best practices in public management, however, has depended less on scientific analysis of operational data—Taylor is famous for his time-and-motion studies of factory workers—than on the close analysis of specific cases, on inferences drawn from experiential information, and on the codification of richly textured folk wisdom.

The popularity of "principles of administration" came under sharp criticism in the late 1940s. Such principles are no more than proverbs, insisted Herbert Simon. "For almost every principle one can find an equally plausible and acceptable contradictory principle. . . . What is needed now is empirical research and experimentation to determine the relative desirability of alternative administrative arrangements."[65] Nevertheless, research that distills managerial principles from personal experiences and case analyses has continued to be one of the most popular genres in the field, both in academic publications, in the prescriptive management literature of consultancies, and in government reports such as those of the Government Accountability Office (GAO). Examples of this literary genre were cited earlier in this chapter.

One example is *Excellence in Managing*, by Harry P. Hatry and several coauthors, which advertises itself as follows:

> An easy-to-use, practical guide to more than 125 actions that will improve management and leadership, this book is particularly responsive to public-sector needs. The authors interviewed personnel, their clients, and elected officials from 18 community development agencies across the country to find out what does and does not work for them. The book is a quick reference tool for managers and their staffs at all levels. The foreword is written by Tom Peters, coauthor of *In Search of Excellence*. Awarded a Certificate of Merit for distinguished research by the Governmental Research Association in 1992.[66]

The largely unhistorical, institutions-are-given approach to public management drew criticism from traditional public administration scholars and other social scientists for its lack of rigor and concern for democratic values. The research on which the identification of best practices is based is controversial because "cases are subject to a wide variety of selection and interpretation biases. Drawing on specific cases, a clever rhetorician can not only confirm the infinite complexity of the world but also can find support for almost any plausible conjecture about that world,"[67] points that echo Simon's critique.

The intuitive appeal of lessons drawn from actual experience accounts for the popularity among practitioners of this source of managerial knowledge. Best practices eventually caught the wave of popularity initiated by the success of the "Japanese management" movement and of Thomas Peters and Robert Waterman's *In Search of Excellence: Lessons from America's Best-Run Companies*.[68] The latter book's no-nonsense principles—a bias for action, close to the customer, productivity through people, simple form, lean staff—inspired numerous public sector–oriented imitators motivated to arrest government's declining popularity following the Nixon-era Watergate scandal, the economic crises of the 1970s, and what many regarded as the ineffectual presidency of Jimmy Carter.

Best practices are gathered and disseminated at the national, state, and local levels of government and by nongovernmental organizations in particular policy areas as shown in the following examples:

Example: Government Accountability Office Publications

The GAO has published extensively on best practices. Its "Selected Initial Implementation Approaches to Manage Senior Executive Performance that May Be Helpful to Other Agencies" included the following:

> **Provide Useful Data**. The agencies disaggregated data from agency-wide customer and employee surveys. In addition, the Bureau of Land Management and Veterans Benefits Administration provide senior executives with objective data through real-time data systems so that executives can track their individual progress against organizational goals.

> **Require Follow-Up Action**. The Internal Revenue Service requires senior executives to develop action plans to follow up on customer and employee issues identified through agency-wide surveys. The Federal Highway Administration requires executives to use 360-degree feedback instruments to solicit employee views on their leadership skills and then incorporate action items into their performance plans for the next fiscal year.

> **Make Meaningful Distinctions in Performance**. The agencies are working at making distinctions in senior executive performance. To recognize varying levels of significance and complexity among executive performance, the Internal Revenue Service established an executive compensation plan that assigns executives to bonus levels with corresponding bonus ranges based on levels of responsibilities and commitments.[69]

Example: Center for Best Practices at the National Governors Association

This Center for Best Practices is a consulting service for governors and their staff. Each of the Center's six divisions addresses a particular area of policy and practice. The environment, energy, and transportation division, for example, provides information, research, policy analysis, technical assistance and resource development for governors and their staff in the areas of energy, environment and transportation sectors. The division focuses on several issues, including improving energy efficiency, enhancing the use of both traditional and alternative fuels for electricity and transportation, developing a modern electricity grid, expanding economic development opportunities in the energy sector, protecting and cleaning up the environment, exploring innovative financing mechanisms for energy and infrastructure and developing a transportation system that safely and efficiently moves people and goods.[70]

Example: The Center for Management Strategies at the International City/County Management Association

In 2012, the International City/County Management Association (ICMA) formed the Center for Management Strategies. Its mission is to "bring forward leading practices" to local governments, and "to make available education and technical assistance . . . on practices that have been proven to work through academic research and by 'early innovators.'"[71] The Center set three criteria that constitute a "leading practice":

Scalability—the practice must demonstrate that it has worked in local governments of all sizes, large and small.

Methodology—the practice must have a process involved that can be followed and replicated to achieve success.

Proven Results—there must be evidence that the practice leads to results.[72]

Through its work, the Center so far has identified five "core leading practices":

High-Performance Organizations

Priority-Based Budgeting

Civic Engagement

Data-Driven Communities

Collaborative Service Delivery[73]

In the following message, the Center calls on localities to learn best practices from others in these areas:

More and more communities are finding that these best or leading practices can be successfully implemented. And as more communities escape the paralyzing mindset that they are too unique to implement creative and successful ideas and concepts, more and more local government communities will benefit from the replicable "*best or leading practices*" that have been thoroughly researched and successfully implemented across the country [emphasis in original].[74]

Example: Nonprofit Organizations as Distributors of Best Practices

Many nonprofits, policy advocacy groups, and foundations identify and disseminate best practices in particular policy areas. For example:

- The National Alliance to End Homelessness disseminates best practices in the form of "Ten Essentials,"—"a guide to help communities identify effective permanent solutions to homelessness. Supported by research and grounded in practical experience, the Ten Essentials serve as a blueprint for communities to follow."[75]
- The United Nations maintains a Peacekeeping Resources Hub where it provides policy and resource guidance. It describes its guidance as follows:

> Organizational learning has been recognized as a vital component of peacekeeping since the mid-1990s. The Organization began collecting good practices and lessons learned since 1995, beginning with a very small dedicated unit.

> By 2000 there was an increasing recognition that to be truly "learned", lessons had to be not only collected, but also transformed into guidance, and operational direction in a systematic manner. In 2003, the DPKO launched a new guidance system that sought to link the identification and sharing of best practices to the development of policies, guidelines and procedures that reflect those lessons. This system was further refined in 2005, to focus more on a strategic approach to performance improvement.

> This approach to "institutional strengthening" was further developed in 2007 through the formation of the Division for Policy, Evaluation and Training (DPET), a shared service of DPKO and DFS. DPET's functions are carried out through the Policy and Best Practices Service, the Integrated Training Service, and the Evaluation and Partnerships Units.[76]

Early best practices research typically involved rich description of "successful" programs or innovations in particular settings. More recently, some best practices or "smart" practices are emphasizing research-based evidence, discussed in the next section.

Scientific Research

Researchers from a wide variety of scientific disciplines, fields, and subfields have systematically studied many of the specific issues and decisions in which public managers participate. Drawing on insights from this research can enlighten public management practice in significant ways. In the United States, the United Kingdom, and elsewhere, interest is growing in evidence-based policy and practice (discussed below).

A **scientific paradigm** affects the questions that researchers pursue, their methods for doing so, and the accumulation of knowledge from research. In his book *The Structure of Scientific Revolutions,* Thomas Kuhn defines a scientific paradigm as general agreement among members of a scientific community as to what is to be observed and scrutinized; the kind of questions that are supposed to be asked and probed for answers in relation to this subject; how these questions are to be put; and how the results of scientific investigations should be interpreted.[77] Kuhn argued that scientific truth-seeking and beliefs become cultural: It is what we do and what we think. A dominant paradigm can change but only after a buildup of contrary evidence raising questions that can no longer be ignored.

Example: The Education Sciences Reform Act of 2002

The Education Sciences Reform Act of 2002 established the Institute of Education Sciences (IES) within the U.S. Department of Education. The mission of the IES is to provide rigorous evidence on which to ground education practice and policy.

(19) According to the Act, SCIENTIFICALLY VALID EDUCATION EVALUATION means an evaluation that—

(A) adheres to the highest possible standards of quality with respect to research design and statistical analysis;

(B) provides an adequate description of the programs evaluated and, to the extent possible, examines the relationship between program implementation and program impacts;

(C) provides an analysis of the results achieved by the program with respect to its projected effects;

(D) employs experimental designs using random assignment, when feasible, and other research methodologies that allow for the strongest possible causal inferences when random assignment is not feasible; and

(E) may study program implementation through a combination of scientifically valid and reliable methods.

(20) SCIENTIFICALLY VALID RESEARCH.—The term "scientifically valid research" includes applied research, basic research, and field-initiated research in which the rationale, design, and interpretation are soundly developed in accordance with scientifically based research standards.[78]

Use of Research by Managers and Policymakers

Historically, research and public administration have been regarded as in symbiotic relationship to each other:

> While in absolutist France . . . politics and administration were considered state monopolies, not to be subject to intellectual inquiry or speculation, for Americans, science [research] seemed to support the cause of liberalism, by breaking the yoke of tradition, questioning authority, and celebrating the individual. . . . Liberalism in turn supported the pursuit of science; freedom of belief, assembly, and association were important prerequisites to unfettered inquiry.[79]

In the 1960s, as noted in Chapter 5, a systematic way of incorporating scientific evidence into public policy-making and management, called the Planning-Programming-Budgeting System, became fashionable following its highly publicized adoption by Secretary of Defense Robert S. McNamara. (Impressed with McNamara's managerialist approach, President Lyndon Johnson mandated its use by all federal agencies. Richard Nixon rescinded the mandate several years later.) At the heart of this management system was a benefit-cost–oriented paradigm that came to be known as **policy analysis.** Political scientist Aaron Wildavsky described "the art of policy analysis":

Analytic tools such as policy planning, program development, and program evaluation—whether done "in-house" or by consultants—are now considered to be essential elements in the management of public agencies.

> Policy analysis must create problems that decision-makers are able to handle with the variables under their control and in the time available . . . by specifying a desired relationship between manipulable means and obtainable objectives. . . . Unlike social science, policy analysis must be prescriptive; arguments about correct policy, which deal with the future, cannot help but be willful and therefore political.[80]

The number of policy analysts in government grew rapidly, and analytic tools such as policy planning, program development, and program evaluation—whether done "in-house" or by consultants—are now considered to be essential elements in the management of public agencies.

It is not surprising that preparation for careers in public affairs at undergraduate and graduate levels includes an emphasis on "social inquiry"—on social science concepts and their applications to public policy and management, on methods of data and policy analysis, and on the uses of research in planning and decision making. The idea is to ensure that policymakers and public managers at all levels of government can be intelligent consumers of research findings.[vii]

Evidence-Based Policy and Practice

Interest in **evidence-based policy and practice** has been accelerating over the past few decades. The movement began in the policy area of health and medicine, marked by the formation in 1993 of The Cochrane Collaboration. Its mission is "to promote evidence-informed health decision-making by producing high-quality, relevant, accessible systematic reviews and other synthesised research evidence."[81] Increasingly, the evidence-based movement is expanding in other areas of public policy and management, a direction supported across the ideological spectrum.[viii] In a memo entitled "Use of Evidence and Evaluation in the 2014 Budget," Office of Management and Budget (OMB) Acting Director Jeffrey D. Zients instructed agencies to "demonstrate the use of evidence throughout their Fiscal Year (FY) 2014 budget submissions, arguing:

> Since taking office, the President has emphasized the need to use evidence and rigorous evaluation in budget, management, and policy decisions to make government work effectively. This need has only grown in the current fiscal environment. Where evidence is strong, we should act on it. Where evidence is suggestive, we should consider it. Where evidence is weak, we should build the knowledge to support better decisions in the future.[82]

The idea behind evidence-based practice is simple: policy and practice should be based on strategies whose effectiveness has been measured in high-quality research (where the gold standard is the random assignment design). This straightforward idea can be difficult to implement in practice, however:

- High-quality research is often limited or nonexistent in a particular policy or practice area.
- Even if high-quality research is available, its generalizability (or applicability or extension) to other settings, populations, or time periods may not be straightforward.

[vii]For a critical assessment of the role of scientific research in policymaking, see Carol H. Weiss, "The Haphazard Connection: Social Science and Public Policy," *International Journal of Educational Research* 23, (1995): 137–150.

[viii]Lawrence W. Sherman, "Misleading Evidence and Evidence-Led Policy: Making Social Science More Experimental," *Annals of the American Academy of Political and Social Science* 589, (2003). The entire volume 589 of *The Annals of the American Academy of Political and Social Science* addresses evidence based policymaking and public management. Jon Glasby, Kieran Walshe, and Gill Harvey, eds., *Evidence & Policy* 3, no. 3, (2007), is a special issue on evidence-based practice. It is an edited selection of papers from the British ESRC (Economic and Social Research Council) seminar series, addressing the question, What counts as "evidence" in "evidence-based practice"? The book by Ron Haskins and Gerg Margolis, *Show Me the Evidence: Obama's Fight for Rigor and Results in Social Policy* (Washington, DC: Brookings, 2015), presents in-depth case studies of six evidence-based policy initiatives during the Obama administration.

- Findings from multiple high-quality studies in a particular area might provide conflicting evidence with regard to effectiveness.
- Policymakers and public managers may not have access to studies and their findings that are relevant to their work.

The last of these challenges is increasingly filled by **research brokers**, or **knowledge brokers**. Over 40 years ago, Brookings Institution political scientist James L. Sundquist coined the term *research broker* to describe the role of packaging research for policymakers.[83] His premise was that potentially useful knowledge is often available in the research community but is inaccessible or unrecognizable to policymakers. Policymaking therefore is often less informed than it might be. By identifying, assembling, and translating relevant knowledge, research brokers perform an essential role in rationalizing policymaking. At the time, research brokerage was largely an insider role that, in Sundquist's view, was greatly in need of strengthening.

These research brokers were not mere technocrats. In *A Government of Strangers,* Hugh Heclo labeled them "reformers." Heclo observed, "Such analysts are often the agency head's only institutional resource for thinking about substantive policy without commitments to the constituents, jurisdictions, and self-interests of existing programs." He added, "their most enduring problem is one of attracting political customers to use their analysis while maintaining constructive relations and access with the program offices being analyzed."[84]

More recently, research brokerage has expanded and occurs in different organizational forms and arrangements. It is supported by independent organizations and collaboratives such as The Cochrane Collaboration in health and funded and supported by state and federal governments. Examples include the following:

- The Coalition for Evidence-Based Policy is a 501(c)(3) nonprofit, nonpartisan organization established in 2001. Its mission is to promote government policymaking based on rigorous evidence of program effectiveness. It lists enactment of the following federal-level initiatives as evidence of its influence:

  o **Evidence-Based Home Visitation Program** for at-risk families with young children (Department of Health and Human Services – HHS, $1.5 billion over 2010–2014)
  o **Evidence-Based Teen Pregnancy Prevention Program** (HHS, $109 million in FY14)
  o **Investing in Innovation Fund**, to fund development and scale-up of evidence-based K-12 educational interventions (Department of Education, $142 million in FY14)
  o **First in the World Initiative**, to fund development and scale-up of evidence-based interventions in postsecondary education (Department of Education, $75 million in FY14)
  o **Social Innovation Fund**, to support public/private investment in evidence-based programs in low-income communities (Corporation for National and Community Service, $70 million in FY14)
  o **Trade Adjustment Assistance Community College and Career Training Grants Program,** to fund development and scale-up of evidence-based education and career training programs for dislocated workers (Department of Labor–DOL, $2 billion over 2011–2014)
  o **Workforce Innovation Fund,** to fund development and scale-up of evidence-based strategies to improve education/employment outcomes for U.S. workers (DOL, $47 million in FY14).[ix]

[ix]"Policy Impact," Coalition for Evidence-Based Policy, http://coalition4evidence.org.

- The Campbell Collaboration, modeled after the Cochrane Collaboration, was established in 2000. It produces systematic reviews of evidence (including unpublished studies), aiming "to bring about positive social change, and to improve the quality of public and private services around the world" in the areas of education, crime and justice, and social welfare. This Collaboration emphasizes "a systematic and rigorous approach to research synthesis."[85]

- The What Works Clearinghouse (WWC), maintained by the U.S. Department of Education's IES, provides five kinds of products:

   o **Practice guides** help educators address classroom challenges.
   o **Intervention reports** guide evidence-based decisions.
   o **Single study reviews** examine research quality.
   o **Quick reviews** give the WWC's assessment of recent education research.
   o The **studies database** contains all WWC-reviewed studies.[86]

   For example, a WWC-funded single study review examined a study of the effectiveness of behavioral nudges regarding financial aid on student persistence through a second year of college. The study rating was "Meets WWC group design standards without reservation."[87] A single study review of another study that examined "increased course structure" rated it "does not meet WWC group design standards." Given this assessment, the site does not report findings from the study at all.[88]

- The Evidence-based Prevention and Intervention Support Center (EPISCenter), based at Penn State University, is funded by two state agencies—the Pennsylvania Commission on Crime and Delinquency and the Department of Public Welfare. With these investments, the state is supporting the identification and distribution of evidence-based programs to reduce youth delinquency and promote positive youth development. To support the use of evidence-based programs, the EPISCenter engages in the following types of activities:

   o **Directs outreach and advocacy efforts** to foster recognition, at federal, state, and community levels, of the value and impact of proven prevention and intervention programs
   o **Provides technical assistance** to communities to improve implementation quality, promote the collection and use of program impact data, and foster proactive planning for long-term program sustainability
   o **Develops and provides educational opportunities and resources** to disseminate current prevention science research and facilitate peer networking
   o **Conducts original research** to inform more effective prevention practice and the successful dissemination of evidence-based programs[89]

- The Council for Exceptional Children (CEC), an organization offering professional development and advocacy for educators of special-needs and gifted children, in 2014 published "Standards for Evidence-Based Practices in Special Education."[90] The standards describe research designs that meet the standards, as well as quality indicators for the study. Possible classifications of the evidence include "evidence-based practice," "potentially evidence-based practice," "mixed evidence," "insufficient evidence," and "negative effects."[91] With regard to research designs, the CEC states:

Although CEC recognizes the important role that correlational, qualitative, and other descriptive research designs play in informing the field of special education, the standards do not consider research using these designs because identifying evidence based practices involves making causal determinations, and causality cannot be reasonably inferred from these designs.[92]

The CEC statement on research designs, and similar ones for other organizations, directly considers what constitutes rigorous, scientifically valid evidence. Scholars regard random assignment designs as the gold standard for high-quality research. In these studies, some subjects—individuals, groups, or organizations—are randomly assigned either to receive a treatment (or intervention) under study or to be part of a control group that does not receive the treatment. The effects of the treatment in relation to the counterfactual represented by the control group can then be identified. Some experts would prefer to accept a broader range of evidence to inform practice. European researcher Bent Flyvbjerg expressed this point of view: "good social science is problem driven and not methodology driven in the sense that it employs those methods that for a given problem, best help answer the research questions at hand."[93]

Different kinds of evidence may serve different purposes. A July 26, 2013 memo entitled "Next Steps in the Evidence and Innovation Agenda" was issued to heads of federal departments and authored by the director of OMB, the director of the Domestic Policy Council, the director of the Office of Science and Technology Policy, and the chairman of the Council of Economic Advisors. Among the suggestions it offered was "tiered evidence grant designs":

"Tiered-evidence" or "innovation fund" grant designs focus resources on practices with the strongest evidence, but still allow for new innovation. In a three-tiered grant model, for example, grantees can qualify for 1) the "scale up" tier and receive the most funding; 2) the "validation" tier and receive less funding but evaluation support; or 3) the "proof of concept" tier and receive the least funding, but also support for evaluation. With a tiered-evidence approach, potential grantees know that to be considered for funding, they must provide demonstrated evidence behind their approach and/or be ready to subject their models to evaluation. The goal is that, over time, interventions move up tiers as evidence becomes stronger. So far five agencies have launched or proposed 13 tiered grant programs in the areas such as education, teenage pregnancy prevention, home visitation programs, workforce, international assistance, and more.

Example: The Department of Education's Investing in Innovation Fund (i3) invests in high-impact, potentially transformative education interventions, ranging from new ideas with significant potential to those with strong evidence of effectiveness that are ready to be scaled up. Based on the success of i3, the Department recently issued proposed regulations that would allow its other competitive grant programs to adopt this three-tiered model.[94]

Data and evidence use guidelines described by a group of researchers in a 1982 book, *Data for Decisions: Information Strategies for Policymakers,* still seem relevant today.[95] The authors identify three overarching issues that arise during policy and program deliberation:

- identifying cause and effect relationships,
- measuring the status quo, and
- predicting the future.

The authors discuss appropriate methods for each type of issue, indicating their strengths and weaknesses. Of experiments, the authors conclude, "The well-conducted controlled trial is the most definitive method of investigating causal relationships both in the laboratory and in the field" and is far less risky in identifying causality than observational studies, although, as others have pointed out, even experiments are not free of threats to their validity. For measuring the status quo, they separately discuss sample surveys, longitudinal and panel studies, case studies, management records, and official statistics. Of case studies, which often are the foundation for best practices, the authors say, "The method has severe biases in even the best of hands because of problems of values, slant, omission, and emphasis." For predicting the future, the authors discuss simulations, forecasting, mathematical modeling, and what they call "introspection and advice," which, they suggest, may be better than nothing if a more effective method is unavailable.

Science or Scientism?

Controversies over the relevance of research from the social sciences and the sciences as a source of knowledge for public management have increased in recent years, especially when the policies concern changing human behavior and improving individual, organizational, community, and social life. This is true even when it comes to managing public policies with significant scientific content, where it might seem that a grasp of the relevant science and its applications would be *sine qua non* to effective public management. In general, sharp tensions have arisen between research and public administration.

> **The relationship of science to policymaking has become a matter of evaluating multifarious claims to possession of scientific truth, to arguments over what constitutes scientific "proof," and to the very meaning and moral status of scientific truth itself.**

Far from being viewed as a matter of bringing scientific truth into the realms of power through the institutions of policy analysis and research brokers, the relationship of science to policymaking has become a matter of evaluating multifarious claims to possession of scientific truth, to arguments over what constitutes scientific "proof," and to the very meaning and moral status of scientific truth itself.

This attitude toward science is strikingly evident when it comes to issues that involve powerful ideological disagreements, such as stem cell research and global warming, where arguments over the science may obscure underlying ideological conflicts. But controversies arise in less morally charged issues as well:

> Too much social science evidence may mislead policy with statistically biased conclusions due to weak research designs, and too little science evidence is presented in a way that allows government to assess the risk of bias. The two problems are related: If governments cannot rely on social science evidence as unbiased, they have less reason to invest in producing more evidence.[96]

The Obama administration's "evidence and innovation agenda," and the efforts of organizations such as the Coalition for Evidence-Based Policy, attempt to articulate and advance standards for high-quality evidence. The Coalition states that it

> advocates many types of research to identify the most promising social interventions. However, a central theme of our advocacy, consistent with the recommendation of a recent National Academy of Sciences report, is that evidence of effectiveness generally cannot be considered definitive without ultimate confirmation in well-conducted randomized controlled trials.[97]

Some critics view science as an ideology in itself; a view known as **scientism.** They claim that scientific researchers are not free of ideological bias. In what they choose to study, in which findings are regarded as worth communicating, and in the reasons they offer in support of policy choices, researchers do not exemplify objectivity toward the world so much as a penchant for selectively choosing findings that produce an ideological fit between research and the policy preferences of researchers. Steven Miller and Marcel Fredericks argue, "We are not suggesting, in some simplistic fashion, that ideological commitments or preferences are always working as 'biasing-filters,' but only that they are an often overlooked factor in *explaining* how social policies are formulated, implemented and evaluated given social science research findings."[98]

Example: Medical Research Findings

For 20 years, research into Alzheimer's disease has been dominated by the idea that the cause is the accumulation of sticky plaques made of beta-amyloid.[99] Researchers who wished to explore alternative explanations of the disease encountered difficulties in getting financial support and publishing their findings in prestigious journals. One researcher referred to those with alternative explanations as "voices in the wilderness" who would "come up with clever ideas, new ways of thinking, and they are just destroyed."[100] Experimental drugs are typically based on the amyloid hypothesis, even though the possibility of alternative explanations has respectable scientific support. Amyloid plaques are, scientists have shown, found in normal brains, and amyloid only weakly correlates with differences in Alzheimer's brains.

The science of secondhand smoke is another example. In July 2006, the U.S. surgeon general was quoted as saying that "there is no risk-free level of secondhand smoke exposure" and "breathing secondhand smoke for even a short time can damage cells and set the cancer process in motion."[101] The scientific problem is that "instant exposures" to secondhand smoke cannot practically be cumulated over time to derive an individual's lifetime exposure. Instead, individuals who had been exposed to secondhand smoke were asked to recall and describe those exposures, producing information that is unreliable at best. Advocates of smoking bans give short shrift to such difficulties, however, and science is said to justify policies when, in fact, it does no such thing.

The discussion in this section cautions public managers that to the extent they rely on scientific evidence, they should acquire the skills to be aware of the potential biases involved in the general approach to the research and with regard to any specific findings that are produced.

Institutions Providing Analysis and Expertise

As governing has become more complex, policymakers and public managers have come to rely on **think tanks,** such as the Brookings Institution, the Heritage Foundation, the Center for Budget and Policy Priorities (CBPP), and the American Enterprise Institute (AEI); nonprofit and for-profit contract research organizations, such as Abt Associates, MDRC, Mathematica Policy Research (MPR), and Rand; and management consultancies, such as Booz Allen Hamilton, Deloitte, and Accenture to provide ideas, expertise, and analysis that public agencies may be unable to produce in-house.[x] Some think tanks, such as Brookings, date back to the 1920s, but their participation and influence began to grow in the 1960s and 1970s and accelerated as government began to outsource numerous functions formerly thought to be inherently governmental, including policy development and planning. Now governments at all levels, including small towns, regularly hire outside consultants to assist with matters such as reorganizations, systems designs, land use planning, policy advice, and opinion surveys.

The expanding role of these types of organizations has drawn both praise and condemnation. Think tanks have been lauded for stimulating the "marketplace of ideas" that is essential to democratic self-government. In contrast, the 1976 book *The Shadow Government: The Government's Multi-Billion-Dollar Giveaway of Its Decision-Making Powers to Private Management Consultants, "Experts," and Think Tanks,* viewed these developments in alarmist terms.[102] More recently, worries have arisen over the extent to which political polarization and the rise

---

[x]Andrew Rich, *Think Tanks, Public Policy, and the Politics of Expertise* (New York, NY: Cambridge University Press, 2004), provides considerable insight into the evolution and role of think tanks in American policymaking. See also James McGann, ed., *Think Tanks and Policy Advice in the United States: Academics, Advisors and Advocates* (New York, NY: Routledge, 2007).

of partisan advocacy groups has compromised the independence of such advisory organizations. Their work at times becomes fodder in partisan policy conflicts, and their experts and conclusions make the news when they are cited in the course of policy debates.

The "wrong" findings are always blamed on "flawed methodology" no matter who produced them. Balanced analysis can become a casualty of such conflicts.[103]

Learning from Others

Public managers communicate with individuals both inside and outside their organizations whose insights or knowledge are unique. Made popular by management gurus Tom Peters and Robert Waterman, the notion of **management by walking around** conveys the value of spontaneous communications, which may occur with employees, important stakeholder groups, or citizens.[104] Although managers who are extraverted and prefer sensory information may be more inclined to learn this way, all public managers may benefit from routine exposure to knowledgeable people in a wide variety of settings.

Informal communications may also be more deliberate. The popular term *networking* conveys the notion that communicating with a group of people who have common interests and relevant expertise is useful both as a source of information as well as a way of building social capital. Hugh Heclo noted the political importance of **issue networks**, highly fluid interactions among emotionally committed and knowledgeable activists inside and outside of government who are determined to shape the content of public policy.[105]

A related concept is the **advocacy coalition**, which links policymakers and public managers, important stakeholder groups, think thanks, academic researchers, media organizations, foundations, influential individuals, and advocates with specialized interests. Paul Sabatier and Hank Jenkins-Smith argue that research findings may be influenced by the competition among such coalitions.[106] Public managers who are political appointees are often members of advocacy coalitions, and their learning is heavily influenced by this involvement. Indeed, membership in an advocacy coalition may be an efficient way for researchers to make contact with or have their findings taken seriously by public officials.

Overall, this section has described a number of ways in which public managers learn about the content of decisions they must make and the potential consequences of their decisions. The sources discussed include best practices, paradigms or ideologies, scientific research, institutions providing analysis and expertise, and insights from individuals inside and outside the organization.

BEING STRATEGIC

A common prescription in the public management literature is that public managers should think and act strategically.[107] In this view, managers create a frame of reference and act consistently with the logic of that framework. By doing so, managers can avoid falling into the habit of making decisions in an ad hoc, unsystematic, and reactive way with little or no appreciation for how issues and decisions are interrelated.

Those who emphasize the extent to which managerial decisions are embedded in political structures and cultures take a different view, however. The combined effects of bounded rationality and political constraints counsel a more modest, but feasible strategy. In his article, "The Science of Muddling Through," political scientist Charles E. Lindblom argued that, in the real world, it is best to be engaged in a process of "successive limited comparisons," by which he meant "building out from the current situation, step by step, and by small degrees."[108] Change in the American political system is typically incremental. This is a result of the politics of bureaucratic structure that is founded on the U.S. constitutional scheme of governance. Because of this reality, the public manager is well advised, the argument goes, to think and act incrementally. In this view, more will be accomplished than by formulating bold visions that become clouded in the course of political bargaining.

What Is Strategy?

A **strategy** is a cognitive structure in the mind of the manager, a frame of reference within which thoughts and actions are formulated and reviewed. Public management scholars Barry Bozeman and Jeffrey Straussman specify four principles that guide **strategic public management**:

- Concern with the long term
- Integration of goals and objectives into a coherent hierarchy
- Recognition that strategic management and planning are not self-implementing
- An external perspective emphasizing not adapting to the environment but anticipating and shaping of environmental change[109]

A strategy may be normative; that is, it may originate in managers' ideologies or beliefs about how things *ought* to be done. Alternatively, a strategy may result from a pragmatic weighing of the substantive, political, and organizational considerations that may affect results or outcomes. Managers of particular types, moreover, may be strategic in ways that are consistent with their inclinations; whether their orientation is ideological or pragmatic, sensing or intuitive, managers may wish to make systematic choices concerning various instruments or tools at their disposal for accomplishing their objectives.

Political contexts, organizational structures and cultures, and individual public managers' proclivities and talents for formulating coherent strategies both enable and constrain the opportunities for strategic public management. Mark Moore observes

> Many different strategies are feasible [for public sector organizations] because at any given moment, the politics of a situation can accommodate many different ideas. Moreover, the politics will change . . . in response to particular events, and sometimes even in response to managerial effort. So, if one looks ahead a little bit, the range of possible sustainable political coalitions can be very broad indeed."[110]

Some strategic choices, moreover, are substantive, related to the goals of public policy; examples include compliance versus cooperation, family reunification versus ensuring the safety of the child, and an emphasis on treatment versus an emphasis on prevention. Other strategic choices are related more to the means for accomplishing goals that may be promulgated in statutes, executive orders, or judicial rulings: punishment versus rehabilitation, mandatory versus voluntary compliance, government provision versus contracting with private providers.

Bozeman and Straussman emphasize, "*Effective* public management and *strategic* public management are not identical."[111] Thus, public managers may be good at particular kinds of tasks or aspects of public management even if they are not particularly strategic about it. The pragmatic adapter to a fluid situation may be just what an ambiguous situation requires, and the strategic thinker may appear to be out of touch with the complexities of particular contexts whose meanings are constantly shifting. Moreover, they say, not all public managers have the qualities of statesmanship that strategic management requires: a broad view, a lively sense of engagement, and intellectual curiosity. Like so many other popular notions, strategic public management is not a panacea.

Example: A Strategy of "Broken Windows"
Enforcement at the Securities and Exchange Commission (SEC)

On April 10, 2013, Mary Jo White was sworn in as Chair of the SEC. Formerly a U.S. attorney in New York, White declared a new strategy for SEC enforcement in speech on October 9, 2013. The new strategy was based on the idea that small infractions could not be ignored, lest these small instances accumulate and support a larger culture of violations.[112] In announcing her strategy, White argued that

> minor violations [in our securities markets] that are overlooked or ignored can feed bigger ones, and, perhaps more importantly, can foster a culture where laws are increasingly treated as toothless guidelines. And so, I believe it is important to pursue even the smallest infractions. Retail investors, in particular, need to be protected from unscrupulous advisers and brokers, whatever their size and the size of the violation that victimizes the investor.

> That is why George Canellos and Andrew Ceresney, our co-directors of the Division of Enforcement, are working to build upon the strength of the division by ensuring that we pursue all types of wrongdoing. Not just the biggest frauds, but also violations such as control failures, negligence-based offenses, and even violations of prophylactic rules with no intent requirement, such as the series of Rule 105 cases that we recently brought.

> But this does not mean we will not continue our vigorous pursuit of the bigger violations. Cases like the ones we brought recently against the likes of SAC Capital, Harbinger, J.P. Morgan, Oppenheimer, and the City of Miami not to mention the scores of significant financial crisis cases have always been, and will continue to be, important cases for us.

> I believe the SEC should strive to be that kind of cop—to be the agency that covers the entire neighborhood and pursues every level of violation.

> An agency that also makes you feel like we are everywhere. And we will do our best not to disappoint.[113]

How might public managers go about making strategic sense of the reality in which they are enmeshed?[xi] How can they create mental models for understanding ambiguity, emergence, and uncertainty, which is the process by which individuals (or organizations) create the understanding necessary to acting in a principled and informed manner? The discussion that follows describes several different heuristics from among the many found in the public management literature that public managers might employ in "sense-making."

Framing and Reframing

In *Reframing Organizations: Artistry, Choice, and Leadership,* Lee G. Bolman and Terrence E. Deal argue that managers often fail because "they bring too few ideas to the challenges they face. . . . When they don't know what to do, they simply do more of what they do know." Managers, they say, must be able to reframe experience in order to identify new and creative possibilities for effective action.[xii]

[xi]The activity of "sense making" is a subject for research in social and cognitive psychology, sociology, decision making, and organizations, among other fields. For further discussion, see Karl E. Weick, *Sensemaking in Organizations* (Thousand Oaks, CA: Sage, 1995).

[xii]Lee G. Bolman and Terrence E. Deal, *Reframing Organizations,* 5th ed. (San Francisco, CA: JosseyBass, 2013), is the best source of additional readings on framing and reframing. The chapter "Bringing It All Together: Change and Leadership in Action" is a case study on how a newly appointed public high school principal uses reframing to assess the problems he faces and potential solutions to them.

Bolman and Deal identify four distinctive frames of reference, each with its own assumptions and logic, from the literature on organizations. By applying each frame and its logic, a public manager can gain insights into a situation: what is happening, why it is happening, and what might be done.

- **Structural frame:** organizations rationally pursue their goals. The purpose of organizational structures is to ensure an efficient division of labor, provide incentives for efficient performance, and facilitate managerial control and coordination. Problems of performance are addressed through realignment of goals, responsibilities, and tasks, typically through reorganizations. Metaphors for this frame are "factory" or "machine." The structural frame is likely to be most useful when goals and information are unambiguous; cause-and-effect relations are clear; technologies and information systems are well developed; conflict, ambiguity, and uncertainty are low; and governance is stable and legitimate.
- **Human resources frame:** organizations and people are interdependent and need each other. Organizations need ideas, effort, and cooperation; people need income, opportunities, and satisfaction in their work. Problems of performance are addressed through maintaining a balance between the needs of employees and of the organization and the maintenance of transparent relationships and of opportunities for personal growth. The metaphor for this frame is "family." The human resource frame is likely to be most useful when employees are empowered; morale and motivation are low or deteriorating; adequate resources are available; and diversity, conflict, and uncertainty are low or moderate.
- **Political frame**: underlying organizational behavior is the distribution of scarce resources and conflicts associated with differing degrees of power and influence. Organizations are coalitions of individuals and interest groups, and goals and actions emerge from bargaining among stakeholders. Problems of performance are addressed through redistributing power and creating new coalitions. A metaphor for this frame is "jungle." The political frame is likely to be most useful when resources are scarce and shrinking; diversity is high or increasing; and the distribution of power and influence is diffuse or unstable.
- **Symbolic frame**: organizations must resolve problems of meaning and value. Events have multiple meanings because people interpret them differently, producing ambiguity and uncertainty. Problems of performance are addressed through creating cultures of shared meanings by means of myths, symbols, ceremonies, and stories. A metaphor for this frame is "theater." The symbolic frame is most likely to be most useful when goals and information are ambiguous; cause-and-effect relations are poorly understood; technologies and information systems are not well developed; and there is considerable cultural diversity within the organization.

Another way of understanding the value of reframing is to compare the different interpretations of standard organizational processes using the logic of the four frames. Table 11.1 summarizes the differing interpretations of organizational processes such as decision making, goal setting, and motivation using the four frames. Public managers should be aware that a given process may be viewed in very different ways by those who observe or participate in it.

Richard Heimovics, Robert Herman, and Carole Jurkiewicz Coughlin conducted an empirical test of Bolman and Deal's views on the importance of reframing.[114] Beginning with the proposition that executives of nonprofit organizations are dependent on their external environment for resources to support their missions, the researchers expected to find that executives with reputations for being effective would be more likely to employ the political

TABLE 11.1 Organizational Processes and the Four Frames

Process	Structural Frame	Human Resource Frame	Political Frame	Symbolic Frame
Strategic planning	Process to set objectives and coordinate resources	Activities to promote participation	Arenas to air conflicts and realign power	Ritual to signal responsibility, produce symbols, negotiate meanings
Decision making	Rational sequence to produce correct decision	Open process to produce commitment	Opportunity to gain or exercise power	Ritual to confirm values and provide opportunities for bonding
Reorganizing	Realign roles and responsibilities to fit tasks and environment	Improve balance between human needs and formal roles	Redistribute power and form new coalitions	Maintain an image of accountability and responsiveness; negotiate new social order
Evaluating	Way to distribute rewards of penalties and control performance	Feedback for helping individuals grow and improve	Opportunity to exercise power	Occasion to play roles in shared ritual
Approaching conflict	Authorities maintain organizational goals by resolving conflict	Individuals confront conflict to develop relationships	Use power to defeat opponents and achieve goals	Use conflict to negotiate meaning and develop shared values
Goal setting	Keep organization headed in the right direction	Open communications and keep people committed to goals	Provide opportunity for individuals and groups to express interests	Develop symbols and shared values
Communication	Transmit facts and information	Exchange information, needs, and feelings	Influence or manipulate others	Tell stories
Meetings	Formal occasions for making decisions	Informal occasions for involvement, sharing feelings	Competitive occasions to win points	Sacred occasions to celebrate and transform the culture
Motivation	Economic incentives	Growth and self-actualization	Coercion, manipulation, and seduction	Symbols and celebrations

Source: Copyright © 2013 by John Wiley & Sons, Inc. All rights reserved. Reprinted here with permission from John Wiley & Sons, Inc.

frame than a comparison group of executives lacking such reputations. Not only did the researchers confirm this expectation but they also found, as expected, that effective executives were significantly more likely to use multiple frames than executives in the comparison group.

Bolman and Deal use their observation of and experience with managerial performance and their analysis of the prescriptive literature to draw two types of conclusions:

- First, in analyzing issues that confront them, managers typically do not use enough frames; often they use only one, and that one is usually the structural frame.
- Second, being able to reframe problems and issues overcomes rigidities of thought and perception; managers should train themselves to see the layers or dimensions of a problem instead of leaping to a conclusion based on preconceptions (which are often misconceptions).

Navigating the Terrain

Several writers have used spatial analogies to make sense of the ambiguous, polycentric worlds of public management. Both Richard Haass and Mark Moore locate public managers at the center of a multipolar space in which challenges and opportunities come from every direction, often simultaneously.

- In *The Power to Persuade,* Haass advises public managers to "imagine that you are holding a compass."
    - "North represents those for whom you work.
    - To the South are those who work for you.
    - East represents colleagues, those in your organization with whom you work.
    - West represents those outside your organization who have the potential to affect matters that affect you."[115]

- In *Creating Public Value,* Moore defines the directions toward which public managers must face somewhat differently:
    - upward, toward those with some measure of authority over what you do;
    - outward, toward those whose voluntary cooperation and resources you may need; and
    - downward, toward those who work for you and on whose efforts you depend for your own and your organization's success.

Public management scholars Laurence J. O'Toole Jr., Kenneth J. Meier, and Sean Nicholson Crotty investigated the relationship to organizational performance of Moore's idea of managing upward, outward, and downward. Based on data from more than one thousand public school districts in Texas, the authors measured the extent to which superintendents interacted with school boards (upward); with local business leaders, other superintendents, state legislators, and the Texas Education Agency (outward); and with school principals (downward). They found that managing outward was consistently associated with higher student performance, but that managing upward or downward had mixed results.[116] Other studies in other types of organizational settings might find different relationships between organizational performance and managerial efforts in each of Moore's directions.

Anticipating How Hard a Problem Will Be

Based on his years of experience as a successful public manager in New York City and the Commonwealth of Massachusetts, Gordon Chase distilled lessons from that experience into a framework that he believed public managers should use to decide how hard it might be to accomplish a goal or objective before they embark on it. Managers should apply this analysis to craft their decisions and their implementation strategies.[117] In Chase's view, obstacles to program implementation come from three sources:

- *Operational demands associated with the program concept.* These include the people to be served, the services to be delivered, distortions and irregularities that come from screening, incentives to select clients most likely to succeed, inequitable administration, and the controllability of the program.
- *The nature and availability of resources needed to operate the program.* These include money and the strings attached to it and the availability and quality of personnel, space, supplies, and technical equipment.
- *The need to share authority in accomplishing program goals.* Issues of shared authority and retention of support include dealings with overhead agencies, other line agencies, elected officials, higher levels of government, private sector providers, special interest and community groups, and the media.

In Chase's view, this way of viewing management challenges has several strategic implications.

1. The toughest obstacles involve dealing with actors whose cooperation is required but whom you do not and cannot control. Get around them by contracting out the program to avoid "the overhead system" (public personnel, budgeting, and auditing organizations), by using public corporations, or by other tools that bypass political and bureaucratic obstacles, such as the appropriation process.

2. Chase urges public managers at senior levels to demonstrate competence, loyalty, and reliability to the elected chief executive. "Little, if anything, is more important," he says. Demonstrated loyalty gives a manager leverage over other actors, allies in struggles over resources and priorities, political clout, and credibility with external groups.

3. Public managers should follow some rules: anticipate difficulties and act accordingly, do not alienate important actors, remember that relationships are long term and be straight and open, orchestrate meetings carefully, keep moving so that others will have to move, and make cooperation easy.

Working from the Ground Up

According to the conventional view, public policies are formulated and enacted by duly authorized policymakers, then implemented—managed, executed, carried out—by public agencies and their administrators. This kind of top-down or command-and-control management assumes that higher levels of an agency can and should have effective control over lower levels, directing what they do. Management begins with a policy objective or objectives, prescribes what must be done if that objective is to be achieved, defines measurable outputs or outcomes that will indicate the degree of success in implementation, and, finally, promulgates the directives and resource allocations that will ensure compliant and effective behavior at each hierarchical level.

Serious problems arise with this strict logic-of-governance view of hierarchy when a large and complex bureaucracy and its numerous agents are expected to produce exactly the intended results and to do so efficiently. Inevitably, "stuff happens," as former secretary of defense Donald Rumsfeld might put it.[118] The writ of policymakers is compromised and weakened as authority is delegated down through various hierarchical levels.

Intended results and efficiency are compromised. Viewing the world exclusively from the top down obscures the numerous pitfalls that lie in the way of policy achievement. This occurs especially when chains of command and delegation linking policymakers and frontline service delivery are long and complex.[xiii]

Richard F. Elmore has proposed a solution to the tendency to view the world from the top down, which he calls **backward mapping**, a concept that although initially applied to public policy design, is equally relevant to public management strategy.[xiv] Backward mapping

- starts with a clear and precise description of the desired outcomes;
- describes operational or street-level actions and interactions that are most likely to achieve those outcomes;
- describes, for successively higher levels in the administrative system, what combination of discretion, rules, and resources are needed to sustain the desired operational activities; and
- delegates appropriate authority and allocates appropriate resources to each level in the organization to achieve the goals.

Success at backward mapping requires a deep grasp of "how to use the structure and process of organizations to elaborate, specify, and define policies."[119] Backward mapping entails a different kind of learning from the top-down, forward mapping described earlier and may reveal different implications.

Example: Backward Mapping in Welfare-to-Work Programs

The concept of backward mapping has proven useful not only as a heuristic for management practice but also as a guide to research design. For example, the administration of public assistance programs is the frequent object of public policy reforms intended to encourage able-bodied welfare recipients to become self-sufficient. Researchers Marcia Meyers, Bonnie Glaser, and Karin MacDonald used backward mapping to determine the extent to which public managers were successful in refocusing the primary public assistance program on promoting work and self-sufficiency.[120] The researchers analyzed what the new policy emphasis would require of welfare workers in their interactions with welfare clients: "transformation" behavior that ensured that clients received full, work-related information and consistent encouragement toward self-sufficiency. What they actually observed was "instrumental" behavior; most workers limited both information and encouragement to what was necessary for efficient claims processing. If policymakers' intentions were to be fulfilled, much more effort would be needed to acquaint workers with the new policies, train them in the complexities of its administration, and support them in taking a more individualized approach to welfare recipients.

Command-and-control managers are less likely to know what can go wrong until it has already gone wrong because they fail to understand the complex organizational dynamics involved in producing desired

---

[xiii]Public management scholars Jodi Sandfort and Stephanie Moulton emphasize this point in their book *Effective Implementation in Practice: Integrating Public Policy and Management* (San Francisco, CA: Jossey-Bass, 2015)

[xiv]Richard Elmore, "Backward Mapping: Implementation Research and Policy Decisions," *Political Science Quarterly* 94 (1979–1980): 601–616. For an example, see Caroline Dyer, "Researching the Implementation of Educational Policy: A Backward Mapping Approach," *Comparative Education* 35(1999): 45–61.

results. Backward mapping assumes that public agencies are complex, that there are strong tendencies toward bureau shaping and other self-interested behavior, and that greater reliance on carefully delegated discretion will increase the likelihood of good performance. As Elmore puts it, "the process of framing questions from the top begins with an understanding of what is important at the bottom."[121]

Entrepreneurship

In their handbook *The New Effective Public Manager: Achieving Success in a Changing Government,* Steven Cohen and William Eimicke argue that effective public management is **entrepreneurial public management**: "active and aggressive effort to overcome constraints and obstacles" inspired by "a positive, can-do attitude. . . . Effective public managers try to make things happen . . . by thinking and acting strategically."[xv] Effectiveness has several aspects:

- hiring and retaining good people;
- developing effective working relationships;
- structuring systems, tasks, and responsibilities;
- gathering, organizing, and using information;
- mastering the budgetary process;
- shaping organizational goals and strategies; and
- dealing with the media, legislatures, and interest groups.

The proposition that public managers should think like entrepreneurs, taking risks in order to create value, is controversial.[122] Critics of the concept have pointed out that entrepreneurial zeal could conflict with values such as due process, accountability, honesty, fairness, justice, and benevolence. It could also lead to rule bending and breaking and to unwarranted manipulation of the political process. Cohen and Eimicke insist, however, that entrepreneurship does not imply an abandonment of ethical guidelines. Others argue that new values such as innovation, quality, and responsive service are not inimical to traditional values, and that entrepreneurs and innovators usually exhibit admirable qualities of commitment to public service and personal integrity.

Precept of Managerial Responsibility

Managerial strategies need not be solely instrumental; they may emphasize general principles that guide practice. One example is the **precept of managerial responsibility** articulated by public management scholars Anthony M. Bertelli and Laurence E. Lynn Jr. This precept is based on axiomatic principles in the classical literature of public administration. It emphasizes institutionalized values that can ensure the exercise of responsible discretion with respect for democratic values. The elements of the precept are

---

[xv]Steven Cohen and William Eimicke, *The New Effective Public Manager: Achieving Success in a Changing Government,* 2nd ed. (San Francisco, CA: Jossey-Bass, 1995). For additional discussion of political entrepreneurship, see Mark Schneider and Paul Teske, "Toward a Theory of the Political Entrepreneur: Evidence from Local Government," *American Political Science Review* 86 (1992): 737–747; Carl J. Bellone and George Frederick Goerl, "Reconciling Political Entrepreneurship and Democracy," *Public Administration Review* 52 (1992): 130–134.

- *judgment*, which indicates discretion or autonomy;
- *balance*, which requires "transparently reasonable" judgment among competing values and which must identify and reconcile "the inevitable conflict among interests, mandates, and desires";
- *rationality*, or the "habitual resort to reason" that "ensure[s] transparent justifications for managerial action"; and
- *accountability*, because "directive activity is definitive when the intent of positive law is clear. When it is ambiguous or incomplete, the public manager must exercise judgment as to what the public interest and professionalism require."[123]

When the possibility for discretion is present, Bertelli and Lynn argue, public managers must employ reasonable judgment informed by professionalism and the public interest. Political scientist David Weimer has noted that the design of governance arrangements for delivering and paying for health care could draw on the precept for understanding what "responsible public management" might mean in such a system.[124]

Bertelli and Lynn argue further that political principals must be able to trust those to whom they delegate authority and to trust them to perform in a reliably responsible way. They define "irresponsible public management" as managerial action (or inaction) that "disavows judgment or that acts without authority or in an arbitrary, self-serving, ill-informed, and nontransparent fashion."[125] An example of a manager who exhibited such behavior is J. Steven Griles, former deputy secretary of the interior, who continued to meet with former clients of his management consulting firm despite having signed a written agreement not to do so when he entered government service. Griles resigned after an 18-month investigation by the department's inspector general. Another example is how Federal Aviation Administration middle managers and supervisors responded when they learned of possible safety problems with airplanes flown by Southwest Airlines. They ignored reports from inspectors and even threatened some employees with retaliatory action if they pursued the reported problems.[xvi]

This section has described what it means for a public manager to be strategic and different types of general strategies a manager can draw on. These include framing and reframing, navigating the terrain, anticipating how hard a problem will be, working from the ground up, entrepreneurship, and practicing consistent with a precept for managerial responsibility.

KEY CONCEPTS

Decision	Psychological biases
Deliberation	Garbage can model of decision making
Rational actor	Double-loop learning
Bounded rationality	Paradigm
Satisficing	Ideology
Prospect theory	Democratic ethos
Framing effects	Best practices/Leading practices
Cognitive dissonance	Scientific paradigm
Groupthink	

[xvi]See, for example, Matthew L. Wald, "Inspectors for F.A.A. Say Violations Were Ignored," *The New York Times,* April 3, 2008.

Policy analysis	Strategy
Evidence-based policy and practice	Strategic public management
Research brokers/Knowledge brokers	Reframing
Scientism	Navigating the terrain
Think tanks	Anticipating how hard a problem will be
Management by walking around	Backward mapping
Issue networks	Entrepreneurial public management
Advocacy coalition	Precept of managerial responsibility

CASE ANALYSIS: PAUL VALLAS: CEO, SUPERINTENDENT

At the beginning of the 2007 school year, Paul G. Vallas assumed responsibility for the New Orleans Recovery School District. The situation he confronted was fraught with exceptional challenges: the aftermath of Hurricane Katrina and the long-standing problems in the New Orleans public schools stemming from poverty and a dysfunctional administration. At the end of the previous school year, fewer than half of the district's students were showing up for school. Said one expert on the Louisiana public schools, "I'm just not sure there's very much room to accomplish anything."[126]

But Vallas was no stranger to the challenges of urban public education. Although he was not a professional educator, he had been superintendent of the public school systems of Chicago and Philadelphia and had earned a reputation as someone who could make public schools work better for students. The belief was widespread that if anyone could accomplish something in New Orleans, it was Paul Vallas.

How does a public manager acquire a reputation described as "gold plated" while undertaking such difficult assignments?[127] First, Vallas was regarded as a nontraditional superintendent. Though he has run for public office, he is more of a political technocrat—described by one observer as "charismatic in a wonky sort of way"—whose roots are in the Daley family political machine in Chicago. "The argument in favor of nontraditional leadership has been that managerial experience is more important to running a school system than educational background."[128] And so is political savvy.[i]

Nationally, public school administration in the 1980s and part of the 1990s was, according to one account, "dominated by the idea of decentralization, of devolving power to the individual school site, its principal, teachers and parents." Vallas and many of his peers began strengthening the power of the central office to gain greater control over standards, curricula, facilities, teacher assignments, and resource allocation. One goal was to prevent bad schools from becoming worse by making them "dumping grounds for those with the least seniority" and restricting their access to resources.[129]

(Continued)

---

[i]For additional discussion of public school reform, see William Ouchi, "Making Public Schools Work: Management Reform as Key," *Academy of Management Journal* 48, no. 6 (2005): 929–934.

(Continued)

Second, Vallas might be regarded as a nontraditional manager. According to someone who observed him and is an admirer,

> Tall and ungainly, Vallas is nonetheless a charming, intellectually imposing man, a charismatic bully. In many situations, he simply steamrolls most of those around him. . . . He does what he wants—sometimes rashly—and bristles at any whiff of opposition. Known to berate underlings, educators, and members of the press alike, Vallas has a leadership style that seems more a product of his Greek roots and intellect than of any management book or bureaucratic experience. . . . Self-assured and capable of torrential speech, Vallas only rarely admits to doubt or fault.[130]

Effective public management does not depend upon having the ideal managerial temperament. His outsized skills, however, have been at the root of many of the controversies he has generated.

Vallas does not conform to stereotypes that emphasize vision, stewardship, compromise, unfailing courtesy, and other platonic virtues. By all accounts charismatic, physical, energetic, and passionate, he self-consciously but for the most part intuitively uses his craft to confront the specific structural and cultural realities of the administrative systems in which he works and to devise strategies that result in measurable improvements. He is an inveterate user of structures and processes to transform dysfunctional public school system cultures.

Chicago

When Chicago mayor Richard M. Daley was given control over his city's public schools by the state legislature in 1995, he appointed Vallas as superintendent, and school improvement became one of the mayor's top priorities. Chicago's public schools had once been described by President Ronald Reagan's secretary of education as the worst in the nation. The 1995 school reform legislation gave the mayor, school board, superintendent, and local parents, teachers, and community members greatly expanded powers over the system and established the structural framework within which Vallas would work.

Vallas had important qualifications for running an urban school district. He had served 5 years as Chicago's budget director. "Budgets were a snap for him, large bureaucracies were not intimidating, and he had no previous allegiances within the school system to hold him back from asking hard questions or demanding new solutions."[131] By the end of his tenure in Chicago, more eighth graders than third graders were meeting national norms—meaning students were performing better the longer they were in the system.[132]

During his tenure, from 1995 to 2001, Vallas racked up a long string of accomplishments that would be the envy of nearly any superintendent. The budget was quickly put in order. Vallas rehabbed old schools and built attractive new ones. Test scores reported to the public rose nearly every year, two union contracts were negotiated without any strikes, and a host of new programs—summer school, afterschool programs, alternative schools, new magnet programs—were all created. Most important, for perhaps the first time in Chicago's history, low-performing schools were pressured to do better, and students and their parents encountered a system that did not just pass everyone through regardless of what they learned.[133]

Despite his accomplishments, "Vallas fatigue" led to criticism. According to one account, he was nearly always battling someone or something. During his time as schools chief, he took on the reform groups, the local school councils, the education schools, the state board of education, and the education research community. His verbal attacks on teachers and the teacher union were not matched by any significant attempts to address problems with teacher quality. At one point, he threatened to cancel all field trips. At another, he threatened not to participate in the state's testing program. The public ate it up, but that kind of endless battle could last only so long.[134]

He says of himself, "I don't burn out. I burn other people out."[135]

Critics argued that Vallas lacked a sophisticated or flexible education vision or ready access to one. Over and again during his last year, the mayor called on Vallas for new ideas, to "think outside the box." But Vallas, "deeply suspicious of the reform groups whom he says 'exploited' failing schools, critical of ed-school policy experts, and antagonistic toward the independent research shop set up at the University of Chicago, seemed to have been focused on political and managerial" rather than the priorities of professional educators. Even after six years running the Chicago schools, Vallas still talked about time on task rather than methods or quality: more kindergarten, double periods of reading for struggling students, summer school, mandatory extended day."[136]

Vallas found himself under fire. Student test scores were rising but not fast enough for the mayor, who eventually decided to replace Vallas.[137] Said someone familiar with the situation, "The most obvious political explanation for his departure was that, from the mayor's perspective, Vallas grew too big for his britches. Like many other deputies before him . . . too much adulation can become a problem. Daley is famous in Chicago for firing staffers who steal his headlines."[138] Vallas's tenure as superintendent in Chicago lasted 6 years. His replacement was 36-year-old Arne Duncan, littleknown at the time but liked by professional educators (and who would later be secretary of education in the Obama administration).

Philadelphia

Vallas became superintendent of the Philadelphia public schools, which had been taken over by the state, in 2002. He immediately became involved in overseeing the biggest privatization effort in any district in the country.[139] Many observers believed that the success of the public-private partnerships would make or break his reputation. His impact turned out to be much broader, however.

Vallas's political background was an evident asset in his new situation. His experience in politics, including campaigning for governor of Illinois after relinquishing his school post there,

> shows in the way he interacts with teachers and parents as he makes his stops around the city. He puts them at ease like an old pol, cracking quick jokes and swapping updates on common acquaintances before handing them a little spiral notebook and asking them to jot down complaints or problems in it. Vallas almost seems more at ease with school kids and strangers than with members of his staff, who sometimes flinch perceptibly when he compliments them, taking his kind words as preludes to bigger work assignments.[140]

Unlike previous school administrators, Vallas got on well with the teachers' union and other critical stakeholder groups.

Vallas was said to hate not only the danger that suffused public schools in Philadelphia but also the way so many of the schools looked: "like dark and ugly penal colonies, small fortresses of concrete and brick with windows that no one can see through." He was said to wonder whether there was a connection between the brutality of the schools' appearance and the brutality that often takes place within them. An observer accompanied him on a visit to one of his schools to celebrate a new mural that had been painted

(Continued)

(Continued)

on a school wall depicting several then-current students surrounded by basketballs, comets, and books. The school was one of 17 where Vallas had commissioned murals. "The schools should be the most impressive buildings in the community," he said, "not the most run-down."[141]

Vallas's moves won praise virtually across the board in Philadelphia, "from Republican state legislators pushing hard for school privatization to city activists who can't stand that part of his program." "I don't remember a superintendent ever being on a honeymoon for three years," said Ted Kirsch, the local union president. He continued:

> He's imposed stricter discipline enforcement and assigned the most unruly kids to alternative facilities, a strategy that has reduced by half the number of Philadelphia schools considered "persistently dangerous" by federal standards. More positively, Vallas expanded the number of children who receive early childhood instruction by about 50 percent, lowering the shelf life of textbooks down to three years, pioneering the idea of a standardized curriculum for high schools, bringing advanced placement and college preparatory classes to every high school— "even where the students don't think they're going to college," he insists—and pursuing the structural reorganization of virtually every middle and high school in the city. All that on top of big changes in finance, human resources, capital planning and technology.[142]

On Vallas's departure from the Philadelphia schools, one observer said,

> I know, he is not a miracle worker [and] any successes of the school district in the last five years may have had more to do with the . . . additional funding to play with after the state takeover than with the guy at the top. . . . But he brought an enormous amount of energy to a job that is known for sapping it right out of your bone marrow.[143]

New Orleans

Reflecting his intuitive grasp of context and culture, in New Orleans Vallas appeared to be convinced that the approaches he had used in Chicago and Philadelphia were ill-suited to his new responsibilities. "There's much deeper poverty here," Vallas said. "So you take deep poverty and then you compound that by the aftermath of the hurricane, by the physical, psychological, emotional damage inflicted by the hurricane. It's like the straw that breaks the camel's back."[144]

In Vallas's view, the culture of New Orleans schools had to change; school personnel needed to accept that they were, in effect, substitute families. "You begin to make the schools community centers," he said. "The whole objective here is to keep the schools open through the dinner hour, and keep schools open 11 months out of the year."[145] Said one New Orleans teacher, "What he brings is high expectations, of course, but also a sense of urgency. You can hear it in his voice."[146] Said Vallas of his strategy in New Orleans, "I've actually prepared a checklist that we're giving to all the teachers and the parents the first week of school." His impact was immediate: Early in his first school year, the truancy rate had already dropped to 15 percent.

Said one observer, "As an educator for the past 14 years, I've heard it all. I've heard promises being made and nothing being the result. Superintendent Vallas is promoting technology in the classrooms. It's here. He's saying every classroom will be painted before students actually come into the school. That is being done. He really has come in with everything that he's promised."[147] Other teachers regarded Vallas's high expectations as naïve and unrealistic, however, and they remained skeptical as to whether he could keep all his promises or if he even understood what he was up against. After almost a year on the job, according to one account, "On one level the transformation has already been total. . . . The schools are being administered with a vigor that would have been unrecognizable here before the storm."[148] Once again, Paul Vallas appeared to be very much in his element.

Vallas's long-term influence in Chicago and Philadelphia is hard to gauge. Individuals who show that "it can be done" often leave elevated expectations concerning what is attainable after they have moved on. Indeed, organizations may outgrow the need for this type of leadership, and a change of managers may be beneficial for all concerned. Leadership that is intense, demanding, and charismatic can also create, as noted above, a kind of fatigue that leads successor administrations to consolidate the gains and manage in a lower key, which may allow some unraveling of earlier accomplishments and the reappearance of old power relationships.

Discussion Questions

The cases of Michelle Rhee and Paul Vallas offer an opportunity to compare and contrast the managerial craft of two different leaders in similar jobs. The following questions can be considered for one or the other leader; or, more fruitfully, by comparing and contrasting each.

1. Analyze the deliberation and decision-making strategies of Rhee and Vallas. In the information presented in these profiles, is there evidence of cognitive dissonance, groupthink, or other psychological biases? What strategies do Rhee and Vallas use, if any, to guard against these biases?

2. How do Rhee and Vallas learn? What are their strategies? Use concepts from the chapter to frame your analysis.

3. Is Michelle Rhee a strategic public manager? Is Vallas a strategic public manager? Use specific concepts and heuristics from the chapter to analyze their strategic orientations. For example,

   a. use the Bozeman and Straussman four principles to construct an argument of whether each is a strategic public manager.

   b. use Bolman and Deal's framing concept to analyze Rhee's and Vallas's frame use and preference. Could Rhee improve her strategy by reframing? Could Vallas improve his strategy by reframing? Be specific in your argument about what frame(s) could benefit them, and what they might learn.

   c. use either Haass's compass or Moore's directions to analyze how successfully Rhee and Vallas navigate their terrains.

   d. how successfully did Rhee and Vallas anticipate how hard their reform efforts would be? What did they do to prepare for these challenges?

   e. did Rhee and Vallas work from the ground up to design their reforms? How does education reform look different from the ground up in contrast to top down?

   f. is Rhee an entrepreneurial public manager? Is Vallas?

   g. does the managerial practice of each comport with a precept of managerial responsibility?

4. Chapter 10 emphasized the importance of fit between managerial personality and the situation. Using concepts from Chapters 10 and 11, analyze the fit between person and situation for both Rhee and Vallas.

NOTES

1. Clay Risen, "The Lightning Rod," *The Atlantic*, November 2008, http://www.theatlantic.com/magazine/archive/2008/11/the-lightning-rod/307058.

2. Ibid.

3. Ibid.

4. Ibid.

5. Ibid.

6. Dan Keating and V. Dion Haynes, "Can D. C. Schools be Fixed?" *The Washington Post*, June 10, 2007, http://www.washingtonpost.com/wp-dyn/content/article/2007/06/09/AR2007060901415.html.

7. Ibid.

8. David Nakamura, "Fenty's School Takeover Approved," *The Washington Post*, April 20, 2007, http://www.washingtonpost.com/wp-dyn/content/article/2007/04/19/AR2007041902376.html.

9. David Nakamura, "Fenty to Oust Janey Today," *The Washington Post*, June 12, 2007, http://www.washingtonpost.com/wp-dyn/content/article/2007/06/11/AR2007061102383.html.

10. "Timeline: Michelle Rhee," *The Washington Post*, http://www.washingtonpost.com/wp-srv/special/metro/michelle-rhee/index.html?sid=ST2009061302085, accessed May 23 2015.

11. Nakamura, "Fenty to Oust Janey Today."

12. Risen, "The Lightning Rod."

13. Ibid.

14. Bill Turque, "Two Years of Hard Lessons for D.C. Schools' Change Agent," *The Washington Post*, July 14, 2009, A01, http://www.washingtonpost.com/wp-dyn/content/article/2009/06/13/AR2009061302073_pf.html.

15. Amanda Ripley, "Can She Save Our Schools?" *Time*, 172, no. 23 (December 8, 2008): 36–44.

16. Ibid.

17. Risen, "The Lightning Rod."

18. Ibid.

19. Ibid.

20. Ibid.

21. Ripley, "Can She Save Our Schools?"

22. Risen, "The Lightning Rod."

23. Ibid.

24. Turque, "Two Years of Hard Lessons."

25. Ibid.

26. Ibid.

27. Risen, "The Lightning Rod."

28. Ibid.

29. Turque, "Two Years of Hard Lessons."

30. Ibid.

31. Ibid.

32. Oxford Dictionaries, s.v. "decision," http://www.oxforddictionaries.com/us/definition/american_english/decision.

33. Herbert A. Simon, "On the Concept of Organizational Goal," *Administrative Science Quarterly* 9 (1964): 21; Herbert A. Simon, *Models of Man* (New York, NY: Wiley, 1957); Herbert A. Simon, "Rationality as Process and as Process of Thought," *American Economic Review* 68 (1978): 1–16; see also Jonathan Bendor, "Herbert A. Simon: Political Scientist," *Annual Review of Political Science* 6 (June 2003): 433–471.

34. S. Kenneth Howard, "Analysis, Rationality, and Administrative Decision Making," in *Toward a New Public Administration: The Minnowbrook Perspective,* ed. Frank Marini (Scranton, PA: Chandler, 1971), 287.

35. John M. Pfiffner, "Administrative Rationality," *Public Administration Review* 20, no. 3 (1960): 125–132.

36. Anthony M. Bertelli and Laurence E. Lynn Jr., *Madison's Managers: Public Administration and the Constitution* (Baltimore, MD: Johns Hopkins University Press, 2006).

37. "Secretary Kempthorne Announces Decision to Protect Polar Bears under Endangered Species Act," U.S. Department of the Interior, May 14, 2008, http://www.doi.gov/news/archive/08_News_Releases/080514a.html.

38. Amos Tversky and Daniel Kahneman, "Rational Choice and the Framing of Decisions," in *Rational Choice: The Contrast between Economics and Psychology,* ed. Robin M. Hogarth and Melvin W. Reder (Chicago, IL: University of Chicago Press, 1986), 67–94.

39. John Billings, "Promoting the Dissemination of Decision Aids: An Odyssey in a Dysfunctional Health Care Financing System," *Health Affairs Web Exclusive,* October 7, 2004, 128–132, http://content. healthaffairs.org/cgi/reprint/hlthaff.var.128v1.pdf.

40. B. J. McNeil et al., "On the Elicitation of Preferences for Alternative Therapies," *New England Journal of Medicine* 306, no. 21 (1982): 1259–62.

41. A. Edwards et al., "Presenting Risk Information—A Review of the Effects of 'Framing' and Other Manipulations on Patient Choice," *Journal of Health Communication* 6, no. 1 (2001): 61–82, cited by Billings, "Promoting the Dissemination of Decision Aids."

42. Paul Krugman, "Quagmire of the Vanities," *The New York Times*, January 8, 2007.

43. L. Festinger, *A Theory of Cognitive Dissonance* (Stanford, CA: Stanford University Press, 1957).

44. John Schwartz, "Facing and Embracing Risk as Return to Space Nears," *The New York Times*, July 10, 2005.

45. Adapted from Laurence E. Lynn Jr., *Managing Public Policy* (Boston, MA: Little, Brown, 1987), 95–97.

46. Tim Weiner, "Naiveté at the C.I.A.: Every Nation's Just Another U.S.," *The New York Times*, June 7, 1998.

47. Daniel Kahneman and Jonathan Renshon, "Why Hawks Win," *Foreign Policy*, October 13, 2009, http://foreignpolicy.com/2009/10/13/why-hawks-win.

48. Shankar Vedantam, "Iraq War Naysayers May Have Hindsight Bias," *The Washington Post*, October 2, 2006, Sec. A.

49. Amit R. Paley, "Ex-Aides Break With Bush on 'No Child,'" *The Washington Post*, June 25, 2007, Sec. A.

50. Shankar Vedantam, "Repeated Warnings Have Diminishing Returns," *The Washington Post*, November 20, 2006, Sec. A.

51. Ibid.

52. Eldar Shafir, "Choosing Versus Rejecting: Why Some Options are Both Better and Worse Than Others," *Memory & Cognition* 21 (1993): 546–556, quoted in Barry Schwartz, "Mr. Bland Goes to Washington," *The New York Times*, November 7, 2006.

53. Daniel L. Schacter, "The Fog of War," *The New York Times*, April 5, 2004.

54. Daniel Gilbert, "I'm O.K., You're Biased," *The New York Times*, April 16, 2006.

55. Daniel Gilbert, "He Who Cast the First Stone Probably Didn't," *The New York Times*, July 24, 2006.

56. Quoted by Jared Sandberg, "Brainstorming Works Best if People Scramble for Ideas on Their Own," *Wall Street Journal*, June 13, 2006.

57. Michael D. Cohen, James G. March, and Johan P. Olsen, "A Garbage Can Model of Organizational Choice," *Administrative Science Quarterly* 17, no. 1 (March 1972): 1–25.

58. Jane Mayer, "The Hidden Power," *The New Yorker*, June 26, 2006, http://www.newyorker.com/magazine/2006/07/03/the-hidden-power.

59. Jim Grieves, *Organizational Change: Themes and Issues* (Oxford, UK: Oxford University Press, 2011), 227.

60. Henry Mintzberg, "Managing Government, Governing Management," *Harvard Business Review* 74, no. 3 (1996): 75–84.

61. Beryl A. Radin, *Challenging the Performance Movement: Accountability, Complexity, and Democratic Values* (Washington, DC: Georgetown University Press, 2006), 19.

62. Linda DeLeon and Peter DeLeon, "The Democratic Ethos and Public Management," *Administration & Society* 34 (2002): 229–250.

63. Eugene Bardach, "From Practitioner Wisdom to Scholarly Knowledge and Back Again," *Journal of Policy Analysis and Management* 7, (1987): 188–199; Giandomenico Majone, *Evidence, Argument, and Persuasion in the Policy Process* (New Haven, CT: Yale University Press, 1989).

64. Frederick Taylor, *The Principles of Scientific Management* (New York, NY: W. W. Norton, 1967), 25; Robert Kanigel, *The One Best Way: Frederick Winslow Taylor and the Enigma of Efficiency* (New York, NY: Penguin Books, 1997).

65. Herbert A. Simon, "The Proverbs of Administration," *Public Administration Review* 6 (November/December 1946): 53, 66.

66. Harry P. Hatry et al., *Excellence in Managing* (Washington, DC: The Urban Institute, 1991).

67. Laurence E. Lynn Jr., "The Budget-Maximizing Bureaucrat: Is There a Case?" in *The Budget Maximizing Bureaucrat: Appraisals and Evidence*, ed. André Blais and Stéphane Dion (Pittsburgh, PA: University of Pittsburgh Press, 1991), 59.

68. Richard T. Pascale and Anthony G. Athos, *The Art of Japanese Management* (London, UK: Alan Lane, 1982); Thomas J. Peters and Robert H. Waterman, *In Search of Excellence: Lessons from America's Best-Run Companies* (New York, NY: Harper and Row, 1982).

69. Government Accountability Office, "Results-Oriented Cultures: Using Balanced Expectations to Manage Senior Executive Performance" (GAO-02-966), 2002.

70. "Center Divisions," *NGA Center for Best Practices*, accessed January 7, 2015, http://www.nga.org/cms/home/nga-center-for-best-practices/center-divisions.html.

71. Cheryl Hilvert, "How Can I leave My Community a Better Place When I am Lucky Just to Keep My Head Above Water?" ICMA Center for Management Strategies, August 28, 2012, http://icma.org/en/icma/knowledge_network/blogs/blogpost/785/How_can_I_leave_my_community_a_better_place_when_I_am_lucky_just_to_keep_my_head_above_water.72. Chris Fabian, "Reconsidering Best Practices in Local Government, *ICMA Center for Management Strategies*, October 22, 2013, http://icma.org/en/icma/knowledge_network/blogs/blogpost/1787/Reconsidering_Best_Practices_in_Local_Government.

73. Ibid.

74. Ibid.

75. "Ten Essentials," National Alliance to End Homelessness, accessed January 7, 2015, http://www.endhomelessness.org/pages/ten-essentials

76. "Evolution of the Guidance System," Peacekeeping Resource Hub, last update may 18, 2015, http://www.peacekeepingbestpractices.unlb.org.

77. Thomas Kuhn, *The Structure of Scientific Revolutions* (Chicago, IL: University of Chicago Press, 1962).

78. Education Sciences Reform Act of 2002, H.R. 3801, 107th Cong., 20 U.S.C. 9501, P.L. 107-279.

79. Lisa Anderson, *Pursuing Truth, Exercising Power: Social Science and Public Policy in the Twenty First Century* (New York, NY: Columbia University Press, 2003), 13.

80. Aaron Wildavsky, *Speaking Truth to Power: The Art and Craft of Policy Analysis* (Boston, MA: Little, Brown, 1979), 16.

81. "About Us," The Cochrane Collaboration, access date January 7, 2015, http://www.cochrane.org/about-us.

82. Jeffrey D. Zients, "Memorandum to the Heads of Executive Departments and Agencies-Subject: Use of Evidence and Evaluation in 2014 Budget," *Executive Office of the President,* May 18, 2012, http://www.whitehouse.gov/sites/default/files/omb/memoranda/2012/m-12-14_1 .pdf.

83. James L. Sundquist, "Research Brokerage: The Weak Link," in *Knowledge and Policy: The Uncertain Connection,* ed. Laurence E. Lynn Jr. (Washington, DC: National Academy of Sciences, 1978).

84. Hugh Heclo, *A Government of Strangers: Executive Politics in Washington* (Washington, DC: Brookings Institution, 1977), 151.

85. "About Us," The Campbell Collaboration, access date January 7, 2015, http://www.campbellcollaboration.org/about_us/index.php.

86. "What Works Clearinghouse," Institution of Education Sciences, access date January 7, 2015, http://ies.ed.gov/ncee/wwc/.

87. "WWC Review of the Report "Freshman Year Financial Aid Nudges: An Experiment to Increase FAFSA Renewal and College Persistence," *What Works Clearinghouse,* December 2014, http://ies.ed.gov/ncee/wwc/pdf/single_study_reviews/wwc_castleman_121614.pdf.

88. "WWC Review of the Report "Getting Under the Hood: How and For Whom Does Increasing Course Structure Work?" *What Works Clearinghouse,* December 2014, http://ies.ed.gov/ncee/wwc/pdf/single_study_reviews/wwc_eddy_120214.pdf.

89. "About Us," EPIS Center, access date January 7, 2015, http://episcenter.psu.edu/aboutus.

90. "Council for Exceptional Children: Standards for Evidence-Based Practices in Special Education," *Council for Exceptional Children,* 2014, http://www.cec.sped.org/~/media/Files/Standards/Evidence%20based%20Practices%20and%20Practice/EBP%20FINAL.pdf.

91. Ibid.

92. Ibid., 2.

93. Bent Flyvbjerg, "Five Misunderstandings about Case-Study Research," *Qualitative Inquiry* 12 (2006): 242.

94. Sylvia Burwell, "Memorandum to the Heads of Executive Departments and Agencies–Subject: Next Steps in the Evidence and Innovation Agenda," *Executive Office of the President,* July 26, 2013, 8-9, http://www.whitehouse.gov/sites/default/files/omb/memoranda/ 2013/m-13-17.pdf.

95. David C. Hoaglin et al., *Data for Decisions: Information Strategies for Policymakers* (Cambridge, MA: Abt Books, 1982).

96. Lawrence W. Sherman, "Misleading Evidence and Evidence-Led Policy: Making Social Science More Experimental," *Annals of the American Academy of Political and Social Science* 589 (2003): 6.

97. "Coalition for Evidence-Based Policy," accessed January 7, 2015, http://coalition4evidence.org.

98. Steven I. Miller and Marcel Fredericks, "Social Science Research Findings and Educational Policy Dilemmas: Some Additional Distinctions," *Education Policy Analysis Archive* 8 (2000), http://epaa. asu.edu/epaa/v8n3.

99. Sharon Begley, "Alzheimer's Field Blocking Research into Other Causes?" *Wall Street Journal,* April 9, 2004, Sec. B; Sharon Begley, "Scientists World-Wide Battle a Narrow View of Alzheimer's Cause," *Wall Street Journal,* April 16, 2004, Sec. A.; Jerome Groopman, "Before Night Falls," *The New Yorker,* June 17, 2013, http://www.newyorker.com/magazine/2013/06/24/before-night-falls.

100. Groopman, "Before Night Falls."

101. Gio Batta Gori, "The Bogus 'Science' of Secondhand Smoke," *The Washington Post,* January 30, 2007.

102. Daniel Guttman and Barry Willner, *The Shadow Government: The Government's Multi-Billion Dollar Giveaway of its Decision-Making Powers to Private Management Consultants, "Experts," and Think Tanks* (New York, NY: Pantheon Books, 1976).

103. James McGann, "US Think-Tanks Casualties in the War of Ideas," *openDemocracy,* December 20, 2005, http://www.opendemocracy.net/ democracy-think_tank/us_thinktanks_3137.jsp.

104. Peters and Waterman, *In Search of Excellence.* See also David Boud and Heather Middleton, "Learning from Others at Work: Communities of Practice and Informal Learning," *Journal of Workplace Learning* 15 (2003): 194–202.

105. Hugh Heclo, "Issue Networks and the Executive Establishment," in *The New American Political System,* ed. Anthony King (Washington, DC: American Enterprise Institute, 1978), 106.

106. Paul Sabatier and Hank Jenkins-Smith, *Policy Change and Learning: An Advocacy Coalition Approach* (Boulder, CO: Westview Press, 1993).

107. John M. Bryson, *Strategic Planning for Public and Nonprofit Organizations,* rev. ed. (San Francisco, CA: Jossey-Bass, 1995); David L. Weimer and Aidan R. Vining, "Thinking Strategically about Adoption and Implementation," in *Policy Analysis: Concepts and Practice* (Upper Saddle River, NJ: Prentice Hall, 2005); Mark H. Moore, "Managing for Value: Organizational Strategy in For-Profit, Nonprofit, and Governmental

Organizations," *Nonprofit and Voluntary Sector Quarterly* 29 (2000): 183–204; Peter Smith Ring and James L. Perry, "Strategic Management in Public and Private Organizations: Implications of Distinctive Contexts and Constraints," *Academy of Management Review* 10, (1985): 276–286.

108. Charles E. Lindblom, "The Science of Muddling Through," *Public Administration Review* 19, no. 2 (Spring 1959): 81.

109. Barry Bozeman and Jeffrey D. Straussman, *Public Management Strategies: Guidelines for Managerial Effectiveness* (San Francisco, CA: Jossey-Bass, 1990), 29–30.

110. Moore, "Managing for Value," 94.

111. Bozeman and Straussman, *Public Management Strategies,* 203.

112. George L. Kelling and James Q. Wilson, "Broken Windows," *The Atlantic*, March 1982, http://www.theatlantic.com/magazine/archive/1982/03/broken-windows/304465.

113. Chair Mary Jo White, "Remarks at the Securities Enforcement Forum," *US Securities and Exchange Commission*, October 9, 2013, http://www.sec.gov/News/Speech/Detail/Speech/1370539872100#_ftn1.

114. Richard D. Heimovics, Robert D. Herman, and Carole L. Jurkiewicz Coughlin, "Executive Leadership and Resource Dependence in Nonprofit Organizations: A Frame Analysis," *Public Administration Review* 53, no. 5 (1993): 419–427.

115. Richard Haass, *The Power to Persuade: How to Be Effective in Any Unruly Organization,* (Boston, MA: Houghton Mifflin, 1995), 2. See also Dan H. Fenn Jr., "Finding Where the Power Lies in Government," *Harvard Business Review* 57 (1979): 144–153.

116. Laurence J. O'Toole Jr., Kenneth J. Meier, and Sean Nicholson-Crotty, "Managing Upward, Downward, and Outward: Networks, Hierarchical Relationships, and Performance," *Public Management Review* 7, no. 1 (2005): 45–68.

117. Gordon Chase, "Implementing a Human Service Program: How Hard Will It Be?" *Public Policy* 27(1979): 385–435. For an example, see L. C. Steenbergen et al., "Kentucky's Graduated Driver Licensing Program for Young Drivers: Barriers to Effective Local Implementation," *Injury Prevention* 7 (2001): 286–291.

118. "DoD News Briefing-Presenter: Secretary of Defense Donald H. Rumsfeld," *Office of the Assistant Secretary of Defense,* April 11, 2003, http://www.defenselink.mil/transcripts/transcript.aspx?transcriptid=2367.

119. Richard F. Elmore, "Backward Mapping: Implementation Research and Policy Decisions," *Political Science Quarterly* 94, no. 4 (1979–1980): 606.

120. Marcia K. Meyers, Bonnie Glaser, and Karin MacDonald, "On the Front Lines of Welfare Delivery: Are Workers Implementing Policy Reforms?" *Journal of Policy Analysis and Management* 17, no. 1 (1998): 1–22.

121. Elmore, "Backward Mapping."

122. S. Borins, "What Border? Public Management Innovation in the United States and Canada," *Journal of Policy Analysis and Management* 19 (2000): 46–74.

123. Anthony M. Bertelli and Laurence E. Lynn Jr., "Managerial Responsibility," *Public Administration Review* 63, no. 3 (2003): 261–262.

124. David L. Weimer, "Medical Governance: Are We Ready to Prescribe?" *Journal of Policy Analysis and Management* 26, no. 2 (2007): 217–229.

125. Bertelli and Lynn, "Managerial Responsibility," 262.

126. Adam Nossiter, "A Tamer of Schools Has Plan in New Orleans," *The New York Times,* September 24, 2007.

127. Ibid.

128. Alan Greenblatt, "The Impatience of Paul Vallas," *Governing Magazine,* September 2005. http://www.governing.com/topics/finance/Impatience-Paul-Vallas.html.

129. Ibid.

130. Alexander Russo, "Political Educator," *Education Next* (Winter 2003), http://www.hoover.org/ publications/ednext/3354931.html.

131. Ibid.

132. Greenblatt, "The Impatience of Paul Vallas."

133. Russo, "Political Educator."

134. Ibid.

135. Adam Nossiter, "Against Odds, New Orleans Schools Fight Back," *The New York Times,* April 30, 2008.

136. Ibid.

137. Greenblatt, "The Impatience of Paul Vallas."

138. Russo, "Political Educator."

139. Greenblatt, "The Impatience of Paul Vallas."

140. Ibid.

141. Ibid.

142. Ibid.
143. "Paul Vallas Leaving," *The Next Mayor,* http://blogs.phillynews.com/dailynews/nextmayor/2007/ 04/paul_vallas_leaving.html.
144. Nossiter, "A Tamer of Schools Has Plan in New Orleans."
145. Ibid.
146. John Merrow, "New Orleans Chief Tackles Rebuilding Shattered System," *The News Hour,* October 2, 2007, http://www.pbs.org/news-hour/bb/education/july-dec07/nola_10-02.html.
147. Ibid.
148. Nossiter, "Against Odds."

PART V | MANAGING IN THREE DIMENSIONS

Reflecting Society's Values, Performing Effectively, Earning Trust

The goal to be sought combines adequate recognition of personal rights as declared in the constitution with effective achievement of great social programs.[i]

—Leonard D. White
Introduction to the
Study of Public Administration

At the outset of this book, the following question was posed: How can public managers ensure that our governments reflect our society's values, perform effectively, and earn the people's trust? This question was raised against a backdrop of widespread public distrust of government. But it was also raised in a spirit of optimism and of respect for the public servants at the local, state, and national levels; in the belief that public management practice *can* meet those goals even in the face of inevitable challenges.

Meeting these goals is not inevitable, however. America's system of governance was designed to restrain the discretion of administrators. The prospects for managerial success can nonetheless, be significantly improved by helping readers of this book—as citizens and as public managers—develop an appreciation of and prepare for its uniquely difficult intellectual and practical demands.

This book has characterized public management as a multifaceted endeavor. It has emphasized the fundamental dimensions—structure, culture, craft—of public management. It has traced the authority of public management to the rule of law, emphasized the importance of systematic analysis as a management tool, and described frameworks and concepts upon which informed citizens and practitioners can draw for gaining insight and taking action. This approach encapsulates public managers' dual roles as both creatures of their political environments and creators of administrative capacity to implement public policies enacted within those environments.

---

[i]Leonard D. White, *Introduction to the Study of Public Administration* (New York: The MacMillan Company, 1926), 455.

This approach encapsulates public managers' dual roles as both creatures of their political environments and creators of administrative capacity to implement public policies enacted within those environments.

For its central argument, the book draws on concepts and methods derived from the social and behavioral sciences and from public policy research and analysis that have proven to be useful in management applications.

Both the routine and distinctive challenges that public managers face will almost always call for choices and actions that involve more than one of the three dimensions of public management. Public managers who are unprepared to master the logic of and manage in all three dimensions are at a disadvantage when dealing with the kinds of problems that have significant political and programmatic ramifications for their effectiveness and reputations. While useful, instinct and experience are not enough.

PUBLIC MANAGEMENT'S PERFECT STORM: HURRICANE KATRINA IN THREE DIMENSIONS

The introductions to Parts II, III, and IV included examples of the roles played by each of public management's three dimensions in the response to Hurricane Katrina:

- **Structure**: Command and communications structures were inadequate to cope with a hurricane of Katrina's magnitude and, in all likelihood, with disasters and terrorist incidents of similar magnitude.
- **Culture**: In some cases the organizational cultures of the entities charged with responding impeded their ability to rise to the enormous challenges. The kinds of coordination and collaboration that could have saved lives were subordinated to narrow agency interests and standard operating procedures. In other cases, organizational cultures enabled and encouraged entrepreneurial and life saving responses by professional staffs facing emergency conditions.
- **Craft:** Numerous officials did not demonstrate appropriate skills and expertise or exhibit adequate leadership. The public had a right to expect that they would—because it was their job.

The story of Hurricane Katrina reveals serious failures of ensuring and directing. Ensuring failures were evident because the necessary authority and organization for an effective response had not been provided. Directing failures were evident because the authority and organization that were provided were used ineffectively by public managers. The preparation for and response to Katrina occurred within the legal and political context of public management in the United States. Katrina's "perfect storm" of public management occurred because public managers were constrained to performing roles as creatures and, in many cases, failed to respond adequately in their roles as creators.

How should policymakers and public managers think about, let alone accomplish, changes in public management as fundamental as those called for by the House report on Katrina? The following questions apply to Katrina but are applicable to many kinds of policies, programs, and situations:

- How should policymakers and public managers address issues raised by legal, command, and organizational structures that fail?

- How should they address the shortcomings of organizational cultures that are risk-averse, with employees who are unwilling to act if doing so will expose them to criticism later?
- How should they encourage and ensure the responsible exercise of initiative?
- How should they address basic managerial issues such as ensuring adequate staffing of operations and timely collection, communication, and dissemination of information essential to effective operations, organizational learning, and system coordination?
- How can policymakers ensure that these interdependent aspects of public management create a system of public management practice throughout the federal system that not only performs the daily work of government efficiently but also responds effectively to extraordinary demands?

The Katrina experience puts in sharp relief both the capacity and incapacity of governments to manage in ways that citizens and their representatives have a right to expect.

PART V OVERVIEW

Part V of the book has one chapter, Chapter 12, which (1) summarizes why and how three-dimensional (3D) public management is an effective analytic framework for both the routine and distinctive challenges of public management as well as the inevitable management conundrums and dilemmas revealed by such analysis, and (2) emphasizes the need for public managers to think institutionally about their work in order to ensure their accountability to the rule of law in America's unique scheme of governance. With these habits of mind and practice, public managers can improve the capacities of governments to make decisions, manage people, and cope with the stresses associated with uncertainty, ambiguous mandates, limits on authority and resources, and political conflict. They also improve their personal capacities to think critically and analytically about what the law, the task, common sense, and collective justice require. By doing so, they are more likely to perform effectively and produce results that earn the public's trust.

This part of the book provides answers to the question:

1. How does 3D public management enable public managers to increase the likelihood that they will earn the public's respect and trust—both for their effectiveness in implementing public policies and for accountability to the rule of law in America's pluralistic, often divisive political system?

12 3D PUBLIC MANAGEMENT

Structure, Culture, Craft

INTRODUCTION

Three-dimensional (3D) public management is an approach to deliberation and decision making that, first, analyzes managerial responsibilities and problems from three angles—structure, culture, and craft—then formulates goals and strategies and actions for achieving them. This 3D approach to public management is proactive rather than reactive, a way of moving forward that creates a framework for planning action and for confronting the exigencies of managerial life. While purposeful action may not require using all three dimensions, the 3D approach enables public managers to avoid the trap of thinking too narrowly or reflexively when deliberating and deciding what to do.

To elaborate on this idea, this chapter draws on the preceding 11 chapters of this book and proceeds as follows. First, a high-profile case of public management reform at the local level—the adoption of CompStat in the New York City Police Department—is described. The next section considers the possibilities and necessities for 3D public management as a response to the distinctive challenges described in Chapter 1 and as an essential tool for situations public managers often encounter:

- Responding to early warning
- Connecting the dots
- Confronting a crisis
- Managing in an impossible job
- Managing people
- Reforming public management
- Measuring performance

Next is a discussion of thorny puzzles, both intellectual and practical, that can arise no matter what type of challenge public managers must confront, difficulties that may be termed the typical "conundrums and dilemmas" of public management.

The penultimate section of the chapter returns to the fundamental theme of accountability to the rule of law, depicting an overarching view of how America's constitutional scheme of dependence on private parties and the courts to define and enforce public laws is at the heart of thinking institutionally about public management. It is, as well, a primary rationale for 3D public management. The chapter then returns to the opening case in Chapter 9—the *Columbia* space shuttle crash and subsequent analyses. It emphasizes the importance of three-dimensional analysis in identifying causal factors contributing to the tragedy and in planning a reform strategy to preclude future disasters in the space shuttle program.

CASE: COMPSTAT IN 3D

Soon after being appointed commissioner of New York City's police department by Mayor Rudolph Giuliani in 1994, William J. Bratton launched a reform initiative that came to be regarded as so successful in reducing crime that the initiative's core elements were replicated in state and local government jurisdictions across the country. In 1996, this initiative, known as **CompStat,** received an Innovation in American Government Award from the John F. Kennedy School of Government even though it had been operational for only 2 years. The Kennedy School Case Program published a teaching case, "Assertive Policing, Plummeting Crime," that is widely used in public affairs education.[1] The Harvard Business School also published a teaching case on Bratton's leadership of the New York Police Department (NYPD).

What Is CompStat?

Commissioner Bratton and his deputy for operations, an experienced police official named Jack Maple, initially adopted the kind of strategy that had been successful for Bratton when he headed the New York Transit Authority. They rejected the community policing strategy of Bratton's predecessor in favor of a strategy involving four elements:

- quality-of-life policing (focusing on those crimes and misdemeanors that affect large numbers of citizens directly or indirectly),
- assertive policing,
- devolving authority to the precincts, and
- the psychological touch.

Bratton publicly announced an ambitious goal of reducing crime in New York City by 10 percent in the first year of the new strategy, thus putting himself on the hook for achieving a specific outcome. The reform initiative encompassed all three dimensions of public management:

- **Structure:** precinct commanders were given real authority to devise and implement strategies appropriate to their jurisdictions, whether in pursuit of citywide anticrime strategies or in response to local "hot spots" and special problems;

(Continued)

(Continued)

- **Culture:** changing the police mind-set from law enforcement to crime prevention; and
- **Craft:** Bratton and Maple and their subordinates became personally and intensely involved in managing all aspects of the CompStat process.

That process centered on creating an accountability mechanism. Bratton and Maple decided they wanted to see the crime statistics by precinct on a weekly basis. However, crime statistics were compiled quarterly and primarily for the FBI Uniform Crime Statistics, not for managerial purposes. Bratton and Maple devised a series of specific steps so the figures could be used as an accountability mechanism:

- make precinct commanders provide briefings to command staff on the weekly numbers, maintain up-to-date pin maps, and prepare acetate overlays;
- bring borough commanders and precinct commanders together on a regular basis to discuss the numbers, and address detailed questions;
- set an ambitious goal on which all personnel would focus: reduce crime by 10 percent;
- institutionalize the weekly meetings: the maps were computerized and became the basis for the discussions, and the name CompStat was coined, referring to computerized comparison crime statistics;
- establish a tradition of tough, unsentimental interactions, resembling interrogations, between command staff and precinct commanders;
- encourage the process to trickle down, so that precinct commanders and tour commanders begin using the process; and, as experience is gained,
- refine the model, focusing on

  o accurate and timely intelligence on crime;
  o rapid deployment of policing resources;
  o effective tactics for addressing problems; and
  o relentless follow-up and assessment.

The four-part refinement became a mantra among CompStat's NYPD leadership. Internal restructuring was essential to this system. As criminal justice scholar Paul O'Connell puts it,

> **Bratton and Maple were skilled craftsmen in translating their new structures and processes into changes in the NYPD culture.**

An emphasis was placed upon the realignment of organizational resources. An ambitious reengineering effort shifted the department from being a centralized, functional organization to a decentralized, geographic organization. A number of centralized, functional units were broken up with their functions (and personnel) redistributed to new geographically decentralized units (precincts). Functional specialists were placed under the command of newly defined geographic managers, thereby moving decision making down the organizational hierarchy.[2]

Bratton and Maple were skilled craftsmen in translating their new structures and processes into changes in the NYPD culture. For example, when challenged if he knew how much time it would take to produce pin maps, Maple responded, "Yes, 18 minutes." He had run a test of the process in the busiest precinct. Faced with complaints that precinct commanders and their staff would be unable to attend meetings, command staff set an earlier time so that no one could claim unavailability. The 10 percent goal for crime reduction was set after weeks of experience with meetings and with detailed analyses of the crime statistics. An extraordinary amount of operational knowledge, credibility, and self-confidence was needed to make the weekly sessions effective. In O'Connell's view, "The department was seeking to institutionalize the organizational learning process."[3]

Why Did CompStat Succeed in New York City?

A number of factors seem to have contributed to the CompStat success story, reflecting structure, culture, and craft dimensions:

- The timely availability of operational numbers (which had to be created from scratch) and the implicit use of performance benchmarking across precincts supported a data-centered process to the problems of crime. Visibility and actionability followed.
- The increased discretion allowed to precinct commanders and the deregulation of policing were the structural enablers of cultural change within the department. Increased discretion empowered precinct commanders in ways they had not experienced before. "Quality of life" policing amounted in effect to deregulation of policing.
- The processes of intense scrutiny of precinct operations, the regularity of the meetings, and the wearing down of resistance and building up of a new value system were undoubtedly helped by the fact that police departments are paramilitary organizations with strong boundaries (everyone inside faces a common mission and a common danger, and there is a chain of command, a system of discipline).
- The objective was unmistakably clear: reduce crime.
- Bratton, Maple, and Chief of Patrol Louis Anemone were unusual in their toughness, competence, and determination; it is unlikely that police officials of ordinary managerial talent could have succeeded so quickly and so well.

In addition to the influence of CompStat, many factors associated with crime reduction could have been moving independently of the reform. Some researchers argued that long-term cycles in illegal drug use, restrictive gun laws dating to the mid-1980s, expanded police departments and prison systems, demographic trends, and the collective influence of family, community groups, and police, not CompStat, were responsible for crime reduction in New York. Criminal justice scholar Dennis Smith and Bratton rebut these claims: demographics—the crime-prone young male population was actually increasing; drugs—no substantial declines in drug use; gun control—decline in gun crimes was probably due to the NYPD strategy, not an exogenous reduction in guns; the economy—improvement in city economy followed, rather than preceded, crime reductions.[4]

Even so, CompStat's apparent success does not mean that its implementation posed no problems or challenges. Quality-of-life policing led to visible and invisible increases in police misconduct, increased tensions with the minority community, and declining confidence in the police department on the part

(Continued)

(Continued)

of the public. High-profile police misconduct and an adversarial relationship between police and civilians became the norm. Though crime fell, complaints and general controversy increased. The implication was that there was a trade-off between a "broken windows" strategy (which punishes routine violations in order to heighten citizen awareness of law enforcement) and police misconduct, especially toward minority young people. Former New York City mayor David Dinkins claimed that the Giuliani administration believed that the ends justify the means, and the public was coming around to the view that police brutality was tolerated.

Certain performance measures, such as gun confiscation, tended to have a corrupting influence on police officers, some of whom, it was said, became unjustifiably more aggressive. Street crime officers were expected to confiscate at least one gun per month. Said one officer: "We frisk 20, maybe 30 people a day. Are they all by the book? Of course not; it's safer and easier to just toss people. And if it's the 25th of the month and you haven't gotten your gun yet? Things can get a little desperate."[5]

Giuliani and Bratton's successor, Howard Safir, responded to such claims with a barrage of statistics, all of which seemed to refute the assertion that the NYPD was out of control. One of the authors of the broken windows strategy said that criticism amounted to an "ideological attack on a successful philosophy of policing." Increases in "misconduct" were held to be a statistical artifact because there was now a Civilian Complaints Review Board, more cops were on the street making more arrests, and few complaints were substantiated. The statistics seemed to have little effect on public perceptions, however.

Will CompStat Work Anywhere?

Bratton claimed you can "CompStat" practically anything and raise performance. Some researchers cautioned that the realities of attempting innovation and change in an urban police department or in any other large bureaucracy are more complex than the arguments of CompStat's advocates acknowledge. According to criminal justice specialists James Willis, Stephen Mastrofski, and David Weisburd,

> A review of the research literature suggests that the glowing accounts of CompStat's success are fueled mostly by studies that rely on anecdotal evidence or concentrate on the NYPD, the nation's largest and, by any measure, most exceptional police department. To date, there has been little systematic analysis of CompStat in U.S. police departments of different size and organization. Very little is actually known about how CompStat operates.[6]

The Police Foundation conducted a study of three city police departments that had attempted to replicate CompStat: Lowell, Massachusetts; Minneapolis, Minnesota; and Newark, New Jersey. According to the study, "CompStat's creators and advocates present it as a way to transform sluggish, unresponsive police organizations into focused, efficient, and smart organizations."[7] The basic transformational elements are

- motivated employees who are guided by a focused mission, disciplined, and stimulated by a rigorous system of direct and personal accountability;
- organizational nimbleness, or a capacity to deliver resources to places and at times that will nip problems in the bud;

- organizational decisions informed by knowledge of the problems that require attention beyond that provided by normal organizational routines and facilitated by sophisticated electronic information management and data-analysis systems;
- problem-solving that reflects collaboration and exchange of ideas among members of an organization, draws on research dealing with successful practices, and acknowledges the experience of other agencies; and
- decision making in an atmosphere that has an elevated tolerance for risk and encourages new approaches to persistent problems.[8]

The study's fieldwork suggested that the alterations to fundamental organizational structures needed to facilitate these changes were not fully in place in the three police departments it examined. For example, CompStat implementation in Lowell

> placed greatest emphasis on mission clarification and internal accountability. Members of the department had a strong sense of the department's crime-fighting goal, and district commanders felt highly accountable for identifying and responding to crime problems. Holding officials responsible for attaining valued objectives embraces existing attributes of bureaucracies that are goal oriented and organized hierarchically. Those elements that did not fit easily with existing bureaucratic structures were much less developed. The department was unable or unwilling to shift substantially toward geographic operational command, flexibility, data-driven analysis, innovations in problem solving, or external accountability. The collective benefits of existing bureaucratic structures—formalization, routine, and functional specialization—make them difficult to surrender for the promise of uncertain gains.[9]

The report's authors further observe, "CompStat . . . was in good part a response to what was seen as bureaucratic dysfunction in the New York City Police Department. However . . . CompStat itself may also be prone to bureaucratic dysfunction, though of a very different type than that which spawned the program."[10]

Public management scholar Robert Behn has analyzed and observed many **PerformanceStat** initiatives over a number of years. He rejects an overemphasis on specifying components of a PerformanceStat system that will guarantee success, observing "if you've seen one PerformanceStat, you've seen one PerformanceStat."[11] Instead Behn stresses the importance of adaptation and a concerted leadership strategy. He identifies 16 leadership behaviors that are likely to be associated with PerformanceStat success, including "Creating targets can specify exactly what needs to be done by when," "Distributing comparative data widely can help every team appraise, without delusions, its own performance," and "Scrutinizing the positive deviants can facilitate everyone's learning."[12]

Will CompStat or reforms like it work in any kind of agency? Its implementation perhaps seemed straightforward. But even within similar settings of other police departments, implementation was difficult. In different settings, such as child protection services, public school systems, or counterterrorism operations, the challenges to extending the model are likely to multiply. Some considerations that bear on the success of replication include

(Continued)

(Continued)

- repetitive operations,
- ease of assembling the chain of command in one location,
- hierarchical managerial control,
- adequate resources,
- adequate, timely data,
- political support sufficient to withstand criticism and opposition, and
- local talent sufficient for the intense demands of the process.

CompStat will not work anywhere, in any jurisdiction, or with any public service unless considerable care is taken to replicate those features of CompStat that were operative in the NYPD. But policy and service improvements may follow from the aggressive use of operational data by managers, by relentless follow-up, and by other actions that were part of the CompStat model.

In subsequent years after CompStat, William J. Bratton would move on to become chief of the Los Angeles, California, Police Department. On January 1, 2014, he began a second stint as commissioner of the NYPD, this time as an appointee of a New York City mayor who was a liberal Democrat. Once New York City's leading crime fighter, Bratton's mission the second time around would be different, reflecting changing times. "We will all work hard to identify why is it that so many in this city do not feel good about this department that has done so much to make them safe—what has it been about our activities that have made so many alienated?"[13]

DISTINCTIVE CHALLENGES OF PUBLIC MANAGEMENT: MANAGING IN 3D

Most managerial strategies, as emphasized throughout the book, are likely to involve two or more dimensions. The need for managerial effectiveness is especially urgent when public managers operate in situations that are extraordinary in scope and consequence. In Chapter 1, such situations were called **distinctive challenges of public management:**

1. Confronting situations where solutions are beyond the manager's span of control

2. Being responsive to powerful actors whose preferences and expectations are in conflict

3. Ensuring accountability when control is lacking

4. Learning about serious problems from outside sources

5. Operating under constant critical scrutiny

6. Making consequential decisions with partial information

7. Contending with employees' ingrained values and beliefs

8. Responding in a timely fashion to shifts in priorities

Examples of these challenges in specific contexts have been offered throughout the book. Further examples include

- ensuring that urban police departments under pressure to control crime also respect the civil rights of the citizens they are sworn to protect;
- changing the missions of federal and state agencies responsible for homeland security from prosecuting criminals to preventing acts of terrorism;
- introducing new information technologies to improve the effectiveness of organizations, when employees might perceive the change as threatening to their security and importance to the organization;
- achieving an appropriate balance between protecting children from harm and strengthening and unifying troubled families in the administration of child welfare policies and programs that call for removing children from homes if circumstances justify it; and
- managing regulatory agencies to achieve a reasonable balance between promoting and negotiating voluntary compliance with regulations and impartially detecting and punishing violators in areas such as airline, mine, and consumer product safety.

Combinations of effective enabling structures, functional organizational cultures, and managerial leadership and skill can result in effective responses to these kinds of challenges. But workable solutions that have a reasonable likelihood of success are usually not obvious:

- Do the policies governing agency operations enable or stand in the way of needed change?
- Are assignments of responsibilities to and within the agency and resources available to the agency—financial, human, and technical—adequate to meeting organizational objectives?
- Will agency personnel accept new directions or must internal resistance be overcome?
- Do public managers have the motivation, knowledge, and skills to discover and accomplish what needs to be done to reach the objectives?

Effective public management analysis, described in Chapter 1 and illustrated throughout the book, will vary by the specifics of the situation. Structural change may not be necessary, cultures may be functional, or subordinates may be experienced and effective, all of which eases the burden of leadership. Diagnosing a situation and making good decisions concerning what kinds of strategies might be appropriate will depend not only on the facts of a situation but also on the public manager's particular temperament and skill set. One manager might decide not to reorganize but to address organizational interdependence through more effective communications, and another might decide that only structural change will provide the capacity to address similar problems that might arise in the future. A manager might be particularly adept at crisis management but less effective in managing day-to-day operations, where a manager with different temperament and skills might excel.

For many, public management analysis is a matter of intuition, of instinctively recognizing the importance of managerial direction and leadership, of appropriate organizational arrangements, and of the taken-for-granted beliefs and values of those who are employed at various levels of governance. But, as discussed in Chapter 11, intuition may not be a reliable foundation for effective action if it is based on a restricted range of experience or a dogmatic certainty that only leadership or only reorganization or only changing hearts and minds will suffice to solve a problem. To guard against faulty intuition, in one's self or one's advisers, the **model deliberative process** described in Chapter 1 can ensure that a full range of possibilities are considered, drawing on the three dimensions of public management.

A number of generic problems or processes that public managers encounter often exhibit at least one of the distinctive challenges and can be aided by three-dimensional management analysis. The following sections discuss these: responding to early warning, connecting the dots, confronting a crisis, managing in an impossible job, managing people, transforming an organization, and measuring performance.

Responding to Early Warning

Public managers may receive early warnings of possible crises or dangers:

- The warnings may be speculative and controversial predictions of possibilities in the distant future for which no specific organization is responsible, such as the earliest concerns about global warming in the 1970s.
- The warnings may be specific but still uncertain regarding events that could materialize at any time and affect specific organizations. Emergency preparedness experts were confident that New Orleans eventually would be struck by a devastating hurricane, but no one could say when.

Analytical journalist Malcolm Gladwell argues that it may be wrong to look backward to see if there were warning signs of a devastating event, and then conclude that if there were, they *should* have been heeded.[14] Many public managers face continuous, repeated warnings of varying degrees of specificity and credibility about a great many potential dangers. The vast majority of them, Gladwell says, turn out to be wrong. Therefore, not all threats can or should be taken seriously. There will always be more warnings than resource. There will always be lots of noise in the flow of information. It is necessary, Gladwell says, to set priorities.

In these kinds of situations, psychological factors come into play, as described in Chapter 11. People are apt to be more sensitive to warnings similar to past failures or warnings of events. They are apt to be biased in their assessments of threats. Gladwell's analysis of why Israeli leaders failed to react to the threat of the Yom Kippur War in 1973 is convincing. Warned on the morning of October 6 that the attack would occur later that day, the Israelis did nothing, and the attack did in fact occur later that day. But many such warnings had been received from the same sources in the past, the Israelis had prepared for an attack, and nothing had happened. Similarly, foam shedding from the space shuttle launch vehicle's external fuel tanks had become such common occurrences that they were not considered to be warnings of impending trouble until trouble happened.

Example: Early Warnings of Global Warming

Beginning in the mid to late 1970s, expert, media, and public opinion on climate change shifted. The new view, that the world was facing the prospect of global warming, constituted an early warning that governments, and especially the Environmental Protection Agency (EPA), would likely be required to take action to reduce greenhouse gas emissions.

A well-respected geochemist, Wallace Broecker, took the lead in 1975, warning in an influential *Science* magazine article that the world might be poised on the brink of a serious rise of temperature. "Complacency may not be warranted," he said. "We may be in for a climatic surprise."[15]

In April 2007, a generation later, the U.S. Supreme Court ordered the EPA to explain why its refusal to regulate carbon dioxide emissions from motor vehicles was in compliance with the Clean Air Act. In December, the EPA responded with a report concluding that greenhouse gases must be controlled. According to a *New York Times* account quoting agency officials, the White House told the agency that "an e-mail message containing the document would not be opened." This meant the report had no official status. In mid-2008, the EPA issued a version of the report that showed how warming might be dealt with and then proclaimed that no action would be taken.

Early warnings and the responses to them are likely to reflect all three dimensions of public management:

- structural and procedural arrangements that either encourage or discourage and impede the communication and interpretation of such warnings;
- cultural factors that predispose employees to react to warnings in certain ways, ranging from shrugging them off to overreacting; and
- inclinations and deliberative skills of public managers, similarly ranging from eye-rolling skepticism to "the sky is falling" zeal.

Prudence suggests, however, that ignoring early warning and its implications altogether is unwise. The magnitude of the risks, the consequences of being wrong, and the possibility of irreversible harm need to be carefully considered.

Connecting the Dots

Public managers may confront situations in which relevant bits of information for identifying a problem are widely dispersed. These bits may appear in known and unknown locations; they may be within or beyond the manager's jurisdiction. If assembled and analyzed, these bits—dots—might reveal a clearer picture of the problem and provide a basis for addressing it. But a particular official may be unaware of what others know. Connecting these dots may be costly and time-consuming.

A well-known example of such a **connecting-the-dots problem** was assessing the terrorist threat prior to the attacks of September 11, 2001. Bits of potentially relevant information were scattered throughout the intelligence community. But because of factors relating to public policy structures, organizational cultures, and managerial craft, they were never assembled for analysis.

Connecting-the-dots problems often arise when criminal suspects or individuals posing threats to homeland security are moving across various surveillance and law enforcement jurisdictions. They arise when individuals suffering chronic mental illness or other debilitating conditions experience acute episodes or become criminal suspects while away from their home jurisdictions and service providers. Service workers, supervisors, and managers must try to assemble information relevant to accurate diagnosis and appropriate intervention.

In the immediate situation, the premium is likely to be on managerial craft: skill in identifying relevant sources of information, eliciting cooperation, and using partial information to create perceptive conjectures or hypotheses as to

In the longer run, three-dimensional analysis comes into play in creating institutional arrangements that ensure timely and effective responses.

the precise nature of the situation. In the longer run, three-dimensional analysis comes into play in creating institutional arrangements that ensure timely and effective responses. Effective diagnosis and intervention require

- structures, such as networks, incident command protocols, resource-sharing agreements, and communications systems;
- attitudes that regard cooperation and information sharing built on trust as normal and taken-for-granted; and
- managerial leadership in mobilizing preexisting structures and cultures on behalf of the immediate challenge quickly and nondefensively.

Example: A 3D Solution to Connecting-the-Dots Problem in the U.S. Department of Veterans Affairs (VA)

A hotline created by the VA to prevent suicides by veterans in distress is an example of 3D response to a connect-the-dots problem. Urged to call the hotline by a VA official, a veteran named Robert told the social worker who answered that he wanted to "just lay down in the river and never get up." According to a *New York Times* account, the social worker "gave an assistant Robert's phone number to find his address and alert local police to stand by. The chain of care resembled a relay race, with one runner trying not [to] let go of the baton until the next runner had it in hand."[16] The hotlines enable counselors for the first time "to instantly check a veteran's medical records and then combine emergency response with local follow-up services." VA leadership saw to it that structures were in place and staffed by those with a cultural commitment to veterans' suicide prevention.

Structural solutions that depend on timely information sharing may encounter privacy issues, such as statutes and regulations that preclude organizations from releasing certain information at all or without consent or court approval.[i] Such concerns arise in counterterrorism and homeland security activities (as described in Chapter 3), law enforcement, medical diagnosis and treatment, the determination of benefits eligibility, and the administration of financial transactions.

Some organizational cultures encourage information sharing, while others emphasize information protection and nondisclosure. In emergency situations, connecting the dots may, therefore, require a high order of leadership skill and timing.

Confronting a Crisis

Public managers may confront the need to manage under emergency conditions where lives and property are at stake. Hurricane Katrina confronted officials at all levels of government with unprecedented demands on their time, resources, and managerial acumen. Many of them lost credibility in the aftermath. Similar demands followed the September 11 attacks. A formerly controversial mayor, Rudolph Giuliani, became a popular hero.

But situations amounting to a crisis may arrive from oblique angles. In November 2007, officials in the District of Columbia, from the mayor on down, were suddenly confronted with the indictment and arrest of two midlevel officials in the Office of Tax and Revenue, who were accused of stealing tens of millions of dollars even though auditors had long warned that something—they did not know what—was amiss in revenue administration.

---

[i]For information on information sharing concerning terrorism, law enforcement, and other aspects of national security, see Information Sharing Environment, http://www.ise.gov/index.html.

If an agency faces a likelihood of crises, contingency planning is a reasonable structural response:

- Crisis scenarios are created and simulated.
- Officials evaluate their responses to the simulated circumstances to determine what additional preparations are needed to ensure an adequate response should an actual crisis occur.
- Plans include the preparation of protocols to allocate responsibilities and guide action in an emergency.
- Preparation may require contentious negotiations:
  - o police and fire departments may disagree over which agency should be the first responder to particular kinds of emergency or what frequencies should be used on radios; or
  - o public and nonprofit agencies may disagree over the sharing of responsibilities and resources.

Example: The National Incident Management System (NIMS)

The Federal Emergency Management Agency (FEMA) oversees the NIMS. It provides a common framework for different kinds of incidents, across different jurisdictions, and aims to improve coordination across both public and private organizations:

> While most emergency situations are handled locally, when there's a major incident help may be needed from other jurisdictions, the state, and the federal government. NIMS was developed so responders from different jurisdictions and disciplines can work together better to respond to natural disasters and emergencies, including acts of terrorism. NIMS benefits include a unified approach to incident management; standard command and management structures; and emphasis on preparedness, mutual aid, and resource management.[17]

Crises may evoke the kinds of pathologies of deliberation and decision making discussed in Chapter 11, prominently including groupthink. Culture conflicts between and within agencies may be exacerbated. The leak of sensitive or embarrassing information may cause officials to become unthinkingly defensive when they should be using deliberation and decision-making processes to address problems.

Unwelcome realities are a test of managerial leadership and craft. Giuliani was widely praised for his leadership—appearing on the scene with inspirational courage—in mobilizing New York City's post-9/11 response. In sharp contrast, the ineffectual responses of Bush administration officials to Hurricane Katrina were widely criticized and had long-lasting political repercussions.

Managing in an Impossible Job

Impossible Jobs in Public Management, an edited volume published in 1990, grew out of the intuition that some public management jobs, especially in state and local government, are so difficult as to be virtually undoable.[18] The volume was edited and partially written by Erwin Hargrove, a political scientist, and John C. Glidewell, a psychologist, along with a group of collaborators. The collaboration produced a model with four dimensions of possibility/impossibility:

- *The legitimacy (or deservingness) of the public manager's clientele*: Children, those in need of medical treatment, veterans, and farmers are usually regarded as deserving of public support, but welfare recipients, suspected and convicted criminals, suspected terrorists, and the chronically mentally ill are viewed, if not as undeserving, at least as intractable.

- *The intensity of conflict among the agency's constituencies*: Should welfare mothers be given income support or forced to go to work? Should prisoners be punished or rehabilitated? Should the mentally ill be hospitalized or sustained in their own communities? Such issues are likely to produce intense, protracted political conflict.
- *Public confidence in the authority of the public manager's profession*: Physicians, agricultural extension agents, and maternal and child health nurses are held in esteem, but inner city school superintendents (Paul Vallas, discussed in Chapter 11, was a clear and arguably rare exception), social workers, and corrections officers have relatively low professional status.
- *The strength of the agency "myth," the extent of sustained public commitment to an ideal worth pursuing and public understanding and acceptance of the difficulties and altruistic sacrifice inherent in providing the service*: Fire departments, public health agencies, and many environmental protection agencies usually enjoy good reputations for serving the public interest, but welfare agencies, many local law enforcement agencies, and urban school boards are often not accorded the benefit of the doubt by a skeptical public.

Impossible jobs are those in which the actors

> must serve irresponsible and intractable clients in intense conflicts with more legitimate clients for public resources; must satisfy multiple and intensely polarized, active constituencies; possess professional, scientific authority that commands little public respect; and are guided by weak, controversial myths that cannot sustain policy continuity.[19]

In contrast, officials with "possible" jobs serve a legitimate clientele with little political conflict and enjoy public respect for the expertise needed to perform their jobs and for the reputation for effectiveness of their agencies.

Example: Rod Hickman and the California Department of Corrections

Roderick Q. Hickman was sworn in as secretary of the California Department of Corrections (CDC) on November 17, 2003, the first day of Governor Arnold Schwarzenegger's administration. A little more than 2 years later, near the end of February 2006, Hickman abruptly resigned.

On their basis of their research, Hargrove and Glidewell might well have warned Hickman about his future. The position of corrections commissioner was, according to their analytical framework, the quintessential impossible job. Still, the circumstances were ripe with possibility.

Hickman seemed ideal for the challenges of his new position. When named to the post, he was serving as the CDC's chief deputy director for field operations. Prior to that assignment, he was assistant deputy director of operations and programs of CDC's Institutions Division. Before that, he was the northern regional administrator for the Institutions Division and was warden of Mule Creek State Prison in Amador County. Hickman began his CDC career in June 1979 as a correctional officer at the California Institution for Men in Chino. At the same time, he earned degrees in public administration, attended courses in leadership development and often spoke to professional and community groups.

Schwarzenegger had campaigned on the promise to solve the problems of overcrowding, violence, rising costs, poor medical care, and high rates of recidivism that were overwhelming California's prison system. Although a system insider, Hickman was committed to shifting the emphasis away from punishment toward rehabilitation. He said his mission was "to bring social sector organizations into prison and parole reform."[20] Corrections employees and advocates for prison reform were optimistic that Hickman would be able to bring about real and constructive change in the agency. His leadership team devoted long hours to crafting the specific measures that they believed would accomplish the governor's and Hickman's reform goals.

Within a year, however, Hickman was under fire from an unexpected quarter: "the labor union that represented him for 20 years. . . . When Gov. Arnold Schwarzenegger appointed [him], correctional officers rejoiced that, finally, one of their own would be running the show. At the same time, skeptics questioned whether he would stand up to the union, a formidable force inside the prisons and beyond." Unexpectedly, union leaders were soon routinely bashing Hickman and labeling him "an embarrassment."[21] A *Los Angeles Times* article reported,

> Hickman said he does not worry about the attacks on his performance, but that he receives many calls and e-mails from officers and supervisors concerned about the criticism and supportive of his work. Pulling out his hand-held computer, Hickman shared two new e-mail messages—one from an associate warden, another from a sergeant— praising a recent videotape he distributed on the code of silence. "We're heading in a new direction," Hickman said. The prison guards union "can get on the train or get left at the station."[22]

On the news of Hickman's departure, a union spokesman said, "Our members are tired, they're demoralized, we have an unclear chain of command, and the management team is in complete disarray. It all happened under Mr. Hickman's watch."[23]

Criticism also began to be heard from the other side: the reform groups that had put their faith in Schwarzenegger and Hickman. In an editorial, the *Los Angeles Times* cited an example of the mounting frustrations:

> In 2004, the state expanded a program begun under Gov. Gray Davis to send nonviolent parole violators to halfway houses, home detention, or jail-based drug treatment programs. It was a badly needed effort to reduce the prison population and cut recidivism by helping addicts get the kind of treatment they weren't getting in prison. A year later, as a victims' rights group, heavily supported by the guards union, was running misleading commercials claiming that the program was endangering the public, Hickman abruptly dropped it. Then he had to revive it two months later under orders from a federal judge.[24]

As a reason for his resignation, Hickman cited dwindling support from the governor and his staff for the reforms he had initiated. California's "political environment and the power of special interests work against efforts to bring about lasting reform."[25] Opposition from the correction officers union, whose contract gave its leaders influence over any change in the workplace, became a particular liability and appeared to cause the governor's office to back away from Hickman's aggressive program. Reform groups in turn expressed disappointment at the slow pace of change. Finally, legislators began weighing in, questioning Hickman's progress. The situation had repercussions nationwide. Said the chief of corrections in Ohio, "Nobody believes you can do your craft there. Nobody is going to come to a place where the environment just makes it impossible to do the business of corrections."[26] (Hickman was replaced by his deputy.)

Following his resignation, even the media distanced itself from the once-popular Hickman. The *Los Angeles Times* editorialized,

Running this state's prisons is a thankless job. On one side are legislators demanding quick fixes to intractable problems and federal courts that are dividing up responsibility over the prisons piecemeal; on the other is a guards union wielding its enormous political clout to squelch most changes. Hickman, standing in the middle, had only one ally he could count on: Gov. Arnold Schwarzenegger, who now seems to have moved on to other things. . . . [Hickman] may be remembered as a man who said all the right things but did few of them, buffeted as he was by competing interests and problems beyond his control.[27]

Often, say Hargrove and Glidewell, the tenure of those with impossible jobs "is short and their accomplishments are limited, but they persist in doing the best they can until they burn out or are fired."[28] Coping, in other words, may be the only way to secure any gains at all when the odds are against you.

But that view is too pessimistic. Jobs with reputations as being impossible need not be entirely beyond the influence of effective managerial leadership, or of the value of deliberation within a model deliberative framework. FEMA, and Alabama's child welfare agencies, regarded at one time as exceedingly difficult (if not impossible) to manage, experienced turnarounds and achieved real excellence after sustained periods of capable management.[ii] Such management will almost invariably be not only three-dimensional but also cognizant of the complex patterns of overlap and interdependence among the three dimensions.

Hickman may have erred by overemphasizing the power of his craft and the efficacy of structural/procedural techniques and underemphasizing the primary importance of the organization's culture and its potential influence on both craft and structure. He persisted in a strategy of aggressive entrepreneurship in circumstances that called for a different strategy—employing the power of professionalism and expertise, which Hickman possessed in abundance. His persistent use of rewards and punishments alienated his most powerful rival, the union, and that alienation was a significant contributor to his undoing. Hickman might also have taken greater care to heed the advice of experts such as Mark Moore and Gordon Chase, discussed in Chapter 11, to spend more time "managing upward" and preserving the all-important support of his boss, the governor.[iii]

> Hickman may have erred by overemphasizing the power of his craft and the efficacy of structural/procedural techniques and underemphasizing the primary importance of the organization's culture and its potential influence on both craft and structure.

But such persistence appeared to be less a matter of miscalculation than of Hickman's temperament. To waste an opportunity to lead by merely coping must have seemed unthinkable to him. More calculation might have helped. Had he successfully practiced 3D management, he might not have achieved all that he hoped for but more than he did.

Managing People

Public managers must decide whether and how to hire, supervise, reward, train, promote, and discipline employees in their organizations. In recent years, management of these tasks has become known as **human resource management** or **human capital management**, reflecting the shift in emphasis from a primarily structural

---

[ii]A history and status of the lawsuit that instigated the child welfare reforms in Alabama is at http://www.youthlaw.org/ publications/fc_ docket/alpha/rcvwally. An assessment of the reforms themselves is *Making Child Welfare Work: How the R.C. Lawsuit Forged New Partnerships to Protect Children and Sustain Families,* Bazelon Center for Mental Health Law, Washington, DC, May 1998.

[iii]See John J. DiIulio, "Managing a Barbed-Wire Bureaucracy: The Impossible Job of Corrections Commissioner," in *Impossible Jobs in Public Management,* ed. Erwin C. Hargrove and John. C. Glidewell (Lawrence: University Press of Kansas, 1990), 49–71.

approach of managing employees to an approach that engages all three dimensions. Reforms to personnel systems have introduced flexibility, managerial discretion, pay for performance, and decentralization, as described in Chapter 5.[29] And with these changes comes the need for three-dimensional management.

The leadership and best practices literatures are both concerned with managing people. Among works mentioned in Chapter 11, Richard N. Haass's *The Bureaucratic Entrepreneur: How to be Effective in Any Unruly Organization* offers down-to-earth, practical advice to managers on, for example, organizing staff, being a successful boss, delegation, and being loyal to subordinates. Not surprisingly, says Haass, treating your people as you yourself want to be treated is a good way to be effective. In *Caught Between the Dog and the Fireplug, or How to Survive in Public Service,* Kenneth H. Ashworth, an experienced practitioner, insists that good bosses figure out a way to work for those under them; they delegate but are accessible for advice and counsel; and they keep people focused on the mission of the organization.[30] Earning respect and loyalty, then, is a matter of showing respect and loyalty to one's own people.

People management is necessarily three dimensional. All three dimensions are evident, for example, in a self-assessment developed by the Government Accountability Office for agency managers to use in weighing their human capital policies and needs:

1. Strategic Planning: Establish the agency's mission, vision for the future, core values, goals and objectives, and strategies.

2. Organizational Alignment: Integrate human capital strategies with the agency's core business practices.

3. Leadership: Foster a committed leadership team and provide reasonable continuity through succession planning.

4. Talent: Recruit, hire, develop, and retain employees with the skills for mission accomplishment.

5. Performance Culture: Empower and motivate employees while ensuring accountability and fairness in the workplace.[31]

An increased focus on the cultural and craft dimensions of management that affect human capital policies is consistent with the ideas of John Brehm and Scott Gates and William Ouchi, discussed in Chapter 9. These ideas emphasize the importance of the hiring function as perhaps the best way to ensure that employees will act in ways consistent with the organization's mission.[iv]

Reforming Public Management

European scholars Christopher Pollitt and Geert Bouckaert define **public management reform** as "deliberate changes to the structures and processes of public sector organizations with the objective of getting them (in some sense) to run better."[32]

From the three-dimensional perspective, policymakers (external actors) and public managers (internal actors) employ their craft—their temperament, skills, and values—to change a structural and cultural status quo, whether

---

[iv]John Brehm and Scott Gates, *Working, Shirking, and Sabotage: Bureaucratic Response to a Democratic Public* (Ann Arbor: University of Michigan Press, 1999); William G. Ouchi, "A Conceptual Framework for the Design of Organizational Control Mechanisms," *Management Science* 25, no. 9 (1979): 833–848. The importance of employee screening and hiring is also emphasized by Anthony M. Bertelli and Laurence E. Lynn Jr., in *Madison's Managers: Public Administration and the Constitution* (Baltimore, MD: Johns Hopkins University Press, 2006).

it be of the government as a whole or of a department, bureau, or program, to engineer a better outcome. These actors typically use structures as leverage for changing results for the better: In contrast to people or cultures, structures are most clearly under their control.

Because they are given significant publicity, deliberate reforms, whether externally or internally generated, are the most visible of the many kinds of changes in public management policies and practices that occur with regularity at all levels of government.[v] Examples of large-scale initiatives discussed in the book include the congressionally initiated Government Performance and Results Act of 1993 (GPRA) (Chapter 6) and the Reinventing Government (ReGo) initiative of the Clinton administration (Chapter 5).

Yet large-scale initiatives are not the only or primary sources of reform. Public management scholar Michael Barzelay observes,

> A focus on initiatives is less helpful in comprehending what governments are actually doing, for two main reasons. First, some changes in public management policy happen without being included in an initiative. . . . Second, focusing on initiatives often permits only a vague understanding of policy content. A clearer understanding requires an effort to specify either the policy instruments or programs of action involved, or both.[33]

Reforms often reflect the efforts of officials operating well below the political radar screen on behalf of specific organizational, programmatic, or personal goals. These might include adoption of

- new tools of action,
- new forms of organization, and
- new ways to perform governmental functions, such as
  - budgeting and budget execution,
  - personnel administration,
  - new techniques of communication and coordination, and
  - new managerial strategies for accomplishing organizational change and performance.

Examples of specific reform initiatives aimed at improving governmental performance include the following:

- The Chief Financial Officers Act of 1990
- The creation of the Department of Homeland Security in 2002
- The creation of the Directorate of National Intelligence in 2004
- State-level reorganizations of child welfare agencies
- Presidential and gubernatorial reorganizations of executive offices and their functions
- Privatization initiatives
- State-level efforts to facilitate college students' transferring credits from one institution to another

---

[v]A useful overview of American federal government reform initiatives is James P. Pfiffner, "The American Tradition of Administrative Reform," in *The White House and the Blue House: Government Reform in the United States and Korea,* ed. Yong Hyo Cho and H. George Frederickson (Lanham, MD: University Press of American, 1998).

- The launching of a website that enables citizens to track government performance measures
- A city program that recruits and trains high school dropouts to work in home construction
- The adoption of strategic planning and performance measurement processes by an agency's management[vi]

Many public management scholars regard the seemingly routine, below-the-radar reforms as cumulatively more significant than the more politically visible initiatives: "The bulk of the improvements in government efficiency that have taken place in recent years have resulted not so much from overt, grandiose reform schemes as from a host of modest, tactical reforms."[34] Such expert-driven reforms often originate in one state or municipality and then quietly diffuse to other jurisdictions through professional networks.

> **Many public management scholars regard the seemingly routine, below-the-radar reforms as cumulatively more significant than the more politically visible initiatives.**

Public Managers as Change Agents

Many public management reforms are internally generated. They are initiated not by legislators, judges, or elected executives but by public managers in departments, bureaus, and offices at all levels of government. For example, as director of FEMA in the 1990s, James Lee Witt earned a reputation for successful agency transformation.[35]

Managers may be motivated by external pressures (such as legislatures or powerful stakeholders), by their own desire to improve organizational performance, or by their desire to strengthen policy control over subordinate officials and offices. Public managers may redesign processes of deliberation and decision making, introduce new administrative technologies or abolish old ones, introduce new best practices, reallocate responsibilities, create new positions not requiring legislative authorization, issue guidelines concerning performance of tasks and functions, or introduce new information technologies and communications methods.

Although these reforms may become as politicized as those initiated by external actors, most do not attract the attention of partisan politics and achieve visibility primarily among experts and specialists. Some of these managerial reforms are primarily structural; others are intended to alter organizational cultures. Some reforms use restructuring as a means of achieving cultural transformation, as discussed in Chapter 9.

Some public managers may proceed with organizational transformation through informal, make-it-up-as-you-go-along activities. Other managers may prefer to conduct a formal or deliberate strategic planning process. A well-known example of a strategic planning process, designed for use in public and nonprofit organizations, is described by public management scholar John M. Bryson. His *Strategic Planning for Public and Nonprofit Organizations: A Guide to Strengthening and Sustaining Organizational Achievement* features a "strategy change cycle," which includes actions such as

- "setting the organization's direction,"
- "making internal and external assessments,"

[vi]These examples are from the website of the "Government Innovators Network," maintained by the Ash Institute for Democratic Governance and Innovation at Harvard University's Kennedy School of Government, http://www.innovations.harvard.edu/.

- "making fundamental decisions," and
- "continually monitoring and assessing the results."[vii]

Real-world strategic planning in political environments is bound to deviate from any specific model procedure. But the model can provide a degree of structure in such situations.

Organizational change often involves all three dimensions of public management, requiring public managers to employ craftsmanship in identifying strategies, including structural changes that will alter organizational cultures toward acceptance of the changes and the adoption of new practices.

Reform as a Political Process

In recent years, dissatisfaction with the status quo and impulses to fix the government have often taken the form of bureaucracy bashing. As political scientist William Gormley has noted, "legislators, chief executives, and judges have beaten up on one another. Even more frequently, they have beaten up on bureaucrats. Not to be outdone, federal bureaucrats have beaten up on state bureaucrats, who in turn have beaten up on local bureaucrats."[36] This kind of punitive reformism, Gormley notes, is in the Madisonian spirit of checks and balances, which make tension and conflict inevitable in American politics and in public management.

Chronic dissatisfaction with the status quo has its costs, however. Public anger toward government can provoke actions by elected officials that are hasty, illconsidered, or opportunistic:

- Meritorious bond issues, ballot initiatives, and tax increases may be impossible to pass.
- Tax caps, term limits, appropriations with restrictive provisions, hiring freezes, denial of appointments, and other antigovernment measures may be approved with little consideration for their consequences.

Public discontent need not have a specific justification, however. Regimes of ordinary competence are also condemned and frequently replaced simply because they become emblematic of "bureaucracy" or of a tiresome status quo: a convenient scapegoat for candidates for office and frustrated voters.

With the ground constantly moving under their feet, public managers may be tempted merely to hunker down: to mollify critics, avoid provocative actions, and manage defensively so as not to jeopardize their careers. The toll on the morale, creativity, and sustained attention to effective service of civil servants can be high. The administrators of public policies face pressures that test and often defeat even the most skilled.

Many reforms also create cross-pressures that result from competing accountability requirements, which public management scholar Robert Behn terms **accountability dilemmas.** He argues that the dilemmas often result in **accountability bias,** in which accountability for finances and accountability for fairness are emphasized

---

[vii]John M. Bryson, *Strategic Planning for Public and Nonprofit Organizations: A Guide to Strengthening and Sustaining Organizational Achievement,* 3rd ed. (San Francisco, CA: Jossey-Bass, 2004). See also Richard D. Young, "Perspectives on Strategic Planning in the Public Sector," http://www.ipspr.sc.edu/publication/Perspectives%20on%20Strategic%20Planning.pdf. For a more critical account of the concept of strategic planning, see Henry Mintzberg, *The Rise and Fall of Strategic Planning* (New York, NY: Free Press, 1994).

because they typically involve more objective, explicit criteria against which to judge than does accountability for performance.[37]

> While management reforms encourage initiative and sometimes even necessitate entrepreneurial behaviors—for example, to continue to provide high levels of service with reduced staff and funding—accountability dynamics continue to reinforce risk-averse rules and process orientations.[38]

At times, reform seems to represent change for its own sake, its methods poorly related to its goals. The inclination to improve the status quo, whether by external or internal actors, is to be expected. If citizens insist, as Americans do, that they are sovereign, and if they differ among themselves as to what the public good requires, then candidates for elective office will compete vigorously to win control over the powers of the state to tax, spend, and regulate economic activity.

The news is not all bad, however. As noted above, public managers may use their own internal authority to become agents of organizational change. If circumstances permit, public managers are likely to be proactive toward their responsibilities and opportunities.

> **Public managers may use their own internal authority to become agents of organizational change. If circumstances permit, public managers are likely to be proactive toward their responsibilities and opportunities.**

In Herbert Kaufman's famous study of federal bureau chiefs, all of them were proactive, goal oriented, and willing to buck the tide.[39] In fact, they were chosen for those qualities. In addition, Kaufman notes, others in their political environments will not allow public managers to be wholly passive; they will make demands and expect responses. The resulting uncertainty of administration is an inevitable concomitant of our political practices and, it can be argued, the price we pay for the long-term stability of our governing arrangements.

The positive legacies of public management reform must also be emphasized. America has been transformed from a sparsely settled agrarian wilderness into a positive state capable of promoting the welfare and security of its citizens and arguably the most powerful nation on earth. Despite extraordinary complexity—America has more government than any nation in the world—the private, nonprofit, and public sectors; federal, state, and local governments; and executive, judicial, and legislative branches somehow contrive to achieve growth, stability, and worldwide influence in a remarkably diverse society.

Measuring Performance

A number of reform efforts at all levels of government feature performance measurement, discussed throughout this book. As a structural mechanism, performance measurement may be imposed by formal authority external to the organization such as the GPRA and the Automated Budget and Evaluation System of Texas (ABEST) or by executive initiatives such as the Clinton administration's ReGo plan and the Bush administration's Program Assessment Rating Tool (PART). Or the structural mechanism can be internally authorized formal authority, as when managers exercise their discretion to implement a measurement system.

While the implementation of a performance management system entails many structural details and concerns, its successful implementation invariably encompasses culture and craft dimensions as well: Performance measurement is inherently a three-dimensional public management challenge.

Among the most visible and important aspects of accountability are concerns with agency, program, and individual performance.[viii] Indeed, "accountability compels some measure or appraisal of performance, particularly of those individuals and agencies with the authority to act on behalf of the public."[40] Robert Behn points out that performance measurement may be used for purposes beyond accountability. Elements of each of the three dimensions can be found in the eight purposes he identifies:

1. evaluate performance
2. control subordinates
3. prepare budgets
4. motivate employees, stakeholders, citizens, and contractors
5. promote the agency to principals
6. celebrate accomplishments
7. learn about what is working and not working
8. improve performance[41]

In a similar vein, performance measurement expert Harry Hatry lists eleven ways that performance information could be used, some of which overlap with Behn's list:

1. Respond to elected officials' and the public's demands for accountability
2. Help formulate and justify budget requests
3. Help allocate resources throughout the year
4. Trigger in-depth examinations of why performance problems (or successes) exist
5. Help motivate personnel to continue improving the program
6. Formulate and monitor the performance of contractors and grantees (performance contracting)
7. Provide data for special, in-depth program evaluations
8. Support strategic and other long-term planning efforts (by providing baseline information and later tracking progress)
9. Analyze options and establish priorities
10. Communicate better with the public and to build trust and support for public services
11. Above all, help provide services more effectively[42]

[viii]In addition to the references cited in this section, see also William T. Gormley and Steven J. Balla, *Bureaucracy and Democracy: Accountability and Performance* (Washington DC: CQ Press, 2008); Donald P. Moynihan, *The Dynamics of Performance Management: Constructing Information and Reform* (Washington, DC: Georgetown University Press, 2008); Rita M. Hilton and Philip G. Joyce, "Performance Information and Budgeting in Historical and Comparative Perspective," in *The Sage Handbook of Public Administration,* eds. B. Guy Peters and Jon Pierre (London, UK: Sage Publications, 2010), 402–412; Office of Management and Budget, Primer on Performance Measurement (Washington, D.: Office of Management and Budget, 1995), http://govinfo.library.unt.edu/npr/library/resource/gpraprmr. html; Colin Talbot, "Performance Measurement," *The Oxford Handbook of Public Management,* eds. Ewan Ferlie, Laurence E. Lynn Jr. and Christopher Pollitt (Oxford, UK: Oxford University Press, 2007), 494–496.

Whether viewed through Behn's or Hatry's lens, different performance measures may be desirable, depending on the purpose of measurement.

In the literature on performance measurement, **performance analysis** refers to the assessment and interpretation of performance measures to ascertain the specific contribution of the organization or managers, independent of other factors, to organizational performance.[43] Performance analysis can be used to help public managers understand how their own policy and management decisions are linked to outcomes and how systemic and situational factors outside of their control also affect performance.[44] **Performance management,** then, is the use of information from performance measures and performance analysis to improve the management and performance of an organization. **Performance budgeting** refers to the use of performance information to set budget allocations and priorities.

Performance may be measured at the levels of the individual, project, program, or agency. Chapter 5 discussed individual performance measurement. Often, public sector measurement efforts at the city, county, state, and federal levels focus on organizational performance, which is the focus of this section.

How Are Performance Measures Reported?

Performance with regard to any specific measure or dimension may be measured

- in its natural metric, such as the average test scores of students in a school or the percentage of welfare recipients working part-time or full-time;
- in relation to an external criterion, such as the percentage of students in a school that attained a "proficient" score on a math test or the percentage of welfare clients working more than 35 hours a week; or
- in relative terms by comparing a particular measure with that of other programs.

Rewards for high performers and/or sanctions for low performers may be based on either relative or criterion-based rankings.

Example: Information to Include in Performance Reports

Legislation authorizing the Workforce Investment Act detailed the types of information that should be included in performance reports for local workforce investment offices.

(d) Information To Be Included in Reports.—

1. In general.—The reports required in subsection (c) shall include information regarding programs and activities carried out under this title pertaining to—

   (A) the relevant demographic characteristics (including race, ethnicity, sex, and age) and other related information regarding participants;

   (B) the programs and activities in which participants are enrolled, and the length of time that participants are engaged in such programs and activities;

   (C) outcomes of the programs and activities for participants, including the occupations of participants, and placement for participants in nontraditional employment;

(D) specified costs of the programs and activities; and

(E) information necessary to prepare reports to comply with section 188.[45]

Performance information, extracted from administrative data, survey data, or subjective or objective assessments, may be compiled by external actors or produced and self-reported within an organization for its own uses. In an effort to enhance accountability of their agents, external authorities may mandate and provide detailed requests for performance information. The GPRA, for example, set forth such requirements.

For internal accountability purposes, organizations may report performance within the context of a **balanced scorecard,** a reporting method developed in the private sector that draws performance information from four perspectives: customers, internal organizational, financial, and innovation and learning.[ix] Now used in public, for-profit, and nonprofit organizations, the balanced scorecard approach is viewed as a strategic management process that moves beyond measuring financial performance alone. Entities external to government may also collect information about performance of public organizations. The Fraser Institute, a free market think tank, produces data on waiting times for medical services under the Canadian single payer health insurance system.[46]

A specific type of performance report compiled by external organizations is the **organizational report card:** a "regular effort by an organization to collect data on two or more *other* organizations, transform the data into information relevant to assessing performance, and transmit the information to some audience external to the organizations themselves."[47] Report cards comparing indicators across states are available in policy areas such as K–12 and higher education, the environment, and economic development and are published by governments, commercial groups, academics, and nonprofits.[48]

Example: Hospital Compare

The Hospital Compare system is a joint effort of the Centers for Medicare & Medicaid Services (in the Department of Health and Human Services) and the Hospital Quality Alliance (a public-private partnership involving a number of nonprofit as well as government organizations). The system reports on process and outcome of care measures, as well as patient survey results regarding quality of care received while hospitalized, for conditions such as heart attacks, pneumonia, and diabetes and for procedures such as heart bypass, gallbladder removal, and back and neck operations.[49] The data reported through this system are based on medical records submitted voluntarily by hospitals.

What Kinds of Performance Are Measured?

Typically, multiple performance measures are collected to provide a broad picture of an organization's efforts and results. **Types of performance measures** include[50]

- *inputs* (human and material resources used, such as number of staff hours or classroom space used to conduct a welfare-to-work program or textbooks used in K-12 classrooms);

[ix]Robert S. Kaplan and David P. Norton, "The Balanced Scorecard—Measures that Drive Performance," *Harvard Business Review* (January–February 1992): 71–79; see also http://www.balancedscorecard.org.

- *outputs* (amount of service, effort, or activity produced or delivered, such as number of clients receiving job training or number of students in advanced placement courses);
- *outcomes* (results or effectiveness of service or effort, such as the number of clients employed at least half time within 6 months of job training or percentage of students who graduate from high school);
- *efficiency or productivity* (amount of output or outcome achieved in terms of input, costs per participant in welfare-to-work programs, or cost per student);

> Specific performance measures that are chosen depend on the reason(s) that performance is being measured and on the intended users of that information; no one performance measure will suit all circumstances.

- *demographic/workload characteristics* (descriptions of persons or groups served, such as gender, race/ethnicity, income, family size characteristics);
- *impacts* (the program's value-added, over and above the outcome that would have happened in the absence of the program, such as the number of clients employed in a special job-training program, compared to the employment rate of similar persons who did not participate in the program).

As Behn and others have pointed out, specific performance measures that are chosen depend on the reason(s) that performance is being measured and on the intended users of that information; no one performance measure will suit all circumstances.[51]

For the purpose of measuring effectiveness, public management scholar Carolyn J. Heinrich suggests choosing a performance measurement system exhibiting the following characteristics:

- performance measures focused on quality, outcomes, or results;
- formal report requirements for comparing actual performance with performance goals or standards;
- multiple levels of performance accountability in decentralized programs; and
- market-oriented provisions such as financial/budgetary incentives for performance, as in the [Job Training Partnership Act] program, and plans to use performance information to promote continuous improvement and increased citizen ("customer") satisfaction.[52]

Challenges of Performance Measurement

A number of challenges arise in performance measurement for public and nonprofit organizations. Addressing these challenges likely requires some combination of structure, culture, and craft:

1. *What can be measured and what can be inferred?* The performance of public and nonprofit sector organizations is widely acknowledged to present performance measurement challenges different from those of for-profit organizations, where the bottom line—the ultimate outcome of interest—is profit. For public and nonprofit sector organizations, outputs may be easier to observe and measure than outcomes. But outputs may be the only type of measure available; outcomes may not be observed until well after management decisions have to be made. The question, then, is to what extent output measures actually correspond to outcome measures?

2. *When is information collected?* Here, the question is whether short-term measures correspond well with longer-term outcomes. These issues are relevant for many public sector organizations such as those concerned with basic scientific research, the environment, health, human services, or national security.

3. *Is the link clear between performance measures and organizational actions?* If organizations are to be held accountable for their performance, then performance measurement must be as accurate as possible. Organizations should not be penalized or held accountable for factors out of their control. For example, job training programs should not be penalized for serving clients who are more difficult to employ or who are looking for jobs during economic downturns. Performance measurement should somehow account for these external factors; such attribution problems are what performance analysis is meant to address. Yet, establishing a clear link between organizational action and any particular measure of performance—taking into account the features of the environment, clients, or other organizational aspects that are out of the control of the manager or frontline workers—can be quite difficult.

4. *What pressures and incentives are created by performance measurement systems?* Especially when accompanied by consequences such as sanctions for poor performance or rewards for high performance, performance measurement creates incentives to change the behavior of managers and organization staff. Some are unintended.

   - **Creamskimming** occurs when agency staff members select clients who are likely to be better performers instead of selecting those who are likely to be poor performers. This is a rational response to incentives to raise the overall level of performance (of either clients or the organization). Poorly prepared students may be reclassified into special education or learning disabled programs, where they are excluded from a school's reported performance. Although incentives for creamskimming may exist, it is possible that managers and street-level bureaucrats will not act on them. Indeed, one study found that job training workers still chose to serve clients who were most in need, regardless of performance incentives that should have led them to do just the opposite.[53]
   - Staff may **suppress information** that would adversely affect a performance measure. Especially when performance information is used to make arguments for or against the support of particular programs—that is, when the information is used for political purposes—only select measures may be conveyed, either by public managers themselves or by their political superiors, in the interests of maintaining support for their programs.

5. *What performance paradoxes or unintended consequences are present?* **Performance paradoxes** may occur when a weak correlation exists between performance indicators and performance itself and when performance measures lose their potency over time by failing to discriminate between strong and weak performers.[54] This response is akin to teaching to the test in school settings: More effort is devoted to the dimensions of performance that are measured and less effort is devoted to unmeasured dimensions. Such a response is consistent with the multitask principal-agent model described in Chapter 6.

   One criticism of performance measurement systems is that efficiency measures tend to be emphasized at the expense of equity concerns. The reason is that equity is difficult to define and measure and, subsequently, to include in performance assessments. Such problems are related to "data issues, problems of the extent of bounding these questions, and—perhaps most important—the conflict within the society about these issues."[55] A counterargument is that equity is improved, although it may not be explicitly measured, as efficiency or effectiveness of a program improves.

Example: Performance Paradox in High School Drop-Out Measurement

Performance paradoxes may result from the manipulation of assessments, which can be mitigated by auditing performance measures or adopting more objective measures. In Houston, Texas, some schools were reporting no high school dropouts at all, even though the dropout problem was substantial. The Texas State Auditor's Office and independent research examined the measurement of dropout rates in Houston's system.[56]

These analyses found that dropouts had been undercounted and students had been assigned to the special education program, which did not test students for achievement reporting purposes. Actual progress of minority groups was minimal, and retention in grade had increased markedly.

In response to these revelations, in 2003, the Texas legislature passed a law that defined how dropout rates must be reported: "dropout rates, including dropout rates and district completion rates for grade levels 9 through 12, computed in accordance with standards and definitions adopted by the National Center for Education Statistics of the United States Department of Education."[57]

6. *How does political rationality affect public organizations?* Performance measurement is, for the most part, regarded as a matter of technical rationality. Yet when performance is used for accountability purposes, especially in public sector programs, political rationality enters the picture: Who wants performance information? How will performance information influence the decisions and actions of political actors? Seldom are policymakers interested in performance, effectiveness, or results in a technical or academic sense. Instead, elected officials want to know how performance will affect their agendas, political bases, districts, constituencies, and reelection prospects. Other constituencies for performance information include inspectors general, auditors, budget examiners, personnel officers, advocacy groups, watchdog groups, and other interest groups. Because of political rationality, production of performance information may be done for its symbolic value rather than as an actual tool for management or budgeting.

   In a related vein, Beryl Radin criticizes what she characterizes as the "unreal and naïve approach" of those who advocate performance measurement and assume that it is mainly a straightforward matter of defining and measuring performance in an objective way, then providing the performance information to policymakers and public managers, who will draw appropriate conclusions from it and act accordingly. She argues that the generation of information for performance measurement is based on the following false assumptions:

   - Information is readily available.
   - Information is neutral.
   - We know what we are measuring.
   - We can define cause-effect relationships in programs.
   - Baseline information is available.
   - Almost all activities can be measured and quantified.[58]

   Radin emphasizes that policies are the product of ideology, interests, and information, and that the use of performance information often depends on whether it is consistent with ideology and interests.

7. *Does measured performance correspond with organizational participants' understandings of performance?* Sociologist Renee Anspach argues that "effectiveness" is a socially constructed phenomenon.

She investigated the "indigenous or folk methods" actually used by administrators, case managers, families, and clients in community mental health centers to understand the effectiveness of their organizations. She identified the following types of methods the groups used to assess effectiveness:

- *Measuring "success" against personal trajectories.* Success was valued most in clients least likely to succeed because it enhanced the case manager's sense of efficacy.
- *Interpreting acts in the context of relationships.* Success was attributable to particular people, not to treatment.
- *Using the dramatic incident.* Dramatic events came to represent the system as a whole, for good or for ill.
- *Relying on the appearance of involvement.* Effort was weighted far more than results; effort stood for progress toward results or for results themselves.
- *Scaling goals to meet shifting constraints.* By lowering expectations, faith can be maintained even in failing programs.[59]

Caseworkers in Anspach's study cited all of these methods for assessing effectiveness, tending to locate sources of failure in the clients or in circumstances but not in the treatments. These understandings of effectiveness may be coping mechanisms in the face of intense frustrations. The downside of such methods is that "promulgating effectiveness and neutralizing ineffectiveness—while securing resources necessary to a program's survival—may protect a program from critical scrutiny, both by outside evaluators and by program participants."[60] Anspach's work illustrates how understanding performance measurement may contribute to or be affected by the culture dimension of public management.

The Role of Culture

Structural tools are the dominant mechanisms under the control of external and internal formal authorities for defining accountability relationships. The culture dimension also plays important roles in shaping these relationships, as discussed in Chapters 8 and 9. These roles range from interactions between culture and structural mechanisms or reforms to the unique contribution of individual values and organizational culture to ensuring responsible action on the part of organizational participants.

For example, creating a **performance culture** may be crucial to the success of reforms to improve performance, where aspects of such a culture include "a focus on performance and performance data, the prospective high compensation levels, and the competitive spirit" with the idea that "when culture makes performance important, it influences the behavior of people at all levels."[61] Reform at the federal, state, and local levels that aim to improve performance often focus a part of their efforts on bringing about cultural change.

Empirical research supports the link between performance and organizational culture. As noted in Chapter 9, interest in organizational culture has been driven in large part by how it relates to organizational performance.[x] One study identified four important elements of an organizational culture that were positively related to performance:

---

[x]See, for example: Guy S. Saffold III, "Culture Traits, Strength, and Organizational Performance: Moving Beyond 'Strong' Culture," *Academy of Management Review* 13, no. 4 (1988): 546–558; Daniel R. Denison and Aneil K. Mishra, "Toward a Theory of Organizational Culture and Effectiveness," *Organization Science* 6, no. 2 (1995): 204–223; George A. Marcoulides and Ronald H. Heck, "Organizational Culture and Performance: Proposing and Testing a Model," *Organization Science* 4, no. 2 (1993): 209–225.

- involvement,
- consistency,
- adaptability, and
- mission.[62]

Elements of organizational culture are prominent in public management scholars Hal G. Rainey and Paula Steinbauer's theory of organizational effectiveness in public organizations.[63] Among the cultural elements the authors identify are

- a "strong" culture linked to accomplishing the organization's mission,
- professionalism, and
- motivation of individual actors related to tasks, mission, and public service.

Using data from the 1996 Merit Principles Survey, collected by the Merit Systems Protection Board, public management scholars Gene A. Brewer and Sally Coleman Selden tested the Rainey/Steinbauer model by predicting employees' perceptions of organizational performance in federal agencies.[64] They found empirical support for the model through significant associations with cultural factors of efficacy, teamwork, concern for the public interest, protection of employees, and task and public service motivation.

The Role of Craft

As emphasized through the book, explicit and implicit delegations of authority may require the practice of managerial craft. Responding to specific structural requirements such as performance measurement may involve discretion and therefore craft. It is not a foregone conclusion that managers will be fully responsive to such requirements. They can undermine accountability requirements by ignoring or subverting them, or they may even use the requirements as leverage for their own agendas.

The early responses across federal agencies to the GPRA (discussed in Chapter 6) illustrate the range of responses to the legal requirement to engage in strategic planning and performance measurement. Beryl Radin has described these responses:

> There are agencies that have engaged in planning as an intellectually rigorous exercise and have taken the requirements both seriously and almost literally. For some agencies, by contrast, the approach might be described as a narrow compliance strategy. In this approach, agencies simply describe what they are already doing but package that description in a way that appears to meet the requirements. Others have used the requirements of GPRA as an opportunity to focus on a specific set of administration or agency initiatives. In this approach, the goals and objectives are crafted as a way to make a case for new, expanded, or refocused policy areas. Still others have focused on measures that will be used for internal management purposes, usually at a program level rather than agency or department level.[65]

This observed variation illustrates how managers, through exercising discretion, may shape responses to external accountability requirements.

Managers may choose to generate performance measurement requirements themselves, as a tool for managing and monitoring their subordinates or for advancing their own agendas.

Example: Promoting Accountability Through CitiStat

The mayor of Buffalo, New York, demonstrating the exercise of managerial craft, implemented a number of reforms intended to increase the accountability of city agencies as part of the city's CitiStat program. Attention to institutionalized values is also evident:

> BUFFALO—Mayor Byron W. Brown today announced the City of Buffalo's Public Integrity and Accountability Plan, which will ensure integrity, transparency, accountability, and ethical behavior in City Hall as well as enhance public confidence in the employees of the City of Buffalo. Since taking office, Mayor Brown has created a written travel policy, and all department heads have had a mandatory ethics training course given by the local Federal Bureau of Investigations office.
>
> "This plan is part of the continuing progress we have made to make City government transparent and accountable through CitiStat Buffalo," said Mayor Brown. "Buffalo is the first city in the nation to televise its CitiStat meetings unedited, so that all citizens can see how their government is functioning and performing. The new Public Integrity and Accountability Plan will enhance policies and procedures that are presently in place."
>
> Details of the Public Integrity and Accountability Plan include the creation of the Office of Inspector General, an independent, centralized office within the Executive Branch that is tasked with addressing government waste, fraud, abuse and complaints. The Office will have the authority to receive and investigate integrity related complaints and incidences of fraud, corruption, and abuse involving city personnel—including elected officials—contractors, vendors and consultants doing business with the City.[66]

For each of the situations discussed in this section—responding to early warning, connecting the dots, confronting a crisis, managing people, reforming, measuring performance—three-dimensional management offers valuable analytical traction. Yet 3D is not restricted to these situations; it might be beneficial or even essential for a number of other situations or tasks that public managers face. For example, policy and management scholar Eugene Bardach has written about the challenges of designing and managing collaborations or interagency networks.[67] His concepts of managerial craftsmanship and interagency collaborative capacity reflect the importance of structure, culture, and craft dimensions. The three dimensions are also evident in the strategic action field approach to policy and program implementation emphasized by public management scholars Jodi Sandfort and Stephanie Moulton.[68] Indeed, across a range of situations and challenges, the model deliberative process can be used as a tool for 3D management.

CONUNDRUMS OF 3D MANAGEMENT

In their comprehensive monograph *Public Management Reform: A Comparative Analysis,* public management scholars Christopher Pollitt and Geert Bouckaert point out that no matter what strategy a public manager may choose, the process of moving forward is seldom straightforward.[69] The book's chapter on "Trade-offs, Balances, Limits, Dilemmas and Paradoxes" discusses a number of the intellectual and practical difficulties that challenge the craftsmanship of any public manager attempting to practice three-dimensional management.

Such difficulties may be termed **conundrums:** intractable or difficult problems that may constitute no-win situations. The types of conundrums identified by Pollitt and Bouckaert include the following:

- *Trade-offs:* Because resources are scarce, achieving more of one good thing means settling for less of another good thing. Decentralizing agency decision making, empowering field offices, and outsourcing functions and responsibilities usually occur at the expense of policy control and accountability. The adoption of "quality of life" policing may lead to reductions in crime but a rising level of citizen complaints because of increased police-citizen interactions.

- *Limits:* Public managers may encounter absolute constraints on what they may do even if it means accepting considerable inefficiency. The Internal Revenue Service was prohibited by arcane budget scoring rules from hiring additional auditors and was forced to hire private contractors to collect delinquent taxes at greater cost. U.S. aid agencies are able to purchase less food to feed victims of drought or civil conflict because of rules requiring the use of U.S.-grown commodities and U.S.-flag transportation, both of which are more expensive than goods and services from abroad.

- *Dilemmas:* Public managers may confront choices between undesirable, often incommensurable alternatives. National Aeronautics and Space Administration (NASA) managers must occasionally choose between canceling a shuttle flight and throwing flight schedules into disarray, which jeopardizes program goals, and allowing a flight to proceed, thereby incurring an unknown risk of a catastrophic accident.

- *Paradoxes:* Public managers may encounter situations with seemingly contradictory aspects that nevertheless may be true. The paradoxes of performance discussed earlier in this chapter are examples. Public managers may face the reality that being opportunistic and disingenuous is politically safer than exhibiting integrity and a commitment to quality. And then there is the adage "We never have time to do it right, but we always have time to do it over."

- *Contradictions:* A contradiction is an extreme trade-off: If you have one desirable thing, you cannot have another desirable thing. For example, allowing interest groups or representative groups of citizens to have a veto over program implementation alternatives may reduce the prospects for technically and economically efficient solutions to near zero. Democracy cancels out efficiency, which are both in the public interest.[70]

To Pollitt and Bouckaert's list the following might be added:

- *Unintended consequences:* Unintended consequences are outcomes of a managerial strategy, usually unanticipated and unwelcome, that complicate, undermine, or nullify the intended consequences. For example,

  In 1692, John Locke, the English philosopher and a forerunner of modern economists, urged the defeat of a parliamentary bill designed to cut the maximum permissible rate of interest from 6 percent to 4 percent. Locke argued that instead of benefiting borrowers, as intended, it would hurt them. People would find ways to circumvent the law, with the costs of circumvention borne by borrowers. To the extent the law was obeyed, Locke concluded, the chief results would be less available credit and a redistribution of income away from "widows, orphans and all those who have their estates in money."[71]

- *Externalities:* As discussed in Chapter 1, externalities occur when the actions of a government agency or a business firm affect the well-being of others in either positive or negative ways. Construction of a hospital or a shopping center, while a benefit to patients and customers, may create aggravating traffic congestion for those who must use nearby roads.

- *A Hobson's Choice*: A Hobson's choice is one that involves a take-it-or-leave-it proposition. Managers in weak bargaining positions may be offered this-or-nothing settlements of disputes.

Public managers may downplay or fail to identify conundrums that they are likely to encounter. They may be motivated by wishful thinking or ideological conviction more than by careful planning or rational anticipation of potential problems. To attract sufficient political support, policymakers often create expectations and demand results that are unrealistic. The result often places their agents, who must deal with the conundrums, in difficult or untenable situations.

Pollitt and Bouckaert describe some specific examples of conundrums in public management.[72] They suggest, for example, that public managers may be directed to

- increase political control of the bureaucracy and at the same time empower subordinates to manage or empower consumers;
- promote entrepreneurship, risk taking, and innovation and at the same time raise citizen trust in the certainty of effectiveness;
- increase efficiency by saving money and at the same time increase effectiveness (the notion that government can cost less and work better);
- improve staff morale and dedication and at the same time downsize and outsource;
- reduce agency complexity and at the same time improve agency coordination; and
- improve quality and at the same time cut costs.

Failure to accomplish incompatible objectives may doom the offending public manager to political reprisals and loss of reputation by whichever side is most aggrieved or maybe by all sides. Such possibilities may be minimized by deliberation that is carefully three-dimensional.

THE RULE OF LAW IN 3D MANAGEMENT

As noted in Chapter 2, in the American scheme of governance, the process of judicial review resolves conflicting claims about managerial discretion. Judicial review of administrative actions is regarded, in a nation born in a rebellion against the arbitrary exercise of administrative authority by a distant monarch, as a bulwark against abuses of power by unelected bureaucrats. The possibility, or even the likelihood, of such abuses flavors American political discourse at all levels of government. Judicial review is how the rule of law in America is enforced.

> Among the most confounding conundrums and dilemmas public managers will encounter is the inevitability of conflicts between what common sense (technical rationality) and political rationality require of them.

Among the most confounding conundrums and dilemmas public managers will encounter is the inevitability of conflicts between what common sense (technical rationality) and political rationality require of them. As noted in Chapter 2, that conflict is played out at the highest court in the land. Supreme Court Justice Sotomayor has argued that "the government must be allowed to handle the basic tasks of public administration in a manner that comports with common sense."[73] Her opinion, however, is not the law of the land, no matter how much public managers wish it were. The ever-present reality for public managers is that they must come to terms with the reality that their every consequential act is potentially reviewable by the courts in response to lawsuits brought by aggrieved parties claiming they have been harmed by managerial actions. They must think and act institutionally, as has been urged throughout this book.

> A 3D approach will increase the likelihood that purposeful, lawful public management will result in success.

Thinking institutionally requires public managers to accept, and act in the light of, what political scientist Robert Kagan has termed "adversarial legalism."[74] Political scientist Francis Fukuyama has argued that, uniquely among the world's liberal democracies, "the enforcement of national law [is] left up to the initiative of private parties and carried out by courts."[75] Thus, conflicts that in other liberal democracies "would be solved through quiet consultations between interested parties in the bureaucracy are fought out through formal litigation in the U.S. court system."[76] Accustomed to the litigiousness of public policy implementation, Americans can scarcely comprehend a political system in which political and policy conflicts are left to "unelected" bureaucrats to sort out.

There is no getting around this reality. The politics of bureaucratic structure, for example, guarantee that judicial conflicts will be built into public policy implementation for reasons discussed at length in Chapter 5. And, in the twenty-first century's second decade, no solution is in sight. The reason, argues Fukuyama, is that America's decentralized political system, rife with what were called in Chapter 4 primary and secondary checks and balances, "is less and less able to represent majority interests and gives excessive representation to the views of interest groups and activist organizations that collectively do not add up to a sovereign American people."[77]

Another institutional reality is equally compelling, however. As noted earlier in this chapter, the political and institutional environment will not allow public managers to be passive. An achievement orientation is essential not just for success but also for survival. And, as numerous examples through the book demonstrate, success is achievable, sometimes for getting it right and often for getting it better. A 3D approach will increase the likelihood that purposeful, lawful public management will result in success.

KEY CONCEPTS

PerformanceStat
CompStat
Connecting-the-dots problem
Impossible jobs
Human resource management/human capital
   management
Public management reform
Accountability dilemmas
Accountability bias
Performance analysis

Performance management
Performance budgeting
Balanced scorecard
Organizational report card
Types of performance measures
Creamskimming
Performance paradoxes
Performance culture
Conundrums
Thinking institutionally

CASE ANALYSIS: THE SPACE SHUTTLE *COLUMBIA* ACCIDENT IN 3D

The opening case to Chapter 9 explored the role played by institutionalized values in the crash of the space shuttle *Columbia*. But fully understanding the accident requires a three-dimensional analysis:

- An analysis might view NASA as an organization with a formal structure that defined functions and assigned responsibilities and rules for performing them. Analysis might focus on the location of the space shuttle program within the NASA chain of command and the relation of the safety-of-flight function to operations management.
- Or analysis might focus on what the Columbia Accident Investigation Board (CAIB) report called NASA's culture (as in Chapter 9)—the beliefs and values of NASA's various employees that, because they came into conflict, jeopardized the mission of the space shuttle program.
- Or analysis might be concerned with the actions and decisions of NASA's administrator, Sean O'Keefe, or of Linda Ham, head of the Mission Management Team, or of flight director Leroy Cain, or of other officials whose priorities and decisions influenced the outcome.

But no one of these perspectives by itself provides an adequate basis for understanding the complex challenges of public management involved in the *Columbia* accident. In fact, the danger in a one-dimensional approach to public management analysis and practice, whether by managers, elected officials, or judges, is the possibility of seriously misdiagnosing the underlying problem and therefore of taking inappropriate corrective measures. An agency might decide to concentrate on hiring better managers instead of tackling problems with norms of conduct that have become dysfunctional. Or it could impose new rules where additional managerial discretion is needed. For this reason, as the CAIB recognized, multiple dimensions of public management must be considered to understand the *Columbia* accident.

Remembering *Challenger*

NASA came under intense scrutiny from Congress, the print and broadcast media, a variety of interest groups, and a shocked public. Many remembered an earlier accident: the explosion of the space shuttle *Challenger* shortly after launch in 1986, which killed its seven-member crew. That accident, too, had been the subject of a detailed investigation resulting in a report. The Report of the Presidential Commission on the Space Shuttle *Challenger* Accident, known as the Rogers Report after its chair, former secretary of state William P. Rogers, recommended numerous changes to improve the safety of manned space flight.[78] The Rogers Report was followed a year later by an evaluation of how well its recommendations had been implemented.[79] How was it possible, many asked about the *Columbia* accident, for history to repeat itself so soon with such tragic consequences?

In the view of Laurence Mulloy, former *Challenger* project leader,

> If—and this is a big if, with big capital letters in red—if the cause of the *Columbia* accident is the acceptance of debris falling off the tank in ascent, and impacting on the orbiter, and causing damage to the tiles—if that turns out to be the cause of the accident, then the lesson we learned in *Challenger* is forgotten, if it was ever learned.[80]

The *Challenger* accident had resulted from mission managers overruling engineers' warnings concerning air temperatures at launch that were lower than design tolerances for launch equipment. Officials responsible for the *Columbia* launch were anxious to forestall similar allegations of ignoring expert advice. But Mulloy's suspicions turned out to be correct.

Immediate Diagnoses

Much of the scrutiny of the *Columbia* accident focused on the technical cause of the orbiter's disintegration. Eighty-two seconds after launch a piece of insulating foam had detached from one of the solid rocket boosters and struck the leading edge of one of the orbiter's wings, creating a hole that would allow super-heated air generated during reentry to penetrate the vehicle's protective shield and cause fatal structural damage. But significant attention was also devoted to what were termed "management issues."

The media soon reported that less than a year before the accident, in April 2002, Richard Blomberg, the former chairman of the NASA-appointed Aerospace Safety Advisory Panel, had reported to NASA officials and to a congressional committee "the strongest safety concern the Panel has voiced in the 15 years I was involved with it." The problem, said Blomberg, "is that the boundary between safe and unsafe operations can seldom be quantitatively defined or accurately predicted. Even the most well-meaning managers may not know when they cross it."[81] Debate was underway regarding the implications for efficiencies, effectiveness, and safety culture of contracting out.[82]

At issue in this was NASA management during the period between the two space shuttle accidents when, in Blomberg's view, the agency had possibly crossed the line into unsafe operations. The CAIB report would later diagnose the problem as the agency trying to accomplish too many missions with too few budgetary and human resources. Thus, it was implied, structural constraints, ingrained behaviors within NASA, and management strategies and actions (or inactions) were all implicated in what appeared to be a repetition of the *Challenger* disaster.

The CAIB as Honest Broker

When it was created, the CAIB was criticized by interest groups such as the nonprofit Freedom of Information Center and the Project on Government Secrecy at the Federation of American Scientists for its lack of independence: Its members were appointed and paid by NASA—that is, they were federal employees—and, for this reason, public law allowed the board to operate in relative secrecy. In fact, Admiral Gehman had to fight with NASA officials to ensure his board's autonomy and adequate resources to support its work. Its report, however, largely dispelled any concerns about its independence. An editorial in the respected British scientific journal *Nature* said,

> The investigative board charged with finding the causes of February's explosion of the space shuttle *Columbia* turned in about as good a report last week as anyone could have asked. In clear, direct language, the panel . . . spelled out what has gone wrong—technically, politically, even sociologically—with the space-shuttle programme since its inception almost 30 years ago. . . . Gehman's report accurately describes the dysfunctional relationship that has developed between the space agency and those in the White House and Congress who fund it. . . . The agency got into the dangerous habit of promising what it could not deliver.

(Continued)

(Continued)

> Meanwhile, NASA's overseers in the White House and Congress, who surely suspected that the agency was stretched too thin, suppressed their own doubts.[83]

In addition to its analysis of technical issues, such as the prevention of foam shedding from the rocket boosters, the CAIB report addressed issues not only of management but also what it called, in scores of references, NASA's "culture." (Chapter 7 of the report is titled "The Organizational Causes.") Some of its observations included the following:

- Shuttle program managers were responsible for schedule, cost, *and* safety of flight. Combining these responsibilities had the practical effect of shifting the burden of proof on flight safety matters from those responsible for operations to those responsible for the safety of a flight. Had safety-of-flight decisions been independent of the management of flight operations, then operations managers would have been required to prove to the independent authority that a mission was safe.
- Bureaucratic distance and rank—that is, the organization of the formal hierarchy—impeded communications among engineers and managers who needed to discuss issues informally with each other; instead, dissonant information was brushed aside, and dissenters were inhibited from "jumping" the chain of command by going over the heads of superiors who had shown no inclination to listen to them.
- Administrative decisions requiring subjective judgments—applying criteria for determining acceptable risk, safety-of-flight status, conditions for mandatory review, and the existence of an anomaly or a deviation from a norm or rule—were manipulated by managers in the interest of maintaining flight schedules. Managers also were found to have failed to properly evaluate past experience or to examine the assumptions underlying recommendations or unanimous opinions.

Of immediate interest to the CAIB investigators were the reactions of NASA officials during *Columbia*'s mission, particularly those officials constituting the Mission Management Team, to the intensely felt concerns of agency and contractor engineers that the orbiter might have been fatally damaged by the foam strike, which would jeopardize the vehicle's reentry unless corrective measures were taken. Evidently, these internecine conflicts and their potentially dire implications never reached O'Keefe or other top officials during the 16 days of the mission. Even if they had, NASA had no contingency plans to rescue a mortally damaged orbiter in flight, possibly explaining mission management's inclinations to downplay the seriousness of the foam strike, because nothing could be done about it. Contributing to this disinclination to take corrective action was that foam strikes had become so common during previous shuttle operations as to be considered normal and, therefore, not safety-of-flight issues.

Structure, Culture, Craft

Considerations of structure enter into the analysis of the *Columbia* accident in the delegation of two responsibilities to shuttle program managers—meeting flight schedules and the safety of flights—instead of giving these functions separate status. As a consequence of this structural arrangement, these managers could on their own authority choose to take chances with the safety of a flight in order to maintain flight schedules and stay within budget. Moreover, there were no authorized communication channels within NASA for dissident views on issues concerning safety. NASA's structure gave senior officials no opportunity to make a different decision about the flight.

Craft enters into the analysis of the *Columbia* accident in the judgments made by individual NASA offi-cials, including the head of the Mission Control Team, to ignore what amounted to dire warnings by the agency's own advisers of threats to the safety of the shuttle program in general and to the *Columbia* flight in particular. Considerations of craft enter into the aftermath of the accident in the efforts of individual NASA officials to restrict the independence of the CAIB and to create an implementation evaluation team that would be sympathetic to NASA.

The CAIB report reflected the concept of three-dimensional awareness of the safety-of-flight issues confronting NASA management:

> Policy constraints affected the Shuttle Program's organization culture, its structure, and the structure of the safety system. The three combined to keep NASA on its slippery slope toward *Challenger* and *Columbia*. NASA culture allowed flying with flaws when problems were defined as normal and routine; the structure of NASA's Shuttle Program blocked the flow of critical information up the hierarchy, so definitions of risk continued unaltered. Finally, a per-ennially weakened safety system, unable to critically analyze and intervene, had no choice but to ratify the existing risk assessments on these two problems.[84]

Public management analysis will typically employ theoretical concepts in evaluating a complex problem. The key to an incisive public management analysis is selecting concepts and ideas that are especially appro-priate for illuminating the problem at hand. The CAIB drew on several theoretical concepts to help interpret the factual evidence, including the following examples:

- NASA management's acceptance of the debris strike (which is not supposed to occur) as a nor-mal occurrence was regarded as what sociologist Diane Vaughan has called the "normalization of deviance," an aspect of NASA's culture that had also been present prior to the 1986 *Challenger* accident.[85]
- The report invoked *high reliability theory* (see Chapter 9 in this book) which argues that "organi-zations operating high-risk technologies, if properly designed and managed, can compensate for inevitable human shortcomings, and therefore avoid mistakes that under other circumstances would lead to catastrophic failures."[86]
- "Additionally, organizational theory, which encompasses organizational culture, structure, history, and hierarchy, is used to explain the *Columbia* accident and, ultimately . . . to produce an expanded explanation of the accident's causes."[87]
- Commentary on this incident also invoked the concept of *groupthink* (see Chapter 11 in this book), that is, collective decision making such as that by the STS-107 Mission Management Team, charac-terized by uncritical acceptance of or conformity to particular points of view.

Public management analysis, then, involves not only the habitual resort to three-dimensional thinking but also the insightful use of a portfolio of theoretical concepts and heuristics that can lead to a more thorough, in-depth understanding of the role of structure, culture, and craft in causing—and addressing— specific management challenges.

(Continued)

(Continued)

Discussion Questions

1. For each of the *distinctive challenges of public management* discussed in Chapter 1, discuss whether it was evident in the *Columbia* case. Analyze the response to each of the relevant challenges, incorporating 3D analysis. That is, analyze to what extent the responses by public managers to the distinctive challenges seem to reflect an appropriate awareness of how considerations of structure, culture, and craft could contribute to an effective response.

2. Propose a performance measurement system for the successful launch and return to earth of a manned space vehicle. In your proposal, consider the three dimensions of public management, as well as the issues that might arise in successfully implementing the proposed measurement system.

3. Discuss tensions between political rationality and technical rationality in the space shuttle program.

NOTES

1. J. Buntin, "Assertive Policing, Plummeting Crime: The NYPD Takes on Crime in New York City," Harvard University, John F. Kennedy School of Government Case Study Program series, #C16-99-1530.0, 1999.

2. Paul E. O'Connell, "Using Performance Data for Accountability: The New York City Police Department's CompStat Model of Police Management," in *Managing for Results 2002*, ed. Mark A. Abramson and John M. Kamensky (Lanham, MD: Rowman and Littlefield, 2001), 179–224.

3. Ibid.

4. Dennis C. Smith, with William J. Bratton, "Performance Management in New York City: Compstat and the Revolution in Police Management," in *Quicker, Better, Cheaper?: Managing Performance in American Government*, ed. Dall W. Forsythe (Albany, NY: Rockefeller Institute Press, 2001): 453–482. See also Appendix A, "Eight Possible Societal Explanations for Crime Decline," in Robert D. Behn, *The Performance Stat Potential: A Leadership Strategy for Producing Results* (Washington, DC: Brookings Institution Press, 2014).

5. David Kocieniewski, "Success of Elite Police Unit Exacts a Toll on the Streets," *The New York Times*, February 15, 1999.

6. James J. Willis, Stephen D. Mastrofski, and David Weisburd, *CompStat in Practice: An In-Depth Analysis of Three Cities* (Washington, DC: Police Foundation, 2003), 3.

7. Ibid., 73.

8. Ibid.

9. James J. Willis, Stephen D. Mastrofski, and David Weisburd, "CompStat and Bureaucracy: A Case Study of Challenges and Opportunities for Change," *Justice Quarterly* 21 (September 2004): 491.

10. Ibid., 493.

11. Robert D. Behn, *The PerformanceStat Potential: A Leadership Strategy for Producing Results* (Washington, DC: Brookings Institution Press, 2014), 232.

12. Behn, *The PerformanceStat Potential*, 264, 272–273.

13. David J. Goodman and Joseph Goldstein, "Bratton Takes Helm of Police Force He Pledged to Change," *The New York Times*, January 2, 2014, http://www.nytimes.com/2014/01/03/nyregion/bratton-stands-before-police-force-with-a-mandate-for-change.html?_r=0.

14. Malcolm Gladwell, "Connecting the Dots: The Paradox of Intelligence Reform," *The New Yorker*, March 10, 2003, 83–89.

15. Spencer Weart, "The Public and Climate Change," in *The Discovery of Global Warming*, July 2007, http://www.aip.org/history/exhibits/climate/Public.htm#L000.

16. Patricia Cohen, "Talking Veterans Down from Despair," *The New York Times*, April 22, 2008.

17. "NIMS Compliance–Frequently Asked Questions," Federal Emergency Management System, last update November 24, 2014, https://www.fema.gov/nims-frequently-asked-questions.

18. Erwin C. Hargrove and John C. Glidewell, eds., *Impossible Jobs in Public Management* (Lawrence: University Press of Kansas, 1990).

19. Ibid., 8.

20. Frances Hesselbein, "Seeing Things Whole," *Leader to Leader* 37 (Summer 2005): 4–6, 5.

21. Jennifer Warren, "Roderick Q. Hickman's Reform Agenda Has Riled the State's Correctional Officers Association," *Los Angeles Times,* November 15, 2004.

22. Ibid.

23. Jennifer Warren, "State Chief of Prisons Resigns after 2 Years on Job," *Los Angeles Times,* February 26, 2006.

24. Editorial, "Prisons and the Brick Wall," *Los Angeles Times,* February 28, 2006.

25. Jennifer Warren, "State Prison Reform in Jeopardy—The Recent Resignation of the Corrections Chief Raises Doubts about the Governor's Commitment to Overhaul the System," *Los Angeles Times,* March 7, 2006.

26. Ibid.

27. Editorial, "Prisons and the Brick Wall."

28. Hargrove and Glidewell, eds. *Impossible Jobs in Public Management,* 25.

29. John J. DiIulio, "Managing a Barbed-Wire Bureaucracy: The Impossible Job of Corrections Commissioner," in *Impossible Jobs in Public Management,* ed. Erwin C. Hargrove and John. C. Glidewell (Lawrence: University Press of Kansas, 1990), 49–71.

30. Richard N. Haass, *The Bureaucratic Entrepreneur: How to be Effective in Any Unruly Organization* (Washington, DC: Brookings Institution, 1999); Kenneth H. Ashworth, *Caught Between the Dog and the Fireplug, or How to Survive in Public Service* (Washington, DC: Georgetown University Press, 2001).

31. Government Accountability Office, "Human Capital: A Self-Assessment Checklist for Agency Leaders," GAO/OCG-00-14G, 2000, 10.

32. Christopher Pollitt and Geert Bouckaert, *Public Management Reform: A Comparative Analysis* (Oxford, UK: Oxford University Press, 2004), 8.

33. Michael Barzelay, "Politics of Public Management Reform in OECD Countries" (paper presented at the II International Congress of CLAD on State and Public Administration Reform, Margarita Island, Venezuela, October 14–18, 1997).

34. George W. Downs and Patrick D. Larkey, *The Search for Government Efficiency: From Hubris to Helplessness* (New York, NY: Random House, 1986), 259.

35. See Patrick S. Roberts, "FEMA and the Prospects for Reputation-Based Autonomy," *Studies in American Political Development* 20, no. 1 (April 2006): 57–87; and James Lee Witt and James Morgan, *Stronger in the Broken Places: Nine Lessons for Turning Crisis into Triumph* (New York, NY: Times Books, 2003).

36. William T. Gormley Jr., *Taming the Bureaucracy: Muscles, Prayers, and Other Strategies* (Princeton, NJ: Princeton University Press, 1989), 224.

37. Robert D. Behn, *Rethinking Democratic Accountability* (Washington, DC: Brookings Institution Press, 2001), 10–12, 11–13.

38. Barbara S. Romzek and Patricia Wallace Ingraham, "Cross Pressures of Accountability: Initiative, Command, and Failure in the Ron Brown Plane Crash," *Public Administration Review* 60, no. 3 (2000): 241; see also Beryl A. Radin, *The Accountable Juggler: The Art of Leadership in a Federal Agency* (Washington, DC: CQ Press, 2002).

39. Herbert Kaufman, "The Confines of Leadership," in *The Administrative Behavior of Federal Bureau Chiefs* (Washington, DC: Brookings Institution, 1981), 91–138.

40. Carolyn J. Heinrich, "Measuring Public Sector Performance and Effectiveness," in *The SAGE Handbook of Public Administration,* ed. B. Guy Peters and Jon Pierre (London, UK: Sage, 2010), 25.

41. Robert D. Behn, "Why Measure Performance? Different Purposes Require Different Measures," *Public Administration Review* 63, no. 5 (2003): 586–606. See also Colin Talbot, "Performance Management," in *The Oxford Handbook of Public Management,* ed. Ewan Ferlie, Laurence E. Lynn Jr. and Christopher Pollitt (Oxford, UK: Oxford University Press, 2007), 491–517.

42. Harry P. Hatry, *Performance Measurement: Getting Results* (Washington DC: The Urban Institute Press, 2006), 196.

43. Lawrence M. Mead, "Performance Analysis," in *Policy Into Action: Implementation Research and Welfare Reform,* ed. Mary Clare Lennon and Thomas Corbett (Washington, DC: Urban Institute Press, 2003); Heinrich, "Measuring Public Sector Performance and Effectiveness."

44. Heinrich, "Measuring Public Sector Performance and Effectiveness."

45. Workforce Investment Act of 1998, H.R. 1385, 105th Congress, 112 Stat. 936, P.L. 105-220, http://www.doleta.gov/usworkforce/wia/wialaw.htm#sec185.

46. The Fraser Institute, accessed January 7, 2015, www.fraserinstitute.org.

47. William T. Gormley Jr. and David L. Weimer, *Organizational Report Cards* (Cambridge, MA: Harvard University Press, 1999), 3.

48. Charles K. Coe and James R. Brunet, "Organizational Report Cards: Significant Impact or Much Ado about Nothing?" *Public Administration Review* 66, no. 1 (2006): 90–100.

49. "Hospital Compare," Medicare.gov, accessed January 7, 2015, http://www.medicare.gov/hospitalcompare/search.html.

50. Hatry, Performance Measurement, 14–24.

51. Behn, "Why Measure Performance?"

52. Heinrich, "Measuring Public Sector Performance and Effectiveness," 29.

53. James J. Heckman, Jeffrey A. Smith, and Christopher Taber, "What Do Bureaucrats Do? The Effects of Performance Standards and Bureaucratic Preferences on Acceptance into the JTPA Program," in *Advances in the Study of Entrepreneurship, Innovation, and Growth,* ed. G. Libecap (Greenwich, CT.: JAI Press, 1996), 191–217.

54. Sandra Van Thiel and Frans L. Leeuw, "The Performance Paradox in the Public Sector," *Public Performance and Management Review* 25, no. 3 (2002): 267–281.

55. Beryl A. Radin, *Challenging the Performance Movement: Accountability, Complexity, and Democratic Values* (Washington, DC: Georgetown University Press, 2006), 97.

56. Walt Haney, "The Myth of the Texas Miracle in Education," *Education Policy Analysis Archives* 8, no. 41 (August 2000).

57. SB 186, 78th Texas Legislature, Texas Education Code § 39.051(b)(2).

58. Radin, Challenging the Performance Movement.

59. Renee R. Anspach, "Everyday Methods for Assessing Organizational Effectiveness," *Social Problems* 38, no. 1 (February 1991): 1–19.

60. Ibid., 16.

61. Howard Risher, *Pay for Performance: A Guide for Federal Managers* (Washington, DC: IBM Center for the Business of Government, 2004), 27.

62. Daniel R. Denison and Aneil K. Mishra, "Toward a Theory of Organizational Culture and Effectiveness," *Organization Science* 6, no. 2 (1995): 204–223;

63. Hal G. Rainey and Paula Steinbauer, "Galloping Elephants: Developing Elements of a Theory of Effective Government Organizations," *Journal of Public Administration Research and Theory* 9, no. 1 (1999): 1–32.

64. Gene A. Brewer and Sally Coleman Selden, "Why Elephants Gallop: Assessing and Predicting Organizational Performance in Federal Agencies," *Journal of Public Administration Research and Theory* 10, no. 4 (2000): 685–711.

65. Beryl A. Radin, "The Government Performance and Results Act (GPRA): Hydra-headed Monster or Flexible Management Tool?" *Public Administration Review* 58, no. 4 (1998): 313.

66. City of Buffalo, Office of the Mayor, "Mayor Brown Announces Public Integrity and Accountability Plan," press release, August 2007.

67. Eugene Bardach, *Getting Agencies to Work Together: The Practice and Theory of Managerial Craftsmanship* (Washington, DC: Brookings Institution Press, 1998).

68. Jodi Sandfort and Stephanie Moulton, *Effective Implementation in Practice: Integrating Public Policy and Management* (San Francisco, CA: Jossey-Bass, 2015).

69. Christopher Pollitt and Geert Bouckaert, *Public Management Reform: A Comparative Analysis,* 2nd ed. (London, UK, and New York, NY: Oxford University Press, 2004). © Oxford University Press. Used with permission.

70. Ibid.

71. Rob Norton, "Unintended Consequences," *The Concise Encyclopedia of Economics*, 2008, http://www.econlib.org/library/Enc/UnintendedConsequences.html.

72. Pollitt and Bouckaert, *Public Management Reform,* 164.

73. *Wheaton College v. Sylvia Burwell*, Secretary of Health and Human Services, 573 U. S. ____ (2014), http://s3.documentcloud.org/documents/1212608/wheaton-vs-burwell.pdf, 16.

74. Francis Fukuyama, "America in Decay: The Sources of Political Dysfunction." *Foreign Affairs* 93, no. 5 (September/October 2014): 13. https://www.foreignaffairs.com/articles/united-states/2014-08-18/america-decay.

75. Ibid.

76. Ibid.

77. Ibid., 12.

78. Presidential Commission on the Space Shuttle *Challenger* Accident, *Report to the President* (Washington, DC: National Aeronautics and Space Administration, 1986).

79. Presidential Commission on the Space Shuttle *Challenger* Accident, *Implementation of the Recommendations* (Washington, DC: National Aeronautics and Space Administration, 1987).

80. John Schwartz and Matthew L. Wald, "Echoes of *Challenger*: Shuttle Panel Considers Longstanding Flaws in NASA's System," *The New York Times,* April 13, 2003.

81. Richard Blomberg, "Statement to the House Subcommittee on Space and Aeronautics," April 18, 2002.

82. Craig Couvait, "Shuttle Shakeup Eyed for Cost, Safety Goals," Aviation Week and Space Technology, September 23, 2002.

83. Editorial, "Honesty and Denial at NASA," *Nature* 425 (September 4, 2003): 1. http://www.nature.com/nature/journal/v425/n6953/full/425001a.html.

84. "Report of Columbia Accident Investigation Board," August 2003, 197.

85. Diane Vaughan, *The Challenger Launch Decision: Risky Technology, Culture, and Deviance at NASA* (Chicago, IL: University of Chicago Press, 1996), in Report of Columbia Accident Investigation Board, 130.

86. "Report of Columbia Accident Investigation Board," 180; Todd R. La Porte and Paula M. Consolini, "Working in Practice but Not in Theory," *Journal of Public Administration Research and Theory* 1 (1991): 19–47.

87. "Report of Columbia Accident Investigation Board," 180.

Appendix

Argument in Public Management

Arguments are made by public managers and officials at all levels of government. They argue about ideas, courses of action, processes, programs, and policies. Some arguments aim to sway or convince internal organizational actors about a policy position or administrative action. Others aim to sway or convince external actors, such as elected officials, interest groups, newspaper editorial boards, or the general public about their organization's needs, direction, or effectiveness. Arguments address topics that range from everyday matters (such as the style and format required for proposals for local garbage collection) to matters literally of life and death (such as whether to mobilize troops for a military intervention or to intervene in a child welfare case).

Effective public management requires the ability not only to think analytically but to communicate persuasively. Through their communications, public managers explain the strategies and options about which decisions must be reached and actions taken.[i]

Discussion of public policies and programs often takes the form of argument: discourse intended to persuade policymakers and stakeholders of a particular point of view and to build political and organizational support for it. Reasoned persuasion is, and should be, a central part of the job for public managers.

More than a half century ago, political scientist Arthur Macmahon pointed to the central role of argument in the public sphere: "The essence of rational structure for any purpose frequently lies in recognizing how far administration is an argumentative as well as a deliberative process that goes on within the frame of legislation."[1] Put differently, arguments made by policymakers and public managers to justify or persuade are fundamental to conducting the public's business in a republican democracy.

Making an argument should not be equated with having an argument. "Having an argument" implies disagreement and efforts to "win." "Making an argument," in contrast, implies effort to ensure engagement on the basis of fair-minded and dispassionate analysis: back-and-forth interaction with other participants in a discourse, whether they are supporters, critics, or the merely curious.

Argument in this sense is integral to reasoning, persuading, and decision making. It infuses rationality into the process of resolving disagreements, overcoming doubts and skepticism, clarifying facts, reaching compromises, and making choices on the basis of just and fair weighing of conflicting evidence or preferences.[2] Even when such exchanges bring out underlying conflicts and

---

[i]In addition to the citations throughout this chapter, see also Christopher Hood and Michael Jackson, *Administrative Argument* (Aldershot, UK: Dartmouth, 1991); Michael Barzelay, "How to Argue about the New Public Management," *International Public Management Journal* 2, no. 2 (1999): 183–216.

Making an argument should not be equated with having an argument.

---

disagreements among actors, doing so need not be contentious or divisive. As Joseph M. Williams and Gregory G. Colomb point out, "the language we use about *having* an argument pictures it as combat. But when we describe *making* one, we sound less like combatants than builders."[3]

Making a sound argument does not guarantee that a manager's desired course of action will be approved or that a proposed action will produce the intended or expected outcome. The absence of sound analysis and argument, however, can substantially decrease a public manager's effectiveness. Making sound arguments and recognizing them when made by others are essential skills for public managers.

MAKING ARGUMENTS

Most arguments made by public managers are intended to accomplish one of three general purposes:

- *The argument may address the need for action to effect change.* Examples include appeals from a local school board to the community for a levy increase or analyses by public officials, scholars, and pundits following Hurricane Katrina arguing for Federal Emergency Management Agency (FEMA) restructuring.
- *The argument may elaborate on the justification or support of a prior decision.* Examples include the Bush administration's defense of the National Security Agency wiretapping or a child welfare agency's documentation that it followed procedures after a publicized incident involving harm to a child.
- *The argument may address the need to maintain the status quo.* An example is a defense of the current system of generic drug approval by the Food and Drug Administration.

The Elements of an Argument

Thinking analytically can be strengthened by reference to a formal logic of argument. One common approach is that of philosopher Stephen Toulmin.[ii] As illustrated in Figure A.1, a complete argument's elements include the following:

- **Claim:** A statement that represents the main point or idea being advanced, what the maker of the argument wants us to accept as true, valid, or necessary. A claim can be thought of as the "topic sentence" of the argument.
- **Reasons**: Statements that support the specific claim. Reasons provide the logic of the argument, that is, why the claim should be believed.
- **Evidence**: Specific facts, data, and other information that support the claim and the reasons for it.

[ii]Our discussion reflects the terminology used by Wayne C. Booth, Gregory G. Colomb, and Joseph M. Williams, *The Craft of Research,* 2nd ed. (Chicago, IL: University of Chicago Press, 2003); Joseph M. Williams and Gregory G. Colomb, *The Craft of Argument,* 3rd ed. (New York, NY: Pearson Longman, 2007); and Joseph M. Williams et al., *The Craft of Argument, with Readings* (New York, NY: Longman, 2003). Stephen E. Toulmin, *The Uses of Argument,* updated ed. (Cambridge, MA: Cambridge University Press, 2003), 89–96, refers to main elements of an argument as "claims," "data," "warrants," "qualifiers," and "backing," where "backing" provides the fundamental justification for a warrant. Stephen Toulmin, Richard Rieke, and Allan Janik, *An Introduction to Reasoning,* 2nd ed. (New York, NY: Macmillan, 1984), 25–27, 85–87, refer to the main elements of argument as "claims," "grounds," "warrants," and "backing." They consider "qualifiers" to be at the "second level of analysis" for an argument. Toulmin's work contains an explicit role for qualifications, but this is not found in Williams and Colomb or in Williams et al., who argue that qualifications may play a part in each element of the argument and therefore are not a separate element.

| **FIGURE A.1** | **Elements of an Argument** |

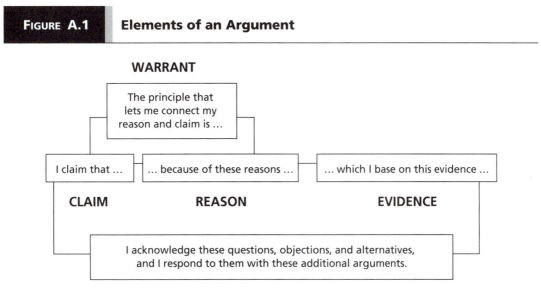

WARRANT

The principle that lets me connect my reason and claim is ...

| I claim that ... | ... because of these reasons ... | ... which I base on this evidence ... |

CLAIM   **REASON**   **EVIDENCE**

I acknowledge these questions, objections, and alternatives, and I respond to them with these additional arguments.

ACKNOWLEDGMENT AND RESPONSE

Source: Joseph M. Williams, Gregory G. Colomb, *The Craft of Argument*, 3rd ed., ©2007, p. 35. Reprinted by permission of Pearson Education, Inc., New York, New York.

- **Warrant**: A statement of a general principle or theory that justifies the linkages between a particular claim and its reasons and evidence. A warrant may draw on a theory or framework and may take the form of a statement such as "this is a case/example/illustration of a principal-agent problem" (for example).
- **Acknowledgment and response:** Statements that respond to the anticipated challenges or objections to the claim. These statements are likely to involve further reasons, evidence, and warrants and often acknowledge limits or qualifications to a claim's generalizability.

Complete arguments are almost always more complex than a single claim, reason, piece of evidence, warrant, and acknowledgment and response. An argument may include multiple instances of each element, and subarguments may be present. Indeed, reasons may themselves become claims for a subargument. As arguments grow more complex, the need to convey clearly one's reasoning and to identify precisely the reasoning of others becomes all the more important and more difficult.

A number of sources provide examples, further elaboration, and practice exercises for creating and using the **elements of a complete argument** (see, for example, the sources in Footnote ii of this Appendix). The remainder of this section considers specific issues for the use of argument in public management practice.

The Importance of Warrants

Warrants are statements that relate a general circumstance to a general inference and can be stated in the following form: "Whenever X, then Y."[4] Often, reasons and evidence can support many claims. The warrant points the analyst to the claims that are most appropriate given the specific circumstances. Put another way, a warrant is a general statement that provides a justification for why *a particular* reason and body of evidence are a basis for making *a particular claim.*[iii]

In some cases, a claim does not require an explicit warrant if the underlying principle is widely accepted or self-evident. In other cases, drawing appropriate conclusions requires articulation of the principles or causal relationships that link the reasons, evidence, and claim. Regardless of whether warrants are made explicit, they play an essential role in argument. As Toulmin put it,

> unless, in any particular field of argument, we are prepared to work with warrants of *some* kind, it will become impossible in that field to subject arguments to rational assessment. The data we cite if a claim is challenged depends on the warrants we are prepared to operate within that field, and the warrants to which we commit ourselves are implicit in the particular steps from data to claims we are prepared to take and to admit.[5]

In private sector management, where the basis for decisions is widely accepted to be the prospect of increased profit, "often the warrants are only implied: they are clearly understood, because all involved are intimately familiar with the organization's goals and values, which determine the operative warrants for most such arguments."[6] Shared, obvious warrants are rare in the realm of public management analysis because of the lack of a single unifying goal or widely accepted theory of why public policies succeed or fail. Specific, clearly explained warrants therefore may be particularly necessary in analysis and argumentation in the sphere of public management.

> Shared, obvious warrants are rare in the realm of public management analysis because of the lack of a single unifying goal or widely accepted theory of why public policies succeed or fail.

To establish warrants that link reasons and evidence to claims, public managers may draw on different sources: opinions or ideologies, experience, authority, general cultural beliefs, methods, logic, articles of faith, and systems of knowledge and beliefs from a great many fields of study.[7] Although no one type of knowledge or understanding will suffice to comprehend complex situations, some of these sources provide stronger backing for warrants than others. Opinions and ideologies are likely to be the most problematic basis for warrants because they tend to be more purely subjective and less confirmable by evidence than other sources. Warrants based on opinion are likely to be contested because they are viewed as arbitrary, and thus provide a weaker justification for linking claims and reasons in any particular context.

Warrants based on systems of knowledge, including academic/empirical findings with theoretical foundations, may hold the most promise for public management analysis. That is, the theories and evidence from the social sciences, their potential for bias notwithstanding, are a resource from which warrants can be developed. By the very nature of social science, theories and hypotheses are subject to scrutiny and to empirical testing in particular settings. The accumulated knowledge from these processes—resulting in the kinds of theories, concepts, and analytic frameworks discussed throughout this book—are a source of generalizable, verifiable warrants that public managers can use in their arguments to link specific claims with specific reasons in specific circumstances.

[iii]Particularly useful resources showing examples of warrants and their use are "The Logic of Your Argument: Warranting Claims and Reasons," in Williams and Colomb, *The Craft of Argument,* 203–231; and "Warranting Claims and Reasons," in ibid., 154–177.

Drawing on theory and research instead of mere opinion for making an argument increases the appeal to reason of a manager's argument. The likelihood increases that the analysis is viewed as trustworthy and dispassionate.

Though arguments with warrants drawn from systems of knowledge reflect rational analysis, the world of public management is most often one of political rationality, not technical rationality, as expressed by Terry Moe and emphasized in this book.[8] Two factors, political pressures and the fact that so many policymakers are lawyers, incline political actors to make strong, partisan arguments meant to sway public opinion. Such arguments are often based on warrants rooted in opinion or ideology rather than bodies of knowledge and fairly weighed evidence. As participants in this system of political rationality, public managers whose arguments solely reflect scientific or technical rationality may fail to persuade or capture the attention of policymakers, politicians, and interest groups. Indeed, such arguments may fall flat. For example, even in the face of seemingly incontrovertible arguments regarding the safety and efficacy of the measles vaccine, some "antivax" parents refuse to have their children vaccinated.[9]

> The accumulated knowledge from these processes—resulting in the kinds of theories, concepts, and analytic frameworks discussed throughout this book—are a source of generalizable, verifiable warrants that public managers can use in their arguments to link specific claims with specific reasons in specific circumstances.

While it may not always be feasible to make a sound, persuasive argument supported by warrants drawn from the knowledge, theories, and frameworks of the social sciences, having the skills to do so enhances public managers' trustworthiness and effectiveness as purveyors of reliable analysis.

Complete and Incomplete Arguments

A well-crafted argument should contain the four or five key elements listed at the beginning of this section. But that does not mean that arguments by public officials always contain these elements. In the realm of public management as it is actually practiced, carefully and completely constructed public arguments are relatively rare. Public arguments made by public officials and public managers often lack reasons, evidence, warrants, or qualifications:

- Claims may be missing (often provoking the response, "What's your point?").
- Assertions (claims) are made that are not supported by any evidence.
- Evidence or reasons may be used selectively to support the particular claim.
- Warrants may be missing, vague, or faulty.
- Potential concerns of critics may be mischaracterized or ignored.

Herbert Simon suggests one reason for incomplete arguments: humans exhibit **bounded rationality**—that is, limited capacity to obtain and assess all possibly relevant information.[10] If this is the case, then arguments constructed on such limited information may be limited or incomplete as well.

Beyond this cognitive constraint, however, it is not surprising that incomplete or flawed arguments are relatively common in a democracy of separated powers and political partisanship. Presenting all relevant evidence or data on both sides of an issue may bring charges of inconsistency—of being a "waffler" or a "flip-flopper" or being "two-handed," as in framing arguments in terms of "on the one hand" and "on the other hand." Offering no evidence may bring

> Regardless of whether the full scope of an argument is conveyed in a particular forum, a skilled public manager will have a firm grasp of the relationship between the claims, reasons, evidence, warrants, and counterarguments and responses that support his or her preferred course of action.

charges of evasion from opponents, but offering any evidence at all may provide a target for dissection and counterargument. Qualifications or acknowledgment of critics' concerns are rarely offered because to do so may be interpreted in the political arena as a sign of weakness. In the light of these risks, the most effective public arguments may be incomplete arguments based on a self-interested selection of elements.

Another reason for incomplete arguments may be the constraints of particular settings or forums in which the arguments of public officials and managers are conveyed, discussed in the next section. Regardless of whether the full scope of an argument is conveyed in a particular forum, a skilled public manager will have a firm grasp of the relationship between the claims, reasons, evidence, warrants, and counterarguments and responses that support his or her preferred course of action. The public manager will be able to identify the elements of argument (and whether they are present or missing) in the arguments he or she constructs as well as in the arguments of others. Figure A.2 describes a continuum of arguments, from weaker to stronger.

FIGURE A.2	**Ranking the Strength of Arguments**

Arguments may be evaluated using the following ranking scheme, presented from the weakest to the strongest type of argument. This ranking scheme might be used to assess arguments made in the context of a public management course for in-class discussions or assignments or as a part of public management practice either for constructing one's own argument or assessing the arguments of others.

The "No argument" argument

A public manager took particular actions. She should have taken other actions instead.

Problem: No reasons, evidence, warrants, or qualifications are supplied to support the claim.

The "Well, of course, but . . . " argument

A public manager took particular actions. She should have acted differently

- for reasons that are obvious in hindsight, such as she had no political support, so she should have mobilized the support she needed; she failed to win over the constituency that ended up defeating her;
- because of principles that, on reflection, always apply, such as always consider the values and feelings of your subordinates.

Problem: Although the argument presents reasons and evidence, it emphasizes hindsight and does not link the evidence and reason to the claim in a way that invokes a general principle in the context of the situation. A warmed-over "counsel of perfection" is conveyed, rather than insight into how to handle complex public management situations.

The "Almost, but not quite" argument

A public manager took particular actions. It would have been better had she taken different actions based on reasoning

- drawn from shrewd observation of the evidence in the case or lessons from personal experience;
- that implies but does not state a more complex theory or concept of general but not universal application. For example, her actions assumed that her subordinates would comply, but they stood to gain more by noncompliance.

Problem: Although the argument presents reasons and evidence, and hints at warrants linking those elements with the claim, the full logic is not articulated and appropriate qualifications are not offered, leaving the argument with holes.

The "I know how to construct an argument" argument

A public manager took particular actions. It would have been better had she taken different actions because this is an example of a theory/framework/model/concept that incorporates cause-effect logic. Appropriate qualifications and acknowledgments and responses are included. The framework is

- used as a source of vocabulary for interpreting the facts in the case;
- used to derive conclusions based on those facts.

Why This Works: The emphasis in these arguments is on applying the logic of analytic models to the facts of cases or real world problems in order to gain nonobvious, nondescriptive insights into how the managerial world works. Theories and frameworks are used to establish warrants, which then drive the linking of evidence, reasons, and claims, noting appropriate qualifications. Counterarguments are acknowledged and responded to.

Forums and Formats for Public Arguments

Skilled public managers will understand how and where to present an argument. They may use a number of different types of formats, forums, and media:

- giving speeches (such as a speech by EPA administrator Gina McCarthy at a conference at Georgetown University);[11]
- testifying before official bodies (such as Assistant to the President for National Security Affairs Condoleezza Rice appearing before the 9/11 Commission);[12]
- writing intra- or interoffice memos or e-mail messages (such as an e-mail message from a local FEMA official, Marty Bahamonde, to FEMA director, Mike Brown, on August 31, 2005);[13]
- writing position papers, reports, or "white papers" (such as an Environmental Protection Agency white paper on nanotechnology);[14]

- issuing commission reports (such as the one issued by President Bush's Commission to Strengthen Social Security);[15]
- issuing or responding to audit reports (such as an audit of management practices of the Los Angeles Fire Department conducted by the city controller's office);[16]
- addressing public forums (such as those held to discuss a school tax levy increase in a local school district); and
- giving interviews to the media, including newspapers, magazines, TV, radio, websites, specialized journals, or newsletters (such as former Federal Reserve chair Ben Bernanke's appearance on *60 Minutes*).[17]

An argument on a particular topic may be presented using different media and in different formats and forums. A particular forum and format may not be well suited to a full presentation of an argument; this is especially true for media accounts and interviews. News sources have limited space or time, and writers' and editors' decisions will always determine what parts of a manager's arguments are conveyed. Even if a manager's argument is "complete" (in the five-element sense), it may not emerge that way in any particular forum, especially when the manager may not have control over the final version, as with a news story. Furthermore, consumers of arguments should keep in mind that a single source or forum will seldom convey the whole argument and that additional research may be necessary.

ANALYSIS AND ARGUMENT AS MANAGEMENT SKILLS

To summarize, a proficient public manager is able to make sound arguments and to understand and critique the arguments of others. This means formulating specific, concise claims; giving the reasons and evidence that sustain the claims; selecting and specifying warrants that provide a causal logic for linking the evidence and reasons to the claims; and acknowledging and responding to potential objections. Scrupulously noting any qualifications on claims, reasons, evidence, warrants, and responses is also fundamental. Arguments constructed in this way are analytical in that they are based on a careful and dispassionate consideration of the facts and issues in a given case. Any preconceptions are put to the test of surviving examination of their consistency with the facts and of their superiority to alternative explanations for those facts.

Being skilled in the method of argument will increase understanding of the actions, statements, and positions of other actors after the fact (*ex post*) and understanding of a situation prior to action in real time (*ex ante*) as a practicing public manager. With greater familiarity and practice in the method of argument and its application in various formats, forums, and media, skills for developing arguments in real time will become stronger.

The model deliberative process described in Chapter 1 prompts readers to strengthen their analytical skills by pushing beyond their initial responses to an issue or situation. After their initial assessments, they can analyze the situation using three-dimensional analysis as emphasized in this book. Then they can formulate a complete and coherent argument by stating clearly their claims, reasons, evidence, warrants, and acknowledgments and responses.

The tools of argument and the three-dimensional framework can be employed as management analysts develop judgment and skill in synthesizing insights from diverse sources. The examples discussed throughout the book and the cases presented in each chapter are intended to provide opportunities for practicing this set of skills.

KEY CONCEPTS

Elements of a complete argument
Claim
Reasons
Evidence

Warrant
Acknowledgment and response
Bounded rationality

NOTES

1. Arthur Macmahon, "Specialization and the Public Interest," in *Democracy in Federal Administration,* ed. Orrin Bryte Conway Jr. (Washington, DC: U.S. Department of Agriculture Graduate School, 1955), 40.

2. Stuart Hampshire, *Justice Is Conflict* (Princeton, NJ: Princeton University Press, 1999), 45.

3. Joseph M. Williams and Gregory G. Colomb, *The Craft of Argument,* 3rd ed. (New York, NY: Pearson Longman, 2007), 133.

4. Williams et al., *The Craft of Argument, with Readings,* (New York, NY: Longman, 2003), 156.

5. Toulmin, *The Uses of Argument,* updated ed. (Cambridge, MA: Cambridge University Press, 2003), 93.

6. Toulmin, Rieke, and Janik, *An Introduction to Reasoning,* 2nd ed. (New York, NY: Macmillan, 1984), 386.

7. Booth, Colomb, and Williams, *The Craft of Research,* 2nd ed. (Chicago, IL: University of Chicago Press, 2003), 179–181.

8. Terry Moe, "The Politics of Structural Choice: Toward a Theory of Public Bureaucracy," in *Organization Theory: From Chester Barnard to the Present and Beyond,* ed. Oliver E. Williamson (New York, NY: Oxford University Press, 1990), 116–153.

9. See, for example, Laura Parker, "The Anti-Vaccine Generation: How Movement Against Shots Got Its Start," *National Geographic,* February 6, 2015.

10. Herbert A. Simon, *Models of Man* (New York, NY: Wiley, 1957); Herbert A. Simon, "Rationality as Process and as Process of Thought," *American Economic Review* 68(1978): 1–16; see also Jonathan Bendor, "Herbert A. Simon: Political Scientist," *Annual Review of Political Science* 6 (June 2003): 433–471.

11. Gina McCarthy, speech at Georgetown University, October 24, 2014, http://yosemite.epa.gov/opa/admpress.nsf/8d49f7ad4bbcf4ef852573590040b7f6/ca425d96d817267585257d7b005c8f40!OpenDocument.

12. Testimony of Assistant to the President for National Security Affairs Condoleezza Rice before the National Commission on Terrorist Attacks Upon the United States, Hart Senate Office Building Washington, DC, April 8, 2004, http://www.9-11commission.gov/archive/hearing9/9-11Commission_Hearing_2004-04-08.htm.

13. Spencer S. Hsu, "Aide Says FEMA Ignored Warnings," The Washington Post, October 21, 2005, http://www.washingtonpost.com/wp-dyn/content/article/2005/10/20/AR2005102000858.html.

14. Nanotechnology Workgroup, Science Policy Council, U.S. Environmental Protection Agency, "Nanotechnology White Paper," February 2007, EPA 100/B-07/001, http://www.epa.gov/OSA/ pdfs/nanotech/epa-nanotechnology-whitepaper-0207.pdf.

15. The President's Commission to Strengthen Social Security, *Strengthening Social Security and Creating Personal Wealth for All Americans,* December 21, 2001, http://govinfo.library.unt.edu/csss/reports/Final_report.pdf.

16. Los Angeles City Controller and Sjoberg Evashenk Consulting Inc., "Review of the Los Angeles Fire Department Management Practices," January 26, 2006, http://controller.lacity.org/stellent/groups/electedofficials/@ctr_contributor/documents/contributor_web_content/lacityp_008196.pdf.

17. Interview with Ben Bernanke, *60 Minutes,* December 3, 2010, http://www.cbsnews.com/news/fed-chairman-ben-bernankes-take-on-the-economy/.

Name Index

Subject Index